AMERICA AND THE SURVIVORS
OF THE HOLOCAUST

Contemporary American History Series
WILLIAM E. LEUCHTENBURG, GENERAL EDITOR

AMERICA AND THE SURVIVORS OF THE HOLOCAUST

LEONARD DINNERSTEIN

COLUMBIA UNIVERSITY PRESS

NEW YORK

Library of Congress Cataloging in Publication Data
Dinnerstein, Leonard.
America and the survivors of the Holocaust.

(Contemporary American history series)
Bibliography:
Includes index.
1. United States—Emigration and immigration
—History—20th century. 2. Jews—United
States—History—20th century. 3. Refugees,
Jewish—Government policy—United States—
History—20th century. I. Title. II. Series.
JV6895.J5D55   325.73   81-15443
ISBN 0-231-04176-4   AACR2
ISBN 0-231-04177-2 (pbk)

Columbia University Press
New York   Guildford, Surrey

To Myra

CONTENTS

PREFACE

The slaughter of 6 million Jews by the Nazis during World War II is the tragedy of modern Jewish history. Many Jews were dismayed that the world, and especially Great Britain and the United States, stood by while Hitler proceeded with his ruthless scheme to rid Europe of all its Jews. Histories such as Bernard Wasserstein's *Britain and the Jews of Europe*, Henry Feingold's *The Politics of Rescue*, Saul Friedman's *No Haven For The Oppressed*, Arthur Morse's *While Six Million Died*, Barbara McDonald Stewart's, *United States Government Policy on Refugees, 1933–1940*, and David Wyman's *Paper Walls*, described the unresponsiveness of British and American government officials who did little to stop the annihilation. Sadly, a similar indifference to the welfare of European Jewry persisted even after the war. In 1946, Judge Simon Rifkind, the Jewish adviser to the American Army in Europe, noted that survivors of the German concentration camps:

> expected the miracle of liberation to be followed by worldwide welcome extended by a repentant mankind which had permitted them to suffer such barbarism. There was no such welcome. Instead they awoke to find themselves in the chilly atmosphere of a displaced persons center with every avenue of escape to a land of freedom and dignity closed to them.[1]

Until now, and aside from contemporary analyses, there have been few investigations of American attitudes towards the displaced persons. Robert Divine devoted two chapters to the Displaced Persons Acts of 1948 and 1950 in his book, *American Immigration Policy*, and two graduate students have done theses on the subject. But these scholars did not have access to documents and manuscript collections that have opened within the past decade. This new material provides the opportunity for a much fuller examination of the displaced persons issue, and the role that the United States played in attempting to solve it.

In analyzing the evolution of the American response to the problem of the displaced persons this study is concerned with several issues. One is the reaction to, and treatment of, those survivors of World War II who could not, or would not, return to their prewar homes. Another centers on the efforts of Great Britain and the United States to find a joint solution for the placement of the Jewish DPs. A third focuses on both the attempts of American Jewry to influence the United States government's treatment of DPs and how the awareness of Jewish concerns and American antisemitism shaped United States military and civilian policy decisions. Finally, the book explores the activities of a well-organized lobby and congressional responses to the campaign designed to alter American immigration laws in order to accommodate a large number of DPs in the United States. The drama that unfolds in answering these questions is both moving and troubling, and has echoes in our own time. It is a revealing tale—and a shocking one, too.

Leonard Dinnerstein

Tucson, Arizona
February 12, 1981

ACKNOWLEDGMENTS

Generous financial support to carry out this project was provided by grants from the American Philosophical Society, the
Herbert Hoover Presidential Library Association, the Immigration History Research Center, the Eleanor Roosevelt Institute, the Harry S. Truman Library, the University of Arizona
Foundation and the University of Arizona Humanities Committee, and the National Endowment for the Humanities.
I am deeply indebted to several people who read the entire
manuscript. The cogent critiques, keen observations, and warm
encouragement that I received from four close friends—Fred
Jaher, Dave Reimers, Bob Schulzinger, and Michael Schaller—
contributed significantly to whatever merit this book may
possess. Bill Leuchtenburg, as everyone who has had the good
fortune to work with him knows, is an editor without peer. His
pointed comments in matters of both style and substance were
absolutely invaluable. Don Weinstein also made many helpful
suggestions.

A number of people, many of whom participated in aspects
of the events described herein, took time from their busy
schedules to talk with me about their experiences. It is a
pleasure to thank them here: Benjamin N. Brook, Abraham
Duker, Irving M. Engel, William Frankel, Henry M. Friedlander, R. Gogolinski-Elston, Amy Zahl Gottlieb, Selma Hirsh,
William Haber, Simon Rifkind, Francis Rosenberger, Harry N.
Rosenfield, John G. Slawson, and William G. Stratton. Jerome
E. Edwards and Bernard Wasserstein shared their findings
with me while Sister Margaret Patricia McCarran discussed her
father's role as she remembered it. William S. Bernard made
himself available on several occasions and commented upon
early articles that derived from this study.

The single most important collection of manuscripts, books, and periodicals used for this study is housed at the American Jewish Committee offices in New York City. Without the AJC materials it would have been very difficult for me to have understood the dynamics involved in the evolution of a United States displaced persons policy. Everyone with whom I dealt at the AJC was helpful. Milton Himmelfarb granted me permission to use the archives. Cyma Horowitz extended every courtesy whenever I chose to use the outstanding Blaustein Library. Ruth Rauch, and her associate Helen Ritter, efficiently and cheerfully made available the AJC's vast, and extremely well organized, archival materials. I am grateful to these women, as well as to Esther Eidensohn in the library and Barbara Schonberg in the archives, for their assistance and their particularly warm welcomes whenever I arrived.

The course of my research also took me to several other libraries and archives where I invariably met knowledgeable and helpful professionals. Their aid contributed to the speed with which I was able to go through a variety of collections. They included Marcia Friedman, American Council for Judaism; Jack Sutters, American Friends Service Committee; Fannie Zelcer, American Jewish Archives; Nehemiah Ben-Zev, American Jewish Historical Society; Rose Klepfisz, American Jewish Joint Distribution Committee; Sybil Milton, Leo Baeck Institute; Mary Jo Pugh, Bentley Historical Library of the University of Michigan; Olla della Cava, Center for Migration Studies; Joel Meyerson and Hannah Zeidlik, Center of Military History; Elizabeth W. Mason, Columbia University Oral History Project; June Gustafson, Cornell University Library; Albert W. Fowler, Friends Historical Library, Swarthmore College; Dwight M. Miller, Herbert Hoover Library, West Branch, Iowa; Adorjan I. deGalffy, Hoover Institution, Stanford University; Paul Spence, Illinois State Historical Society; Rudolph Vecoli, Immigration History Archives, University of Minnesota; William B. Liebmann, Herbert H. Lehman Papers, Columbia University; Nancy Bressler, Seeley G. Mudd Manuscript Library, Princeton University; Marilla B. Guptel, Harry W. John, and William J. Walsh, National Archives; Frederick C. Gale, Nevada

State Archives; Jane N. Ramsay, The Presbyterian Historical Society; William R. Emerson, Franklin D. Roosevelt Library; Dennis Bilger, Philip Lagerquist, Erwin J. Mueller, and Warren Ohrvall, Harry S. Truman Library; Alf Erlandsson, United Nations Archives; Peter Gottlieb, West Virginia Collection, West Virginia University; Nancy Lankford, Western Historical MSS. Collection, University of Missouri; June Witt, Western History Collections, University of Oklahoma; Josephine L. Harper and Katherine Thompson, Wisconsin State Historical Society; Elizabeth Eppler, World Jewish Congress, London; Mark Friedman, World Jewish Congress, New York City; Marek Web, YIVO; Sylvia Landress, Zionist Archives and Library, New York City; and finally, Andrew Makuch and many others at the University of Arizona library.

During the course of my many research trips I enjoyed the hospitality of Sharon and Bill Lowenstein in Kansas City; Martha and Leonard Helfenstein, Diane and Jack Zeller, and Barbara and Archibald Stewart in Washington, D.C.; Irene and Ben Rosenberg in Philadelphia; Rita and Levon Kabasak-alian, Josette and George Lankevich, Marcia Benewitz, Sydney and Dan Ratner, and Marilyn and Philip Yablon in New York; Jerome Edwards in Reno, Nevada; Linda and Dick Kerber in Iowa City; and R. Larry Angove in West Branch, Iowa.

A number of other people provided timely assistance, advice on sources available, and/or editorial suggestions. They include Stephen Ambrose, William Aydelotte, Richard A. Baker, Robert Claus, Naomi W. Cohen, William Carpenter, Robert Dallek, Russell H. Dorr, Seymour Drescher, Bernard Gronert, Donna Guy, Robert Hathaway, Kathryn Allamong Jacob, Wolfgang Jacobmeyer, Jana Johnson, Kay Kavanagh, Julie M. Koch, Ursula Lamb, Maudi Mazza, John McKean, Ralph Melnick, Amikam Nachmani, Phileo Nash, Gemma Mae Newman, Roger Nichols, James Patterson, Von V. Pittman, Jr., Dan Rylance, David Schoenbaum, Duncan Sellers, Ken Stein, Steve Stone-man, Mel Urofsky, Richard Weiss, and David S. Wyman. Major Irving Heymont graciously sent me a copy of "After the Deluge," an unpublished collection of letters that he had written to his wife while he was commander of the Landsberg

DP assembly center in the fall of 1945. Joan Schwartz and Leslie Bialler carefully edited the manuscript for Columbia University Press.

I must also acknowledge the aid given to me by the staff of the History Department at the University of Arizona. Dawn Polter, Dorothy Donnelly, Valla Galvez, and Marilyn Bradian provided a large number of office services which were far beyond what any faculty member has a right to expect. In addition, Marilyn Bradian skillfully and speedily typed more drafts of the manuscript than either she or I could possibly recollect. The friendliness, efficiency, and productivity of these women have facilitated my progress enormously.

My greatest debt is to my loving family: my wife, Myra, who read the entire manuscript, and my children, Andrew and Julie, who read none of it.

AMERICA AND THE SURVIVORS
OF THE HOLOCAUST

"The last chapter in the Nazi persecution of the Jews was written in the displaced-person camps and in the emigration of survivors during the years after the war in Europe."

Robert W. Ross
So It Was True: The American Protestant Press and the Nazi Persecution of the Jews

AMERICA, JEWS, AND REFUGEES

The advent of Adolf Hitler to power in Germany, in January 1933, marked the beginning of the tragedy of European Jewry. In his famous autobiography, *Mein Kampf,* the Nazi dictator indicated his intentions to eliminate Jews from the German scene. Once in power Hitler began to carry out his plans. Ultimately, he ordered the obliteration of all European Jewry but before he attempted this final solution hundreds of thousands of Jews and Gentiles emigrated from Germany.

As German Jews fled their homeland in the 1930s a majority of Americans feared that the refugees would overrun the United States. In March 1938, only 17 percent of those polled favored admitting "a larger number of Jewish exiles from Germany," and in November of that year, after the savage attacks of *Kristallnacht,* when Germans systematically destroyed Jewish stores, indiscriminately beat individual Jews, and arrested 20,000 Jewish citizens, the percentage of Americans who wanted to relax existing immigration laws to admit more German Jews increased to only 21.[1]

Although American Jews never suffered the kind of legal harassments and treatment endured by their coreligionists in Germany, they lived in a country where antisemitism was widespread.[2] After the Bolsheviks triumphed in 1917, several American patriotic and fundamentalist organizations feared that Russians and other foreign radicals might attempt to undermine traditional values in the United States and they specifically linked Jews with the "Red Menace." Another popular American stereotype connected Jewish bankers to economic problems. In other words, as sociologist Arthur Liebman so aptly put it, "Jews were both bomb-throwing, beared Bolsheviks and money-grasping Shylocks. These themes were picked up and broadcast throughout the nation." Added to this, there were many religious Protestants and Catholics who still viewed the Jews as Christ-killers who not only had murdered the Savior but who also refused to accept the "true faith." Popular hero Henry Ford was the most prominent American antisemite of the 1920s. His newspaper, the *Dearborn Independent,* described the existence of an "international Jewish conspiracy," a belief shared by millions in the United States. Some Americans displayed their biases by establishing quotas limiting Jewish entry to institutions of higher education, by refusing to hire Jews in their concerns, and by restricting Jewish entry to hundreds of desirable residential neighborhoods throughout the country.[3]

Antipathy toward Jews contributed, in part, to American governmental inaction concerning refugees fleeing from Germany. Officials made few attempts to aid German Jews or to modify existing immigration policies. In fact, responding to both historical and contemporary prejudices, functionaries of the State Department outdid themselves to prevent the distribution of an excessive number of visas to Jews who might otherwise have qualified for admission under the large German quota. The most common device barred entry to people "likely to become a public charge." Ironically, in 1930, President Herbert Hoover had ordered stringent enforcement of this clause of the immigration laws as a humanitarian endeavor to prevent unknowing immigrants from flooding the depressed American economy. Franklin D. Roosevelt succeeded to the presidency in 1933 but did not alter the established procedures. At the end of the decade, when humanitarians concerned with providing assistance for German Jewish refugees sought the President's assistance, he hid behind the laws and public attitudes claiming that he could do little by himself. Roosevelt was also unwilling to alienate congressmen and senators whose votes he might need for other measures by pushing legislation to aid refugees. In the late 1930s, when the refugee problem became more acute, the President, though aware of antisemitism among State Department career officials, made no attempt to appoint more sympathetic administrators to American consulates where foreigners had to obtain visas to enter the United States. Even Secretary of State Cordell Hull, although married to a woman of Jewish birth, did not interfere in immigration matters.[4]

The particularly inopportune appointment of Breckinridge Long as Assistant Secretary of State in January 1940 proved especially troublesome to Hitler's victims looking for sanctuary in the United States. Long, later characterized by Congressman Emanuel Celler as the person "least sympathetic to refugees in all the State Department," supervised 23 of the department's 42 divisions, including the all-important visa section. If he had any concern for the Jews or any understanding of their travails in trying to escape from Europe, his performance in the State Department failed to reveal it. Shortly after Long took office he ordered stiffer security precautions and instructed all diplomatic and consular officials to reject any applicant about whom they had "any doubt whatever"; President Roosevelt tacitly endorsed this decision. Ambitious foreign service officials, therefore, noted that lax enforcement of visa requirements might undermine their opportunities for advancements, while rigid adherence to established guidelines would in no way hurt them.[5]

The Jews' difficulty in getting into the United States would not necessarily have been catastrophic except that no other nation in the world wanted them either. In a major international conference concerning the plight of the refugees, held in 1938 at Evian, France, no national spokesman offered them haven; but the delegates did establish an intergovernmental committee to help solve the problem. Five years later, however, James G. McDonald, former League of Nations High Commissioner for Refugee Affairs, charged that "the intergovernmental organizations have almost never faced the realities of the tragedy of the refugees but that instead they have been guilty of face-saving maneuvers while millions of innocent men and women have been needlessly sacrificed."⁶

The nature of that sacrifice became increasingly apparent as World War II went on and the horrifying news of the German concentration camps and extermination centers filtered into the United States. In January 1943, a Protestant newspaper, *The Brethren Missionary Herald,* informed its readers that Jewish

> men are forced to dig their own graves, then are tortured to death and thrown in. Young Jewesses by the thousands are shipped to Germany for use in brothels. The young men are moved to defense plants to slave under indescribable cruelty to make war equipment. In Poland alone 8,000 die of starvation daily and are buried like dogs. Hitler boasts, and not without reason, that no Jews will remain in Europe after 1943.

Rational people refused to believe the rumors and reports. The editor of the *Christian Century* challenged the accuracy of Stephen Wise's charge that Hitler was paying money for Jewish corpses to be "processed into soap fats and fertilizer." The allegation, the editorial continued, was "unpleasantly reminiscent of the 'cadaver factory' lie which was one of the propaganda triumphs of the First World War." Ultimately, the weight of the evidence and the variety of the sources convinced first Jews and then others, that "the Mass Murder of Jews in Europe," was, in the words of the *Federal Council Bulletin,* another Protestant newspaper, "beyond anything the civilized imagination can picture."⁷

In 1942 President Roosevelt questioned congressional leaders about the possibility of bringing more European Jews to the United States but received unsympathetic responses. By January 1944, however, political pressure to aid the surviving Jews in Europe had broadened beyond that of American Jewry. A new group called the National Committee Against Nazi Persecution, headed by United States Supreme Court Justice Frank Murphy, former Republican presidential nominee Wendell Willkie, and Vice-President Henry A. Wallace, called for "sustained and vigorous action by our government and United

Nations to rescue those who may yet be saved." With such distinguished Americans speaking out, Roosevelt felt impelled to listen carefully to Secretary of the Treasury Henry Morgenthau, Jr., who in December 1943, brought him detailed information about the Nazi atrocities. The next month the President established the War Refugee Board to rescue as many Europeans as possible. As a result of the agency's efforts thousands who might have been killed were saved.[8]

The end of the war created new difficulties. No longer was it necessary to make special efforts to keep people alive. Allied concerns centered on finding homes for the uprooted who could not, or would not, return to their homelands. At first the problem of the displaced persons (as the refugees were called) was not perceived as a significant issue. But as world Jewish leaders became increasingly alarmed about the fate of the war's survivors, they brought their plight to the attention of government officials. However, such patriotic groups as the Daughters of the American Revolution, the American Legion and the Veterans of Foreign Wars—fearful of a large influx of refugees to the United States—called for a ban on all immigration to this country for periods of five to ten years. For despite the Nazi slaughter of 6 million Jews, in 1945 many Americans seemed no more inclined to welcome newcomers than they had been a few years earlier. The Jewish periodical *Opinion* was incensed not only over what had occurred, but also over the continued neglect of European Jewry:

> The most shocking [activity] of the war, indeed of all history, is the extermination of close to five million European Jews! Almost equally shocking is the indifference of the civilized world. If the Nazis had murdered five million dogs or cats under similar circumstances, the denunciations would have risen to the high heaven, and numerous groups would have vied with one another to save the animals. Jews, however, has [sic] created hardly a stir![9]

Antisemitism, more than any other factor, conditioned the response of Americans to the survivors of the Holocaust. Polls indicated that a majority of the people harbored some degree of antisemitic feelings, did not want to go to school with Jews, live in the same neighborhood with them, or work in the same offices. To the question "Do you think Jews have too much power in the United States?" those answering affirmatively rose from 41 percent in March 1938, to 48 percent in October 1941, and to 58 percent in June 1945, one month after the war had ended in Europe. During most of America's involvement in World War II, in fact, more than 40 percent of the public indicated that it would support or sympathize with a campaign against Jews. And, according to sociologist C. H. Stember, "as late as 1945 and 1946, well over half the [American] population said they would not be influenced against a Congressional candidate by his being anti-Semitic, and almost a quarter declared they would find him more attractive for being so—considerably more than had expressed this view during the prewar period." The intensity of the emotion varied widely but Laura Z. Hobson captured its essential spirit in her best selling novel, *Gentleman's Agreement,* published in 1947; Bruce Bliven documented its extensiveness in a series of articles in *The New Republic* that same year.[10]

The continued existence of antisemitism in the United States did not surprise American Jews but their reaction to it differed markedly from their prewar responses. In the 1930s Jewish leaders had been timid, disorganized, and afraid of provoking more intense American hostility, so they had done little to prod the government to act on behalf of the refugees. But the Nazi atrocities brought together an otherwise disorganized American Jewry in 1942. For the first time in American history practically every major Jewish organization in this country supported a demand for a homeland in Palestine—the goal of Zionists since Theodore Herzl had proposed the idea in 1896. These Jewish organizations proclaimed a Zionist commitment that tolerated no deviation from the "party line." Almost all had, or knew people who had, relatives in Europe who had been killed by the Nazis during the war. American antisemitism added further evidence that the Jews could feel safe in no other place than a homeland of their own. Thus the American

Zionists emerged unified, strong, and ready to do battle in 1945 to obtain their objective of a Jewish state in Palestine.[11] Although most Jews in the United States were Zionists or supporters of Zionism, non-Zionists and anti-Zionists constituted about 10 percent of American Jewry. These were the predominantly wealthy German-American members of the foremost Jewish defense group in the United States, the American Jewish Committee (AJC), and its offshoot, the American Council for Judaism (ACJ). Relatively small in numbers, the ACJ originated in 1943 in reaction to the American Jewish Conference's absorption of the Zionist demand for a Jewish homeland in Palestine. The ACJ exerted little influence upon most of America's Jews but it appeared powerful to outsiders because it included Lessing Rosenwald, the former chairman of the board of Sears, Roebuck, and Athur Hays Sulzberger, publisher of *The New York Times,* among its members and backers.[12]

The American Jewish Committee, founded in 1906, stood out as the prestige organization in American Jewish circles until World War II. It sought to protect the civil rights of Jews throughout the world. Composed of many distinguished, accomplished, and wealthy Jews of Central European background, the organization and its leaders wanted acceptance from the larger American community. Despite the Committee's involvement in protecting Jewish rights at home and abroad, the organization shunned activities that stressed parochial concerns. From 1912 through his death in 1929, Louis Marshall served as AJC president and he possessed a keen sense of how to defend the rights of Jews while not alienating otherwise friendly Americans in prestigious positions. After his death the AJC suffered through a string of weak leaders for the next twenty years. Judge Joseph M. Proskauer, the AJC president during most of the 1940s, felt priviliged to be consulted by members of the State Department and other American influentials and tried to reflect their views in his judgments.[13] Alone among the major Jewish organizations, the AJC walked out of the American Jewish Conference in 1943 when that group adopted the Zionist platform.[14] (The ACJ had not yet been founded). Not until 1946, in fact, did the AJC come around to supporting a Jewish homeland in Palestine.

Despite the fractured nature of institutionalized American Jewry in 1945, all of the groups agreed that the survivors of the Holocaust required special care and assistance. Therefore they sought entry into the Holy Land for the European Jews most in need. When this goal failed to be achieved by the summer of 1946, the Zionists and non-Zionists parted ways and worked for different programs. The Zionists continued their quest for a national homeland; the non-Zionists focused their efforts on bringing survivors to America. In this endeavor they had the quiet acquiescence of most Zionists but little of their zeal or financial backing.[15]

Given the strong feeling in the United States against bringing in more Jews during the Depression, and aware of similar sentiments in the 1940s as well, it is unlikely that any Jewish group wanted to be in the forefront seeking alterations in American immigration policies after the war. But their overriding concern for the welfare of Europe's remaining Jews, and the dreadful conditions in which the survivors of the Holocaust dwelled, propelled the non-Zionists to act. They saw that other nations seemed disinclined to welcome many of their coreligionists and thus they took it upon themselves to shoulder the burden of resettlement for those European Jews who survived the most inhumane episode that the civilized world had ever experienced.

I

THE ARMY AND THE
DISPLACED PERSONS

A T THE END OF World War II the Allied armies faced the staggering problem of dealing with over 7 million displaced persons in the occupied territories. They included former slave laborers brought in to work Germany's farms and factories, former concentration camp inmates and prisoners-of-war (POWs), and Eastern Europeans who either came voluntarily in the early 1940s to help the German war effort, or who fled as the Russian armies advanced in 1944. Approximately 7 million DPs constituted only about one-quarter of the 20 to 30 million Europeans uprooted as a result of the war, but millions of others either perished or were located outside the realm of Allied military territory. During the war the Russians had taken in over 2.5 million Poles and Czechs. After the war, and as a result of the Potsdam Agreement in July 1945, the Eastern Europeans began expelling 12 million "ethnic Germans."[1]

The problems encountered by the occupying troops in handling so many diverse groups and individuals found no parallel in previous military history. The logistics of processing, moving, feeding, clothing, and communicating with these disparate groups boggled the mind. Nevertheless the reality of the situation required immediate attention. From May through September 1945, the military, while dismantling its own forces, repatriated almost 6 million refugees. Another million and a half refused to, or could not, return to their former homes, and they required care. While the repatriation accomplishments deservedly won a great deal of admiration for the military, the handling of those who chose to remain in Germany, Austria, and Italy left much to be desired. The Army's gross inadequacies as custodians of the homeless bordered on the inhumane and resulted in an investigation of their activities by a presidential commission in July 1945.

The mishandling of the displaced persons did not occur because of lack of foresight. The military had devised plans earlier for dealing with the displaced persons who remained in central Europe at the end of the war. The subject of their handling arose at Roosevelt's cabinet meeting on October 29, 1942, and frequently thereafter. On November 29, 1943, forty-four Allied governments met in the White House and agreed to the establishment of the United Nations Relief and Rehabilitation Administration (UNRRA), an organization intended to provide food, clothing, medical supplies, and other types of relief to those awaiting repatriation. A refugee section appeared shortly thereafter within the Government Affairs Branch of the Civil Affairs Division of the Supreme Headquarters of the Allied Expeditionary Forces in Europe (SHAEF), which was renamed the Displaced Persons Section in January 1944. Once the magnitude of the problems became evident to the military, the DP section expanded and, on May 1, 1944, began functioning as a separate branch of the G-5 division of the American Army. UNRRA worked as an administrative and subordinate branch of the military.[2]

By the fall of 1944 the Allied forces were making full-scale plans to repatriate homeless citizens of any United Nations country and to relieve their distress while they awaited transport. In October, a SHAEF guide detailed the procedures and kinds of anticipated services that it assumed the DPs would require: registration, housing, food, counseling, recreation, special arrangements for the aged and orphans, etc. A month later SHAEF and UNRRA signed a pact outlining their mutual commitments but gave no assurance that UNRRA personnel would be utilized. According to this agreement the Army would provide food, shelter, clothing, medical supplies, and security to the assembly centers housing the DPs; UNRRA's tasks included administering these camps, and providing supplementary supplies, recreational facilities, health and welfare services, and amenities such as tobacco and toilet articles. Self-help programs and vocational guidance also came under the UNRRA banner. Furthermore, UNRRA recruited the necessary professional and technical personnel who ministered to the DPs awaiting repatriation. Another agreement, concluded on February 19, 1946, required UNRRA to operate a records office and tracing bureau, prepare statistics and research reports, and supervise educational programs, while the Army retained ultimate authority for DP care, movements of United Nations' citizens and DPs, and overall management of the camps.[3]

The military structure was bewilderingly complex. SHAEF went out of existence on July 13, 1945, and the British, French, and Americans took over responsibilities for DP centers in their respective zones. (Russia acknowledged no DP problem in its areas of occupation.) A Combined Displaced Persons Executive (CDPX) representing the three Western powers, UNRRA, and the Intergovernmental Committee on Refugees (IGC), an international and almost useless organization set up in 1938 to help find homes for refugees, was then established to coordinate DP affairs and ease the administrative transition. The CDPX ceased functioning on October 1 when care for the homeless became the responsibility of the commanding generals in each of the occupied zones. The DP centers in Italy remained under joint allied jurisdiction. At that time UNRRA supposedly would have taken over most of the functions of the CDPX, but its lack of personnel adequate to handle the task left the burden upon the respective military commanders.[4] On paper the organizational plans seemed impressive but, especially at the beginning, almost nothing worked out as planned.

When the war ended in May 1945, hundreds of thousands more DPs remained in Germany and Austria than had been anticipated. Assembly centers established to hold 2,000 to 3,000 people contained over 10,000. The military requested 450 UNRRA teams but the organization could not supply the requisite number. Each UNRRA team should have had thirteen persons; at first each contained only seven people and not until July did the component increase to ten. One unit was originally intended to work with 2,000 DPs but sometimes had to deal with four or five times that number. With more than a million people to handle this proved impossible. Former New York Governor Herbert H. Lehman, the Director-General of UNRRA, hoped for 5,000 to 6,000 workers that summer, but only 2,656 were on the job in July.[5]

Hurriedly recruited and poorly trained, too many of the original UNRRA workers lacked competence. Confused policies, inadequate supervisors, uncoordinated programs, generally poor administration, and inability to get along with the military stigmatized UNRRA. A Canadian major represented the organization in SHAEF but in the rank-conscious military, superior officers paid him scant attention. Individual UNRRA teams found themselves directionless, broken up, and reshuffled; their supervisors rarely knew where all their subordinates were deployed in Germany. The best UNRRA personnel came from France, England, Holland, Norway, and Poland, where they had experienced the savageries of war, understood the problems of the DPs, and knew Nazi terrorism. The worst of the UNRRA people spoke none of the DP languages, had not even heard of Dachau, and profiteered from black market activities. By December officials dismissed more than 1,000 of the original employees for such reasons as incompetence, inefficiency, lack of adaptability, and misconduct. The quality of operations began to improve thereafter, but Colonel Stanley R. Mickelson, chief of the United States Army's Displaced Persons Division in Germany, nonetheless regarded the organization as "chaotic." Thirty years later Judge Simon Rifkind, who served as the Army's Adviser on Jewish Affairs in Germany in 1945–46, dismissed the UNRRA people as "a bunch of social workers."[6]

The failure of UNRRA to take over as anticipated in May 1945 forced the military to fill the vacuum, a task for which it lacked training. Soldiers know how to fight, to maintain discipline, and to obey orders. If they had knowledge of how to handle Holocaust survivors they generally failed to display it. Although the commanding generals often, but not always, had achieved their positions because of political acumen as well as military skill, as one went down the ranks the level of acuity decreased and the instances of a rigid military outlook increased. These characteristics were present throughout the military-DP involvement.

Before the war ended, SHAEF handbooks detailed the nature of DP care. "Military Government action should stress treatment of Jews equal to that of other citizens of the Reich," an American War Department pamphlet stipulated in 1944. "As a general rule," it continued, "military Government should avoid creating the impression that the Jews are to be singled out for special treatment, as such action will tend to perpetuate the distinction of Nazi racial theory." A SHAEF memo of April 16, 1945, ordered ex-enemy nationals persecuted because of race, religion, or activities on behalf of UN countries to be accorded the same care as UN DPs but this was generally ignored, as were several memorandums in a similar vein that regularly went out to field commanders. This meant that German Jewish concentration camp inmates did not receive the same consideration as others persecuted by the Nazis but were, in fact, treated by Allied soldiers as Germans and thus former enemies. Hungarian and Austrian Jews were handled in the same fashion.

On the other hand, the Army herded Jewish concentration camp survivors of non-enemy states together with non-Jewish DPs, many of whom had been their former guards and tormentors, or with Nazi collaborators, because SHAEF memoranda proclaimed that non-German nationals who cooperated with "the enemy" should be treated as DPs if they did not desire to return to their homelands, even though UNRRA regulations prohibited assistance for those of German, or ex-enemy, nationality. Moreover, the military at first refused welfare organizations the right to minister to the needs of any of the DP camp inmates.[7]

Army officials had little understanding of DP needs and even less sympathy for their desires. So many ill-conceived directives filtered down to those who actually dealt with the displaced persons that several UNRRA workers began to "wonder if anyone around those top-level round tables had ever seen a DP." Within the centers both the military and

UNRRA employed Germans to assist them. To be sure, many of the former concentration camp inmates could not work, but officers made no effort to find DPs whose talents could be used or other persons who would treat the DPs fairly. Hence, in one place a former professor, in charge of distributing clothing to DPs even though everyone but the American military knew he had been a Nazi, refused to give clothes to the DPs on the grounds that returning German POWs would need them. In another DP center, in Rentzschmule, an ex-Nazi supervised the activities of former Jewish concentration camp victims. He paid no attention to their needs, and his charges had to walk 16 miles to the Army base to protest his actions.[8]

Redeployment of forces and reorganization of the military structure led to a continual change in personnel. Army men had no sooner developed some knowledge of DP circumstances when they were transferred and replaced by raw recruits. In one assembly center, military commanders changed six times between May 6 and June 9, 1945. Each new officer reorganized his predecessors' procedures and reallocated UNRRA workers and their responsibilities. Even as late as October, an UNRRA official at Wildflecken complained that

> The "new broom" officers came through camp and made sug-
> gestions that kept us crazy for weeks at a time, undoing past
> work, redoing it in the new way and revamping all reports to fit
> the orders in the sheaves of directives which we had to study at
> night because we still had fifteen thousand people to take care
> of during the day.[9]

Turnover of personnel led not only to confusion but to harassment as well. Military men who preferred order to laxity did not understand that DPs could not be treated as merely another battalion. On one tour of a Polish DP camp, in September 1945, the inspecting generals showed extreme displeasure with what they saw. Like so many other officials they expected the DP centers to be run "with military disci-pline," and were upset with lax management. Immediately after this particular inspection one of the generals promulgated new regulations for the "Concentration Camp at Wildflecken." Obligatory reveille would be at 8 A.M., and, "under surveillance of an armed guard," cleanups would take place. "Malefactors" caught throwing paper in the streets or on the stairways would immediately "be imprisoned without food." A committee representing the 15,000 residents of the compound complained to the UNRRA director that "our camp is occupied more rigorously than were concentration camps during the war or German cities since the peace." DPs were also penned in behind barbed wires and required to obtain passes before leaving the premises. One day an American woman witnessed a particularly painful scene at the Jewish DP Camp in Foehrenwald. Two children wanted to get out but only one had a pass. So he left and then smuggled the pass back to a friend. A German who witnessed the incident reported it to the guards, and both children were imprisoned for two days for their "crime."[10]

Some soldiers protested against the lack of humane treatment given to the DPs. Fifty individual American servicemen signed their names to a letter which they distributed to several American periodicals as well as to every United States congressman and senator. Dated January 13, 1946, it purported to reflect their collective experiences and to reproduce typical orders from army officials. They accused their commanding officers of callous behavior to those housed in the assembly centers and environs, and willful disregard of human decency. Officers, they charged, used DPs as menials and domestics, refused them adequate recreational facilities, and prohibited easy fraternization between the soldiers and the inmates. DPs and GIs could not eat meals together, movie theaters frequently remained off-limits, and even the almost empty buses taking soldiers to church would not carry DPs. American soldiers allegedly responded to the GIs' protests with remarks like, "We are not running a nursery. This is an Army base. We are in charge, and want them to know it." Another American officer allegedly informed a sergeant one day, "Tell them [the DPs] to take the lead out of you know where or some disagreeable changes [will] take place toute de suite." The GIs who signed the letters assured their recipients that

> if this were an isolated instance of the attitude toward and management of Latvian and Lithuanian, Polish and Rumanian,

Yugoslavian, Turkish and Russian DPs, an officer or enlisted man observing the scene might find some assurance in the thought that conditions were better elsewhere. But he knows it is not so; his buddies from every part of the American Zone of Occupation report to the contrary.

One year later an observer wrote in the *Lithuanian Bulletin,* "DPs are treated as rightless slaves in an arbitrary lawlessness."[11]

The exasperated officers may have behaved as they did because of the enormous burdens thrust upon them. Without sufficient preparation, personnel, or supplies, they had to deal immediately with caring for, feeding, clothing, registering, and housing the hundreds of thousands, if not millions, of people, who spoke a wide variety of languages and who had had an incredible number of ghastly experiences. So many people entered the American zone of Germany in May 1945, that the military ordered bridges blown up to cut down on the flow. Many of the wanderers clogged the roads preventing the movement of men and equipment, while others expressed their joy at liberation by pilferage, raping German women, and creating other disturbances. Added to these problems, the Army found itself with a severe personnel shortage and an inadequate and ever-shifting number of forces untrained in social welfare. Faced with such conditions, officials fell back upon the things they knew best: maintenance of law and order and rigid discipline within the more than 500 hastily set up assembly centers.[12]

Not all Army groups functioned in the same manner. The Seventh Army, in Northern Germany, attempted to deal with DPs in a humane fashion. Residents of the assembly centers could come and go at will, disturbances were few, and morale seemed relatively good. In the Third Army in Southern Germany, which contained most of the DPs in the United States zones, General George S. Patton, Jr. insisted that every camp be surrounded by barbed wire and manned by armed guards to watch over the detainees as if they were prisoners. Patton's behavior cannot be attributed solely to crowded conditions and a shortage of soldiers. He wrote in his diary on

September 15, 1945, that others "believe that the Displaced Person is a human being, which he is not, and this applies particularly to the Jews who are lower than animals." When confronted with the issue of treating the DPs as prisoners, he explained that "if they were not kept under guard they would not stay in the camps, would spread over the country like locusts, and would eventually have to be rounded up after quite a few of them had been shot and quite a few Germans murdered and pillaged."[13]

Patton also ignored directives from SHAEF commander General Dwight D. Eisenhower to continue admitting stateless and nonrepatriable individuals to the assembly centers. In July, on his own initiative, he ordered the entire Munich area cleared of DPs not in camps. People were then rounded up and taken against their will to repatriation centers for shipment back to Eastern Europe. The Vatican protested that Croats, Slovenes, Slovaks, and Hungarians might be involuntarily forced back to Communist dominated areas. Tales circulated that American soldiers, in implementing Patton's orders, beat up Polish Jews and then threw them into trucks and trains with sealed cars and shipped them back to Poland. A London newspaper, *The Jewish Chronicle*, reported that American troops, "just like Hitler's S.S.," drove Jews out of their huts and indiscriminately attacked women and children. Members of the local German population aided the GIs, and when the Jews protested "against the Americans allowing Germans to manhandle them, they were told that this was the only way to deal with Jews." One scholar who wrote about Patton's disregard of Eisenhower's order to set up facilities for stateless refugees, noted, "at the same time he was not as severe in his treatment of the German population as required by Army directives."[14]

Fifty-two nationalities, comprising over 1 million people, were represented in over 900 Displaced Persons Assembly Centers run by the Allied Armies, UNRRA, and social service voluntary agencies in Germany, Austria, Italy, France, North Africa, and elsewhere. Perhaps another 300,000 registered DPs chose to live near the assembly centers. Among the DPs, in and out of the camps, were Hungarians, Rumanians, Soviet nationals and dissidents, Greeks, Albanians, and Spanish Republicans unwilling to return to a Spain governed by Franco. DPs mingled with Nazi collaborators, POWs, and ethnic Germans uprooted, or expelled, from Eastern Europe. The Poles numbered anywhere from 270,000 to 800,000 depending on whose count, and which census date, was accepted, and also whether Polish Jews and Ukrainians were included within that total. Neither the 100,000 to 150,000 Ukrainians nor the 50,000 to 100,000 Jews in or out of the assembly centers, regardless of place of birth, chose to identify themselves as "Polish." There were 150,000 Yugoslavs, mostly in UNRRA camps in Italy and Austria, and perhaps 150,000 to 200,000 Balts (Latvians, Estonians, and Lithuanians, in roughly 3:2:1 proportions to the whole, respectively), which rounded out the major groups of DPs. Almost all of the non-Jewish East Europeans refused repatriation because they hated and feared communism, and their own governments had been taken over by the Communists. In addition to the ideological abhorrence, members of each of the groups had their own unique reasons for choosing to remain wards of the Allies.[15]

The Poles constituted a plurality, or about 40 percent of the DPs; 75 percent of these people were farmers and unskilled laborers. Most were brought or came voluntarily into Germany, and then, influenced by officers in General Wladyslaw Anders' London-based Polish Army, accepted the information about the horrendous conditions in a Communist-dominated Poland. Stories about violence and disorder in Poland, advice from their priests, a desire to avoid military service, food shortages, and fear of the harsh winter in their home country also contributed to their reluctance to return. The *Times* of London asserted that the Poles remained in Germany because they believed that they would be less well off in Poland than in the assembly centers, which provided minimal care. A scholarly observer offered another opinion:

> Some of the younger men among the Polish DPs allowed themselves to be persuaded to serve in the German army labor forces, generally under duress and in fear of being sent to concentration camps for "liquidation" if they refused; these men,

too, as well as their families, are frightened to return to Poland lest they be branded as traitors or collaborators.[16]

The Ukrainians, frequently identified as Poles, constituted a second major group. American military forces initially refused to recognize Ukrainian as a separate nationality and classified them as Russians, Poles, Czechs, Rumanians, or "stateless," depending upon their place of birth, residence on September 1, 1939 (the first day of the war), their personal wishes, or the whim of the soldier doing the classification. Many Ukrainians were descendants of Germans who had settled in the Ukraine in the 1760s, and hated the Russians. During World War II they volunteered to work for the Germans and helped massacre Poles and Jews. Afterwards they changed both their names and identification papers to avoid repatriation. Among the occupations one found large numbers of farmers, engineers, and skilled workers.[17]

Over 100,000 Yugoslavs and more than a million Russians also refused repatriation. Many of the Yugoslavs, mostly supporters of King Peter's royalist government, had become "very good Nazis" during the war, one American consulate official observed in 1948, and their friendship with the Germans would, no doubt, have resulted in dire consequences had they returned to Yugoslavia.[18] The Russians were in the same boat, having voluntarily joined forces with the Nazis. According to the Yalta agreement, however, bona fide Russian citizens had to be returned home, willingly, or otherwise. Many of these people, with good reasons, feared death or Russian labor camp assignments, and either committed suicide or unavailingly struggled against forced repatriation.[19]

Many, if not most, of the 150,000 to 200,000 Balts among the DPs had left for Germany voluntarily; some to enrich themselves with better jobs, others to flee the oncoming Russians in 1944. In 1940 the Russians had taken over Latvia, Estonia, and Lithuania and deported more than 60,000 persons to the East. The Russians were particularly brutal with the elites of these countries. The Germans assumed control of the Baltic states in 1941, when the Nazi armies invaded Russia, and the Balts seemed truly appreciative. Many Latvians and

Lithuanians had, in fact, signed a petition "to the Führer" in 1939, "to come and rescue [us] from the Bolshevik terror." Large numbers of Balts, especially the Estonians, sympathized with Hitler and his policies. And, in turn, they received better treatment than several other foreign groups living in Germany under the Third Reich. During the war the Germans had welcomed back to their country kinsmen whose ancestors had moved deeper into Eastern Europe, some as many as seven centuries earlier. Many had retained the German language and culture. For some, including the Balts, one scholar tells us, "the National Social regime outdid itself in kindness, consideration, and decency." Heinrich Himmler, for example, considered the Estonians racially indistinguishable from the Germans and members of one of the "few races that can, after the segregation of only a few elements, be merged with us without any harm to our people." Significant numbers of the Balts enjoyed living in Germany and sought permanent residence there. An Army report of August 4, 1945, noted that 200,000 of those in DP camps had applied for German citizenship before the war ended. These were people of "German blood who had lived in colonies outside of the Reich and who had voluntarily returned to Germany during the war years and applied for German citizenship." Some of the Balts had also voluntarily joined Hitler's elite guard, the Waffen SS, and, according to one authority, "fought grimly to the end" of the war. Others were conscripted under duress for Nazi service or forced by devious means into the German army. A more poignant explanation came from a former Estonian history professor then living in a DP camp. He wrote:

> War and peace deprived me of my native country, my family, my home, my work and my life. . . . I am now a European outlaw, one of those who, because they are called DPs are forced to live in Germany in the most hateful conditions. For a man willing and capable of rebuilding his life with his own hands it is abhorrent to be forced to eat the bitter bread of UNRRA's charity.[20]

The Balts constituted the gentry among DPs because they were well educated, well groomed, and a generally cultured and sophisticated people. Large numbers enjoyed friendships with Germans. The majority of the Latvians, for example, did not live in the assembly centers but in homes in the nearby towns, where they got on well with their German neighbors. They went to the DP camps daily, though, to pick up their rations. An Americans Friends Service Committee worker in Germany wrote in January 1946, "one of the many surprises of this work has been the type of displaced person whom UNRRA is helping over the winter. Instead of all being victims of Nazi aggression one finds that great numbers of the Baltics, Poles, Ukranians [sic], Hungarians, Czechs, and Yugoslavs came here because of the occupation of their homelands by the Russian armies. . . . Instead of great animosity between the DPs and the native German population one frequently finds definite friendliness and cooperation."[21]

Camps housing Balts and Ukrainians became the showplaces to which officials brought visitors and whose residents made an excellent impression upon the tourists. Everything in these centers seemed to run like well-oiled machines and the Army won plaudits for its accomplishments. Adjoining their homes one found gardens of gooseberry and raspberry bushes and exquisite landscaping. Viewers praised the floral designs of marigolds, pansies, and begonias displaying the national crests and colors of Latvia, Lithuania, and Estonia. After touring these camps in 1946 the American chargé d'affaires in London reported to the Secretary of State that the Balts would "make excellent settlers." He added: "Morale is good, [the] percentage who work is relatively high, education is well organized, knowledge of skilled crafts is unusually extensive, standard of cleanliness is high; self-government is carried further and seems more efficient than amongst most other groups. There is no doubt that if those who favored Germans could be eliminated, the remainder would make most desirable immigrants." A year and a half later Congressman Frank Chelf of Kentucky, investigating conditions among the DPs, noted in his report that "the great majority of these Balts also were unmistakably intelligent, conscientious, industrious, energetic, and showed every sign of having come from good stock and good breeding."[22]

Other observers were not as favorably impressed. The historian Koppel S. Pinson, who worked as the American Jewish Joint Distribution Committee (JDC) educational director for displaced persons in Germany and Austria from October 1945, through September 1946, wrote that "a large group of Poles, Ukrainians, Russians and Balts, who are not DPs in any real sense at all," resided in the DP assembly centers although they "are just as deserving of trial by the Allies as war criminals as are German Nazis. Among them are some of the bloodiest henchmen of the S.S. and the Gestapo." Ira Hirschmann, Fiorello LaGuardia's personal emissary, on an inspection tour of the DP camps while the former New York City Mayor served as Director General of UNRRA in 1946, also reported that the "hard core" of the non-Jewish DPs "has been proved to be a criminal and Fascist group, many of whom left their countries voluntarily to work for Hitler." A year earlier, in May 1945, an American journalist estimated that 50 percent of the DPs had voluntarily entered Germany during the war years to aid the Nazis. A more recent history of the American occupation of Germany has also charged that "most" of the Balts entered Germany on their own accord and had actually been members of the Nazi party.[23]

The accusations occurred so frequently, and from such a variety of sources, that they cannot be ignored. The accusers included a number of DPs, UNRRA and military personnel, the head of England's National Catholic Welfare Conference in London from 1943 to 1962, a later American Displaced Persons Commissioner, and other historians. Some Jewish writers in *The DP Express,* an assembly center newspaper, thought it "outrageous to the living genuine D.P.'s to know that many a murderer of their kin, of their parents or brothers or sisters had not only escaped punishment, but is also leading a life in many respects better than their own, that he gets the very same advantages and besides, more often than not, enjoys a superior emigration quota. And it is an offense of the memory of the dead." These same writers regretted that so many of the assembly centers "were transformed into regular shelters and unexcelled hiding places for more than one 'veteran' of fascism." "Just ask a Jew from Latvia," an article in *The DP Express* read, "who he dreaded more, the German S.S. or the local nationalists, the answer in most cases will be that the Germans were 'angels' in comparison." Another writer, comparing the German concentration camp guards and the Ukrainian *Polizei*, commented, "It is hard to say who brutalized the prisoners worse." The chief American repatriation officer in Germany noted on September 12, 1945, after having toured the UNRRA DP camps, that "almost all these Ukrainians were collaborating with the Germans or served in the so called Vlasov Army fighting against Russia." The following month Drew Middleton wrote in *The New York Times* that at least one-third of the Balts in the DP camps had been collaborators. Most of them spoke English and therefore made a good impression upon the American Military Government personnel, "many of whom are only too willing to believe their anti-Russian propaganda." Even where Army officials readily acknowledged the presence of dubious "displaced persons," a spokesman announced that the "United Nations still were pledged to feed the Balts and Poles who do not want to go home even though they have been found to be pro-Nazi." "It is easy to forget," one Army colonel wrote to his wife, that most of the Balts "came to Germany voluntarily and worked to help feed and clothe the people who were shooting us and the people who were making the shells and equipment being used against us."[24]

The most savage attack on these DPs came from Abraham G. Duker, who based his analysis on a careful study of the Nuremberg trial materials. Dr. Duker had worked as a member of the American team headed by U.S. Supreme Court Justice Robert Jackson at Nuremberg after the war and he claimed to have examined hundreds, if not thousands, of original German documents. He pointed out that "many . . . Estonians, Latvians, and Lithuanians, in conjunction with Ukrainians and Croats, were especially egregious collaborationists." During World War II, Duker continued, in hundreds of towns and villages, "it is the Ukrainians who guided the SS men, searched the ghettos, beat the people, assembled and drove them to the places of slaughter." Many had been assigned to the concentration camps as "guards and tormentors," where they brutalized the inmates.[25]

The last significant group of DPs, the Jews, had lost more from the war than any of the others and no one accused them of having collaborated with Hitler. Nazi barbarism had practically decimated Europe's Jewish population. Of 500,000 Jews in Germany in 1933, only 30,000 could be found in 1949; of 3 million Jews in Poland in 1939, only 100,000 or so remained ten years later. At first the 50,000 to 100,000 Jewish DPs constituted only 5 to 8 percent of the DP population. During the next two years their numbers increased. Some came out of hiding; many who had returned to their former homes in Eastern Europe found life intolerable there and returned to Germany. More than 150,000 Polish Jews had fled to Russia when the Nazis advanced in 1939. They were released in 1946 and a majority made their way either to Palestine or to the DP assembly center in Central Europe.[26]

Those who had lived in Russia had not been treated differently than citizens of the country but the survivors of the concentration camps looked like the living dead. Those who did not die shortly after release revealed their extreme psychological trauma in almost everything they did. They could not concentrate, they rambled when they spoke and stopped in midsentence without explanation, they angered quickly and often over minor or misunderstood words or actions.[27]

An American Jewish chaplain "found no one" in the military "genuinely and basically sympathetic" to their needs. "From top to bottom," he wrote, their problems were "just one grand nuisance, so far as the Army is concerned." The military disliked having to deal with DPs and some soldiers carried their antisemitic prejudices with them to Europe. One American Army officer gratuitously told a survivor in Vienna, "The lowest thing in my country are [sic] the Negroes and the next lowest are the Jews. . . . We allow them to live but we don't like them."[28]

The soldier's prejudices accurately reflected the views of a considerable number of Americans but it in no way compared

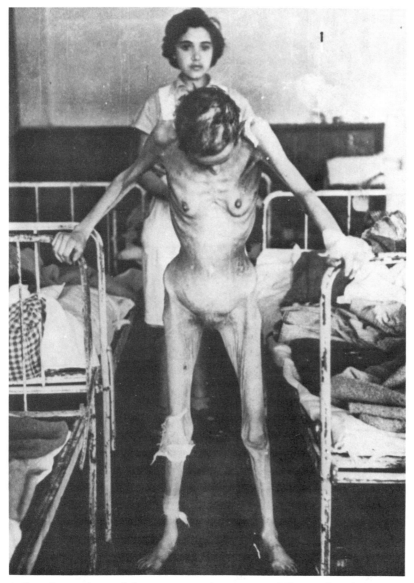

A female survivor of the concentration camps. (The National Archives)

Intolerable filth surrounds patients in "hospital" at Buchenwald concentration camp near Weimar. Disease, malnutrition above all, plus incessant torture, resulted in approximately 200 deaths a day. (Signal Corps photograph from file of Fleur Fenton. Courtesy Harry S. Truman Library)

to the bestiality of the Nazis who slaughtered millions and who forced most of them to live through unspeakable tortures before murdering them. Examples of inhumane and perverse conduct abound. A physician remembered that 36,000 people had entered Auschwitz concentration camp on the night that she arrived. Within a day, 34,000 of them had been killed. The guards in the camp demonstrated their sadistic perversity in numerous ways. The physician saw them force all of the women to strip—and then they whipped those with particularly beautiful bodies. Sometimes the Germans exhumed and burned corpses, then crushed the bones with machines and used them for fertilizer. In some camps Germans scalped Jews. Seven thousand kilos of hair were found in a warehouse after the war. Other sadistic Nazis hung people on meathooks and left them to die. They first pushed their victims through 4- by 4-foot holes to a 15-foot drop on cement floors, tying nooses around the necks of the survivors and hanging them on hooks until they expired. If any were still living after a while their skulls were cracked with a mallet. Some Jewish children were put to labor in forests while Germans shot at them for sport or hunted them with dogs. In the Mauthausen concentration camp in Austria, the German commandant allowed his 11-year-old son to amuse himself by shooting inmates with a rifle from the porch of the main administration building. An Army report detailed another method of annihilation in the same place:

> No one in Mauthausen camp who was guilty of a disciplinary offence was to be allowed to die in a natural manner. For killing these people special bloodhounds had been trained. Three of those hounds were let loose on each victim and tore him to pieces. The mutilated bodies were laid out in front of the row of prisoners during roll-call to act as a deterrent.

One man who survived had deep scars on his legs from having been shackled to his oven for 18 months so that he could cook for SS troups. Another recalled having been forced to throw his parents into an incinerator, while a third saw his six-year-old daughter tossed into the crematorium and his wife sold for six kilos of sugar. A fourth wrote:

> Crying children and babies were seized by the S.S. and their
> heads bashed against the lorry, or sometimes taken by one foot,
> like poultry, the head hanging down, and killed by a blow with
> a club. The sight of these weeping children, with their tear-
> stained cheeks even more rosy in the summer sun, slaughtered
> or stunned on the spot, like ducks, broke my heart.[29]

Sixty thousand Jews, mostly single survivors of exterminated
families, walked out of the concentration camps. Within a week
more than 20,000 of them had died. Three-quarters of the
remainder were "physical and mental wrecks. With swollen
feet, gloomy eyes, no teeth and dry hair they present[ed] a
gloomy picture."[30]

Allied authorities officially opposed religious discrimination
and assured these survivors that they would be treated in
exactly the same fashion as others of their nationality. Hence
the German Jews were regarded as former enemies. However,
since Hitler had already singled out the Jews for special
attention and had annihilated over 6 million of them, "equal"
care for survivors translated itself into callousness; the Jews
needed more than the others. But the British feared that any
special consideration for Jews might imply that they had some
particular rights that other DPs did not possess, and this in
turn would give them an extra reason for being admitted to
Palestine, which His Majesty's Government (HMG) did not
sanction. The Americans also saw no reason to provide for the
unique needs of the surviving remnant. "I can assure you," the
European theater commander, Dwight D. Eisenhower, cabled
Secretary of War Henry L. Stimson, on August 10, 1945, "that
this headquarters makes no differentiation in treatment of
displaced persons."[31]

The fact that "no distinction is made between persons, mostly
Jewish, who have long years of concentration camp experience
and D.P.'s of other countries who have been working, for
instance, in Germany," aroused comment at an American
Friends Service Committee meeting later that summer. "Army
officials admit that the former group [the Jews] needs special

Inmates of Amphing concentration camp, liberated by Third Army troops. Out of the camp's 4,500 prisoners, 2,500 died of starvation. The bodies were piled six high in a ditch and covered over with dirt. (From file of Fleur Fenton. U.S. Army photograph. Courtesy Harry S. Truman Library)

This 23-year-old Czech victim of dysentery in Nazi camp at Flossen-
burg, Germany, was found by the 97th Division of the U.S. Army.
May 4, 1945. (U.S. Army photograph)

Concentration camp survivors. (The National Archives)

care . . . but at the moment this cannot be given," a summary of the meeting's minutes indicated. The minutes noted as well that "as long ago as June 20 SHAEF urged special camps for the non-repatriables or those whose repatriation is likely to be deferred, but the army officials in charge of D.P.'s have not set this up." The policy of nondiscrimination on religious grounds was carried to such absurd lengths that German Jews released from concentration camps in Poland and Czechoslovakia were denied ration cards on the grounds that they were "German" and not entitled to any consideration. Austrian Jews received no help from UNRRA because they were not citizens of UN nations while the Austrian government refused aid to Jews because they had only been racially, and not politically, persecuted. The British, on the other hand, rounded up Austrian Jews from the Buchenwald concentration camp and placed

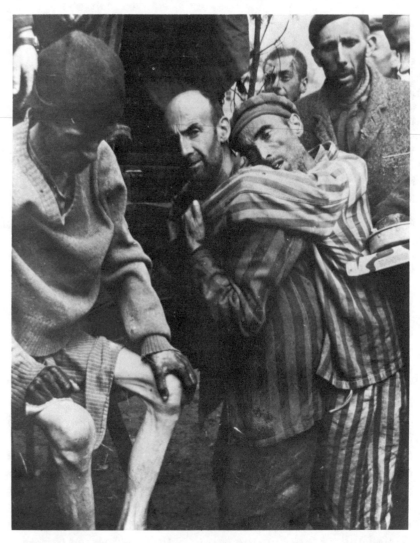

Former prisoners of the Germans being taken to a hospital for much needed medical attention after being starved nearly to death. (U.S. Army photograph. Courtesy of the Harry S. Truman Library)

those able to work in labor battalions, "along with non-perse-cuted enemy and ex-enemy nationals."[32]

The released German Jews who did not regard themselves as "stateless" were turned over to German civilian authorities for care while the others, as well as the East Europeans not forcibly repatriated, were kept in or near the same concentration camps, often housed with their former guards who now claimed displaced persons status, and given about the same quantity of food—bread and watery soup or coffee—as they had received before the war ended. "It is unbelievable," Chaim Finkelstein, the head of the World Jewish Congress' Displaced Persons division in New York, wrote to a colleague in London. "The German murderers, the ones who have strangled [and] . . . burned our brothers, will come to live in the place of their crimes, where there are still a few thousand of their victims [sic]. And this is called the triumph of humanity and civilisation."[33]

Some of the survivors of the camps along with other displaced persons who appeared on the scene went to hastily put up assembly centers. In Landsberg, 6,200 Jews were confined to an area which the Allies had rejected as unfit for German prisoners of war. In Turkheim 450 Jews remained behind the double barbed wire fence which still retained "the deadly electrical apparatus." Supplies and amenities were almost non-existent. DPs lacked shoes, underwear, handkerchiefs, toilet paper, and toothbrushes. In one camp for 500 women there were only five or six combs, no nail files, and "no sanitary supplies for the girls, and no means of obtaining them here."[34]

To top it all off, the Allies put Germans—ex-Nazis—in charge of the DP camps while the inmates were held as virtual prisoners with armed guards surrounding the centers. Even Dachau, a camp whose name symbolized the most barbarous activities, lacked Jewish representatives on the newly formed internal camp committee because the authorities did not recognize religious divisions. Requests made by Jewish social agencies for permission to enter the camps to minister to the survivors were routinely turned down. One historian wrote that, "the Army tended to see in any civilian intrusion, an unwelcome complication in a situation that was already difficult enough."[35]

Word about the nature of the assembly centers reached government officials quickly. Jewish leader Chaim Weizmann complained to British Prime Minister Winston Churchill that "the position of the Jews in liberated countries is desperate," but the American ambassador in England, John G. Winant, discounted the general allegations about the DP camps being badly run because the war had been over only two weeks and operations had not had time to solidify. American Jews did not share the ambassador's equanimity. As early as April a Jewish chaplain wrote that Jewish welfare organizations ought to get in to help the survivors as quickly as possible. An American Army captain collected and sent about one hundred letters from a Jewish group in Theresienstadt, Czechoslovakia, to the National Council of Jewish Women in the United States to forward to the relatives of these Europeans because military policies prohibited mail to and from persons in the assembly centers. Letters also went out from others about the treatment of Jewish survivors.[36]

The rumblings greatly disturbed several American Jewish leaders who were concerned about saving the remnants of European Jewry. Thousands of Jews in the United States felt themselves morally bound to lead and finance the work of rehabilitation and resettlement of the Holocaust survivors. The continued maltreatment of their coreligionists in the assembly centers enraged them. Knowledgeable about the ways of getting governmental action, the leaders of organized Jewry mobilized their forces. Congressman Emanuel Celler gathered together other Jewish members of the House of Representatives and they collectively protested to the War Department. So, too, did several leading American Jewish organizations. In addition, two prominent members of the World Jewish Congress, Rabbi Stephen S. Wise and Nahum Goldman, contacted George Warren, the State Department's adviser on refugees and displaced persons, requesting that "urgent attention" be given to the disturbing reports about conditions in the German camps. At about the same time Henry Morgenthau, Jr., Secretary of the Treasury, approached President Harry S. Truman with the suggestion that a Cabinet-level committee be established to deal with the problem of the displaced persons; but Truman thought little of the idea and rejected the proposal.[37]

Undaunted, Morgenthau contacted the State Department about the stories that he had heard and urged an immediate investigation. He recommended that the State Department appoint Earl G. Harrison, formerly United States Commissioner of Immigration and then both dean of the University of Pennsylvania Law School and the American representative to the Intergovernmental Committee on Refugees (IGC), to conduct the inquiry. Joseph C. Grew, the acting Secretary of State, pursued the subject further. He asked George Warren to meet with Harrison and John Pehle, a close associate of Morgenthau's who also presided over the War Refugee Board, to discuss the matter.[38]

Pehle proved ideally suited for this task. As head of the WRB, he could discuss the enormous pressure that had been brought to bear upon that agency from the Zionists to investigate conditions in the assembly centers. He also detailed the difference between Morgenthau's main concern—the needs and treatment of the displaced persons—and that of the Zionist groups who focused primarily on the issue of the Jewish survivors being allowed to enter Palestine, which, they claimed, had been promised to them in the British Balfour Declaration in 1917. This distinction, between those Jews in the United States who wanted to help their coreligionists return to a normal life somewhere and the Zionists, was blurred among government officials and almost all non-Jews except those who were either involved with the various Jewish organizations, or who had studied the situation carefully. A misunderstanding of these distinctions would continue for years in the minds of the public, the military, and the politicians, and would lead to considerable problems. Pehle, however, thought that his analysis could be digested by Warren and Harrison, two men whose work necessitated a keen awareness of the divisions within the immigrant and refugee populations.[39]

The explanation, combined with Morgenthau's appeal to

Grew, as well as the political necessity of responding in some fashion to the representative spokesmen of the nation's Jewish constituents, resulted in action. The acting Secretary of State contacted Truman and informed him that the Department was sending Harrison to survey the conditions of the displaced persons, "particularly the Jews," in Europe. "Mr. Harrison has also been directed to determine in general the views of the refugees with respect to their future destinations," he wrote. The note added that Harrison's mission had been approved by SHAEF and that "an expression of your interest will facilitate the mission and reassure interested groups concerned with the future of the refugees that positive measures are being undertaken on their behalf. Attached is a letter for your signature addressed to Mr. Harrison expressing such interest." Truman accepted the suggestion and signed the letter.[40]

The President may not have been interested in establishing a Cabinet committee to examine DP problems in May but he certainly did not desire to have the abuses of the past continued by American military personnel. A basically decent man, Truman wanted all of the war's survivors dealt with in as humane a manner as possible under the trying conditions that existed in Europe at that time.

It is also probable that domestic political considerations at home motivated the President's decision to endorse the letter authorizing Harrison's investigation. Truman had no sooner taken over after Roosevelt's death, on April 12, 1945, when Zionist spokesmen alerted him to their goal of obtaining a Jewish homeland in Palestine and their desire that he help surviving European Jews get there as quickly as possible. He discovered, as well, that many individual Jews possessed considerable influence with David K. Niles, Roosevelt's adviser on minority affairs, whom Truman invited to remain in the White House, as well as with several of the more important elected and appointed officials.[41]

The so-called Jewish lobby did not really exist until after World War II began. Then, when the horrible news about the extermination of European Jewry reached American shores, the Zionists organized an overwhelming majority of their coreligionists in the United States who, in 1943, united behind the goal of a Jewish homeland in Palestine. The inclusion of a plank endorsing this view in both the Republican and Democratic national platforms in 1944 probably indicated a sympathetic reaction to the plight of European Jewry as well as an acknowledgment of the Zionists as a potent political force. Despite Republican support, however, the Jews had a much greater attachment to the liberalism of Franklin Roosevelt and in 1944 more than 90 percent of those Jews who voted marked their ballots for the President.[42]

Such political loyalty to the Democratic Party alone warranted presidential recognition of Jewish concerns, but Truman also knew of their large cash contributions to national, state, and local candidates, as well as their significance in close elections. Jews, in turn, believed that their financial assistance entitled them to be heard seriously at the highest levels of government. Moreover, Jews also voted in much greater proportion than their 3 percent of the population might indicate, especially in Democratic primaries, and in four or five states, and on key issues—such as Palestine—they could count on the backing of 75 to 90 percent of their coreligionists. A cohesive and politically conscious segment of the American voting public, Jews provided the margin of victory in states like New York and Illinois, and occasionally in Pennsylvania and Ohio as well. Wealthy Jews also made donations to "friendly" candidates both within and outside of their own communities, and many congressmen and senators throughout the country depended on these funds to conduct election campaigns. Several Jews, whose names few people would have recognized, made sizable contributions to politicians in states as remote from New York as Iowa, Oklahoma, Arizona, and Oregon. Bernard Baruch in the East helped line the coffers of Democrats as far away as Pat McCarran in Nevada. Though these funds did not "purchase" votes or tip officials against their constituents' wishes, they often ensured access to congressmen and senators. Finally, despite the pervasiveness of antisemitism in the United States, no large-scale anti-Jewish political force existed. Hence Truman could attempt to please the Jews without serious adverse consequences.[43]

Thus the appointment of Harrison seemed justified by both political and humanitarian considerations. The establishment of the mission to examine conditions in the DP camps demonstrated the President's concern and indicated as well that the administration recognized the need for responding positively to representatives of organized Jewry. Then, during a summer in which most Americans celebrated the war's end, Harrison and his associates toured the DP camps to check the veracity of the accumulated tales and rumors about life among the survivors. It took only three weeks to discover that the unsubstantiated accounts were in fact understatements of the truth.

2

THE HARRISON REPORT—
AND AFTER

THE HARRISON REPORT hit the leaders at the highest level in Washington like a bombshell and led to a scurry of activity for change. At the outset no one would have believed that the findings of the investigators would be as devastating as they turned out. But Harrison and his entourage uncovered conditions within the DP camps that only the most heartless and indifferent bureaucrat could have ignored. In fact, none of the responsible political and military officials who read about them failed to implement changes. Ultimately, the Harrison report affected American diplomatic relations with Great Britain and led to the movement for ameliorative legislation by Congress. Its immediate impact, though, resulted in the reorganization of the assembly centers, the appointment of a special adviser for the Jewish DPs, and a renewed plea by President Truman for the British to open the gates of Palestine to the survivors.

Harrison left for Europe in early July with Dr. Joseph J. Schwartz of the American Jewish Joint Distribution Committee (JDC), Patrick M. Malin, Vice-Director of the IGC, and Herbert Katzski of the War Refugee Board. The State Department informed its European ambassadors of the mission and Secretary Morgenthau sent out several letters to Treasury representatives in London and on the continent introducing Harrison, "who is on a special mission to Europe to ascertain the facts in regard to displaced persons, particularly Jews."[1] With this kind of endorsement Harrison and his fellows had no difficulty in seeing and doing whatever they chose. They visited about thirty DP camps, often in separate groups, and because the military officials had no qualms about their policies and procedures, observed existing conditions. What they saw and heard outraged them. They found 14,000 DPs at Wildflecken under heavy guard, Jews in Celle living in horse stalls, and 14,000 DPs still in the old concentration camp buildings in Bergen-Belsen. The crematorium had been burned down but "all the rest of Belsen remains much as the Nazis left it." Several military officials with whom they spoke expressed the view that "maybe Hitler had something with reference to the Jews."[2]

Interim impressions went back to Washington and on August 24 the final document reached the President. Divided into five sections and typed on ten legal sized pages it stated:

> Many Jewish displaced persons and other possibly non-repatriables are living under guard behind barbed-wire fences, in camps of several descriptions (built by the Germans for slave-laborers and Jews), including some of the most notorious of the concentration camps, amidst crowded, frequently unsanitary and generally grim conditions, in complete idleness, with no opportunity, except surreptitiously, to communicate with the outside world, waiting, hoping for some word of encouragement and action in their behalf.

The document detailed the inadequacy of housing, medical, and recreational facilities, and pointed out the lack of any efforts to rehabilitate the internees. Although some camp commandants obtained clothing "of one kind or another for their charges, many of the Jewish displaced persons, late in July, had no clothing other than their concentration camp garb—a rather hideous striped pajama effect—while others, to their chagrin, were obliged to wear German S.S. uniforms. It is questionable which clothing they hate the more."

Another observation noted that "the most absorbing worry of these Nazi and war victims concerns relatives—wives, husbands, parents, children. Most of them had been separated for three, four or five years and they cannot understand why the liberators should not have undertaken immediately the organized effort to re-unite family groups." In places where "infor-

mation has been received as to relatives living in other camps in Germany, it depends on the personal attitude and disposition of the Camp Commandant whether permission can be obtained or assistance received to follow up on the information."
Harrison also

raise[d] the question as to how much longer many of these people, particularly those who have over such a long period felt persecution and near starvation, can survive on a diet composed principally of bread and coffee, irrespective of the calorie content. In many camps, the 2,000 calories included 1,250 calories of a black, wet and extremely unappetizing bread. I received the distinct impression and considerable substantiating information that large numbers of the German population—again principally in the rural areas—have a more varied and palatable diet than is the case with the displaced persons.

Meal at DP camp at Landeck Area, Austria. The girl with the pot is drawing rations for her entire family of five. (U.S. Army photograph)

The section of the report labeled "Needs of the Jews" estimated that the "top figure" of Polish, Hungarian, Rumanian, German, and Austrian Jews probably did not exceed 100,000 while "some informed persons" thought the total was "considerably smaller." Harrison believed that "the first and plainest need of these people is a recognition of their actual status and by this I mean their status as Jews." Their present conditions were "far worse than that of other groups." They had been more severely victimized and came out in much weaker conditions than other survivors. "Refusal to recognize the Jews as such has the effect, in this situation, of closing one's eyes to their former and more barbaric persecution, which has already made them a separate group with greater needs."

Most Jews wanted to "be evacuated to Palestine now, just as other national groups are being repatriated to their homes." They did not want to wait in Germany for this to happen. Only in Palestine, they believed, could Jews have an equal opportunity to start life anew. A small percentage of the DP Jews had friends or relatives in Great Britain or the United States and chose those countries as suitable future homes. Therefore, Harrison emphasized, there was "great need" for "prompt development of a plan to get out of Germany and Austria as many as possible of those who wish it."

In section 3 of the report, Harrison exposed the deficient care that had already been given. "Relatively little beyond the planning stage has been done . . . to meet the special needs of the formerly persecuted groups," he stated. Several camp commandants seemed reluctant to use UNRRA personnel, while UNRRA, on its part, sent inadequate staff members to work under the military. Lack of coordination between UNRRA and the army meant that good proposals submitted by knowledgeable voluntary agencies were ignored. "The military authorities," Harrison continued, "have shown considerable resistance to the entrance of voluntary agency representatives, no matter how qualified they might be to help meet existing needs of displaced persons."

In his fourth section, "Conclusions and Recommendations," Harrison advised that Jews should receive the "first and not last attention." They should be evacuated from Germany as quickly as possible and allowed to enter the Holy Land. Harrison recommended modification of Britain's 1939 White Paper which restricted Jewish immigration to the Middle East. The United States should also permit "reasonable numbers" of the DPs into the country although the total of those who wanted to cross the Atlantic was "not large."

The denunciation of the American occupying forces could not have been more scathing. "As matters now stand," Harrison wrote, "we appear to be treating the Jews as the Nazis treated them except that we do not exterminate them. They are in concentration camps in large numbers under our military guard instead of S.S. Troops. One is led to wonder whether the German people, seeing this, are not supposing that we are following or at least condoning Nazi policy." Jewish DPs "have found it difficult to obtain audiences with military government authorities because ironically they have been obliged to go through German employees who have not facilitated matters." Harrison also commented on the enforced idleness of the DPs, whose skills were not utilized by the military. He denounced "the continuance of barbed-wire fences, armed guards, and prohibition against leaving the camps except by passes," and the quality of military personnel who "are manifestly unsuited for the longer-term job of working in a camp" with DPs.

In an especially revealing paragraph, the report uncovered the crux of the problem:

> At many places . . . the military government officers manifest the utmost reluctance or indisposition, if not timidity, about inconveniencing the German population. They even say that their job is to get communities working properly and soundly again, that they must "live with the Germans while the dps . . . are a more temporary problem." Thus . . . if a group of Jews are ordered to vacate their temporary quarters, needed for military purposes, and there are two possible sites, one a block of flats (modest apartments) with conveniences and the other a series of shabby buildings with outside toilet and washing facilities, the burgermeister readily succeeds in persuading the Town Major to allot the latter to the displaced persons and to save the former for returning German civilians.

To lessen the devastating revelations of the report, Harrison then threw in a few concluding words of praise for the military. He expressed admiration for its handling of the 4 million persons who had already been repatriated and noted that some individual soldiers were working well with the DPs and helping them adjust to their new status. But in his final paragraph he reiterated the point that all nonrepatriable Jews should be moved: "It is inhuman to ask people to continue to live for any length of time under their present conditions."[3]

Some of the findings of the investigation reached Washington even before Harrison left Europe. On July 28, 1945, he sent a telegram from Zurich to the Secretary of State: "In general found complete confirmation of disturbing reports concerning Jews in SHAEF Zone of Germany." The details followed and the words spread. Fred Vinson, who succeeded Morgenthau as Secretary of the Treasury in early July, received the essentials of Harrison's report by August 1 and wrote to Joseph Grew at the State Department about them. "Matter is urgent from United States point of view," an August 3 British Foreign Office cable read, as "high level pressure has been brought to bear on State and War Departments." Although the President did not receive the final version officially until August 24, two dispatches preceeded the document and the War Department summarized their contents in an August 4 message to General Eisenhower in Europe. Furthermore, Secretary of War Henry L. Stimson declared, "I want to emphasize the importance we attach to this problem and request that everything possible be done to improve present situation."[4]

Eisenhower answered with alacrity albeit angrily. "The tenor of that report," he wrote to Stimson, "is completely different to that submitted verbally by Mister Harrison to this headquarters." But he did admit, just as Harrison had indicated, "that this headquarters makes no differentiation in treatment of displaced persons." Moreover, he executed a rapid turnabout. The Commanding General issued a series of directives aimed at improving an extraordinarily difficult problem. Subordinates were told to segregate Jewish refugees, requisition housing for them even if it meant displacing Germans, increase their daily rations to 2,500 calories, twice that of German civilians, give DPs priority in employment over Germans, treat German Jews as UNDPs, set up a tracing bureau to help reunite families, provide facilities for recreation and rehabilitation, and cooperate with voluntary agencies and officials. In addition he ordered frequent inspections to see that his commands were being carried out. After Truman wrote to Eisenhower about the Harrison report, on August 31, 1945, the General responded honestly, but defensively:

> When it is realized that the Army in this area has been faced with the most difficult types of redeployment problems; has had to preserve law and order; furnish a multitude of services for itself and the thousands of people it employs, and on top of this has had this question of displaced persons with unusual demands upon transportation, housing, fuel, food, medical care and security, you can well understand that there have been undeniable instances of inefficiency. Commanders of all grades are engaged in seeking these out and I am confident that if you could compare conditions now with what they were three months ago, you would realize that your Army here has done an admirable and almost unbelievable job in this respect.

Eisenhower did not slacken the pace of his efforts once the letter went out to Truman. He continued zealously striving to improve the difficult lot of the DPs. One Army colonel admitted to some journalists that as a result of the Harrison report "the heat" had been turned on and he had been getting orders fired at him so fast that he had been unable to keep up with them.[5]

The SHAEF commander also requested that an adviser for Jewish affairs be added to his staff. Although Eisenhower had at first opposed the idea, the impact of the War Department cables altered his judgment and immediately he temporarily detailed Chaplain (Major) Judah P. Nadich to the position. The General suggested to Stimson, though, "that if the War Department should like to choose some broadgauge Jewish representative to serve here as an investigator and advisor to me he will be acceptable and we will facilitate his work." This offer coincided with the views that five major Jewish organizations*

* American Jewish Conference, American Jewish Committee, American Jewish Joint Distribution Committee, Jewish Agency for Palestine, and World Jewish Congress.

had been presenting to the Departments of State and War
since May. Jacob Blaustein of the American Jewish Committee
(AJC) had discussed with the Acting Secretary of State, Joseph
Grew, the need for a Jewish liaison officer to advise the Army
of problems relating to Jewish DPs. The adviser, it was suggested, might stand as a buffer between the DPs and the
military and could serve as a conduit for reports and complaints
between both sides. At first Grew took the matter under
advisement. After receipt of the Harrison report at the end of
July, however, politically astute government officials embraced
the suggestion and made the appointment. The Jewish organizations were required to pay the adviser who, technically,
would serve under the auspices of UNRRA. Through the
influence, and recommendation, of the AJC, Judge Simon
Rifkind of New York received the position.[6]

Eisenhower, and his successor, General Joseph T. McNarney,
who took over as SHAEF Commander in November 1945,
showed Rifkind every courtesy. In his introductory note to the
Judge, General Eisenhower referred to him as "my Personal
Advisor" and indicated that he was to have whatever assistance
he needed in personnel and transport. The General also stated:

> I am particularly anxious that wherever you discover errors in
> detail of execution of approved policies, you bring the matter,
> on the spot, to the attention of the responsible person, and at
> the earliest possible moment report the matter to the appropriate
> District Commander. I assure you that District Commanders will
> welcome consultation with you at any time.[7]

Eisenhower's orders had the desired effect in some quarters.
By the fall there were separate assembly centers for Jews, Poles,
and Balts in the American zone. An American brigadier general
in Austria reported that "all of the Jewish" refugees were
comfortably housed in well-established hotels and apartment
houses "including some of the finest hotels in such famous
resorts as Bad Gastein." In Landsberg, the largest DP camp in
Bavaria, with a population of about 5,500, the Joint was actively
participating in camp administration, while in Feldafing, another assembly center for about 4,000 DPs, the Harrison report

and the Eisenhower visit resulted in the addition of 30 new houses with family accommodations, a new 1,000 bed hospital, and expanded cultural and welfare programs. Harvey D. Gibson, president of the Manufacturers Trust Company, surveyed seven camps at Eisenhower's request in September and October, and returned to the United States to proclaim that "the Army has done a fine job" and "all should be satisfied with present conditions." British officials, who refused to alter their policy against recognizing the Jews as a separate national group, also noted the change. "The Americans take very great trouble with all Jewish refugees," the UK political representatives in Vienna informed the Foreign Office in March, 1946, "and woe betide any U.S. officer who leaves himself open to a complaint." Thirty years later a historian wrote how the Harrison report prodded the military to act with the result, among other things, that the JDC "for all practical purposes, was put in charge of the Jews in the United States zones."[8]

But other commentators stressed those aspects of DP life which remained unchanged. Rabbi Judah Nadich toured the assembly centers and discovered that "many of General Eisenhower's policies were pigeon-holed and, in some instances, deliberately overlooked by commanders in the field." In the Third Army area, under General Patton's command, Jews escaping from Poland were not being accepted into the DP camps but non-Jewish Poles were. General Eisenhower and his deputy, General Walter Bedell Smith, found themselves constantly reminding Patton to treat the DPs decently. Patton believed, however, that the "Jewish type of DP is, in the majority of cases, a sub-human species without any of the cultural or social refinements of our time." While inspecting a DP camp with Eisenhower, on September 17, 1945, Patton told his superior about how he intended to utilize a nearby deserted German village: "I'm planning to make it into a concentration camp for these goddamn Jews."[9]

Patton's comments may have been more extreme than those of his associates but his values and attitudes coincided with those of other American military officials; he only expressed them more openly. His biographer, Martin Blumenson, wrote that the General "simply reflected a parochial interpretation of the non-American world, a vision that was middle-American, populist, and the essence of Babbittry and conformity, where anyone who was different was undoubtedly bad. . . . He shared whatever endemic anti-Semitism existed in America, in the U.S. army, and among the rich and fashionable." In the American Army, where 99 percent of the officers, between 1910 and 1950, were native born, 88 percent were Protestant, and an overwhelming majority came from small-town or rural America and were of British or German stock, it is not surprising that there was a similarity of outlook and belief. It is also understandable why many of those trained to obey orders and uphold traditions also internalized the antisemitic attitudes prevalent in the United States during their lifetime.[10]

With such views pervasive in the Army, some subordinate officers showed little inclination to improve the lot of Jewish DPs. One general refused to sanction more spacious housing accommodations for DPs as long as thirty-six square feet of building floor, the minimum required for soldiers in barracks, existed in the assembly centers. But the room layout in the DP assembly centers made it impossible to adhere to this rule and still separate the sexes or give adequate privacy to families. Major Irving Heymont, the Landsberg military commander, wrote to his wife that "the present population and space ratio figures seem to be derived from an Ouija board." He also believed "that if the Army really wants to give the Jewish DP accommodations equal to those of the Germans, they should abolish the DP camps and move the Germans into the barracks and the DPs into private dwellings." A journalist who toured Germany in October and November acknowledged that the quality of the food had improved, that guards had disappeared from the gates, and that the residents could come and go at will, but he also likened each person's quarters to "the width of a coffin," contrasted the real beds and real linens of the Germans to the straw mattresses of the DPs, and concluded that "to compare the living conditions inside the camps with those of average Germans living in towns is to make a mockery of the word *priority.*" Six months later an UNRRA report read:

> Insofar as it has affected and continued to effect the D.P. situation, we can state authoritatively that the U.S. military establishment has broken down completely. The directives of General Eisenhower have not been and are not being properly implemented in the field. The majority of officials are woefully ignorant of the problem and the few officers remaining who have knowledge of, and sympathy for, it are unable to make their influence felt at the troop level.[11]

In short, many military officials failed to adhere to the spirit, as well as the letter, of the Eisenhower directives. In part, they abdicated responsibility by employing Germans to assist them in some of the most sensitive areas of concern, thereby aggravating the DP problem. As early as October 18, 1945, General Lucius D. Clay hoped that German police would be armed and able to assist the occupying forces in handling DPs by the end of December. Clay expressed the opinion that the DPs "must obey German laws, and that it is only through aid of an efficient German police force that the small occupation Army can control Germany." Armed German police, along with "disaffected Poles and Yugoslavs," many of whom were acknowledged antisemites, patrolled the assembly centers. The German police were said to have been "brutal" with the DPs, breaking into their homes on pretexts, and "always" being more severe with them than with arrested Germans. "In almost every instance" of a DP being arrested, "the German police aggravated the situation by beating up the culprit and claiming that the individual resisted arrest or insulted the officer." The worse incident occurred at Stuttgart on March 29, 1946, when 200 armed German policemen, accompanied by their dogs and a few noncommissioned MPs, raided a Jewish assembly center in search of black market goods. They killed one DP, a concentration camp survivor who had recently been reunited with his wife and two children, and wounded three others. The adverse publicity created by this incident resulted, on April 4, in General McNarney's suspending the right of German police to enter the DP enclaves, and he removed the DPs from German jurisdiction.[12]

The black market was well-nigh universal in the European postwar economy, both inside and outside of the camps, and keeping German officials beyond the borders of DP centers in no way altered that fact. To be sure, there were widely exaggerated stories concocted about DP black marketeering which resulted in the military, self-righteously and periodically, raiding the assembly centers, often in the middle of the night, to search for contraband. Cigarettes served as the customary medium of exchange in the black market and most of the illegal trades involved bartering them for meat, butter, fresh eggs, milk, toilet articles, sheets, pillowcases, clothes, and books. A British social worker thought that "the ceaseless quest for extra food and clothes . . . was inextricably mixed with the effort to maintain something better than the mere existence which was all the official rations would have sustained." As a result of these activities, the DPs, especially the Jews, developed a reputation for notorious profiteering. The American Army turned out to have a large number of participants. The head of the military police detail in Landsberg, who was charged with controlling black market activities, sold dollars illegally to DPs. In November 1945, *Stars and Stripes* reported that American soldiers sent home approximately $11 million more than they drew in salary. A year later a former UNRRA worker commented about the military's vigor and its attempts "to restrict, detect, and penalize black market operations among the displaced persons. How Americans manage to keep their righteous halo floating over their heads has been a constant source of amazement to me." Black market activities kept the European economy functioning. A relatively small number of profiteers, however, made a fortune from this kind of work, and the authorities had every reason to be concerned with the large dealers.[13]

Other crimes and looting existed as well. In May and June 1945, the Army picked up bands of Russians and Poles accused of rape, theft, and robbery; in November a group of Polish DPs looted areas near the Landsberg camp; and in December, a U.S. Army investigation concluded that "many Balts were enjoying a haven by day and raiding and murdering by night. The G2 investigation pointed to them as to a large extent responsible for the crimes which have been the main source of disorder in the American zone."[14] No references appear to Jews having been significantly engaged in any other criminal activity aside from black marketeering.

Except for those engaged in illegal trading operations, DP criminality, in general, did not loom as a major problem. An American congressional committee found, in 1947, "that the crime rate among displaced persons is notably low in comparison to other elements in the territories concerned." This contrasted sharply with the report of the military governor in the American zone in August 1946, which stipulated that crime and lawlessness among the DPs was at a "relatively high level." Among the crimes listed was that of a DP wearing an American uniform; another involved scuffles between DPs and MPs. In 1945 two DPs received three-month jail terms for trivial offenses. One stole a pound of butter, the other exchanged an Army shirt for cigarettes. "Someone in Munich, where the trials took place," Major Heymont wrote, "is insane. These sentences are outrageous." (The American MP who headed the black market operations in Landsberg was also locked up for three months but allowed to keep all of his profits.)[15]

It is difficult to evaluate the level of "criminal" activity with such evidence. An UNRRA report, however, describing the "crimes" of the following people who were arrested after a raid on the Forstner Kaserne DP Assembly Center, suggests the kind of people and activities which the military regarded as warranting punishment:

1. a mother of two who the Army said had excess soap and chocolate
2. a mother of six who had excess soap, chocolate, and cigarettes
3. a father who had a flashlight
4. a camp leader who had four tins of cookies
5. a teacher who had cigarettes, food, and chocolate.

The UNRRA report concluded, "It is significant that three days later all food was returned to the camp and all charges were dropped." Nevertheless, the rule remained that anyone who possessed more than two packages of cigarettes would be arrested.[16] If this experience was representative of the "relatively high level" of crime, then it would also indicate the nature of DP "lawlessness." Though some of the "crimes" struck several observers as ludicrous, the fact that a DP had a "criminal record" would loom large in the minds of a number of employees of the Displaced Persons Commission screening applicants for admission to the United States in 1948 and thereafter, as well as with several senators considering a revised Displaced Persons Act in 1950.

Some other contacts that the military had with the DPs, however, especially Jewish concentration camp survivors in 1945, warranted more serious concern. These encounters tried the patience and exceeded the comprehension of both enlisted men and their officers. For example, the average GI, emerging from a sheltered American adolescence, found it difficult, as the War Department publication *Army Talk* acknowledged, "to understand and like people who pushed, screamed, clawed for food, smelled bad, who couldn't and didn't want to obey orders, who sat with dull faces and vacant staring eyes in a cellar, or concentration camp barrack, or within a primitive cave, and refused to come out at their command." Even Major Heymont, sympathetic to the DPs and their plight, noted that when he arrived in Landsberg he found the place "filthy beyond description." Superior officers authorized him to cut food rations a third if necessary to force the inhabitants to tidy up their quarters. "The camp was considered a scandal," the Major wrote his wife. He then added, "It seemed that some civilian VIP named Harrison had inspected DP camps for President Truman and had some harsh things to say. . . . Landsberg . . . was one of the reasons Harrison had 'burned' the Army." It did not take Heymont long to find out why that "VIP" had reacted so vehemently or why American soldiers could not stomach their charges. "The toilets beggar description," Heymont informed his wife. "About half the bowls were inoperative but full of excrement. Toilet seats were smeared with excrement or wet with urine." In another letter two weeks later the exasperated Major again described his bewilderment:

Even after concentration camp life it is not too much to expect people to flush toilets that are in working order. Is it too demanding to ask that they use the urinals in the latrines and not the floors? When a garbage can is provided, is it unreasonable to expect them to put the garbage into the can and not on the ground next to the can?[17]

Partly as a result of experiences like the aformentioned, and others equally draining emotionally, the Army wanted to be rid of the DPs and made no bones about it. Save for the "persecutees" (Jews, who had suffered too much to be thrown out in the cold again), officials sought in early 1946 to eliminate the assembly centers and let all of the inhabitants out to fend for themselves. Twice, on February 25 and April 22, 1946, General McNarney wrote to Eisenhower, who was then chief of staff in Washington, urging that the facilities be closed. The British government, UNRRA, the Federal Council of Churches in America, the National Catholic Welfare Conference, the American Federation of Labor, and the Congress of Industrial Organizations opposed the idea. Both the Secretaries of War and State, Robert Patterson and James F. Byrnes, respectively, ignored these protests and endorsed McNarney's recommendation. Byrnes even announced the closing of the camps, but Truman cancelled the order. The President feared a domestic imbroglio and wanted alternate accommodations found before taking such a step. The Catholic Church and the Poles "particularly," Truman warned, "are simply going to have a spasm if we close out these camps without some sort of arrangement to take care of the people who can't go back."[18]

The military focused its attention on rebuilding Germany. General Lucius D. Clay, successor to Eisenhower and McNarney, acknowledged, "My orders are to reconstitute the German economy without delay." But the presence of DPs thwarted that mission. As the military saw it, sheltering the DPs taxed German-American relations and retarded the development of a strong friendship between the United States and Germany. By 1946 American political officials, industrialists, and military men viewed Russia as the "enemy," and they saw the need for a strong German ally to aid the West against the "Communist menace." One lieutenant colonel argued "that denazification would drive the German people into the hands of the Communists, that we did not destroy one dictatorship in order to build another, that we must preserve a bulwark against Russia." The presence of "disgruntled," "uncooperative," and even "criminal" elements in the DP camps thwarted the more important goal of wooing Germans. Furthermore, officers, who generally held conservative political opinions, believed that "most of the [Jewish] DPs are inclined to a strong leftist tendency." Unable to fulfill its role of rebuilding Germany without the irritating presence of and responsibility for DPs, military officials behaved harshly toward those helpless individuals who would not return to the lands of their birth but who were not permitted to enter any of the countries where they would have liked to start anew.[19]

At the same time upper echelon officers continued to treat the American Jewish advisers, all of whom had the ear of influential Americans, respectfully and, on occasions, deferentially. A British official explained the reason for this seemingly contradictory behavior. "Americans," Sir George W. Rendell informed his superiors in the Foreign Office, "are haunted by the fear of Jewish opinion in the United States." Any "official" adverse policies adopted, he continued, might stimulate "an immediate outcry from the New York Jews, with possible political reactions in the United States."[20]

The average officer and soldier, though, seemed little concerned with official policies. Their own personal needs took precedence. In January 1946, 3,000 GIs demonstrated in front of General McNarney's headquarters and chanted "We wanna go home" for forty minutes in the cold. This incident symbolized the deterioration in morale that had taken place within the armed services. The editor of one of the military newspapers thought that early 1946 marked the "lowest ebb" of the occupation Army's "morale and discipline." "The average soldier in Germany learns only two things from his occupational experience," the editor wrote, "He learns how to drink and how to pick up a fräulein."[21]

The fräuleins, and other Germans, seemed irresistible to the GIs, as well as to the officers. Meek, obsequious, and obedient, they addressed the Americans correctly and deferentially. Unlike the DPs, they possessed what one American called "a passion for cleanliness." Therefore, by late 1945, the American soldiers preferred the company of Germans to that of the dirty, destitute, and argumentative, if not depressed, DPs, who were always making demands upon them. "How can we hate the Germans?" the newly arrived GIs asked after seeing the nice, clean-looking, inhabitants who obeyed the law, tidied their homes, respected their parents, loved their children, and lavished affection on pets.[22]

The Germans, who displayed "a terrifying nostalgia for the good old days of Nazi splendor," despised the Jewish DPs and the American military accepted the German version of many events. One Jew wrote a friend, in September 1947:

> I tell you nothing new when I report that anti-semitism is as rife now in Germany as when Hitler was in power. . . . But you cannot really understand and appreciate what those things are, what they mean in daily life, what they can do to the minds of men, yes even of children, unless you visit Germany and its DP camps. . . . You must talk to the residents of the camps, to the remnant of German liberalism, to American civilians working in the area, to military government officials to understand the full devastation of what has occurred and in which our co-religionists who came through the horrors of Auschwitz, Bergen-Belsen and Dachau must still linger and travail.

The viciousness of some of the Germans rivaled the excesses of their conduct during the war. A children's camp at Indersdorf adjoined a blacksmith's shop. The blacksmith had "fixed an electrified barbed wire fence between his land and the children's camp (ostensibly to prevent the theft of fruit) without even providing an appropriate warning notice. When officials . . . took him to task, he is supposed to have said that this wire was intended for Jewish children."[23]

American troops frequently expressed attitudes toward the DPs shockingly similar to those mouthed by the Germans. In February 1946, one officer observed, "The DPs have food and clothes and a camp to live in. What more do they want? They should be grateful. If they are not satisfied let them go back where they came from." Two months later an Army Captain told an UNRRA worker "that UNRRA would not be needed in Kreis Pfarrkirchen because he was soon going to have all D.P.s in jail." In the summer of 1945 Earl Harrison had discovered that the military men "were quite impatient with any form of political dissidence," and the idea "that people might be 'stateless' was talked about as though it were a loathsome disease. They seemed to think that the people in the camps were there because of wrongdoing, and failed utterly to realize that they were there simply because they were Jews." Soldiers associated the term *Zionism* with *communism* because they did not know what it meant. In one poll "a very high proportion" of GIs indicated that "Hitler was *partly right* in his treatment of Jews." By February 1946, the military instituted an educational program for the newly arrived GIs including tours of the concentration camps (See Appendix C). Many of the men believed that the exhibits they saw had been faked or exaggerated for propaganda purposes. "Do you believe what I have told you?" one former Dachau inmate asked a JDC visitor after taking her around the camp.[24]

It would be perhaps too much to expect military personnel, who deeply resented the DPs, to treat them with the dignity and sympathy to which survivors of the Holocaust had every right. But assembly centers varied and the attitudes of the military commanders largely determined how they functioned. If the officers showed warmth and understanding, then these feelings reflected themselves in the operation. If they were, as a majority unfortunately appeared to be, rigid and unsympathetic, or if they expected the DPs to live according to strict military regimentation, life was more difficult.

The basic task of running a camp required a unique combination of skills. Operations were exceedingly complex. They necessitated interaction between and among the military,

UNRRA or its successor, the International Refugee Organization (IRO), the residents, their delegated representatives, and the numerous visiting dignitaries and investigating committees. Administrators dealt with immigration, morale, care and maintenance, supply and distribution, work and vocational training, black marketeering, and, in some cases, an almost continuous flow of transient residents. It took great skill to juggle all of the requirements of the job. As the American chargé d'affaires in London remarked after inspecting facilities on the continent, "running a DP camp is an art."[25]

DP assembly centers in the United States zones existed mainly in Berlin, Munich, Frankfurt, Stuttgart, Regensburg, Vienna, Rome, Milan, and Naples (fig. 2.1). The size of the camps varied. Smaller ones contained 50 to 500 people; others held more than 5,000. Of the 300 to 500 establishments, which opened and closed according to population needs at any given time, about 80 housed only Jews. The assembly centers, for Jews and non-Jews alike, included former Army barracks and training facilities, industrial worker sites, a former airport, a former Luftwaffe headquarters, temporary tent colonies, requisitioned hotels, apartment houses, resorts, garages, stables, former POW and slave labor camps, a monastery, and institutional structures like hospitals, schools, and sanitoria. Of all these, former German troop barracks predominated. Basic responsibility for care of the residents rested with the Army, but UNRRA teams and DP camp committees engaged in the day-to-day administration. The Army estimated that the actual cost, which included food, clothing, medical supplies, linen, etc., amounted to $23.90 per DP per month. When there were over 1 million DPs, which was the case through early 1947, the monthly cost to the American government exceeded $23 million. Thousands of registered DPs—estimates place the numbers at about 15 to 25 percent of the total—came to the assembly centers only to pick up their food rations; they chose to live in nearby communities. Some got on well with the indigenous population; others simply could not tolerate further confinement.[26]

Almost all of the assembly centers were overcrowded, more

Figure 2.1. Displaced Persons Assembly Centers.

so on December 31, 1946, when the official DP population peaked at 1,243,263 in the western zones. People slept in barracks, huts, and horse stalls, on bundles of straw, or two to three in a bunk. A chaplain described one group as living "like a litter of puppies crowding under the body of their mother," while a 22-year-old, who shared one room with fourteen other DPs of several families, told how she reacted to this situation. "When I undress at night, I can't help feeling everybody's looking at me. Sometimes mother holds the blanket in front of me; but sometimes she's too tired." The woman related her apprehensions of finding a man in the washroom whenever she entered, or that one might follow her in. Ira Hirschmann, UNRRA Director Fiorello LaGuardia's emissary on a tour of these camps, described one place in Munich: "1800 Jewish DPs most former concentration camp inhabitants were massed in a parking garage. Only three repeat three toilets for all men, women and children."[27]

The man who served as UNRRA team director of Wind-

DP Living Accommodation Unit, Germany. Summer 1947. (Courtesy YIVO Institute of Jewish Research)

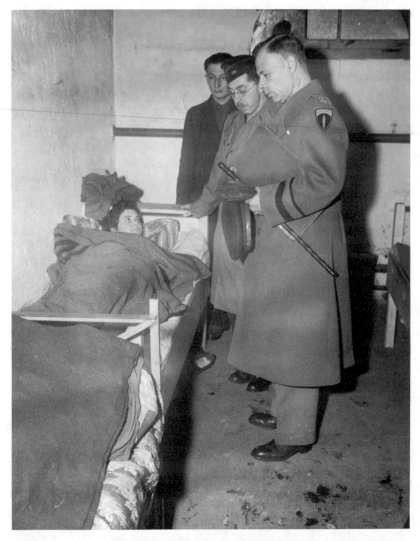

Lieutenant General W. Bedell Smith (holding cap), chief of staff, U.S. Forces in the European theater, and Judge Simon H. Rifkind (wearing cap), inspect living quarters of displaced persons at Landsberg, Germany. December 6, 1945. (U.S. Army photograph)

sheim, another Jewish Assembly Center, from July 1946 to May 1947, related the "unbelievable squalor, misery and unrest [which] filled the camp. People slept in attics and on the bare earth in cellars. The theft of toilets and washbowls made it impossible to satisfy adequately even the most fundamental of human needs." He discussed the difficulties of having to cook without fuel, or sporadic food distributions, and of "sullenly obdurate German bakers" who failed to turn out enough bread for the populace. The director noted as well that the Germans evicted from the Herman Goering apartment buildings to make way for DPs, in the spring of 1946, stripped the tenements of all plumbing, heating, and lighting fixtures and strewed garbage throughout the corridors. He added: "The military government detachment (4 men) did little to combat the destruction; they had fought the UNRRA requisition, realizing that the additional population would increase their administrative difficulties." A few weeks later contingents of Jewish DPs occupied these apartments.[28]

There were also "good' assembly centers where a semblance of a normal life could be maintained. Landsberg had two indoor cafes, an outdoor cafe, a 1,300-seat theater, a radio station which broadcast music and international news of concern to Jews, and a camp newspaper. The Freiman Seidlung camp housed and fed people in family groups, not at mess halls like most of the others, and allowed for a wide variety of cultural, recreational, and social activities. With only 1,700 people living in a facility designed for 1,200 it was one of the least overcrowded centers. The hotels and resorts requisitioned housed a small minority of DPs in truly luxurious accommodations.[29]

It was SHAEF policy, however, to return sequestered private homes and buildings to their owners as quickly as possible, and the DPs did not long retain their improved facilities. Starting in the summer of 1946 the better apartments were transferred first for use of Army personnel and their families, then back to their owners. But while this transfer occurred, work also proceeded to improve the quality of the buildings housing DPs. On September 1, 1947, the Army reported, "today one witnesses a complete change in the life and nature within the displaced persons assembly center. Buildings have been repaired; people have been transferred to better accommodations; necessary facilities and furniture have been added to the camp. Although a complete life of normality has not been restored, considerable progress has been made in that direction." But in January 1948, several voluntary agencies, including the Red Cross and the World Council of Churches, made an international appeal for those DPs in "absolute despair." "Millions of people," they asserted, "find themselves without a home. They live in wooden huts or in the cellars of ruined houses, a prey to starvation and sickness. Innumerable children are orphaned. There are no beds or hospital equipment for the sick. Adolescents, their health already undermined, have neither the will nor the strength to face the difficult future. How will the unfortunates survive the privation of the coming winter?"[30]

The assembly centers ran the gamut from good to bad. Striking differences appeared between those that housed Jews and those for Gentiles. "On the whole," a journalist from *The Manchester Guardian* wrote, "the non-Jewish camps give a healthier, cleaner, and happier appearance. The general atmosphere of Jewish camps is one of apathy, greyness, and despair." The Balts and Poles surrounded themselves with neat gardens, green lawns, and pretty flowers.[31] They also appeared, according to *The Manchester Guardian* dispatch, to "have, in most cases, managed to bring with them different sets of clothing, jewelry, valuable rugs, and other belongings." Similarly, a British social worker noted that "some of the Balts had been able to bring a surprisingly large number of valuables and money with them in their flight."[32] The Jews, on the other hand, were "invariably shabbily dressed." "The reason for this marked difference is complicated," the journalist continued, and was rooted in the fact that the Jews were victimized to a greater extent by the war and could not bear to remain in Germany but longed for Palestine, while the non-Jews "beyond knowing where they do not wish to go . . . have no definite aim. In consequence they are relatively content with their present living conditions and take pride in cleanliness, orderliness, and in their occupations."[33]

But in those Jewish camps with collectives (*kibbutzim*) morale was almost always high. Zionist leaders organized everyone and trained them for life in Palestine. They brought the orphans and other children under their wing and restored their zest for life. They instilled discipline and patriotic values. They told endless tales about Palestine, taught spirited songs, and drilled the youths in marching battalions. The Jewish Agency from Palestine also sent in workers to revive and uplift the remnant of Jewry, and those who responded to the Zionist program recovered their emotional equilibrium much faster than other Jewish DPs. "Zionism" according to the UNRRA director at Windsheim, "exercised an all-pervasive influence second only to the unifying force of Jewish culture."[34]

Although the military and observers referred to the Jewish DPs as one group—and in many ways they were one—there were several component parts. Survivors of the concentration camps constituted one segment, adults and children who had been hidden during the war made up another, while Polish infiltrees—those who had either spent the war in Russia or who had returned to Poland in 1945 but found conditions unbearable and therefore made their way back to Germany— constituted a third. Poles made up at least two-thirds of all of the Jewish DPs. Hungarians, Rumanians, Germans, and Italians constituted much smaller proportions. Jews of Hungarian and Rumanian nationality, formerly more assimilated into their countries, spoke their native tongue, as did the western Europeans. Most Polish Jews, on the other hand, generally of a lower socioeconomic class than the others, rarely spoke the language of their native country. They emphasized their feelings of estrangement from Poles by conversing with one another in Yiddish, the East European Jewish vernacular. Problems of assimilation as well as group differences led to continual friction.[35]

Religious and political differences also created stress among Jews. The most religiously orthodox proved totally inflexible.

"Compromise is an unknown word in their vocabulary," Major Heymont wrote. Nothing mattered to them as much as strict compliance with religious teachings and no problems had any meaning for them unless they interfered with observances.[36] The orthodox, who trusted in God, along with the nonreligious but otherwise equally zealous Zionists, recovered most quickly from the war's deprivations. The moderately or indifferently religious survivors suffered most. The orthodox had little use for them, the Zionists gave up on them once they realized they could not be converted to the cause, and they had little to engage them while trying to readjust to a new life.

The people with no devout religious or political affiliations endured the most severe emotional crises. They, especially, needed rehabilitation centers, psychiatrists, and social workers but not until late 1945 did UNRRA provide any. Many of these DPs exhibited characteristics of restlessness and impotence, engaged in threats and tantrums, and seemed to have no emotional control. They could not concentrate; they could not work. A psychiatrist who later lived in one DP center under-statedly described the behavior of the residents as "asocial." The myriad number of soldiers and voluntary officials, along with visitors from several walks of life, thought "bizarre" a more appropriate term. An American woman who went through the Jewish camps in September 1945 seemed totally unprepared for what she found. She reported: "I would say 90% of the camp inmates are neurotics. *How* they speak, *how* they roll their eyes, *how* they wallow in their sufferings, *how* they repeat and repeat their stories."[37]

Simple and rational requests sometimes evoked unantici-pated reactions which only those knowledgeable about mental illness might comprehend. Many of the original field workers and servicemen failed to recognize the psychological disturb-ances. They could not understand the DP resistance to authority or hysterical responses to what others considered normal procedures. For example, in one camp the DPs were asked to line up for the distribution of clothing. Although they had been assured that there would be enough for everyone the residents fought for first place in line and a riot ensued with

A member of a dusting team applies DDT powder to a newly arrived displaced person at the camp at Heidelberg, June 19, 1945. (U.S. Army photograph)

people using knives, clubs, and fists to claim their positions. Unbelieving officials did not know what they had done wrong. Thousands of DPs also dreaded showers and innoculations, which brought back terrible memories of torture by the SS, yet it was routine to innoculate them against disease, delouse them with DDT, and have them take a shower. One UNRRA worker recalled the difficulties of getting "these people to take a steam bath voluntarily." He seemed not to have known that that was the method used for gassing Jews in the concentration camps. He wrote how women screamed and "quite a few . . . had to be forcefully pushed or carried in." The UNRRA worker also noted that "German medical corps attendants brushed each person down with a stiff brush and probably were not any too gentle with some of the patients." This was in June 1945, before anyone thought it amiss to have Germans working in such close contact with DPs.[38]

The non-Jewish DPs presented other, but fewer, problems and complications. Although individually some may have suffered as much as the Jewish survivors, most of the remainder had had different kinds of wartime experiences. The non-Jewish groups also established some kind of viable community life and did not seem to have the emotional complexities, highs and lows, associated with the Jews. More family groups of Gentiles than Jews remained together, and some among them settled down very well in and near the assembly centers. An American Friends Service Committee worker seemed quite surprised, in January 1946, that the Gentile DPs among whom he worked got on so well with the Germans and even invited them to their numerous social functions. "Each celebration," he wrote

> is the excuse for a huge banquet and each time one wonders where the food comes from—soups, sandwiches, hors d'oeuvres, jellies, hot and cold meats, vegetables, salads, fruit compotes, layer cakes, and all kinds of bread and pastry are served on such occasions to say nothing of the equally plentiful but less delectable *schnapps*, wine, beer, and coffee. . . . Because some of these displaced persons came from wealthy homes and had time to bring part of their possessions with them it is not uncommon to

be served on gilt-edged porcelain and to find most of the company dressed in beautiful clothes.[39]

Such banquets described by the American Friends Service Committee employee contrasted with the reports from most of the other assembly centers where the amount and quality of the food provided for DPs seemed a constant irritant. The U.S. zone in Germany contained a region ordinarily short of the food necessary to feed its population, even in good times. The normal population was 13 million and 20 percent of the food had been imported. On January 1, 1947, however, the population approximated 16 million plus another million in Berlin which the Army had to feed. In 1946, DPs had received between 1,500 and 2,500 calories per day on paper, but those rations were not always met. The Harrison report resulted in the establishment of special kosher kitchens for Jews wherever possible. But the rations provided by the Army invariably came out of tins and packages and one found a constant shortage of fresh vegetables and milk, butter, onions, fish, chickens, eggs, jam, sugar, honey, cocoa, chocolate, canned fruits and juices, rice, and other body-building foods. The basic diet of soup, bread, coffee, and dehydrated foods remained monotonous; it provided enough food for people to survive but not enough for them to thrive. The menu in the Deggendorf DP camp for the period July 20–29, 1945, read:

> breakfast: coffee or tea (substitute)
>
> dinner: soup (potato or pea)
>
> supper: soup

In addition, the daily distribution to each resident included 13 oz. of black bread, 3/4 oz. of butter, little more than 1/2 oz. of cheese, and about 6 oz. of milk. The total daily ration came to 1,100 calories and was served to 700 Jewish men, women, and children aged 14 to 70. Twenty-four people fled the camp on August 1, and as punishment for this deed the administrator ordered that all the remaining inmates be deprived of their suppers that night. The rations in Mauthausen consisted of 3.3

Transient displaced persons sitting down to a meal. Mattenberg Camp, Kassel, Germany. (U.S. Army photograph)

ozs. of bread and one portion of soup daily, while in Mittenwald the DPs received one piece of bread and coffee for breakfast, soup and beans for their second meal, and no third meal. (German POWs, however, received the same rations as American GIs.) The German population was supposed to have provided half of the food, but they asserted that they did not have enough for themselves, so the military did not press them. In early October 1945, *Stars and Stripes* reported that the fresh food supply to the DPs had to be cut because "such demands have dangerously reduced the German civilian food stocks." DPs in some Polish assembly centers complained that they had had more to eat under German rule than they had in the American zone after the war. Major Heymont, in Landsberg, wrote his wife that he could not help but "wonder if the people of the camp are aware of how their inspectors eat. The whipped

cream cake and ice cream desert from lunch had a bad after taste now when I think of the monotonous starchy diet of the camp."[40]
The first shipments of clothing to the DPs were also found wanting. Well into the winter of 1946–47 there were still shortages of shoes, underwear, and outer garments. To meet the clothing needs of some Jews shipments of SS trousers and coats went out, along with other items of ex-Wehrmacht uniforms. An UNRRA official estimated in September 1945 that 10 million pounds of used clothing would be needed for all the DPs in Germany, but not until 1947 did the relief organizations get sufficient quantities to these people.[41]
Once the voluntary agency personnel arrived, education and vocational training proved to be areas of strength in the DP centers. The agencies helped educate the children, provide

Two displaced persons make dolls and toys of scrap materials. Hanau, Germany. These products were sold to visitors. (U.S. Army photograph)

skills to the young adults, and retrain the more mature residents. The JDC, the Jewish Agency for Palestine, and the World ORT found their way into practically every one of the Jewish camps. They set up schools, provided materials where possible, and brought in teachers. They taught everything imaginable. In one Bavarian center people learned carpentry, auto repair, tailoring, hairdressing, metal work, radio technology, electrical engineering, and nursing. In a non-Jewish camp, a group of Ukrainians turned out exquisite sweaters, mittens, pillowcases, table covers, and dolls. The artisans bartered for needles, thread, embroidery, cloth, silk, and other necessary materials. When appropriate goods could not be found people improvised. Discarded military equipment was often employed, German uniforms were dyed and altered, ropes of Nazi flags were unravelled, parachute and airplane fabrics became clothes or soft toys, old tires were torn apart and used to fix shoes, and bicycle spokes emerged as knitting needles. In 1947 the IRO, successor to UNRRA, also started vocational courses but on a limited scale. By December 1948, it was training only 15,000 DPs; shortages of lumber, wool, clay, leather, and metals limited the effectiveness of the program.[42]

People eagerly sought retraining because they hoped to utilize newly acquired skills after resettlement. No matter how bleak camp life appeared, or how enjoyable some moments or days might have been, practically all of the DPs expected that life would eventually start anew in another country. The Zionists had no doubt that one day Palestine would be universally recognized as the Jewish homeland. Some prominent American military officials probably hoped for the same thing because they helped Jewish DPs escape to the Middle East.[43]

But limits remained upon what Army personnel, anxious to see the DPs on their way, could do. Responsible officials responded to the Harrison report with somewhat more humane policies than had previously existed in the DP assembly centers. Harrison himself acknowledged as much only a month after the publication of his findings. But he was, in fact, quite dismayed by what had occurred. "What we need," he told reporters, "is more action in getting the people out of the camps and less talk about improving conditions within the camps."[44] Yet while the military might wholeheartedly have agreed with Harrison on this point, the transference of populations to other countries required political decisions by the nations' leaders; officers did not set national policies and could not organize the dispersal of people. Thus the DPs remained in their assembly centers longer than they or their supervisors wanted them to while in London and Washington, British and American diplomats endeavored to work out some kind of accord to help the most discontented leave Europe.

3

THE ANGLO-AMERICAN
COMMITTEE OF INQUIRY

THE HARRISON REPORT not only led to improved conditions for the DPs but it also stimulated President Truman to make some attempt to change the British position on limiting Jewish entry into Palestine. On August 31, 1945, Truman urged Prime Minister Clement Attlee to allow 100,000 displaced European Jews into Palestine.[1] But the Prime Minister was not willing to move quickly. Just as before the war, the British government would admit only a token number of Jews into the Holy Land. Nevertheless, Great Britain had suffered heavy losses during the conflagration, needed American friendship, and could not ignore requests from the President of the United States. Thus, to forestall action, buy time, and perhaps win American assistance for a joint Palestine policy, the British government ultimately suggested that the two nations collectively explore the possibilities for helping DPs resettle outside of Europe. President Truman accepted the proposal.

In one sense, Truman really had no choice but to go along with the inquiry because of the course of action taken by Franklin D. Roosevelt before him. The new President could not precipitously overturn foreign affairs decisions made by an extremely popular and highly respected predecessor without severe political consequences. And he had learned, shortly after entering the White House on April 12, 1945, that Roosevelt had straddled the fence by encouraging both Arabs and Jews to believe that their wishes about the future of Palestine would be carefully considered in the White House.

While Franklin Roosevelt lived, both Jews and Arabs regarded him as a friend. In March 1944, the President, after a meeting in the oval office, authorized Zionist leaders Abba Hillel Silver and Stephen S. Wise to state "that the American government has never given its approval to the White Paper of 1939. The President is happy that the doors of Palestine are today open to Jewish refugees, and that when future decisions are reached, full justice will be done to those who seek a Jewish National Home." Actually Palestine admitted only 1,500 Jews monthly, much too small a number for the Zionists, who sought unlimited entry. In 1945 the President, who usually told callers what they wanted to hear, informed Wise that he favored the Zionist program. At about the same time Roosevelt confessed to Colonel Harold B. Hoskins of the State Department that a Jewish state in Palestine could only be "installed and maintained . . . by force." Unknown to the Jews, the President also pledged to King Ibn Saud of Saudi Arabia and to the heads of other Arab governments that the United States would not undertake new policies toward Palestine without consulting them first.[2]

It is possible, of course, that President Roosevelt did not actually give differing assurances and that his words might have been misinterpreted. It must also be acknowledged that the President, otherwise occupied by World War II and in an impossible situation vis-à-vis conflicting Arab, British, and Jewish demands, may only have been treading water until the time came when a firm decision about Palestine would have to be made. Nonetheless, no matter what the circumstances surrounding his remarks, existing documents leave Roosevelt open to attack. Members of the future Anglo-American Committee of Inquiry later read the various State Department files on Palestine and found them shocking. The American chairman of the committee labeled FDR "a duplicitous son-of-a-bitch," while another member, Bartley C. Crum, wrote, "I was to find, on what is commonly called the highest level, instances of duplicity and intrigue which would seem almost incredible to the ordinary masses of decent citizens elsewhere."[3]

Roosevelt's deceptiveness did not hurt him; he died before the war ended, and his allegedly conflicting promises did not become public until October 1945. Shortly after Roosevelt's death, however, State Department officials informed the new

President of his predecessor's actions. Truman thereupon reaffirmed American commitments to the Arabs.[4]

Coming from Missouri, a state where Jewish opinions did not carry much weight, the new President was at first not attuned to their political significance. It did not take him long to learn. By the end of the summer Truman knew that a homeland in Palestine was the first priority among most of the Jews in the United States, that admission of 100,000 Jewish DPs into the Holy Land would be an initial step toward that goal, and that Jewish spokesmen possessed considerable political influence with many of the more important elected as well as appointed governmental officials.[5] The President did not have the power to translate Jewish goals into British policy, but he did listen to the Jewish representatives.

What Truman heard obviously struck a responsive chord. The tales about Jewish suffering no doubt affected his course of action. Thus, although he had turned down a proposal of a Cabinet level committee to deal with DP problems in May, the President dispatched Earl Harrison on his fact-finding tour in June. During the summer several Jews communicated their sentiments about opening Palestine to the refugees, and the governors of 37 states endorsed that proposal. When Truman went to Potsdam in July for a Big Three conference on the problems of postwar Europe, he urged Prime Minister Churchill to lift all British restrictions on Jewish immigration to Palestine. A few days later the British electorate repudiated the Tory Party and Labour Party leader Clement Attlee became Prime Minister. Truman reiterated his views to Attlee and proclaimed them publicly upon returning to the United States in August. The receipt of Harrison's report at the end of the month propelled the President further, and he made a written request that the British allow 100,000 Jews into the Holy Land.[6]

Attlee, Prime Minister for only six weeks when Truman's letter arrived, did not respond immediately. Aside from the numerous domestic problems that had to be handled more quickly, foreign policy issues and the unexpected end of the war with Japan also made demands upon his time. The Labour Party had not anticipated its huge victory at the polls in July

1945, and its leaders assumed responsibility for government without having given much original thought to major areas of British concern, including the Middle East. Palestine would almost immediately prove to be one of the thorniest issues of contention.

Serious British involvement in Palestine had not begun until the First World War. Anticipating victory against the Germans and their allies in Austria and Turkey, the British and French signed the secret Sykes-Picot agreement in 1916, dividing between themselves long-coveted territories of the Ottoman Empire in the Middle East. The French took Syria and Lebanon; Palestine went to the British. In the hopes of getting world Jewry to support the Allied cause, and for a variety of other tactical and long-range strategic reasons, Foreign Secretary Sir Arthur J. Balfour issued his famous declaration in 1917 indicating that "His Majesty's Government view with favour the establishment in Palestine of a national home for the Jewish people." Although American officials and leading Jews were consulted extensively before the issuance of the declaration, there is no evidence of talks with the Arabs despite their having occupied the land for centuries. A League of Nations mandate in 1920 acknowledged "the historical connection of the Jewish homeland." A Jewish state in Palestine thus had firm roots in *Western* international law, but it did not have the approval of the Arabs who dwelled there. In fact, Arabs opposed the Balfour Declaration and the promise of a Jewish homeland from the first because they feared, correctly, ultimate Jewish domination and the emergence of a Zionist nation.[7]

The Zionist movement, with its dedication to reestablishing a Jewish state in Palestine, may be dated from the 1896 publication of Theodore Herzl's *Der Judenstaat*, although Jews over the centuries, and especially in the late nineteenth century with its growth of nationalism, spoke and dreamed of returning to the land of Israel. Although Herzl himself did not originally stress Palestine as *the* place, other Jews quickly pointed to the Holy Land as the only country where Jews could obtain true freedom. The rise of Pan-Slavism and pogroms in Eastern

Europe in the 1880s, and the Dreyfus affair in France in the 1890s, convinced many of the most thoughtful East European Jews that they had no place to go but Zion.[8] At first only a few intellectuals and zealots pursued the idea. The European upheavals wrought by World War I, and the rise of Hitler, then began to convince other Jews that the Zionist goal provided their only hope for security.

Jews did not immediately flock to Palestine in the numbers hoped for by the Zionists. Although there were about 65,000 of them in the Holy Land at the end of World War I, the figure increased to only about 180,000 in 1932. The advent of Hitler in 1933, however, led to a huge exodus of Jews from Germany, and Palestine was one of few areas where they were able to go. In eight years the Jewish population there more than doubled, totaling 463,535 by 1940. The massive influx both infuriated and frightened the Arabs, who saw their worst fears realized. The Jews, on the other hand, came to Palestine because almost every other nation in the world had tightened its immigration restrictions.

The Jews brought with them to Palestine Western ideas of industrial and agricultural development and the capitalist's views of expropriation and expansion. They bought and cultivated land. Their presence changed Palestine from a traditional Muslim community to a modern industrial European outpost. The alterations created tensions and led to increased skirmishes and battles between Arabs and Jews. Both sides proclaimed the righteousness of their cause. The Jews pointed to the Balfour Declaration and League of Nations mandate which stipulated that a Jewish national home should be provided in the Holy Land. Jews swelled with pride when talking about the agricultural developments and prosperity they helped create. The Arabs, on the other hand, resented the encroachment upon their lands, the changed direction of society, and the resultant "progress." Trying to placate both sides and protect its own imperial interests at the same time, the British government sent several investigating committees to suggest means for bridging the gap, the most distinguished being the Peel Commission of 1937, which found the possibilities for reconciliation hopeless and recommended partition. Both Jews and Arabs rejected that solution.[9]

In May 1939, facing the ever-growing threat of an expansionist Germany and fearful of losing Arab allegiance, Britain issued a controversial White Paper which restricted Jewish land purchases in, and immigration to, the Holy Land. His Majesty's Government calculated that the Jews could never support Hitler but that the Arabs might, and therefore the wishes of the latter had to predominate in the Middle East. The League of Nations declared the White Paper incompatible with the terms of the mandate, and Winston Churchill, along with members of both the Liberal and Labour parties in England, denounced the restrictions on Jewish immigration to Palestine. The Conservative Cabinet of Neville Chamberlain, however, knew no other way to buy Arab good will, curtail pro-Axis sympathy in the Middle East, and maintain its pipeline to Arabian oil and imperial possessions. The issuance of the White Paper occurred only a few months before the outbreak of World War II. Despite many pleas by those anxious to save the Jews from being exterminated later in the war, the British government refused to alter its policy. In 1945, the Labour Party, which had affirmed its support for a Jewish national home in Palestine eleven times previously, once again took a stand. Hugh Dalton, voicing strong opposition to the existing policy at a party conference in May 1945, asserted that "it is morally wrong and politically indefensible to impose obstacles to the entry into Palestine now of any Jews who desire to go there." No Labour Party spokesman challenged Dalton's remarks.[10]

The Labour Party victory in July 1945 raised Zionist hopes, and President Truman's letter to Attlee, a few weeks later, forced the new Cabinet to make some response. Attlee and Foreign Minister Ernest Bevin retained most of the senior civil servants in the Foreign Office who had advised Churchill's War Government and previous Conservative Cabinets. Strongly pro-Arab, these men urged that existing policies be continued because of Britain's dependence upon Middle Eastern oil, its need to control the Suez Canal as a route to imperial possessions in Asia, and fear of Russian encroachment into the area. Attlee had been Prime Minister for less than a week when he received a memo from the Foreign Office informing him that a Jewish state in Palestine would have a deplorable effect on Anglo-Arab relations. Whitehall declared that His Majesty's Government had vital strategic interests in the Near and Middle East and that the preservation of these interests depended largely on the good will of the Arab peoples. The communiqué added that it would be desirable to have the United States cooperate with the British in that part of the world.[11]

In Truman's letter about the DPs Attlee saw an opportunity to involve the American government in British strategy, without at first altering any of his positions. On September 16, 1945, the Prime Minister responded cautiously to the President. He suggested two North African camps as places which might be used to alleviate the overcrowding in the European DP centers and advised Truman that "we have the matter under urgent examination. . . . I shall be very happy to let you know as soon as I can what our intentions are in this matter."[12]

The British Cabinet discussed Truman's request several times during the late summer and fall, and the members agreed on basic issues. Everyone seemed to feel that admitting 100,000 Jews to Palestine might lead to an explosion in the Middle East without solving any of the Jews' difficulties in Europe. Nevertheless, since so many refugees still lived "in conditions of great hardship" no public announcement should ignore that fact. The Foreign Secretary stressed, however, that "it was essential to broaden the basis of British influence in the Middle East" and that HMG should develop an economic and social policy which would insure prosperity and contentment in the area as a whole. Bevin had no intention of antagonizing the Arabs but did suggest a fresh inquiry into the whole Middle East question. He thought Britain and the United States might investigate the problems of the Jews in Europe, see how many immigrants Palestine could take, and "examine the possibility of relieving the position in Europe by immigration into other countries, including the United States and the Dominions."[13]

The Cabinet liked the idea of bringing the United States

into partnership in the Middle East. Members of the British public as well as the government resented Americans urging them to open up the gates to Palestine while refusing to allow any of the DPs into the United States. "America's request would be more impressive," commented *The New Statesman and Nation*, "had she herself opened her doors wide to Hitler's victims." In agreeing to invite the United States to join in an Anglo-American inquiry, members of the Cabinet expressed the opinion that Britain's ally would "thus be placed in a position of sharing the responsibility for the policy which she advocates. She will no longer be able to play the part of irresponsible critic." Furthermore, the new government had been looking for ways of involving the Americans in British imperial concerns and the joint inquiry was seen as a means for advancing this interest. To get that support, Cabinet members agreed not to resist further expansion of American oil concessions in the Middle East. A Labour MP, Richard Crossman, afterward recalled that the Cabinet seemed "to consider its primary concern the dragging of a reluctant America into Middle Eastern Affairs." For these reasons Bevin and Attlee were encouraged to propose a joint Anglo-American Commission of Inquiry into the problems of the displaced persons and the capacity for Palestine to absorb them. While the proposed committee conducted its investigation, and until its report was received, the British government could further delay action.[14]

On October 19, 1945, Lord Halifax, the British ambassador to the United States, brought Bevin's proposal for a joint Anglo-American Committee of Inquiry to Secretary of State James F. Byrnes, who promptly discussed the matter with Truman. Lord Halifax had informed Byrnes that HMG regarded the Palestine situation as a "terrible legacy," found the American "approach to the problem . . . most embarrassing," and could not accept "the view that all of the Jews or the bulk of them must necessarily leave Germany, and still less Europe. That would be to accept Hitler's thesis." The President, still holding to the position he expressed in his August 31 letter to Attlee, nevertheless accepted the proposal with modifications. Bevin had specifically failed to mention Palestine by name as one of the places that might absorb the DPs, and the Americans insisted that it be spelled out. The British wanted 14 members on the committee while the President wanted 10; they compromised on 12. The British wanted an indefinite inquiry with no cutoff date; the President held out for, and got, a provision requiring a report in 120 days. As Truman later wrote, "I did not want the United States to become a party to any dilatory tactics."[15]

Truman probably welcomed the opportunity for the inquiry because of the conflicting stands that Roosevelt had taken and the differing advice that he received about which course of action to pursue. Zealots like the American Zionists demanded the admission of 1 million Jews to the Holy Land as rapidly as possible. The State Department responded with words suggesting more deliberation and the avoidance of precipitous decisions. One communiqué neatly summarized the views prevailing within the department:

It is very likely that efforts will be made by some of the Zionist leaders to obtain from you at an early date some limited Jewish immigration into Palestine and the establishment there of a Jewish state. As you are aware, the Government and people of the United States have every sympathy for the persecuted Jews of Europe and are doing all in their power to relieve their suffering. The question of Palestine is, however, a highly complex one and involves questions which go far beyond the plight of the Jews in Europe.

There is continual tenseness in the situation in the Near East largely as a result of the Palestine question, and as we have interests in that area which are vital to the United States, we feel that this whole subject is one that should be handled with the greatest care and with a view to the long-range interest of the country.

Those officials who subscribed to the ideas highlighted in the memorandum were particularly concerned about American oil and aviation interests, and worried about the possibility of increasing Russian influence in the Middle East should the Western powers force Jews into the Holy Land against Arab wishes. Thus with pressures from a major voting bloc, the Jews, on one hand, and the State Department officials who favored the Arabs and feared Russian encroachment on the other, Truman was probably just as glad as the British to buy time with the appointment of the Anglo-American Committee of Inquiry.[16]

Political considerations, however, delayed public announcement of the investigation. The British ambassador in Washington informed Secretary of State Byrnes that the Foreign Secretary wished to inform Parliament of the decision on October 25. Byrnes vetoed that move. He observed to the ambassador, "Quite frankly, I am thinking of the New York City election the following Tuesday and when this [proposal] is submitted to the President he has to think about that." The Secretary of State obviously feared that any perceived delaying tactics in moving Jews to Palestine would arouse New York Jewry and possibly impair the Democratic Party's chances of recapturing City Hall from LaGuardia's fusionists, who had been in power for twelve years. Then, and for the next few years, every major American decision about Palestine and displaced persons was considered with an eye toward the Jewish voters. The British, and especially Bevin, criticized the Americans for "running a pro-Arab policy in the Middle East, where Standard Oil is master, and a pro-Jewish policy at home, where two million Jews can decide the election results in New York State."[17]

Bevin's remarks, then and afterward, showed a lack of sensitivity to the concerns of world Jewry. After the announcement of the inquiry, on November 13, reporters in Britain questioned the Foreign Secretary about previous Labour Party pledges. Bevin replied with two equivocal comments. "There is not one resolution carried by the Labour Party that I know of," he asserted, "that promised a Jewish state. If ever it was done, it was done in the enthusiasm of a Labour Party Conference." To American reporters Bevin cautioned, "If the Jews, with all their sufferings, want to get too much at the head of the queue you have the danger of another anti-Semitic reaction through it all." The Foreign Secretary's tactless remarks drew a fiery response from Stephen Wise, head of the

American Jewish Congress. "There is no reason for expecting anything but unfairness from Mr. Bevin," Wise wrote to a colleague. "He is an enemy of the Jewish people; he is a foe of human justice."[18]

The President, aware of the strong feelings many Jews harbored against Bevin and the British government, wanted his choice of members of the Anglo-American Committee of Inquiry to show good faith on his part, and also to win the support of those people who viewed the new investigation as another delaying tactic. To this end he requested lists of nominees from his counsel in the White House, Samuel Rosenman, and Secretary of State Byrnes. Both complied, but neither man recommended any Jews.[19] The Secretary of State in particular also opposed professional advocates of either the Arab or Jewish position, as well as elected officials. "It really is not a friendly service to a Senator or Congressman to appoint him to this Commission," Byrnes wrote. "It may embarrass him." The President weighed the recommendations and then decided that he would like these men, "in the order listed":

1. John W. Davis	6. Learned Hand
2. Charles E. Hughes, Jr.	7. Frank W. Buxton
3. Frank Aydelotte	8. Walter Loudermilk
4. Mark Ethridge	9. James G. McDonald
5. Bartley C. Crum	10. Archibald MacLeish

But the President could get only four of his first ten choices. Byrnes declined to ask Hand, who was ill; he eliminated Crum because of his supposedly "leftist" leanings; and dropped Loudermilk because he had just written a book about Palestinian agriculture highly favorable to the Zionists. Ultimately, the State Department composed a delegation but "it was no secret," Richard Crossman wrote, "that President Truman had found it difficult to collect six men willing to accept all the risks of serving on this committee."[20]

Although the joint announcement of the investigation occurred on November 13, 1945, not until December 10 did the two governments reveal the names of the twelve-member committee. The Americans included Joseph C. Hutcheson as chairman, Buxton, McDonald, Aydelotte, William Phillips, and O. Max Gardner. Gardner, the former Governor of North Carolina, accepted but suffered a gallstone attack during his first week on the job and resigned. Crum replaced him. A San Francisco attorney, Crum had been a campaign manager for Wendell Willkie, hoped for a future political career, and clearly indicated where his sympathies lay. During the course of the investigation he established close personal relations with the accompanying Jewish correspondents. Chairman Hutcheson, a judge of the Fifth United States Circuit Court in Houston, started out virtually ignorant about Arab-Jewish problems and with strong feelings against any form of Jewish state. McDonald, a New Yorker, had been League of Nations High Commissioner for Refugees in the early 1930s and had subsequently devoted himself to finding a place where Europe's Jewish outcasts could feel secure. The British regarded him "as hopelessly pro-Zionist." Both Crum and McDonald were friends of David Niles, Truman's adviser for minority affairs in the White House, and all three allied themselves with several important Jewish organizations in the United States. Niles favored the Zionist cause and both his friends and concerned members of the State Department knew it. One British member also thought that Buxton, a friend of United States Supreme Court Justice Felix Frankfurter and editor of the Boston *Herald*, possessed strong Zionist proclivities. Aydelotte, formerly president of Swarthmore College and, at the time of his appointment, director of the Institute of Advanced Study in Princeton, candidly admitted that he had been "strongly anti-Zionist" at the start of the mission. Along with Phillips, former Undersecretary of State and ambassador to Italy, he often appeared to sympathize with the British in their affection for the Arabs. Aydelotte and Phillips were both Anglophiles whose past expressions showed no particular affection for Jews. Aydelotte's biographer quoted him as having written, "The Jews have exhibited genius in many forms but . . . one of the commonest forms is the genius for getting themselves disliked." Phillips had referred to a Russian diplomat in 1923 as "a perfect little rat of a Jew, born in Buffalo, and utterly vile." The views of the two American secretaries, Leslie L. Reed and Evan M. Wilson, reflected prevailing sentiments in the State Department but I have found no indication that they contributed significantly to the positions eventually taken by the six-member delegation.[21]

If the Americans included some representatives who favored the Zionist point of view, the British contingent did not. Attlee had let it be known that "Zionist pressure was very irritating" while his Foreign Secretary perhaps tipped his hand when he asked Richard Crossman, one of his appointees to the Inquiry Commission, a rather strange question. "Ernest Bevin in a three minute conversation," Crossman later noted in his diary, "confined himself to asking me whether I had been circumcised." Other British appointees included Sir John Singleton, chairman of the delegation and Judge of the King's Bench Division of the High Court of Justice, London. This "John Bull in our midst," William Phillips noted, possessed a "touch of pomposity which was not altogether appreciated even by his own colleagues." James McDonald evaluated another member of the committee, Labour MP Lord Morrison (Robert Creigmyle, Baron Morrison), as "the most British of the group; even more sensitive than Sir John about any possible questioning of 'the infallibility' of British officialdom." Another member, Sir Frederick Leggett, former deputy secretary of the Ministry of Labour and National Service, struck Crossman and McDonald as a natural conciliator. Wilfred Crick, economic adviser to the Midland Bank of London, proved Leggett's opposite in temperament. His colleagues on the committee found him "unnecessarily obstinate." The sixth member, Major Reginald E. Manningham Buller, a barrister and Conservative MP, also appeared "stubborn as a mule," pro-Arab, and anti-Jew. Yet when the deliberations ended the following April, all of the Americans, save Hutcheson (who had already departed) and Phillips, concluded that Manningham Buller "was the best, ablest, most substantial of the Englishmen" (Phillips characterized Leggett in that way). Crossman, generally considered the most brilliant person in the group, served as an editor of *The New Statesman and the Nation*, had taught at Oxford University, and in the summer of 1945 won election to Parliament on the Labour ticket. He later declared that all of the British members "had been chosen either because of their strict impartiality—which was only possible if they were totally ignorant of the problem—or because they were anti-Zionist, which was also regarded as impartiality."[22] The British delegation included two staff members, H.G. Vincent and Harold Beeley, who represented the defenders of the British pro-Arab policy in the Middle East, and whose views coincided with those of the chairman, Sir John Singleton.

The members of the commission began their investigation by holding hearings in Washington, D.C. Individuals and groups wishing to make statements were given the opportunity to share their views with the commission. The leading American Jewish organizations sent spokesmen who recalled the history of the Balfour Declaration, the promise of a national home for the Jews, the despicable introduction of the White Paper curtailing Jewish immigration to the Holy Land, the millions killed by the Nazis during World War II, and the world's obligation to provide a homeland for the refugees. These presentations, for the most part, struck the Englishmen as Zionist propaganda and they displayed a guarded hostility toward those individuals who showed little appreciation for the complexities of the Palestine problem. Richard Crossman found himself "irritated during the Washington hearings by the almost complete disregard of the Arab case," even though Dr. Philip Hitti, a Christian Arab representing the Institute of Arab American Affairs, attacked Jewish immigration into Palestine as "an attenuated form of conquest." Hitti also expressed the opinion that Arabs might accept some Jewish DPs if the Western powers did so as well. Crossman believed that Western diplomats shared Hitti's opinion on this matter but "hardly anyone," the Englishman continued, thought that the United States would modify its restrictive immigration laws.[23]

After concluding their work in Washington, the twelve men moved to London to continue the inquiry. In the British capital Jews were fewer and therefore more restrained, the Arab case received a more forceful presentation, and a Syrian asked

Judge Hutcheson, "Why don't you give the Jews part of Texas?" The Foreign Secretary, Ernest Bevin, pledged that he would follow the advice of a unanimous committee recommendation. Yet little material emerged. By the end of the inquiry, a journalist, writing for *Commentary* magazine, observed, "In its hearings in Washington and London, the Anglo-American Committee of Inquiry turned up little that it could not have found in a public library."[24]

After London the delegation split up, ventured to different parts of the Continent to gather first-hand impressions about the DPs, and discovered that the remaining Jews could no longer be comfortable in Europe. Almost all of the committee members learned that Zionism for the Jewish DP was the expression of the most primitive urge, the urge for survival, and recognized as well that the vast majority of the DPs would have to emigrate or perish. Every official with whom they spoke agreed that the Jews could not return to their former homes in Eastern Europe because they had no homes to go to. The committee members found that antisemitism pervaded all of Europe; Poland appeared to be a Jewish graveyard. A renewed Jewish community in Germany seemed out of the question. Both Crossman and Crum revealed in their narratives of the Anglo-American Committee experiences that the Bishop of Vienna's solution for the Jewish problem "was the conversion of the Jews to the true faith." An officer in charge of the DPs and POWs in the British zone of Vienna observed that "it's too bad the war didn't last another two or three months. They'd [the Jews] all have been done away with by then. We'd have had no problems."[25]

Their findings moved all of the members of the committee. Sir Frederick Leggett, who had been hostile to the Jews at the outset, became emotionally exhausted by the trip and resolved to do something to help those who had survived. He even started greeting everyone with the term "Shalom." Sir Frederick told his colleagues, "Unless we can do something and do it soon, we shall be guilty of having finished the job Hitler started: the spiritual and moral destruction of the tiny remnant of European Jewry." It seemed obvious to everyone that only

Palestine's Jews would accept these people, and consequently the committee favored an interim report urging the immediate admission of 100,000 Jews. But Judge Hutcheson received calls from Washington telling him that both the President and the State Department preferred to have no provisional statements made. The Judge, therefore, adamantly opposed the majority position taken by both British and American members, and he prevailed.[26] From the Zionists' point of view, Hutcheson's actions thwarted what might have been a strong statement in support of their goals. As the weeks passed the ardor of several of the Englishmen cooled and their evaluation of the situation would be much more dispassionate in April, when they prepared their report, than it had been in February when they toured Poland and the DP centers.

After Vienna there were stops in Cairo and Jerusalem. Once again hearings were held but in Palestine members of the committee also visited different parts of the land. They observed Arabs living as they had been for centuries and Jews utilizing Western concepts of development. No one disputed that the Jews improved the per capita income of the country and the general standard of living. The committee members found the Middle Eastern portion of the trip extremely informative. Aydelotte, who had left Washington opposed to the Zionist position, admitted that his views had changed. "When you see at first hand what these Jews have done in Palestine," he wrote in his diary, "you cannot . . . vote to destroy it. They are making . . . the greatest creative effort in the modern world." "But the Arabs," Aydelotte continued, "do not understand it, are not equal to anything like it, and would destroy all that the Jews have done and are doing if they had the power. This we must not let them do."[27]

The Arabs regarded the Jews as the vanguard of Western imperialism who would eventually encroach on their territories and force them out. They frequently asked American committee members why, if their country was so concerned about Jews, they did not take them into the United States. "We found that question," Aydelotte later wrote to Earl Harrison, "difficult to answer." The Arab leaders feared Jewish immigration because it promised to undermine their way of life. The Jews did not dispute this point. "Our aim," David Ben-Gurion, head of the Jewish Agency in Palestine, told the Anglo-American Committee, "is a Jewish state."[28]

British officialdom in Palestine, according to Richard Crossman and others, favored the Arabs and disliked the Jews. The former accepted, while the latter rebelled against, the status quo. The British, Crossman wrote to his wife, felt superior to the Arabs but recognized the Jews as "a great deal abler than we are. And the Jews don't often permit us to forget it." The Arab intelligentsia and upper class, a small minority of the population, exhibited a sophisticated, amusing, and "civilized" manner which beguiled British leaders. The Jews, on the other hand, struck Palestinian officials as too intense, too enthusiastic about socialism, and devoid of either charm or breeding. Crossman found these sentiments of his countrymen "utterly nauseating." To his wife, he castigated the British officials as "snobbish, cliquy, second rate and reactionary. They like the Arabs because they are illiterate, inefficient, and easy to govern. They dislike the Jews because Jewish leaders are ten times as able as they are."[29]

When the committee finished in Jerusalem the members flew to Lausanne, Switzerland, for a few days of rest and then the arduous task of preparing their report. On April 1 they resumed working. Judge Hutcheson began by suggesting a framework for their conclusions. Arguing for unity, he outlined a program where neither Arabs nor Jews would dominate the country but where each group might develop independently. The Judge noted the Jewish contributions to modernization and wanted "nothing done to check the normal development of the Jewish homeland." He also favored renewed immigration "on a substantial emergency scale" and regularly thereafter. The American chairman also proposed a binational state and then concluded his introductory remarks by stating that they were merely a basis for discussion and that he would alter "his conclusions if the reasons on which they were based were successfully challenged." McDonald considered the proposal "a masterly statement which I can confess amazed me because it was so out of keeping with many of his private comments and his questions during the public hearings. In his analysis he showed no influence of prejudice or dislikes." Sir John, on the other hand, countered with a speech strikingly reminiscent of the White Paper. Then each of the others spoke in turn. By the end of the first day, McDonald wrote, "it was clear that there were basic differences . . . on almost everything."[30]

The committee members spent the next two weeks arguing and refining their individual positions. The Americans unanimously supported entry of 100,000 Jews to Palestine. The British, with the exception of Crossman, favored either lowering the number or attaching clauses which would have made such entry impossible. Everyone except Buxton agreed that Palestine should be dominated by neither Arabs nor Jews. The Boston *Herald* editor probably won no friends nor influenced colleagues when he warned the British that "the finger of God was guiding the Jews to mastery of Palestine." Crossman, Crum, and McDonald opted for partition. Most of the British members, less emotionally involved with the DPs than they had been after their tour of the assembly centers two months earlier, thought that their country should be freed from the obligations of the Balfour Declaration and the League of Nations mandate which reinforced it. They wanted the opportunity to start again with a clear slate. In effect that would have meant an Arab Palestine with no hope for further Jewish immigration. Moreover, Sir John and Manningham Buller were particularly emphatic in demanding that the local, unauthorized, Jewish army, the *Haganah*, be condemned and disbanded. The committee members knew, however, that this was impossible. The *Haganah* had, in the words of a British Cabinet member, "in some part originated as a protection against Arab violence," and at the time "was the most formidable fighting force in the Middle East because it was not a private army but simply the whole Jewish community organized" to defend itself. Neither the Jewish Agency in Palestine nor American political leaders would accept a proviso requiring its abolition. Certainly, Crossman later wrote to Attlee, "such a recommendation, if made against the unanimous view of six

Americans, would range all American public opinion against us and force the President to back the Zionists against the British government." Members of the British team also thought that the American government should help enforce the policies adopted. None of the Americans envisaged sending troops to Palestine. They rejected that recommendation.[31]

From their expressions in Lausanne it appears that in reaching their conclusions the British members were most impressed by the opinions of their compatriots in Palestine, the recognition of the fact that despite the desperate need of the Jews, Arabs had inhabited the Holy Land for more than a millennium, and Foreign Office policies of favoring Arabs and protecting Middle East possessions. The Britishers still agreed that something should be done to help remove the Jews from the DP assembly centers, but they were not convinced that unlimited immigration to Palestine was the answer.

Resentment, bitterness, and acrimony handicapped the working relationships among the committee members and aggravated the taxing nature of their responsibilities. Most of the men got on each other's nerves, and their belligerency resulted in needless conflicts over trivialities. The two chairmen, according to Aydelotte, talked too much, and Crossman found himself getting "sick to death being told how Texas Judges prepare their judgments." He disagreed with Hutcheson who proclaimed that "you had to reach your conclusions first and then choose the facts which supported them: this was judicial procedure." Sir John Singleton also disturbed his junior colleague because he consorted only with Manningham Buller and staff member H. G. Vincent. The three of them "work[,] eat, drink and for all I know sleep in the same bed," Crossman complained to his wife. Buxton disliked Manningham Buller who, along with Crick, disparaged Crossman who, in turn, found Bartley Crum "a great disappointment. He reads nothing, drinks too much and changes his mind according to the last newspaper he receives from the States." Aydelotte also thought that the San Franciscan "formed his opinions on pretty slender evidence." In addition, Aydelotte loathed Sir John whom he characterized as "a perfectly impossible person," and found only William Phillips, among the Americans, a congenial colleague. He dismissed Hutcheson as "hopeless," Buxton as "the most maladroit of our members," and McDonald as "not any too useful." Neither Sir John, Manningham Buller, nor Vincent got on with any of the Americans, who always opposed the British chairman's suggestions, and the three of them, Crossman concluded, disliked "their British compatriots even more than the Americans."[32]

By the end of the first week it seemed to Crossman that his five colleagues would make one report, the Americans another, and he, himself, a third. "But Morrison, Leggett and I were convinced that it would be disastrous if conflicting reports were issued," Crossman wrote. So he "talked to Phillips, Phillips talked to Aydelotte, Aydelotte talked to Morrison, and finally Aydelotte and Leggett played golf on Sunday. Result—a nucleus of a middle group which will try to mediate between the obstinate intransigence of the two judges." Crossman showed less appreciation for the fact that the American chairman also wanted to avoid a minority report. President Truman had, in fact, cabled Judge Hutcheson during the deliberations in Lausanne, expressing the hope that the committee would produce a unanimous verdict. Unlike Crossman, Buxton, McDonald, and Phillips shared Bartley Crum's conclusion that "it was the leadership of Judge Hutcheson which kept us all together. He would not permit our initial differences to result in a breakup of the committee into American and British groups. It is not an oversimplification to say that had it not been for him, the final report would not have been unanimous."[33]

The final recommendation of the Anglo-American Committee, in a document which ran over 40,000 words, tried, but failed, to placate Arabs, Americans, Jews, and Englishmen. Spokesmen for these groups and government officials rejected a substantial amount, if not all, of the report which suggested that the entire world, not just Palestine, open its doors to the DPs; that 100,000 Jews be allowed into Palestine, and that that country should be dominated by neither group; that the British maintain the mandate until the UN executed a trusteeship agreement; that Arab economic, educational, and political advancement was necessary and measures should be taken to these ends; that Jews should be allowed to purchase lands proscribed in the White Paper; that Jews and Arabs should cooperate with one another for economic development; that compulsory education should be introduced; and that violence and terrorism by both sides should be suppressed.[34]

Although each of the twelve men signed the report, the British members appeared less happy with their recommendations than did the Americans. Some of the latter even speculated about why the British had all affixed their signatures. Perhaps the British thought that their government desired a unanimous report? Allegedly Philip Noel Baker, Minister of State in the British Foreign Office, had gone to Lausanne with a message from Ernest Bevin to Sir John urging unanimity. In light of the later exchange between Crossman and Attlee, however, this seems unlikely. Perhaps the British members intended to communicate their privately held reservations independently to members of the Cabinet? Or perhaps they thought that modifications would certainly be made by the British government in any case? Crum recalled, in fact, British staff member Harold Beeley saying to him in Lausanne, "Well, after all, we certainly won't implement any such program as this," and Sir John pontificating, "You know, Crum, these are only recommendations." To Manningham Buller, Sir John "revealed considerable bitterness" over the final product more openly, and voiced his concern that the British had "given way to American pressure." At a farewell dinner, which he hosted, Sir John, having had perhaps a bit much to drink, "launched into a bitter attack on Hutcheson," and, McDonald added, "I am afraid that what [he] said at this dinner represented what he really felt, nor am I surprised because the resolutions were clearly a defeat of his policies."[35]

If the British delegation faltered under American pressure, the British government certainly had no intention of doing so. While Hutcheson flew to Washington to present a copy of the report to President Truman, Sir John immediately returned to London to inform the Prime Minister of the commission's conclusions. Neither a unanimous verdict nor one recommending admission of 100,000 Jews to Palestine had been anticipated. Most British officials regarded the report "as a sellout to the Americans." Prime Minister Attlee made no effort to hide his displeasure. He had expected support for existing British policies and labeled the document that he received "grossly unfair to Great Britain." Furthermore, he wanted a recommendation that would have included the American government in any actions taken. Crossman was aghast. He had not known that Attlee wanted "to push responsibility on to America. If I had been told that that was your wish," he commented, "I would of course have declined to serve." "You've let us down," Attlee replied, "by giving way to the Jews and Americans."[36]

The British Cabinet discussed the report at length. According to Crossman, "a flow of fantastic misinformation" from the chiefs of staff and Foreign Office officials convinced Bevin that "a general Arab rising in Palestine would follow" its implementation. In actual fact, the commission had been informed, and so related to both Bevin and the Prime Minister, that the reverse was true. A majority of the Anglo-American Committee members thought that the Arabs would accept the new policy, and no additional troops would be required in the Holy Land. Failure to follow through on the recommendations, however, would lead to a Jewish uprising. Crossman made several unsuccessful attempts to convince members of the Cabinet that their beliefs had little basis in fact. Nonetheless, the Cabinet stuck to its guns, agreeing that to allow 100,000 Jews into Palestine in 1946 would incur Arab wrath, imperil the British position in the Middle East, and therefore allow the Russians greater influence in the area. "The essence" of British policy, Cabinet members decided, "should be to retain the interest and participation of the United States government in this position." Attlee's announcement that the report would not be put into effect without American support, and until the "illegal armies" in Palestine had been disbanded, disturbed many Americans.[37]

The stand taken by the British government, in fact, outraged Jews on both sides of the Atlantic. The feisty American reporter

I. F. Stone commented, "What Mr. Attlee wants in effect is American help in disarming the Jews of Palestine." Congressman Emanuel Celler wrote Crossman, "The attitude taken by Prime Minister Attlee in imposing conditions on the immigration of 100,000 Jews into Palestine is utterly indefensible," while London's usually docile *Jewish Chronicle*, a newspaper that went out of its way to support the government's policies, editorialized that Attlee's reference to the "illegal armies"

> was lamentable. What genius it must be wondered, prompted the drafting of that monumental specimen of diplomatic clumsiness and political left-handedness. Surely Mr. Attlee himself cannot have become so unperceptive and unimaginative as not to realize that all the trouble in Palestine . . . sprang basically from one fact—the utter and final breakdown of confidence in the British Government's honour and good faith as regards Palestine. . . . For 20 years the British Government failed persistently and consistently to afford the Jews in Palestine . . . the elementary right of security for life and limb. . . .
>
> To give the appearance of trying to "pull a fast one" at this stage was a blunder quite incredible in a world which still remembers the Sudetenland cession and its consequences.[38]

While the British took a position which made implementation impossible, Truman publicly committed himself to only one of the recommendations: the immediate admission of 100,000 Jews into Palestine. To this end he ordered the Secretary of State to begin consultations with both Arabs and Jews, since he had pledged to consult with the Arabs before any change occurred in Palestinian policy, and then to speak with British representatives about emptying the Jewish displaced persons camps. The American government did not object to assuming financial and technical responsibility for getting the Jews to Palestine, but it had no intention of sending troops there.[39]

In the United States, 78 percent of the public and most of the newspapers approved admitting 100,000 Jews to Palestine. Some of the more prominent journals like *The New York Times*, the New York *Sun*, the New York *Post*, the Philadelphia *Record*, the Baltimore *Sun*, the Washington *Star*, and the members of the Hearst chain endorsed the entire report. Two the major dailies, the *Times* and the New York *Herald-Tribune*, even backed substantial American assistance in enforcing the recommendations. "The United States is too powerful to give advice and insist on action unless we are ready to help in all the ways necessary . . . to put into effect the policy we demand," the *Times* editorialized. The *Tribune*, almost repeating the words of the British Cabinet, declared:

> To this newspaper it seems impossible for American spokesmen to go on much longer trying to make political capital out of the miseries of the Jews and the tragedies of the Palestine dilemma without accepting any responsibility in the premises. If this nation's influence is to produce anything save catastrophe, then it will have to place its power, prestige and if need be its troops behind the basic solutions which it is prepared to advocate.[40]

Several senators and congressmen also endorsed the Anglo-American Committee's conclusion that Palestine should immediately receive 100,000 Jewish DPs but vigorously objected to other aspects of the report. Representative John McCormack (D., Mass.) and Senators Edwin C. Johnson (D., Colorado), Owen Brewster (R., Maine), and Robert F. Wagner, Sr. (D., N.Y.) joined the most ardent Zionists in denouncing all of the other provisions. Senator Wagner perhaps expressed their opinions best when he announced how "elated" he was that the report recommended the admission of so many Jews to the Holy Land but felt "grievously disappointed . . . in the Committee's long-range recommendations as to the political future of Palestine. These latter recommendations appear completely at variance with the overwhelming American sentiment for a Jewish Commonwealth in Palestine."[41]

Most other Americans who gave the subject any thought at all probably shared Wagner's conclusions. Frank Buxton explained why in Lausanne, when he likened the Jewish penetrations of Palestine to the American "conquest of the Indians and the inevitable giving way of a backward people before a more modern and practical one." "There was such a thing as an international law of eminent domain," Buxton argued, and "ultimately the worthy, the enterprising, the improvers, were bound to displace the backward folks." Crossman elaborated upon this theme in a talk at Chatham House, London, in June 1946. He pointed out that few Englishmen could understand "that for Americans the Jewish adventure in creating their National Home by emigrating from their countries of origin is nothing mysterious or strange, as it is to Englishmen." Jews were simply doing what Americans had done. They pioneered in the wilderness and turned an agricultural society into an industrial one. Americans thought of the Arabs as "Red Indians," Crossman continued, and they "would find a certain embarrassment in too repeated a reminder that the rights of the indigenous population must at all costs be preserved against the needs of the colonist!" Americans of all backgrounds were mostly sympathetic to the Jewish position about making Palestine a Jewish homeland and they deplored the White Paper, which they regarded "as an obvious crime." Arabs, on the other hand, appeared "as a human obstacle in the way of a great colonizing achievement."[42]

Another explanation for why Americans supported a plan to get Jews into Palestine came from Ernest Bevin. Unflattering to the United States, and inelegantly expressed, it nonetheless had the ring of truth. At the annual conference of the Labour Party at Bournemouth, June 12, 1946, the Foreign Secretary declared, "Regarding the agitation in the United States, and particularly in New York, for 100,000 to be put into Palestine. I hope it will not be misunderstood in America if I say, with the purest of motives, that that was because they do not want too many of them in New York." Zionists as well as a number of the eastern newspapers denounced the crassness of Bevin's remarks. A Washington *Post* Columnist, Barnet Nover, claimed, "No British statesman of modern times ever before reached so low and despicable a level. . . . His statement stands revealed as an outright anti-Semitic outburst that would have gladdened the heart of the late Adolf Hitler." But the Jewish periodical *Commentary* put a different twist on it. "The readiness of the United States to tell others what they ought to do, while doing little or nothing itself," the journal commented, "had long been one of its less endearing characteristics in the eyes of other nations. Britain, an especially favored recipient of this country's unsolicited advice, had never learned to live with it." President Truman, on the other hand, did not regard Bevin's remark as insulting to the American people. Truman claimed to understand the British Foreign Minister blowing up "because he is often tempted 'to blow up' himself because of the pressure and the agitation from New York."[43]

Arabs, too, resented the self-serving American position. One spokesman labeled the Anglo-American Committee's report "inhuman and harsh" while another declared, "Arabs and Moslems will not take it lying down if these monstrous recommendations are sought to be implemented." Abdul Rahman Azzam Pasha, Secretary-General of the Arab League, announced what everyone knew—but which only Bevin had had the audacity to proclaim publicly—that the 100,000 Jews could be much more easily absorbed in the United States than in the relatively small area of Palestine.[44]

Britain's High Commissioner in Palestine, Sir Alan Cunningham, thought that if the Arabs saw other nations admitting the Jewish DPs they might also be willing to take some as well, but their present attitude was "Why should we, who had no responsibility for the conditions which caused the Jewish Displaced Persons problem, be the only people asked to solve it?" Richard Crossman, as usual one of the more perceptive commentators, may have summed up the dilemma in a letter which he wrote to one of the London dailies:

> The tragedy of Palestine is that our obligations to the Jews and the Arabs are contradictory. We cannot do justice to the one without doing injustice to the other and at the moment we are doing grave injustice to both.
>
> When I weighed up the political objections of the Arabs against the human needs of the homeless survivors of Polish Jewry I felt that the issuing of 100,000 certificates was a lesser injustice than the refusal to do so.[45]

Crossman's perspicacious comments, however, did little to advance the welfare of the Jewish DPs. A year after the war ended in Europe, eight months after Truman had received the Harrison report, and six months after both the British and

American governments agreed to the establishment of the Anglo-American Committee of Inquiry, the world's leading governments had made no significant strides toward the emptying of the DP assembly centers. In fact, as the summer of 1946 approached, the population in the DP camps increased. But in June few people could have anticipated the future occurrences that by mid-August dictated an entirely different American approach to resettlement of the DPs.

4

PALESTINE, POLAND, AND POLITICS

UNANTICIPATED EVENTS in Europe and the Middle East in the summer of 1946 led to a serious reevaluation of the American policy toward displaced persons. At the beginning of June few people in the United States, aside from the Jews, thought much about either the DPs or the report of the Anglo-American Committee of Inquiry. Truman still clung to the hope that the British government would not only allow 100,000 Jews into Palestine but would also agree to postpone decisions on the committee's other recommendations. And in June, despite private conversations indicating otherwise, the President declared publicly that he had no intention of asking Congress to alter the United States immigration laws so that DPs could be admitted. By August everything had changed. Stories from and about Palestine dominated summer newspaper headlines, the British government made demands which would have been politically suicidal for Truman to accept just to get 100,000 Jews into the Holy Land, and the number of Jewish DPs in Central Europe more than doubled. As a result of these changed circumstances Truman embarked upon a new course of action in August to help alleviate the distress of Europe's displaced persons.[1]

The first decision President Truman made in June 1946, with regard to DPs was to accept the advice of Loy Henderson, head of the Department of State's Near East desk, that a Cabinet committee be established to work with the British in implementing the recommendations of the Anglo-American Committee. As a result, on June 11, 1946, the President issued Executive Order 9735 creating the Cabinet Committee on

Palestine and Related Problems, composed of the Secretaries of State, War, and the Treasury. The appointees had no desire to belong to such a committee and delegated responsibility to alternates who, collectively, served as the negotiating team with the British delegation. Secretary of State Byrnes chose Henry F. Grady to represent him and act as chairman of the American group; Secretary of War Robert P. Patterson selected Goldthwaite H. Dorr in his stead, while Secretary of the Treasury John M. Snyder dawdled a bit before anointing Herbert E. Gaston. Grady and Dorr began their preparations immediately. Gaston, who did not receive his appointment until just before the delegation left for London, did not have much background for his task. One American, J. C. Hurewitz, did good staff work for the group in Washington but was not invited to accompany the others to the meeting in London because the commissioners feared that including a Jew might offend the British.[2]

In July the American team, known colloquially as the Grady Commission, crossed the Atlantic to negotiate with its British counterpart. Attlee and Bevin were particularly anxious that the meetings be held in London because they thought that a better settlement would be obtained at home insulated from the Jewish lobby. They were right. Being away from Washington, where they would have had access to a variety of knowledgeable individuals, and lacking familiarity with Zionism, Palestine, and the DPs handicapped the Americans, whom historian Herbert Feis would later dub "rather indifferent officials." More specifically, Richard Crossman wrote, these Americans "knew virtually nothing of Palestine and were singularly ill-equipped to face the real experts of the British Colonial Office on the other side of the table." The British negotiators, headed by Lord Herbert Morrison, took advantage of the Americans' ignorance and placed before them an old Colonial Office plan prepared even before the Labour Government had come to power, which the Anglo-American Committee had already rejected. Dorr, a practicing attorney, knew that a certain advantage existed with the individual or group that got its working paper on the table first; hence he realized the handicap placed upon the Americans who immediately began reacting to proposals rather than presenting their own for discussion. Thus, Dorr recalled, the Grady Commission received a "set of papers" in which the British "had analyzed out, with great care, the various recommendations of the Joint Committee of Inquiry, and I must say there was no weakness or ambiguity in these recommendations." As a result, the Grady Commission accepted the British suggestions without modifications. *The New York Times* reported that it had obtained "incontrovertible evidence" that American staff members had filed written objections to the British proposals but that Grady had ignored these protests and "acted contrary to directives that had been agreed to in Washington prior to the departure of the mission."[3]

An examination of the Morrison-Grady agreement indicates a wide departure from anything that the members of the Anglo-American Committee had recommended. The new plan called for a division of Palestine into separate Arab and Jewish provinces, and separate districts for Jerusalem and the Negev, all under a British central government. The plan envisioned local autonomy combined with British-appointed Speakers of the House for the provincial assemblies, whose approval would be necessary for the enactment of all legislation. In addition the central (British) government retained control of defense, foreign relations, customs and excise taxes, the courts, prisons, police, post office, civil aviation, and broadcasting. In case of differences between the Arabs and the Jews on immigration matters, British officials would decide. Most of the territory went to the Arabs but, according to Grady, the areas assigned to the Jews included 85 percent of all citrus lands, almost all of the industries, railroads, and deep water ports, most of the Mediterranean coast, and practically all of the water resources. As part of the plan 100,000 Jewish DPs would be admitted to the Jewish province if the United States transported them from Europe and paid for their food during their first two months in the Holy Land; thereafter, the Jewish Agency officials would have to guarantee their support.[4]

The British government reacted quite differently to the Morrison-Grady agreement than it had to the report of the

Anglo-American Committee of Inquiry a few months earlier. The Cabinet found this program splendid and singled out chief negotiator Sir Norman Brook for special praise and "appreciation of the skill which [he] has shown in conducting to so successful a conclusion the negotiations with the United States Delegation." One British official called the agreement "a beautiful scheme. It treats the Arabs and the Jews on a footing of complete equality in that it gives nothing to either party while it leaves us a free run over the whole of Palestine."[5]

Even Truman, who after having been President for 15 months should have shown more political sensitivity, applauded the Morrison-Grady proposals. One might have thought that an American President, anxious to woo Jewish constituents, would have recognized that the new presentation tightened British controls, limited Jewish access to wide areas of Palestine, and did nothing to promote an independent Jewish state. But the President claimed that the Grady Commission implemented "to the letter" the report of the Anglo-American Committee, and he regarded the suggestions as eminently fair. Averell Harriman, the United States Ambassador to Great Britain, and three Cabinet Members—Byrnes, Patterson, and Clinton Anderson of Agriculture—agreed with him.[6]

Those most knowledgeable about Jewish attitudes and desires, however, vigorously protested. American Zionist leader Abba Hillel Silver attacked the Grady Report as "a conscienceless act of treachery" and orchestrated nationwide protests. Every American member of the Anglo-American Committee of Inquiry, recalled to Washington for comments upon the new recommendations, opposed the agreement, with Judge Hutcheson denouncing it as a "sellout." Congressional leaders including Ohio Republican Senator Robert A. Taft and Brooklyn Democratic Representative Emanuel Celler led the outcries from Capitol Hill. The chairman of the New York Democratic Party wired Truman, in a statement which underscored the enormous impact of domestic pressures on American foreign policy, to say that if this new plan went into effect it would be useless to nominate a slate of candidates in the Empire State that fall. With such opposition the President reluctantly dropped his support for the Morrison-Grady agreement. To Bronx political boss Ed Flynn he complained, "I have done my best to get" the 100,000 Jews into Palestine, "but I don't believe there is any possible way of pleasing our Jewish friends."[7]

Yet continue to try and please them he must. Jewish groups in the United States were well organized and had friends strategically located. Their defense organizations hired top lawyers, publicists, and community relations personnel to promote group interests and thwart potentially unfavorable legislation and executive actions. An indication of their success is that they never seemed to have had any difficulty reaching people at the highest levels of government. A case in point took place in July 1946, when both the Secretaries of State and War advised Truman to close the West German border to further infiltration from East Europeans. To prevent this action the Jewish lobby orchestrated counterpressure. Representatives of the American Jewish Conference met with Patterson and Undersecretary of State Dean Acheson on July 22 to present the views of their constituents who believed that closing the border "to refugees escaping for their lives" violated humanitarian principles. Massachusetts Democrat John McCormack, the majority leader in the House of Representatives, wrote Truman opposing the move. Two Democratic Senators, Joseph Mead of New York and Joseph Guffey of Pennsylvania, telephoned the President. Guffey urged him to consult with Judge Rifkind, the former adviser to the military on Jewish affairs in Europe, before proceeding further. Secretary of Commerce Henry Wallace visited the President to buttress the Zionist position and to provide answers to any doubts he might still entertain. Then David Niles, Truman's special assistant for minority affairs, who represented Jewish organizations as well, came in to explore the issue further. As a result of these contacts Truman kept the West German border open and East Europeans continued to flock into the DP centers.[8]

The very fact that Truman retained Niles as his adviser on minority affairs reflected the President's concern with issues important to Jews. Almost everything that went into the Oval Office about Jews and Palestine filtered through Niles. As Loy

Henderson put it, Niles "felt that it was his duty to maintain the Zionist support, and through the Zionists, the Jewish support of the President, and he acted accordingly. Furthermore, his personal sympathies lay with the Zionist cause." Niles aided those Jews seeking a homeland in Palestine and would later work very closely with leaders of the American Jewish Committee in 1947 and 1948 to help obtain passage of ameliorative displaced persons legislation. Thirty years after these events occurred Judge Rifkind paid Niles the highest compliment when he described him as a *mentsch*, a Yiddish word which, roughly translated, means a person of fine character.[9]

Thus boxed in by the realities of strategically located representatives, congressional and executive influences, and, as a British Foreign Office official observed, "the practically irresistible force of Jewish opinion in the United States," Truman did not enjoy the luxury of indulging in his exasperation with the relentless pressure that he felt from the Jews, except in private. But in private he exploded! At a July 1946 Cabinet meeting he observed, "Jesus Christ couldn't please them when he was here on earth, so how could anyone expect that I would have any luck?" On another occasion the President remarked, "I think that a candidate on an anti-Semitic platform might sweep the country." Despite these outbursts, Truman did sympathize with the plight of the Jews and publicly fought for their issues as best he could.[10]

Occasionally, championing Jewish concerns presented difficulties, especially given the nature of illegal activities in Palestine. The *Haganah*, the underground Jewish army in the Holy Land, had not engaged in any unusual or major disturbances while the Anglo-American Committee of Inquiry deliberated during the winter and spring. Once Attlee refused to implement the report, however, Jewish militants reacted vehemently. As a result, the British began to crack down on activist Jews in Palestine. In late May and June troops searched Jewish settlements and seized a cache of weapons. Members of the *Haganah*, and the *Irgun*, an even more militant Jewish defense organization, then retaliated by blowing up strategically located bridges and railroad junctions, which practically crippled Army communications in Palestine. About ten days later, on June 29, the British rounded up and jailed 3,000 Jewish leaders and made another intensive search for weapons. But the Jewish militants could not be suppressed. On July 22, 1946, several members of the *Irgun*, disguised as milk delivery men, placed cans with gelignite in the basement of the King David Hotel, the British military headquarters in Jerusalem. After 25 minutes the cans exploded damaging the hotel, wounding 45 people, and killing 91 Britishers, Arabs, and Jews in the building.[11]

The repercussions of the explosion spread far beyond Jerusalem. The British responded with curfews, martial law, arrests, hangings, and deportations of illegal immigrants to Germany. In addition HMG established detention camps in Cyprus to contain the Jewish DPs who were trying to enter Palestine illegally. The news of the bombing reached the White House on July 22, two days before Grady cabled Byrnes of the completion of his mission. The tragedy shocked the President and intensified his concern with the Jewish problem.[12]

Summer developments on the Continent compounded the dreadful news from Palestine. Earlier that month, on July 4 and 5, more than 75 Jews were beaten and another 41 massacred in and around Kielce, a small city 120 miles south of Warsaw. The pogrom, the worst in Poland since the end of World War II, began after a nine-year-old boy, who had disappeared for three days, returned and asserted that he had been kidnapped by Jews and taken to a cellar where he saw 15 other Christian children murdered. The American ambassador in Poland, Frederick Lane, later learned that the Kielce pogrom had been deliberately planned, and the boy himself eventually confessed that he had fabricated the entire story. The Poles in Kielce—men, women, and children—beat Jews mercilessly, squeezed their genitals, crushed bones, broke legs, tore off limbs, and mutilated bodies in the most barbaric fashion. Not all the violence was confined to Kielce. A 70-year-old Jewish woman was dragged from the train in Piekuszow and stoned to death; six other Jews were killed in that town. The police and local militia aided the rioters and officials of the Catholic Church declined to intervene.[13]

The Roman Catholic Church had a history of antisemitism in Poland and no church official spoke against the pogrom until July 19, when Augustus Cardinal Hlond, Archbishop and Primate of Poland, discussed "the highly regrettable events at Kielce." His explanation for the assaults centered on the points that "Jews today occupy leading positions in Poland's Government and are endeavoring to introduce a government structure which the majority of Poles do not desire. This is harmful, as it creates a dangerous tension. In the fatal battle on the political front in Poland, it is to be regretted that some Jews have lost their lives. But a disproportionately larger number of Poles have lost theirs." London's *Jewish Chronicle* correspondent asserted that the Cardinal's statement "will be eagerly pounced on by every anti-Semite in Poland since he repeatedly and implicitly gave his sanction to the half-truth which anti-Semites had been spreading for months." The Cardinal obviously spoke for Poland's Catholic Church. Only one priest, Father Henryk Werynski of Cracow, denounced the Kielce pogromists from the pulpit. That very week Cracow Archbishop Adam Cardinal Sapieka relieved Werynski of his post and barred him from exercising his ecclesiastical duties.[14]

The Kielce pogrom reflected not only hostility toward Jews but the nation's aversion toward the existing government. Poland, more than any other East European country, seemed particularly disrupted by the war and its aftermath. The new Communist government, however, appeared unable to cope with the apparently insurmountable problems with which it had to deal. One issue which it faced squarely, however, was antisemitism. Four Jews received appointments in the new Cabinet and all observers agreed that the government was free of religious intolerance. But fascist and semi-fascist dissidents used the issue of Jews-in-government to rally the antisemitic masses against an extremely unpopular regime. For many Poles, Jew was synonymous with Communist. Thus, antisemitism became a vehicle for anticommunism, and anticommunism could be disguised as antisemitism.[15]

Jews returning to Poland after the war, in search of relatives and with the idea of regaining confiscated properties, found few loved ones and many hostile Poles unwilling to relinquish what had been theirs for the past five years. Persecution commenced as if it had never been interrupted. The British ambassador wrote, "The Poles appear to be as anti-Semitic as they were twenty five years ago." A Jew expressed the opinion that "if the stones of Poland had feelings they would be anti-Semitic feelings." Indiscriminate murders occurred daily, mostly in the Radom and Kielce districts, but also in and around Warsaw, Lublin, Bialystock, and elsewhere. Between September and December 1945, Jews recorded 26 minor pogroms. Antisemites ransacked synagogues in Cracow, shot patients in a Lublin hospital, and randomly pulled Jews from trains and stoned or killed them. On January 9, 1946, the British ambassador estimated that about 300 Jews had been murdered in Poland since the previous May. Jewish sources counted more.[16]

Despite the incontrovertible evidence of discrimination, a bizarre and unfortunate event occurred at the beginning of 1946. On January 2, Lieutenant General Sir Frederick E. Morgan, the British head of UNRRA DP operations in Germany, told a group of reporters that there was a "well organized" Jewish exodus under way from Poland, sponsored by a secret Jewish force. The newcomers appeared to Morgan to be "well dressed, well fed, rosy-cheeked and have plenty of money." They all repeated the "same monotonous story about pogroms," which the General found less than convincing. Sir Frederick's remarks made international headlines. American entertainer Eddie Cantor took out an advertisement in *The New York Times* excoriating the General and entitled it, "I Thought Hitler Was Dead." "Tell me Sir Frederick," Cantor inquired, "are you one of those 'humanitarians,' who believe that the only good Jews are dead Jews?"[17]

Sir Frederick's comments, made only days before the opening of the Anglo-American Committee of Inquiry hearings in

Washington, outraged UNRRA officials in London who demanded his resignation. Sir Robert Jackson, deputy director of the organization, found the statements particularly infuriating because the previous summer he had instructed the General never to say anything publicly about the Jews. Sir Frederick disobeyed orders and Sir Robert fired him. "If he'd bloody well done that in the Army," Sir Robert later recalled, "he would have been court-martialed on the spot and out." But UNRRA director Herbert H. Lehman countermanded the move because Zionist leaders feared that the dismissal might lead to new waves of antisemitism in Germany. The General seemed cocky about the reprieve, and six months later spoke too freely again. He told reporters that UNRRA in Germany served "as a cover for Soviet espionage, black marketeers and dope peddlers." This time Fiorello LaGuardia, Lehman's successor as head of UNRRA, removed him immediately.[18] Sir Frederick's remarks left a dangerous and inherently false impression with military and UNRRA personnel who had to cope with the newcomers, mostly Jewish, in the already overcrowded DP centers.

What actually did exist, in Poland and throughout most of Europe, was a semiclandestine Jewish organization from Palestine, *B'riha*, which helped Jews get out of Eastern Europe. Some went to the DP centers, others fled directly to the Middle East. *B'riha* received generous support both from the Jewish Agency in Palestine and from the American Jewish Joint Distribution Committee (JDC). *B'riha* recruited workers from Palestine and Europe, including a large percentage of DPs themselves. Working quietly, and using legal and illegal means, they led parties of Jews into Central Europe and then on to the Holy Land. The Polish borders were alternately opened and closed, and the same was true for Czechoslovakia. Sometimes frontier guards were bribed or circumvented, and on more than a few occasions *B'riha* provided false documents to those who needed them. Many Polish Jews received Greek papers; the frontier patrols mistook the Hebrew language, which some of the emigrants spoke, for Greek, and let the Jews through. After a time Greek authorities, unaware that such a large "Greek" colony existed in Poland, wondered why none of these people reached Greece. The reason, of course, was that most of the Polish Jews had no intention of going there or remaining in Europe. Between the end of the war in 1945 and the establishment of Israel on May 14, 1948, *B'riha* claimed to have transported almost 250,000 Jews from the Continent to Palestine.[19]

Jews fleeing Eastern Europe took one of several routes. Some went from Poland through Czechoslovakia into Austria and then into American DP camps in Germany, or through the Alps into Italy and then by boat to Palestine. Another stream went from Bucharest through Hungary and into Austria. A third path led from Poland into Berlin and then to British or, more likely, American DP assembly centers. *B'riha* obtained the necessary documents—forged papers were a commonplace in Europe at the time—and "borrowed" whatever supplies, equipment, and trucks it needed to get the Jews on the way to more congenial communities. In early 1946 *B'riha* officials convinced Foreign Minister Jan Masaryk to legitimize the path through Czechoslovakia and thereafter movement proceeded along legal channels.[20]

The new refugees went to DP centers in the occupied zones of Germany and Austria. They were labeled "infiltrees" by the military and UNRRA because they "infiltrated" after having already returned home. Their presence threatened to wreak havoc. More people exacerbated tensions and contributed to making camps even more overcrowded than they already were. By January 1946, more than 40,000 Jewish infiltrees swelled the population of the American zones, and there seemed no end in sight. Another 150,000 had spent the war years in Russia and were due to be released in the spring, with most expected to continue westward through Poland and into the DP camps. In addition, non-Jews, released POWs, and others with no permanent homes made their way into the DP assembly centers in 1945–46. The influx, as well as the anticipated numbers, frightened both military and UNRRA personnel. After the Harrison report was published and General Patton transferred to the command of the Fifteenth Army in October

1945, Third Army officials made greater efforts to accommodate the almost continuous flow of DPs arriving into the camps.
But despite directives of December 16, 1945, and March 1946,
mandating the admission of all of the newcomers into the
assembly centers, in the spring of 1946 most UNRRA and
military government personnel were refusing to obey the
orders.[21]

With the arrival of warmer weather in the spring of 1946
the Jewish stream from East Europe increased; after the Kielce
pogrom, it turned into a torrent. During the summer months
more than 100,000 Jews left Poland. From August 1 to 6, over
10,000 entered the western zones of Germany; on one of those
nights 3,900 crossed the Czechoslovakian border. Many only
passed through on their way to Palestine, but the majority went
to DP centers where facilities had to be found for them.
Physically and psychologically unprepared for the massive
invasion, the military belatedly added to its capacity and
accommodated thousands of the infiltrees in makeshift tents
on swampy terrain. On July 31, 1946, General J. H. Hilldring,
Assistant Secretary of State for Occupied Areas, complained to
Moses A. Leavitt, secretary of the JDC, about "the mounting
difficulties which the displaced person problem is causing the
U.S. Army."[22]

The exodus from Eastern Europe, combined with the failure
of the American and British governments to reach an accord
in regard to Palestine, necessitated major decisions in the White
House. The President had to decide what to do with the DPs
and, as before, Truman took what he considered to be the just
and humane course of action. The Secretaries of State and
War tried to persuade him to close the DP centers to further
entrants but he rejected their advice. The President, according
to all accounts, including his own, sympathized with the DPs
and wanted to help them. He had dispatched Earl Harrison to
investigate the DP camps in 1945 and had written to Attlee
afterward about admitting more Jews to Palestine. Although
Truman acceded to British wishes about establishing an Anglo-
American Committee of Inquiry, he did hope that something
fruitful would result. Then, just before Christmas 1945, the

President issued a directive mandating preferential treatment for all displaced persons, especially orphans, within the existing United States immigration laws. Leaders of several Jewish organizations, including the American Jewish Committee and the American Council for Judaism, had been urging Secretary of State Byrnes to designate the unused immigration slots that had accumulated during the war for DP utilization. The Truman Directive resulted, in part, from this request. The President also allowed 900 refugees, who had been kept isolated since August 1944 in a camp at Fort Ontario in Oswego, New York, to leave the country and re-enter as immigrants. "The immensity of the problem of displaced persons and refugees," Truman declared when he issued the order, "is almost beyond comprehension. . . . This period of unspeakable human distress is not the time for us to close or to narrow our gates."[23]

Truman announced his preferential policy for DPs within the immigration quota system on December 22, 1945. During the preparation of congressional displaced persons legislation in 1948 that date would emerge as a crucial demarcation line. At the time it was hailed as the President's "Christmas present" to the DPs. In reality it helped the DPs only slightly. The entire yearly quota for all of the East European nations, the source of most DPs, amounted to only 13,000; another 26,000 quota places were reserved exclusively for Germans. The number of DPs in Europe, however, hovered around 1 million. Furthermore, such administrative complexities as obtaining visas, passing screening and health examinations, and obtaining transport complicated the problems enormously for the would-be immigrants. American consular officials also demanded appropriate documentation from DPs who had been robbed of all of their possessions and whose birth and marriage certificates remained locked away in Communist countries whose governments would not cooperate. As a result, the more documentation Americans required, the more forged papers they received. Preparation of documents flourished in postwar Europe and knowledgeable individuals discovered ways of obtaining whatever certificates they needed. The Truman Directive also provided for the "corporate affidavit" which allowed voluntary agencies to sponsor individuals and guarantee that an immigrant would not become a public charge. For the first time in American history the government sanctioned the idea that social agencies could accept responsibility for receiving and resettling newcomers.[24]

The President's efforts to aid the DPs impressed few observers. The British Foreign Office recognized immediately "that the number of displaced persons that can be dealt with under the scheme will be quite small, and the statement amounts to little more than a gesture." But gesture or not, the House of Representatives Immigration Committee opposed the directive. Democratic Congressman John Lesinski of Michigan, speaking for his colleagues, wrote the President, "The Committee feels that immigration at this time should not be encouraged." Lesinski's opinion represented a widespread outlook. The Congress and the country were in an anti-immigrant mood and had no desire to lower the barriers. A Gallup Poll, conducted between December 7 and 12, 1945, asked interviewees: "Should we permit more persons from Europe to come to this country each year than we did before the war, should we keep the number the same, or should we reduce the number?" They responded as follows:

More— 5%
Same—32%
Fewer—37%
None at all—14%
No opinion—12%[25]

Public and congressional opinion notwithstanding, for almost a year, Truman had given thought to how more of the DPs might be welcomed in the United States. In June 1946, he indicated to the Grady Commission that it could, if necessary, commit this country to accepting 50,000 refugees if the British would allow 100,000 of them into Palestine. Truman also examined the possibility of getting DPs into Latin America and the British dominions. He held preliminary conferences with Latin American representatives as well as with members of the House and Senate Immigration Committees during the summer. As a result, few legislators appeared surprised when on

August 16 the President announced that he would seek congressional legislation to bring an unspecified number of DPs to the United States. Although he had contemplated recommending as many as 300,000, publicly he stipulated no figure.[26]

Legislative leaders may have been aware of the President's announcement beforehand, but they neither shared his concern nor anticipated passage of any ameliorative legislation. The Democratic chairman of the Senate's Committee on Immigration, Georgia's Richard Russell, called the possible alteration of the quota system a "dangerous precedent." Other senators and congressmen also disliked the idea of bringing more DPs to this country. A Massachusetts representative believed that "too many so-called refugees pouring into this country bringing with them communism, atheism, anarchy and infidelity" could not be tolerated. Texas Congressman Ed Gossett not only announced vigorous opposition to the entrance of more immigrants but indicated as well that he would introduce legislation to cut quotas in half, something he had done earlier that year and was prepared to do again.[27]

Others in the United States also thought the President's humanitarian gesture misguided. Some of the more ardent Zionists, unable to speak out publicly, regarded the announcement "as a declaration of collapse on Palestine by this administration," and frowned upon the idea. They feared that bringing DPs to the United States would weaken the pressure to establish a Jewish homeland in Palestine. Furthermore, a national majority continued to oppose increased immigration. In late August pollsters questioned Americans: "President Truman plans to ask Congress to allow more Jewish and other European refugees to come to the United States to live than are allowed under the law now. Would you approve or disapprove of this idea?" Only 16 percent of the respondents answered affirmatively; 72 percent disapproved; 12 percent had no opinion.[28]

On the other hand, Truman's tenuous pledge won immediate approval from *The New York Times*, the Washington *Post*, and leaders of non-Zionist Jewish organizations. Before his announcement no Jewish spokesman or prominent American leader, with the exception of Dean Virginia Gildersleeve of Barnard College, publicly suggested the possibility of amending the immigration laws. The *Times* praised the President's move and added, "We must assume our fair share of responsibility for the whole program of the refugees." Two leading Jewish spokesmen, Joseph Proskauer and Lessing Rosenwald, respective presidents of the American Jewish Committee and the American Council for Judaism, also applauded the statement.[29]

Thus, as the summer ended, a new phase in the efforts to assist DPs began. To Truman, and some of the leading non-Zionist Jewish spokesmen, it became obvious that the United States would have to help bring pressure on Great Britain to open the gates to Palestine. At the same time it was also apparent that getting Congress to enact ameliorative legislation would be no easy task. But politically sensitive American Jews, grasping at Truman's tentative proposal, embarked upon a new plan in the fall. Carefully designed, well organized, and adequately financed, it ultimately provided the vehicle for emptying the European DP centers.

5

THE FORMATION OF
THE CITIZENS COMMITTEE

TRUMAN'S DECISION to seek congressional approval for the admission of more DPs to the United States drove deeper the wedge between Zionist and non-Zionist American Jewish organizations. Before August 1946, all of the Jewish groups supported the proposal to bring 100,000 Jewish DPs to Palestine. The Zionists saw it as a first step toward a Jewish state. The non-Zionists viewed it merely as a move to help the survivors start anew. But when it seemed that the President had abandoned hope of getting the DPs into the Holy Land, the American Zionists and non-Zionists moved in different directions. The Zionists, headed by Rabbis Abba Hillel Silver and Stephen S. Wise, intensified their efforts for a Jewish commonwealth; the non-Zionists, represented by the American Jewish Committee (AJC) and the American Council for Judaism (ACJ), started working to bring 100,000 Jews to the United States. The latter two organizations, cognizant of the tremendous task involved, established a nondenominational Citizens Committee on Displaced Persons (CCDP) to make public and congressional opinion more receptive to such a move. During the next three and a half years Irving Engel of the AJC directed the operation; Lessing Rosenwald of the ACJ and members of his family provided the bulk of the financing; and William S. Bernard, a University of Colorado sociologist who had been brought to New York a year earlier to work for an organization promoting postwar immigration, oversaw day-to-day operations of the new lobby, to which Earl G. Harrison lent his name as chairman.[1]

The idea of bringing 100,000 Jews to the United States simply could not arouse Zionists as did the drive for a Jewish Palestine. To be sure, the American Jewish Conference, organized in 1943 to speak for American Jewry on matters concerning the rights of European Jews and in regard to Palestine, "wholeheartedly" supported the goal of getting the Jewish DPs into the United States. Some Zionists even sat on the board of directors of the CCDP. But a powerful minority of Zionists thought that bringing DPs to this country meant sabotaging the ultimate goal of the Jewish state. They believed that more than 100,000 suffering Jews in Europe stood as a constant reminder of the world's inhumanity and their presence there buttressed the argument for a Jewish Palestine. Fortunately, this minority did not undermine the efforts of those working with the CCDP.[2]

Before the AJC and the ACJ took any specific action, however, others in the United States called for the admission of some DPs. The Federal Council of the Churches of Christ in America, the nation's largest body of Protestant churches, officially endorsed the idea of bringing more refugees to this country, as did the Catholic weekly, Commonweal. Then, in a full-page editorial in its September 23, 1946, issue, Life magazine became the first national journal of general interest to urge a new policy. The editorial took a strong stand, declaring: "The most shocking fact about the plight of these displaced persons is not that they are interned. It is the fact that the U.S. government and people have the means to open the door for many of them but have not done so." Life's editorial, along with demands from New York state politicians, spurred Truman to another public commitment. On October 4, 1946, he reiterated his pledge to recommend that Congress pass ameliorative legislation to help DPs.[3]

Similar stirrings occurred in Jewish circles as well. Two days before Truman's announcement, Alan M. Strook of the AJC's administrative committee urged upon his colleagues the need for a campaign of public education and persuasion. Strook summarized the history of the Jewish DPs, the numerous attempts made to get them into Palestine, their increased flow westward after the pogroms in Poland, and the disappointing results after the Truman Directive. Although the President had mandated favorable treatment for DPs under the immigration laws the previous December, ten months later only 2,400 Jews had benefited from the order. The key problem, Strook pointed out, centered on the national origins quota system written into the American immigration laws. The countries from which most of the Jews emanated had very low quotas. Hence, although Eastern Europeans of all faiths constituted more than 95 percent of the United Nations DPs, the annual allotments for their countries provided little hope that these people would ever see American shores. He then presented figures to indicate the annual quota limit of each of these nations:

Poland	6,524
Latvia	236
Estonia	116
Lithuania	386

Therefore, Strook continued, any significant effort to help the DPs would require congressional modification of existing restrictions. Mindful of the tremendous opposition to liberalizing the immigration laws, Strook nevertheless believed that the task could be accomplished and urged that the AJC assume leadership in this endeavor. The members of the administrative committee agreed with the suggestions and put the AJC on record as favoring the admission of more DPs to the United States.[4]

The AJC, along with other Jewish organizations, had thought about changing the restrictive immigration laws while World War II was still going on, and collectively several groups laid the groundwork for future action. In 1944 the American Council of Voluntary Agencies for Foreign Services (ACVAFS), established the National Committee for Postwar Immigration Policy (NCPI), after several Jewish groups decided upon its need. Both the ACVAFS and the NCPI were nonsectarian, funded primarily by Jewish organizations to promote good will among Americans, and to foster a liberal immigration policy.

These nonsectarian associations existed because many Jews believed that their goals would be unobtainable if they were identified as such. The leading Jews in the country recognized that widespread antisemitism and anti-immigrant feeling existed in the United States and argued that unless steps were taken to combat such hostility Congress might bar all immigration after the war. Ostensibly a nonsectarian and unified association, the NCPI included the AJC, the American Jewish Congress, B'nai B'rith, the Hebrew Sheltering and Immigration Aid Society (HIAS), and token representatives from Protestant and Catholic groups among its members. The NCPI goal was to promote the entry of more Jews to the United States under the guise of doing a "scientific review" of American immigration policy. Throughtout its six-year lifespan, until the publication of *American Immigration Policy* in 1950, the Jewish groups backed it strongly and, not surprisingly, the NCPI concluded that this country did need more immigrants. Earl Harrison accepted the post of NCPI chairman and, after his tour of the DP camps for Truman in the summer of 1945, also helped the ACVAFS to commission a study of the DP problem. That agency's report, in June 1946, timidly recommended the establishment of a new intergovernmental agency to handle DP problems but never once mentioned the Harrison report by name or suggested that the United States alter its immigration policies to admit DPs.[5]

But Lessing Rosenwald, president of the American Council for Judaism, found the ACVAFS' recommendations timorous, and he wanted to proceed with a more concrete plan. By the spring of 1946 Rosenwald had already decided to investigate the possibilities of finding new homes for Jewish DPs in the United States. In September, after Truman's announcement, the ACJ chairman established a committee to explore the chances of getting the DPs into this country. Rosenwald, who lived in Jenkintown, a suburb of Philadelphia, knew Earl Harrison and asked him to chair a national citizens committee which would undertake the necessary efforts in the United States. Rosenwald also approached the major Jewish organizations about working in concert. When he discovered that

AJC operations were also in the embryonic stage, Rosenwald accepted Irving Engel's invitation to cooperate.[6]

Rosenwald, a member of the AJC as well as president of the ACJ, knew that the senior organization had 40 years of experience and that, although it did not win every campaign or always change public policies, it had a reputation for professional competence. The AJC employed well-qualified administrators, including experts in community and public relations, research, finance, and political analysis. Necessary skills not possessed by AJC members and employees were provided by outsiders.

The AJC Administrative Committee had already established an immigration subcommittee under the stewardship of Irving M. Engel, a New York attorney, when Rosenwald made the initial contact. Engel, John G. Slawson, AJC executive vice-president, and Selma G. Hirsh, another AJC official, worked as a team on the DP issue. None of them sought individual publicity because each one recognized that too much Jewish identification with proposed immigration changes would undermine the purpose of their efforts. Rosenwald also devoted himself to the cause but kept out of the limelight.[7]

The AJC began operations quickly, even before it had coalesced with the ACJ. Its department of public education and information prepared and mailed a brochure on the immigration problem which contained ideas concerning the liberalization of American laws. Statements in support of the program were obtained from respected public figures. The brochure served as the opening volley in the campaign to admit Jewish DPs and was distributed, significantly, with no indication of the organizational source. Then and later Jews did not want to be too visibly identified with the movement to bring in DPs. AJC staff and officials also approached congressmen and senators; alerted and distributed suitable materials to the mass media; and sought out sympathetic individuals to proclaim their cause.[8]

They relied heavily upon their contacts with important national figures like David Niles. From the White House, Niles kept them abreast of the President's current attitudes and problems, frequently advising about timing and courses of action. For example, in September 1946, he recommended that "the best procedure to follow at the moment is to undertake a campaign of letter writing to the President asking for a firmer stand on the lowering of immigration barriers." Later Niles met regularly with Engel and his "strategy committee."[9]

Engel also sought out others whose assistance was deemed vital. The November 1946 congressional elections swept the Republicans into majority control of both houses. As a result, Engel visited GOP Senate leader Robert Taft of Ohio in Washington. Taft promised Engel that the Republican steering committee would appoint a committee to investigate the DP problem. Engel met as well with Catholic Bishop J. Francis A. McIntyre, a close associate of Francis Cardinal Spellman of New York City, and other church officials. Although the Catholics on the East Coast did not appear to want DP legislation, a week or so after the Engel-McIntyre discussion the Catholic Bishops of the United States issued a statement saying that DPs have "the right of refuge—a right that is sacrosanct in our history and culture." Through Bishop Mc-Intyre, Engel secured the backing of William Green, President of the American Federation of Labor (AF of L).[10]

The most important meeting occurred at a luncheon of an AJC subcommittee in early November where the groundwork and strategy for the entire campaign emerged. The conferees agreed with Rosenwald's idea that a broadly based national citizens committee, composed of prominent Christian, and perhaps a few Jewish, leaders from the ranks of the ministry, business, labor, education, and social welfare should be formed. It would serve as a "political action and propaganda group which could . . . swing public sentiment in favor of relaxing immigration laws in order to admit a fair share of displaced persons in this country." Thus, in the classic tradition of lobbying, a narrow humanitarian interest (aiding Jewish DPs) would take on an expanded focus (helping all DPs, 80 percent of whom were Christian), and would strive for widespread support.[11]

The new Citizens Committee on Displaced Persons (CCDP)

would have an executive and advisory board composed of a cross-section of important individuals, and would be carefully balanced politically and geographically. Most of its members would be political conservatives, non-Jewish, and would represent major national organizations. All American groups favoring liberalized immigration laws or emergency legislation to aid DPs would be encouraged to work through the new CCDP. It was also decided that Earl Harrison should be asked to invite about forty prominent people to meet at a strategy session launching the new organization. The AJC, and it was hoped other Jewish and non-Jewish groups, would lend their facilities to achieve the desired goals. Before the luncheon meeting ended, the AJC representative to both the NCPI and the American Council of Voluntary Agencies for Foreign Services received instructions to broach the idea of a proposed citizens committee at his next meeting with these groups.[12]

While plans went forward to establish the CCDP, the AJC Immigration Committee members discussed the kind of legislation they wanted. They remembered the figure of 100,000 Jewish DPs first mentioned in the Harrison Report and repeated in the Anglo-American Committee of Inquiry recommendations. But Jews constituted only 20 to 25 percent of the European DPs in the fall of 1946. To bring 100,000 of them to the United States, the proposed law would probably have to stipulate four times that amount if a proportionate number of non-Jewish DPs were also incorporated into the legislation. Hence the AJC Immigration Committee opted for legislation calling for the admittance of 400,000 *European* DPs over a four-year period with no monthly or annual limitations. Aware of congressional and public affinity for the immigration quotas and cognizant of the fact that William Green, President of the AF of L, whose support was thought to be vital, indicated that his organization would under no circumstances agree to tampering with the quota system, the AJC stressed that the proposed legislation should be pushed as an emergency humanitarian measure. The Immigration Committee members knew that thousands of alleged Nazi collaborators in the DP camps might receive visas if such legislation ultimately passed, but they believed that "a calculated risk . . . should be taken since it was unavoidable if a haven were to be found in this country for any really significant number of displaced Jews."[13]

AJC leaders knew that perhaps 12 to 15 million displaced persons roamed the globe. At least 2 million Chinese had been displaced in Asia during the war. The Potsdam Agreement, in the summer of 1945, resulted in the expulsion of about 12 million *Volksdeutsche*, people of German descent, from East Europe although most of these people could trace their residence back several centuries. In addition, other Europeans, Africans, and Asians had been forced from their homes before, during, and after the war and still had not been properly settled. But the Jewish leaders felt little sympathy for expelled Germans, knew almost nothing about the Africans and Asians, and believed strongly that to help 100,000 Jews the campaign had to be narrowly and sharply focused on those people uprooted by the war in Central and Eastern Europe. Aside from the Jews, no other well-organized and well-financed American group thought enough about the homeless millions to take concerted action on their behalf. As a result, the American public learned only about the 850,000 or so DPs in or near the German, Austrian, and Italian assembly centers, and received almost no education about the other several million for whom the Jewish leaders felt no sense of responsibility.

Most of the work done by the AJC and its immigration committee members remained unknown to the public and to the distinguished Americans whom Earl Harrison invited to a strategy session at the Waldorf Astoria hotel in New York City on December 20, 1946. The AJC assumed primary responsibility for preparation of the CCDP organizational meeting. Letters on Harrison's personal stationery over his signature were typed and mailed by AJC staff members who also sifted lists of distinguished persons who were to receive invitations. The 32 people who accepted the invitation included such notables as former Supreme Court Justice Owen Roberts; Charles P. Taft, president of the Federal Council of the Churches of Christ in America; Dr. Samuel McCrea Cavert, executive director of that organization; Major General William

J. Donovan, former head of the Office of Strategic Services; Bishop McIntyre; and a few Jewish leaders from business, labor, politics, philanthropy, and religious organizations. The AJC did not think it politically important to include representatives of Polish, Latvian, Lithuanian, Estonian, Ukrainian, or Yugoslav organizations in this meeting although their compatriots made up the overwhelming majority of the DPs. Sensitive to American antipathy toward immigrants and foreigners at that time, the AJC wanted to avoid including minorities in the forefront of the battle. The Jewish leaders believed that new legislation would emerge only if a significant number of respected Protestants called for it. Later on, the CCDP welcomed the backing of a wide variety of ethnics to supply additional names on the list of supporters for the proposed modifications in the immigration statutes. But in the beginning, the AJC utilized only "important" and "distinguished" Americans.

At the Waldorf meeting on December 20, Harrison explained its purpose. He reviewed the DP problem, suggested that the more prosperous nations of the world should take their "fair share" of DPs for permanent settlement, and indicated that the United States must assume the lead. Dr. Bernard then spoke to the group and explained that our "fair share" would be about half of the remaining "hard core of non-repatriable displaced persons," which he estimated at 800,000. Bernard claimed that the "fair share" quota of 400,000 for the United States was selected because the country had "51 percent of the combined population of the major potential immigrant-receiving countries." The explanation seems simplistic, but no one questioned him. Thereafter, the CCDP would cling to the 400,000 as our "fair share" although the number of DPs fluctuated; moreover, the definition of "eligible DP" remained a subject of significant controversy among those familiar with the situation in Europe.[14]

The discussion that took place after Bernard had finished his presentation revealed virtually unanimous support for the purposes of the CCDP. Dr. Cavert pointed out that it would be difficult to obtain the necessary legislation but "often what had been considered impossible had been accomplished, particularly if public opinion has been properly organized." Jacob Potofsky of the Amalgamated Clothing Workers Union thought that this was the time to act since severe economic problems did not exist; thus the United States had "a great opportunity to demonstrate its moral leadership." After several others had spoken in the same vein, the group elected Harrison chairman of the CCDP and authorized him to establish the necessary organizational and administrative committees. Dr. Chaim Finkelstein of the Jewish Theological Seminary moved that the CCDP "transmit to President Truman a statement of its existence and purposes and interest in his program." His motion carried unanimously. Harrison officially accepted the chairmanship, and promised to make further reports to the members whenever appropriate.[15]

From the AJC standpoint the meeting had gone perfectly. A number of eminent Americans had met and agreed to help pave the way for significant new legislation to bring DPs to the United States. Only a few Jews had participated, and everything appeared to have been done openly and democratically. It was, as far as everyone could see, a consensus of some important and knowledgeable American leaders. Shortly thereafter, Eleanor Roosevelt, Fiorello LaGuardia, William Green, Edward R. Stettinius, Jr., the former Secretary of State, and Charles P. Taft lent their names as vice-chairmen to the CCDP letterhead.

Although representatives of various professions and religious bodies ostensibly teamed up to establish the CCDP, very few of the non-Jews made, or induced their organizations to make, substantial financial contributions to the new lobby. Over 90 percent of the financing of the CCDP came from individual Jews, Jewish groups, and their friends. Lessing Rosenwald and his family contributed over $650,000 to the CCDP's million-dollar budget. Prominent Jews like Judge Proskauer, Herbert Lehman, and Ben Lazrus, founder of Benrus Watches, continually solicited funds from friends.[16] Furthermore, the AJC and other Jewish organizations recruited members for the CCDP and provided it with contacts, speakers, and ideas.

The CCDP, subsequently recognized as one of the largest

and best-run lobbying groups in the nation in 1947 and 1948,[17] demonstrated considerable ingenuity in its operations. William S. Bernard, the executive secretary, organized and directed the staff, which included a Washington counsel (the AJC had its own political representatives in Washington), a publicity division, a field organization section which coordinated the work of the national CCDP with state and local groups, and a department which maintained contact with, and provided materials to, important national associations. CCDP representatives went to national and local conventions, spoke with key leaders, inspired letter-writing campaigns, organized local groups, analyzed the nature of various committees, decided which individuals and congressmen to isolate for special attention, and sent out mailings. The home office kept records on different cities and states along with tabulations of possible congressional votes. Both local and central offices distributed thousands of flyers to citizens and newspapers, wrote radio scripts, suggested magazine articles, and drew mats and posters. According to one authority, "almost all editorials on the displaced persons problem appearing in the press of the nation were inspired, if not written, by the Committee" (see Fig. 5.1).[18] CCDP also furnished speakers and films and made its services available to local, prominent people who might be helpful to the cause. By May 1948, nearly 600 radio stations used its materials, and millions of Americans had seen the film *Passport to Nowhere* (prepared with professional actors and technicians) on the plight of the DPs, which RKO distributed nationally. Almost every major American organization, except for the Daughters of the American Revolution, eventually endorsed the goals of the CCDP. The strongest newspaper supporters included *The New York Times*, the New York *Herald-Tribune*, the Louisville *Courier-Journal*, the St. Louis *Post-Dispatch*, and the Washington *Post*.[19]

At the outset of its campaign the CCDP merely tried to inform the public of the facts, present the possible alternative solutions, and then indicate the only judgment it deemed feasible. Thus the lobby emphasized that 80 percent of the approximately 850,000 DPs in Europe were Christian, which

VE-DAY EDITORIAL
Suggested by the

CITIZENS COMMITTEE
ON DISPLACED PERSONS

39 East 36th Street
New York 16, N.Y.

1710 Rhode Island Ave., N.W.
Washington, D.C.

The Editorial herewith submitted should be accepted as a suggestion. If your newspaper is the sole publication in your community this editorial may be reproduced without the risk of conflicting publication. Date of publication should be on or about V-E Day plus two years—May 8, 1947.

"Send These, The Homeless, Tempest-Tossed, To Me!"

A bill now before Congress possesses the authority to remove a disgraceful blot from America's postwar record.

This bill, introduced by Rep. William G. Stratton Jr., Republican Representative-at-large from Illinois, asks for temporary emergency legislation to permit 400,000 driven, despairing, homeless, persecuted individuals to enter the United States in the next four years.

The emergency legislation does not request special privileges for these persons. During the past nine years more than twice 400,000 could have come to America except for the misfortune of war. Their quotas disappeared in the smoke of the battle. The bill merely asks for temporary legel machinery so that these men and women—and the children—without a country may find a home here.

And they won't take urgent housing from anyone because they will live with relatives and those without relatives will be settled by welfare groups in rural areas where housing is available on farms for agricultural workers.

Who are these people? They are the "displaced persons." More than 75 per cent of them are victims of one or another of European dictators, no matter under what cause or name the dictatorship flourished—communist or fascist. They are, these 80 per cent, of the Christian faith, a good many of them Polish and Baltic Catholics. Another portion of them, by far the smallest number, only one out of five, is of the Jewish faith. Some of them are political exiles, and since fascism is nominally dead in Europe today, this means that some of them are exiles from countries now controlled by communism.

Out Statue of Liberty, standing majestically above the waters of New York City's Upper Bay, carries at its base a famous quatrain:

"Send these, the homeless, tempest-tossed, to me!"

Congressman Stratton's bill would at least abolish the hypocrisy of this invitation at the base of our world-famous Statue of Liberty, which under our present laws means so little since the "homeless, tempest-tossed" are at present barred from entry here.

Write your Congressman to support this bill and make the invitation meaningful in this human emergency.

A typical editorial sent out to newspapers throughout the country by the CCDP.

Source: William G. Stratton MSS. State Historical Society of Illinois.

was not widely known at that time. CCDP literature also discussed the fact that at the end of World War II there were several million uprooted people in Europe but most had been repatriated. There remained about a million or so "hard-core" DPs, mainly from Eastern Europe, who did not return home either because they feared persecution, or because their families and former lives had so disintegrated that they would not return. According to flyers and brochures distributed, the choices for those peoples were as follows: to be repatriated against their will, to remain in DP camps indefinitely, to be dumped into the shattered European economies and left to fend for themselves, or to be resettled elsewhere. CCDP leaders concluded, "The last was the only humanitarian as well as realistic solution."[20]

The organization's publicity took several liberties with the facts. "Do You Know That?" one of the CCDP's most widely distributed handouts, suggested that most of the DPs were "survivors of Nazi concentration camps and of slave labor battalions." That was patently untrue. Father Walter Dushnyck of the Catholic periodical *America* criticized the CCDP's "tactical error . . . which failed to emphasize in its campaign the real reasons of the plight of displaced persons in Europe—namely, that the greatest majority of them are fleeing Soviet totalitarianism." Father Dushnyck was correct as far as most of the Protestant and Catholic DPs were concerned. The majority of the Balts, Ukrainians, and Poles had fled from Stalin, not Hitler. Few, if any, of the Balts had been incarcerated in concentration camps or placed with slave labor battalions. Furthermore, most of the Jewish concentration camp survivors had already left the DP assembly centers by early 1947. But the remaining Jewish DPs suffered from postwar European antisemitism. Polish Jews who left Russia in 1946 could not start anew in Poland. Jews who had hidden out during the war also found no hospitable community afterward. CCDP leaders, however, may have thought that complete honesty about the DPs required complex explanations. They may also have decided that getting their message across sharply and quickly, like a good advertisement, necessitated a rearrangement of the facts. "Do You Know That?" highlighted some "of the organizations which have gone on record as favoring the admittance of a fair share of displaced persons" and mentioned by name, in the following order, the Federal Council of the Churches of Christ in America, the National Catholic Welfare Conference, Catholic War Veterans, the United Council of American Veteran Organizations, the National Conference of Union Labor

Legionnaires, the American Federation of Labor and Congress of Industrial Organizations. But the Jewish supporters remained unspecified and were identified only at the end as "the major national Jewish organizations" and lumped together in the same sentence with "many other civic, educational and religious groups."[21]

So desirous was the CCDP to play down those aspects of the DP portrait that might suggest association of the term *DP* with Jew, that its most publicized flyer carefully avoided emphasizing occupations of the European refugees that people sometimes thought of as possibly Jewish, such as tailor, physician, or attorney. Instead the lobby highlighted the facts that "*There are some 90,000 agricultural workers among them; some 21,000 are construction workers; some 22,000 are domestics; about 32,000 are professionals;* hundreds of others are artisans." When the United States Senate ultimately prepared a bill giving preference to agricultural workers among the DPs, both the CCDP and the Jews complained about discrimination, since only 2 percent of the Jews fell into that category. But by that time it was too late. Emphasizing certain facts for public consumption while they were trying to get legislation passed, and then condemning legislators afterward for having acted upon them, resulted in the Jewish groups being hoist by their own petard, a fact which certain Zionists would later pounce upon.[22]

Along with attempts to arouse an apathetic and prejudiced populace went concrete proposals. The CCDP prepared a bill, based on AJC recommendations, for the United States to accept its "fair share" of DPs. AJC and CCDP leaders had decided earlier that to receive the widest possible support their legislation should be introduced in Congress by a member of the majority party from the Midwest. Hence they approached, in turn, Republican Senators Homer Ferguson and Arthur H. Vandenberg of Michigan, and then Robert Taft of Ohio, but each refused to sponsor the measure. Then they went to the House of Representatives where they had to make do with William G. Stratton, Representative-at-Large from Illinois. A later in-house AJC memo indicated that "Mr. Stratton would not have been our choice." Efforts were made to find a

Judiciary Committee member, but "the feeling was so adverse at the time no one cared to 'stick his neck out' by introducing such a bill."[23]

Congressman Stratton was one of the many non-Jews who had a sincere desire to help alleviate the DP problem. A midwesterner who aligned himself with the conservatives of his party on most political issues, he felt an "urgent need" to do something to help the refugees. He also thought that it was "good foreign policy" to assist in emptying the DP camps because it would show the world that our actions reflected the nation's humanitarian beliefs. Finally, as a congressman-at-large, he represented the entire state of Illinois; he counted among his constituents large groups of people who felt a kinship with the Poles, Jews, and others remaining in the assembly centers.[24]

On April 1, 1947, Representative Stratton introduced a bill to allow 400,000 DPs into the United States during the next four years. Most congressmen, knowing little about the DPs, could not understand why they had not gone home after the war, and feared a possible economic depression if a large number of immigrants arrived. In February 1947, about five weeks before Stratton proposed the legislation, Eleanor Roosevelt remarked that "every representative in Congress with whom I have talked has told me that the general feeling is that they wish to stop all immigration." Democratic Senator Burnet R. Maybank of South Carolina probably expressed the dominant sentiment when he wrote to a constituent on January 16, 1947, "We have too many foreigners here already and I think we should get rid of them rather than bring in additional ones." President Truman thought Stratton's figures preposterous. "The idea of getting 400,000 immigrants into this country," he wrote David Niles, "is, of course, beyond our wildest dreams. If we could get 100,000 we would be doing remarkably well." Truman knew, better than Stratton, that mail to the White House and to Congress ran 7–1 against allowing DPs into the United States, and few knowledgeable Washingtonians ever tried to legislate against such overwhelming public sentiment.[25]

The correspondents provided a variety of reasons for constituents' feelings. The housing shortage, insufficient job opportunities, opposition to Jews, Communist infiltration, and the threat to the "American way of life" constituted the most frequently stated objections. Scattered letters stipulated fears about "radicals and undesirables," "riffraff," and "the scum of Southern and Eastern Europe," terms which might have been used to cover up prejudices against Jews. Some of the more explicit letter writers, though, left nothing to the imagination. One wrote, "the word 'refugee' is synonymous with *Jew*, and the *latter* is synonymous with Red!" Another opposed "Communistic Hebes, new dealers of the rankest kind." A third claimed that DP legislation would result "in a flood of Jews coming to the United States. We have too many Jews." *Newsweek* reported that many Americans asked, "Weren't the DP's *Jews?* Didn't they come from Eastern Europe? And didn't that mean that most of them were probably Communists?"[26]

Misperceptions about the number of Jews among the DPs continued well into 1948. For example, while it was endlessly stressed that the majority of DPs were Christians, many Americans failed to digest the information and continued to equate the term "DP" with "Jew." In June 1947, two months after the introduction of the Stratton bill and five months after the CCDP inaugurated its campaign, newscaster Fred Van Devanter of radio station WOR in New York announced that the proposed legislation would admit 400,000 "*Jewish* displaced persons" to the United States. "What will 400,000 Jews do when they get here?" a constituent of Congressman Stratton's inquired. A year later *New York Times* columnist Anne O'Hare McCormick wrote, "although it has been explained a thousand times, Americans are slow to realize that 80 per cent of the displaced persons . . . are non-Jews."[27]

Despite CCDP efforts to present relatively accurate statistics on the proportion of Jews and Gentiles among the DPs in Europe, Executive Secretary Bernard acknowledged in December 1947 "that the average unthinking and uninformed American is all too prone to categorize DPs as Jewish, and to use that fiction as an excuse for apathy, delay, or hostility to our program." The conviction that refugees were Jews existed among members of the public and church organizations as well. When a Jewish agency publicized some aspect of its work with DPs, the CCDP problem increased "a hundred fold," its publicity director informed Bernard. No margin existed for error or awkward publicity. Shortly after a November 1947 newspaper article appeared indicating that a Jewish organization was raising $13 million to bring Jewish DPs to the United States, the CCDP representative in Minnesota

> met stiffened resistence among the church groups. One church leader told him quite frankly that it was because everyone thought that this was a Jewish problem that the church leaders shied away from assisting the campaign morally or financially. On Thanksgiving Day, the Minneapolis morning paper ran a story about "A Jewish DP grateful for his holiday in America," adding that this boy got into America with forged credentials posing as a Catholic. Another church leader contacted Mr. Armstrong and accused him of using the entire problem as a cover for Jewish organizations.[28]

Awareness of these attitudes no doubt stalled congressional activities and affected the President as well. After stating the previous August and October that he would recommend to the Congress that it pass a measure to bring some DPs to the United States, Truman restricted the suggestion to the pallid comment in his 1947 State of the Union address: "Congressional assistance in the form of new legislation is needed. I urge the Congress to turn its attention to this world problem, in an effort to find ways whereby we can fulfill our responsibilities to these thousands of homeless and suffering refugees of all faiths."[29] Truman did not utter another public word on the subject for the next six months. He neither endorsed the Stratton bill nor sent any measures to the Congress for consideration.

Lack of public enthusiasm, however, did not indicate lack of concern or lack of activity on the administration's part. Within the White House John H. Steelman, one of Truman's top aides, read a report from the Attorney General's office which concluded, "the strongest argument in favor of the admission of a fair share of displaced persons lies in the fact that all other alternatives are probably less desirable." Then David Niles, who, according to his assistant Phileo Nash, "acted at the President's direction," continued meeting with and advising AJC strategists. Niles also sent word to Congressman Stratton that although Truman would not endorse his bill publicly, the President nonetheless supported it. The chairman of the President's Council of Economic Advisers also informed Stratton that 400,000 immigrants over a four-year period "would not be a large number to be assimilated," while the National Housing Agency head thought that admission of 100,000 persons a year "would not result in a demand for that many additional housing units."[30]

The State Department also favored entry of DPs into the United States. Assistant Secretary John Hilldring had his staff at work on two possible proposals for the President to submit to Congress. (Truman never used either one of them.) One called for the admission of 150,000 DPs, or the U.S. "fair share," while the other added up the unused immigrant quotas for the years 1942–45, a total of 571,057, and allocated them solely for the use of DPs. In the fall of 1946, the State Department also hired Goldthwaite Dorr, who had been the Secretary of War's alternate on the Grady Commission the previous summer, to help promote congressional approval of American membership in the new International Refugee Organization (IRO) which had as its stipulated goal the resettlement of DPs. The State Department's position marked a strong shift from previous years when Breckinridge Long suspected a Nazi fifth columnist in every German Jewish applicant who sought admission to the United States. But cold war considerations, and blocking the establishment of a Jewish Palestine, which the Department still believed necessary, made the support of DP legislation almost mandatory.[31]

Outside the administration, the CCDP continually recruited influential individuals and organizations to join its efforts but even when it won public endorsements the enthusiasm, especially from religious organizations, frequently lacked intensity. In April 1947, the Bishop in New Orleans refused to do anything for the cause because he had not received "orders from above." Two months later Francis Cardinal Spellman, the most important Catholic prelate in America, finally came out for admission of DPs to the United States. But not until April 1948 did the *Catholic World*, published in New York City, even mention the DP situation. CCDP Executive Secretary Bernard later acknowledged that the strongest Catholic interest came from the Midwest, not the East, and that Cardinal Spellman did not really back the organization's goals. The Protestant spokesmen, according to both the executive secretary of the Federal Council of Churches and one AJC official, were also "less than dynamic" in their efforts for the DPs, thereby leaving the Jews with the overwhelming responsibility for promoting the CCDP and its issue.[32]

The AJC and the ACJ, with their eye continually on the best plan of action to influence Congress, shouldered the burden along with several individuals who sincerely believed in the need to help DPs. At the CCDP Harrison and Bernard dedicated themselves to completing their mission. Eleanor Roosevelt, Herbert Lehman, Herbert Bayard Swope, and others provided guidance on political strategy while Lessing Rosenwald could always be depended upon for still another contribution.[33] Yet such people could at best arouse and educate the public, alert officials, and marshal political support. What was needed in addition was ameliorative legislation. But the congressmen and senators, not oblivious to the workings of the CCDP, carefully waited until favorable public sentiment crystallized before embarking upon a new course in immigration policy.

6

THE SCENE SHIFTS
TO CONGRESS

TRYING TO GET Congress to move proved an almost insuperable task. The CCDP aimed its efforts both at the public, thereby hoping to stimulate concern which would reach the legislators, and at the lawmakers themselves. Such lobbying efforts as publicity, contacts by prominent hometown acquaintainces, and direct access to individual congressmen and senators continued throughout 1947 and 1948. Unfortunately the 80th Congress, the first in sixteen years with a Republican majority in both houses, did not consider immigration legislation among its priority items. Continued public and administrative pressure ultimately convinced the legislators that some bill on the subject of DPs should emerge. The nature of that law, however, would be dictated by the predilections of some of the most reactionary men in Congress.

The advocates of emergency DP legislation faced severe handicaps. First, President Truman, a weak legislative leader in domestic affairs, failed to rally his allies in Congress behind any specific proposal. Nor did the President attempt to cultivate public opinion, provide a draft bill, or work closely with either Republican or Democratic party officials in Congress. In other words, Truman did not use the full range of his powers on behalf of the displaced persons. Yet even if he had been extraordinarily energetic, legislation to aid DPs faced formidable barriers. Nativist sentiment remained strong and pervaded the Congress as well as the nation. A CCDP Washington attorney reported earlier in the campaign that "the general sentiment in Congress at the present . . . [is] still too hostile, particularly because of the feeling that too many Jews would come into the country if immigration regulations were relaxed." Democratic Senator Carl Hatch of New Mexico expressed the same point publicly when he admitted, "I have heard it said— and I am ashamed to say that frequently it is said in the Halls of Congress: They are nothing but Communists, nothing but Jews—hated, despised, unwanted spawn from the Old World."[1]

Besides lackluster presidential leadership and nativism the DP relief program faced other obstacles. Several more compelling issues confronted the 80th Congress in foreign affairs— such as aid to Greece and Turkey and the Marshall Plan. On the domestic side, the Taft-Hartley labor bill, tax and budget cuts, housing, medical care, universal military training, the extension of social security, the revision of the minimum wage law, and the development of other river valley authorities patterned along the lines of the Tennessee Valley Authority struck many legislators as much more worthy subjects of consideration than DP legislation.[2]

Finally, the Republican leaders in both houses of Congress, Taft and Vandenberg in the Senate, and Joe Martin, Speaker of the House, were supremely indifferent to promoting the DP cause. Martin, according to reporter Tris Coffin, voted "down the line for the world of fifty years ago" and stubbornly resisted change. The Senate leaders gave their attention to other matters and specifically refused CCDP requests to introduce ameliorative legislation. Taft called the tune on domestic matters while colleagues looked to Vandenberg to show the way in foreign policy. The nominal Republican chief in the Senate, Wallace H. White of Maine, served, according to one student of Congress, as "majority leader in name only. On the Senate floor he often openly turned around to receive signals from Taft."[3]

The Ohio Republican, like all senators, specialized in only a few issues and relied on colleagues he respected for guidance in their areas of expertise. Taft, however, wanted the Republican presidential nomination in 1948, and therefore took the lead on issues of concern to his conservative colleagues while being careful not to venture into areas where they opposed action. Immigration counted among the latter. Although Taft emerged as a spokesman in the congressional movement to establish a Jewish homeland in Palestine, he felt no urge to bring more Jews to the United States. In this sense he was in agreement with most other senators. The New York City Yiddish paper, the *Forward*, quoted him as saying, in April 1947, that he would support the admission of 400,000 DPs; in September of that year, before a student body at Corvallis, Oregon, Taft declared, "I have not absolutely opposed any admission of displaced persons, but I think it certainly should be carefully limited and very carefully screened to the extent that we are willing to cooperate in that general problem." Taft's equivocation on this matter left several individuals baffled and angry. Irving Engel, State Department consultant Goldthwaite Dorr, and DP Commissioner Harry N. Rosenfield all considered him "untrustworthy."[4]

Taft was responsible for the appointment of his Republican colleague from West Virginia, William Chapman Revercomb, to investigate DP conditions in Europe. Engel had secured Taft's word in November 1946 that an investigation would be made, and the Ohioan brought the matter before the Republican Steering Committee, which chose the West Virginian to assume the task. Goldthwaite Dorr thought that Taft may have designated Revercomb "by accident rather than with malice aforethought," but the choice was nonetheless devastating. Revercomb, characterized by a Senate Judiciary Committee staff member as a "Know-Nothing type," harbored the most conservative and nationalist viewpoints on a variety of issues. In the 80th Congress he voted for the Taft-Hartley law, opposed the extension of rent and price controls, and voted against both the Truman Doctrine and the Marshall Plan. He made no secret of the fact that he had "been a foe of immigration all his lifetime," and soon after receiving the assignment to head the Senate Judiciary Committee's Subcommittee on Immigration* allegedly confided to colleagues, "We

---

* The Congress reorganized its committee system beginning with the 80th Congress. The old immigration committees emerged as subcommittees of the Judiciary Committee in both the House and the Senate.

could solve this DP problem all right if we could work out some bill that would keep out the Jews."[5]

Revercomb did investigate the DP situation, but his report reflected many of his own predispositions. He opposed admitting too many refugees because of purported Communist influences, and because of the possibility of another economic depression. He thought it "very doubtful that any country would desire these [Jewish] people as immigrants." Like everyone else, however, Revercomb admired the well-educated and well-mannered Estonians, Latvians, and Lithuanians. The West Virginian concluded his report with the following observation:

> Many of those who seek entrance into this country have little concept of our form of government. Many of them come from lands where communism has had its first growth and dominates the political thought and philosophy of the people. Certainly it would be a tragic blunder to bring into our midst those imbued with a communistic line of thought when one of the most important tasks of this Government today is to combat and eradicate communism from this country.[6]

In response to Revercomb's conclusions the Washington *Post* editorialized that if the Republicans allowed themselves to be guided by the West Virginian's views, "there will be little of either charity or understanding in our treatment of Europe's refugees." The editorial also condemned some of Revercomb's other conclusions. "It is a strange sort of reasoning that labels as Communists the refugees from Communism," it said. Besides, many of the DPs suffered because of the Nazis. "But can Senator Revercomb mean that to be undesired by the Nazis makes them undesirable to the United States," the *Post* asked.[7]

The Washington *Post* spoke for the liberals but not the lawmakers. There existed a general belief among congressmen and the nation at large, *Fortune* magazine observed, "that D.P.'s were mostly Jews or Communists or both." That was one of the reasons many legislators opposed the Truman Directive of 1945 and resisted the President's suggestion that the United States admit more DPs.[8] The taint of communism clung to the cause of the DPs throughout the late 1940s. By 1947 Americans had become wary of Communists, and few thought clearly on the subject.

The issue of communism had first stirred Americans after World War I, and then again in the 1930s. In 1938 the House of Representatives had set up its Un-American Activities Committee under the chairmanship of Martin Dies to discover which Americans followed the party line. Our wartime commitments to Russia blunted the attacks of American anti-Communists, but during the election of 1946 the subject reemerged. To be sure, Americans were made aware of rifts in the wartime alliance in 1945 and Winston Churchill did go to Fulton, Missouri, in March 1946 to deliver his famous "Iron Curtain" speech. But during the election campaigns it surprised many politicians to hear the word *communism* whooped up so frequently. Catholics, especially, spurred the battle cry. In the November 1946 issue of *Cosmopolitan*, Cardinal Spellman wrote, "Every Communist is a potential enemy of the United States and only the bat-blind can fail to be aware of the Communist invasion of our country." That winter Truman acknowledged that "people are very wrought up about the Communist 'bugaboo.'" Probably in response to existing national concern about communism, the President, in March 1947, established a federal loyalty program to weed out subversives in the government.[9]

The public suspected that Jews, in particular, were likely offenders. Although most Jews were not Communists a large number of Communists were Jewish. A former UNRRA worker later wrote that the United States should be careful about taking in Jewish DPs who were "Trotskyites at heart. They are the kinds of people that would most likely vote for a Henry Wallace or a Vito Marcantonio."[10] That was one of the reasons the CCDP could not find a suitable legislator to introduce its proposed bill to bring DPs to the United States.

Another reason why the CCDP bill was not introduced in the House of Representatives before April 1 is because the sponsors did not want their measure presented until after the Senate had approved American membership in the IRO. The United Nations Assembly established the IRO on December

15, 1946, to replace, and assume the functions of, the Inter-governmental Committee on Refugees, UNRRA, and American Army operations in regard to DPs. Primarily charged with resettling the DPs into permanent abodes, the IRO would commence operations as the Preparatory Commission (PCIRO) as soon as eight member states joined, and would be fully operational as soon as fifteen UN countries agreed to participate in it. Everyone knew, however, that unless the United States became a member the new organization had little chance of success.[11]

Getting IRO approval from the United States Senate required delicate maneuvering. The State Department hired Goldthwaite Dorr to help guide the bill to passage, and Michigan's Senator Vandenberg, generally responsive to State Department experts, took the lead in the upper chamber. But many Senators regarded UNRRA as having been an inefficient, spendthrift organization whose staff had contained "pinks" and "leftists," and feared the IRO would be more of the same. Revercomb and Republican Kenneth Wherry of Nebraska led the opposition forces. They believed that the new organization might in some way infringe on American immigration laws and therefore saw to it that the bill agreeing to United States membership included an amendment with, according to Vandenberg, "language so airtight and copper-riveted that there can be no remote possibility of any change in our immigration laws as a result of the particular action proposed." The Revercomb amendment, which the Senate approved, stipulated that American acceptance of IRO membership would in no way "have the effect of abrogating, suspending, modifying, adding to, or superseding any of the immigration laws or any other laws of the United States." The passage of the Revercomb proposal, and Vandenberg's astute understanding of his colleagues' needs, paved the way for Senate acceptance of the IRO on March 25, 1946.[12] A week later Stratton introduced his bill in the House of Representatives.

It took another two months before the Immigration Subcommittee of the House Judiciary Committee, under the chairmanship of Frank Fellows of Maine, commenced public hearings. The CCDP did not expect much from the Fellows Committee but nonetheless hoped that the growing public pressure and the eloquence of both public and administrative witnesses might result in a favorable report. In February, AJC Washington representative Marcus Cohen confided to the New York headquarters, "The Committee is stacked against us." Fellows had "a terribly conservative" record, while Kentucky members John Marshall Robsion and Frank Chelf were "no better." (Cohen later proved to have been mistaken about Chelf.) The Texas member, Ed Gossett, had repeatedly introduced legislation to cut immigrant quotas and on several occasions had shown no hesitation in denouncing foreigners. Pennsylvanian Louis E. Graham allegedly possessed "a rather sour anti-administration voting record." "Some Machiavellian brain purposely put [Emanuel] Celler," a Brooklyn partisan on the committee also, "knowing beforehand," Cohen continued, "that he is generally disliked and frequently has the effect of people voting against things merely because he is for them." Celler's behavior on the committee confirmed Cohen's misgivings. According to Goldthwaite Dorr, the congressman "made himself just as offensive as he can make himself . . . sticking pins into the other members whose support he had to have."[13]

To face these six committeemen both the AJC and the CCDP marshaled a notable array of witnesses, carefully including only two Jews: Rabbi Philip S. Bernstein, a former adviser on Jewish affairs to the army in Europe, and Herbert H. Lehman. Dorr opposed using the former UNRRA director but Lehman regarded himself as a "mouthpiece and leader" and the Jewish organizations insisted that he take the stand. Dorr believed that Bernstein did "everything that could be done usefully, and that with the anti-Semitic susceptibilities which tend to run through, unhappily, so much of American life . . . we'd better stop there." Although Dorr objected to Lehman, the former governor handled himself creditably. His remarks probably neither helped nor hurt. Congressman Stratton spoke on behalf of his own legislation and submitted lists of public and newspaper backers. Charles Rozmarek of the Polish American Congress, William Green of the AF of L, Earl Harrison, Owen J. Roberts, and spokesmen for the Catholics, Lutherans, and Federal Council of Churches followed and pledged their adherence to the proposed measure. Dr. Samuel McCrea Cavert, executive secretary of the Federal Council of Churches, had written to the CCDP indicating that he would "welcome any tentative draft, or some paragraphs for inclusion in my statement," and the CCDP obligingly prepared a speech for him to read at the congressional hearings.[14]

The administration also came through solidly by sending Assistant Secretary of Labor Philip Hannah, Assistant Secretary of State John H. Hilldring, Ugo Carusi, Commissioner of Immigration and Naturalization, and three Cabinet members: Secretary of State George C. Marshall (who had succeeded Byrnes the previous January), Secretary of War Robert P. Patterson, and Attorney-General Tom Clark to testify on behalf of the Stratton bill. The most effective speaker, or at least the person who seemed to have the most influence among the legislators, was Lieutenant Colonel Jerry M. Sage. Colonel Sage served as second in command to Colonel Stanley Mickelson, Chief, Civil Affairs Division, European Command, and had been recalled especially to present the views of the DPs from the military vantage point in Europe. Although Sage's remarks, like those of the other administration witnesses, repeated the arguments already propagated by the CCDP he did an effective job, according to Goldthwaite Dorr, of creating congressional understanding of the DP situation.[15]

General John H. Hilldring, Assistant Secretary of State for Occupied Areas, also provided useful information although, judging from comments made later by the legislators, his testimony did not have much effect on the committee members. He pointed out that 40 percent of the DPs were employable and of that number 80 percent had regular jobs in or near the assembly centers. Hilldring also discussed the cost to the American taxpayers for maintaining DPs, $130 million in fiscal 1947, and indicated the savings that would accrue if the refugees emigrated to the United States and elsewhere. General Hilldring next proceeded to the Communist issue. "Let us be frank about it: the question is often asked, are they communistic? I want to meet this issue squarely. Any statement or innuendo or intimation that the displaced persons in Germany, Austria, or Italy are communistic flies in the face of the basic facts of the situation."[16]

The opponents of DP legislation sounded familiar themes, in some cases ignoring testimony that had already been given, at other times contradicting it without sufficient evidence to support their conclusions. With or without data, however, their testimony reflected real fears, real concerns, and blatant prejudice. Among those who protested passage of the Stratton bill were spokesmen for conservative and/or right-wing fringe groups like Charles E. Babcock of the Junior Order, United American Mechanics; John Trevor of the American Coalition; and Merwyn K. Hart of the National Economic Council. They argued that enough had been done already to help the DPs, warned of potential subversives entering the country, and argued that future unemployment problems and tight housing conditions inevitably would follow the admission of more immigrants. A closer look at their presentations reveals some other apprehensions as well. Trevor announced that "we have taken 23.5 percent of the Jewish refugees" while Canada, Australia, and South Africa had only taken 1 percent each. He warned that "our political institutions could not survive further dilution of the basic strain of our population," while those "for whose benefit [the Stratton bill] was devised [are] peculiarly susceptible to the absorption of socialistic propaganda." Hart paraphrased much of Trevor's argument but also added the piquant note that the Federal Council of Churches, whose executive secretary had supported the proposed measure on behalf of his organization, "is recognized widely throughout the country as definitely left-wing."[17] Hart's conclusion had no basis in fact.

The most frequent, articulate, and outspoken opponent, however, was not a witness but one of the questioning congressmen, Ed Gossett. Often he interrupted testimony to express his opinions and observations. He reminded listeners that 75 percent of the visas granted under the Truman Directive, an order he considered illegal, had gone to Jews, that some of the DP camps in Europe, "are just small universities of subversives and revolutionary activities," and that the "sustaining force back of this movement is our Jewish friends." Nonetheless, Congressman Gossett observed, if the Veterans of Foreign Wars and the American Legion endorsed the Stratton bill, he would probably vote for it. It appears that Gossett spoke for a majority of his colleagues, for when the hearings concluded Speaker Martin counted fewer that 100 members of the House of Representatives willing to stand up for DP legislation. Even the CCDP, keeping its own tallies, could uncover only 120 congressmen taking its side.[18]

But the groundwork had been laid. The CCDP did its job well and by the summer of 1947 large numbers of Americans began to respond in the desired fashion. As a result of letters from Earl Harrison to the governors of every state, the Stratton bill won endorsements from the chief executives of Illinois, Maine, New York, Arizona, and Wyoming, and from the Mayors of New Orleans, Minneapolis, and Baltimore, as well as Stamford, Connecticut; Schenectady, New York; and Passaic and Atlantic City, New Jersey.[19]

National and local organizations also lent their prestige to the movement to bring DPs to the United States. Such bodies as the General Federation of Women's Clubs, the American Library Association, and the Chamber of Commerce were contacted by CCDP field representatives and they too responded affirmatively. Names and addresses of all of the state and local presidents of the various clubs or groups were obtained and then letters or circulars explaining the CCDP position went out to all of the people. At all levels (national, state, regional, local) organizations having conventions or meetings were asked whether they would like to have CCDP speakers or literature provided free of charge. As a result of these efforts the American Library Association offered to hand out literature in libraries throughout the country; the Business and Professional Women's Clubs invited a CCDP speaker to one of their conventions; and the Chamber of Commerce agreed to distribute brochures in its offices. By the time Congressman Stratton testified before the Fellows Committee he could report that 94 national organizations as disparate as the AF of L, the Congress of Industrial Organizations (CIO), the Catholic War Veterans, the Home Missions Council of North America, the Methodist Federation for Social Action, the international board of YMCA, the American Association of University Women, the American Association of Social Workers, the American Lithuanian Council, the National Peace Conference, the Order of the Sons of Italy, the Marine Corps League, the National Council of Negro Women, the Girl Scouts, the Seventh-Day Baptists, the Syrian Antiochian Orthodox Church, the Unity of Bohemian Ladies, the Western Slavonic Association, and the major bodies of the Catholic, Protestant, and Jewish faiths in the United States favored the goals of his proposed bill. Six months later a CCDP field worker wrote Bernard, "this is the most comprehensive and heterogeneous group of organizations ever to sponsor a particular cause."[20]

Individuals were encouraged to speak out. The usual CCDP tactic was to send field workers into communities throughout the nation looking for civic and church leaders to spark their neighbors into concerted action. Participants were chosen with care by the CCDP so that each local committee, William Bernard later wrote, "was composed of or contained persons known to and bearing weight with the particular Senator or Congressman whose position on the DP issue needed strengthening." Senator Alexander Wiley of Wisconsin, for example, complained to Bernard at one point that "he could not walk down the streets of his home town without someone like his banker, butcher, or former Sunday School teacher stopping him and saying, 'Senator, why aren't you a good Christian? Why are you against DPs?'" Congressman Frank Fellows also protested, in May 1947, that he and other Immigration Subcommittee members had been the objects of "a very definite propaganda movement from all over the country" to pass the Stratton bill. It appeared, Fellows continued, to be the work of a very strong and well-paid lobby. "They're putting on tremendous pressure of the type I don't like," he told reporters. "We've been receiving armfuls of telegrams, letters, postcards; many of them alike."[21]

As a result of the public's response four of the six Immigration Subcommittee members "realized that sooner or later they must report out favorably some bill," Dorr wrote his friend William Hallam Tuck, the first head of the IRO. Two of the subcommittee members, Gossett and Robsion, struck CCDP observers as hopeless and they counted on nothing from these men. Celler supported DP legislation without reservations. But Fellows, Chelf, and Graham, though they could not back the Stratton measure, apparently felt impelled to do something to admit a number of DPs to the United States. Dorr, on behalf of the administration, tried to bring Fellows around but the chairman argued that the Stratton bill, by giving preferences to relatives, disciminated against the poor and the friendless while favoring the rich and those with connections—the very opposite of a humane bill. Graham stated, more deliberately, that the "unjust priority system" proposed by Stratton seemed designed to help "a favored group." Bernard interpreted these comments to mean that Congressmen Fellows and Graham "have in mind that these priorities are discriminating against the Baltic people and favor the Jews," because the Stratton bill stipulated that preferences be given to relatives of American citizens. Many American Jews, therefore, might bring in family members. Fewer persons of Estonian, Latvian, or Lithuanian ancestry possessed American citizenship; therefore those groups would be handicapped by the proposed legislation. Chelf, who also opposed the Stratton bill, nonetheless favored some form of assistance. In a thoughtful letter to Secretary of State George C. Marshall, the congressman wrote:

> Certainly, if it is necessary, under the "Truman Doctrine," to appropriate $400,000,000 for economic aid to Greece and Turkey to stem the tide of communism, it is likewise imperative that the homeless victims of World War II be assisted in their fervent hope to establish a new home in a new land away from the hateful and scornful eyes of the German Nazis (where they are now located) and the possible influence of the Commuists, both of whom they hate and despise.[22]

At the same time that House members considered ways to handle the DP problem, Republican Senator Homer Ferguson of Michigan, along with eight colleagues, introduced another version of the CCDP proposal in the upper chamber on July 2.[23] Why Ferguson took the lead and acted as he did while the House subcommittee was still holding hearings on the Stratton bill is difficult to explain. The Senator claimed that he offered the measure because he did not think that the House of Representatives would approve the Stratton bill; Goldthwaite Dorr wrote his friend William Hallam Tuck that Ferguson had blown "hot and cold on the matter and finally," through the influence of their mutual friend, Senator H. Alexander Smith of New Jersey, plunged ahead. Two political scientists, Stephen K. Bailey and Howard D. Samuel, later wrote that considerable pressure from Polish groups in Michigan may have nudged Ferguson to work for DP legislation but they offered no evidence to support their position.[24]

One might speculate that the cumulative pressure from newspapers and periodicals combined to influence Ferguson and his colleagues. The Washington *Star* had run a series of articles from May 8 through June 4, 1947, entitled, "Our Duty, and a Haven, for 'DPs,'" and then collected and distributed the columns in booklet form. More than one hundred editorials endorsing American legislation to aid DPs had also appeared in newspapers like the Minneapolis *Tribune*, the Washington *Post*, the Baltimore *Sun*, the Chicago *Sun*, and *The New York Times*, while at the same time periodicals like *Life*, *Reader's Digest*, *The Saturday Evening Post*, *Survey Graphic*, and the *Yale Review*, published material indicating that the time had come for the United States to welcome more DPs to our shores. The Denver *Post*, in recommending that this country take in a substantial number of DPs, made two statements which summarized the views expressed by several publications. The first was that "President Truman is doing no more than accepting the responsibilities which this nation must face in its new role of internationalism," and the second indicated that "The United States owes it to the world to accept its share of the problems of the world."[25]

The changing sentiment of public mail to Congress, which even in May had run against admitting DPs, may also have served as a catalyst. Raymond Wilson of the American Friends Service Committee in Philadelphia informed former New York Senator James R. Mead that "on few bills has there been as much favorable support from the press, high government officials, and the people in general," as the ones intended to aid DPs. Republican Senator James P. Kem of Missouri received a letter from two constituents which was perhaps typical of the many that expressed sympathy for a law to bring DPs to the United States. "We are Christians," the correspondents wrote, "active in one of the Baptist Churches in St. Louis and our conscience would be hard to live with if we did not write you as our representative to do everything possible to improve this legislation so that more displaced persons would make homes in our country and so they would be allowed to enter without regard to race or religious faith."[26]

Whatever the reasons Ferguson and the others had for introducing their bill in the Senate the effort attracted attention, especially from those observers curious about the difference between the Senate and House versions of almost the same proposal. Careful analysis of the Ferguson and Stratton bills indicates only slight variations. Whereas the congressman had called for admission of 100,000 DPs per year over a four-year period, the Ferguson measure merely stipulated 400,000. Stratton included DPs currently resident in Germany, Austria, and Italy, while Ferguson offered no such restriction. The Senator gave first priority to war orphans and second priority to relatives of American citizens whereas Stratton listed relatives first. Other differences were equally minor except for a provision in the Senate version which, if accepted and passed by the Congress, would cover practically every applicant for admission to the United States. Listed as a third priority, the clause favored people who possessed "special trades, skills, professions or aptitudes as will meet the needs of the United States and contribute to its cultural, religious, economic or industrial welfare and prosperity."[27]

Less than a week after the introduction of the Ferguson bill, the President reentered the fray. On July 7 he sent a special message to Congress urging the passage of legislation admitting "a substantial number" of DPs into the United States but did not mention the Stratton or Ferguson proposals. A week later Truman met with congressional leaders and apparently for the first time told them in person about his concern. Later in the month Undersecretary of State Robert Lovett wrote Republican Senator Alexander Wiley of Wisconsin, chairman of the Senate Judiciary Committee, that the Department of State was "wholeheartedly in favor" of a suitable DP bill. In August the President transferred Ugo Carusi from the Immigration and Naturalization Service to the State Department for the purpose of making a thorough survey of all phases of the DP problem. Dorr thought Carusi had conducted himself well before the House during the hearings on the Stratton bill, and he assured his friend William Hallam Tuck that "his knowledge of the present Immigration laws and their administration . . . will be invaluable in working out practical methods for the selection and screening of D.P.'s to be admitted into the United States." Dorrs's remarks indicated that the administration anticipated future action from Congress.[28]

Irving Engel of the AJC, and others, were less sanguine. Although Engel acknowledged on July 1 that "the change that has taken place in public opinion [on bringing DPs to the United States] has been very little short of miraculous," a transformation which he attributed to the work of Bernard and his CCDP staff, he nonetheless recognized the problems still to be faced. A bedrock of resistance to any new immigration bill remained and, at a time when rumors of antisemitism in Congress persisted, hostility to Jews exacerbated this anti-immigrant sentiment. Dorr observed that opponents of the proposed legislation tended "to ascribe the whole pressure for DP admissions to the Jewish interest in it" while a military official claimed that several legislators thought that "if there were no Jews in the displaced persons camps, the problems would be solved in no time." Irving Engel warned members of the AJC in August 1947:

Both in the country and in Congress there is a stubborn opposition reflecting distrust of foreigners in general and, to a shocking extent, of Jews in particular. It is to be feared that, if the legislation cannot be sidetracked entirely, an attempt may be made so to shape its terms as to reduce the number of Jewish DPs who could benefit by it.[29]

Existing apprehensions were well grounded because of the predilections of the senators who would control the preparation of any immigration bill. Chapman Revercomb chaired the Senate Immigration Subcommittee and Democrat Patrick McCarran of Nevada who, according to Dorr, "was as hostile as Revercomb" to DPs, served as the only other member. The organizational structure of the Senate made it almost impossible to take the DP measure away from the West Virginia Senator. Custom dictated that chairmen assume a wide latitude in determining the nature of legislation, its position on the agenda, and the timing of hearings. Since Revercomb refused to cooperate with those seeking DP legislation or hold hearings on the Ferguson measure, the Michigan Senator's proposal came to the floor of the Senate as an amendment to another bill. And although for a brief time it appeared as if there might be enough votes for passage of the Ferguson bill, Revercomb argued vehemently against any kind of precipitous action. As a result, the Senate approved an investigation of the whole immigration system and DP problems in general.* Although this was seen as a delaying tactic by many observers, Revercomb carried the day. He hoped the investigative committee would consist solely of McCarran and himself, but liberal elements managed to get two of the cosponsors of the Ferguson measure, Democrat J. Howard McGrath of Rhode Island and Republican John S. Cooper of Kentucky, along with Republican Forrest C. Donnell of Missouri included as well. At the time Donnell had not yet committed himself on the refugees and much was expected of him. In late July Dorr acknowledged that although "we are taking a licking on immediate legislation admitting DP's" we "have laid the foundations for next session."[30]

---

* This authorization became the basis for the wider Senate Judiciary Committee examination of immigration which culminated in the McCarran-Walter Immigration Act of 1952.

Dorr knew, of course, that Revercomb had a mandate to investigate DP conditions and report back to the second session of the 80th Congress. The European trip had to be made and the DP camps had to be inspected. A relatively accurate appraisal was necessary because several others would make similar journeys at the same time and look at the same assembly centers.

The military in Europe had an almost constant stream of official visitors touring the DP camps in the fall of 1947. The President sent Ugo Carusi as well as Paul Griffiths, the national commander of the American Legion; Secretary of War Patterson dispatched Goldthwaite Dorr; the House of Representatives authorized three liberal congressmen, James G. Fulton of Pennsylvania, Jacob Javits, and J. L. Pfeiffer of New York City, along with Kentuckian Frank Chelf, to look into the DP situation; and the Senate Foreign Relations Committee assigned H. Alexander Smith to join the Revercomb Committee on its investigation and make a separate report.[31]

With so many legislators marching through the DP camps, "action at the next session of the Congress is going to depend very largely on the results of the observations of members who will be in Germany between now and then," Dorr wrote to General Lucius D. Clay, McNarney's successor as military commander in Germany. Dorr urged Clay to see to it that the lawmakers "get a full and fair view of the displaced persons work" and suggested that Colonel Sage, who had earlier been recalled to Washington to testify during the hearings on the Stratton Bill, "would be extremely good . . . for this work." In addition, Dorr thought "it would be equally important for [Sage] to contact other members of Congress who are in Germany on other errands so as to give them at least a little information as to the DP situation which will be helpful on their return." Frank Schilling of the American Consulate in Germany later confirmed that Clay followed instructions. "If that large group of Senators who visited the Munich D.P. camps knew how well the stage had been set and the play rehearsed," Schilling wrote Ugo Carusi, "they would crawl into holes."[32]

Members of the Senate Judiciary Group touring the European Command arrive at the Rhine Main Airport from Paris. Left to right: Senators Harry P. Cain (R, Washington), Forrest C. Donnell (R, Missouri), Chapman Revercomb (R, West Virginia), and J. Howard McGrath (D, Rhode Island). (U.S. Army photograph)

The "large group of Senators" included Revercomb, Donnell, McGrath, Smith, Democrat Olin Johnston of South Carolina and Republican Harry Cain of Washington. McCarran did not go to Europe because of illness, and Cooper remained in Kentucky for a political campaign. The traveling legislators visited the assembly centers and some of Europe's leading cities—Paris, Frankfurt, Stuttgart, Berlin, Vienna, Geneva, Rome, and London—speaking with consular officials, immigration authorities, military personnel, and the DPs themselves. In London, the British had been alerted beforehand by Lord Inverchapel, the ambassador in Washington, to the unsavory qualities of some of the senators. "Revercomb and Donnell,"

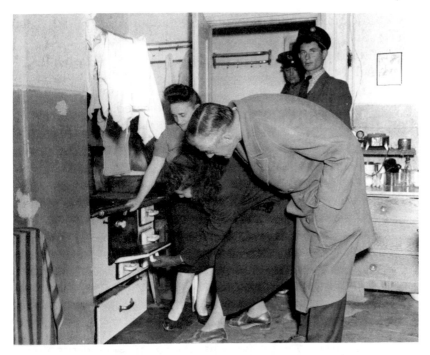

Senator Leverett Saltonstall (R., Massachusetts) peers into an oven where dinner is being prepared by a family at the Zielsheim DP Camp, Wiesbaden. October 19, 1947. (U.S. Army photograph)

one communication indicated

are Conservative Republicans disposed to view European problems with a sceptical eye. Johnston is a loudmouthed, Isolationist Southern Democrat. Cain is a young opportunist, who although fond of posing as a Progressive and an Internationalist is apt to vote with the Republican leaders who seem to him at any given moment to be on the ascendant. He is therefore worth cultivating.

Members of the British Foreign Office, in turn, lost no opportunity to impress upon their visitors the importance of passing the Stratton or some similar bill as "the most effective means of solving the refugee problem." One in-house memo for the British Secretary of State, Eastern Department, read, "There are indications that these representations have not been ineffective."[33]

The touring legislators learned a great deal. Staff members who had both preceded and accompained them had done considerable research on the historical evolution and current state of the DP problem. Statistics indicated over 1,660,000 refugees in Europe and the Far East eligible for DP status, with about 1,125,000 in the Allied zones in Germany, Austria, and Italy. The American zones alone housed over 800,000 in and outside the camps. The legislators also discovered that about 50 percent of the Jews who had been in Germany in 1945 had already left for Palestine and other nations, while more than 100,000 of the Jewish DPs in the assembly centers had either been released from Russia in the spring of 1946 or had fled from Polish antisemitism and pogroms in the summer of that year. Only 10,000 of the Jews then in the camps had arrived before December 22, 1945.

The Revercomb Committee's findings confirmed what others had already described. The assembly centers remained over-crowded; three to eight persons per room seemed the norm. Inmates received about 2,000 calories of food a day; Jewish DPs obtained about 15 to 25 percent more in supplementary rations from the JDC. Black market operations still flourished. Almost 37 percent of the DPs (61.9 percent of the employables), were gainfully employed but most engaged in only routine occupations. Despite Revercomb's assertions to the contrary the previous winter, when he traveled without his peers, his current report clearly stated that communism in the camps, "so far as overt activity is concerned, is not manifest."

The Senate Investigating Committee also surveyed repatriation and resettlement possibilities and the kinds of people who had already been relocated. Some countries like Britain, Belgium, and France had begun to recruit DPs for their labor-short economies and to Revercomb and his colleagues it appeared that "all selections have been from the 'cream' of the labor potential among all displaced persons." What seemed most alarming to the senators was that "more nonquota immigrants were admitted into the United States in the last two fiscal years (156,217) than were admitted nonquota in the course of the preceding eight fiscal years (154,829). The numbers admitted have been disproportionately from less assimilative stock." This made a particular impression upon Revercomb who, while in London, told IRO director Tuck that the IRO ought not to be responsible for the care of the 1946 influx from Eastern Europe, who were mostly Jews.[34]

The Fulton Committee, composed of three liberal congressmen, represented the House Foreign Relations Committee. The members, favorably disposed toward helping the DPs, visited approximately 150 camps, interviewed 5,000 refugees,

Congressman Frank L. Chelf (wearing hat) and a party of DP Camp officials leave one of the buildings in the DP camp at Eschwege, Germany. The men and boys in the background are Jewish DPs. The words in Hebrew above the entrance read: "Kibbutz: The Ghetto Fighters." September 8, 1947. (U.S. Army photograph)

and held spontaneous discussions with the DPs, military personnel, and others knowledgeable about the subject of their investigation. Military or IRO preparations for their visits could not be made because the congressmen did not announce their schedules until the mornings of their journeys. As a result they probably saw things that they would not have seen had their plans been publicized well in advance, and they commented upon these in their report. For example, the Fulton Committee document include the sentence, "Barbed-wire entanglements are inappropriate in the approaches to displaced persons camps." Their written conclusions also stressed the need for ameliorative legislation, and resettlement in the United States and elsewhere as "the only permanent solution of the problem." The congressmen declared, "If the Jewish facet of the problem could be cleared up, the solution of the remainder of the problem would be greatly facilitated. The opening up to Palestine to the resettlement of Jewish displaced persons would break the log jam." Congressman Fulton also told representatives of the Joint that pictures showing DPs engaged in constructive activities at work or while being rehabilitated should be sent to him in Washington "where they could be displayed in the lobbies of Congress and play an important role in giving our representatives a good visual picture of the constructive features of the programme for DPs."[35]

The European inspection by the American Legion national commander, Paul Griffiths, also augured well for DP legislation. Griffiths toured the DP camps and returned home to announce that his organization now favored the United States accepting its "fair share" of DPs. The trip alone did not produce the dramatic turnabout but it climaxed months of lobbying efforts within the Legion itself. Credit for the change should be given primarily to behind-the-scenes maneuvering by the American Jewish Committee. Irving M. Engel belonged to the American Legion and got his post to endorse the idea of special temporary legislation to allow DPs into the United States. Similarly, other Jews affiliated with the organization worked through their local chapters. A Jew in Dallas confessed that he prepared a statement "in accordance with" a suggestion from an AJC staff member and then

> read it to our Post meeting last night, and much to my surprise and pleasure, it was unanimously passed and accepted.
> Frankly, I was somewhat hesitant about presenting this resolution for fear it would be turned down or politely tabled because of the dislike of "foreigners." I did a little politicing [sic] and trading before the meeting and all went well.

Events like this occurred throughout the country. A member of the American Legion's Americanization Committee frankly admitted to an AJC official that his group opposed the Stratton bill

> because they did not want this country flooded with Jews. When [the AJC spokesman] told him . . . the statistics about the DP camp population, and also emphasized the fact that most of those Jews in the DP camps want to go to Palestine and not to the USA, [the AJC spokesman] was told that if this information could be imparted immediately to the chairman of the Americanization Committee, the Legion's whole attitude might change.

Then Griffiths himself confirmed the overwhelming number of Christians among the refugees and the Legion withdrew its opposition. That switch, Dorr informed Tuck, was "very important" because "opposition of the Legion . . . was one of the greatest handicaps to the passage of any legislation here."[36]

A number of other events also increased the prospects for DP legislation. In August 1947, the Maine legislature passed a resolution inviting Baltic DPs to settle there and engage in agricultural and lumbering activities. This, no doubt, influenced Maine Congressman Frank Fellows. In October, Lessing Rosenwald met Henry Luce, publisher of *Time, Life*, and *Fortune* magazines, for lunch and walked away believing "there is every prospect that further support of the Stratton bill will be forthcoming." Then, led by Minnesota, several midwestern states established commissions on the resettlement of displaced persons and made efforts to find out where homes and jobs existed for the Europeans. On November 28, the St. Louis *Post-Dispatch* editorialized on the need for the north-central breadbasket states (North Dakota, South Dakota, Wisconsin,

Minnesota, Nebraska, Iowa) along with Missouri, Kansas, Colorado, and Wyoming to recoup the million or more people they had lost since 1940. "Those from the Baltic countries, in particular," the editorial observed, "are ideally suited to take over as farm hands and other agricultural workers. . . . The DPs need America, but no more than America needs the DPs." That very day the St. Paul *Pioneer Press* published an almost identical editorial giving rise to the suspicion that their views may have been inspired by a canned version distributed by the CCDP (see fig. 5.1).[37]

In the fall, the CCDP itensified its publicity and programs throughout the nation. Tired of repeatedly referring to the "displaced persons," William Bernard substituted the term "delayed pilgrims," which projected a favorable connotation. The national CCDP publicity department cooperated with the main researcher for the October *Fortune* article on DPs and other staffers worked closely with *Look* for a scheduled picture story in the January 8, 1948, issue. Attending a meeting in Chicago, Irving Engel received some good news and passed the word along. "We learned that as a result of the work of the Texas Citizens' Committee on Displaced Persons," Engel informed Bernard, "it was expected that approximately half the Texas delegation in Congress would vote for the Stratton bill." In November, the Washington, D.C., Committee on DPs held a meeting attended by the legislative representatives of 24 national organizations where they mapped out political strategy for the coming year. Participants from the American Association of University Women and the National Federation of Women's Business and Professional Clubs indicated that their organizations were undertaking special efforts in Indiana, especially in the district of House Republican Majority Leader Charles A. Halleck. On December 6, the CCDP organized the Great Lakes Regional Conference on Displaced Persons. "The chief purpose of the conference," field worker Helen Shuford wrote William Bernard, "is planning political action in the districts of Congressmen from the states covered by the conference." The sum total of CCDP endeavors continued to please its progenitors. In February 1948, Engel again praised

Bernard and his staff to others in the AJC. The CCDP "has done a really magnificent job, both in educating the general public on the DP issue, and in securing support for emergency legislation from a very large number of the country's most important national organizations," Engel's letter read. "As a result," it continued, "there is today no strong organized opposition to our cause. Nevertheless, Congressional resistance is strong, and the battle is by no means won."[38]

The task ahead for 1948, therefore, was to deal with this congressional resistance. In January that did not appear to be an insurmountable problem. On October 29, 1947, a delegation of concerned citizens had held a meeting with Senator Taft and once again solicited his aid. How much this session influenced the Ohioan is difficult to say but in November he called for "immediate action" to bring some DPs to the United States. Furthermore, the congressional tours of DP assembly centers the previous fall had made an impact. Those "who really took a good look at the camps," Colonel Sage observed to Goldthwaite Dorr, "came away impressed with the need and desirability of opening our doors to some extent." Truman's 1948 State of the Union message urged Congress to admit DPs who would "add to the strength of this nation" and one week later the Federal Council of Churches in America passed a resolution strongly endorsing the President's position.[39] Thus the second session of the 80th Congress began in a public climate more favorable to admitting DPs than had existed during the first session in 1947.

7

CONGRESS ACTS

DURING THE FIRST SESSION of the 80th Congress the lawmakers had to be educated about the DP problem; in the second session they were expected to act upon it. Most congressmen and senators sensed that some kind of legislation would emerge from the House and Senate immigration subcommittees and both chambers knew that stronger opposition existed in the Senate. The House of Representatives was not prepared to pass any bill unless favorable action seemed likely in the upper house. An assistant to Nevada's Democratic Senator, Pat McCarran, stated the case succinctly in a telegram to her boss: "STRATTON BILL IS BEING HELD ON ICE UNTIL HOUSE COMMITTEE SEES WHAT SENATE WILL DO IN MATTER."[1] Thus CCDP staffers and others anxiously awaiting favorable results kept their eyes on Senator Revercomb and his committee.

As everyone knew, the disproportionate number of Jewish DPs who had arrived under the provisions of the Truman Directive particularly alarmed the West Virginian and many of his colleagues as well. According to the Revercomb Committee report, not only was the normal German immigration quota "available almost exclusively to the Jews," but as of June 30, 1947, about 22,950 visas had been issued to DPs in Germany. Of that number (and no one disputed the accuracy of the statistics), the religious breakdown read as follows:

Jews	15,478
Catholics	3,424
Protestants	2,968
Others	1,080

Not all of these people had reached the United States by the end of June but of those who had, three-quarters settled in urban areas, half in New York City alone. The legislators did not like the fact that Jews, who the CCDP kept reminding everyone constituted no more than 20 percent of all the DPs, made up such an overwhelming proportion of those arriving in the United States. Furthermore, they knew that the Stratton bill incorporated no provision to prevent this kind of lopsided distribution. Publicly, however, the lawmakers commented only about the numbers going to urban areas and kept their reservations about the religious breakdowns relatively quiet. But, responding to what the senators said in private, Dorr warned his friend William Hallam Tuck that unless assurances could be made that the DPs would be "fairly distributed" and scattered throughout the country, "we are not apt to get any legislation."[2]

In January 1948, the Revercomb subcommittee began preparing a bill for the Senate's consideration. The enlarged five-man group (Revercomb, McCarran, Donnell, Cooper, and McGrath) split three to two over most issues, with Cooper and McGrath in the minority. The majority wanted only 50,000 DPs over a two-year period, and restrictions which would have limited eligibility virtually to Balts alone. Supposedly Revercomb was determined to "keep out the Jews." The subcommittee chairman also wanted assurances that the DPs would resettle in all parts of the nation, that they would displace no one from a house or a job, and that none would become a public charge. The Immigration Subcommittee talked for days but could not reach agreement so the proposals went before the parent Judiciary Committee for consideration.[3]

The chairman of the Senate Judiciary Committee, Alexander Wiley, possessed a "pronounced Revercombish point of view," and had, in fact, appointed the West Virginian to his Immigration Subcommittee chairmanship over the protests of the CCDP.[4] Not much could be expected from him. CCDP observers anticipated that Oklahoma Republican E. H. Moore and Mississippi Democrat James Eastland could also be expected to join Wiley, Revercomb, McCarran, and Donnell, thereby giving six potential votes to the restrictionists. Cooper and McGrath, however, shared views with Ferguson and Democrats Harley Kilgore of West Virginia, Warren Magnuson of Washington, and J. William Fulbright of Arkansas. That left North Dakota Republican William Langer as the swing vote on close decisions.

Senator Langer, of German ancestry, represented a state where the German-Russians (Germans who had settled in Russia in the early nineteenth century but who had retained their native culture) counted as the leading ethnic group. Langer had started his political career in the German areas of central and southwestern North Dakota, and those counties supported him heavily at the polls. He had great affinity with the German people and according to two Washington reporters, Robert S. Allen and William V. Shannon, his pro-German proclivities during the early 1940s had "strong Nazi and anti-Semitic overtones." A staff member of the Senate Judiciary Committee later recalled the North Dakotan as being "almost pro-Nazi." Despite these allegations Langer fit no prescribed label and had, in fact, engaged in activities which suggested generous humanitarian instincts. In 1947 and 1948 he favored broad social welfare programs to aid the underpriviliged in the United States and in October 1945, the North Dakota senator had written to President Truman indicating that he "felt very strongly that we are repudiating the very principles for which we fought when we do not insist that the Jews be allowed admittance to Palestine." He had also indicated in a public meeting in Beulah, North Dakota, on November 9, 1947, that he planned to vote for the Stratton bill. Therefore the CCDP assumed that he would be with them in the Judiciary Committee deliberations.[5]

But the CCDP guessed wrong. Langer would support DP legislation only if the Senate Judiciary Committee incorporated his proposal to include the *Volksdeutsche* among the beneficiaries of the proposed measure. But a majority opposed this recommendation.[6] Therefore, Langer joined the restrictionists at crucial points.[7] Thus, with Eastland and Magnuson absent for the final tally of the committee measure, the restrictionists (Wiley, Revercomb, Moore, Donnell, McCarran, and Langer) outnumbered the proponents of a more liberal bill (Cooper,

Ferguson, Kilgore, Fulbright, and McGrath) six to five and carried the day for their version.[8]

The Wiley-Revercomb DP bill (Wiley added his name to the measure reported on the floor of the Senate) proved to be everything Irving Engel had feared. It called for admitting 100,000 DPs over a two-year period, confined eligibility to those who had been in the DP camps in the American, British, and French zones of Germany, Austria, and Italy on December 22, 1945, reserved 50 percent of the visas for agricultural workers and 50 percent for former residents of the Baltic States and Eastern Poland which had been annexed by Russia after the war. (In other words, only people in these categories would qualify for consideration!) It also established a DP Commission to administer the bill. In addition eligible DPs would have to meet all other requirements of the existing immigration statutes, except the quota provisions, and have their characters thoroughly screened before obtaining an entry permit. Furthermore, no DP could be admitted who did not have a guaranteed place to live and a job for the family breadwinner. Langer, alone, then voted against reporting any bill out of committee.[9]

On a superficial level, aside from its lack of generosity, the Wiley-Revercomb bill seemed logical. By using the December 22, 1945, cutoff date, it ostensibly favored those people who had suffered displacement the longest. Giving preference to individuals whose countries had been annexed indicated concern for those who could not return to their homes because of fears of political reprisals, and by stipulating a sizable proportion of agricultural workers, it gave recognition to the needs of the American economy, especially in the Midwest where states hungered for farm hands.

But in a more profound way the Wiley-Revercomb proposal reflected the lawmakers' desire to exclude Jews. That date stipulation resulted in the automatic exclusion of more than 100,000 Jews who were released from Russia in the spring of 1946 and/or who fled the Polish pogroms that summer. The Revercomb entourage discovered on its 1947 European tour, and noted accordingly in its report, that most of the Jewish

DPs in the camps in 1945 had already left for Palestine and other countries. Therefore the cutoff date, possibly the idea of staff assistant Richard Arens or Senator McCarran, both of whom helped frame the legislation, carefully but without ostensible prejudice discriminated against the Jewish DPs, six-sevenths of whom arrived in the western zones afterward. In February 1949, after many of those who might have gone to the United States had settled in Israel instead, the DPC estimated that changing the cutoff date to April 21, 1947, would then make 95,000 more DPs, 78,000 of whom were Jewish, eligible for consideration for visas to the United States.[10]

A second discriminatory provision favored people whose countries had been annexed by a foreign power. The State Department did not recognize any such annexations, but the senators obviously meant Estonia, Latvia, and Lithuania, as well as eastern Poland, which the United States government did acknowledge and which was the home of the Ukrainians, "all" of whom, according to Dr. R. Gogolinski-Elston, head of London's National Catholic Welfare Conference from 1943 to 1961, had fought in the German army.[11]

The third discriminatory clause in the Wiley-Revercomb measure, the agricultural stipulation, also worked against Jewish DPs, most of whom were not farmers. A 1948 JDC analysis estimated that only 3.7 percent of the Jews in the American zones and 6.1 percent of those in the British zones might qualify as "agriculturists." On the other hand, the percentage of farm workers among all DPs totaled approximately 16.9 percent in the American zones and 31.5 percent in the British-controlled territories.[12] The Jews, thought of as the archetypal urban dwellers, and "unassimilable" within American society, could be more easily kept out, therefore, if the legislation required a large percentage of agriculturists.

Finally, it must be kept in mind that about half of the American population exhibited some antisemitic prejudices. During and after the war pollsters and psychologists characterized 5 to 10 percent of Americans as rabidly antisemitic and 45 percent as mildly so.[13] The Revercomb subcommittee and the whole Judiciary Committee split three to two and six to five, respectively, against liberalizing the proposed DP act. Whether the senators were motivated by feelings of antisemitism when they voted is impossible to say definitely. (Langer, for example, apparently cared more about bringing the *Volksdeutsche* into this country than he did about excluding Jews) but the closeness of the tallies reflected, to a considerable degree, the cleavage in American society. Even those who most fervently supported the CCDP approved of the line emphasizing that 80 percent of the DPs were Christian because they, too, recognized the impossibility of obtaining legislation designed primarily to bring Jews to the United States.

The combination of restrictions in the Wiley-Revercomb proposal outraged those who had most strongly sought an adequate bill. Irving Engel indicated that he "would rather have no bill than see this measure pass in its present form." The editors of the *New York Times* wondered "whether its sponsors sat up nights to be certain of producing the worst possible offer for DP's." Senator Taft wrote Lessing Rosenwald, "I fully agree with you that the bill is very inadequate. I will work with those who are preparing amendments and do my best to see that they are adopted." Senate Democrat Scott Lucas of Illinois acknowledged that the proposal was "discriminatory" and in need of amending while William Phillips, who had served on the Anglo-American Committee of Inquiry, thought the measure "a most unfortunate piece of legislation." AFL President Green regarded the bill as "wholly inadequate."[14]

The State Department, in no uncertain terms, also indicated its displeasure. Undersecretary of State Robert A. Lovett wrote to Revercomb indicating the administrative difficulties that would be encountered if the December 22, 1945, cutoff date remained. The American consuls in Europe had been using April 21, 1947, the day General Clay ended DP admissions to American assembly centers in Germany, as the date of eligibility for DP status. Records simply did not exist proving entry before December 22, 1945. Lovett noted further, "I should like to point out that almost all of the Jewish displaced persons who remain in Germany, Austria, and Italy arrived in those countries after December 22, 1945." The Undersecretary also recommended doubling the number admitted to 100,000 per year and eliminating the priorities for agricultural workers and for peoples from "annexed" areas since the United States did not recognize these acquisitions. Lovett wrote this letter in response to Revercomb's request for the Department of State's views on his bill but the West Virginian did not share the Undersecretary's response with all of his colleagues on the Judiciary Committee.[15]

Some senators agreed with the harsh criticisms and thought about altering the bill when it reached the Senate floor. On April 28 Republicans Wayne Morse of Oregon, Leverett Saltonstall of Massachusetts, Ferguson, Cooper, and Smith met in Senator Cooper's office to devise a strategy for changing the offensive Wiley-Revercomb DP proposal. They had received folders and exhibits from the State Department designed to aid them with their floor presentations. Specifically, they decided to offer amendments increasing the numbers to be admitted, eliminating the Baltic preference, and substituting a provision requiring a "fair cross section" of DPs, and changing the cutoff date from December 22, 1945 to April 21, 1947. Each of the senators assumed responsibility for introducing, and trying to round up votes for, at least one of the proposals.[16]

A month later debate commenced in the Senate. (Senator Revercomb had to contend with a primary fight in West Virginia and did not want the Senate to deal with DP legislation until after he won it on May 12.) Revercomb and Wiley presented their proposed bill and received staunch support from Senators Eastland and Donnell. The two sponsors defended the measure as nondiscriminatory although Wiley did urge his colleagues "to be careful about letting displaced persons into this country. He said he want[ed] 'good blood' to come here and added: 'We don't want any rats. We've got enough of them already.'"[17]

The liberalizing amendments were introduced but only one, which would increase the totals from 100,000 to 200,000 over a two-year period, passed, by a vote of 40 to 33. Interestingly, former President Herbert Hoover had been in Washington a few weeks earlier lobbying for just that number.[18] His views may have influenced some of the Republican Senators. The other key amendments failed. Revercomb"demanded" the retention of the Baltic preference because the Balts really were stateless whereas many of the other DPs had not fled from persecution. The Polish government, Revercomb asserted, had "leaned over backwards" to induce its nationals to return home. Senator Taft supported his West Virginia colleague in this contention, and the two of them carried the majority with them, 40 to 31.

The most important amendment, from the point of view of CCDP supporters as well as members of the Senate who recorded the largest tally against it of any of the proposed changes, concerned the cutoff date. The liberals wanted April 21, 1947, thereby preventing the automatic exclusion of the 78,000 or more Jews who might otherwise qualify. Revercomb, arguing against its passage, claimed that the cutoff date was "indeed the heart of the bill." Most of his colleagues seemed to agree with him and the amendment mustered only 29 favorable votes against 49 negative ones.[19]

Thirteen Republican Senators (Bricker, Buck, Cain, Capper, Ecton, Flanders, Knowland, Martin, Millikin, Thye, Vandenberg, Wherry, Wilson, and Young) and one Democrat (Fulbright) who had voted to increase the total number of DPs from 100,000 to 200,000 voted against changing the date while three Republicans (Brewster, Cooper, and Taft) and one Democrat (Hayden) who had voted for the earlier amendment did not vote on the later one. Four Republicans (Hawkes, Jenner, Reed, and Watkins) and three Southern Democrats (Hoey, McClellan, and Umstead) who had not been recorded on the increased numbers amendment voted against changing the cutoff date. In other words, whereas 14 Republicans (12 from the middle or far West) and 19 Democrats (all from the South except Chavez, McFarland, and Tydings)[20] opposed increasing the total number of DPs, more than twice as many Republicans, 31, and about the same number of Democrats, 18 (all from the South except McFarland and Tydings), opposed changing the cutoff date. There can be no doubt that the key reason for this opposition was the Republicans' objection to the entry of more *Jewish* immigrants, since shortly afterward the Senate passed by a voice vote Langer's amendment to allow the *Volksdeutsche*, those ethnic Germans expelled from Eastern Europe, who entered the western zones of Germany by July 1, 1948, to be given half of the normal German and Austrian quotas. Strictly speaking, the term *"Volksdeutsche"* refers to ethnic Germans beyond the borders of the German empire. But most of those who passed under this category were, in fact, German citizens in the conventional sense, who had lived in Pomerania, Mecklenburg, East Prussia, Silesia and other areas of Eastern Europe and who were displaced because much of East Germany was assigned *de facto* to Poland and the Soviet Union after the end of World War II. Senator Langer argued, however, that the *Volksdeutsche* were "much worse off than the so-called displaced persons," most of whom he assumed "are related to residents of New York City."[21]

Several Senators, including Saltonstall, Smith, Morse, Mc-Grath, and Claude Pepper (D., Fla.), commented about how the proposed legislation discriminated against Jews, but to no avail. Senators Pepper and McGrath were perhaps the most eloquent. Pepper spoke of the "appalling inadequacy of the bill, which gave a majority of places to a minority of the DPs," yet limited "if not by design at least by effect" the slots available for Jews. McGrath lamented, "We come to this sad moment in the Senate of the United States when we probably shall have to write into the law of this country the principles of narrowness, intolerance, and bigotry. The date of December 22, 1945 was deliberately written into this bill because that date prohibited Jews from taking part in this program." Senator A. Willis Robertson informed a constituent a few days later, however, that "if the bill had gone as far as Senator McGrath proposed, it would not have passed the Senate." The Wiley-Revercomb bill won Senate approval by a vote of 63 to 13. Twelve Southern Democrats, not including Robertson, and Republican Albert W. Hawkes of New Jersey constituted the minority.[22]

The Senate's action shocked Earl Harrison and he responded with a scathing critique. The CCDP head called the measure a "booby trap" and urged the House of Representatives, which

had not yet passed the Fellows bill, introduced in April, to
undo the "monstrosity of Senate action," which not only
discriminated on religious, national, and occupational grounds,
but which contained the special provision admitting "*Volksdeutsche*, the notorious Nazi Fifth column. The bill's racist
character makes all decent Americans hang their heads in
shame." He then spelled out his opposition in greater detail.
That the *Volksdeutsche* "should be handed special privileges over
the victims of Nazi oppression, is a mockery of American
justice. For the first time in American history, immigrants can
now be classified not by nationality, but by 'race.' Thus, do we
not only admit our former enemies, but we accept Hitler's
twisted philosophy of blood."[23]

Harrison's statement expressed the views of most of the
members of the CCDP and AJC executive boards but it did
not affect the outcome in the House of Representatives which
proceeded to discuss its version of the DP bill as soon as the
Senate concluded deliberations. Frank Fellows, chairman of
the House subcommittee on immigration, prepared his own
DP bill which passed the Judiciary Committee with only two or
three dissenting voice votes. The proposal called for the
admission of 200,000 DPs over a two-year period, and gave
preference to DPs whose occupational skills could be utilized
in the United States and to those who had close relatives in this
country. It also set the cutoff date at April 21, 1947. This
indicated, of course, that the bill writers consciously decided to
allow the Jewish DPs who had left Russia in the spring of 1946,
as well as those who had fled from Poland before and after the
Kielce pogrom that summer, to qualify for admission to the
United States under the provisions of this special legislation.
In addition, the House bill would have allowed 15,000 uprooted
Europeans already in the United States on student, tourist, or
other nonpermanent visas to apply for immigrant status. But
the key clause in this version charged 50 percent of the DPs to
future immigration quotas for their countries of birth. Hence,
any number of Latvians, for example, might enter the United
States but 50 percent of them would be subtracted from their
nation's yearly quota of 236. Officials estimated that if the bill

passed as proposed, the Latvian quota would be mortgaged for the next hundred years. Without the mortgaging provision, however, many of the more conservative members of the House Judiciary Committee would have withheld their support, thereby making the bill's passage unlikely.[24]

With the clause, the bill sailed through the subcommittee, the Judiciary Committee, and the House itself. Some congressmen, like Democrats Eugene Cox of Georgia and Ed Gossett of Texas, felt impelled to speak out against the DPs in the debate. Cox called them "the scum of the earth," while Gossett characterized many of the DPs as "bums, criminals, subversives, revolutionists, crackpots, and human wreckage." An amendment offered by Representative Charles J. Kirsten, similar to the Langer proposal passed by the Senate, to include the *Volksdeutsche* among the beneficiaries of the bill failed, but another by Nebraska Republican Karl Stefan, to admit 2,000 Czechoslovakians victimized by the *coup* the previous February, received majority support. A third, also approved, proposed by Pennsylvania Democrat Francis Walter added 3,000 orphans to the 200,000 figure. Then the House passed the measure by a vote of 289–91. All but two of the opposing Democrats resided in the South, while 27 of the 39 negative Republicans votes hailed from the Midwest.[25]

Supporters of a liberal bill hoped that the House-Senate Conference Committee would eliminate or modify the most offensive provisions of both versions. Six of the seven House conferees (Fellows, Graham, Celler, Chelf, Boggs, and Chadwick) and two of the three original Senate representatives (Ferguson and Kilgore) favored a less restrictive bill. Only Gossett and Revercomb could be expected to oppose more humanitarian provisions. But before the group met, Senator Wiley, in a surprise move, left a committee meeting one afternoon, went to the floor of an almost empty Senate, and asked unanimous consent for adding Senators Eastland and Donnell, two restrictionists, to the Conference Committee. The move caught most people unawares, and since no one in the Senate immediately objected the majority of the Senate conferees changed complexion. No explanation ever came forth as to what motivated the Wisconsin Senator to act as he did but observers speculated that Wiley did not want a more liberal bill, that Revercomb had encouraged him to take this action, and that neither Taft nor Vandenberg, the acknowledged Republican leaders, cared enough about the subject to thwart Wiley's move. Concerned Jews were certain that Wiley had loaded the dice against the DPs and sabotaged their cause.[26]

In the conference, the three Senate restrictionists remained adamant against accepting provisions which might help Jewish DPs. They gave the House members an ultimatum: either something resembling the Senate measure or nothing. One of the House conferees, Frank L. Chelf, later claimed "they had a gun barrel at our heads and that gun was the legislative rush." As a result, the conferees went along with modified aspects of the worst features of both the House and Senate bills: the mortgaging provision of the Fellows measure was retained, the 50 percent Senate provision for DPs from the Baltic countries was cut to 40 percent, and the 50 percent preference for farmers was cut to 30 percent. "The real bone of contention" Fellows noted, the cutoff date, remained December 22, 1945, and the *Volksdeutsche* qualified for admission to the United States if they entered Germany by July 1, 1948, the effective date of the bill. Other provisions called for the admission of 3,000 orphans and 2,000 Czechs who had fled their native land after the Communist coup in early 1948. And 15,000 DPs temporarily in this country were allowed to apply for residence status. In addition, the DPs, but not the *Volksdeutsche*, would have to have guarantees of jobs and housing in the United States before receiving their visas. Finally, the group established a Displaced Persons Commission to administer this law which would allow 205,000 immigrants into the country. The report so displeased some of the conferees that four refused to sign it. Congressman Celler later wrote about the compromise, "it wasn't 'half a loaf'; it wasn't even half a slice."[27]

Despite the fact that many members of both Houses of Congress believed that the bill was deliberately intended to exclude Jews, President Truman reluctantly signed it while denouncing the measure in a manner which suggested that his speech might have been drafted at the offices of the CCDP. He called it "flagrantly discriminatory," speculated "whether this bill is better or worse than no bill at all," and charged "it must be frankly recognized . . . that this bill excludes Jewish displaced persons . . . also many displaced persons of the Catholic faith." On this last point Truman received erroneous advice. Catholics predominated among both the displaced persons and the *Volksdeutsche*.[28]

The bill passed with the discriminatory provisions because antisemitism in the United States waxed strong, and its existence proved too formidable a barrier to overcome. Senator Revercomb and his allies knew exactly what they were doing when they inserted the December 22, 1945, cutoff date, and contemporaries criticized them for it. Even Democratic Congressman James C. Davis of Georgia, who voted against the bill because he feared admitting Communists to the United States, acknowledged that "the Wiley bill was palpably and obviously discriminatory in its terms, and I will not knowingly discriminate against good people of any creed or religion or race."[29] Although Revercomb bore the brunt of the criticism for those clauses in the Displaced Persons Act which discriminated against Jews, it is possible, if not probable, that he represented the views of a significant number of senators who were glad not to be publicly identified with discriminatory provisions they wholeheartedly endorsed. Their prejudices were immediately apparent when they accepted a provision allowing the *Volksdeutsche* to be considered under the German quota and to apply for a United States visa if they reached West Germany by July 1, 1948.

In the summer of 1948, during the brief session of the recalled 80th Congress, both President Truman and the Republican presidential nominee, Governor Thomas E. Dewey of New York, urged Revercomb to get the cutoff date changed to April 21, 1947, but the West Virginia senator refused. Although several Republican senators also pressed Revercomb to alter the date, he had the support of two members of his immigration subcommittee, Donnell and McCarran, and they constituted a majority. They probably represented dominant sentiment in the Congress as well as in the nation. After all, the cutoff date change lost by a decisive majority during the Senate debates and a Roper–Fortune public opinion poll, conducted in September 1948, confirmed public support of that position. Although 53 percent of those questioned favored admitting more DPs to this country 59.8 percent of those answering affirmatively also responded "yes" to the follow-up question, "If most of these refugees turn out to be Jews, do you think we should put a special limit on the number of them we let in."[30]

Most American Jews were outraged by the 1948 DP Act. The president of the oldest Jewish fraternal order wrote that "in the 105 years of its existence, B'nai B'rith has never witnessed proposed congressional action so violative of American principles of equality and fair play. The vice of the bill is aggravated by its sanctimonius pretensions." An editorial in the HIAS bulletin, *Rescue*, found

> the unashamed cynicism displayed in legislating ostensibly for the relief of those who suffered most from the last war, while actually locking the doors of the United States against them . . . almost beyond the understanding of civilized men and women. . . . The act of specifically refusing to grant relief to the terror-stricken and homeless who are shut out from their native countries by the threat of murder and mob violence is an instance of deliberate and cold-blooded legislative cruelty.

From Europe, William Haber, the Jewish adviser to the army that year, wrote, "It is the most anti-Semitic Bill in US history."[31]

Several Jews also thought that the CCDP had failed in its endeavors. "All it has to show for its vast expenditures," wrote Will Maslow, a member of the CCDP executive committee, "is a law which many of its members will agree is worse than no law at all." One AJC staff member thought that an investigation should be made to see where the Jews had gone wrong. "One of the questions I should like to see the study address itself to," this member wrote, "is the aspect of the strategy of always getting up a non-Jewish front to press for Jewish causes." George J. Hexter of the AJC expressed his organization's general feelings when he admitted, "We took a calculated risk. We nearly won. Actually we lost—lost heavily. Does it follow that we should never have tried?"[32]

The most explosive critique came from the pen of an American Zionist, Abraham Duker, who had worked for the Nuremberg Trials Commission where he had amassed a considerable amount of material on Ukrainians and Balts. He claimed to have examined hundreds, if not thousands, of original German documents, and pointed out that many of the Balts and Ukrainians "were especially egregious collaborationists" who "guided the SS men, searched the ghettos, beat the people, assembled and drove them to the places of slaughter." These same East Europeans also served as "guards and tormentors" within the concentration camps.[33]

One New York City Yiddish language newspaper, the *Day*, forwarded copies of Duker's analysis and accusations to several congressmen and senators in early June 1948, in order to stiffen the provisions of the not-yet-passed DP Act. The summary page read, in part, "The enclosed documented study contains authentic proof that many of the Baltic and other Displaced Persons . . . are former Nazi collaborators."[34] But this information made no impact upon the lawmakers who instead wrote in a special provision to bring the *Volksdeutsche* to the United States. After the bill passed, Duker lashed out at both the Jewish organizations that had worked hardest to achieve the legislation, and the CCDP.

In an article entitled "The DP Scandal Reviewed," Duker excoriated the "self-delusion" of those Jewish organizations which still refused "to see the indecency, the shame and the danger of rewarding the killers and their kin by admitting them to these hospitable shores." The Jews were doing well enough under the Truman Directive, Duker argued, and should not have agitated for additional legislation. He berated the CCDP for repeatedly and erroneously emphasizing that the DPs constituted "the survivors of Nazi concentration camps" and were "victims of all forms of religious and political persecution, of barbarism, and Nazi terror." Duker declared "that members of the 15th Latvian Police Battalion and the other quislings who killed men, women, and let us not forget, 1,200,000 Jewish children under the age of 14, are not survivors of 'the concentration camps.' The Committee's propaganda utilized the feelings of mercy built up by the sufferings of Nazism's victims to make propaganda for all DP's, including the murderers, by its indiscriminate plea for all." His resentment, which expressed the views of the mostly Zionist and East European Jews in the American Jewish Congress, the Jewish Labor Committee, and the Jewish War Veterans, appeared in another piece for the *Reconstructionist* in October 1948. In "Admitting Pogromists and Excluding Their Victims," he again asserted that "many, if not most, of the non-Jewish DPs are former German collaborationists, past killers, present fascists and anti-Semites."[35]

Several Jews responded angrily to the accusations. Officials within the AJC dubbed Duker's remarks "misleading propaganda" harmful to relations between Christians and Jews. George Hexter, the AJC representative to the CCDP, thought it "the height of irresponsibility" for Duker to have publicized "the fact that the Citizens Committee was maintained so largely with Jewish funds." From Europe William Haber reported that "perhaps with the exception of the Baltic group," the blanket indictment of all or most non-Jews "is a dangerous generalization." If the purpose of attacks like Duker's, Haber wrote, is intended to prevent the entry of antisemites to the United States, "then we had better prohibit all immigration for most immigrants from Europe have a good deal of anti-Semitism."[36]

But AJC officials knew that Duker's statements could not be entirely dismissed. They objected to his charges because they undermined good intergroup relationships between Jews and Gentiles in this country. Members of the AJC and ACJ, especially, wanted to promote harmonious exchanges among American Jews, Protestants, and Catholics to minimize antisemitism and foster tolerance. Through the CCDP they met, and for the first time in the memory of most American Jews, worked in concert with people from various denominations.[37] Duker's impolitic accusations threatened the very development of those cooperative endeavors that the assimilated Jewish Americans desired.

This feeling that Jews should work well with, and avoid antagonizing, Gentiles is perhaps best illustrated by examining how the ACJ, the archetypal Jewish assimilationist organization in the United States at that time, reacted to the new law. Instead of directing an attack against the men who actually wrote and promoted the legislation, an ACJ editorial speculated "as to what different measure might have been passed if the powerful mass support which Zionists have rallied" for a Jewish homeland in Palestine, "had been utilized in support of a better D.P. bill. . . . With a fraction of the energies that went into the Jewish nationalist struggle in this country, a far more adequate bill might very well have been passed."[38]

In other quarters the DP Act was received with far greater equanimity. A variety of groups and individuals looked at the DP problem from a wider perspective and found some good in the measure. Spokesmen for the Federal Council of Churches and the National Catholic Resettlement Conference condemned the restrictive aspects of the bill but supported its passage nonetheless. In deference to the views of the Jews with whom they worked on the CCDP they called for an amended version in the future. New Jersey's Senator Smith, a strong proponent of a more generous version, did not feel badly about what had happened because "we did put over the increase to 200,000, and also at least got the machinery started so that we can find out the weak spots in the present legislation." He believed "that we are well on the way to a sound and final solution to this whole difficult problem." The Senate's Republican leader, Robert Taft, claimed that he was sorry about some of the bill's provisions, "particularly the [cutoff] date." (According to Bernard and Engel, Taft had promised to vote against the December 22, 1945, cutoff date but stepped off the floor of the Senate when the amendment came up for a roll call.) On the other hand, the senator explained to a constituent, "the provision which gives some special consideration to those who came from behind the Iron Curtain seems to be a proper distinction to make. These are the people who can never go back, whereas there is still reasonable hope of restoring many D.P.'s to Poland and Czechoslovakia." Monsignor Thomas J. O'Dwyer, in Los Angeles, agreed with Taft. "It is only just," he wrote, "that the first consideration should be given to those people who have been homeless for the longer time. The Balts, Poles, and Ukrainians east of the Curzon line were the first victims of the Nazi and Communist aggression."[39]

Although a majority of Jewish groups, primarily those of a Zionist bent like the Anti-Defamation League of B'nai B'rith and the American Jewish Congress, wanted the bill vetoed, there was no Jewish consensus. The AJC and the ACJ, the two Jewish organizations that had originally committed themselves wholeheartedly to bringing DPs to the United States, thought that the act should be signed by the President. Despite the obvious antisemitic drawbacks they recognized that the law did provide some help. Moreover, some Jews argued that it would be easier to amend a bad bill than to start from scratch the following year. Finally, after having supported the goals of the CCDP, which had emphasized that 80 percent of the DPs were Christian, it would have been politically unwise for Jewish organizations to demand that no one receive any assistance because Jews were being discriminated against.[40]

For obtaining any DP Act at all, credit must be given primarily to Lessing Rosenwald, Irving Engel, William Bernard, and others associated with the ACJ, AJC, and CCDP, whose unstinting efforts and finances were crucial. While Rosenwald, Engel, and their associates worked privately and behind the scenes, the CCDP made no effort to disguise its activities. Its outstanding lobbying generated an outpouring of concern which had prompted Congress to act. In less than two years the negative attitudes of a majority of both the public and the Congress toward liberalization of the immigration laws were reversed. It is possible that without the intensive efforts of the CCDP, Congress might have further restricted opportunities for entry into the United States. When President Truman first called for the admission of DPs to this country, in August 1946, few Washingtonians thought that such a proposal had any chance for success. "Apathy, not to say hostility," the President of the AJC reminded its members, "was rife in both the country and in the Congress. Only a vigorous and extensive program of public education made possible the passage of any such legislation at all."[41] Knowledgeable Jews realized that had it not been for their efforts, contacts, and especially finances, there would have been no Displaced Persons Act. The measure that passed therefore was ironic: those who had done the most, because they wanted to help Jewish DPs, ultimately wound up supporting a bill which circumscribed opportunities for Jews to emigrate to the United States.

There was a double irony in the 1948 DP Act. Not only did it discriminate against Jews but it undercut the advantages that had accrued to them under the provisions of the Truman Directive. Between May 1946, when the first boatload of refugees to be given preference under the President's order arrived, until June 29, 1948, Jews constituted about two-thirds of the 41,379 people admitted under the program. On July 1, 1948, when the new law went into effect, 23,000 European DPs (mostly Jews) who had received preliminary approval to enter the United States had their priorities wiped out because the act had specifically repealed the Truman Directive. Disconsolate American Jews estimated (incorrectly, as it turned out) that only about 30,000 of the Jewish DPs then in Europe would qualify for admission to this country.[42]

In and around the European assembly centers the new law upset many DPs as well as those who ministered to their needs. It not only dashed the hopes of resettlement in the United States for hundreds of thousands but it complicated the tasks of people who had crossed the ocean to help refugees rebuild their lives. An American social worker on the Continent wondered how she would "explain to a Jewish DP in Germany that under the present DP Act, the Balts, who he knew, voluntarily came to Germany to help Hitler in his war effort, had preference for admission to the States over him, the Jew, who suffered from the Hitler regime, not since the beginning of the war, but since 1933. And that *this* preference was the very expression of American democracy and humanitarianism."

After they heard the provisions of the legislation large numbers of DPs made no effort to hide their bitterness. They grumbled about the cutoff date and resented the fact that people whom they considered Nazis had a greater opportunity to obtain a visa than they did. One spokesman reflected the prevailing feeling when he observed, "Anybody who hates Communism has a good chance of going to America, but nobody seems to care now whether or not you hated Hitler."[43]

Although the seriously flawed measure that came out of Congress cruelly and intentionally discriminated against Jews, the humanitarian implications cannot be denied. The Displaced Persons Act of 1948 must be recognized as a landmark in the history of American immigration policy. By breaking precedent with existing legislation and mortgaging future quotas, it laid the groundwork for granting asylum to escapees from repressive, especially Communist, governments thereafter. It was the principle of helping the politically dispossessed that eventually allowed the United States to assist Hungarian, Cuban, and Vietnamese refugees in the 1950s, 1960s, and 1970s, respectively. It also provided for the first time a specific agency, the Displaced Persons Commission, to facilitate immigrant entry into the United States.

Jews who anticipated few positive effects from the 1948 Displaced Persons Act would be quite surprised to see how the new law was administered. They considered the legislation restrictive and could have no way of knowing in June that the commissioners later appointed by the President in August would be imaginative in their interpretations of the bill's provisions. In fact, the DPC was so creative in its operations that many legislators would later wonder how the bill that they had voted for contained so many loopholes.

8

RESETTLEMENT

THE DISPLACED PERSONS COMMISSION (DPC) began formal operations on August 27, 1948, and continued in existence until
August 31, 1952. During its four-year lifespan it helped resettle
more than 339,000 DPs in the United States. Aided by a large
number of social service agencies sponsored primarily by
religious organizations and state governments, it was the first
American immigrant resettlement agency established by the
federal government. The accomplishments of the Commission
set a pattern for accommodating subsequent refugee groups.
The activities of the DPC also showed how a government
bureau could change the intent of a law by the nature of its
administration. Congress passed a complex and restrictive
measure in 1948. The DPC, however, sought every loophole
and stretched every ambiguity to help bring people to the
United States under the terms of that act. A different set of
commissioners, with views similar to those of Senator Revercomb, would have been devastating to Jewish DPs seeking entry
to the country.

President Truman appointed the three commissioners on
August 2, 1948. He chose Ugo Carusi, a former United States
Commissioner of Immigration and a Protestant from Vermont,
to head the agency; Edward M. O'Connor, the director of the
War Relief Services of the National Catholic Welfare Conference (WRS-NCWC), who had been engaged in welfare work
for the previous 15 years; and a Jew, Harry N. Rosenfield, a
former American delegate to UNESCO and then assistant to
Oscar Ewing in the Federal Security Administration. Truman
deliberately appointed a Protestant, a Catholic, and a Jew on
the advice of many of the voluntary agencies which told him

that the Commission required a religious balance. Carusi undertook overall authority for administration and also supervised the overseas division. O'Connor specialized in dealing with those groups helping to bring DPs to the United States. Rosenfield oversaw the legal aspects of their work, prepared the annual reports, and functioned as the DPC legislative liaison with Congress. To some extent, of course, their managerial responsibilities overlapped. Moreover, all major policy decisions required their acquiescence or at least the approval of two of them.[1]

At the outset the commissioners established a system which reflected their liberal biases and undercut the letter and spirit of the law passed by the Congress. They also hired senior and middle-level staff people who had formerly worked for UNRRA, the IRO, and the voluntary agencies, and these administrators for the most part shared their outlook. The commissioners instructed DPC employees to find the means to remove people from the assembly centers and get them on the boats. The State Department consulates and the Immigration and Naturalization Service bureaus, on the other hand, accustomed to finding reasons to exclude prospective immigrants, continued making it difficult to obtain American visas. As a result of the DPC's more flexible processing procedures, the agency later became embroiled in controversy with Senator McCarran's immigration subcommittee.

The commissioners worked in a tense atmosphere. Rosenfield later recalled that everything had to have been done "yesterday." Many of the DPs had been awaiting the exodus for more than three years. Passage of the 1948 DP Act quickened their hopes, and they resented time-consuming administrative delays. The commissioners sympathized with these feelings, but their anxieties did not hasten the processing and several organizations complained about the slowness of DPC operations. The most serious problems encountered during the early months were insufficient public education about what the DPC was doing, long and complicated procedures, and poor coordination among the several government agencies overseas.[2]

To help eliminate some of these problems the commissioners established an advisory committee, composed of the heads of several of the state DP commissions and representatives of the major voluntary agencies. They also decided to allow, if not encourage, the major voluntary agencies to prepare corporate affidavits whereby these organizations guaranteed placement of the DPs and pledged that they would not become a public charge. The corporate affidavit was first used in bringing people to the United States under the Truman Directive and since it worked well the DPC continued its use. The Commission had enough to do without investigating each American sponsor for the more than 200,000 people the law would allow into the United States in the first two years of its operations.[3]

The DP groups with whom the DPC had to deal were, in order of size, Poles, Ukrainians, Latvians, Lithuanians, Yugoslavs, and Estonians. The law prohibited selection on a religious basis. On the other hand, the American agencies initially accredited to prepare corporate affidavits included primarily those with religious affiliations: American Hellenic Educational Progressive Association (AHEPA), American Federation of International Institutes, American Friends Service Committee, American National Committee to Aid Homeless Armenians, Church World Service, HIAS, International Rescue and Relief Committee, Mennonite Central Committee, National Lutheran Council, Unitarian Service Committee, United Service for New Americans (USNA—Jewish), United States Committee for the Care of European Children, United Ukrainian American Relief Committee, and the War Relief Services—National Catholic Welfare Conference.[4]

The rigidities of the law provided innumerable frustrations. Forty percent of the DPs had to have come from annexed areas (Fig. 8.1), 30 percent had to have been engaged in "agricultural pursuits," and all had to have entered Germany, Italy, or Austria between September 1, 1939, and December 22, 1945. But only 19 percent of the DPs actually came from "annexed areas"—which, according to State Department directives, ultimately included, in addition to the Baltic states, eastern Poland, Silesia, Bessarabia and Moldavia, the former free city of Danzig,

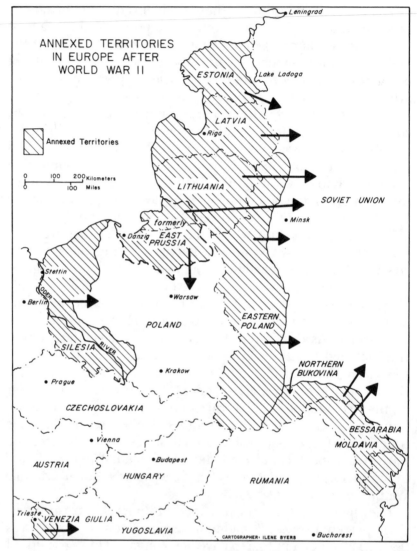

Figure 8.1. Annexed Territories in Europe After World War II.

and what was once East Prussia. Only 20 percent of the DPs had engaged in "agricultural pursuits." The DPC then broadened the definition of "agricultural pursuits" to include not only farming, dairying, horticulture, and gardening, but cotton ginning, lumbering, and preparation for marketing or delivery to market of farm products. Despite the wide latitude, in the first six months of the DPC's existence only 20 percent of the DP applicants were Balts (the major group from the annexed areas) and only 11 percent were agricultural workers.[5]

The main administrative stumbling block, however, concerned the December 22, 1945, cutoff date. Thousands of people were unable to prove their eligibility. Accurate records of DP residents went back only to 1946 or in some cases only to April 21, 1947. In the confused situation of 1945 not all centers maintained records, and many files could no longer be found.[6]

Further complications existed. Government agencies responsible for interpreting the 1948 DP Act and proving the eligibility of the DPs included the United States Immigration and Naturalization Service, the United States Public Health Service, and the State Department's Visa Division. Each interpreted its responsibilities under the law differently. Some officials could not always distinguish between their own prejudices and their legal obligations. In the summer of 1948, in particular, the visa agency proved obstructionist. Many of its personnel, for example, required people to whom they had already given visas under the Truman Directive, but who had not used them before July 1, 1948, when the Truman Directive became inoperative and the DP Act went into effect, to reapply for visas and be completely reprocessed. Moreover, consular officials did not hire sufficient additional staff to handle the larger number of applicants who applied because of the law. At the end of August 1948, a *New York Times* reporter wrote:

> The almost universal opinion of refugee experts who have observed procedures in Germany is that consular officials make it much more difficult for displaced persons than for Germans emigrating to the United States. This is a matter of their personal attitudes as much as anything else, observers feel. . . . As matters stand, it is easier for a former Nazi to enter the United States than for one of the Nazis' "innocent victims."[7]

The Immigration and Naturalization Service hurdles proved even more difficult for the Jewish DPs to surmount than those put up by the visa division. For example, where

"Surprising How Many Of Them Don't Come In"

From *The Herblock Book*. (Beacon Press, 1952)

DPC employees would pass along applicants who had been convicted of minor theft and/or black marketeering, INS officials would not. DPC personnel also looked less searchingly at documents presented and sometimes waived them if the DPs presented sufficiently good reasons for not having the appropriate papers. INS people scrutinized applications meticulously. Wendell Tripp, the INS Commissioner in Europe, conducted what Arthur Greenleigh, Head of the Jewish agency United Service for New Americans (USNA), regarded as a "witch hunt" to prove Jewish individuals inadmissible. The JDC head in Europe wrote his supervisor in New York, "I think it would be a very good idea to have the INS transfer Mr. Tripp to Idaho."[8]

In 1951 Greenleigh sent the DPC records of several typical cases which he believed the INS mishandled. In one, the INS held up clearance for an individual who had been denounced in an anonymous letter as an NKVD (Russian secret police) agent who had also spent time in Israel. The applicant denied both charges but had difficulty in clearing up the matter since he had no idea of who had accused him. A second case involved a woman charged with villainy by another correspondent. The letter arrived ten months before the accused woman learned of its existence. When finally informed of it her husband recalled an incident in which his wife had quarreled with another person who then vowed that the family would never get to the United States. When Greenleigh wrote to the INS about the problem it had already been pending for almost a year with no solution in sight. A third case involved a man whose wife had lived under an assumed Aryan name in Poland during World War II. The INS held up granting him a visa from July 1949 to March 15, 1951, because the consul would not accept the valid explanation that one had a better chance to survive in Nazi-occupied Poland without a Jewish name.[9]

These prejudices and obstructionist practices combined with the law's complexities to create a lag of approximately nine months from the time an ordinary application originated until a DP reached the United States. A HIAS information bulletin of January 3,1949, outlined the steps necessary to bring one DP to this country:

1) An affidavit from a voluntary agency sponsor promising to provide housing and a job had to be executed and sent to the DPC in Washington.

2) The DPC validated the assurance and then sent it along to the DPC coordinator in Frankfurt.

3) In Frankfurt, the DPC office prepared an index card listing all of the family members.

4) The index cards were then separated according to which voluntary agency was supporting the applicant.

5) The cards were assembled weekly according to voluntary agency and given to that organization's representative to have the appropriate forms filled out.

6) The forms were then given case numbers, separated into jurisdictional areas, and then sent to the DPC representative in the different jurisdictional cities in Germany and Austria.

7) The IRO was then asked to prepare a dossier on each case and include the following documents where available, and if appropriate:

> 7 passport photos
> 2 copies of birth certificates
> 2 copies of marriage certificate
> 2 copies of divorce certificate
> 2 copies of death certificate
> 2 police character certificates from either the DP assembly center or the German police
> 2 documents proving residence in Germany, Austria, and/ or Italy for any period between September 1, 1939 and December 22, 1945.

8) After the IRO assembled the dossier it was returned to the local DPC representative.

9) The DPC representative approved the documents and forwarded them to his supervisor who, in turn, sent them along for security clearance.

10) The Counter Intelligence Corps (CIC) of the United States Army conducted a security check and returned the dossier to the DPC where an analyst reviewed the file, prepared a report, and made a recommendation about acceptance. He then returned the dossier to the local DPC representative at the individual DP camp who, in turn, informed the IRO coordinator that the case had been approved or disapproved. If approved, the IRO representative would then arrange for a physical examination by the U.S. Public Health doctor.

11) The IRO coordinator next informed the IRO sub-area representative to notify the individual DP and members of his family, if any, to report for a physical examination.

12) If the DP passed the physical he was sent to a U.S. Consul to apply for a visa. When the visa was obtained the senior DPC representative was notified. He would then inform the IRO coordinator that a visa had been granted. The IRO coordinator would subsequently relate that information to the appropriate voluntary agency.

13) The IRO coordinator also informed the IRO movement officer that the DP had received a visa and advised him that transportation to Bremen, the port of embarkation, should be arranged.

14) Upon arrival in Bremen, the DP was given another physical examination—this time by the INS inspector—and if he passed, awaited his turn to board an IRO ship destined to the United States.

To comply with the law, the DPC originally tried to see that four of every ten DPs came from the annexed areas, but this made everything more difficult and slowed down the "pipeline"—as the process was called—still further. The Geneva correspondent of the *Christian Century* thought it a "miracle that *any* displaced persons have arrived in America . . . in the face of all the obstacles placed in their way." He then observed that "the entire complicated process is confusing, humiliating and brutal."[10]

After a few months at work the DPC recognized that its procedures needed streamlining if the agency were going to bring 200,000 DPs into this country by June 30, 1950, the date on which the DP Act would expire. Therefore the commissioners decided to ignore the mandates of the law and process whatever cases came along. It hoped to meet the specific quotas of the 1948 DP Act by the end of the second year but thought that to try to balance the various priorities on a weekly or monthly basis made no sense. The commissioners also encouraged subordinates to keep the immigrant flow moving and communicated the sense of a "steady pressure on everybody to pass everything no matter how." One employee complained that the DPC appeared

more interested in filling the quota than in the quality of the processed applicants. Consequently, people who have falsified documents and who have much to hide in their personal history records have their cases pushed along without much of an investigation to ascertain the validity of their documents. Thus many persons are finding their way with completely false information about themselves.

As a result of such practices, the number of DPs processed increased considerably. Whereas only 40,000 had arrived by June 30, 1949, during the next six months 81,968 more reached this country.[11]

But even with the expedited procedures the screening process remained a serious source of frustration and contention. Individuals and organizations differed over which DPs qualified for assistance. Which people had or had not voluntarily supported the Nazis during the war or might have been sympathetic to the Communists afterward could never be agreed upon. Despite valiant efforts made by the American Army, those closest to the screening process questioned the results. Since the end of the war in 1945 there had never been enough trained personnel to determine accurately who should be given DP status. From the first, qualified individuals were denied DP care and fraudulent claimants were accepted. Persecuted German Jews were originally treated as "Germans" and therefore former enemy aliens, rather than "Jews." Many Ukrainians, Poles, and Balts, on the other hand, who had voluntarily contributed to the German war effort, had no difficulty obtaining DP classifications. Many others who claimed Ukrainian or Polish nationality were sometimes considered "Russians" by American troops and therefore forcibly repatriated. The American Army sometimes refused to recognize "stateless" or "Ukrainian" as separate categories until several months after the war ended. Even as late as August 2, 1946, long after official policy acknowledged such demarcations, 250 Ukrainians were denied entrance to the Augsburg DP camp on the grounds that they were Soviet citizens.[12]

Formal screening in the DP camps to weed out war criminals, collaborators, illegal U.S. zone residents, voluntary immigrants into West Germany, enemy and ex-enemy nonpersecutees, and other impostors began in April 1946. It was interrupted and begun again several times because of questionable policies, procedures, and personnel. Most frequently, Army youths between the ages of 18 and 23 were given twelve hours of training before being sent out to determine eligibility. In this short period they were taught about European minorities and dialects, national enmities, German occupation policies, Russian government methods, ploys, guises, and tricks, and the differences between false and genuine documents. In one and a half days they were expected to learn what it had taken more experienced individuals years to master.[13]

As a result of this "training," Army personnel often failed to distinguish properly among those eligible and ineligible for DP care. Many could not recognize individuals who had been coached before appearing at their desks. Nor did they always know when their translators accurately conveyed individual replies. Since each screening team usually interviewed 50 to 80 DPs a day it is not surpising that a number of bizarre episodes occurred which made others question the accuracy of the process. In one group of 20 Latvians there were 12 former SS officers who bore the SS mark on their arms. All were approved for DP status. Each of the men claimed that he had received this identical mark from a burn, a wound, or an accident, and the American interrogator accepted the explanation. In another case an American officer interrogated people with a revolver on his desk. Whenever he did not like an answer he menacingly picked up the pistol and threatened the DP with it. In some cases brothers and sisters with identical backgrounds were separated, one being eligible for DP status, the other not. Children too young to have been able to make rational decisions were declared to have come "voluntarily" to Germany, and were therefore ineligible for DP status, while their parents, as former forced laborers, qualified. Many Latvian women in their sixties were said to have "voluntarily" accompanied husbands conscripted for forced labor during the war. Screeners found them ineligible for care while their husbands, who came "involuntarily," could remain in the DP camps. Technically, this should not have happened since married women were to receive the same status as their husbands and German women who married DPs acquired their spouses' classifications. Several Estonians complained that "the decisions of the US Screening Boards and their motivations for disapproval differentiate very widely and often are in plain contradiction to each other." In 1947, of the 318,000 non-Jewish DPs screened (all Jews were considered *ipso facto* eligible for DP status after the publication of the Harrison Report) 39,000 were found ineligible.[14]

As the years passed the screening became more arbitrary and slipshod. A captured document center in Berlin, under control of the U.S. Army after the war, allegedly contained the record of every person who had ever been affiliated with the Nazi organization or who had applied for German citizenship. The names of all DPs were supposedly checked against these files. But people changed their names or their spellings and they did not show up in the records. Moreover, the DPC archives contain files of numerous individuals with dubious backgrounds for whom the Berlin Document Center found no listings. Case #EC 48233 detailed the experiences of a member of the Latvian Legion, an officer, and a staff director of a concentration camp who later assaulted a DP policeman. Case #EC 34658 indicated that the applicant had lied about a previous application for admission to the United States and that his wife had earlier been denied a visa. Nevertheless, the Army's CIC cleared both cases for admission.[15]

The CIC's methods continually frustrated and exasperated several DPC staff members. In November 1950, one employee wrote Commissioner Rosenfield, "A day hardly passes here without my getting into an argument with . . . respect to these unfair C.I.C. reports." He then appended two quite similar cases in which the CIC recommended that the Jewish subject be denied a visa while the non-Jew be given one. The report on the Jew, case #EC 107770, dated September 5, 1950, read:

> Subject when interviewed by an agent of this Section on 22 August 1950 admitted that he was a member of the 1st Polish Army from May 1944 to May 1945, holding the rank of Private in the 1st Panzer Division. Subject stated further that he had been discharged in September 1945. Subject further stated he had Russian Officers and that the Army was Russian dominated.

The CIC finding then concluded:

Based upon the sources available to this organization at this time, it *appears* that subject adheres to or advocates, or followed the principles of any political or economic system or philosophy directed towards the destruction of free competitive enterprise and the revolutionary overthrow of representative governments.

In the case of the non-Jew, #EC 105606, dated October 23, 1950, the report indicated:

Subject stated that in June 1944 when the Russian Army came to Poland he was drafted in the Polish Army sponsored by the Russians. He became a Sergeant in the 3rd Armoured Regiment of the 2nd Polish Russian Army and fought against the Germans. He remained with the unit until October 1945, at which time he was demobilized in Glurvitz, Poland where he had been doing occupation duty. After his release from the Army he went to Austria and obtained work as a farmer.

Attention is directed to the attached Work Card which was the only document subject possessed to substantiate his story. It is noted that the number 2 typed after "Geburtstag" is of a different type than the 2 in the date of issuance. The day and month (20 December) appear to have been typed over an erasure. When questioned regarding above mentioned discrepancies subject denied any knowledge of alterations being made on the card or that card was falsified.

For this subject the CIC recommended:

Based upon the sources available to this organization at this time, it does *not appear* that subject adheres to or followed the principles of any political or economic system or philosophy directed towards the destruction of free competitive enterprise and the revolutionary overthrow of representative governments.[16]

The apparent arbitrariness of evaluations such as the above carried over into other areas of screening and approving DPs. The idiosyncrasies of DPC employees, consular and public health officials, and other Army and IRO personnel were allowed to affect decisions on which papers needed to be shown. Thus requirements varied from group to group, and sometimes from individual to individual. As a result, document factories sprang up to provide whatever forms and authorizations a DP needed to produce. Many Balts and Ukrainians, for example, came to Germany with official government stamps and stationery. The American Army traveled with huge supplies of paper, ink, machines, etc., and black marketeers somehow found access to these materials. Sometimes, with or without these items, individuals used local craftsmen skilled in various types of forgeries. Some voluntary agency personnel also engaged in these illegal practices to speed the departure of DPs out of the assembly centers. Several thousand people had survived the war living by their wits, and the use of false papers did not strike them as improper. Most DPs regarded their own case as worthy, and if it simply meant changing a name, date, or place of birth or arrival to be accepted in the United States, they saw no harm in doing so.[17]

When the DPC began its processing in the fall of 1948 it encountered many problems that had confronted the Army earlier as well as several others which cropped up because of the new law. Section 13 of the DP Act, for example, specifically indicated:

> No visas shall be issued under the provisions of this Act to any person who is or has been a member of, or participated in, any movement which is or has been hostile to the United States or the form of government of the United States.

While this statement might appear self-explanatory to some, Carusi asked for greater clarification from Admiral R. H. Hillenkoetter, Director of the Central Intelligence Agency (CIA). Carusi sent over a list of suspect organizations and inquired whether membership in any of them constituted sufficient reason to bar individuals from admittance to this country. Admiral Hillenkoetter's reply suggested that new national concerns should be considered in implementing Section 13:

> It is definitely worth pointing out, in connection with many of the organizations listed, that a curious anomaly has developed since the end of the war. Several of these organizations (for example, the Melnik and Bandera groups and the Lithuanian

Partisans) sided with the Germans during the war not on the basis of a pro-German or pro-Fascist orientation, but from a strong anti-Soviet bias. In many cases their motivation was primarily nationalistic and patriotic and their espousal of the German cause determined by their national interests. Since the end of the war, of course, these opportunistically pro-German groups remain strongly anti-Soviet and, accordingly, find a common ground with new partners. This position of similar groups with a highly fascist, rather than middle-of-the-road, political program presents an even more subtle problem. They similarly array themselves on the anti-Soviet side, but the degree or nature of their actual hostility to the United States or its form of government will continually vary with conditions in their own country and with the changing international situation.

In other words, while some DPs might have belonged to organizations which in the past were hostile to the United States, the fact that they were primarily anti-Soviet, rather than pro-German, might have to be taken into consideration. The three commissioners discussed this problem several times. Rosenfield argued that membership in a pro-German or fascist organization during the war required a declaration of ineligibility under the DP Act, but in September 1950, Carusi and O'Connor voted against their colleague's stand. Thereafter, the DPC took the position that the Latvian Legion and Waffen SS Units were separate in purpose, ideology, and activities from the German SS and therefore "not [considered] to be a movement hostile to the Government of the United States under section 13 of the Displaced Persons Act."[18]

DPC policies toward alleged Nazi partisans particularly concerned others who believed it wrong to harbor former enemies or fugitives from justice. Several Jewish organizations formally complained to the DPC that too many Nazis were receiving clearance to go to the United States. Congressman John A. Blatnik, a Minnesota Democrat, objected to such people even being housed in the assembly centers. Although an Army intelligence report of May 1949 confirmed that "hundreds, if not thousands, of Nazi collaborators have been and still are residing in DP camps," and a DPC employee pointed out to

Commissioner Ugo Carusi that the "majority of displaced persons coming from [the] Baltic countries, [along with] Polish Ukrainians, Rumanians, Hungarians, Slovakians and Croatians, have records of treachery, complete Nazi collaboration, and in many cases have committed atrocities," little was done to eliminate these individuals from being processed through as DPs eligible for admission to the United States.[19]

The screening process disturbed almost all of the organizations that dealt with DPs but, in general, did not retard the pace of the exodus. The DPC, the IRO, and the voluntary agencies existed to resettle people, not to help prolong their stay in Europe. In addition, the American Army also wanted the DPs removed and military officials did whatever they could to facilitate the migration out of Germany.[20] Thus the atmosphere in Central Europe in 1948 and after contributed to speeding up the work and getting the job done. Each of the groups had different reasons for moving the occupants, and all had their favorites, but none wanted to obstruct or slow down the tempo. A scrupulous adherence to the provisions of the 1948 DP Act would have choked the movement.

The major agency promoting DP emigration was the International Refugee Organization. Established on December 15, 1946, by the General Assembly of the UN to replace UNRRA and the Intergovernmental Committee on Refugees (IGC, which had been in existence since 1938), the IRO inaugurated operations on July 1, 1947. Technically, it did not come into existence until fifteen UN participants had ratified and accepted membership in the organization; hence, until August 30, 1948, when Denmark became the fifteenth nation to join, it functioned as the Preparatory Commission of the International Refugee Organization (PCIRO). Although it succeeded UNRRA as administrator of the DP assembly centers and coordinator of the work of the voluntary agencies, its main charge was to resettle DPs in new homes, and to achieve this goal it did not always check people's backgrounds carefully.

The IRO sought openings for the refugees in European and other nations and pointed out to several governments how DPs could replenish depleted labor supplies. Many nations, in fact, sent delegations to the DP assembly centers to pick those who best met their needs. By allowing receiving countries to choose from among the most skilled and physically able Protestants and Catholics in the camps, the IRO helped move people to permanent homes.

Most countries preferred unmarried, well-built, non-Jewish adults.[21] In 1947 Belgians chose 20,000 Baltic and Ukrainian males to work in the coal mines. That same year the British inaugurated their "Westward Ho!" policy seeking single men and women of these same ethnic groups to serve as domestics, textile workers, coal miners, agricultural employees, and steel processors. By November 1947, the British had taken about 30,000 DPs. Other nations also sought young, strong, single, males. The French accepted the *Volksdeutsche* but, to avoid antagonizing the Russians, neither Balts nor Ukrainians. Within the Commonwealth, Britishers were preferred as immigrants but ultimately over 275,000 DPs were taken. Australia wanted to swell her population with growing familes but specified that 75 percent of those referred must be non-Jews. "Fairly good teeth, a lot of youngsters, and knowing how to sign your name," a reporter later wrote, "qualified you for Operation Kangaroo."[22]

The IRO respected the various requests but occasionally came across some unusual people and circumstances. One man and woman, accompanied by their six children, were all set to go to Australia when it was discovered that they had never been married. IRO officials indicated that a wedding ceremony had to be performed before departure, but the man was upset. "Marry her?" he exclaimed, "but I don't even like her!" Nonetheless, the marriage took place and the family went off to Australia. Another unmarried woman with a child had difficulty getting into Brazil. When the IRO persuaded the Brazilian consulate to accept them she was again pregnant. Confronted with this discovery, the woman indignantly accused IRO personnel of causing her troubles. "If you had worked faster on my papers," she told them, "there would not have been time for this to happen. But I will overlook it if you send me and my lover to Brazil as soon as possible." On another occasion a Polish DP, asked to sign his name, whipped out a rubber stamp, blew on it, and banged it on the paper, upside down. Told about the discrepancy, the man blew on the stamp again, turned it around, and affixed the signature rightside up. The IRO representative shipped him out on the next transport for resettlement overseas.[23]

Several nations that wanted no Jews received them anyway. Ships destined for such places as Brazil, Venezuela, and Canada listed passengers by religion. Specific numbers of Roman Catholics, Greek Orthodox, and Protestants of various denominations were spelled out along with a category called "orthodox." Under this guise the IRO included many "orthodox" and not-so-orthodox Jews.[24]

On the other hand, the IRO made it extremely difficult for Jewish DPs who desired assistance in getting to Israel. Britishers not only constituted 38 percent of the employees of the PCIRO but held 216 of the 435 administrative positions in October 1947. This made the organization, according to Hirschmann and others, "the instrument of British politics." Consequently staffers thwarted attempts of Jewish DPs to get into Palestine. After the establishment of Israel on May 14, 1948, the British-dominated international resettlement agency refused to assist Jewish DPs who wished to go there on the grounds first, that all member nations of the UN did not recognize Israel, and then because the IRO claimed that it could not send DPs to "belligerent" countries in the Middle East. Yet the IRO did not hesitate to aid Jews in evading American immigration laws. Along with the voluntary agencies, IRO staffers prepared documents for those in need, especially for people who claimed to have arrived in Germany before December 22, 1945.[25]

In getting Jews and others on their way the IRO relied upon the assistance of voluntary agencies from all over the world. These groups aided with resettlement, vocational training, religious needs, jobs, rehabilitation, retraining, and repatriation. Voluntary agency personnel worked both in Europe and in their own countries; the Jewish agencies predominated in the American zones of Germany, Austria, and Italy, and in the United States. In January 1948, for example, the PCIRO listed

710 employees of thirteen voluntary agencies in Germany for that month. The list was representative of the efforts that each group had been making for the previous years. The following list indicates the agencies named and the number of employees that each one had. More than 60 percent of both agencies and workers were Jewish:

American Jewish Joint Distribution Committee (JDC)	266
American Friends Service Committee	6
American Polish War Relief	8
Czechoslovakian Red Cross	5
HIAS	34
International Rescue and Relief Commission	14
Italian Red Cross	1
Jewish Agency for Palestine	92
Jewish Committee for Relief Abroad	12
National Catholic Welfare Conference	52
Netherlands Red Cross	2
Polish Red Cross	31
U.S. Committee for Care of European Children	5
United Ukrainian American Relief Committee and Ukrainian Canadian Relief Fund	3
Vaad Hatzala (Orthodox Jews)	12
Church World Service & affiliates	15
World Organization for Rehabilitation Through Training Union (ORT)	59
World's YMCA/YWCA	57[26]

The Jewish agencies were on the scene first, had the largest resources of money and personnel, and the greatest interest in helping the survivors of the Holocaust. In June 1945, employees of the JDC were the first to get into the DP assembly centers. Their teams included social workers and child care specialists, health personnel and educators, and simply interested and knowledgeable Jews willing to help out. In addition to providing food and clothing, they established schools, distributed books and religious articles, set up hospitals and health care facilities, and helped trace friends and relatives of the DPs. (The American military would not permit DPs to send or receive mail until November 1945, and in the interim voluntary agency personnel served as the intermediaries.) JDC workers spoke Yiddish, German, or both, and they frequently intervened for the DPs and UNRRA and Army officials. They also helped Jews depart for Palestine and other places. No other voluntary agency, Jewish, Gentile, or nonsectarian, could compare with the JDC in accomplishments. In 1945 it fed 200,000 Jewish DPs, in 1946, 349,000, and in 1947, 411,800. Between 1946 and 1950 it shipped over 154 million pounds of food, 750,000 pairs of new shoes, 500,000 coats, 250,000 new suits, 300,000 dresses, and 2 million pieces of underwear. Its medical clinics treated more than 2.5 million cases and its kitchens and canteens distributed more than 42 million hot meals. Between 1945 and 1950 the agency provided cash relief to between 180,000 and 200,000 Jews, and its total expenditures in the postwar period exceeded $200 million. As one chronicler put it, "The performance of the JDC as a private, voluntary agency has set a new mark in the peacetime history of international social service."[27]

HIAS ranked second to the JDC in importance to the Jews in Europe. Established at the end of the nineteenth century to help newly arrived Jewish immigrants adjust to the United States, HIAS is still doing the same kind of work today. After World War II its personnel engaged in activities similar to those of the JDC and was particularly active in Poland. The fact that the JDC existed did not preclude HIAS from conducting its tasks. It is not uncommon for Jewish agencies to overlap in their services because there are so many people in need, and also because slight variations in goals occasionally seem like major differences. HIAS, too, spent millions of dollars helping the DPs and, outside of Germany, was probably the key agency aiding the emigration of Jews from Central and Eastern Europe. It also helped European Jews on their way to Palestine, then Israel, and after passage of the DP Act, it combined operations with the JDC to assist those who wanted to get into the United States. Both organizations pooled their efforts with the major Jewish resettlement agency in the United States—USNA—to avoid duplicated, and hence wasted, efforts.[28]

The United Service for New Americans (USNA), carefully

named to avoid any reference to the fact that it was Jewish and worked with Jewish newcomers, originated as a result of a merger of the National Refugee Service and the National Service to Foreign Born of the National Council of Jewish Women in the summer of 1946. Designed primarily to help the DPs resettle in America, at the time that the 1948 DP Act passed, it employed over 800 people. Like the JDC and HIAS, USNA spared no expense, and at one point purchased the Hotel Marseilles on New York City's upper west side to house temporarily the newcomers awaiting trains or buses to the hinterlands. The following annual expenditures suggest the magnitude of its commitment:

Year	Dollars
1946	3,000,000
1947	9,153,253
1948	10,462,141
1949	7,926,778
1950	2,341,059
1951	1,455,168
1952	783,673[29]

USNA, reflecting the fears of the older and more assimilated non-Zionist American Jews who controlled the key positions in the voluntary agencies, tried to disperse the foreigners all over the country and actively worked against allowing any DP Jews but those who had close relatives in New York to remain there. There had been too much talk in Congress about how the Jews would continue to congregate in the urban ghettos and many Americanized Jews believed the newcomers would assimilate faster where fewer coreligionists dwelled, therefore lessening the possibility of antisemitism. Lessing Rosenwald expressed the prevailing view when he wrote, "Naturally I am opposed to [DP] resettlement in large urban areas."[30]

After the Jewish organizations, the Catholic agencies were most active but they were slow in getting their operations started. The premier Catholic agency in the field, the War Relief Services of the National Catholic Welfare Conference (WRS-NCWC), had all but ignored the DPs in 1945. At the time of the Truman Directive, on December 22, 1945, it had only five relief workers in all of Central and Eastern Europe. Not until May 1946 did the hierarchy designate a Catholic Committee for Refugees to handle visa applications for coreligionists who qualified under the President's order. The lackluster Catholic interest is perhaps best illustrated by the remark of a Catholic DP who complained that while Jewish representatives were "all over the place," he could not find one other DP in Germany who had ever been in contact with a Catholic social worker. Even at the end of August 1946, the Catholic Committee for Refugees had no idea of how many Catholic personnel were engaged in relief work overseas or how many corporate affidavits had been offered by Catholic organizations. As a result, Catholics resettled relatively few people under the directive. Although no two sources agree on how many quota visas were issued because of Truman's order, one count, which ignored the atheists and those with unknown affiliations, indicated the following religious breakdown among the beneficiaries between March 31, 1946 and June 30, 1948:

Jews	25,594
Catholics	5,924
Protestants	2,091
Other	1,906
Total	35,515[31]

Once the Catholics realized, however, that 80 percent of the DPs were Christians, and most of those people adhered to the Roman Catholic faith, they increased their efforts. By January 1948, Monsignor Edward E. Swanstrom, executive director of the WRS-NCWC, was stating that the American immigration laws should be changed to admit 50,000 to 100,000 "individuals of Christian denominations." At about the same time the Roman Catholic Church indicated that it would inaugurate a far-reaching program to assist in the relocation of DPs. Catholic DP resettlement committees were to be set up in 118 dioceses and 19,000 parishes throughout the United States. After the DP Act of 1948 passed every Catholic bishop in America received instructions to appoint a diocesan resettlement director. These preparations made the Catholic agencies as ready as the Jewish ones to assist in the movement of DPs out of Europe. It is not surprising, therefore, that of the 82,000 DPs admitted to the United States between July 1, 1948 and September 1949, 75,000 arrived under the auspices of agencies of these two faiths.[32]

The Protestants, except for the Lutherans, showed the least interest in resettling the refugees. There were several reasons for this. Protestants had the fewest numbers of coreligionists in the European assembly centers and hence lacked sufficient motivation to help. Samuel McCrea Cavert, the general secretary of the National Council of Churches, suggested another reason. He wrote that the constituent groups in his organization included many people with, as he phrased it, "racial and national prejudices," who did not want most of the DPs to come to the United States. David Lloyd, an assistant to President Truman, later put this sentiment somewhat differently when he commented, "I suspect that one of the motives for Protestant opposition to continuing participation by voluntary groups in the immigration process is a dislike of immigration from . . . Roman Catholic areas." Certainly when the DPC inaugurated operations in 1948 the Protestant agencies seemed particularly inept. A State Department spokesman observed "that the group of Protestant welfare agencies which had undertaken to perform their share in the matter of settling DPs in this country has 'fallen on its face' in such a way as to cause 'grave concern' to the State Department and the DP Commission." That same spokesman confessed further to an interviewer that "since the program got under way the Protestant group has shown poor organization and an inability to raise the necessary money." In 1948, when USNA provided over $10 million for refugee aid, Church World Service allocated $1 million. The following year CWS budgeted only $600,000, but *Christian Century* thought it "extremely unlikely that that amount will be anywhere near realized." A few weeks later the same journal noted that with the exception of the Lutherans, the Protestant "record reflects, if indeed it does not contribute to, the callous indifference of the nation at large" toward DPs. That September the Protestant

Episcopal Bishop of Massachusetts called upon coreligionists to "assume their responsibility for resettling European DPs." At the time, only three of the 101 Protestant Episcopal dioceses had guaranteed havens for ten or more families, forty had sponsored nine or fewer people, while the other 58 had taken none. Ultimately the Protestants resettled almost 60,000 of the more than 400,000 DPs and *Volksdeutsche* who reached America between 1945 and 1953. Lutherans, especially, showed a willingness to help. They aided over 30,000 people, mostly Balts. One leader of the Lutheran Church in South Dakota "expressed the desire," according to a DPC employee, "of obtaining displaced persons from the Baltic Waffen SS Units." A Baptist group in Maine also made special efforts to house and retrain Baltic DPs.[33]

Working with the agencies of the major religious denominations, as well as those representing such nationality groups as the Poles and Ukrainians, the DPC carefully selected an appropriate mixture of people to arrive on the first boatload under its auspices. Eight hundred thirteen DPs came ashore when the Army transport *General Black* docked in New York City on October 30, 1948. Most of the passengers had already been processed under the Truman Directive, and therefore could get through the "pipeline" quickly, and the mix satisfied various political needs and constitutencies in the United States. Among the arrivals, Poles numbered 338, Balts 214, Czechs 53, the remainder, stateless. There were 491 Roman and Greek Catholics, 161 identified themselves as Jews, 75 were Russian and Greek orthodox, 67 belonged to various Protestant denominations, 18 had no sectarian affiliation. One-quarter of the passenger list consisted of children under sixteen—there were 197; 83 farmers headed for the Midwest made up a plurality of those divided according to occupation. The press made a great fuss over this first boatload, took numerous pictures, and an appropriate number of American dignitaries including Ugo Carusi, Attorney-General Tom Clark, Francis Cardinal Spellman, Rhode Island Senator J. Howard McGrath, and New York City Mayor William O'Dwyer, turned out to greet them. One of the DPs made the political response exactly appropriate to the occasion:

> It seems to us that we have arisen from the dead. Not so long ago we were tortured in forced labor battalions. Only a short while ago we were living from day to day in the expectation of being burned alive in the Nazi stoves. Today, we begin a new life. How beautiful this is for us. Thank you America.[34]

Subsequent arrivals received less attention, except when particularly newsworthy events occurred. An alleged ex-Gestapo agent, along with his wife and children, came in on one ship that landed just before Christmas. A fellow passenger accused this man (who had allegedly changed the spelling of his name from Danilov to Daniloff) of having beaten him and burned him with a lighted cigarette in the Riga concentration camp during the war. The Church World Service brought the Daniloffs to the United States but disclaimed any responsibility

A DP family that arrived in the U.S. under the auspices of HIAS. (The National Archives)

A DP family arrives in the U.S. under the auspices of the auspices of the United Service for New Americans. (Courtesy American Jewish Committee)

since it sponsored the family only after the members had been screened and cleared by the State Department, the IRO, the DPC, and the CIC. Another ship brought a couple with their five-year-old daughter. The two adults claimed to have met, fallen in love, married and had their child in a slave labor camp, where they had remained for three years until liberated in 1945. The newspaper reporter neither questioned, nor explained, how two people might court, marry, consummate a relationship, and raise an infant in a "slave labor camp." In 1945, Katherine F. Lenroot, chief of the United States Department of Labor's Children's Bureau, wrote that "there are almost no Jewish children between the pre-school age and adolescence in Germany." And the DPC final report explicitly stated that the "opportunity for bearing children and for marriage . . . was lacking during the period of persecution and forced labor." A third ship that docked in Boston in May 1949 not only included 221 children, an unusually large number for a DP grouping, but also thousands of family heirlooms. Customs officials wondered how "displaced persons" could have acquired such riches. Incidents such as these brought to mind the *Manchester Guardian* reporter's observations in February 1946 that the non-Jewish DPs "have, in most cases, managed to bring with them different sets of clothing, jewelry, valuable rugs, and other belongings. The Jews are invariably shabbily dressed."[35] In 1950 the DPC chose "a frail Latvian" woman to be honored as the 200,000th DP and newspapers pictured her with four healthy looking children, born between 1939 and 1944. Published information of this sort also helped substantiate Abraham Duker's accusations that one of the ways to identify the collborationists was to see which ones had their children with them. Those who had been taken as slave laborers had been separated from their families.[36]

Despite such occurrences the press emphasized the wholesomeness of the newcomers and the positive aspects of the DP program. A *Collier's* reporter wrote in July 1948, "It is doubtful if the endless 'screenings' by military and civil agencies have left a single criminal undiscovered among those who still qualify as DPs." Both the CCDP and the Informational and Educational Division of the DPC, anxious to get the 1948 Act amended, did not want to give publicity to individuals who might not have qualified for admission but who nonetheless made it to the United States. Thus, they made zealous efforts to stimulate the proper kinds of newspaper and magazine stories which would show happy, contented, foreigners thankful for their

New York City. December, 1950. Mrs. Zinaida Supe of Latvia, the 200,000th person brought to the United States under the Displaced Persons Act of 1948, and her four children, aboard the U.S. Navy Transport, *General Sturgis*. Reverend Edward E. Swanstrom (right), executive director of the War Relief Services, National Catholic Welfare Conference, is shown welcoming the family. Left to right: Richard, Marguerita, Mrs. Supe, Edmund, and Irene. The family, sponsored by the Catholic Daughters of America, was taken to New York City Hall for a greeting by Mayor Vincent Impellitteri and later flown to Colorado Springs, Colorado, where they planned to live. (The National Archives)

opportunities in this country. To this end they arranged interviews, suggested pictures, and provided numerous opportunities for "upbeat" human interest stories. Most reporters and journalists welcomed the opportunity to cooperate.[37]

The favorable narratives and pictures about a few, lavishly spread across the pages of periodicals like *Collier's, Life,* and the *Ladies' Home Journal,* helped contribute to the public receptiveness for a broadened, and less discriminatory, DP Act, while at the same time masking the more serious problems of adjustment which many of the newcomers faced. Hence, stories abounded about DPs ever-so-anxious to become citizens, thrilled that they could go places without having to produce "their papers," and quickly adjusting to American life. Smiling men were shown seated on tractors, women appeared using washing machines and going to beauty parlors, children were described as "completely adapted to such Americanisms as cowboy movies, comic books and baseball." One journal pictured a baby alongside a comment from a North Dakota community leader: "Forget that term 'displaced persons' quickly. When they come into their new country they're no longer displaced. They're in the right place. They're home. They're new neighbors!" One resettled Latvian, when asked about how things were going, replied, "*Das geht* OK."[38]

Despite the pictorial and journalistic euphoria the trauma of resettlement cannot be overlooked. Eventually, most of the DPs who arrived in the United States blended into middle class anonymity, but they grappled with many of their own anxieties in the process. In 1946, when several National Refugee Service employees caring for Jewish orphans separated infants from older children, the latter became quite upset. "The babies have been taken to the gas chambers," the agitated youths told one another and they accepted no reassurances to the contrary until they were allowed to see the little ones in their new quarters. In Detroit, high incidences of motor accidents occurred among refugees. This resulted not only from ignorance of traffic laws but from the immigrant's almost instinctive "desire to outwit the policeman;" therefore the refugee turned left when told to turn right. An English teacher showed her class of recently arrived upper-middle-class professionals a

picture of voting day in a small New England town. The picture
bewildered them. They could not understand how a group of
people could stand around talking in an apparently relaxed
manner while waiting their turn to vote, with a policeman lazily
tilting back in his chair. The Europeans distrusted policemen
and law officers and found it difficult to comprehend the
Americans' indifference to them.[39]

Aside from the psychological adjustments, serious problems
faced those DPs misplaced in rural areas or on menial jobs; 27
percent of the DPs admitted to the United States received
classifications as "agricultural workers." In December 1951,
however, fewer than 3.4 percent remained in that occupation.
Balts and Poles with little or no farm experience found
themselves on plantations in Louisiana and Mississippi where
they were treated in the same fashion as local blacks. Not even
in the DP camps had they been so humiliated and degraded.
Overworked, poorly fed, and rigidly supervised, the newcomers
experienced lives which seemed more like those of medieval
serfs than of residents of the world's wealthiest industrial
nation. Newspapers and periodicals in the North excoriated
the southern exploiters of these DPs. A southern sociologist in
attempting to give a partial explanation of the difficulty, wrote
that the DPs seemed unwilling "to accept the simpler kind of
plantation workers' quarters as permanent abodes. In their
native culture rural housing standards were higher than those
of plantation workers in the Deep South."[40] Recent arrivals
also preferred the association of compatriots in the northern
cities who hailed from the same region of Europe, spoke their
language, and shared cultural values. Hence, they left the
farms in droves.

Other refugees also struggled with placements for which
they lacked appropriate backgrounds. DPs in the Boston area
obtained menial jobs although they had received training in
Europe as physicians, dentists, lawyers, and teachers. One
Latvian, a former professor of medieval history and a scholar
with a knowledge of several languages, first worked in the
United States as a dishwasher. Many other professionals also
resented being downgraded in employment on assembly lines
and in industrial plants.[41]

The experiences of foreigners in the same occupation differed from state to state. Physicians are a case in point: 17 states would not allow DP doctors to practice until they became United States citizens; 21 states prohibited foreign-trained doctors from practicing at all. New York, the most hospitable of all the states, allowed the immigrants to take their licensing examinations with only a minimum of further schooling. Refugee physicians needed only a year of internship before proceeding with examinations in Illinois. In Delaware they might work in hospitals but not in private practice, and only citizens could become licensed. In Indiana foreign physicians served only as orderlies. The North Dakota and Minnesota boards of medical examiners, inspired by their state DP commissions, changed their rules, however, so that DP doctors could find work in those states.[42]

Thirty-six states established their own DP commissions to help the newcomers with a wide variety of services but the impact and worth of their efforts varied considerably.[43] For the most part they prepared information lists of available community agencies, jobs, and housing facilities, coordinated the efforts of numerous public and private agencies, and helped establish local planning bodies. In general, the upper Midwest had the most active and efficient state DP agencies while New England and the South had the least effective ones. An outstanding executive secretary ran the Michigan commission while the Minnesota DP establishment, which distributed a pamphlet to all of the newcomers, entitled "Welcome New Neighbor," ranked as the best in the country, according to one DP investigator. Illinois provided a vast array of services. Among other things the state DPC traced lost baggage and long lost relatives. In Iowa, DPs received cooking lessons and met regularly with one another to air their problems and complaints. "The thought that these displaced persons could criticize without being punished," an employee of the DPC noted, "fascinated them." The Oklahoma DPC also functioned well, and there one full-blooded Indian, who owned a 20,000 acre ranch, sponsored 31 immigrant families. Delaware, another state where the commission did "a marvelous and very thorough job," operated on a high level despite the lack of cooperation from the voluntary agencies. Wisconsin, too, had an active and successful commission but its workers occasionally became frustrated with foreigners' language handicaps. One of them suggested to the national DPC that more appropriate expressions be taught in the orientation program after hearing a DP, in his new home on an upstate farm, proudly enunciate the only English phrase he knew, "Mr. and Mrs. Smith are in the drawing room."[44]

Not all of the states helped DPs, despite the existence of a commission. In Wyoming, where lumber camp owners allegedly exploited the newcomers, the state DPC appeared "somewhat anti-Catholic." Maryland, which received mostly Ukrainians, had a commission that barely functioned and the same could be said of those in the states of Connecticut, Rhode Island, North Carolina, Mississippi, and Tennessee.[45]

That these commissions existed at all can be attributed to the continuing efforts of the CCDP and the DPC to facilitate the adjustment of the foreigners. Their endeavors in this area—sparked, of course, by genuine humanitarian concerns—also had legislative overtones. Neither the CCDP nor the DP commissioners regarded the 1948 DP Act as satisfactory, and both agitated for revisions. Promoting the adjustment and the assimilation of the DPs into American society, they thought, would reinforce the campaign to bring more refugees into the United States.

The CCDP continued its efforts to change the cutoff date and eliminate the preferences for agricultural workers and people from annexed territories. The DPC agreed with these proposals and in its first semiannual report to Congress requested these and other changes. The Commission complained to Congress that the DP Act was uneconomical and difficult to administer with its cutoff date, rigid preferences, priorities, and requirements for job and housing assurances. The DPC suggested an April 21, 1947, cutoff date, an expansion of the program to admit 400,000 DPs over a four-year period, financial aid to voluntary agencies to help defray their costs of assisting and transporting the DPs in the United States, special provision for political refugees, denial of visas to anyone "who advocated or assisted in persecution of others for reasons of race, religion, or national origin," and a transference of the *Volksdeutsche* group to some other bureau.[46]

As a government agency, the DPC had both the right and the responsibility to recommend to Congress legislation which would improve the quality and efficiency of its work. The commissioners expected that a revised DP bill, eliminating the more awkward provisions of the original act, would be approved in 1949.[47] In fact, the DPC predicated many of its policies—including the temporary bypassing of the 40 percent requirement for people from annexed areas and the stipulation that 30 percent of the places had to be reserved for people enagaged in agricultural work—on the assumption that these stumbling blocks would be eliminated. Thus, as the 81st Congress prepared to inaugurate operations the DPC looked ahead with confidence. But the commissioners did not anticipate the tests to which the DPC would be subjected.

9

PAT McCARRAN AND THE
AMENDED DP ACT

THE NOVEMBER 1948 ELECTION results buoyed the hopes of the supporters of a revised DP bill. Not only did Truman emerge victorious but the public elected an overwhelmingly Democratic Congress as well. More important for displaced persons legislation, several conservative Republican Senators including Revercomb, Buck of Delaware, and Brooks of Illinois were replaced by people sympathetic to the cause. According to one source, "the victory that the Democrats pointed to with the greatest of pleasure was that of . . . [Matthew Neely] over Senator Revercomb in West Virginia."[1]

The President had campaigned for changes in the DP bill as did Democratic Senators-elect Paul Douglas (Illinois), Guy Gillette (Iowa), Hubert Humphrey (Minnesota), Matthew Neely, and Republican Margaret Chase Smith of Maine. The New York *Post* surveyed the newly elected members of the 81st Congress and found that "a large majority" favored liberalization of the existing law. *Life* magazine informed its readers that revision of the DP Act "stands high on the priority list of the 81st Congress." And in December 1948, Rhode Island Senator J. Howard McGrath announced that he would lead the fight for corrective amendments to the bill. Therefore, as Irving Engel observed in a letter to Herbert Bayard Swope, "it seems fairly certain that the inequities and unworkable provisions in the displaced persons act will eliminated."[2]

But the initial expectations of favorable change had been made without considering the importance of Nevada's senior senator, Pat McCarran, who succeeded to the chairmanship of the Judiciary Committee. The Nevadan shared Revercomb's

views during the previous session of Congress and was, if
anything, even more determined to keep DPs out of the United
States than his West Virginia colleague had been. With enhanced authority, McCarran shrewdly used his power to stifle
bills that he opposed. In fact, his campaign literature assured
voters in Nevada that although a committee chairman could
not always secure passage of desired legislation "he can almost
always kill the bill if he wants to do so." Since McCarran headed
the Judiciary Committee, which passed on all immigration
matters, all federal judicial appointments, and all U.S. attorney
nominations, and chaired the appropriations subcommittee,
which doled out money to the Departments of State, Commerce,
and Justice, few knowledgeable Washingtonians cared to court
his displeasure. A Nevada historian would later write, "Mc-
Carran was so powerful he could introduce a bill calling for
the execution of the president and get twenty votes."[3]

McCarran was an isolationist Democrat who considered
himself responsible for safeguarding the national interest. He
frequently voted differently from the internationalists in his
party. At one time he had opposed selective service, Lend-
Lease, and aid to Britain and France. Except for the Basques,
who tended sheep in Nevada, few immigrants merited his
enthusiastic welcome. He distrusted the United Nations and
regarded its presence in New York City "as an open door for
foreign spies and Communists," whom he opposed with a
vengeance. The Senator also believed that "too many" DPs
entering the country "are active subversives . . . who have no
other purpose than to undermine our American way of life."
To his daughter, he complained about "ten thousand illegal
voters in the Ladies Garment district in New York."[4]

Pat McCarran had grown up in the open spaces and moun-
tainous region of Sparks, Nevada (a suburb of Reno), and
never understood the needs and aspirations of the Jewish
immigrants in the crowded eastern cities. As did so many of
his contemporaries, he equated Jews with a slew of negative
images and characteristics. Simple in his unbridled patriotism,
and simplistic in his understanding of the kinds of people who
congregated in and near the DP assembly centers, the Nevada

Senator Pat McCarran (Courtesy the National Archives)

Senator intended to use the vast powers of his office to prevent a speedy revision of the 1948 act. His delaying tactics would have the effect of prolonging the suffering of the survivors of the Holocaust.

Patriotism and prejudice, however, were not the only sources for McCarran's opposition to DP legislation. The Senator had never gotten along with President Truman; their enmity dated back to clashes in the 1930s over the establishment of the Civil Aeronautics Board. McCarran had favored an independent commission while Truman had wanted the agency in the executive branch, responsible to the President's wishes. The Nevadan, therefore, was not one of those senators who the President might phone or invite over for a drink to discuss legislation informally.

Furthermore, McCarran displayed extreme sensitivity to personal effronts and resented the fact that Senators McGrath and Neely had introduced the administration's revised DP bill without first consulting him, the chairman of the committee that would have to prepare the legislation. Since McGrath, as the Democratic Party's national chairman, represented the President's views in the proposed bill, McCarran knew exactly how he would handle it. "Each request from the President for swift committee action received long and careful study," one reporter wrote. "The more urgent the request, the more elaborate the study."[5]

The knowledgeable Nevadan made extensive use of all of the power available to a committee chairman. He decided that he himself would head the special subcommittee established to consider revisions of the DP bill, and added three others who shared his views: Eastland, Donnell, and Republican William Jenner of Indiana. Only McGrath, who completed the five-man group, displayed any sympathy for the DPs. McCarran's control of the time and agenda of subcommittee meetings, his astute use of delaying tactics, and the support he received from one of the largest and most dedicated staffs on Capitol Hill further enhanced his power.[6]

Richard Arens, the "bitterly antisemitic"[7] chief of the immigration subcommittee staff, firmly ruled one of the busiest committees in Congress. A conservative Missouri Republican who had worked for Governor Donnell and then came to Washington with him in 1945, Arens shared the views of both Revercomb and McCarran. The Nevada senator had originally appointed Arens in 1945, and later retained him when the

Democrats resumed control of the 81st Congress. Another staff member remarked many years later that if Revercomb was a conservative then Arens was "icing on the cake."[8] The Washington *Post* observed in 1949 that "few elected members of the upper chamber wield the influence that he seems to in determining whether legislation which the House has approved but which he does not approve shall come before the Senate." Arens' power stemmed, in considerable degree, from his close relationship with McCarran. It was the committee chairman's custom to place a special subordinate on each proposal that concerned him, and Arens was assigned the DP bill. The two would ride to work together each day and discuss the proposed item. People correctly assumed that in his official actions the staff director represented McCarran's thinking.[9]

In addition to his staff, the Nevada Senator also counted numerous backers outside of Congress. The Mobile (Alabama) *Press Register* advised its readers: "Unless the American people are willing to see their country become dangerously infested from abroad by a new motley horde of stinkers they had better begin listening more carefully to the warnings of such men as United States Senator Pat McCarran of Nevada." Columnists like Westbrook Pegler and newspapers including New York City's *Daily News* also stood solidly with the Senator. Furthermore, a host of letter writers, especially in the West, backed further restriction rather than liberalization of existing statutes. Two people warned that the United States should not become "a dumping ground;" another correspondent opposed populating the country "with Rotten Apples (Communists, and subversives of all kinds);" while a Texan informed his senator that "a great many of the persons coming into this country are disguised as displaced persons and are mostly Catholics or Jews. It seems to me that we ought to protect what we have and stop the scum of the earth . . . from coming into this country."[10]

But, according to the signs extant, those who opposed liberalization of the DP Act apparently constituted a minority. The major newspapers in the country favored such ammendments as did most of the correspondents of the senators and the congressmen. The CCDP spearheaded the movement for change but this time it had a wider range of self-interested supporters. The commissioners of the DPC, especially Harry Rosenfield, lobbied for more workable and liberal legislation in the Congress and the numerous state DP commissioners also called for a revised bill. Furthermore, because passage of the first act suggested possibilities for bringing more people to the United States, several ethnic groups attempted to obtain special consideration in the proposed amended version. The Greek AHEPA organization sought to include 55,000 Greeks fleeing communism among the beneficiaries of a revised bill. The Steuben Society of America wanted the Germans expelled from East Europe by the Potsdam Agreement placed on an equal footing with the DPs, and it inspired a tremendous amount of congressional mail supporting its position. The group secretary of the Federation of American Citizens of German Descent, Inc. protested the "barbarous treatment shown our group and the favoritism shown other groups." Jewish leaders wanted the 7,000 or so of their coreligionists who fled to Shanghai after the disastrous *Kristallnacht* attacks in Germany in November 1938 also given consideration in the revised bill.[11]

The administration's measure, which had been prepared by the DPC, did not specifically include any national groups, but it did call for elimination of the blatantly discriminatory features originally included by the previous Congress. The proposed bill also incorporated a provision granting financial aid to the voluntary agencies to help them transport the newcomers from the docks to their homes in the United States, and recommended, as well, that allowances be made for "recent political refugees."[12] In general, the new suggestions received the backing of the proponents of the original DP Act. They also opened up cleavages, some not unexpected, between and within the major religious groups.

Among the Jews, discussion ensued as to whether any more legislation was even necessary. The more assimilated Jews, represented by the AJC and ACJ, were primarily concerned about erasing an antisemitic statute from the books, keeping out the most avid Nazi collaborators, and maintaining a good working relationship with the Catholic Church and the various Christian groups of East European background with whom they had cooperated to get the first law passed. They also wanted to admit more Jews. But a segment of the orthodox Jews, and the Yiddish press in general, did not want to bring any more DPs to the United States. The establishment of Israel in 1948 had provided refuge for coreligionists and the orthodox feared that another bill would simply bring more pogromists and Nazis into this country. They were supported in this view by Major Abraham Hyman, the Jewish adviser to the army in Europe in 1949, and Chaplain Louis Barish, who thought it a mistake for the Jews to work for revision. Hyman and Barish argued:

> It is highly questionable whether the Jewish organizations should press for the admission of an additional 200,000 DPs in order to make possible the admission of 10,000 Jews. It must be remembered that the non-Jewish DPs are, at very best, a potentially anti-Semitic element and are certainly not worthy of even an ounce of Jewish effort on their behalf. We are of the opinion that American Jewry is courting trouble when it urges the admission of 190,000 non-Jewish DPs in order to accommodate 10,000.

(Later immigration tallies proved Hyman and Barish much too conservative in their estimate. A total of approximately 27,000 Jewish DPs entered the United States in the fiscal years ending in June 1951 and June 1952.)[13]

Unspoken publicly, but in the air privately, was the Zionist concern that fewer European Jews would resettle in Israel if the possibility existed of getting to the United States. Since many of the orthodox and Yiddish speaking American Jews shared a Zionist outlook, it is difficult to separate one group from another on this point. Within the American political arena, however, the desires of the AJC and ACJ on the subject of revision prevailed. Their members controlled impressive sums of money and commanded a certain respect from journalists and legislators (but definitely not from the Zionists or the more traditional Jews). Consequently, the views of the

Zionists, the less assimilated Jews, and the Yiddish press made no impression on the national scene.

Catholics, on the other hand, exhibited no serious internal dissension. The WRS-NCWC head possessed the authority to speak for all. But in his position Monsignor Swanstrom did not ignore the different viewpoints among Catholics. The nationality divisions, including the Poles, the Lithuanians, and the Czechs, wanted the amended bill to have proportional representation of the various elements among the DPs in Europe. The hierarchy found this suggestion difficult to resist because more than half of all European DPs were Catholic although fewer than half of those who had already arrived in the United States adhered to the faith. At one point Catholics called for proportional representation in the revised act and some congressmen backed this position. Both groups feared that without this provision a disproportionate number of Jews might continue to swell the totals. "Whether or not this is actually the case as far as the Catholics are concerned," a member of the AJC wrote, "there can be no doubt but that this fear is felt in Congress, and proponency of this provision by the Catholics may be all that is needed to confirm McCarran and other members of the Immigration Committee, as well as a considerable number of members of the Senate and House generally, in their reluctance to pass a liberal bill." But since the legislation came first before Emanuel Celler's House Judiciary Committee, and since Celler represented the views of his staunch allies in the Jewish community who vigorously opposed any such delineation on the ground that Jews would be short-changed by it, the "groups and elements" provision never saw the light of day.[14]

The Democratic victory the previous November had put Celler of Brooklyn into the House Judiciary chairmanship, just as it had elevated McCarran to the same position in the Senate. The New Yorker's position diametrically differed from the Nevadan's on DP legislation. Just as McCarran had chosen an immigration subcommittee whose majority wanted to block further immigration, Celler's choices for the House Subcommittee on Immigration reflected his desire to liberalize the law.

Of the four Democrats (Francis Walter, Pennsylvania, chairman; Michael Feighan, Ohio; Frank L. Chelf, Kentucky; and Ed Gossett, Texas) and three Republicans (Louis E. Graham, Pennsylvania; Frank Fellows, Maine; Clifford P. Case, New Jersey) chosen, only one, Gossett, opposed broadening the provisions of the 1948 DP Act. Congressmen Fellows and Chelf had originally been wary of the Stratton bill but they did favor a more recent cutoff date and the elimination of the agricultural and annexed territories stipulations forced upon them by the Senate conferees during the last days of the 80th Congress.[15]

The subcommittee held expeditious hearings in March 1949 on a bill that Celler had introduced. The Brooklyn Democrat and DPC chairman Ugo Carusi provided most of the testimony and both argued for the goals previously enunciated in the Stratton bill. The subcommittee also permitted brief courtesy appearances by three Republican Congressmen—Carl Curtis of Nebraska, John Davis Lodge of Connecticut, and Jacob K. Javits of New York—who spoke in favor of ammendments to the bill that they favored. Eighty-two groups submitted written statements to the subcommittee; all but three endorsed bringing more DPs into the United States. Even Wisconsin's Senator Wiley, a staunch supporter of the restrictionist legislation of 1948, wrote the House subcommittee reversing his earlier position and indicating his desire for more humanitarian changes. Behind the scenes Commissioner Rosenfield of the DPC and the President himself paid a great deal of attention to Congressman Walter and helped him prepare a bill that the CCDP, the DPC, and the administration could wholeheartedly endorse.[16]

Chairman Celler put his name on the bill which the whole Judiciary Committee reported but which had essentially been written by Congressman Walter. The proposed measure called for the admission of an additional 179,000 DPs (over and above the original 205,000 stipulated in the 1948 Act) plus 56,623 *Volksdeutsche*. Special provisions were made for 18,000 members of the Polish Army then residing in Great Britain (followers of General Anders who refused to return to Communist Poland after the war), 4,000 refugees in Shanghai, 5,000 nonquota orphans, and 15,000 recent political refugees. Quota mortgaging and housing and job assurances of the 1948 Act remained, but the new bill dropped the provisions for 40 percent from annexed territories and 30 percent agricultural workers. One section specifically prohibited discrimination against any of the DPs on the grounds of race, religion, or national origin, and the cutoff date was advanced to January 1, 1949, a date which almost everyone supported. The new cutoff date made it clear "that refugees from communism as well as those who suffered from the Nazis should be offered equal opportunities for immigration into the United States."[17]

Three southern members of the Judiciary Committee— Gossett of Texas, Joseph R. Bryson of South Carolina, and Boyd Tackett of Arkansas—appended a minority report. Among the reasons given for opposition they noted that since 1946 "120,000 Jews flocked into our [DP] camps. . . . Bear in mind these were not German Jews. . . . They came from behind the iron curtain and are correctly described as Russian Jews. These Jews differ fundamentally from other Jews and many of them are Communists." The December 1945 cutoff date should have remained, the southerners argued, because that date "would, of course, eliminate most of the Russian Jews." The minority position did not affect the outcome in the House of Representatives which passed the bill by acclamation after only three hours of debate.[18]

Hopes for similar expeditious treatment in the Senate proved fruitless. The House no sooner passed the bill in June 1949 than Senator McCarran let it be known that he had no intention of holding hearings on the Celler measure at that time, that he did not know when he would begin, and that under no circumstances would a revised DP bill be reported by his committee that year. Newspaper columnist Robert S. Allen, who had interviewed the Nevada senator earlier that month reported, "McCarran makes no bones of his determination to strangle the House bill. He should have no trouble doing that with the subcommittee he has carefully handpicked. It's loaded for that purpose."[19]

McCarran's obduracy did not go unnoticed or even unchal-

From *The Herblock Book* (Beacon Press, 1952)

lenged in the Senate. By April, the Senate's impatience began to show and Republicans Irving Ives (N.Y.), Wayne Morse (Oregon), H. Alexander Smith, Homer Ferguson, and Leverett Saltonstall (Mass.) made public a letter that they wrote to the Judiciary Committee chairman "respectfully urging" him to go forth with the revised DP bill. (The fact that five Republican senators publicly called for action probably meant that they were interested in embarrassing the Democrats as well as getting the legislation through.) McCarran responded in a conciliatory fashion by telling reporters that the DP bill "would not be pigeonholed. It is not going to be delayed. It will be put forward." A few weeks later, true to his word, McCarran introduced legislation calling for the admission of an additional 302,000 DPs over a four-year period, a cutoff date of January 1, 1949, and retention of all of the other restrictions and complications of the existing act. At executive sessions of his committee, however, it turned out that no one else supported McCarran's proposal and it was buried. Observers speculated that McCarran's efforts had been mere delaying tactics. He probably knew that his bill had no chance of passage, but he wanted to muddy the waters. The AJC later received information based on "unimpeachable authority" that the McCarran committee would ultimately present the Senate with "very broad all-inclusive legislation. The theory behind this maneuver will be to cause such confusion and such a debate that a specific amendment to the DP Act would literally be lost in the shuffle. As you might expect, the all-inclusive legislation will be quite bad and restrictive." The Senate majority leader, Scott Lucas (D., Illinois), observed that "the silver Senator from Nevada never wanted a DP bill, except his own. He never wants any bill except his own."[20]

But the most vocal proponents of a revised DP Act would not bow to McCarran's recalcitrance, obstructionism, or perversion of their intent. In June, Senator Ives took the floor of the Senate to denounce the "deplorable lack of action" on a revised bill. A discussion ensued with Senator Ferguson backing Ives and Senator Taft calling upon Democratic leaders to force the measure out of the committee. Senator McCarran defended himself and his committee and intimated that hearings on the Celler bill might not begin until the fall.[21]

On July 26, however, and for no apparent reason, the McCarran subcommittee resumed interviewing people who wanted to be heard on the DP situation. Ugo Carusi had already appeared before the subcommittee on March 25 and April 8 but not until July 26 did anyone else testify. From then until mid-October the subcommittee conducted nineteen sessions, interviewing primarily those who thought that more German expellees, Greek DPs, and Arab refugees from Palestine should be brought to this country. Others spoke on behalf of Europeans from Hungary, Rumania, and Czechoslovakia, while representatives of the JDC appealed for consideration of refugees in Shanghai. Congressman Celler and DPC Commissioners Rosenfield and O'Connor also testified.[22]

The subcommittee's accelerated pace, however, did not prevent Senate liberals from moving forward. Majority leader Lucas had promised action on the bill that session and he did everything he could to get it. Lucas told the members of the Majority Policy Committee that "the Republicans had been needling him," and they threatened to make a motion on the floor to discharge the Judiciary Committee from further consideration of the bill. Unwilling to allow Republicans to take credit for such an action, Lucas indicated that the Democrats might do so first. But before proceeding further they attempted to cajole the stubborn Nevadan. At the very meeting where the issue of the discharge petition arose, fellow Democrats provided McCarran with a huge birthday cake, hoping, in the words of Senator Lucas, that "a birthday party might produce in the distinguished Senator a mellow mood, and while in that mood he would consider the bill. . . . The cake had no effect upon the Senator from Nevada whatever. It was a large cake, too. It was a delicious cake."[23]

Since the celebration failed to achieve the desired goal, Lucas switched tactics. On August 10, two days after the birthday party, he accompanied Senator Ives to a Republican Policy Committee meeting and together with the Senate's GOP leaders agreed to remove the bill from the subcommittee. Five days later a bipartisan group of senators announced that they would prepare a discharge petition. But one last effort was made within the Judiciary Committee itself. Senator Ferguson moved to discharge the subcommittee from further consideration of the revised DP bill; the motion lost by a vote of 2–5, Kilgore siding with Ferguson; McCarran, Eastland, Langer, Donnell, and Jenner constituted the majority. The Ferguson move having failed, on August 24 Senator Lucas introduced the resolution to discharge the bill from the Judiciary Committee. Fourteen senators, including Lucas and Taft, affixed their signatures to the petition. They anticipated no difficulty in finding 35 others willing to support them.[24]

The ploy did not result in McCarran's yielding to the will of the leaders, the petitioners, or the proponents of a revised bill. He had not yet played all of his tricks and he countered, three weeks later, with a bold stroke. On September 12 the Nevadan requested, and received, permission from the Senate to take a three-week leave of absence to investigate conditions in the European DP camps and other matters that came within the jurisdiction of his committee assignments. Although granting the leave, Lucas also warned McCarran that the DP bill might be brought before the Senate in his absence. The Nevadan did not seem concerned. He informed the Senate that it would take a "long, long time" to discuss the Celler bill that had already passed the House. In interpreting McCarran's remark for its readers, the Washington *Post* observed, "in Senate lingo, extended debate often means filibuster." McCarran's unanticipated trip caught the supporters of a revised bill by surprise and added to the difficulties of those who wanted quick action. The Washington representative of the AJC informed the New York office:

> As long as Senator McCarran is absent, I think the odds for getting through the discharge petition are lessened. It's one thing to slap McCarran in the face while he is in town, but I think there would be an understandable reluctance to knife him in the back while he is out of town. In fact, McCarran's associates seem rather smug about his absence from the city which may be interpreted to mean that his absence is calculated to discourage action on the petition.[25]

Being away, however, did not prevent McCarran from inflicting himself and his views about DPs upon his colleagues. On October 7 he wrote to Senator Tom Connally of Texas, that "there is no necessity for any immediate change in existing laws." That same day he cabled Senator Herbert O'Conor of Maryland (he had replaced McGrath on the subcommittee when the President elevated the Rhode Island senator to the Attorney-Generalship) that he had found "misrepresentation, maladministration, and violation of law" on the part of DPC employees, and he cautioned the Senator that liberalizing the bill at that time would be a "serious mistake." Unfortunately, he misquoted and misrepresented the views of several people with whom he had talked, and cables went out from Joseph J. Schwartz of the JDC, J. J. Norris of the NCWC, and Paul M. Lindberg of the Lutheran World Federation disavowing the words and thoughts that the Senator had attributed to them. Norris' telegram read, "We do not agree with a single statement in the message of Senator McCarran."[26]

McCarran continued to take liberties with the truth. Less than a week later he sent Senator Edwin C. Johnson of Colorado a speech which he wanted read on the Senate floor. In the prepared text that the Colorado Democrat obligingly read, McCarran asserted that "the ultimate objective" of those seeking a bill was "to tear down our immigration barriers to the end that this country will be flooded with aliens." He accused Earl Harrison, head of the CCDP, of having been "notoriously" lax in administering the immigration laws while he had been Commissioner of Immigration, 1942–44, and also of having accepted an award in 1942 from the American Committee for the Protection of the Foreign-Born, "a Communist-front organization." McCarran warned further that "present immigration methods" allow people who are "prejudicial to our way of life" to enter the United States and he asserted, without factual substantiation, that 75 percent of the 90,000 DPs admitted to the United States since 1945 have been "infiltrees from Iron Curtain areas and others who do not properly belong to the displaced persons group." Finally, the Nevadan's speech concluded: "This bill would not embrace as a displaced person a single Greek displaced person, a single displaced person of German blood, a single displaced person of Arab extraction, or displaced person of other equally deserving groups."[27]

McCarran's pleas and observations were duly noted but his own Judiciary Committee, under the acting chairmanship of Harley Kilgore of West Virginia, nonetheless voted 7–3 to remove the immigration measure from the subcommittee and to report the Celler bill without any recommendation. The senators in Washington had taken advantage of the chairman's absence and Eastland's attendance at a funeral to get the favorable vote. Kilgore, Ferguson of Michigan, and Lucas had all agreed that it would be better for the Senate Judiciary Committee to report the bill than for a discharge petition to be used to dislodge it.[28]

Once on the floor, however, the measure met determined opposition. Republican Harry Cain of Washington, along with Senators Langer, Donnell, Jenner, and Eastland led the successful fight against its consideration while the chairman remained in Europe. By a vote of 36–30 a majority of the Senate returned the bill to the committee with instructions to bring it out again no later than January 25, 1950.[29]

Senatorial courtesy, fear of reprisals, and effective politicking by McCarran and his friends convinced enough members of the upper chamber to delay positive action on the DP bill. Many of the Nevadan's colleagues, especially the westerners, supported the revised measure but they did not want to offend McCarran, the chairman of the Conference of Western Senators. They, along with others, also hesitated to appear to be going behind the chairman's back by repudiating him during his absence because the Judiciary Committee still had pending several judgeships and U.S. attorney nominations, along with private bills, that McCarran might later bury. The proposal also lost votes because of its late place on the Senate calendar, the senators' desire to adjourn, and the absenteeism of supporters who had already left Washington. Rumors circulated afterward that McCarran had privately persuaded a few senators who favored the proposed legislation to absent themselves during the vote. Finally, as California's Democratic Senator

Sheridan Downey noted,

> I do not believe that in the closing hours of the session, when all
> Senators are tired and worn out, and in the excitement now
> surrounding the bill, with no real report from the Committee,
> with no recommendation from the Committee, with no printed
> hearings, that any Senator can properly express himself upon
> the bill itself.

Mindful of these various factors, McCarran pulled the Senate
strings from Europe as effectively as he had done while in
Washington.[30]

On December 7, 1950, McCarran returned from Europe
and repeated his charges of fraudulent operations in the DPC
and once more questioned the need for a new law. In January,
he rose on the floor of the Senate and in a speech interweaving
fiction and fantasy maligned the DPs, the DPC, and those
working for a revised bill. McCarran claimed, with absolutely
no basis of fact, that "of the hundreds of thousands of DPs
who were admitted to the United States, it is reliably estimated
that approximately four-fifths were of the Jewish faith." Even
the statistics which accompanied his assertion contradicted the
statement. According to McCarran, the number of persons, by
religious affiliation, admitted to the United States between July
1, 1948, and November 30, 1949, included 33,479 Jews, 53,402
Catholics, 20,279 Protestants, 19,283 Greek Orthodox, 1,423
religion unknown.

The Senator also claimed that there had been "a complete
breakdown" in the administration of the law and accused the
DPC of carelessly screening individuals and thus allowing entry
to this country of people "who will become ready recruits of
subversive organizations to tear down the democracy of the
United States." He charged the CCDP, without identifying the
organization by name, of having spent $1 million "solely for
the dissemination of propaganda designed to influence legislation to repeal the safeguards of our immigration laws."[31]

McCarran's opposition to liberalizing the DP Act was already
well known before his presentation. By reiterating his views he
hoped perhaps to convince a few wavering senators or inspire

other opponents of the bill to be more outspoken. Perhaps he was responding to political advice from Nevada. Due to stand for reelection in 1950, McCarran might have been developing a campaign base. Although victory was never in doubt, a close associate, Pete Peterson, urged him "to emphasize the fact that the Jews were after you. I don't think that particular race is too well thought of in this state. . . . It may not be a bad idea to create the impression that there are certain Jews after you for their own selfish purposes."[32]

Liberals reacted unfavorably to McCarran's speech and accusations. James J. Norris, European Director of the NCWC, found it "discouraging to see him repeating the same old baseless charges again." *The New York Times* considered McCarran's remarks replete with "distortion and misrepresentation." And the editors of *Christian Century* asserted: "Only desperate fear that a more humane and generous displaced persons law was about to be passed could have occasioned Senator Pat McCarran's charges that administrators of the present act had ignored Army warnings and admitted Communists."[33]

The adverse criticism in no way dissuaded the senior Senator from Nevada who followed up his charges by resuming committee hearings. Determined to prove the accusations, he brought several disgruntled DPC employees over from Europe as well as the European director of the Immigration and Naturalization Service, to testify about the alleged fraud and misrepresentation within the agency. Most of the testimony dealt with documents of doubtful validity about a displaced person's residence on or before December 22, 1945, and the possibility that people lacking good moral character might have been declared eligible for a visa to the United States under the 1948 Act. Considerable amounts of time were consumed in presenting allegations that some of the DPs were Communists and that the DPC was lax in processing those so accused, as well as black marketeers. According to the committee's material people in both categories were invariably Jewish.[34]

McCarran and Arens, the subcommittee staff director who conducted most of the questioning during the hearings, seemed particularly anxious to pursue the issue of how many Jews might be entering the United States illegally. At one point the following colloquy between Arens and a DPC employee, John Wilson Cutler, Jr., took place:

Arens: Is there any particular element or group among the displaced persons which has a greater percent, proportionately, of the fraud and false documents as compared to other groups?

Cutler: Yes. Those cases I gave you referred completely to all, I would say, over 95 percent to one group.

Arens: What group is that?

Cutler: That was the Jewish group.[35]

None of the witnesses brought before McCarran's committee could document more than a handful of even "doubtful" cases that had cleared, although one who testified in executive session estimated, without any corroborative evidence, that 50 percent of the applicants in his working area of Germany presented fraudulent documents. He also speculated that "a great many of them, particularly one race . . . are coming from Israel," and he affirmed that "the blackmarket operation is conducted solely by one class of DP's."[36]

Several disgruntled employees accurately claimed that the DPC, in favoring quick processing and ignoring minor or unsubstantiated accusations, was following neither the letter nor the restrictionist spirit of the 1948 Act which placed the burden of proof of eligibility on the DP. Cutler, the most vigorous critic of the DPC, acknowledged that "it is very hard . . . to prove any man an out-and-out Communist, or connected in any way with the Communist Party, or even subversive," but he sincerely believed that in questionable cases the proof of eligibility must be produced by the applicants, with all doubts resolved in favor of exclusion.[37]

According to one DPC employee who testified, the bulk of suspect materials came from individuals sponsored by two Jewish agencies, USNA and HIAS, and involved the issue of a person's presence in Germany, Austria, or Italy by December 22, 1945. Those DPC employees who wanted to foster entry allegedly went over the documents less carefully than those desirous of keeping Jews out. Apparently every example given by Cutler of cases of falsification of documents, black market activities, and alleged immoral character involved a Jew.[38]

An abundance of evidence existed that some non-Jews also presented questionable documents, dissembled about their wartime and postwar experiences, and participated in black market activities. By the time of the subcommittee hearings in February 1950, several indicators suggested that some Nazi collaborators still remained in the camps and had been given DP status. DPC employees testified that alleged Nazi collaborators were cleared for visas to go to the United States. It was also readily acknowledged that Ukrainians and Poles from territories annexed by Russia, residing in DP assembly centers in 1945, had changed their names and disguised their previous activities to prevent repatriation.[39] Neither the senators nor Arens investigated these matters, whereas the real and alleged episodes of Jewish chicanery and DPC culpability for pushing Jews who were possibly Communists through the "pipeline" received extensive attention from the subcommittee.

The danger of communism emerged as a major domestic political concern between 1947 and 1950, and the subcommittee majority, although probably antisemitic and hostile to increased immigration in any case, expressed the real fears of the day. The senators seemed particularly anxious to thwart the progress of communism in this country. The trials of Alger Hiss, who allegedly passed classified materials to the Communists in the 1930s, the "loss" of China, and the detonation of the atomic bomb by the Soviet Union in 1949 reinforced the anxieties of those who suspected foreigners and Jews of plotting to undermine American institutions. George F. Kennan's October 1949 opinion that the "appeal" of communism "is relatively strong to maladjusted groups: in our country—Jews, Negroes, immigrants—all those who feel handicapped in the framework of a national society,"[40] legitimized existing apprehensions, and apparently justified the actions of those who believed that restricting the number of Jews entering the United States in effect meant curtailing the expansion of Communist activities in America.

Although in their own minds the members of the McCarran Committee may have thought that by the nature of their inquiry they were protecting this nation from an influx of subversives, in actuality it seems that they, and staff director Richard Arens in particular, desired to expose the alleged inadequacies of the DPC. Arens so infuriated Congressman Celler that he charged "that man" with having "created more havoc than dozens of men in Washington in reference to immigration and naturalization." By nuance, by slight misstatements, by careful selection of certain phrases, Arens conveyed his views. Some of his questions were suggestive as well as misleading. The staff director asked DPC chairman Ugo Carusi, "Do you know whether or not the International Refugee Organization maintains a unit of lawyers for the purpose of obtaining paroles or pardons for convicted displaced persons so as to enable them to become eligible for immigration to the United States?" After Carusi responded, "It does not," the staff director followed up with, "Do you know whether or not certain employees of the Displaced Persons Commission have solicited or caused to be solicited pardons or paroles for displaced persons to enable them to be eligible for immigration to the United States under the displaced persons laws?" Again, Carusi claimed to have found no evidence of the alleged activity. A third suggestive question from Arens to Carusi concerned settlement in the United States. "What percentage of your displaced persons who have thus far been admitted into the United States pursuant to the present law, have settled in New York City?"[41] Carusi did not know the answer and Arens did not inquire about resettlement in other American cities.

Of one of the disgruntled employees in the DPC, Arens inquired whether "the security risk to this Government and to the people of the United States [would] be increased or decreased" if the cutoff date were advanced from December 22, 1945. The witness responded "that the security risk would be increased because of the vast number of individuals coming in from behind the iron curtain." While questioning another DPC employee, Frank B. Vaughan, Jr., Arens and Senator Donnell devoted time to showing that Commissioner Rosenfield and a senior DPC officer in Europe had tried to secure a pardon for "convict" Frank Dastich, to make him eligible for an American visa. The conversation went as follows:

> Arens: What was the crime?
> Vaughan: Theft.
> Arens: [Dastich] had been convicted of theft?
> Vaughan: Theft of 14 eggs.
> Senator Donnell: Mr. Vaughan, the theft of food over there is a pretty serious thing, is it not?
> Vaughan: I think at that time it was more serious than today.
> Senator Donnell: It was at that time. Eggs are not as plentiful there as they are in this country?
> Vaughan: No.
> Senator Donnell: It was Mr. Rosenfield who wanted the Dastich case expedited?
> Vaughan: That is correct.[42]

At some time during the hearings each member of the "McCarran bloc" on the subcommittee managed to bring out information which the questioner thought denigrated the DPC and its operations. Although figures indicated that less than a fraction of 1 percent of the 135,000 DPs already admitted to the United States had arrived illegally, Senator Jenner engaged the European director of the Immigration and Naturalization Service in a conversation to suggest that the estimates were too low. Almanza Tripp admitted that he had kept no record of how many people might have been "fraudulently" admitted to the United States but Jenner led him on anyway:

> Senator Jenner: There is no question about it that we are bringing in subversives, Communists, robbers, criminals of all kinds, black-marketeers, perjurers, defrauders. There is no question about that, is there, Mr. Tripp?
> Tripp: There is no question but what a number of people of those categories are being admitted.

Two days later, Senator Eastland went after a DPC senior officer, Meyer D. Bashein, for following orders as to who qualified for consideration:

Senator Eastland: You have stated that your policy was that in black-market cases you overlooked black-market activities. Now, those were criminal activities; were they not?

Bashein: Small black-market cases.

Senator Eastland: But yet you passed Stein.

Bashein: I said, sir, that that was an error.

Senator Eastland: You say small black-market activities. Those were criminal acts; were they not?

Bashein: No, sir. It has been held that small black marketing by——

Senator Eastland: Held by whom?

Bashein: Laid down to us as policy by headquarters.

Senator Eastland: Do you mean by the Commission here? Is that what you mean?

Bashein: By the Commission in Frankfurt.

Senator Eastland: By Squadrilli?*

Bashein: Yes, sir.

Senator Eastland: That you would overlook small black-market activities?

Bashein: Yes, sir.

Senator Eastland: But yet the responsibility was on you, was it not, to enforce this law?

Bashein: Yes, sir.

Senator Eastland: And this law placed the burden of proof on the applicant and he was to be a man of good moral character, we he not?

Bashein: Yes, sir.

Senator Eastland: Yet you condoned criminal activities; that is what you are saying, is it not?

Bashein: Small black-market activities are not considered criminal.

Senator Eastland: Are they criminal acts? Answer my question "yes" or "no."

Bashein: No. Small black-market activities are not criminal acts.

Senator Eastland: Is it in violation of the law?

Bashein: Yes, sir.

* Alexander Squadrilli was the European director of the DPC.

Senator Eastland: They are criminal acts, then, are they not? You know the difference between right and wrong, Mr. Bashein, and you can answer that question.

Bashein: Yes, sir.

Senator Eastland: Then they are criminal acts, are they not?

Bashein: Yes; in the same sense that a violation of an ordinance is a criminal act.

Senator Eastland: I certainly disagree with you there, sir.[43]

The innuendos and attitudes of the "McCarran bloc" were criticized in the liberal press. One journalist penned the observation, "It is not considered proper to write publicly about the intolerance and scarcely veiled Know-Nothingism exhibited in Congress during committee hearings on such matters as a D.P. bill." "The Know-Nothingism of the Congressmen," he continued, "can be observed in the sly wording of a question, an ironic observation which no one can prove is anti-Semitic, an amiable statement of appreciation for a witness's prejudical contribution."[44]

Toward the end of the hearings Commissioner Carusi complained about the committee's tactics. "We talk about one thing, and then bring in another," he said. The Berlin Document Center contained records of Nazis, not Communists. Yet Arens and the Senators continually referred to those people that the BDC suggested needed follow-ups as Communists and subversives. Another point that arose frequently during the hearings concerned the "doubtful dateline cases," of individuals who may not have been in the requisite areas of Europe on or before December 22, 1945. But "doubtful dateline cases," Carusi explained did not mean "doubtful security risks," as Senator Jenner had asserted on the Senate floor. On the subject of "crime" and its relationship to people's moral character, Carusi also made some revealing comments. Sometimes, he pointed out, a DP might have accepted a $2 tip from a GI, got caught with the American money which DPs were not allowed to possess, and received a six-month prison sentence. Carusi indicated that such occurrences happened "very frequently," but that the DPC did not regard the convicted individuals as "criminals." "You have to consider that rule [of criminality] in the light of the circumstances as you know them," he stated. In regard to black marketeering, Carusi made the clearest public statement to that date regarding the DPC's attitude. "It is possible," he anounced,

> for a person to be technically guilty of black marketing [sic] and still be a person of good character. He can exchange a shoe for a can of soup because he needs the soup. He can exchange a figurine or object of art for foodstuffs or clothing. He can give to a GI some little knicknack and get back a package of cigarettes. He can do those things and still be, in our judgment, a person of good moral character.[45]

Carusi, and then Commissioner Rosenfield, defended the DPC and its work, acknowledged that any human organization would be subject to occasional error or misjudgment, but stated that they were conscientiously trying to do a good job. Both men indicated their displeasure with Dick Arens' conduct and methods, and Rosenfield, in particular, condemned the Senate staff director. The previous September Arens had accused the DPC of condoning fraud within its ranks but never provided the agency or the public with any specifics. Hence, the DPC could not inquire further into the matter. "There has been a lot of phoney talk not based on fact," Rosenfield asserted.[46]

In rebutting Rosenfield, Arens not only incriminated himself further in the eyes of those who questioned his character, motivations, and obvious partiality, but summarized, as well, the views of the majority of senators on the subcommittee: McCarran, Eastland, Jenner, and Donnell. For some inexplicable reason he also interjected his personal opinion that

> every patriotic American in this country ought to get on his knees every night and thank the Good Lord that we have the senior senator from Nevada who had been waging this fight against tremendous odds and against a million dollar lobby [CCDP], that has been defaming him from one end of the country to the other.

Arens then revealed that Rosenfield's charges against him were not without substance when he averred, "There is no question but what there is a complete breakdown in the administration of this law, so that black marketeers, subversives, criminals, undesirables, are gaining admission into this country." In no uncertain terms, he went on to denounce the DPC, which, "instead of discharging its duties in Europe . . . has turned the operation over to former UNRRA employees, social workers, persons of that caliber, who are not concerned primarily with the best interests of the United States of America." And finally, he announced that there were "hundreds, if not thousands, of cases of fraudulent documents" which the DPC did not check properly, a charge which was probably accurate but for which Arens apparently lacked documentation.[47]

The staff director's assertions explain why the "McCarran bloc" wanted to thwart the progress of any amended version of the 1948 DP Act. But the previous fall the majority of the Senate had instructed the Judiciary Committee to produce a bill by January 25, 1950, and despite the fact that the subcommittee prolonged the hearings through March, McCarran and his associates complied with the order. By a vote of 10–3, the Judiciary Committee members reported out McCarran's revised DP Act. Athough most of the men preferred more liberal terms than the chairman had written, they supported his proposal to get something on to the Senate floor. Like the Celler bill passed by the House, it advanced the cutoff date to January 1, 1949, made provision for 5,000 orphans and 18,000 members of General Anders' army in London who chose not to return to Poland, and increased the total number of DPs to be admitted to the United States to approximately 320,000. But there the agreement between the Celler measure and the Senate Judiciary Committee bill ended.

The differences between the two versions attracted more attention than did the similarities. Although the Senate committee proposal called for 10,000 Greeks to be incorporated among the beneficiaries of the proposed law, it deleted the House provision to aid the refugees in Shanghai, and retained the 40 percent preference for persons from annexed territories and 30 percent for agricultural workers. It also changed the definition of a DP from those people victimized by the Nazis to anyone forced to flee his last residence because of persecution or fear of persecution between September 1, 1939 and January 1, 1949. In effect, the new definition added 12 million *Volksdeutsche* expelled from Eastern Europe and Czechoslovakia after World War II to the pool, and thus diluted the number of places available to the DPs already registered. Senator Kilgore pointed out that the broadened definition would really allow fewer DPs into the country because the other clauses would give preference to *Volksdeutsche* agricultural employees expelled from the "annexed territories" of Eastern Europe.[48]

As expected, the liberals condemned the Judiciary Committee's offerings. In the most charitable evaluation of the bill, the Washington *Post* called the provisions "less pernicious than might have been expected from Senator McCarran's expressed prejudices," but nonetheless, "harsh and discriminatory." Congressman Celler denounced the measure as "a sham," while New York's newly elected Democratic senator, Herbert H. Lehman, lamented that the committee's real object was "to change the entire nature of the program from one of relief for displaced persons to one of relief of German expellees." Many senators, Lehman thought, regarded the expellees as DPs and could not distinguish between the experiences of the two groups. McCarran himself acknowledged that his critics' contentions bore considerable resemblance to the truth when he admitted that his proposals were intended to make the DP Act more restrictive.[49]

A minority of the members on the Judiciary Committee—Kilgore, Ferguson, and Democrat Frank Graham of North Carolina—not only dissented from the majority opinion but, led by the West Virginian, backed more generous and humane legislation. Both President Truman and Senator O'Conor, the lone member of the subcommittee sympathetic to the DP plight, believed that Kilgore, second in seniority to McCarran on the Judiciary Committee, should do something to counteract the chairman's position. The West Virginian agreed and, with the aid of Commissioner Rosenfield, prepared another bill, similar to that passed by the House. The Kilgore substitute won the support of four additional Judiciary Committee members, Senators Magnuson, Estes Kefauver, (D., Tenn.) Wiley, and O'Conor, then of fourteen other senators who, along with the three original dissenters and Magnuson, cosponsored the new proposal in the Senate. The basic issue, Kilgore declared when the debate over a revised DP Act began in the Senate on February 28, 1950, is "do we want a fair and workable displaced persons law, or do we not?"[50]

In their efforts to thwart the passage of what Kilgore referred to as a "fair and workable displaced persons law," McCarran and his associates used arguments by now familiar to those who had observed the subcommittee hearings. The Nevada senator accused the DPC of having "violated the intent and spirit" of the 1948 Act, and he also verged close to the truth when he charged that "a certain voluntary agency" helped DPs evade the law. Denying that prejudice guided any of his thoughts or actions, McCarran told colleagues that "some of his most intimate friends, some of his best friends in all the world belong to the Jewish faith."[51]

Some of the views expressed by McCarran's allies distorted the truth and slandered people dedicated to fostering humanitarian goals. Oklahoma's Senator Elmer Thomas believed that "many, if not a majority, of those who have been brought to this country are either persons with prison records or persons who got out of prison through either parole or pardon in order to come to America." Eastland, with Arens sitting at his side in the Senate, called the administration of the DPC "shocking" and labeled the three commissioners "guilty of moral treason, because they have set up a system there, as a result of which they know that Communist saboteurs and agents and officers of the Russian secret police have been filtered into the United States."[52]

Senator Eastland, however, was not a man totally devoid of compassion. Although he did not exhibit warm feelings toward the survivors of the Holocaust, he told colleagues that the *Volksdeutsche*, "the real displaced persons," had been slighted by the Kilgore substitute because they were not given equal consideration with other groups. "One of the greatest crimes in all history," the Mississippian asserted, was "uprooting . . . people . . . whose only offense was that through their veins flowed Germanic blood. . . . They were turned out into the cold and snow, driven like cattle across eastern and central Europe into Germany, where many of them died on the march like flies. I say that is one of the greastest crimes in all human history."[53]

The Kilgore bloc did not dispute the crime of the removal of 12 million people of German ancestry from their homes in Eastern Europe and Czechoslovakia, but these senators viewed it as a problem separate from that of the Nazis' victims. Throwing in the *Volksdeutsche* muddied the waters and delayed action. Several liberals thought that Eastland, McCarran, and others who displayed such intense concern for expelled Germans were, in fact, doing so to stall for time and make the new measure so complex as to give some of its backers pause before they voted. On the other hand, in 1950 the Kilgore group was willing, as the Congress had done in 1948, to set aside some places in its bill for people of German ethnic origin who fled, or were expelled from, Eastern Europe after the war ended.[54]

Kilgore and his supporters had not intended to take any specific action for the *Volksdeutsche* alone or even write new legislation. Recognizing the power of McCarran's subcommittee to call witnesses and direct the flow of questions, as well as the traditional hesitation of the Senate to undermine a powerful committee chairman, Kilgore and the liberals moved slowly in 1949 while waiting to see what kind of measure would be produced. Only after the restrictive version came out of the Judiciary Committee in January 1950, did the West Virginian and his allies put together another kind of bill. Meeting almost daily in the offices of Kilgore or the Senate secretary, Leslie Biffle, a tightly knit group charted its course. DPC Commissioner Rosenfield attended these sessions and provided guidance in strategy and facts to counteract the McCarran Committee's accusations. The senators also benefited from the presence of Herbert Lehman, who answered questions about UNRRA's activities and the role of the International Refugee Organization.[55]

Those working to revise the bill also received the continuing support of the CCDP, the National Catholic Welfare Conference, the major Jewish organizations, Church World Service, the AF of L and the CIO, and certain prominent Americans. *The New York Times*, the New York *Herald-Tribune*, the Washington *Post*, and other important newspapers also favored a more liberal bill. In addition, the backing of the President and the Senate majority leader, the stipulations in the 1948 Democratic platform, and the passage of the Celler bill in the House buttressed the position of the Kilgore bloc. The support was periodically reinforced by letters from the public, and in February, just before the DP legislation reached the floor of the Senate for consideration, telegrams signed by Lucius D. Clay, Mrs. Franklin D. Roosevelt, Jim Farley, Monsignor Edward E. Swanstrom, Clarence Krumbolz of the National Lutheran Council, and others urged approval of the Kilgore substitute. Whereas in 1948 liberals had assumed that a bill which they could support would emerge from the House-Senate conference committee and therefore made no special efforts to be diligent, in March 1950, the key people worked together to prevent slip-ups and to block parliamentary maneuvers that might bury the legislation.[56]

Opponents of liberal legislation, on the other hand, took advantage of every stratagem available to delay a vote. In addition to speaking against the Kilgore substitute they kept a watchful eye for additional opportunities. One day Senator Langer noticed an almost empty Senate and proposed adjournment. Senator Jenner agreed, and before Louisiana Democratic Senator Russell Long, a supporter of Kilgore's bill, realized what had happened the Senate had adjourned. On March 7, McCarran, with the backing of Republican Senators Langer and Kenneth Wherry of Nebraska, asked to have the vote on the DP bill delayed because his subcommittee was still conducting hearings and a printed record would not be available until the end of the month. Their ally, Senator Donnell, proposed that the vote be held on April 4. McCarran claimed that he would have made such a motion but, "of course, if I were to make the motion, then the Committee and some others would say I was stalling. . . . I have never stalled this bill. I have tried to work it through, to bring it on the floor. But the bill cannot be properly considered by the Senate unless the record is printed and is before the Senators." Majority Leader Lucas did want an earlier date but could not get it. By "gentleman's agreement," the factions agreed to a vote on April 3, a day earlier than Senator Donnell had originally proposed.[57]

The senators primed themselves for the showdown. Discussions began on March 30 and a fierce struggle ensued. The agreed upon voting day passed with senators still talking. Opponents and proponents repeated established arguments. Throughout the debate McCarran fought bitterly. He offered 130 amendments to his committee proposal, which New York's Irving Ives denounced as a "prejudice-laden piece of legislation," and which the Senate quashed. Then the Nevadan tried to append the same amendments to the Kilgore substitute. He apparently wanted to drive a wedge among the liberals or simply wear them out. But his efforts were to no avail and the Kilgore version won approval by a count of 49–25. Once that happened the liberals relaxed. In the final tally, taken on April 5, 58 senators voted for the measure while only 15 (seven Republicans and eight Southern Democrats)[58] formally opposed it. Several men who had no liking for the Kilgore substitute, including McCarran, supported the amended bill. The Nevadan did so to insure a place for himself on the House-Senate conference committee; others may have seen no political benefit in being on the defeated side. From the lopsided margin of approval one would have never guessed that only a few weeks earlier doubts remained about the final outcome. Senator Lehman, for example, wrote Irving Engel on March 13, 1950, "It is hard to gauge the situation at this time but for your confidential information, I am not as hopeful as some of my colleagues are."[59]

In its amended form, the Senate bill stipulated a total of 344,000 DP admissions (including the 205,000 already agreed to in 1948), 54,744 *Volksdeutsche* expellees, and 20,000 nonquota war orphans. The preferences for people in agriculture and from annexed territories were eliminated, the cutoff date was advanced to January 1, 1949, and provision was also made for 18,000 members of General Anders' Polish army in London,

10,000 Greeks, 4,000 Europeans in Shanghai, and 5,000 refugees from Venezia-Giulia (territory on the Italian border that Yugoslavia had annexed). The Kilgore substitute adopted by the Senate bore a striking resemblance to the original Stratton bill which had been introduced in the House three years earlier. The quota-mortgaging provision stood out as the only significant departure from Stratton's proposal.[60]

Immediately after the final vote Senator McCarran, apparently undaunted, recommended a conference committee including himself, Eastland, Langer, Donnell, and Jenner—all of whom had worked against the bill that passed—to serve with Kilgore and O'Conor as the Senate representatives. But Lucas and Donnell opposed the idea, the Missourian asserting that "the committee should represent the dominant point of view arrived at by the Senate." McCarran then withdrew his suggestions. Vice-President Alben Barkley did include McCarran on the committee delegated to meet with the representatives of the House but added four strong proponents of the version that the Senate passed: Kilgore, O'Conor, Wiley, and Ferguson.[61]

McCarran left the Senate that night a dejected man. In the elevator he unexpectedly met CCDP Executive Secretary William S. Bernard who had been in the gallery during the vote. Neither acknowledged the other. The two men left the building and walked down the Capitol steps with McCarran in the lead mumbling to himself. Suddenly he turned around to face Bernard and exploded: "You son of a bitch!" Bernard responded, "Thank you, Senator." Then McCarran turned and walked away, his head sinking lower and lower as he went. Two days later he wrote his daughter, "I met the enemy and he took me on the DP bill. It's tough to beat a million or more dollars and its something worth while to give the rotten gang a good fight anyway, and they know they have been to a fight for its [sic] not over yet."[62]

McCarran meant what he said. Traditionally, the Senate chairman of the Conference Committee calls the House chairman to arrange for a meeting. But the Nevadan procrastinated. Finally Celler, who had appointed himself along with four other strong proponents of a liberal bill, Congressmen Feighan,

Fellows, Graham, and Walter, to represent the House, threatened to call the meeting and McCarran capitulated. Within the
conference McCarran once again tried to shape the final
product. Although he failed, he nonetheless slowed the negotiating process.[63]

On June 1 the conferees reached agreement. The bill that
they approved, just as in 1948, bore a striking resemblance to
the Senate version. Both houses of Congress endorsed it, and
the President, who hailed the bill as a measure which "corrects
the discrimination inherent in the previous act," signed it into
law. Its provisions, as compared to the 1948 legislation are
shown in table 9.1. The bill also extended the life of the DPC
to June 30, 1951 (the next Congress changed it to August 31,
1952), provided a cutoff date of January 1, 1949, and allowed
consuls and the Immigration and Naturalization Service equal

Table 9.1 Immigration Acts of 1948 and 1950, Compared

	Numbers Allowed In	
	1948 Act	1948 Act as Amended in 1950
IRO DPs	200,000	301,500
German expellees[a]	27,377	54,744
General Anders' Army	—	18,000
Greek DPs	—	10,000
Europeans in Shanghai	—	4,000
Venezia-Giulia refugees	—	2,000
DP orphans	3,000	5,000
Adopted orphans	—	5,000
Recent refugees	2,000 (Czechs)	500
Adjustment of status in U.S.A.[b]	15,000	15,000
	247,377	415,744

[a] German expellees were those people of German heritage born in Eastern Europe or
Czechoslovakia who were charged to the German quota and admitted under normal
immigration procedures under the 1948 Act, but who were charged to their country
of origin under the 1950 Act.
[b] Adjustment of status referred to people already in the United States under tourist,
student, or other temporary visas who were allowed to apply for admission under
normal immigration procedures and whose visas would be charged to the countries of
their birth.

authority with the DPC to rule on the eligibility and admissibility of individuals who applied for entry to the United States. Quota mortgaging was also retained.[64]

Ten days after the President signed the bill the Korean conflict began. If McCarran had succeeded in delaying the progress of the legislation a few more weeks he might have achieved his goal of blocking passage of the liberal measure. Even after the appearance of the conference report, which he signed, the Senator warned his colleagues that the new cutoff date would be "an open door for the infiltration into this country of subversives," and that under this bill, "the only limitation on the number of Communist agents who will be sent into the United States will be the number which the Kremlin wants to send to this country."[65] When repeated after the outbreak of the Korean War at the end of June, this argument was to receive a more careful hearing from colleagues.

In retrospect, it appears that though McCarran "lost the legislative battle, he had won the administrative fight." His visits to DPC offices in Europe the previous fall and the nature of his subcommittee hearings in the winter unnerved the commissioners and their subordinates. According to Charles Jordan, European head of the JDC, the DPC took "very seriously" the criticisms hurled at it by some of the senators. Snags developed in the agency's operations and backlogs increased. Pro-refugee attitudes turned to anti-refugee biases. Screening procedures tightened; processing of applicants slowed. Jordan observed that the once friendly DPC now "goes hunting for ways to exclude Jews." Morale among DPC personnel was shattered. Two of the senior officers who appeared as witnesses before the McCarran Committee returned to their jobs in Europe and, Jordan wrote, "antagonized everybody." They maintained, he continued, "the worst possible relations with their staff." By July, thirty people had resigned and Alex Squadrilli, the European DPC director, complained about receiving conflicting instructions from each of the commissioners. In August Squadrilli resigned. A DPC advisory council committee went over to Europe to survey the scene and reported "deep concern" about the operations. Privately, Walter H. Bieringer, chairman of the Massachusetts DP Commission and head of the investigating team, informed the three commissioners that European operations had broken down, that the staff was divided and demoralized, and that the personnel no longer had any confidence in Carusi. In October Carusi resigned. President Truman replaced him with John W. Gibson, the Assistant Secretary of Labor. A rebuilding job would have to take place.[66]

McCarran also achieved another of his goals by keeping the number of Jews down. Whereas Jews numbered between twenty and twenty-five percent of the DPs at any given moment in 1946 and 1947, the final breakdown of the 365,233 American visas issued to DPs between July 1, 1948 and June 30, 1952 showed these religious demarcations: Roman Catholics, 47 percent; Protestants and Orthodox, 35; Jews, 16; Other, 2 percent.[67] All told fewer than 100,000 Jewish DPs reached the United States as a result of the Truman Directive and the two DP acts. An exceedingly rough breakdown of the statistics would suggest that approximately 28,000 Jews benefited from the Truman Directive while perhaps another 68,000 reached the United States as a result of the DP Acts of 1948 and 1950. Data that I have seen on Jewish arrivals for the years 1949 through 1952 show these numbers: 1949, 31,381; 1950, 10,245; 1951, 13,580; 1952, 13,508.[68] Thus McCarran's numerous tricks and ploys were effective. Jews who might otherwise have chosen the United States as their place of resettlement went to Israel or to whatever other nation would have them. In one sense, delay itself dictated the course of events. The slowness of the congressional process helped to shape the direction of DP resettlement.

In addition to discouraging Jews from waiting for a visa, McCarran also succeeded in tightening American security. Less than three months after the Korean War began the Congress enacted the Nevada Senator's internal security proposal. Designed to keep out Communists and subversives, the measure prohibited the United States from admitting any aliens who had belonged to totalitarian or Communist organizations. Furthermore, it required Communists already in the United

States to register with the Attorney-General's office and provided for the establishment of concentration camps to detain
subversives, spies, and saboteurs in times of emergency. United
States Attorney-General McGrath called McCarran's proposal
a sign of domestic "hysteria" but the Senate passed the bill by
a vote of 51–7, the House by 312–20, and after Truman vetoed
it, both chambers passed it a second time by more than the
necessary two-thirds majority.[69]

Table 9.2 DPs Admitted to the United States May 1946 to August 1952

Period	Number	Number of Jews	Cumulative Number Under Dp Acts	Cumulative Total
May 1946 to June 30 1948 (Truman Directive)	41,379	28,000[a]		41,379
Oct. 30, 1948 to Dec. 31, 1948	2,499	834	2,499	43,878
Jan. 1, 1949 to June 30, 1949	37,549	10,836	40,048	81,427
July 1, 1949 to Dec. 31, 1949	81,968	20,003	122,016	163,395
Jan. 1, 1950 to June 30, 1950	42,385	NA[b]	164,401	205,780
July 1, 1950 to Dec. 31, 1950	43,150	NA	207,551	248,930
Jan. 1, 1951 to June 30, 1951	42,161	NA	249,712	291,091
July 1, 1951 to Dec. 31, 1951	63,155	NA	312,867	354,246
Jan. 1, 1952 to June 30, 1952	80,675	NA	393,542	434,921
July 1, 1951 to Aug. 31, 1952[c]	11,695	NA	405,616	446,616

SOURCE: *The DPC Report*, February 1, 1949, p. 37, August 1, 1949, p. 8, February 1,
1950, p. 7, August 1, 1950, p. 18, February 1, 1951, p. 37, August 1, 1951, p. 43;
Vernant, *The Refugee in the Post-War World*, p. 525; *The DP Story*, p. 336; "D.P.
Commission Makes Final Report," *Christian Century* (September 10, 1952), 69:1020;
folder, "Legislation—1950," box 22, DPC MSS.
[a] Rough estimate based on approximately two-thirds of the beneficiaries of the Truman
Directive being Jewish.
[b] Figures not available.
[c] The DPC completed its operations on August 31, 1952.

In the overall picture, however, McCarran's roadblocks were hurdles to be gotten over rather than insuperable barriers. Congress did pass a generous bill in 1950 and, ultimately, the full allotment of DPs reached the United States. Snags produced by McCarran's visits to the European centers in 1949, the concern that he and other members of the Senate expressed regarding DPC operations, and the reshuffling of DPC personnel in 1950 reflected themselves in the lowered numbers of DPs being cleared for entry into the United States. But after John Gibson took over the DPC chairmanship in late 1950 he recharged the agency and the staff again moved full speed ahead. So much so, in fact, that to complete its business Congress had to twice extend the life of the agency. When the DPC finally closed its doors on August 31, 1952, it took pride in having helped more than 400,000 Europeans resettle in America. The final statistics, broken down for six-month periods (see table 9.2) demonstrated its accomplishments.

THE DELAYED PILGRIMS AT HOME

The passage of the 1950 act culminated the lobbying efforts on behalf of the DPs. William Bernard supervised the dismantling of the CCDP, and the AJC and ACJ ceased their quest for special legislation. They were pleased with their accomplishments. Congress postponed the termination of the DP program twice, into 1952. In 1953 the legislators passed another emergency refugee act which admitted 214,000 more Europeans, mostly the homeless who fled from Communist nations after the war. By the end of 1952 more than 400,000 Europeans had arrived in the United States as a result of American efforts at resettlement. The *Saturday Evening Post* estimated that the government had invested $250 million in the DP program, including $11,897,000 for the DPC. A spokesman for the DPC calculated that placing all of the DPs who reached the United States cost $100,601,000 or $1.93 per taxpayer. Thus, the United States efforts on behalf of the DPs and refugees proved more generous than those of any other western nation in terms of money spent and people received.[1]

In Europe, the passage of the American DP acts led to mass migrations out of the assembly centers. The 1950 act came too late to help most of the Jewish DPs who had already gone to Israel or to other countries that would have them. On the other hand, several nations contributed to the end of the DP plight by accepting substantial numbers. Israel took about 136,000 Jews, Australia welcomed over 175,000 Gentiles and Jews, Great Britain received slightly more than 100,000 DPs, Canada brought in about 80,000, while approximately 40,000 found homes in France, and about 36,000 went to Belgium.[2]

In 1951 the West German government took over the operations of the camps, which still contained about 2,500 Jews. Two years later 2,200 remained. Of these, 800 were considered "hard-core": they had TB, were mentally or physically disabled, or were simply too demoralized to move again. Another 400 who wanted to get into the United States could not pass a security check because of a false statement on an application for a visa or a one-time membership in a radical organization. Almost 1,000 of the other DPs had returned disillusioned from Israel. The West German government finally began moving people out of the assembly centers in late 1953. The last DP camp, at Foehrenwald, closed on February 28, 1957.[3]

Too little is known about what happened to Jewish and Gentile DPs after they left the camps to permit any sweeping judgments about their experiences. The few surveys that do exist, however, show that except for those originally placed on farms the DPs adapted well. One study of the 404 refugees who came on the first boatload of people to benefit from the Truman Directive in 1946 indicated that 89 percent of the breadwinners were employed, and 75 percent of those eligible to apply for citizenship had done so. *The New York Times* traced the passengers of the first ship that docked in New York under the auspices of the DPC in 1948 and found 10 percent of them a decade later. Almost all of this fraction had become citizens, were employed, and regarded themselves as financially comfortable. The AJC Oral History project conducted 250 interviews with Holocaust survivors in the United States in the 1970s. Of this group 85 percent married (63 percent to other survivors), with most considered "successful" by ordinary standards. The largest number of those employed were professionals, the next largest were small business proprietors.[4]

But marriage, employment, and regular incomes do not necessarily reflect contentment, adjustment or success. Several accounts of DPs in the early 1950s praised their adaptive qualities and new lives even though, in retrospect, one wonders how the immigrants actually fared. Sixty-eight DPs, mostly Latvians, resettled in Ripon, Wisconsin. The town seemed more exciting with the arrival of the newcomers. The residents were proud of the efforts that they had made on behalf of their new neighbors and how well these people apparently fit into the community. A 1951 magazine story indicated that 43 of the 68 were employed, 16 attended school, 7 women kept house for their families, and 2 individuals were incapacitated by illness. The Europeans who occupied professional and high status positions in their own lands took on menial and unskilled jobs in the Wisconsin town. A school principal in Hungary worked as a cookie packer on the night shift in a local plant. A former magazine writer and radio commentator in Latvia baked pies in the Ripon College dining hall kitchen, while a compatriot, who had taught mathematics and foreign languages overseas, now did other people's laundry in America. Whether these DPs ultimately changed their occupations is difficult to say becase studies do not exist treating their subsequent American experiences but one American physicist, born in Estonia in 1939, told an interviewer in 1975 that the "dislocation" affected his parents severely. "Going from being upper middle class to lower middle class . . . hurt them a great deal."[5]

The new occupation which almost all of the DPs avoided seems to have been farm work. It was foolish for Congress to have stipulated in the 1948 law that 30 percent of the DPs had to be agrarian workers because so few of the refugees possessed the necessary skills. The kinds of people who were sent to agricultural jobs, moreover, reflected how easily DPs could circumvent the intent of the law. More than 90 percent of those originally placed in agricultural jobs left as soon as they could. "You just can't make them believe that a cow has to be milked twice a day, 12 hours apart, seven days a week," an American dairyman complained. An Oklahoman, while generally praising several DPs, confessed, "We had many doctorates of law, and skilled men coming in that just weren't too happy on the farm." And in North Dakota a Lutheran spokesman acknowledged, "Our big trouble has been misrepresentation. We get farmers who are not farmers." Many farm laborers switched jobs several times until they found something suitable.

In Wisconsin, a man resettled four times until placed with a butcher. Then he was happy. He had been a butcher in Europe.[6]

Outside of agriculture there are several bits of information that indicate many individuals adjusted quickly to their new circumstances and, in fact, did well in their original placements. A Baltic woman who had been an orphan admitted in 1952, "I have made for myself a good life here." The acting archdiocese resettlement director in Milwaukee, Wisconsin, claimed that the Catholic DPs assimilated well and could not be distinguished from others in the community less than a year after their arrival. He knew of only two cases of marital discord among 1,600 recently arrived families, and only one case of juvenile delinquency. "On a percentage basis," he asserted, "I believe that the immigrants were more self-sufficient, healthier, and maintained better family relationships than any other cross section of our general population." In St. Louis, one spokesman for a Jewish agency told a presidential commission about several DPs who were occupationally set and financially well off.[7] A Jewish DP living in Rochester, New York stated: "For us it is good as it is. We are happy to be half and half Americans, but our children, for them it is all American. They will be free Americans, college professors, lawyers, doctors, anything they want." And in the 1970s, a Holocaust survivor expressed her enthusiasm to an inquiring writer: "I cannot tell you what it meant to us to come to America; this was the freedom we had never known before. To speak freely, to be without fear, to think as you like. It did not take us long to see what this country was. Americans do not know, they cannot understand, what they have here. Yes, we have had some hard times, some varied times, but I am telling the truth: we have been happy from the day we came here."[8]

Yet for others the adjustment came slowly or not at all. "Our first two years in New York were the hardest," a refugee later told a New York Times reporter. "There were personal problems at first. We had lost everything—our culture, our language, our family." But then the woman came to terms with reality. "You learn what you must do and you just do it," she said. One couple that landed in New Orleans was shocked by the signs "white" and "colored" in public places. The wife read English and translated the words for her husband. Some people could drink at a water fountain, others could not. Some might be served in one restaurant while others would be turned away. "The signs were the greatest shock to us," she later revealed. "They struck a terrible chord. Even long before we were arrested and taken away to camps, there had been these signs forbidding Jews to sit in the park, or to walk certain places. My husband and I were frightened at the regime in the South the moment we saw this, and we decided, as soon as we could, to get out of there whatever we had to do. We left after six months, and came North; there was no use trying, we could never be comfortable, because racial laws meant only one thing to us." Another DP became dejected and despondent after his placement in Michigan. His sponsor unknowingly subscribed to a Communist foreign language newspaper, published in Boston, and gave it regularly to the newcomer assuming that he was being helpful to the man. Finally, the DP had a complete nervous breakdown. "He was under the impression," a DPC employee later wrote, "that the Communists had captured Boston, Massachusetts, and, because he had a son living there, there was no question in his mind that his son would be killed or placed in a slave labor camp." The 1949 annual report of the Lutheran Resettlement Service also discussed the hardships encountered by a small percentage of the DPs with whom they worked. "Unhappy family situations, difficulties among children, school failures, unemployment, mental difficulties, alcoholism, physical and mental illness, exploitation and all the many trials which beset any group of people have beset the resettled persons," the report read. The Home Mission Council of North America, another Protestant organization, also received word about old people, the unemployed, and those simply in need of fellowship: "Despair, frustration and bitterness are the result for many."[9]

What seems most apparent about the DPs, and their children, however, is that as a well-defined group they no longer exist. There are Holocaust survivors whose memories of past horrors cannot be dimmed, and many of their children believe that their parents' unique experiences shaped their own development.[10] But aside from these people one cannot point to any organized or prominent American group or movement that has received attention because of its DP associations. When studies were made of college activists, protesters against the war in Vietnam, and members of the Ku Klux Klan, no one wrote about the DPs, or DP children among them. They may have participated but they were described as college youths, left- or right-wingers, hard-hats, or bigots.

Although some Nazis and collaborators undoubtedly reached the United States as a result of the DP acts of 1948 and 1950, few have been identified in America. How many came and how many are still alive is impossible to say. In 1948 Abraham Duker feared an influx of large numbers of Nazis as a result of the DP Act. However, during the 1970s only about 200 or so alleged war criminals were being investigated by the United States Attorney-General's office.[11] Although many more Nazi criminals may have entered, there is no available evidence that other collaborators are at large in the United States.

From the bits and shreds of information that we do have, it is understandable why the DPs have chosen to fade into the anonymous mass of people in this country. Some individuals, Jews as well as Gentiles, misrepresented their wartime or their postwar experiences. One Jewish DP observed that not a single refugee on the ship that brought him to the United States told the entire truth about his or her background. Yet a "willfull" misstatement "for the purpose of gaining admission into the United States as an eligible displaced person," the United States Supreme Court noted in *Fedorenko* v. *U.S.* (1981), sufficed to make the applicant inadmissible.[12]

There are two examples of non-Jews who either "misrepresented" their past or whose families dissembled for the purpose of gaining admission to the United States. How representative they are of 400,000 people would be absurd even to guess at. But the two tales are indicative of the fact that the screening process of DPs in the late 1940s was not foolproof. The first case is of the Ukrainian Feodor Fedorenko who applied for a visa to the United States in October 1949. At the time he lied about his birthplace and nationality, and concealed the fact that he had served as a guard in the Treblinka concentration camp during the war. Fedorenko received the visa in 1949 but not until the 1970s, when former inmates of the concentration camp saw him in Florida, was he identified. The United States government attempted to revoke his citizenship and deport him on the grounds that he had lied in his application for admission to this country. In defense, Fedorenko asserted that he had been forced into his concentration camp role and had not served voluntarily. But Kempton Jenkins, a government witness and career foreign service officer who had served as a vice-consul in Germany after the war and who had processed applicants for visas under the DP act, contradicted Fedorenko's assertion that he had served involuntarily. On the basis of his and fellow workers' experiences reviewing more than 5,000 visa applications, Jenkins observed that concentration "camp guards invariably admitted that their service was voluntary," and that no "known concentration camp guard was found eligible" for a visa under the DP act. By a majority of 7–2 the United States Supreme Court ruled that the government had the right to deport Fedorenko for misrepresentation on his application for admission to the United States.[13]

The other example of a known discrepancy came from a man born in Estonia in 1939. Today an American physicist, in 1975 he related how he and his family reached the United States. (The man chose not to reveal his name.) They left their homeland in 1944. "We went on a ship which was evacuating Germans from Estonia. My godfather was an official in the German-sponsored government, and he arranged for us to get on this ship." When they reached Germany his father "went to the government officials there and presented himself as being a refugee from the German-dominated country of Estonia and essentially asked for a job working with forests. He received a job as an assistant forester somewhere in Bavaria." The family then moved to the town of Everdorf where they remained for a year or two before entering a DP camp. "In order to get into the camp, we had to claim that we were forcibly taken from

Estonia by the wicked Germans." In 1949 the family came to the United States and settled first in North Dakota, then Minnesota. After a while they discovered that "people kind of forget that you've come recently. You live just like everybody else." And so those members of the family who chose to do so simply faded into whatever communities they resided.[14]

Experiences like the two just mentioned suggest that many people who sympathized with, and worked for, the Nazis while in Europe in the 1940s, quickly adapted themselves—at least in public—to the prevailing tone in the United States after they arrived. Antisemitism in the United States came under widespread attack in the late 1940s.[15] Since 1950 American incidents of antisemitism have declined despite sporadic outbursts from groups like the Ku Klux Klan and the American Nazi party. It is entirely probable, therefore, that the DPs who may have both collaborated with the Nazis or harbored deep-seated antagonism toward Jews, may have been influenced by the officially tolerant attitude of the American government, the growing acceptance of Jews, and the more circumscribed behavior of even many prejudiced Americans.

In evaluating the effects of the Displaced Persons Acts of 1948 and 1950 it is possible to point to both their positive and negative results. Both acts reflected an American sympathy for the plight of the DPs and a desire to help them rebuild their lives in America. Those who were most concerned, especially the non-Zionist Jews, were instrumental in seeing that the legislation was passed. But so great were longstanding prejudices and antisemitism in the United States that the first law did not fully meet the needs of the survivors of the Holocaust. Both bills did, however, set precedents for a renewed American involvement with refugees which, ultimately, proved to be the outstanding accomplishment of the legislation.

Most of those originally eligible for admission to the United States as DPs were not Jews. Indeed, the first DP Act of 1948 was so riddled with restrictions that Will Maslow of the American Jewish Congress characterized the measure as one that "might appropriately be entitled a bill to exclude DPs, particularly Jews, and to admit Hitler's collaborators."[16] Only after a bitter fight and after most of Europe's displaced Jews had gone to Israel did Congress eliminate the law's ugly antisemitic provisions.

Of course, antisemitism alone does not explain the restrictions of the original DP Act, for many Americans were reluctant to welcome displaced persons regardless of their ethnic origin. Moreover, by the late 1940s the cold war was a grim reality that further politicized immigration policy and the granting of visas to America. Still, the situation was ironic. A movement begun to aid the survivors of the Holocaust succeeded in helping others, including some who had been among the strongest Nazi supporters.

In retrospect, one might question whether a more vigorous effort on the part of the President would have made a significant difference. I doubt it. Truman's accession to the presidency coincided with the height of antiforeign and antisemitic feelings in this country. Between 1944 and 1946 several American patriotic groups, most notably the Daughters of the American Revolution, the American Legion, and the Veterans of Foreign Wars, voted to ban immigration to the United States for a five- to ten-year period and most of the Congress saw no reason to challenge them on this issue. Antisemitism in the United States also peaked at just about the time that Truman moved into the White House.[17] Consequently, not only non-Jews, but many Jews as well, refused to seek alterations in the existing statutes. With such antagonism on the part of national organizations and hesitancy from the Jews whose strong support would have been needed to begin a campaign to bring European refugees to the United States, Truman did not move boldly to change immigration policies in 1945. Nonetheless, he did order that the DPs be given preference within the existing statutes just before Christmas of 1945. As a result of the Truman Directive approximately 41,000 DPs reached the United States, two-thirds of them Jewish.

Truman also tried to get the refugees into Palestine and for a time worked with Great Britain to obtain that goal. When their efforts failed to produce a solution that both countries could endorse the President encouraged Congress to modify the immigration laws. But while he wanted to aid DPs, they did not constitute a major priority. They were one among many problems with which he had to deal, and which he hoped, but did not really expect, that Congress would act upon. Truman's actions in regard to DP legislation reinforces Susan Hartmann's observations about him. In her book, *Truman and the 80th Congress*, she points out that the President was characteristically a weak and inconsistent legislative leader. He would call for congressional action but would rarely commit himself on details or support a specific proposal already under consideration. Hartmann's comment fits perfectly Truman's handling of the DPs and the Stratton bill.[18]

The President's own appointments, however, always reflected his desire to see the DP problem identified and solved in a humane fashion. He dispatched Earl Harrison to Europe in the summer of 1945, appointed Ugo Carusi as a special adviser on DPs in 1947, and later put three liberals on the DPC in 1948 (four, if one counts John Gibson, who replaced Carusi in 1950). Moreover, in the White House and behind the scenes, Truman encouraged his assistant for minority affairs, David K. Niles, to let Congressman Stratton know that the administration supported his bill. He also signaled his concern by having Niles communicate frequently with important American Jewish leaders. At no time was there any evidence that Truman wanted to sabotage or undermine efforts to aid the DPs.

The President's attitude is also indicated by the fact that Cabinet members and White House subordinates worked diligently and, when appropriate, openly for DP lesgislation. The State Department in particular presented a strong case in behalf of bringing DPs to the United States—a change from its prewar attitude. General Hilldring and special adviser Goldthwaite Dorr spoke frequently with the legislators, and Undersecretary of State Robert Lovett reiterated the administration's position in a letter to Senator Revercomb in the spring of 1948. Truman signed, but denounced the discriminatory provisions of, the 1948 act, supported a plank in the

Democratic party platform that year for a revised bill, and then after his surprise election "buttered-up" Congressman Walter while encouraging him to write a more generous bill in the 81st Congress.

Despite Truman's activities more might have been done for the DPs had the military and the President made greater efforts on their behalf. At first, military officials in Europe, perhaps overwhelmed by the myriad concerns of government, made little attempt to provide decent havens for survivors. Those displaced persons who refused repatriation were poorly treated, their diet and housing inferior to both the American soldiers' and the German prisoners'-of-war. German civilians, aside from suffering the consequences affecting a defeated nation, usually lived better than those who had endured the ravages of war in concentration and slave labor camps. Neither General Patton, who regarded the Jewish refugees as animals, nor his subordinates, argued strongly for humanitarian measures. Even General Eisenhower resented the suggestion that Jews might need special care.

The President and many of the generals had other priorities and viewed the displaced persons as an additional burden. Truman's messages to Eisenhower and the General's order to subordinates resulted in some improvement, but keeping people in assembly centers without adequate food, clothing, shelter, and occupational activities, and making only minimal attempts to find them new homes, showed how little the displaced persons counted in American postwar concerns. With the war won the United States could easily have undertaken relief measures with no strains on its resources. The Army Corps of Engineers had accomplished extraordinary feats during the war. Its talents might have been utilized to build more comfortable and commodious accommodations for the survivors; the DPs might have been put on the same rations as the American soldiers and prisoners-of-war; PX facilities might have been made available to them; they need not have been prevented from having any money in their possession; sufficient clothing could have been shipped from the United States. Though President Truman could not single-handedly alter

American immigration laws, he could have seen to it that the displaced persons were treated with dignity and respect. Enough supplies could have been shipped from the United States to improve the quality of life in the DP centers.

Such a policy, however, was never considered. Political and military officials hesitated to make conditions comfortable for the DPs because they thought that this might discourage them from leaving the assembly centers. UNRRA employees tried numerous devices to get the DPs to return to their native countries. In 1946, in fact, UNRRA offered an extra 60 days' rations to anyone who voluntarily repatriated himself.

Most officials believed that the Jews constituted the most serious challenge and that until they were resettled little headway would be made in solving the DP problem. Truman's attempt to get Britain to allow the Jews into Palestine failed because Americans lacked the leverage to influence HMG's Middle East policy. The Americans and British feared Russian encroachment in the area and courted Arab friendship. Neither country wanted to antagonize those who controlled the Middle Eastern oil fields, the Mediterranean ports, and the Suez Canal. Both the United States and Great Britain thought that Russia would benefit if the Western powers pushed the Arabs too far.

The Communist issue also began to affect domestic politics. In the fall of 1946 it emerged as a concern of a number of voters and in early 1947 Truman established his loyalty program for federal employees. Fear of expanding communism contributed to congressional passage of aid to Greece and Turkey, and the establishment of the Marshall Plan, in 1947. A number of Americans thought that subversives would be admitted among the displaced persons if immigration barriers were lowered. Republican conservatives and southern Democrats, especially, represented constituents who opposed any additional immigrants, particularly Jews and other East Europeans. The potency of antisemitism and anti-immigrant sentiment in the United States combined with fear that the Jews and other East Europeans who came from countries behind the iron curtain would bring Russian ideology to these shores. Such thoughts carried considerable weight with legislators who shared their constituents' hysteria and ignorance.

Everyone concerned with immigration, displaced persons, and the plight of the Jewish survivors was mindful of these widely held attitudes. Their existence dictated the way that the AJC and ACJ, through the CCDP, embarked upon their campaign to bring some DPs to this country. The CCDP had to dispel the fears of those who believed that most of the DPs were Jews and/or Communists. William Bernard acknowledged as much in October 1948, when he wrote, "Anti-Semitism opposed our efforts at every step."[19]

The main thrust of the lobbying efforts aimed at those hundreds of thousands, if not millions, of Americans horrified by the Holocaust and the consequent displacements in Europe. Jewish organizations recognized that without the strong backing of influential Protestants like Earl Harrison, Samuel McCrea Cavert, and Eleanor Roosevelt, favorable legislation would have been impossible. Moreover, once the CCDP began operations, William Bernard and his staff deliberately worked through local church and community leaders who, once alerted and educated, exerted themselves on behalf of the cause.

The CCDP proved the catalyst. It mobilized its own forces, alerted those most receptive to its message, and made an impact upon the Congress. Congressmen and senators learned a good deal about the DPs from the CCDP's educational campaign and many of them began to recognize the need for some modification of the immigration laws. Reports from legislators who toured the assembly centers in 1947, the influence of the State Department and other government officials, along with a widespread letter-writing campaign and contacts from prominent and concerned constituents, contributed as well to the lawmakers' decision to help the DPs. Although unanimity was not achieved, and huge sections of the nation, particularly in the South and the West, opposed bringing more foreigners to the United States, a sufficiently large and positive response to the CCDP message did make an impact in Congress.

But Senators Revercomb and McCarran, aided by the immigration subcommittee staff director Richard Arens, prepared legislation explicitly designed to discriminate against the Jews. In this action they no doubt represented the dominant sentiments in the Congress and in the nation. Once the Congress decided to aid displaced persons, in fact, the original Stratton bill calling for admission of 400,000 people would have sufficed as a humanitarian gesture. But the December 22, 1945, cutoff date and the agricultural and annexed territories preferences were tailor-made to exclude Jewish DPs. The discriminatory aspects of the 1948 act were further underscored when that same bill made provision for victims of the Czechoslovakian coup in 1948 and for the expelled *Volksdeutsche* from Eastern Europe, who would qualify for admission to the United States if they entered the western zones of Germany, Austria, or Italy by July 1, 1948.

The Revercomb committee had discovered during its European tour in the fall of 1947 that most of the Jews who might have qualified under the 1945 cutoff date had already left for Palestine and other countries. They knew, too, that the majority of those entering the United States under the 1945 Truman Directive were also Jewish. An unqualified DP law, merely stipulating a maximum number, they feared, would flood the nation with Jews. Few congressmen or senators openly expressed these anxieties but a majority of senators refused to change the cutoff date from December 22, 1945, to April 21, 1947, when an amendment to the Revercomb bill came up for a vote in June 1948. Changing the cutoff date, the senators well knew, meant making more than 100,000 Polish Jews who reached the DP camps in 1946 eligible for American visas. Thus, while Congress wanted to allow some DPs into the United States, it effectively limited the number of Jews among them.

But the law was not without merit. For the first time in American history Congress recognized its responsibilities for housing some of the world's refugees in the United States. The precedent, once set, would be built upon in future decades. Furthermore, the legislation provided the basis for admitting DPs and established the machinery for processing them into the country.

The DP Act of 1948, in fact, worked better than many had originally anticipated because of the men that Truman appointed as commissioners of the DPC. Carusi, O'Connor, and

Rosenfield reflected the President's desire to resettle as many DPs as possible in the United States. The policies that they adopted and the tone of their operations encouraged staff members to facilitate migration. The accomplishments of this agency showed how a government bureaucracy could undermine the thrust of congressional legislation.

Moreover, the DPC emerged as one of the key elements in the drive for more liberal legislation in 1949 and 1950. The November 1948 elections resulted in an astonishing victory for the President and swept the Democrats back into control of Congress. Early journalistic surveys indicated that a majority of the new legislators favored a more generous DP bill. The DPC then joined with the CCDP in lobbying to help the 81st Congress accomplish that goal.

But in the 81st Congress Senator McCarran led a minority determined to prevent the passage of too liberal a bill. McCarran and Richard Arens knew how carefully the 1948 law had been prepared to prevent large numbers of DPs from entering the United States, and the DPC's interpretations seemed treacherous. The Nevadan at first stalled before holding hearings, then decided to tour the European DP centers himself, and finally brought back witnesses to expose the DPC's lax administrative practices.

Ultimately McCarran failed. Unlike 1948, when Senator Wiley changed the complexion of the conference committee by slipping in Eastland and Donnell at the last minute, the liberals remained vigilant in 1950. Thus they prevented the sabotaging of a bill that a majority of the Senators favored.

The fight for DP legislation demonstrated anew the importance of a well-organized, well-financed lobby in the American political system. Although the accomplishments and impact of the CCDP, like other lobbying groups, are not easily measured, that organization was probably responsible for galvanizing the public and the Congress. By bringing the subject of DPs and their plight to the attention of thoughtful Americans, the CCDP helped set into motion the activities that eventually resulted in the passage of more legislation. The CCDP carefully enlisted the support first of the most influential citizens in the community, next of the prestigious organizations, and finally, of the public, and provided each with a sufficient amount of material to buttress its humanitarian arguments. Simultaneously the CCDP, AJC, and ACJ, and their newly won supporters, approached the newspapers and the Congress.

Not everyone, of course, favored setting aside the immigration quotas, even temporarily, and hundreds of thousands, including supporters of a more generous bill, had fears about the kinds of people who might enter the United States as a result of the legislation. We now know that their apprehensions were groundless. Followers of Senators McCarran, Eastland, et al., were convinced that Communist subversives would surely arrive and work to bring the American government down, while thousands of Jews dreaded the entry of former Nazis and collaborators. But in the thirty years since the passage of the legislation no untoward events have occured because of the presence of these newcomers. Like immigrants of previous generations they have blended with the rest of society and have done nothing to bring attention to themselves as a group.

The passage of the DP acts in the face of enormous anti-Jewish and anti-refugee sentiment is a tribute to the bedrock of humanitarianism in the United States. Powerful minorities in Congress thwarted the progress of the bills and almost scuttled them altogether. Nevertheless, most Americans wanted to help some of the displaced persons. Pressure from the CCDP, leading ethnic and religious organizations, and the commissioners of the DPC reflected this sentiment. The CCDP and the Jewish organizations, in particular, capitalized upon existing humanitarianism. In 1950 liberal Senators like Kilgore, Ives, and Lehman asserted themselves vigorously on behalf of a broadened bill and carried a majority of their colleagues with them.

The efforts of the various groups on behalf of the DPs, therefore, not only blended self-interest with justice, but also paved the way for the more generous and understanding refugee relief acts of subsequent years. During the past three decades special interest advocates, frequently anti-Communist zealots, have used the precedent of the DP bills to help bring particular refugees to this country in times of international turmoil. Hungarians, Cubans, and Vietnamese, among others, have become the beneficiaries.

In sum, strong national prejudices, procrastination in Congress, and less than dynamic leadership from the White House combined to prolong the miseries of those Jews who survived the Holocaust. The CCDP fought for a revised DP Act in 1949 and 1950 because leaders of the AJC and ACJ wanted a law that they considered antisemitic eradicated from the statutes, not because they had any hopes of bringing large numbers of Jews to the United States. Passage of the DP acts helped non-Jews more than it did those who had suffered and survived the Holocaust. Finally, and this point cannot be emphasized too strongly, although the DP acts of 1948 and 1950 established fine precedents, and in the long run benefited refugees the world over, they failed to meet the needs of the majority of the Jewish DPs in Europe.

A STATISTICAL SYNOPSIS

The number of displaced persons has never been accurately assessed. Estimates in 1945 ranged from 5 to 10 million in Germany, and up to 30 million throughout Europe. Included among the various totals were prisoners-of-war, deserters, wanderers, Eastern Europeans fleeing the Russians and/or accompanying Germans on their retreat westward, forced and voluntary laborers, concentration camp victims, Spanish Republicans driven out of Spain when Franco came to power in 1939, and an assortment of uprooted people who could not be classified under the headings listed. *Life* magazine gave the total as 9.5 million (fig. A.1) on May 14, 1945. By September, somewhere in the neighborhood of 5 to 6 million had returned to their homelands. Also, in the fall of 1945 Germany and Austria were divided into zones governed independently by the United States, Great Britain, France, and Russia, and each authority compiled its own statistics. Russia controlled East Germany and claimed that its area contained no displaced persons, a statement simply unbelievable given the turmoil that existed after the war. A million, and perhaps more, DPs probably wandered through Russian-controlled territories. The American Army listed 3,230,531 for the United States zones in Germany and Austria (fig. A.2), with only about 600,000 remaining by December 1945. Britain and France contained lesser totals for the year and fewer remaining in December.

The problem of counting people properly plagued officials for the next several years. Who was, or was not, a displaced person, or one eligible for care by UNRRA and its successor, the IRO, could not be agreed upon by the major powers. Technically, all UN member nations' citizens, away from their home countries, were eligible for DP status, but many former prisoners-of-war, Nazi collaborators, and *Volksdeutsche* expelled from Eastern Europe after the war managed somehow to obtain it. Russian citizens, by the Yalta agreement, had

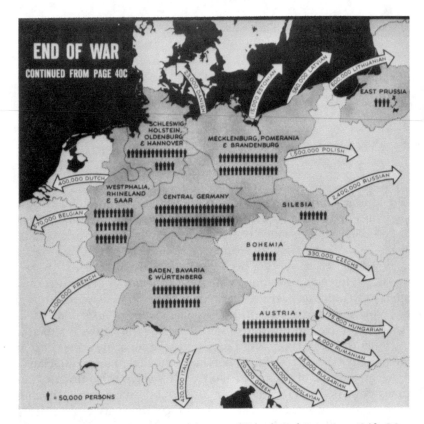

Figure A.1. *Life* Magazine's Estimate of Displaced Persons. (*Life*, May 14, 1945, p. 88A. Anthony Sodaro/Frank Stockman, *Life* Magazine, Copyright © 1945, Time Inc.)

to be returned voluntarily or involuntarily, but Ukrainians, White Russians, Cossacks, and people who despite their birth in, or in territories annexed by, the Soviet Union, and who claimed the status of political persecutees or statelessness, constituted a gray area of dubious qualifications. The individual military officer or UNRRA official in charge frequently made the lasting determination. Germans were not eligible for UNRRA care but German Jews, as persecutees, were. Nevertheless, immediately after the war German Jews freed from the concentration camps were turned over to German authorities for care.

The American Army technically closed the DP assembly centers to new registrants on August 1, 1945, but subsequently this date changed

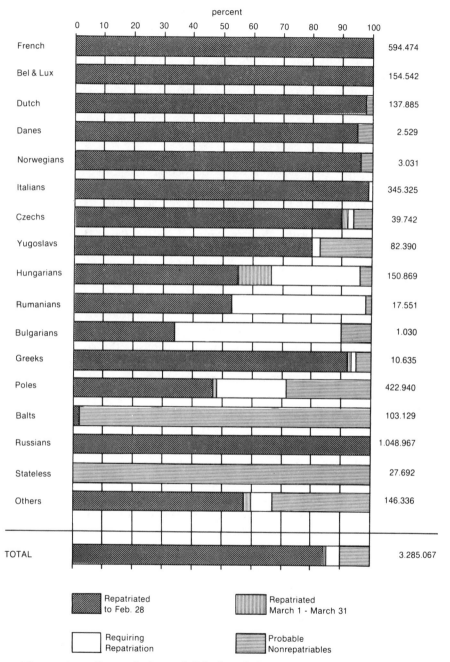

Figure A.2. Repatriation of Displaced Persons, March 1946 (U.S. Zone). (Monthly Report of Military Governor. U.S. Zone, April 20, 1946)

several times before the final official closing on April 21, 1947. Again, some camp commandants allowed new entrants during the official closed periods while others did not.

The British and American governments kept their own statistics, which did not always correlate with one another, and categorized the DPs somewhat differently. Officially, the British listed groups only by nationality and not by religion while the Americans also classified by nationality but listed Jews separately. In their respective zones in Germany and Austria, therefore, the people are listed differently. But in Italy, where there were no separate American and British zones, refugees were sometimes categorized according to the British way and sometimes according to American calculations. Furthermore, in all zones, there were military camps, UNRRA (later IRO) camps, and voluntary agency assembly centers, run mostly by the JDC for Jewish refugees. Consequently, the tables and figures that follow have different headings and demarcations based on who collected which statistics.

Moreover, the statistics are not entirely reliable. In fact, they frequently are at variance, although they purport to count the identical people in the same situation. Obviously, the counters and their techniques lacked refinement. In 1949 one U.S. Senate investigating committee observed in its report that, "during the course of its examination of the IRO, the subcommittee found that many of the Organization's statistics are inaccurate and misleading."[1] A year later, William Bernard, CCDP Executive Secretary, acknowledged:

> The statistics picture is not easy to ascertain because the IRO figures do not always square with those of the Displaced Persons Commission. Moreover, IRO figures themselves are usually in a state of flux both because their statistical techniques are being constantly refined and because there is constant change in the numbers through repatriation or resettlement.[2]

Keeping this in mind, along with JDC head Paul Baerwald's 1947 assessment that "figures for displaced persons are highly fluid, and are subject to continuous changes," one may proceed with caution to examine the following statistics.[3]

The generally accepted estimate is that about 7 of the 8 or 9 million displaced persons found in Germany and Austria in May had been repatriated by September 1945. Table A.1 based on British figures which frequently showed fewer people than the American count, shows the statistics on DPs for September 30, 1945. Because the

Table A.1 European DPs by Claimed Nationality and Location: September 30, 1945
(Excluding German Nationals and Ethnic Germans)

Area or Country Where Located	Total		Balts	Czecho-slovaks	Greeks	Italians	Poles	Soviet Nationals	Yugo-slavs	Jews	Western Euro-peans	Bulgar-ians	Hungar-ians	Ruma-nians	All Others
	Numbers	Per Cent													
Total	1,888,401	100.0	178,904[a]	25,482	33,123	34,802	1,055,701	54,846	124,618	69,098	15,063[b]	1,535	122,182	58,560	114,533
Per cent	100.0		9.5	1.3	1.6	1.8	56.0	2.9	6.6	3.7	0.8	0.1	6.5	3.1	6.1
Austria	210,374	11.1	5,130	6,942	709	1,387	26,069	7,458	53,318	9,492	364	989	17,855	46,607	34,054
United States Zone	110,421	5.9	2,943	3,216	267	940	15,197	1,115	41,263	6,056	1	329	7,963	13,425	17,706
British Zone	59,816	3.1	979	471	128	67	6,525	6,203	8,280	2,812	73	353	7,010	15,416	11,499
French Zone	24,847	1.3	1,208	344	8	17	3,588	140	1,894	615	30	164	2,512	12,565	1,762
Soviet Zone	15,290	0.8	—	2,911	306	363	759	—	1,881	9	260	143	370	5,201	3,087
Belgium	2,763	0.1	52	173	128	38	1,748	221	64	—	192	3	2	137	142
Denmark	10,391	0.6	2,772	—	—	—	5,735	659	—	—	—	—	511	—	577
France	153,460	8.1	213	10,000	100	18,000	100,000	11,149	4,724	—	185	151	6,525	892	1,521
Germany	1,202,446	63.7	133,701	3,090	908	10,446	816,012	33,146	27,699	22,580	7,145	373	95,904	10,456	40,986
United States Zone	488,908	25.9	77,092	1,530	597	1,643	253,981	27,932	13,531	10,417	2,354	223	85,245	3,469	10,894
British Zone	648,784	34.4	50,572	1,251	253	8,681	510,328	3,397	14,092	11,758	4,018	136	8,643	6,677	28,978
French Zone	64,754	3.4	6,037	309	58	122	51,703	1,817	76	405	773	14	2,016	310	1,114
Greece	3,200	0.1	—	—	2,700	—	—	—	500	—	—	—	—	—	—
Italy	75,487	4.0	122	1,032	4,271	—	7,554	1,382	28,076	21,250	6,125	—	419	194	5,062
Norway	18,969	1.0	—	—	—	—	14,050	41	497	—	20	—	—	—	4,361
Sweden	48,634	2.6	36,650	838	—	—	10,275	289	—	—	582	—	—	—	—
Switzerland	17,724	1.0	264	407	152	1,163	9,258	501	1,486	—	404	19	966	274	2,830
Albania	23,000	1.3	—	—	22,000	1,000	—	—	—	—	—	—	—	—	—
China	15,776	1.0	—	—	—	—	—	—	—	15,776	—	—	—	—	—
East, Central, and South Africa	20,000	1.1	—	—	—	—	20,000	—	—	—	—	—	—	—	—
India	5,000	0.2	—	—	—	—	5,000	—	—	—	—	—	—	—	—
Iran	40,000	2.1	—	—	—	—	40,000	—	—	—	—	—	—	—	—
Middle East	38,177	2.0	—	—	4,855	68	—	—	8,254	—	—	—	—	—	25,000
Palestine	3,000	0.1	—	3,000	—	—	—	—	—	—	—	—	—	—	—

Source: Proudfoot, *European Refugees: 1939–1952*, pp. 238–39.

[a] Comprised of 54,844 Estonians; 72,922 Latvians; and 51,138 Lithuanians.

[b] Comprised of 2,086 Belgians; 233 Danes; 6,558 Frenchmen; 5,902 Netherlanders; and 284 Norwegians.

British did not count Jews separately, the number for Jews is probably too low. It is completely out of range of the figures given in the Harrison Report which estimated somewhere between 50,000 and 100,000 Jews in German assembly centers in July 1945.

The exodus of Jews from Poland began in the summer of 1945 and continued for more than a year, climaxing with a mass rush after the Kielce pogrom in the summer of 1946. The numbers in table A.2 detail the Jewish count in the western zones of Germany, Austria, and Italy in February, July, and November 1946, and in the summer of 1947, after most of them had arrived from Eastern Europe. Blank spaces indicate no figures available for that place and/ or period. These figures correlate well with the official American Army totals of 207,788[4] Jews in and out of the assembly centers in the western zones of Germany and Austria and the Allied areas in Italy on December 31, 1946, and with the JDC estimate of 231,500 Jewish DPs in these areas in February 1947.[5]

Twenty to 30 percent of the Jewish DPs lived outside of the assembly centers in Germany but received displaced persons status. Table A.3 shows a JDC nationality breakdown of the Jews *in the camps* on September 26, 1947.

An occupational survey made in January 1947 found only 2.8 percent of the Jews in farm related activities, 48 percent in industry and transportation, and 28 percent without any occupational classification.[6] These figures were also given to members of the Revercomb

Table A.2 Jewish Displaced Persons, 1946–1947

	February 1 1946	July 1 1946	November 1946	Summer 1947
Germany	69,739	105,927	173,592	182,000
U.S. Zone	46,084	71,963		157,000
British Zone	17,000	19,249		15,000
French Zone	1,655	1,616		10,000
Berlin (western sector)	5,000	13,099		
Austria		8,000		44,000
U.S. Zone				20,000
British Zone				11,000
French Zone				1,000
Vienna (western sectors)				12,000
Italy		16,000		19,000

SOURCE: Proudfoot, pp. 339, 341.

Table A.3 Percentage of Jewish DPs in
the Assembly Centers, By Nationality
September, 26, 1947

Polish	81
Hungarian	6
Czech	4
Lithuanian	3
Russian	2
German	1
Other	3
Total	100

SOURCE: Boris M Joffe to Lazard Teper, September 26, 1947, JDC Mss.

committee who toured the camps in October 1947. They knew, therefore, when they prepared the DP bill in 1948, that only a small percentage of Jews would qualify as having been engaged in agricultural pursuits.

Table A.4 shows the official tallies released by the Army concerning the total numbers of DPs cared for by the Allied powers in Western Europe on December 31, 1946. Table A.5 breaks them down according to national groups in the United States zones in Germany and Austria, only, and for the allied areas of Italy. Table A.6 shows the official statistics nine months later, on September 30, 1947.

The International Refugee Organization (IRO) inaugurated operations on July 1, 1947. Its composite figures for the total number of displaced persons in Germany and Austria, in and out of camps, for August 1947 showed a somewhat higher number than did the aforementioned British and American figures. The IRO figures are shown in table A.7.

The IRO, which replaced UNRRA as the custodians of the DPs, began operations as the Preparatory Commission of the IRO (PCIRO) because only eight UN members had agreed to join the new organization by the time it commenced activities and its constitution required that fifteen members acquiesce before it could stand on its own. The fifteenth member, Denmark, joined in August 1948, and the *PC* disappeared from the IRO letterhead. Otherwise the organization functioned in the same way. Its main purpose was to resettle DPs throughout the world. The following statistics show approxi-

Table A.4 DPs, December 31, 1946

	U.S. Zone			U.K. Zone			French Zone			Allied (U.S. & U.K.)	Totals		
	In Camp	Out of Camp	Total	In Camp	Out of Camp	Total	In Camp	Out of Camp	Total	In Camp	In Camp	Out of Camp	Total
Germany	375,931[a]	142,419	518,350	271,088	15,675	286,763	35,494	10,167	45,661		682,513	168,261	850,774
Austria	23,046[b] / 21,887[c] / 44,933	24,867	69,800	9,412[b] / 12,518[c] / 21,930	40,531	62,461	2,849[b] / 3,744[c] / 6,593	9,010	15,603		73,456	74,408	147,864
Italy	Not Allocated By Zones								13,591[b.d] / 25,175[e] / 38,766	38,766	38,766		38,766
Totals	420,864	167,286	588,150	293,018	56,206	349,224	42,087	19,177	61,264	38,766	794,735	242,669	1,037,404

[a] Not including 34,018 recruited from Polish DPs and employed by U.S. Army in Guard and Service Units
[b] In ARMY Camps
[c] In UNRRA Camps
[d] Includes 3,000 (est.) Royal Yugoslavs [now] employed by British Army. To revert to DP status upon termination of employment
[e] In UNRRA Camps, exclusively UNRRA responsibility

Table A.5 DPs in U.S. Zones of Germany and Austria, and the Allied Zones of Italy, December 31, 1946

Nationality	Germany			Austria				Italy			Combined Total
	In Camp	Out of Camp	Total	In UNRRA Camps	In Military Camps	Out of Camps	Total	In Allied UNRRA Camps[a]	In UNRRA Camps	Total	
Polish	114,397	39,788	154,185	1,357	50	2,762	4,169	2,579	765	3,344	161,698
Baltic	88,125	14,690	102,815	1,643	13	991	2,647	275	16	291	105,753
Jewish	124,572	28,231	152,803								
Jewish (permanent)				5,074	372	751	6,197	[b]	21,288	21,288	204,888
Jewish (transient)				4,759	19,841	0	24,600				21,005
Soviet	8,128	11,805	19,933	219	0	533	752	248	72	320	21,005
White Russian				4,103	0	2,326	6,429				6,429
Ukrainian	6,240	11,684	17,924	4,344	0	5,096	9,440	116	0	116	9,556
Yugoslav				362	1,512	4,168	6,042	6,947	902	7,849	31,815
Royal Yugoslav[c]								3,000	0	3,000	3,000
Belgian and Lux	45	1,627	1,672								1,672
Czech	408	5,967	6,375								6,375
French	38	3,114	3,152								3,152
Norwegian	16	178	194								194
Albanian								707	0	707	707
Austrian[d]								22	162	184	184
Greek								73	768	841	841
Stateless	11,115	10,974	22,089	129	0	1,708	1,837				23,926
Others and Classified	22,847	14,361	37,208	121	99	559	779	1,246	1,183	2,429	40,416
Total	375,931	142,419	518,350	23,046	21,887	24,867	69,800	15,328	25,175	40,503	628,653

SOURCE: Displaced Persons Statistics, Box 17, McGrath Mss.

a Figures of November 12, 1946. Later figures not available.
b Separate Jewish breakdown not available. Included in nationality.
c Employed by British Military. Will revert to DP status.
d Many Jews stopped in Austria on their way to the U.S. zone in Germany or before attempting to gain entry into Palestine.

Table A.6 DPs in Allied Zones, September 30, 1947

	In Camp	Out of Camp	Total
U.S. Zone			
Germany	329,243	150,800	480,043
Austria	58,820	175,600	234,420
British Zone			
Germany	176,100	70,800	246,900
Austria	9,000	105,300	114,300
French Zone			
Germany	32,400		32,400
Austria	6,200		6,200
Italy	32,000	150,000[a]	182,000
Totals	643,763	652,500	1,296,263

SOURCE: Revercomb Committee, pp. 12, 14, 15.
[a] The official British totals for April 21, 1947, in Italy listed perhaps 130,000–160,000 estimated displaced persons outside of the camps; 11,000 (mostly Jews) in the UNRRA camps; 10,984 in joint U.S.-British care in Allied camps (including 7,071 Yugoslavs; 1,021 Poles; 618 Albanians; 295 Hungarians; 292 Greeks; 274 Balts; 256 Russians); and 21,000 (including 11,760 Yugoslavs and 8,734 Ukranians) in British custody. FO 271 66661/WR1644.

mately how many people the IRO moved and the period in which the resettlement occurred. Table A.8 covers estimated resettlement from the end of the war in May 1945, two years before the IRO commenced functioning, through June 30, 1947, as well as those placed by the IRO itself from July 1, 1947 through February 1, 1949. Table A.9 picks up with the summary total as of June 30, 1949, and carries the statistics through June 30, 1951. The IRO terminated operations on December 31, 1951.

The totals of "official" IRO tallies, listed in tables A.8 and A.9, are reported slightly differently in the semiannual reports of the Dis-

Table A.7 Displaced Persons in Allied Zones August, 1947

	Germany	Austria	Total
Total	837,700	376,800	1,214,500
United States Zones	556,000	191,000	747,000
British Zones	246,900	114,000	360,900
French Zones	34,800	71,000	105,800

SOURCE: Revercomb Committee, p. 13.

Table A.8 Estimated DP Resettlement May 1945–June 30, 1947

Argentina	26,402	Norway	404
Australia	18,260[a]	Palestine	86,384[a]
Belgium	34,989	Panama	48[a]
Bolivia	587[a]	Paraguay	7,186
Brazil	14,205	Peru	2,198[a]
Canada	53,473[b]	Southern Rhodesia	87[a]
Chile	1,740[a]	Sweden	3,197
Colombia	355[a]	Switzerland	252[a]
Costa Rica	121[a]	Syria	275[a]
Cuba	326[a]	Tanganyika	153[a]
Dominican Republic	95[a]	Turkey	1,698
Ecuador	219[a]	Union of South Africa	243
Egypt	151[a]	United Kingdom	98,443[b]
France	29,858	United States of America	47,539[c]
French North Africa	1,563	Uruguay	594[a]
Guatemala	234[a]	Venezuela	14,091
Italy	176[a]	Miscellaneous[d]	603[a]
Mexico	257[a]	Not Reported	1,320[a]
Netherlands	4,065[a]		
New Zealand	95[a]	Total	451,886

SOURCE: *United States Relations With Organizational Organizations. III. The International Refugee Organization.* 81st Congress, 1st Session, Senate. Report No. 476. Committee on Expenditures In the Executive Departments. June 8, 1949. Appendix V. This table was prepared by the Department of State. It reflects the total number of displaced persons resettled since the end of World War II and includes displaced persons resettled prior to the commencement of IRO operations.

[a] Since July 1, 1947. Indicates either (a) lack of resettlement prior to that date, or (b) lack of statistics concerning such resettlement.

[b] Author's note: these figures are grossly exaggerated and indicate why the statistics furnished must be used with great caution. On November 2, 1947, *The New York Times* published a map entitled, "The Problem of Europe's DP's—Which Nations Will Take Them?" indicating that between 1945 and November, 1947, the United Kingdom had taken approximately 24,000 DPs and Canada had received about 3,000. Clipping, Herbert Hoover Presidential Library, Post-Presidential Files, Subject—Refugees.

[c] Of this number, approximately 44,000 persons were admitted under a presidential directive, dated Dec. 22, 1945, and other executive authority. Approximately 3,500 were admitted under the Displaced Persons Act of 1948 (Public Law 744, 80th Cong. 2d sess).

[d] Includes countries in which small numbers of refugees have been resettled.

Table A.9 Estimated DP Resettlement, June 30, 1949–June 30, 1951

	7-1-49 to 6-30-51 (percents)	7-1-47 to 6-30-51	1-1-51 to 6-30-51	7-1-50 to 12-30-50	1-1-50 to 6-30-50	7-1-49 to 12-30-49	as of 6-30-49
USA	29.1	302,500[a]	44,800	53,100	35,500	81,700	87,400[a]
Australia	17.0	176,100	16,700	13,600	41,600	50,200	54,000
Israel	13.1	136,000[b]	1,100	2,400	2,700	6,400	123,400[b]
Canada	10.9	112,700	14,700	8,600	9,600	11,200	68,600
United Kingdom	10.1	104,300	800	3,100	500	800	99,300
France	4.1	42,400	200	800	500	1,800	39,100
Belgium	3.4	35,700	200	100	500	100	35,200
Argentina	3.2	33,400	700	1,400	1,400	1,100	28,800
Brazil	2.7	28,500	1,300	800	800	3,300	22,300
Venezuela	1.8	19,200	1,000	1,700	1,100	1,100	14,300
Others & Not Reported	4.6	47,200	3,300	6,100	500	5,200	32,100
Totals	100.0	1,038,000	84,800	91,700	94,300	162,900	604,500

SOURCE: *The DPC Report*, August 1, 1949, p. 5, February 1, 1950, p. 6; August 1, 1950, p. 7, February 1, 1951, p. 7
[a] These include people admitted to the United States under the Truman Directive as well as those who arrived under the provisions of the 1948 DP Act.
[b] These include estimates of how many people went to Palestine after the war as well as those admitted to Israel after it became a state on May 14, 1948.

placed Persons Commission and Malcolm Proudfoot's book, *European Refugees*. Table A.10 shows the two sets of statistics. I am inclined to accept the lower figures reported by Proudfoot for the United Kingdom and Belgium. The beginnings of the IRO coincided with the efforts of these two nations to recruit DPs to fill severe labor shortages. Their efforts had mixed results since the sturdiest and best laborers were taken by most of the recruiting nations in 1947 and 1948. Thereafter these two countries chose fewer DPs for their labor markets. In addition, the male Balts selected by Belgium for coal mining were dissatisfied with working and living conditions and many chose to return to the displaced persons areas in Germany and Austria for a different placement. The passage of the DP Act of 1948 led to a massive exodus from the camps. The Balts, whom the Belgians and British both favored, found that entry to the United States was just as easy for them and they seemed to prefer it. Many Balts also chose to relocate in South America.

As the nations of the world started recruiting from the DP areas in 1947, the numbers of refugees cared for began to dwindle. Table A.11 shows the changing statistics as reported to the Displaced Persons Commission. The United States admitted 41,379 people under the Truman Directive and another 405,616 persons afterward. Table A.12 shows the division of people admitted as of June 30, 1952.

Table A.10 IRO RESETTLEMENT
July 1, 1947–December 31, 1951

	DPC[a]	*Proudfoot*[b]
USA	302,500	328,851
Australia	176,000	182,159
Israel	136,000	132,019
Canada	112,700	123,479
United Kingdom	104,300	86,346
France	43,400	38,455
Belgium	35,700	22,477
Argentina	33,400	32,712
Brazil	28,500	28,848
Venezuela	19,200	17,277
Others and not reported	47,200	—
Totals	1,038,900	992,623

[a] *The DPC Report*, August 1, 1951, p. 10
[b] Proudfoot, p. 425.

Table A.11 United Nations DPs in Western Zones in Germany,
Austria, and Italy

Date	In-camp	Out-of-camp	Total
Nov. 30, 1945	1,166,000[a]	—	—
Dec. 31, 1946	828,700	342,700	1,171,400
Nov. 30, 1947	637,800	325,400	963,200
Dec. 31, 1948	501,400	267,900	769,300
June 30, 1949	385,600	245,300	630,900
Dec. 31, 1949	271,200	146,600	417,800
June 30, 1950	209,700	148,400	358,100
Dec. 31, 1950	64,600	209,800	274,400
June 30, 1951	47,800	73,100	120,900

SOURCE: The DPC Report, August 1, 1949, p. 4, February 1, 1950, p. 3, August 1, 1950, p. 4, February 1, 1951, p. 5, August 1, 1951, p. 6.
[a] Does not include numbers in Allied military camps in Italy, nor the French zones of Austria.

Table A.12 Immigrants Admitted Under DP Act by Class of Admission
June 30, 1952

Class of Admission	Percent	Number
All immigrants	100.0	393,542
DPs	(85.7)	(337,244)
DPs from Western Germany, Austria, and Italy	78.0	306,785
Recent political refugees		162
Venezia Giulia refugees	.5	2,000
European DPs from Far East	.8	3,312
Ex-Polish soldiers from Great Britain	2.7	10,487
Native Greeks and preferentials	2.3	8,977
Out-of-zone refugees	1.4	5,521
German expellees	(13.6)	(53,448)
Orphans	(.7)	(2,838)
IRO orphans	.3	1,356
Greek orphans	.2	550
War orphans	.2	932
Adopted children of German Ethnic origin[a]	—	(12)

SOURCE: The DP Story, p. 366.
[a] Less than 1/20 of 1 percent.

Within the United States most of the displaced persons settled in the largest states, with about 30 percent of all of them going to New York, and three quarters of the latter remaining in New York City (see Table A.13).

Jews constituted about two-thirds of the DPs admitted under the Truman Directive, but only 16 percent of those who arrived under the DP Acts. The final totals generally reflected a closer approximation of the relative religious breakdowns in Europe than did the earlier statistics, primarily because most Jews resettled in 1948 and 1949, and most of those who could not get into the United States went to Israel. The religious percentages, according to DPC figures, looked like this for those whose religions were known are shown in table A.14.

All told, 137,450 Jews arrived in the United States between May 1945 and December 1952. Most qualified under the Truman Directive and the DP Acts of 1948 and 1950, but some came in under regular immigration quotas. Table A.15 show the breakdowns, as far as they are known, and the percentage that originally settled in the New York City area:

Tables A.15 and A.16 show occupational distributions of the DP breadwinners who reached the United States between October 1948 and the end of December 1951, and the age breakdown of the

Table A.13 DP Resettlement in the United States, in Percents

States[a]		Cities[b]	
New York	31.3	New York	24.3
Illinois	11.0	Chicago	7.8
Pennsylvania	7.3	Philadelphia	2.9
New Jersey	5.9	Detroit	2.7
Michigan	5.3	Cleveland	2.1
Ohio	5.1	Los Angeles	0.8
California	4.1	Pittsburgh	0.7
Massachusetts	3.3	Washington, D.C.	0.4
Connecticut	2.7	St. Louis	0.4
Wisconsin	2.3		
Total, May 31, 1952	78.2	Total, 1950 Census	43.2

[a] *The DP Story*, pp. 243, 367.
[b] Ibid., p. 244.

Table A.14 Religious Affiliations of DPs Who Arrived in the United States
October 30, 1948 to June 30, 1952, in Percents

	Catholic	Jewish	Protestant and Other
October 30, 1948 to			
March 22, 1949	41	40	11
February 17, 1950	46	26	26
December 31, 1950	45	21	34
June 30, 1952	47	16	35

SOURCE: Harry N. Rosenfield to Richard Arens, March 24, 1949, folder "Legislation—
1949," Ugo Carusi to Arens February 21, 1950, folder "Legislation—1940," box 22,
DPC Mss.; *The DPC Report*, February 1, 1951, p. 51; *The DP Story*, p. 248.

Table A.15 Postwar Jewish Immigration to the United States

Dates	Total	DPs	Non-DPs	To NYC Area	To Rest of Country	Percent NYC Area	Percent Rest of Country
1945:							
May–Dec.	4,000			2,800	1,200	70.0	30.0
1946	15,535			10,870	4,665	70.0	30.0
1947	25,885			18,116	7,769	70.0	30.0
1948	15,982			11,187	4,795	70.0	30.0
1949	37,700	31,381	6,319	20,571	17,129	54.6	45.4
1950	14,139	10,245	3,894	8,861	5,278	62.7	37.3
1951	16,973	13,580	3,393	8,416	8,557	49.6	50.4
1952	7,236	13,508	3,728	4,307	2,929	59.7	40.3
Totals							
1945–1952	137,450			85,128	52,322	62.0	28.0

SOURCE: *Third Annual Report*, folder, "New York Association for New Americans," p.
7, box 55, Kurt Grossman Mss., Leo Baeck Institute, New York City; folder, "USNA
Correspondence Misc. 1944–55," box 148, Central Jewish Federation and Welfare
Funds Mss., American Jewish Historical Society, Waltham, Mass.

Table A.16 Occupations of DPs Arriving in United States October
1948–December 1951

	Percents	
Occupational Group (Based on 1950 Census Classifications)	Sponsored occupation (1948–51)	Current occupation
Farmers and farm laborers	27.6	3.4
Private household workers	16.0	4.7
Laborers, except farm and mine	15.8	24.5
Operatives and kindred workers ("semiskilled")	14.5	30.6
Craftsmen, foremen, and kindred workers ("skilled")	10.2	13.7
Service workers, except private household	8.7	10.3
Clerical and kindred workers	3.4	3.7
Professional, technical, and kindred workers	2.6	6.5
Sales workers	0.8	0.8
Managers, officials and proprietors, except farm	0.4	1.8
Total	100.0	100.0

SOURCE: *The DP Story*, p. 372.

newcomers at the time of arrival, compared with those of similar age
distribution in the United States at the time. Table A.16 is important
because it indicates how few people originally classified as agricultural
workers actually remained in that occupation. Table A.17 points out
how few people born between 1933 and 1945 arrived in this country.
Another significant omission, since I have been unable to find the
necessary statistics, is the breakdown according to number of children
per ethnic group. If a considerable discrepancy could be shown, it
might suggest the nature of the wartime experiences of the different
peoples.

Table A.17 Ages of DPs on Arrival Compared with U.S. Population
(in Percents)[a] 1948–1951

All ages (years)	Immigrants under DP Act			U.S. Population		
	Both sexes 100.0	Males 54.4	Females 45.6	Both sexes 100.0	Males 49.5	Females 50.5
Under 5	12.6	6.5	6.1	10.8	5.5	5.3
5 to 9	6.4	3.2	3.2	8.8	4.5	4.3
10 to 14	5.0	2.6	2.4	7.6	3.8	3.8
15 to 19	5.5	2.9	2.6	7.1	3.5	3.6
20 to 24	8.4	4.0	4.4	7.5	3.6	3.9
25 to 29	14.1	7.1	7.0	8.0	3.9	4.1
30 to 34	9.7	5.6	4.1	7.7	3.8	3.9
35 to 39	10.4	6.5	3.9	7.4	3.6	3.8
40 to 44	8.8	5.4	3.4	6.7	3.3	3.4
45 to 49	6.7	3.9	2.8	6.0	3.0	3.0
50 to 54	5.4	3.1	2.3	5.5	2.7	2.8
55 to 59	3.3	1.9	1.4	4.8	2.4	2.4
60 to 64	1.8	1.0	.8	3.9	2.0	1.9
65 to 69	1.0	.4	.6	3.4	1.6	1.8
70 to 74	.5	.2	.3	2.3	1.1	1.2
75 and over	.4	.1	.3	2.5	1.2	1.3
Median age	29.3	30.8	27.9	30.1	29.9	30.4

SOURCES: In *The DP Story*, p. 368. From Displaced Persons Commission and the Department of Commerce.
[a] Percentages of U.S. Population adjusted to add to totals.

APPENDIX B

THE HARRISON REPORT

REPORT OF EARL G. HARRISON

Mission to Europe to inquire into the condition and needs of those among the displaced persons in the liberated countries of Western Europe and in the SHAEF area of Germany—with particular reference to the Jewish refugees—who may possibly be stateless or non-repatriable.

London, England

The President,
The White House,
Washington.
My Dear Mr. President:
Pursuant to your letter of June 22, 1945, I have the honor to present to you a partial report upon my recent mission to Europe to inquire into (1) the conditions under which displaced persons and particularly those who may be stateless or non-repatriable are at present living, especially in Germany and Austria, (2) the needs of such persons, (3) how those needs are being met at present by the military authorities, the governments of residence and international and private relief bodies, and (4) the views of the possibly non-repatriable persons as to their future destinations.

My instructions were to give particular attention to the problems, needs and views of the Jewish refugees among the displaced people, especially in Germany and Austria. The report, particularly this partial report, accordingly deals in the main with that group.

On numerous occasions appreciation was expressed by the victims of Nazi persecution for the interest of the United States Government in them. As my report shows they are in need of attention and help. Up to this point they have been "liberated" more in a military sense

The Department of State Bulletin (September 30, 1945), 13:456–63.

than actually. For reasons explained in the report, their particular problems, to this time, have not been given attention to any appreciable extent; consequently they feel that they, who were in so many ways the first and worst victims of Nazism, are being neglected by their liberators.

Upon my request, the Department of State authorized Dr. Joseph J. Schwartz to join me in the mission. Dr. Schwartz, European Director of the American Joint Distribution Committee, was granted a leave of absence from that organization for the purpose of accompanying me. His long and varied experience in refugee problems as well as his familiarity with the Continent and the people made Dr. Schwartz a most valuable associate; this report represents our joint views, conclusions and recommendations.

During various portions of the trip I had, also, the assistance of Mr. Patrick M. Malin, Vice Director of the Intergovernmental Committee on Refugees and Mr. Herbert Katzski of the War Refugee Board. These gentlemen, likewise, have had considerable experience in refugee maters. Their assistance and cooperation were most helpful in the course of the survey.

I. GERMANY AND AUSTRIA

CONDITIONS

(1) Generally speaking, three months after V–E Day and even longer after the liberation of individual groups, many Jewish displaced persons and other possibly non-repatriables are living under guard behind barbed-wire fences, in camps of several descriptions, (built by the Germans for slave-laborers and Jews) including some of the most notorious of the concentration camps, amidst crowded, frequently unsanitary and generally grim conditions, in complete idleness, with no opportunity, except surreptitiously, to communicate with the outside world, waiting, hoping for some word of encouragement and action in their behalf.

(2) While there has been marked improvement in the health of survivors of the Nazi starvation and persecution program, there are many pathetic malnutrition cases both among the hospitalized and in the general population of the camps. The death rate has been high since liberation, as was to be expected. One Army Chaplain, a Rabbi, personally attended, since liberation, 23,000 burials (90% Jews) at Bergen Belsen alone, one of the largest and most vicious of

the concentration camps, where, incidentally, despite persistent reports to the contrary, fourteen thousand displaced persons are still living, including over seven thousand Jews. At many of the camps and centers, including those where serious starvation cases are, there is a marked and serious lack of needed medical supplies.

(3) Although some Camp Commandants have managed, in spite of the many obvious difficulties, to find clothing of one kind or another for their charges, many of the Jewish displaced persons, late in July, had no clothing other than their concentration camp garb— a rather hideous striped pajama effect—while others, to their chagrin, were obliged to wear German S.S. uniforms. It is questionable which clothing they hate the more.

(4) With a few notable exceptions, nothing in the way of a program of activity or organized effort toward rehabilitation has been inaugurated and the internees, for they are literally such, have little to do except to dwell upon their plight, the uncertainty of their future and, what is more unfortunate, to draw comparisons between their treatment "under the Germans" and "in liberation". Beyond knowing that they are no longer in danger of the gas chambers, torture, and other forms of violent death, they see—and there is—little change. The morale of those who are either stateless or who do not wish to return to their countries of nationality is very low. They have witnessed great activity and efficiency in returning people to their homes but they hear or see nothing in the way of plans for them and consequently they wonder and frequently ask what "liberation" means. This situation is considerably accentuated where, as in so many cases, they are able to look from their crowded and bare quarters and see the German civilian population, particularly in the rural areas, to all appearances living normal lives in their own homes.

(5) The most absorbing worry of these Nazi and war victims concerns relatives—wives, husbands, parents, children. Most of them have been separated for three, four or five years and they cannot understand why the liberators should not have undertaken immediately the organized effort to re-unite family groups. Most of the very little which has been done in this direction has been informal action by the displaced persons themselves with the aid of devoted Army Chaplains, frequently Rabbis, and the American Joint Distribution Committee. Broadcasts of names and locations by the Psychological Warfare Division at Luxembourg have been helpful, although the lack of receiving sets has handicapped the effectiveness of the program. Even where, as has been happening, information has been

received as to relatives living in other camps in Germany, it depends on the personal attitude and disposition of the Camp Commandant whether permission can be obtained or assistance received to fellow up on the information. Some Camp Commandants are quite rigid in this particular, while others lend every effort to join family groups.

(6) It is difficult to evaluate the food situation fairly because one must be mindful of the fact that quite generally food is scarce and is likely to be more so during the winter ahead. On the other hand, in presenting the factual situation, one must raise the question as to how much longer many of these people, particularly those who have over such a long period felt persecution and near starvation, can survive on a diet composed principally of bread and coffee, irrespective of the caloric content. In many camps, the 2,000 calories included 1,250 calories of a black, wet and extremely unappetizing bread. I received the distinct impression and considerable substantiating information that large numbers of the German population— again principally in the rural areas—have a more varied and palatable diet than is the case with the displaced persons. The Camp Commandants put in their requisitions with the German burgomeister and many seemed to accept whatever he turned over as being the best that was available.

(7) Many of the buildings in which displaced persons are housed are clearly unfit for winter use and everywhere there is great concern about the prospect of a complete lack of fuel. There is every likelihood that close to a million displaced persons will be in Germany and Austria when winter sets in. The outlook in many areas so far as shelter, food and fuel are concerned is anything but bright.

II. NEEDS OF THE JEWS

While it is impossible to state accurately the number of Jews now in that part of Germany not under Russian occupation, all indications point to the fact that the number is small, with one hundred thousand probably the top figure; some informed persons contend the number is considerably smaller. The principal nationality groups are Poles, Hungarians, Rumanians, Germans and Austrians.

The first and plainest need of these people is a recognition of their actual status and by this I mean their status as Jews. Most of them have spent years in the worst of the concentration camps. In many cases, although the full extent is not yet known, they are the sole survivors of their families and many have been through the agony of witnessing the destruction of their loved ones. Understandably, therefore, their present condition, physical and mental, is far worse than that of other groups.

While SHAEF (now Combined Displaced Persons Executive) policy directives have recognized formerly persecuted persons, including enemy and ex-enemy nationals, as one of the special categories of displaced persons, the general practice thus far has been to follow only nationality lines. While admittedly it is not normally desirable to set aside particular racial or religious groups from their nationality categories, the plain truth is that this was done for so long by the Nazis that a group has been created which has special needs. Jews as Jews (not as members of their nationality groups) have been more severely victimized than the non-Jewish members of the same or other nationalities.

When they are now considered only as members of nationality groups, the result is that special attention cannot be given to their admittedly greater needs because, it is contended, doing so would constitute preferential treatment and lead to trouble with the non-Jewish portion of the particular nationality group.

Thus there is a distinctly unrealistic approach to the problem. Refusal to recognize the Jews as such has the effect, in this situation, of closing one's eyes to their former and more barbaric persecution, which has already made them a separate group with greater needs.

Their second great need can be presented only by discussing what I found to be their

WISHES AS TO FUTURE DESTINATIONS

(1) For reasons that are obvious and need not be labored, most Jews want to leave Germany and Austria as soon as possible. That is their first and great expressed wish and while this report necessarily deals with other needs present in the situation, many of the people themselves fear other suggestions or plans for their benefit because of the possibility that attention might thereby be diverted from the all-important matter of evacuation from Germany. Their desire to leave Germany is an urgent one. The life which they have led for the past ten years, a life of fear and wandering and physical torture, has made them impatient of delay. They want to be evacuated to Palestine now, just as other national groups are being repatriated to their

homes. They do not look kindly on the idea of waiting around in idleness and in discomfort in a German camp for many months until a leisurely solution is found for them.

(2) Some wish to return to their countries of nationality but as to this there is considerable nationality variation. Very few Polish or Baltic Jews wish to return to their countries; higher percentages of the Hungarian and Rumanian groups want to return although some hasten to add that it may be only temporarily in order to look for relatives. Some of the German Jews, especially those who have intermarried, prefer to stay in Germany.

(3) With respect to possible places of resettlement for those who may be stateless or who do not wish to return to their homes, Palestine is definitely and pre-eminently the first choice. Many now have relatives there, while others, having experienced intolerance and persecution in their homelands for years, feel that only in Palestine will they be welcomed and find peace and quiet and be given an opportunity to live and work. In the case of the Polish and the Baltic Jews, the desire to go to Palestine is based in a great majority of the cases on a love for the country and devotion to the Zionist ideal. It is also true, however, that there are many who wish to go to Palestine because they realize that their opportunity to be admitted into the United States or into other countries in the Western hemisphere is limited, if not impossible. Whatever the motive which causes them to turn to Palestine, it is undoubtedly true that the great majority of the Jews now in Germany do not wish to return to those countries from which they came.

(4) Palestine, while clearly the choice of most, is not the only named place of possible emigration. Some, but the number is not large, wish to emigrate to the United States where they have relatives, others to England, the British Dominions, or to South America.

Thus the second great need is the prompt development of a plan to get out of Germany and Austria as many as possible of those who wish it.

Otherwise the needs and wishes of the Jewish groups among the displaced persons can be simply stated: among their physical needs are clothing and shoes (most sorely needed), more varied and palatable diet, medicines, beds and mattresses, reading materials. The clothing for the camps too is requisitioned from the German population, and whether there is not sufficient quantity to be had or the German population has not been willing or has not been compelled to give up sufficient quantity, the internees feel particularly bitter about the state of their clothing when they see how well the German population is still dressed. The German population today is still the best dressed population in all of Europe.

III. MANNER IN WHICH NEEDS ARE BEING MET

Aside from having brought relief from the fear of extermination, hospitalization for the serious starvation cases and some general improvement in conditions under which the remaining displaced persons are compelled to live, relatively little beyond the planning stage has been done, during the period of mass repatriation, to meet the special needs of the formerly persecuted groups.

UNRRA, being neither sufficiently organized or equipped nor authorized to operate displaced persons camps or centers on any large scale, has not been in position to make any substantial contribution to the situation. Regrettably there has been a disinclination on the part of many Camp Commandants to utilize UNRRA personnel even to the extent available, though it must be admitted that in many situations this resulted from unfortunate experiences Army officers had with UNRRA personnel who were unqualified and inadequate for the responsibility involved. Then, too, in the American and British zones, it too frequently occurred that UNRRA personnel did not include English-speaking members and this hampered proper working relationships.

Under these circumstances, UNRRA, to which has been assigned the responsibility for co-ordinating activities of private social welfare agencies, has been in awkward position when it came to considering and acting upon proposals of one kind or another submitted by well qualified agencies which would aid and supplement military and UNRRA responsibilities. The result has been that, up to this point, very few private social agencies are working with displaced persons, including the Jews, although the situation cries out for their services in many different ways.

It must be said, too, that because of their preoccupation with mass repatriation and because of housing, personnel and transport difficulties, the military authorities have shown considerable resistance to the entrance of voluntary agency representatives, no matter how qualified they might be to help meet existing needs of displaced persons.

IV. CONCLUSIONS AND RECOMMENDATIONS

1. Now that the worst of the pressure of mass repatriation is over, it is not unreasonable to suggest that in the next and perhaps more difficult period those who have suffered most and longest be given first and not last attention.

Specifically, in the days immediately ahead, the Jews in Germany and Austria should have the first claim upon the conscience of the people of the United States and Great Britain and the military and other personnel who represent them in work being done in Germany and Austria.

2. Evacuation from Germany should be the emphasized theme, policy and practice.

(a) Recognizing that repatriation is most desirable from the standpoint of all concerned, the Jews who wish to return to their own countries should be aided to do so without further delay. Whatever special action is needed to accomplish this with respect to countries of reception or consent of military or other authorities should be undertaken with energy and determination. Unless this and other action, about to be suggested, is taken, substantial unofficial and unauthorized movements of people must be expected, and these will require considerable force to prevent, for the patience of many of the persons involved is, and in my opinion with justification, nearing the breaking point. It cannot be overemphasized that many of these people are now desperate, that they have become accustomed under German rule to employ every possible means to reach their end, and that the fear of death does not restrain them.

(b) With respect to those who do not, for good reason, wish to return to their homes, prompt planning should likewise be undertaken. In this connection, the issue of Palestine must be faced. Now that such large numbers are no longer involved and if there is any genuine sympathy for what these survivors have endured, some reasonable extension or modification of the British White Paper of 1939 ought to be possible without too serious repercussions. For some of the European Jews, there is no acceptable or even decent solution for their future other than Palestine. This is said on a purely humanitarian basis with no reference to ideological or political considerations so far as Palestine is concerned.

It is my understanding, based upon reliable information, that certificates for immigration to Palestine will be practically exhausted by the end of the current month (August 1945). What is the future to be? To anyone who has visited the concentration camps and who has talked with the despairing survivors, it is nothing short of calamitous to contemplate that the gates of Palestine should be soon closed.

The Jewish Agency of Palestine has submitted to the British Government a petition that one hundred thousand additional immigration certificates be made available. A memorandum accompanying the petition makes a persuasive showing with respect to the immediate absorptive capacity of Palestine and the current, actual man-power shortages there.

While there may be room for difference of opinion as to the precise number of such certificates which might under the circumstances be considered reasonable, there is no question but that the request thus made would, if granted, contribute much to the sound solution for the future of Jews still in Germany and Austria and even other displaced Jews, who do not wish either to remain there or to return to their countries of nationality.

No other single matter is, therefore, so important from the viewpoint of Jews in Germany and Austria and those elsewhere who have known the horrors of the concentration camps as is the disposition of the Palestine question.

Dr. Hugh Dalton, a prominent member of the new British Government, is reported as having said at the Labour Party Conference in May 1945:

"This Party has laid it down and repeated it so recently as last April . . . that this time, having regard to the unspeakable horrors that have been perpetrated upon the Jews of Germany and other occupied countries in Europe, it is morally wrong and politically indefensible to impose obstacles to the entry into Palestine now of any Jews who desire to go there. . . .

"We also have stated clearly that this is not a matter which should be regarded as one for which the British Government alone should take responsibility; but as it comes, as do many others, in the international field, it is indispensable that there should be close agreement and cooperation among the British, American and Soviet Governments, particularly if we are going to get a sure settlement in Palestine and the surrounding countries. . . ."

If this can be said to represent the viewpoint of the new Government in Great Britain, it certainly would not be inappropriate for the United States Government to express its interest in and support of some equitable solution of the question which would make it possible for some reasonable number of Europe's persecuted Jews, now homeless under any fair view, to resettle in Palestine. That is their wish and it is rendered desirable by the generally-accepted policy of permitting family groups to unite or reunite.

(c) The United States should, under existing immigration laws, permit reasonable numbers of such persons to come here, again particularly those who have family ties in this country. As indicated earlier, the number who desire emigration to the United States is not large.

If Great Britain and the United States were to take the actions recited, it might the more readily be that other countries would likewise be willing to keep their doors reasonably open for such humanitarian considerations and to demonstrate in a practical manner their disapproval of Nazi policy which unfortunately has poisoned so much of Europe.

3. To the extent that such emigration from Germany and Austria is delayed, some immediate temporary solution must be found. In any event there will be a substantial number of the persecuted persons who are not physically fit or otherwise presently prepared for emigration.

Here I feel strongly that greater and more extensive efforts should be made to get them out of camps for they are sick of living in camps. In the first place, there is real need for such specialized places as (a) tuberculosis sanitaria and (b) rest homes for those who are mentally ill or who need a period of readjustment before living again in the world at large—anywhere. Some will require at least short periods of training or retraining before they can be really useful citizens.

But speaking more broadly, there is an opportunity here to give some real meaning to the policy agreed upon at Potsdam. If it be true, as seems to be widely conceded, that the German people at large do not have any sense of guilt with respect to the war and its causes and results, and if the policy is to be "To convince the German people that they have suffered a total military defeat and that they cannot escape responsibility for what they have brought upon themselves," then it is difficult to understand why so many displaced persons, particularly those who have so long been persecuted and whose repatriation or resettlement is likely to be delayed, should be compelled to live in crude, over-crowded camps while the German people, in rural areas, continue undisturbed in their homes.

As matters now stand, we appear to be treating the Jews as the

Nazis treated them except that we do not exterminate them. They are in concentration camps in large numbers under our military guard instead of S.S. troops. One is led to wonder whether the German people, seeing this, are not supposing that we are following or at least condoning Nazi policy.

It seems much more equitable and as it should be to witness the very few places where fearless and uncompromising military officers have either requisitioned an entire village for the benefit of displaced persons, compelling the German population to find housing where they can, or have required the local population to billet a reasonable number of them. Thus the displaced persons, including the persecuted, live more like normal people and less like prisoners or criminals or herded sheep. They are in Germany, most of them and certainly the Jews, through no fault or wish of their own. This fact is in this fashion being brought home to the German people but it is being done on too small a scale.

At many places, however, the military government officers manifest the utmost reluctance or indisposition, if not timidity, about inconveniencing the German population. They even say that their job is to get communities working properly and soundly again, that they must "live with the Germans while the dps (displaced persons) are a more temporary problem". Thus (and I am ready to cite the example) if a group of Jews are ordered to vacate their temporary quarters, needed for military purposes, and there are two possible sites, one a block of flats (modest apartments) with coveniences and the other a series of shabby buildings with outside toilet and washing facilities, the burgomeister readily succeeds in persuading the Town Major to allot the latter to the displaced persons and to save the former for returning German civilians.

This tendency reflects itself in other ways, namely, in the employment of German civilians in the offices of military government officers when equally qualified personnel could easily be found among the displaced persons whose repatriation is not imminent. Actually there have been situations where displaced persons, especially Jews, have found it difficult to obtain audiences with military government authorities because ironically they have been obliged to go through German employees who have not facilitated matters.

Quite generally, insufficient use is made of the services of displaced persons. Many of them are able and eager to work but apparently they are not considered in this regard. While appreciating that language difficulties are sometimes involved, I am convinced that, both within and outside camps, greater use could be made of the personal services of those displaced persons who in all likelihood will be on hand for some time. Happily in some camps every effort is made to utilize the services of the displaced persons and these are apt to be the best camps in all respects.

4. To the extent that (a) evacuation from Germany and Austria is not immediately possible and (b) the formerly persecuted groups cannot be housed in villages or billeted with the German population, I recommend urgently that separate camps be set up for Jews or at least for those who wish, in the absence of a better solution, to be in such camps. There are several reasons for this: (1) a great majority want it; (2) it is the only way in which administratively their special needs and problems can be met without charges of preferential treatment or (oddly enough) charges of "discrimination" with respect to Jewish agencies now prepared and ready to give them assistance.

In this connection, I wish to emphasize that it is not a case of singling out a particular group for special privileges. It is a matter of raising to a more normal level the position of a group which has been depressed to the lowest depths conceivable by years of organized and inhuman oppression. The measures necessary for their restitution do not come within any reasonable interpretation of privileged treatment and are required by considerations of justice and humanity.

There has been some tendency at spots in the direction of separate camps for those who might be found to be stateless or non-repatriable or whose repatriation is likely to be deferred some time. Actually, too, this was announced some time ago as SHAEF policy but in practice it has not been taken to mean much for there is (understandably if not carried too far) a refusal to contemplate possible statelessness and an insistence, in the interests of the large repatriation program, to consider all as repatriable. This results in a resistance to anything in the way of special planning for the "hard core", although all admit it is there and will inevitably appear. While speaking of camps, this should be pointed out: While it may be that conditions in Germany and Austria are still such that certain control measures are required, there seems little justification for the continuance of barbed-wire fences, armed guards, and prohibition against leaving the camp except by passes, which at some places are illiberally granted. Prevention of looting is given as the reason for these stern measures but it is interesting that in portions of the Seventh Army area where greater liberty of movement in and out of camps is given there is actually much less plundering than in other areas where people, wishing to leave camp temporarily, must do so by stealth.

5. As quickly as possible, the actual operation of such camps should be turned over to a civilian agency—UNRRA. That organization is aware of weaknesses in its present structure and is pressing to remedy them. In that connection, it is believed that greater assistance could be given by the military authorities, upon whom any civilian agency in Germany and Austria today is necessarily dependent so far as housing, transport and other items are concerned. While it is true the military have been urging UNRRA to get ready to assume responsibility, it is also the fact that insufficient cooperation of an active nature has been given to accomplish the desired end.

6. Since, in any event, the military authorities must necessarily continue to participate in the program for all displaced persons, especially with respect to housing, transport, security, and certain supplies, it is recommended that there be a review of the military personnel selected for Camp Commandant positions. Some serving at present, while perhaps adequate for the mass repatriation job, are manifestly unsuited for the longer-term job of working in a camp composed of people whose repatriation or resettlement is likely to be delayed. Officers who have had some background or experience in social welfare work are to be preferred and it is believed there are some who are available. It is most important that the officers selected be sympathetic with the program and that they be temperamentally able to work and to cooperate with UNRRA and other relief and welfare agencies.

7. Pending the assumption of responsibility for operations by UNRRA, it would be desirable if a more extensive plan of field visitation by appropriate Army Group Headquarters be instituted. It is believed that many of the conditions now existing in the camps would not be tolerated if more intimately known by supervisory officers through inspection tours.

8. It is urgently recommended that plans for tracing services, now under consideration, be accelerated to the fullest extent possible and that, in this same direction, communication services, if on open postal cards only, be made available to displaced persons within Germany and Austria as soon as possible. The difficulties are appreciated but it is believed that if the anxiety of the people, so long abused and harassed, were fully understood, ways and means could be found

within the near future to make such communication and tracing of relatives possible. I believe also that some of the private agencies could be helpful in this direction if given an opportunity to function.

V. OTHER COMMENTS

While I was instructed to report conditions as I found them, the following should be added to make the picture complete:

(1) A gigantic task confronted the occupying armies in Germany and Austria in getting back to their homes as many as possible of the more than six million displaced persons found in those countries. Less than three months after V–E Day, more than four million of such persons have been repatriated—a phenomenal performance. One's first impression, in surveying the situation, is that of complete admiration for what has been accomplished by the military authorities in so materially reducing the time as predicted to be required for this stupendous task. Praise of the highest order is due all military units with respect to this phase of the post-fighting job. In directing attention to existing conditions which unquestionably require remedying, there is no intention or wish to detract one particle from the preceding statements.

(2) While I did not actually see conditions as they existed immediately after liberation I had them described in detail sufficient to make entirely clear that there has been, during the intervening period, some improvement in the conditions under which most of the remaining displaced persons are living. Reports which have come out of Germany informally from refugees themselves and from persons interested in refugee groups indicate something of a tendency not to take into account the full scope of the overwhelming task and responsibilities facing the military authorities. While it is understandable that those who have been persecuted and otherwise mistreated over such a long period should be impatient at what appears to them to be undue delay in meeting their special needs, fairness dictates that, in evaluating the progress made, the entire problem and all of its ramifications be kept in mind. My effort has been, therefore, to weigh quite carefully the many complaints made to me in the course of my survey, both by displaced persons themselves and in their behalf, in the light of the many responsibilities which confronted the military authorities.

(3) While for the sake of brevity this report necessarily consisted largely of general statements, it should be recognized that exceptions

exist with respect to practically all of such generalizations. One high ranking military authority predicted, in advance of my trip through Germany and Austria, that I would find, with respect to camps containing displaced persons, "some that are quite good, some that are very bad, with the average something under satisfactory". My subsequent trip confirmed that prediction in all respects.

In order to file this report promptly so that possibly some remedial steps might be considered at as early a date as possible, I have not taken time to analyze all of the notes made in the course of the trip or to comment on the situation in France, Belgium, Holland or Switzerland, also visited. Accordingly, I respectfully request that this report be considered as partial in nature. The problems present in Germany and Austria are much more serious and difficult than in any of the other countries named and this fact, too, seemed to make desirable the filing of a partial report immediately upon completion of the mission.

In conclusion, I wish to repeat that the main solution, in many ways the only real solution, of the problem lies in the quick evacuation of all nonrepatriable Jews in Germany and Austria, who wish it, to Palestine. In order to be effective, this plan must not be long delayed. The urgency of the situation should be recognized. It is inhuman to ask people to continue to live for any length of time under their present conditions. The evacuation of the Jews of Germany and Austria to Palestine will solve the problem of the individuals involved and will also remove a problem from the military authorities who have had to deal with it. The army's ability to move millions of people quickly and efficiently has been amply demonstrated. The evacuation of a relatively small number of Jews from Germany and Austria will present no great problem to the military. With the end of the Japanese War, the shipping situation should also become sufficiently improved to make such a move feasible. The civilized world owes it to this handful of survivors to provide them with a home where they can again settle down and begin to live as human beings.

Respectfully,
Earl G. Harrison

APPENDIX C

"ARMY TALK"

The following publication on "Displaced Persons," issued by the United States Army for use by troops in Europe, is indicative of the type of material distributed by the War Department in an effort to improve the troops' understanding of the plight and backgrounds of the displaced persons.

WAR DEPARTMENT, WASHINGTON 25, D. C.
30 NOVEMBER 1946

ARMY TALK

151

Note to Discussion Leader:

This ARMY TALK deals with the important subject of Displaced Persons—D. P.'s—and the reasons why American military personnel should adopt a sympathetic attitude in their official and unofficial dealings with Displaced Persons. The discussion group should be made thoroughly aware of the rigors, hardships, and brutalities suffered by Displaced Persons at the hands of the Nazis. The brutalities practiced upon Displaced Persons were two of the five counts in Justice Jackson's summation of the charges leveled against the Nazi hierarchy at the Nuremberg War Crimes Trials. Discussion leaders should emphasize that the overwhelming majority of Displaced Persons are nationals of our former allies, and that now, more than ever, there is need for clear and correct thinking when our military personnel meet Displaced Persons. The pictorial material is for your use to emphasize graphically the number of persons involved. The map should be enlarged so that the discussion group may see it to advantage.

DISPLACED PERSONS

Europe's Displaced Persons have been moving about for years in the most tremendous population dislocation in all recorded history. To restore as many of them as possible to health and sanity, to make them self-supporting, to give them confidence in the future, to return them to their native lands with the physical means for economic, social, and religious

The job of human salvage.

rehabilitation, has been the most tremendous job of human salvage ever
to be attempted.

Where do soldiers meet D. P.'s?

In Germany, American military personnel—on and off duty—will meet   **Where D. P.'s are met.**
the D. P.'s in motor pools, kitchens, road gangs, special communities and
cantonments, in hospitals, service centers, and in the cities and towns.

What caused Displaced Persons?

Technically, scientifically, and psychologically, the Nazis planned World   **The Nazi plan**
War II so that at the end of the war Germans would be the strongest
physically, and mentally the most alert civilian population in all of continental Europe. Fundamentally a nation is as strong as its people, and the
greatest ruin in Europe was not the wreckage of cities, not the burned and
scorched forests and earth, not the twisted and scarred bridges and
railroads, not the gutted shambles of factories, mills, and mines—it was   **Europe's greatest ruin—**
the human wreckage systematically produced in Nazi-occupied and dom-   **human beings.**
inated Europe.

After 6 years of the world's most brutal war, most of the peoples of
Europe were clad in rags.

For countless millions there was no future but that of cold, exposure,   **Cold, exposure, and starvation.**
starvation, and death.

And the only role that others would play would be that of companions   **Famine and pestilence.**
of the Pale Horseman—carriers of famine and pestilence.

How many D. P.'s were there in the beginning?

From 1933 to 1945, in the 13 years that Germany terrorized Europe,   **The history of Displaced Persons**
people packed the highways carrying their household effects in crazy   **began in 1933.**
bundles that they abandoned as they fled across borders, across rivers,
through forests, over mountains. They moved at night, in fog, rain, and
snow, whenever the weather was at its worst, for then it was safest to travel.
Men and women, old and young, this human flotsam and jetsam swept
along, forever fleeing from the Nazis—but few escaped from Nazi-domi-
nated Europe.

When it all started in 1933, they were only a few hundred thousand, but
by the time Germany had met defeat, no one could more than venture a
guess at what constituted the total number during the years.

The strength on V-E Day was approximately thirty million Displaced   **Number of D. P.'s on V-E Day**
Persons in Europe. This number was equal to 23 percent of the United   **equaled 23 percent of United States**
States population. Just imagine then that 23 percent of Americans were   **population.**
forcibly moved from their homes—it would include the people of virtually
all of the western half of the United States.

No one knows the fate of all the wanderers. The world is only dimly
aware of the significance of the Lidices, the Maidenecks, and the Belsens
to the total picture. Deliberate murder of nations is known as genocide—
and to the mastering of this technique the Nazis applied all of their
thoroughness, efficiency, industrial know-how, and scientific methodology.

Population of shaded area represents original number of Displaced Persons in Europe on V-E Day.

The pattern widened in 1939 as Poland fell, as the Balkans were invaded by the Nazis and Italians, as the quislings and fifth columnists in Nazi-occupied Scandinavian countries began to persecute minorities and to lure and deport slave labor to Germany.

The pattern widens.

Thus millions of persons were dispersed throughout continental Europe; not haphazardly, but with the precise technique of the Nazis. Czechs were sent to Norway; Norwegians to Germany; Netherlanders to the Ukraine; Greeks to France; Frenchmen to Poland; Belgians to the Rhineland; Italians to Yugoslavia; Yugoslavs to Italy.

They were scattered.

Nearly 2½ million Russians, who have been accounted for, were deported as slave laborers or prisoners to almost every part of Europe.

There were persons of other nationalities: Chinese, Albanians, Portuguese, Syrians, South Americans, Swiss, people whose devious routes across the unfriendly continent were lost in the fury of movement. They, too, were found in the concentration camps, in the slave labor battalions.

More nationalities involved.

The majority of Europe's Displaced Persons are not Jews. On V-E Day, Jews were a little more than 3 percent of the 30 million Displaced Persons in Europe. At the present time they comprise approximately 28 percent of the total number remaining.

Majority of D. P.'s are not Jews.

The Civil Affairs Division of the War Department has grouped Displaced Persons in the following major classifications:

Categories of Displaced Persons.

1. *United Nations Displaced Persons*: The millions of United Nations citizens who were held in Nazi prisons and concentration camps within Germany and Nazi-occupied territories. This includes slave laborers and populations moved from their homes by

Figure C.1. If the Number of Displaced Persons on V–E Were in the United States, Their Numbers Would Have Equaled the 1945 Population of the Shaded Area on the Map. (*Army Talk*, U.S. War Department [November 30, 1946], no. 151)

order of the *Wehrmacht*. It also includes
prisoners of war held by the Nazis.

2. *Persecutees*: Persons persecuted because of race, religion, or political belief or activities in favor of the United Nations.

3. *Stateless Persons*: Persons who, in law or fact, lack the protection of any government.

4. *Refugees*: German civilians located in Germany, who, by reasons of the war, are either temporarily homeless or distant from their home.

5. *Expellees*: Persons of German descent who are being or who have been deported from areas in new Poland, Czechoslovakia, Austria, and Hungary, and who are to be resettled in Germany. This category also includes Axis civilians who were in United Nations' territory on V-E Day.

What was the American soldiers' first reaction to D. P.'s?

Our troops came across the Mediterranean Sea and across the English Channel to fight their way through Italy, France, Belgium, and Holland, through the shattered and crumbling remains of cities, towns, and villages. We were dirty but we met people who were dirtier, who were disease-ridden and starving, who grubbed in garbage cans for our waste, and who smelled like the holes in which they existed.

Our troops breach "Fortress Europe."

But we saw and understood the reasons for the dirt, disease, filth, and squalor. The American soldier offered his strength, his assistance, his kindness, his rations, clothing, and medicine—and to millions of unfortunates this was the first kindness, the first humane act, that had been extended to them in ten or more years.

The American soldier understood.

As the Allied Armies thrust toward Germany, the tide of liberated displaced persons swelled from hundreds to thousands and finally to 30 million. As the Germans fled toward Berlin the liberated persons began to move in wild disorder toward their homelands.

The Allies enter Germany.

Wild disorder.

What was reaction of replacements?

Then most of the soldiers who had experienced combat were redeployed to the United States in the fall of 1945 and the spring of 1946. Fresh American military personnel, who had just left the solid, clean and substantial comforts of our fine homes and towns, arrived in Europe and Germany. Their understanding of the results of the many forces that had been at work in Europe over the several preceding years, naturally was limited.

New military replacements enter Germany

The new GI's found it difficult to understand and like people who pushed, screamed, clawed for food, smelled bad, who couldn't and didn't want to obey orders, who sat with dull faces and vacant staring eyes in a cellar, or concentration camp barrack, or within a primitive cave, and refused to come out at their command.

D. P.'s did not make good impression.

When people are reduced to the animal level their reaction to suggestion and situations is on that level. When some of the Displaced Persons were liberated they gave first priority to retaliation against their one-time masters rather than to cooperation with the Allied civil affairs authorities. Thus, in later months, when American soldiers compared the law-and-order attitude of the Germans with the lawlessness of some Displaced Persons, their attitude toward Displaced Persons was not improved. They failed to make the essential distinction between a people disciplined in defeat and these

Slave labor retaliation.

The GI reaction.

others, most of whom might property hope to be treated as friends and allies.

What are some of the reasons why Displaced Persons are not efficient workers?

A United States Senate report of conditions in Nazi-controlled concentration camps (Senate Document No. 47, 79th Congress, 15 May 1945) revealed that the inmates received a daily food ration of 500 to 700 calories per day. The first daily meal consisted of a cabbage or other leaf vegetable soup and a 3-inch square of bread.

(The discussion leader should have a 3-inch square of cardboard to illustrate the size of this bread ration.)

The second daily meal consisted of another 3-inch square of bread.

There were no meats, fats, fresh fruits, or vegetables.

Red Cross food packages which were sent to the camps to supplement the prisoners' diets often were confiscated by the camp commanding officers and distributed to SS personnel.

A report concerning a Nazi internment camp published in *News Digest* on 17 January 1945, states in part as follows:

". . . . I acted as interpreter in the factory. . . . We worked from 0700 to 1800 hours with a half-hour's rest at noon. Our meals consisted of bread with a little butter or lard, soup with roots or other vegetables, never any meat although we were entitled to some occasionally. The food was quite insufficient considering the long hours of trying work; hence we suffered from undernourishment and consequent diseases. The number of sick workers was very large but no leave was granted unless the worker fainted, which happened daily. . . ."

The average caloric ration for slave laborers was 1200 to 1500 per day, and this did not constitute all the elements of a balanced diet.

On 7 March 1946, *The New York Times* reported the findings of Dr. Ancil Keys, Director of the Physiology Laboratory at the University of Minnesota, where he had supervised a study in human starvation. Thirty volunteers were fed a low protein diet of 1,700 calories a day for a period of 6 months.

Each volunteer lost 40 percent of his body weight. When he reached this weight loss, starvation set in. Hearts shrank in size and all the volunteers displayed psychoneurotic symptoms. Dr Keys concluded that the tests proved that a year of balanced diet ranging from 2,700 to 3,600 calories per day would be necessary to restore those persons, and the systematically starved persons of Europe, to health.

But Dr. Keys' volunteers received 1,700 calories per day and did *not* work. Slave laborers worked a minimum of 11 hours per day on 1,500 calories; persons in concentration camps received a maximum of 700 calories per day.

In the United States moderately active military personnel receive a minimum diet of 3,600 calories per day. In oversea theaters active troops receive a minimum of 3,900 calories per day.

Fritz Sauckel, recently executed Nazi plenipotentiary general for the utilization of labor, and one of the defendants at the Nuremberg War Crimes Trials, was authority for the statement that "out of five million foreign workers who arrived in Germany, not even 200,000 came voluntarily." It was officially reported to defendant Alfred Rosenberg, who also was executed, that in his territory "recruiting methods were used which probably have their origin in the blackest period of the slave trade. . . ."

There is little wonder that the resultant product of this systematic starvation and enforced slavery should present a picture of apathy, chronic weakness, lack of coordination, and warped mentality.

Are all Displaced Persons disorderly or criminal?

It is unnecessary to whitewash the D. P.'s who commit misdemeanors and felonies. Crime is always a cause for concern, and there never has been a valid excuse for lawlessness.

The Displaced Person and crime.

D. P.'s who steal food, military supplies, patronize the black market, assault German civilians, and commit other breaches of good conduct must be apprehended and punished. But we must be aware of three points:

1. The D. P.'s have lived within a lawless atmosphere for many years.

Why some D. P.'s are lawbreakers.

2. Some of them have lived only for revenge, and now lack the emotional balance of those who have not shared their experiences.

3. The destructive and criminal element among the D. P.'s is only a small percentage of the D. P. population.

Most Displaced Persons attempt to cooperate with our military government in the occupied zones of Europe, and they themselves do not condone the lawless activities of their nationals. However, the man who is law-abiding seldom comes to our attention, whereas, the lawbreaker often does. We are not reasoning logically if we condemn large groups of people because of the illegal activities of a small minority.

Most Displaced Persons cooperate with our officials.

Lawbreakers stand out

Are there any other reasons why D. P.'s refuse to work?

In Germany we found destroyed cities that the Germans were rebuilding energetically. Germany is their homeland: Their goal is definite—to repair and rebuild.

Why Germans work.

But the Displaced Persons cannot understand why they should perform any work by which Germany may benefit directly or indirectly. Germany was a nation that attempted to enslave them. The Displaced Persons are in a land which has been and still is unfriendly to them. It is well nigh impossible to persuade the D. P.'s that Germany is worthy of any rehabilitory assistance.

The D. P.'s do not want to rebuild Germany.

Many of the Displaced Persons properly feel that we are forgetful of the more than a decade of suffering, disease, starvation, and death that they have endured because they believed and fought for the right to live decently, in the democratic manner.

The D. P.'s resent our forgetfulness of their suffering.

What has been done to help the D. P.'s?

The job of human salvage and rehabilitation had to start from scratch. We were working with people that somehow had resisted all the brutality and cruelty of a nation that had deliberately planned their exploitation or slaughter. Now they are husks of people; they have lost hope, distrust everyone, have neither will nor strength; they are people bereft of human dignity. Our Army worked unceasingly against time to save as many as possible of these unfortunates. Reception areas were organized and thou-

Starting from scratch.

sands of rest homes were established. Health and welfare services, as important as food and shelter, were disbursed. Approximately 22,000 Displaced Persons a month continue to receive extensive medical care and hospitalization.

Medical care.

By 15 September 1946, 3,512,435 Displaced Persons had been repatriated and resettled from United States controlled areas. This total includes 485,924 ex-enemy Displaced Persons ("intruders")—Bulgarians, Hungarians, Italians, Austrians, and Rumanians.

Repatriation and resettlement.

What can we do?

We must remember that D. P.'s are human beings, despite everything that the Nazis did to them and that they are a product of conditions over which they had little control.

D. P.'s are human beings.

They are living in an unfriendly and alien country which they do not wish to help rebuild.

They need more than food, clothing, and hospitalization. They need tolerance, patience, kindness. They need to know that we are aware of their previous hardships and the tortures that they and their families have endured. They need confidence in the future. They need assurance that we know the score.

What the D. P. needs—a chance for a better future!

We have a moral obligation to give these people the chance that they deserve, and as we give them the chance to regain their health, their strength, their confidence in the future, we will be helping to solve one of the most distressing problems existing in the world.

Prepared by Army Information Branch, Information and Education Division, War Department Special Staff.

ORGANIZATIONS SUPPORTING
THE GOALS OF THE CCDP
March 1, 1948

On March 1, 1948, the CCDP issued a partial list of 128 national organizations supporting the admission of DPs to the United States. They included:

VETERANS
American Legion
American Veterans Committee
Catholic War Veterans
Jewish War Veterans
National Conference of Union Labor Legionnaires
National Council of American Veteran Organizations

LABOR
American Federation of Labor
Congress of Industrial Organizations
Amalgamated Meat Cutters & Butcher Workmen of North America
   (AFL)
Amalgamated Clothing Workers of America (CIO)
Barbers and Beauty Culturists Union of America (CIO)
Brotherhood of Railway Clerks (AFL)
Commercial Telegraphers Union (AFL)
Glass Bottle Blowers Association of the United States and Canada
   (AFL)
Hotel and Restaurant Employees International Alliance and Barten-
   ders International League of America (AFL)

Industrial Union of Marine and Shipbuilding Workers of America (CIO)
International Association of Machinists
International Brotherhood of Paper Makers (AFL)
International Brotherhood of Pulp, Sulphite & Paper Mill Workers (AFL)
International Ladies Garment Workers Union (AFL)
International Longshoremen's Association (AFL)
International Printing Pressmen and Assistants Union of North America (AFL)
Jewish Labor Committee
National Federation of Post Office Clerks (AFL)
National Maritime Union of America (CIO)
National Women's Trade Union League
Oil Workers International Union (CIO)
United Automobile Aircraft—Agricultural Implement Workers of America (CIO)
United Brotherhood of Carpenters and Joiners of America (AFL)
United Cement, Lime and Gypsum Workers International Union (AFL)
United Hatters, Cap and Millinery Workers International Union (AFL)
United Mine Workers
United Office and Professional Workers of American International Union (CIO)
United Steel Workers of America (CIO)
United Textile Workers of America (AFL)

RELIGIOUS
American Friends Service Committee
American Unitarian Association
Congregational Christian Churches: Council for Social Action
Disciples of Christ: International Convention
Evangelical United Brethren Church
Evangelical and Reformed Church: Commission on Christian Social Action
Federal Council of Churches of Christ in America
Friends Committee on National Legislation
Home Missions Council of North America
Knights of Columbus
Mennonite Central Committee

Moravian Church
National Association of Schools and Colleges of The Methodist
    Church
National Catholic Rural Life Conference
National Catholic Welfare Conference
National Lutheran Council
Northern Baptist Convention
Presbyterian Church USA
Presbyterian Church
Presbyterian Church in the United States
Protestant Episcopal Church: General Convention
Russian Orthodox Greek Catholic Church of North America
Serbian Eastern Orthodox Diocese for the United States of America
    and Canada
Southern Baptist Convention
Synagogue Council of America
Unitarian Service Committee
United Presbyterian Church of North America
United Synagogue of America
Universalist Church of America
World Alliance for International Friendship Through Churches
YMCA: International Board

WOMEN
American Association of University Women (in accordance with
    Legislative Program for 1947–49)
Associated Women of the American Farm Bureau Federation
Catholic Daughters of America
General Federation of Women's Clubs
Hadassah
League of Women Voters
National Council of Catholic Women
National Council of Jewish Women
National Council of Women of the United States
National Federation of Business and Professional Women's Clubs
National Federation of Congressional Christian Women
National Federation of Temple Sisterhoods
United Council of Church Women
United Order True Sisters, Inc., Grand Lodge
Women's Action Committee for Lasting Peace
Women's American ORT

Women's Auxiliary of the Protestant Episcopal Church
Women's Division of the Methodist Church
Women's International League for Peace and Freedom (U.S. Section)
YWCA: National Board
Zonta International

SOCIAL, CIVIC, WELFARE, AND OTHERS
American Association of Social Workers
American Association for the United Nations
American Civil Liberties Union
American Council for Judaism
American Council of Voluntary Agencies for Foreign Service: Committee on Displaced Persons
American Farm Bureau Federation
Americans for Democratic Action
American Federation of International Institutes
American Federation of Jews from Central Europe
American Jewish Committee
American Jewish Conference
American Jewish Congress
American Lithuanian Council
Association of Immigration & Nationality Lawyers
B'nai B'rith
Common Council for American Unity
Council of Jewish Federations and Welfare Funds
Federation of Americans of Central and East European Descent
Hebrew Sheltering and Immigrant Aid Society
International Social Service
International Rescue and Relief Committee, Inc.
Lithuanian Alliance of America
National Association for the Advancement of Colored People
National Association of Jewish Center Workers
National Community Relations Advisory Council
National Conference of Jewish Social Welfare
National Congress of Parents and Teachers: Board of Managers
National Council for Jewish Education
National Federation of Settlements
National Jewish Welfare Board
National Peace Conference
National Social Welfare Assembly: International Committee
Order of the Sons of Italy

Polish American Congress
Polish National Alliance
Russian American Union for Protection and Aid to Russians Outside
  Russia
Russian Children's Welfare Society
Self-Help for Emigres from Central Europe, Inc.
Tolstoy Foundation
Ukrainian Congress Committee
United Lithuanian Relief Fund of America, Inc.
United Roumanian Jews of America

ABBREVIATIONS AND LOCATIONS OF SOME OF THE MANUSCRIPT COLLECTIONS

ACJ	American Council for Judaism
ACJ MSS., Madison	American Council for Judaism manuscripts, State Historical Society of Wisconsin, Madison, Wisconsin.
ACJ MSS., New York	American Council for Judaism manuscripts, the ACJ offices in New York City.
ACVAFS	American Council of Voluntary Agencies for Foreign Services
AJC	American Jewish Committee
AJC Library	Blaustein Library, American Jewish Committee, New York City.
AJC MSS.	AJC offices, New York City.
AJC Oral History	William E. Wiener Library of Oral History, AJC, New York City.
AJ Conf	American Jewish Conference
AJ Conf MSS.	American Jewish Conference MSS., Zionist Archives, New York City.
Aydelotte Diary	Frank Aydelotte MSS., Series 6, Anglo-American Commission, Box 2, File, "Palestine Diary." Swarthmore College Library, Swarthmore, Pa.
Aydelotte MSS.	Same as above except in box 1.
Baruch MSS.	Bernard Baruch MSS., Seeley G. Mudd Manuscript Library, Princeton University, Princeton, N.J.
BDC	Berlin Document Center
Bernard interview	Interviews with William S. Bernard. New York City. June 28, 1977, November 15, 1979, November 8, 1980.

Bernstein MSS.   Philip A. Bernstein MSS., American
                                 Jewish Archives, Cincinnati, Ohio.
Brook interview   Interview with Ben Brook, former
                                 director of JDC in Italy (1945–48).
                                 Tucson, Ariz. November 5, 1978.
CAB 128   Minutes of the British Cabinet
                                 Meetings, 1945–46. Public Record
                                 Office, Kew, England.
CAB 129   Cabinet Papers. Ibid.
CCDP   Citizens Committee on Displaced
                                 Persons
CCDP MSS.   CCDP MSS., located among
                                 American Council for Nationalities
                                 Services MSS., Immigration History
                                 Archives, St. Paul, Minn.
Celler Committee   "Amending The Displaced Persons
                                 Act of 1948," *Hearings Before
                                 Subcommittee No 1 of the Committee of
                                 the Judiciary on H.R. 1344*, House of
                                 Representatives, 81st Congress, 1st
                                 Session, March 2, 4, and 9, 1949.
Chelf Report   Appended at the end of the Fulton
                                 Committee report.
CIA   Central Intelligence Agency
CIC   Central Intelligence Corps, United
                                 States Army
Clark Report   Dorothy K. Clark, "UNRRA
                                 Headquarters and the Displaced
                                 Persons Operation," UNRRA MSS.
                                 United Nations Archives. Executive
                                 Offices. Office of the Historian.
                                 Subject File, 1943–48. Monographs,
                                 1943–48. Box 798.
Cohen Address   Address by Henry Cohen to
                                 European Advisory Committee,
                                 World Jewish Congress, November 7,
                                 1946. Folder 65, DP Collection,
                                 Germany. YIVO Institute of Jewish
                                 Research. New York City.
Cohen Report   "Report on Visit to Germany" from
                                 Meyer Cohen to F. LaGuardia, June
                                 21, 1946. UNRRA MSS., United
                                 Nations Archives, New York City.
                                 Executive Offices. Office of the

	Director General. Country File, 1943–48. Germany (G-1).
"Confidential Report"	"Confidential Report on General Situation, Dp's & UNRRA, [April ?] 1946," UNRRA MSS. United Nations Archives. New York City. Germany Mission, U.S. Zone. Office of the Director, 1945–47. Displaced Persons. General. Box #66,480.
Connally MSS.	Tom Connally MSS., Library of Congress, Washington, D.C.
CP	Same as CAB 129.
CR	*Congressional Record*
CRC	National Community Relations Advisory Council. A network of Jewish organizations.
Crossman Diary	Richard Crossman Papers. Oxford University. St. Antony's College. Middle East Library. Diary kept by Crossman of his Anglo-American Committee of Inquiry experience.
Crossman MSS.	Same as above without the diary.
Crump MSS.	Doris Crump MSS. Western Historical Collections. University of Missouri. Columbia, Mo.
Cunningham MSS.	Sir Alan Cunningham Papers. Oxford University. St. Antony's College. Middle East Library. Box V, File 2.
CWS	Church World Service
Dorr Memoir	Goldthwaite Higginson Dorr Oral History Memoir. Columbia University Oral History Collection. New York City.
DP (DPs)	Displaced Persons
DP Report #2	"Report—Relations With Military-D.P. #U.S.-2," UNRRA MSS., United Nations Archives, New York City. Executive Offices. Office of the Historian. Monographs, 1943–48. Box 799.
DPC	Displaced Persons Commission.
DPC MSS.	National Archives, Washington, D.C. Diplomatic Branch. Series 1, Central

	Subject Files, are in boxes 1–39; Commissioner Rosenfield's papers are in boxes 45–55; Commissioner O'Connor's files are in box 56; and the files of the Information and Editorial Division are in boxes 81 and 82.
DPC Report	The DPC made six semiannual reports to the Congress. In the notes they are listed with the date.
DPs-Collaborators	"Displaced Persons—Collaborators, Volksdeutsche and German Balts," UNRRA MSS., United Nations Archives. New York City. Executive Offices. Office of the General Counsel. Subject File, 1943–46. Displaced Persons. Box 234.
Duker analysis Duker report	Abraham Duker, "Many Among DP's in European Camps are Collaborationists." Extension of remarks of Hon. Arthur G. Klein of New York in the House of Representatives, August 2, 5, 6, 1948. *Appendix To The Congressional Record*. 80th Cong., 2d sess., vol. 94, pt. 12, pp. A4891–4892.
Duker Interview	Interview with Abraham Duker. New York City. August 1, 1978.
Edwards interview	Interview with Jerome E. Edwards. History Department. University of Nevada. Reno, Nevada. November 28, 1978.
80C1	Eightieth Congress, First Session.
80C2	Eightieth Congress, Second Session.
81C1	Eighty-First Congress, First Session.
81C2	Eighty-First Congress, Second Session.
Eisenhower MSS.	Dwight D. Eisenhower MSS., Eisenhower Library. Abilene, Kansas.
Engel interview	Interview with Irving M. Engel. New York City. August 21, 1978.
Engel Memoir	Oral History Memoir of Irving M. Engel. William E. Wiener Oral History Library, American Jewish Committee. New York City.

FDR MSS.	Franklin D. Roosevelt MSS., FDR Library, Hyde Park, N.Y.
Feldmans MSS.	Jules Feldmans MSS., Hoover Institution, Stanford University, Palo Alto, Calif.
Fellows Committee	"Permitting Admission of 400,000 Displaced Persons into the United States," *Hearings before Subcommittee on Immigration and Naturalization of H.R. 2910*, 80th Congress, 1st Session (Washington, 1947).
FO	Foreign Office. All FO references are FO 371, which is the classification for the Foreign Office Papers that I used in the British Public Record Office, Kew, England. The reference, cited as FO 371 55619/WR892, means foreign office classification, folder, and cited document in that folder.
Frankel interview	Interview with William Frankel. London. April 5, 1978.
Frenkel MSS.	"Displaced Persons Camps" by Lawrence Frenkel. Typescript of unpublished manuscript, written in 1945. Lawrence Frenkel MSS., Hoover Institution, Stanford University, Palo Alto, Calif.
Friedlander interview	Interview with Henry Friedlander. Tucson, Ariz. October 10, 1978; San Francisco, December 28, 1979.
FRUS	Department of State. *Foreign Relations of the United States, Diplomatic Papers.*
Fulton Committee	"Displaced Persons and the International Refugee Organization," *Report of a Special Subcommittee of the House Committee of Foreign Affairs*, 80th Congress, 1st Session (Washington 1947).
Gogolinski-Elston interview	Interview with Dr. R. Gogolinski-Elston. London. May 28, 1978.
Gottlieb interview	Interview with Amy Zahl Gottlieb. New York City. August 5, 1977.
H	House of Representatives (in *Congressional Record* citations).
Haber interview	Interview with William Haber. Ann

	Arbor, Michigan. November 14, 1979.
Hayden MSS.	Carl Hayden MSS. Library of Arizona State University. Tempe, Ariz.
Henderson Memoir	"Oral History Interview with Loy W. Henderson," by Richard D. McKinzie. Washington, D.C. June 14 and July 5, 1973. Copy in Truman Library.
HIAS	Hebrew Sheltering and Immigrant Aid Society
Hickenlooper MSS.	B. B. Hickenlooper MSS., Herbert Hoover Presidential Library, West Branch, Iowa.
HMG	His Majesty's Government
IGC	Intergovernmental Committee on Refugees
IME	Irving M. Engel. All letters to and from IME not otherwise identified are in his manuscript collection which is extraordinarily well organized in chronological fashion.
IME MSS.	Irving M. Engel MSS. American Jewish Committee. New York City.
Immigration History Archives	Immigration History Archives, St. Paul, Minn.
INS, I & NS	Immigration and Naturalization Service
IRO	International Refugee Organization
Ives MSS.	Irving M. Ives MSS., Cornell University, Ithaca, N.Y.
Jackson Memoir	Columbia University of Oral History. Memoir of Sir Robert G. A. Jackson.
Jacoby Report	Gerhard Jacoby. "The Story of the
Jacoby Story	Jewish 'DP,'" folder 2205, DP Collection, Germany. YIVO Institute of Jewish Research, New York City.
JC	*The Jewish Chronicle*, London.
JDC	American Jewish Joint Distribution Committee
JDC Memo	JDC Memo from Leo W. Schwarz, U.S. Zone Director to Joseph Schwartz, chairman, European Executive Council on "Summary

	Analysis of JDC Program in the U.S. Zone of Occupation, Germany." January 13, 1947. DP Collection, Germany, YIVO.
JDC MSS.	American Jewish Joint Distribution Committee MSS., New York City.
Jewish Advisors' Reports	Unpublished "Reports of the Advisors on Jewish Affairs To The United States Command in Germany and Austria, 1947–1950," in AJC Library, New York City.
Joint, The	JDC
Kem MSS.	James P. Kem MSS., Western Historical Collections. University of Missouri, Columbia, Mo.
Kilgore MSS.	Harley M. Kilgore MSS. One part is in the FDR Library, Hyde Park. The other is in West Virginia State University Library, Morgantown, W. Va.
Langer MSS.	William Langer MSS. The Orin G. Libby Manuscript Collection. Chester Fritz Library. The University of North Dakota. Grand Forks, N.D.
Lehman MSS.	Herbert H. Lehman MSS. Columbia University, New York City.
Lloyd MSS.	Files of David D. Lloyd. Correspondence and General File. Immigration-I & NS. Boxes 3 & 4. Truman Library.
Lucas MSS.	Scott W. Lucas MSS. Illinois Historical Society. Springfield, Ill.
Marcantonio MSS.	Vito Marcantonio MSS. New York Public Library. New York City.
Marrovitch report	Report of conditions in DP Camps by Shalom Marrovitch, June 1, 1945. In folder, "Joint Committee of Inquiry," box 100, World Jewish Congress MSS. London, England.
Maybank MSS.	Burnet R. Maybank MSS., College of Charleston, Charleston, S.C.
McCarran Committee	"Displaced Persons," *Hearings Before the Subcommittee on Amendments To The Displaced Persons Act of the Senate Committee on the Judiciary*, 81st

	Congress, 1st and 2nd Sessions, 1949–50.
McCarran interview	Interview with Sister Margaret Patrick McCarran. Sparks, Nevada. November 28, 1978.
McDonald Diary	James G. McDonald MSS., Herbert H. Lehman MSS., Columbia University, New York City. Diary of Anglo-American Committee of Inquiry experiences.
McDonald MSS.	Same as above without the diary.
McGrath MSS.	J. Howard McGrath MSS., Truman Library, Independence, Mo.
MG reports	Military Government of Germany. *Displaced Persons Stateless Persons and Refugees.* Monthly Report of Military Governor, U.S. Zone. 1945–47.
Military Report	Same as DP Report #2.
MP	Member of Parliament
NA	National Archives
NCPI	National Committee on Postwar Immigration; name changed in 1946 to National Committee on Immigration Policy.
NCWC	National Catholic Welfare Conference
NCWC MSS.	U.S. Catholic Conference (formerly National Catholic Welfare Conference). Department of International Affairs. Division of Migration and Refugee Service (formerly Immigration Bureau). Center for Migration Studies. Staten Island, N.Y.
NLC	National Lutheran Council
OMGUS	Official Military Government of the United States
OMGUS MSS.	OMGUS. National Archives Record Center. Suitland, Md. Record Group 260. Civil Affairs Division. For the OMGUS records there are three cartons for each number. Hence the boxes might be labeled 169 1/3, 2/3, or 3/3, which means box number

	169, first, second, or third of three boxes.
OMGUS Reconnaissance Report	"Report of Reconnaissance in Germany," July 23, 1945, Box 172 3/3. Ibid.
ORT	Organization for Rehabilitation Through Training
Phillips Diary	Diary of William G. Phillips. Phillips MSS. Harvard University. Houghton Library. IX. Palestine (1945–46).
Phillips MSS.	Same as above without the diary.
POW, POWs	Prisoners of War
PPF	President's Personal File, Truman MSS., Truman Library.
PPP	*Public Papers of the Presidents*
PREM 8	Prime Minister Clement Attlee's Official Records. British Public Record Office, Kew, England.
President's Commission	*Hearings Before the President's Commission on Immigration and Naturalization.* 82nd Congress, 2nd Session, House of Representatives. Committee on the Judiciary. September 30, 1952-October 29, 1952.
PRO	Public Record Office, Kew, England
PSF	President's Secretary's Files. *Subject File.* Truman Library.
Revercomb Committee	*Report of the Senate Committee on the Judiciary Pursuant to S. Res. 137.* 80th Congress, 2nd Session, Report No. 950.
RG	Record Group
Rifkind interview	Interview with Simon Rifkind. New York City. July 24, 1978.
Robertson MSS.	A. Willis Robertson MSS., SWEM Library, College of William and Mary. Williamsburg, Va.
E. Roosevelt MSS.	Eleanor Roosevelt MSS., FDR Library, Hyde Park, N.Y.
Rosenberger interview	Interview with Francis Rosenberger. July 31, 1978. Washington, D.C.
Rosenfield interview	Interview with Harry N. Rosenfield. Washington D.C. December 20, 1978.

Rosenfield MSS.   Harry N. Rosenfield MSS., Truman
                                    Library, Independence, Mo.
Rosenman MSS.   Samuel I. Rosenman MSS., ibid.
Rosenman OH   Oral History memoir of Samuel I.
                                    Rosenman, William E. Wiener Oral
                                    History Library, AJC, New York
                                    City.

S   Senate (in *Congressional Record*
                                    citations).
Schwartz Report   Joseph Schwartz's Report of his trip
                                    to Germany, dated August 19, 1945.
                                    Folder 61, DP Collection, Germany.
                                    YIVO Institute for Jewish Research,
                                    New York City.
Sender Report   "Report by Sadie Sender," February
                                    20, 1946. ibid.
SHAEF   Supreme Headquarters, Allied
                                    Expeditionary Forces
Smith MSS.   H. Alexander Smith MSS. Seeley G.
                                    Mudd Manuscript Library. Princeton
                                    University, Princeton N.J.
Squadrilli Report   "Current Status of Displaced Persons
                                    in The U.S. Zone in Germany,"
                                    prepared by Alex E. Squadrilli, May
                                    25, 1946. UNRRA MSS., United
                                    Nations Archives, New York City.
                                    Executive Offices. Office of the
                                    Director General. Country File,
                                    1943–48. Germany (G-1).
Stratton interview   Interview with William G. Stratton.
                                    Chicago, Illinois. October 29, 1980.
Stratton MSS.   William G. Stratton MSS. State
                                    Historical Society of Illinois.
                                    Springfield, Ill.
Study #35   Report of the General Board, United
                                    States Forces, European Theater,
                                    "Displaced Persons, Refugees, and
                                    Recovered Allied Military Personnel,"
                                    G-5 Section, Study #35, n.d. (*ca.*
                                    December, 1945 ?). Eisenhower
                                    MSS., Eisenhower Library, Abilene,
                                    Kansas.
Taft MSS.   Robert A. Taft MSS., Library of
                                    Congress, Washington D.C.

Thomas MSS.

Tobey MSS.

Truman MSS.

Tuck MSS.

UK

UN
UNRRA

UNRRA-Report of the Director
#3
UNRRA #3

USNA
Vandenberg MSS.

Vitales Report

Wagner MSS.

Wallace Diary

Wasserstein interview

Wiener Library

Wiener Library Clipping File

Wiley MSS.

Elmer Thomas MSS. Western
History Collection. University of
Oklahoma, Norman, Okla.
Charles W. Tobey MSS. Dartmouth
College Library. Hanover, N.H.
Harry S. Truman MSS. Truman
Library, Independence, Mo.
William Hallam Tuck MSS. Herbert
Hoover Presidential Library. West
Branch, Iowa.
United Kingdom of Great Britain
and Ireland
United Nations
United Nations Relief and
Rehabilitation Administration
"Report—Field Operations—D.P.
#U.S.—3," UNRRA MSS. United
Nations Archives. New York City.
Executive Offices. Office of the
Historian. Monographs, 1943–48.
Box 799.
United Service for New Americans
Arthur H. Vandenberg MSS. Bentley
Historical Library. Ann Arbor, Mich.
H. Vitales, "Report on Visit to
Germany," May 11, 1946 (visit took
place January through April 1946).
Folder 55, DP Collection, Germany.
YIVO Institute for Jewish Research.
New York City.
Robert F. Wagner MSS. Georgetown
University. Washington, D.C.
Henry A. Wallace Oral History.
Columbia University, New York City.
Interview with Bernard Wasserstein.
London. April 6, 1978.
Institute of Contemporary History
and Wiener Library. London,
England.
Clipping file on Displaced Persons.
Ibid.
Alexander Wiley MSS. State
Historical Society of Wisconsin.
Madison, Wisc.

Wise MSS.	Stephen S. Wise MSS. American Jewish Historical Society. Waltham, Mass.
WJC	World Jewish Congress
WJC MSS.	World Jewish Congress MSS. London, England.
WO	War Office 202 (WO 202). British Public Record Office. Kew, England.
Wolfsohn MSS.	Joel D. Wolfsohn MSS. Truman Library.
WRB	War Refugee Board
WRB MSS.	War Refugee Board MSS., FDR Library. Hyde Park, N.Y.
Wright Report	"Midwinter Report of Edward Needles Wright to the American Friends Service Committee From Vilsbiburg, Bavaria, Germany." January 14, 1946. American Friends Service Committee MSS. Philadelphia.
WRS	War Refugee Services of National Catholic Welfare Conference
YIVO	YIVO Institute for Jewish Research. New York City.
ZA	Zionist Archives. New York City.

NOTES

PREFACE

1. Simon Rifkind, *The Disinherited Jews of Europe Must Be Saved.*

PROLOGUE

1. David S. Wyman, *Paper Walls*, p. 210.
2. There is no adequate history of American antisemitism. A collection of several articles on the subject is Leonard Dinnerstein, ed., *Antisemitism in the United States.*
3. Arthur Liebman, *Jews and the Left*, pp. 420–426.
4. Wyman, *Paper Walls*, pp. 69, 168, 210–12; Robert Dallek, *Franklin D. Roosevelt and American Foreign Policy, 1932–1945*, pp. 445–46, cited hereafter as *FDR*; Fred L. Israel, ed., *The War Diaries of Breckinridge Long*, p. 118.
5. *The War Diaries of Breckenridge Long*, pp. xxiv, 114, 115, 130, 154, 161, 173–74, 335, 336–37; Wyman, *Paper Walls*, pp. 166, 172, 172; Dallek, *FDR*, p. 446.
6. James G. McDonald to Ben Cohen, November 30, 1944, McDonald MSS.
7. Robert W. Ross, *So It Was True*, pp. 157, 178, 182.
8. Dallek, *FDR*, p. 446; Henry L. Feingold, *The Politics of Rescue*, p. 241; Naomi W. Cohen, *Not Free to Desist*, p. 247; Henry Morgenthau, Jr., "The Morgenthau Diaries, VI. The Refugee Run-Around," *Collier's* (November 1, 1947), p. 65.
9. Quoted in Ross, *So It Was True*, pp. 222–23.
10. Samuel H. Flowerman and Maria Jahoda, "Polls on Anti-Semitism," p. 83; Charles Herbert Stember, ed., *Jews in The Mind of America* (New York: Basic Books, 1966), pp. 121, 132, 133. Laura Z. Hobson, *Gentleman's Agreement* (New York: Simon and Schuster, 1974); Bruce Bliven, "U.S. Anti-Semitism Today," pp. 16–19.
11. Wyman, *Paper Walls*, pp. 23–26; David Brody, "American Jewry, The Refugees, and Immigration Reaction (1932–1945)," in Abraham J. Karp., ed., *The Jewish Experience in America* (5 vols.; Waltham, Mass.: American Jewish Historical Society, 1969), vol. 5, pp. 320–48.
12. Zvi Ganin, *Truman, American Jewry, and Israel, 1945–1948*, pp. 10–11.

13. Jerold S. Auerbach, "Joseph M. Proskauer: American Court Jew," p. 111.

14. Ganin, *Truman, American Jewry, and Israel*, p. 11.

15. Bernard Interview.

1. THE ARMY AND THE DISPLACED PERSONS

1. Earl F. Ziemke, *The U.S. Army in the Occupation of Germany*, p. 284; W. B. Courtney, "Europe's Hangover," p. 18; Richard Mayne, *The Recovery of Europe*, pp. 35–36; Report of the General Board, United States Forces, European Theater, "Displaced Persons, Refugees, and Recovered Allied Military Personnel," G-5 Section, Study no. 35, n.d. (*ca.* December 1945), p. 35, Eisenhower MSS., cited hereafter as Study no. 35; *New York Times*, April 7, 1945, p. 1, April 10, 1945, p. 7.

2. Study no. 35, p. 12; Ziemke, *The U.S. Army in the Occupation of Germany*, p. 52; John George Stoessinger, p.49; W. Arnold-Foster, "Displaced Persons In Germany: UNRRA's Cooperation With The Armies," p.241, cited hereafter as *Army Quarterly*; *Congressional Digest* (January 1948), 27:16; Jean Edward Smith, ed., *The Papers of General Lucius D. Clay. Germany, 1945–1949*, p. 187, cited hereafter as *Clay Papers*; F. S. V. Donnison, *Civil Affairs and Military Government, Central Organization and Planning*, pp. 189, 193.

3. Study no. 35, p. 13; *Army Quarterly*, p. 242; PRO WO 202 601; UN Archives, Executive Office, Office of the Director General, Country File, 1943–1948, Germany (G-1), "Current Status of Displaced Persons in the U.S. Zone in Germany," prepared by Alex E. Squadrilli, May 25, 1946, cited hereafter as Squadrilli report; Yehuda Bauer, *Flight and Rescue: BRICHAH*, p. 190; Malcolm J. Proudfoot, *European Refugees: 1939–1952*, p. 236; R. L. Fisher, "The Army and Displaced Persons," p. 4; UNRRA, *Report of the Director General To The Council* for the period 1 July 1947 to 31 December 1947 (Washington, D.C., 1948), p. 144; Kurt R. Grossman, "Refugees, DP's, and Migrants," p. 133; Oliver J. Fredericksen, *The American Military Government Occupation of Germany*, p. 73; *Jewish Chronicle* (London), August 23, 1946, p. 1, cited hereafter as JC; Military Government of Germany, *Displaced Persons, Stateless Persons and Refugees* (Monthly Report of Military Governor, U.S. Zone) (Cumulative Review, May 8, 1945–September 30, 1946), no. 15, p. 4, cited hereafter as MG Reports.

4. "Report on Displaced Persons in US Area of Control, Germany," prepared by Civil Affairs Division (Headquarters, European Command, Frankfurt, Germany, 1 September 1947), p. 2, in H. Alexander Smith MSS.; MG Reports, (August 20, 1945) no. 1; Fred K. Hoehler, "Displaced Persons," in George B. deHuszar, ed., *Persistent International Issues*, pp. 49–50; UNRRA, Executive Offices, Office of the Historian, "Monographs, 1943–1948"; box 798, Dorothy K. Clark, "UNRRA Headquarters and the Displaced Persons Operation," p. 67; PRO WO 202 620.

5. "Occupation Forces In Europe Series, 1945–1946, Displaced Persons"

(Unpublished manuscript in files of Center Of Military History, Washington, D.C.), p. 39; Study no. 35, p. 18; *Army Quarterly*, p. 245; *New York Times*, March 9, 1945, p. 8; Herbert H. Lehman to John R. Lehman, May 5, 1945, Lehman MSS., UNRRA PERSONAL, folder, "John R. Lehman"; "Displaced Persons Operations" (SHAEF/G5/DP/2711/5, June 10, 1945), Eisenhower MSS.; FO 371 51096/WR 2141; Squadrilli report.

6. UNRRA, Executive Offices, Office of the Historian, Monographs, 1943–48, box 799, "Report—Relations With Military—D.P. #U.S.-2," pp. 33–35; *Army Quarterly*, pp. 240–42; "Experiences of DPs in Foehrenwald, February, 1946," in Institute of Contemporary History and Wiener Library, London, File no. IV. Fate of Survivors; Ilja M. Dijour, "Changing Emphasis In Jewish Migration," pp. 78–79; *Stars and Stripes* (Germany edition), December 3, 1945, p. 4; Ira A. Hirschmann, *The Embers Still Burn*, p. 67; interview with Simon Rifkind, New York, July 25, 1978, cited hereafter as Rifkind interview.

7. U.S. War Department Pamphlet no. 31-121, *Civil Affairs Guide, Military Government and Problems With Respect To The Jews In Germany* (July 29, 1944), pp. 1, 4; Karen Gershon, *Postscript*, pp. 30, 34; Judah Nadich, *Eisenhower and the Jews*, 1953), p. 41; JC July 6, 1945, p. 9; FRUS (1945) 2:1158; Fredericksen, *American Military Government Occupation of Germany*, p. 73; FO 371 51118/WR 1908.

8. Kathryn Hulme, *The Wild Place*, p. 45; FO 371 51098/WR 2287; Emanuel Gruss, "In A Camp for Displaced Persons," p. 12; Ladislas Farago, *The Last Days of Patton*, pp. 172–73.

9. UNRRA, Box 799, "Report—Relations With Military—D.P. #U.S.-2," pp. 37, 44; Box 798, Clark, "UNRRA Headquarters and the Displaced Persons Operation," p. 69; Squadrilli report; Hulme, *The Wild Place*, p. 144.

10. UNRRA, "Report—Relations With Military—D.P. #U.S.-2," p. 137; George Masset to J. H. Whiting, September 13, 1945, and September 17, 1945, UN Archives, Box 22156; "Two Reports by Jewish Relief Workers in Germany, November 1945," Wiener Library, London.

11. "Communications: Displaced Persons," p. 502; *Lithuanian Bulletin* (January-February, 1947), 6:18.

12. UNRRA, Germany Mission, U.S. Zone, Office of the Director, 1945–1947, Displaced Persons, General, box 66480, folder, "Displaced Persons Assembly Centers, June 45–July 45"; Nicholas Bethell, *The Last Secret*, p. 65; UNRRA, Clark, "UNRRA Headquarters and the Displaced Persons Operation," p. 74; "Occupation Forces In Europe Series, 1945–1946, Displaced Persons," p. 36; Study no. 35, p. 19; Fredericksen, *American Military Government Occupation of Germany*, p. 73; *New York Times*, April 22, 1945, 4:4, May 20, 1945, 1:6; Irving Heymont, "After The Deluge: The Landsberg Jewish DP Camp, 1945," Davidson Sommers to J. W. Pehle, July 6, 1945, WRB, box 9, folder, "Earl G. Harrison Mission."

13. "Jews in Germany Today . . . August 28, 1945," JDC; Joseph Schwartz's Report on his trip to Germany, August 19, 1945, pp. 20–31, folder 61, in

DP Collection, Germany, YIVO Institute for Jewish Research, New York City, cited hereafter as YIVO; Martin Blumenson, *The Patton Papers, 1940–1945*, p. 751.

14. FRUS (1945) 2:1176; Louis Lipsky to John J. McCloy, September 24, 1945, folder, "Overseas: 1943–1945 Displaced Persons in Ger.," ZA; Lev Zelmanovits to Nahum Goldman, September 21, 1945, WJC, box 70, folder, "New York—Jan.–Dec., 1945"; JC, September 28, 1945, p. 9; Sister M. Madeline Lorimer, "America's Response to Europe's Displaced Persons, 1948–1952: A Preliminary Report," p. 63. See also Nadich, *Eisenhower and the Jews*, pp. 154, 207–8; Leo W. Schwarz, *The Redeemers*, pp. 25, 27; Bauer, *Flight and Rescue*, pp. 69–70.

15. Stoessinger, *The Refugee and the World Community*, p. 55; Joseph A. Berger, "Displaced Persons: A Human Tragedy of World War II," p. 51; AJC, *Thirty-Seventh Annual Report* (1943), p. 202; Sidney B. Fay, "Displaced Persons in Europe," pp. 199–200; Walter Dushnyck, "The Importance of the Problem of Displaced Persons," p. 286; "Midwinter Report of Edward Needles Wright to the American Friends Service Committee from Vilsbiburg, Bavaria?, Germany," January 15, 1946, American Friends Service Committee, Philadelphia; Nathan Reich, "The Last Million," p. 110; U.S. House, Displaced Persons, pp. 6–7; Francesca Wilson, "Displaced Persons—Whose Responsibility?" pp. 10–12; Hirschmann, *The Embers Still Burn*, p. 227; Joseph Schwartz's report, YIVO; Earl G. Harrison, "The Last Hundred Thousand," p. 469; *Time*, July 23, 1947, p. 37.

16. Kathryn Close, "They Want to be People," p. 393; MG Reports, June 20, 1946, p. 1; FRUS, 1946, V, 145–46; "Displaced Persons In Germany," p. 15; Meyer Cohen, "Report on Visit to Germany," June 21, 1946, UN Archives, Executive Offices, Office of the Director General, Country File, 1943–1948, Germany (G-1); Franklin M. Davis, Jr., *Come as a Conquerer*, p. 184; Jan Sargiello, "I Saw Polish D/P Camps In Germany," *Polish Review* (March 7, 1946), 6:11, 14; Clark, "UNRRA Headquarters and the Displaced Persons Operation"; MG Reports, December, 1945, p. 1; Hirschmann, *The Embers Still Burn*, p. 140; *Times* (London), April 4, 1946, p. 5; Berger, "Displaced Persons," p. 52.

17. Margaret McNeill, *By the Rivers of Bablyon*, pp. 56, 68; Wright report; Lorimer, "America's Response to Displaced Persons," pp. 33, 36; McCarran Committee, p. 487; Leonard W. Finder to Charles W. Tobey, March 22, 1952, folder, "Displaced Persons Commission, 1951–1952," Tobey MSS.; "Report on Michigan DP Commission," November 25, 1950, DPC MSS., series 1, box 2, folder, "Advisory Committee on Resettlement of Displaced Persons"; *Current Affairs* (June 28, 1947), pp. 10–12.

18. "Confidential Memo of a Visa Conference held at American Consulate Club in Stuttgart," January 22, 1948, DPC MSS., series 1, box 22, folder, "Legislation–1948"; *Current History* (March 1946), p. 202; *Social Research* (March 1947), p. 53; *Times*, (London) February 12, 1946, p. 4.

19. There have been a number of works on the subject of involuntary

repatriation of the Russians after the war. Few of these refugees evoked American governmental concern in the evolution of this nation's displaced persons policy; hence, they will not be dealt with in this book. For those interested in the topic, see Bethell, *The Last Secret*; Nikolai Tolstoy, *Victims of Yalta*, and Mark Elliott, "The United States and Forced Repatriation of Soviet Citizens, 1944–47," pp. 253–75.

20. Interview with Harry N. Rosenfield, Washington, D.C., December 20, 1978; letter from E. H. Ein, et al., attached to Johannes Kaiv to Arthur H. Vandenberg, February 20, 1947, Vandenberg MSS.; George H. Stein, *The Waffen SS*, pp. 138, 175–76, 194; Robert L. Koehl, *RKFDV*, pp. 91, 247; McCarran Committee, pp. 486–87; "Report of Investigation of Target (Records of German Immigration Office) at Solnhoffen, August 4, 1945," in box 172–2/3, folder, "Reports, Liaison Offices," OMGUS, RG 260, Civil Affairs Division; Harry W. Lielnors to Harry N. Rosenfield, August 3, 1950, in DPC MSS., box 47, folder, "Latvian Relief, Inc."; FRUS (1945) 2:1155; clipping from *New York Times*, February 1, 1947, Clipping File on Displaced Persons, Wiener Library, London.

21. McCarran Committee, p. 487; Hirschmann, *The Embers Still Burn*, p. 122; J. Westerman to A. E. Squadrilli, November 7, 1945, UNRRA, box 66, 484, folder, "Latvia, Esthonia [*sic*], Problems"; Wright Report.

22. Hulme, *The Wild Place*, pp. 166–67; FRUS (1946) 5:150; Blumenson, *The Patton Papers*, p. 753; PSF, folder (Palestine–Jewish Immigration), Chelf Report, October 13, 1947, box 184, Truman MSS.

23. Koppel S. Pinson, "Jewish Life in Liberated Germany: A Study of the Jewish DP's," p. 102; Hirschmann, *The Embers Still Burn*, pp. 122–23; *Collier's*, July 28, 1945, p. 19; Edward N. Peterson, *The American Occupation of Germany— Retreat to Victory*, p. 295.

24. Interview with Dr. R. Gogolinski-Elston, Mission Director of National Catholic Welfare Conference (NCWC), Great Britain and Ireland, 1943–62, in London, May 28, 1978. Dr. Gogolinski-Elston told me that "all" of the Ukrainians had been Nazis. When I informed Harry N. Rosenfield of Dr. Gogolinski's remark, Rosenfield responded with a hearty laugh and observed: "Oh, no. I wouldn't agree with that. Maybe only 90 percent were." Rosenfield interview. Eisenhower's first adviser for Jewish affairs, Chaplain Judah Nadich, wrote that the Ukrainians and *Volksdeutsche* "were Nazis to the very core of their being." Nadich, *Eisenhower and the Jews*, p. 188. Other sources expressing these sentiments are *The DP Express* (Munich), November 19, 1947, p. 1; David W. Nussbaum, "DP Camps Swarm with Pro-Nazis; IRO Shrugs It Off," New York *Post* ("Home News" edition), November 21, 1948, p. 5; clipping in Harry N. Rosenfield MSS., folder, "New Clippings, Nov. 1948," box 25; Aleksandr M. Nekrich, *The Punished Peoples*, p. 7; A. Bedo to V. R. Kennedy, September 12, 1945, Jules Feldmans MSS., box 5, folder, "Displaced Persons"; *New York Times*, October 19, 1945, December 31, 1945, p. 5; Washington *Post*, December 31, 1945, p. 3; Heymont, "After The Deluge," pp. 47–48; Stoessinger, *The Refugee and the World Community*, p. 58;

Duker report; P. E. Brown to J. H. Whiting, August 2, 1946, UNRRA, box 66,480, folder, "Displaced Persons Camps—1 July"; *Current History* (March 1946), p. 202; William Haber's final report, December 20, 1948, in "Reports of the Advisors on Jewish Affairs to the United States Command in Germany and Austria, 1947–1950," in AJC Library, New York City; JC, May 23, 1947, p. 11; "Reports-Congressional Committee," Memo to Col. Messec from Lt. Col. James P. Abbott, September 24, 1947, OMGUS, RG 260, box 172 2/3; Laurence Frenkel, "Displaced Persons Camps," p. 7, in Laurence Frenkel MSS., Marvin Klemme, *The Inside Story of UNRRA*, pp. 114–15; *Stars and Stripes* (Germany edition), January 3, 1946, p. 7, (European edition), August 12, 1946, p. 2; "Displaced Persons," February 13, 1946, McDonald MSS.

25. Duker report.

26. Henry Carter, *The Refugee Problem in Europe and the Middle East*, pp. 11–12.

27. Vitales Report, YIVO.

28. "Chaplain Rachman's Report to the Interim Committee, September 20, 1946," ZA, American Jewish Conference, Minutes of the Interim Committee; "O.H.H.S.," Wiener Oral History Library, pp. 25–26.

29. Myron Emanuel, "Back Page Story," pp. 12–15; clipping from PM, September 23, 1946, p. 8 in YIVO, folder 65; Jewish Survivors Report, May 1945, and a letter to his cantor from Jerry Himelfarb, August 9, 1946, in JDC "News," Wiener Library, London; Dorothy McCardle, *Children of Europe*, p. 117; "Report from Mauthausen Concentration Camp," in "Displaced Persons Operations," Eisenhower Library, Appendix E, June 1945; William Phillips, *Ventures in Diplomacy*, p. 48; "Today's Facts and Figures on the Joint Distribution Committee," February 1, 1946, in JDC General Files on Displaced Persons; Vitales Report, YIVO.

30. Gershon, *Postscript*, p. 22; *Congress Weekly*, June 29, 1945, p. 12.

31. *Eisenhower Papers*, 6:267.

32. "Conference with Earl Harrison and Displaced Persons Committee of the American Council," n.d. [*ca.* August 30, 1945], American Friends Service Committee MSS., Philadelphia, folder, "Committees and Organization," 1945; Schwartz Report, YIVO; "Report of Reconaissance in Germany," July 23, 1945, OMGUS, box 172 3/3; Memo no. 2829, June 12, 1945, NA, Modern Military Section, RG 331, SHAEF, G-5 Division; FO 371 57690/WR 1069.

33. Chaim Finkelstein to Alex Eastermen, August 30, 1945, WJC MSS., box 70, folder, "New York—Jan.–Dec., 1945."

34. Gershon, *Postscript*, pp. 31–32; Shalom Marrovitch, report on conditions in DP Camps, June 1, 1945, WJC, box 100, folder, "Joint Committee of Inquiry"; Vallian Nichols of UNRRA Unit no. 135 to JDC, NYC, June 3, 1945, YIVO, folder 62.

35. *Survey Graphic*, (December 1945) 34:471; Marrovitch report, WJC, box 100; Vitales Report; JC July 20, 1945, p. 1; Philip S. Bernstein, "Displaced Persons," *American Jewish Year Book*, (1947–48) 49:521; Individual News

Reports, WJC, box 100, folder, "Joint Committee of Inquiry"; Two Reports by Jewish Relief Workers in Germany, Nov., 1945, Wiener Library, London; Proudfoot, *European Refugees*, p. 324; *Congress Weekly*, June 29, 1945, p. 12; Bauer, *Flight and Rescue*, pp. 52–53.

36. Zvi Ganin, "The Diplomacy of the Weak," p. 76; FRUS, 1945, II, 1158; "Excerpts from Chaplain Samson M. Goldstein's Report," April 1945, JDC, General Files on Displaced Persons; F. R. Adlerstein, "How Europe's Lost Are Found," p. 487; FO 371 51118/WR 1852; Joseph C. Hyman to Jacob Pat, June 12, 1945, YIVO, folder 62.

37. FO 371 45399/E4741; J. A. Ulio to Emanuel Celler, May 29, 1945, Ulio to Herman Muller, June 14, 1945, M. Grossman to Louis Lipsky, May 10, 1945, Arthur G. Klein to Emanuel Celler, May 14, 1945, Arthur G. Klein to Meir Grossman, May 15, 1945, Louis Lipsky to Thomas M. Cooley II, June 15, 1945, Louis Lipsky to Herbert Lehman, July 5, 1945, M. Grossman to General Luther L. Hill, July 5, 1945, M. Grossman to Samuel Dickstein, July 5, 1945, ZA, folder, "Overseas: 1943–1945 Displaced Persons in Ger."; Stephen Wise and Nahum Goldman to George Warren, June 12, 1945, NA, Records of the State Department, Decimal File 1945–1949, 840.48 Refugees/ 6-1245; Truman to Morgenthau, June 2, 1945, OF 127, box 552, Truman MSS.; Kenneth Ray Bain, *The March to Zion*, pp. 71–72.

38. Morgenthau to Grew, n.d., WRB, box 2; Memorandum to the President from Joseph C. Grew, June 21, 1945, OF 127, box 552, Truman Library.

39. Memo, no author, June 12, 1945, WRB, box 9, folder, "Earl G. Harrison Mission."

40. Grew to Truman, June 21, 1945, ibid.; Harry S. Truman, *Memoirs: Years of Trial and Hope*, 2:137.

41. FRUS (1945) 8:754–55; Dorr Memoir, p. 165.

42. Dorr Memoir, pp. 172, 186; Zvi Ganin, *Truman, American Jewry, and Israel, 1945–1948*, pp. 10–12, 14; Lawrence H. Fuchs, *The Political Behavior of American Jews*, p. 43.

43. Lawrence H. Fuchs, *The Political Behavior of American Jews*, pp. 72–73; *New York Times*, August 1, 1946, p. 10, August 2, p. 8; Richard Crossman, *Palestine Mission*, p. 52; John Snetsinger, *Truman, The Jewish Vote, and the Creation of Israel*, pp. 12, 72; *The Forrestal Diaries*, ed. by Walter Millis, pp. 309, 323, 344–45; Francis Williams, *Ernest Bevin*, p. 259; Eleanor Roosevelt to Bob Hannegan, November 14, 1945, E. Roosevelt MSS., box 3761; FO 371 52651/E12398.

2. THE HARRISON REPORT—AND AFTER

1. Henry Morgenthau, Jr., to Gardner Patterson et al., June 21, 1945, Morgenthau Papers, folder 856.

2. *Survey Graphic* (December 1945), 34:470–72.

3. *New York Times*, September 30, 1945, pp. 1, 38. The copy that I worked

with came from the Eisenhower Library and included Eisenhower's penciled comments in the margin.

4. Harrison to Secretary of State, July 28, 1945, Fred M. Vinson to Joseph C. Grew, August 1, 1945, WRB, box 9, folder, "Earl G. Harrison Mission"; FO 371 51098/WR 2341; WO 202 620; Truman MSS., PSF, box 184, folder (Palestine-Jewish Immigration); "Jews in Germany Today"; *Eisenhower Papers*, p. 267.

5. *Eisenhower Papers*, pp. 266–67, 357–61; WO 202 620; YIVO folder 54; "Occupation Forces in Europe Series, 1945–1946," Center for Military History, pp. 75–76, 79–82; *Stars and Stripes* (Germany edition), October 3, 1945, p. 1.

6. *Eisenhower Papers*, pp. 266, 267, 269; American Jewish Conference, Minutes of the Executive Committee, May 16, 1945, July 5, 1945, Davidson Sommers to Louis Lipsky, July 28, 1945, folder, "Overseas: 1943–1945 Displaced Persons in Ger.," ZA; Thomas Philip Liebschutz, "Rabbi Philip S. Bernstein and the Jewish Displaced Persons," AGWAR SIGNED WARCOS to USFET, October 10, 1945, Eisenhower Library; Cohen, *Not Free to Desist*, p. 285; Grew to Jacob Blaustein, July 26, 1945, folder "Emig-Immig, Displaced Persons, West Germany, 1945–1954," AJC; *39th Annual Report*, p. 53, AJC; Memo to Grew from Blaustein and George Medalie, July 23, 1945, State Department Decimal File, box 5598, item no. 7-2345, NA; F. R. Sweney to Rabbi Abraham Kalmanovitz, August 1, 1945, WRB, box 50, folder, "Cooperation With Other Agencies: Other Government Agencies."

7. *Eisenhower Papers*, p. 470.

8. "Occupation Forces," p. 73; Brig. Gen. Edgar Erskine Hume to Maj. Gen. John H. Hilldring, October 30, 1945, Modern Military, Civil Affairs Division, Executive Offices, Administrative Section, Decimal File 383.7, RG 165, box 211–Austria (Oct. 3, 1945–June 10, 1946), NA; Gottlieb Interview; "Report of AJDC Staff Conference," folder 11, YIVO; *New York Times*, October 26, 1945, p. 6; *Eisenhower Papers*, p. 456; W. B. Mack to Sir George Rendell, March 20, 1946, FO 372 57689/WR 850; Proudfoot, *European Refugees*, p. 330; Farago, *The Last Days of Patton*, p. 174.

9. Nadich, *Eisenhower and the Jews*, pp. 118, 154, 207–8; Blumenson, *The Patton Papers*, p. 787.

10. *The Patton Papers*, pp. 759–60; Morris Janowicz, *The Professional Soldier*, pp. 82–98 *passim*.

11. Heymont, "After the Deluge," pp. 77, 94; Victor H. Bernstein, "Aides Ignore Eisenhower Order to Help Jews," *PM*, November 11, 1945, clipping, box 732, folder 32, Wagner MSS.; "Confidential Report," UNRRA, box 66,480.

12. "Policy Book," OMGUS, box 169 3/3; JC, February 8, 1946, p. 1; Mrs. Churchill to Mr. L. G. Wielezynski, April 8, 1946, "Confidential Report," UNRRA, box 66,480; Squadrilli Report; McNarney to CG Third and Seventh Armies, April 4, 1946, OMGUS, box 169 3/3; Samuel Gringauz, "Our New German Policy and the DP's," p. 510.

13. Pritchard, "Social System of a DP Camp," p. 49; Heymont, "After the Deluge," pp. 175, 176, 209; *Stars and Stripes* (Germany edition), November 12, 1945, pp. 1, 2; Cohen Address, November 7, 1946, YIVO; *New York Times*, May 30, 1948, 6:42; "Final Report of Major Abraham A. Hyman," folder, "Germany Jewish Adviser–H. Greenstein," folder, "Emigration–Immigration, Germany, West, Advisor on Jewish Affairs, Bernstein, Philip, 1947" AJC; "Confidential Report," UNRRA; *Survey Graphic* (1946), 35:234; Squadrilli Report; William Haber report, October 6, 1948, in "Reports of the Advisors on Jewish Affairs," AJC Library; William Haber to Meir Grossman, February 24, 1948, May 26, 1948, JDC, General Files on Displaced Persons; "Foreign Relations Committee—Displaced Persons," box 99, Smith MSS.; Sandulescu, *Hunger's Rogues*, pp. 18, 19, 21; PSF, Subject File, box 184, folder (Palestine–Jewish Immigration), Chelf Report, October 13, 1947, Truman MSS.; McNeill, *By the Rivers of Babylon*, p. 84; Davis, *Come as a Conqueror*, p. 173; Bauer, *Flight and Rescue*, pp. 273–74; Rifkind interview; *American Jewish Year Book*, (1948–49), 50:469; clipping New York *Herald-Tribune*, August 11, 1947, Wiener Library, London, clipping file on displaced persons.

14. *Stars and Stripes* (Germany edition), September 1, 1945, p. 2, January 3, 1946, p. 7; Heymont, "After the Deluge," p. 208.

15. Fulton Committee, pp. 30, 37; MG Reports, August 20, 1946; Heymont, "After the Deluge," pp. 117, 229.

16. "Confidential Report," UNRRA.

17. "Army Talk," (November 30, 1946), no. 151, pp. 4–5, copy in ACJ MSS., box 104, folder, "Relief Organizations—Citizens Committee on Displaced Persons, 1947"; Heymont, "After the Deluge," pp. 9, 10, 13, 61. A public health nurse wrote, "The greatest problem of all was how to teach proper use of the latrine. For several years, these people had lived and been treated as animals, and they did not understand the great interest of our Army in the disposal of human waste. The utmost patience and tact were necessary in educating them in the proper use of toilet facilities." Catheren M. Schneider, "The Displaced Person as a Patient," p. 691.

18. McNarney to Eisenhower, April 22, 1946, OMGUS, box 169 3/3; Sir George Rendell to J. F. Byrnes, March 15, 1946, FO 371 57760/WR 762, WR 828; JC March 22, 1946, p. 9; Truman to Byrnes, April 17, 1946, OF 127, Truman MSS., Cohen, *Not Free to Desist*, p. 285; Lorimer, "America's Response to Europe's Displaced Persons," p. 45.

19. Hirshmann, *The Embers Still Burn*, pp. 105, 176; Hirschmann to Fiorello LaGuardia, June 16, 1946, box 2739, folder, "I. Hirschmann," LaGuardia MSS.; "Confidential Report," UNRRA, box 66,480; George Vida, *From Doom to Dawn*, p. 65; David Bernstein to John Slawsen, May 26, 1947, AJC, folder, "Emigration-Immigration, Germany, West, Advisor on Jewish Affairs, Bernstein, Philip, 1947"; and Joel Wolfsohn to John Slawsen, May 21, 1948, AJC, folder, "Displaced Persons, Germany and Austria."

20. FO 371 66654/WR 289.

21. Russell Hill, *Struggle For Germany*, pp. 112, 117.

22. Union O.S.E., *Report on the Situation of the Jews in Germany (Geneva, 1946), October/December, 1945, p. 118;* Herbert Agar, *The Saving Remnant*, p. 170; WO 202 620; *Stars and Stripes* (Germany edition), December 11, 1945, p. 2; David Bernstein, "Europe's Jews: Summer, 1947," p. 105.

23. *Commentary* (August 1947), 4:101; Joel D. Wolfsohn to Abe Olshein, September 7, 1947, box 19, Wolfsohn MSS., Truman Library; Gershon, *Postscript*, pp. 46–47.

24. Sender Report, YIVO; "Confidential Report," UNRRA, box 66,480; *Survey Graphic* (December 1945), 34:471; Bernstein to Slawsen, May 26, 1947, AJC; JC, August 23, 1946, p. 5, March 1, 1946; Bauer, *Flight and Rescue*, p. 51.

25. FO 371 51098/WR 2287; Pritchard, "The Social System of a Displaced Persons Camp," p. 79; FRUS, 1946, V, 146.

26. Thomas J. Davis, "The Problem of Displaced Persons In Europe: A Factual Resume," box 17, McGrath MSS.; Revercomb Committee, p. 16; Grossman, "The Jewish DP Problem," pp. 29–30; Hirshmann, *The Embers Still Burn*, p. 26; Ephraim Dekel, *B'RIHA: Flight to the Homeland*, p. 76; Rifkind, "The Disinherited Jews"; Gerhard Jacoby, "The Story of the Jewish 'DP,'" YIVO, folder, 2205; Bauer, *Flight and Rescue*, p. 281; "Report— Relations With Military-D.P. #U.S.-2," UNRRA; Davis, *Come as a Conqueror*, p. 183; Fulton Committee, p. 28; Squadrilli Report; United Service for New Americans, "Special Information Bulletin" (December 31, 1947) ser. 2, no. 19, p. 9; Pritchard, "Social System of a DP Camp," p. 58; "Report on Displaced Persons," Smith MSS.; *Social Research* (March 1947), 14:47.

27. Revercomb Committee, pp. 12–15; "Shocking State of Jewish D.P.," JC, December 14, 1945, pp. 1, 9, October 31, 1947, p. 5; Fulton Committee, p. 29; report of R. Peter Straus, OMGUS, Manpower Division, June 17, 1946, Truman MSS. OF 198-B; clipping, January 15, 1949, Wiener Library, London; Hirschmann to LaGuardia, June 16, 1946, LaGuardia MSS., box 2739, folder "I. Hirschmann"; "Address by Henry Cohen to European Advisory Committee, World Jewish Congress, November 7, 1946," in YIVO, folder 65.

28. Pritchard, "Social System of a DP Camp," pp. 1, 2.

29. Leo Srole, "Why The DP's Can't Wait," p. 19; Hirschmann, *The Embers Still Burn*, p. 99.

30. Peterson, *The American Occupation of Germany*, pp. 295–96; Squadrilli Report; Fredericksen, *The American Military Government Occupation of Germany*, p. 77; "Report on Displaced Persons," Smith MSS., Hirschmann to La-Guardia, June 16, 1946, LaGuardia MSS., box 2739, folder "I. Hirschmann"; JC, January 23, 1948.

31. Clipping, *Manchester Guardian*, February 25, 1946, folder 2205, YIVO; *Commentary* (August 1947), 4:107.

32. McNeill, *By the Rivers of Babylon*, p. 84. Displaced Persons Commission officials would later express surprise when DPs disembarking in Boston in May 1949 arrived with an array of riches.

33. *Manchester Guardian*, February 25, 1946.

34. Richard Crossman, *Palestine Mission*, p. 81; FRUS (1946) 5:146; Gershon, *Postscript*, p. 42; Jon and David Kimche, *The Secret Roads*, pp. 77, 82; Herbert Fensterheim and Herbert G. Birch, "A Case Study of Group Ideology and Individual Adjustment," p. 715; Jacoby, "The Story of the Jewish DP," YIVO, folder 2205; Bauer, *Flight and Rescue*, p. 201; Pritchard, "Social System of a DP Camp," pp. 32–33.

35. Pritchard, "Social System of a DP Camp," p. 26; Paul Friedman, "The Road Back For The DP's," p. 503.

36. Heymont, "After the Deluge," p. 137.

37. Vitales Report; *Journal of Abnormal and Social Psychology*, October, 1950, pp. 712–13; Joel D. Wolfsohn to Abe Olshein, September 7, 1947, box 19, Wolfsohn MSS.; "Two Reports by Jewish Relief Workers in Germany," November, 1945, Wiener Library, London.

38. *Journal of Abnormal and Social Psychology* (October 1950), 45:713; "Report on Displaced Persons," Smith MSS.; Experiences of DPs in Foehrenwald, February, 1946, Wiener Library, London; *Persistent International Issues*, p. 53; Klemme, *The Inside Story of UNRRA*, pp. 93–95, 98; *Commentary* (December 1948), 6:502.

39. Wright Report.

40. "Report on Displaced Persons," Smith MSS.; Simon H. Rifkind, "They Are Not Expendable," *Survey Graphic*, p. 234; *Survey Graphic* (December 1945), 34:471; Cohen Address; *New York Times*, November 2, 1947, section 4, p. 5; Hirschmann, *The Embers Still Burn*, p. 156; Sandulescu, *Hunger's Rogues*, p. 18; Fulton Committee, p. 32; clipping, JC, June 6, 1947, Wiener Library; clipping, *The Record*, October 1945, p. 12, U.S. Catholic Conference (formerly National Catholic Welfare Conf.), Department of International Affairs: Division of Migration and Refugee Services (formerly Immigration Bureau), Center for Migration Studies, Staten Island, New York, box 59, folder, National Committee on Postwar Immigration Policy; *Stars and Stripes* (Germany edition) October 8, 1945, p. 3; Heymont, "After the Deluge", p. 82.

41. Nadich, *Eisenhower and the Jews*, p. 214; UNRRA MSS., Executive Offices, Office of the General Counsel, subject file, 1943–46, Displaced Persons, box 234, folder, "Displaced Persons—Collaborators, Volksdeutsch and German Balts"; Lehman to Roy F. Hendrickson, September 17, 1945, Lehman MSS., UNRRA PERSONAL, folder, "Interoffice Memos, 1945–1946," Lehman MSS.; Jacoby Story; Fredericksen, *The American Military Government Occupation of Japan*, p. 77.

42. Harold Nicolson, "Marginal Comment," p. 733; Gershon, *Postscript*, p. 39; Cohen Address; "Schools In The 'Displaced Persons Centers' of Germany," p. 384; Squadrilli Report; Alexander M. Dushkin, "The Educational Activities of the JDC In European Countries," p. 445; JC, March 7, 1947, pp. 1, 9; Heymont, "After the Deluge," p. 15; *Stars and Stripes* (European edition), September 9, 1946, p. 11; *Deggendorf Center Revue* (November 1945), p. 4, Deggendorf folder, Leo Baeck Institute, New York City; "Two Reports

by Jewish Relief Workers in Germany," Wiener Library, London; DPC MSS., box 19, History, ORT; *Current Affairs* (June 28, 1947), p. 9; clipping, *Christian Science Monitor*, December 14, 1948, Rosenfield MSS., box 25, "Newspaper Clippings, Dec. 1948," PSF, folder, (Palestine-Jewish Immigration), Chelf Report, October 13, 1947, box 184, Truman MSS.

43. Pritchard, "Social System of a DP Camp," *passim*; Haber interview.

44. JC, October 25, 1945, p. 5.

3. THE ANGLO-AMERICAN COMMITTEE OF INQUIRY

1. FRUS (1945) 8:737–38.

2. Crossman, *Palestine Mission*, p. 44; John Morton Blum, *The Price of Vision: The Diary of Henry A. Wallace, 1942–1946*, p. 313; Carl J. Friedrich, *American Policy Toward Palestine*, p. 1; Herbert Parzen, "The Roosevelt Palestine Policy, 1943–1945: An Exercise in Dual Diplomacy," p. 44; Philip J. Baram, *The Department of State In The Middle East, 1919–1945*, p. 295; CAB 129, CP (45) 216, p. 50; FRUS (1945) 8:2–3, 694–95, 698, 705–7, 709, 754–55.

3. FRUS (1945) 8:2–3, 694–95, 698; Crossman Diary, January, 1946, p. 2; Bartley C. Crum, *Behind the Silken Curtain*, p. viii.

4. FRUS (1945) 8:705–707, 709, 754–55; Truman, *Year of Decisions*, pp. 68–69.

5. FRUS (1945) 8:754–55; Dorr Memoir, p. 165.

6. AJC, *Thirty-Ninth Annual Report*, pp. 53–54; *New York Times*, July 5, 1945, p. 14; Truman to Attlee, August 31, 1945, PREM 889; Esco Foundation for Palestine, Inc., *Palestine*, p. 1188.

7. "Memorandum On The Administration of Palestine Under the Mandate," prepared for the Anglo American Committee, February, 1946, p. 6, Cunningham MSS.; William R. Polk, *The U.S. and the Arab World*, p. 187.

8. Melvin I. Urofsky, *American Zionism From Herzl To The Holocaust*, pp. 1, 14, 18, 20, 22.

9. Nadav Safran, *The United States and Israel*, p. 30; Urofsky, *American Zionism*, p. 378.

10. Crossman, *Palestine Mission*, pp. 4, 52–53; *Palestine*, p. 186; Safran, *The United States and Israel*, p. 31; W. N. Medlicott, *British Foreign Policy Since Versailles, 1919–1963*, p. 277; Bernard Wasserstein, *Britain and the Jews of Europe, 1939–1945* (New York: Oxford University Press, 1979); *Times* (London), May 3, 1945, p. 3.

11. Safran, *The United States and Israel*, p. 31; Crossman, *Palestine Mission*, pp. 50, 54–55, 113; John Snetsinger, *Truman, The Jewish Vote and the Creation of Israel*, p. 45; FO 371 45378.

12. Clement Attlee to Harry S. Truman, September 16, 1945, NA, General Records of State Department, Office of Near Eastern Affairs, RG 59, General Records, box 1.

13. CAB 128 #38 (October 4, 1945), #40 (October 11, 1945); CAB 129, CP (45) 216, October 10, 1945.

14. Frankel Interview; *New Republic* (December 31, 1945), p. 448; *New York Times*, September 24, 1945, p. 1; *New Statesman and Nation* (September 29, 1945); J. C. Hurewitz, *The Struggle For Palestine*, p. 230; Medlicott, *British Foreign Policy*, p. 270; Crossman to David Horowitz, June 28, 1945, Crossman MSS.; CAB 128 #26 (August 30, 1945), #38 (October 4, 1945), #40 (October 11, 1945); CAB 129, CP (45) 216, October 10, 1945; Noah Lucas, *The Modern History of Israel*, p. 224.

15. FRUS (1945) 8:772, 775, 785–86, 788–90, 819–20; CAB 128 #52 (November 13, 1945), 7; PSF, box 184, folder (Palestine-Jewish Immigration), Truman Library; *Jewish Social Studies* (January, 1973), pp. 63, 68–69; Henderson Memoir, p. 160; Truman, *Years of Trial and Hope*, p. 142.

16. Truman, *Years of Trial and Hope*, pp. 68–69; Bain, *March to Zion*, p. 39; Henderson Memoir, pp. 104–5; Memo of July 8, 1946, PSF, box 184, folder on (Palestine-Jewish Immigration), Truman Library; Snetsinger, *Truman, the Jewish Vote*, pp. 16, 55; Frank Buxton to Felix Frankfurter, June 17, 1946, box 40, Frankfurter MSS.; Rosenmann OH; Baram, pp. 72, 260–61; Crum, *Behind the Silken Curtain*, pp. 7–8; John A. DeNovo, "The Culbertson Economic Mission and Anglo-American Tensions in the Middle East, 1944–1945," pp. 924–25; Feingold, *The Politics of Rescue*, p. 158; Crossman, *Palestine Mission*, p. 46; McDonald Diary, p. 12; Kermit Roosevelt, "The Partition of Palestine: A Lesson in Pressure Politics," p. 2.

17. *Jewish Social Studies* (January 1973) pp. 65, 68; FRUS (1945) 8:777, 782; R. H. S. Crossman, "Mr. Bevin and Mr. Truman," *Statesman and Nation*, p. 11.

18. JC, November 16, 1945, p. 6; *Palestine*, p. 1193; Ganin, "Diplomacy of the Weak," p. 130.

19. Rosenman's list included Summer Welles, Archibald MacLeish, R. L. Buell, Reinhold Niebuhr, Bartley C. Crum, Mrs. Franklin D. Roosevelt, Fiorello LaGuardia, James McDonald, Walter Laudermilk, Senators Wayne Morse (R., Oregon), Robert A. Taft (R., Ohio), Robert F. Wagner (D., New York), and James Mead (D., New York). Box 3, Palestine file, 1945, memo dated November 19, 1945, Rosenman MSS. Byrnes proposed John W. Davis, Learned Hand, Frank Aydelotte, Charles E. Hughes, Jr., Mark Ethridge, Frank Buxton, Harold W. Dodds, James P. Baxter III, Judge Charles E. Clark, Judge Joseph C. Hutcheson, O. Max Gardner, and William Thomas Laprade. James F. Byrnes, "Memo for the President," November 21, 1945, PSF, box 184, folder on Palestine 1945–47.

20. Truman, "Memo for Secretary of State," November 27, 1945, *ibid.*; Aydelotte Diary, December 3, 5, 1945; Henderson Memoir, pp. 104–5; Crossman, *Palestine Mission*, p. 50.

21. Frank Buxton to Felix Frankfurter, December 14, 1945, box 39, April 19, 1946, box 40, Frankfurter MSS.; O. M. Gardner to Harry S. Truman, December 14, 1945, OF 204b, box 775, Truman MSS.; Aydelotte Diary, December 14, 1945, April 11, 1946; William Phillips, *Ventures in Diplomacy*, p. 448; McDonald Diary, pp. 12–13; Crossman Diary, January, n.d., 1946, pp. 6–7, and April 8, 1946; Crum, *Behind the Silken Curtain*, pp. 34–35; Bain,

March to Zion, pp. 94–104; Frances Blanshard, *Frank Aydelotte of Swarthmore*, p. 372; Robert D. Schulzinger, *The Making of the Diplomatic Mind* (Middletown, Conn.: Wesleyan University Press, 1975), p. 131; Evan M. Wilson, *Decision on Palestine*, pp. 69–70.

22. Crossman Diary, January, 1946, pp. 7–8; Phillips, *Ventures in Diplomacy*, p. 448; McDonald Diary, p. 12, and April 8, 1946; Phillips Diary, April 14–April 18, 1946; Buxton to Frankfurter, April 19, 1946, Frankfurter MSS.; JC, May 2, 1947, p. 17; U.S. Senate, *Admission of Jews to Palestine*, p. 47.

23. Transcript of "Hearings Before The Anglo-American Committee of Inquiry," in Blaustein Library, AJC; W. J. Gold to J. G. Slawsen, February 5, 1946, folder, "Federalization Plans, AACofI, Hearings, Israel, Palestine, 1946," AJC; Crum, *Behind the Silken Curtain*, pp. 12–23, 26; Crossman, *Palestine Mission*, pp. 24–28, 33, 37, 45, 46.

24. Crossman, *Palestine Mission*, p. 52; Horowitz, *State in the Making*, p. 62; Crum, *Behind the Silken Curtain*, p. 61; Phillips Diary, January 30, 1946; Crossman to Clement Attlee, May 7, 1946, PREM 8 302/XM 03323; James G. McDonald, *My Mission In Israel* (New York: Simon and Schuster, 1951), pp. 23–24; Sidney Hertzberg, "This Month in History," *Commentary* (March 1946) vol. 1; Nicholas Bethell, *The Palestine Triangle*, p. 223.

25. Joseph C. Hutcheson, Jr., "Memorandum," February 1946, in McDonald MSS.; Crossman, *Palestine Mission*, pp. 81–82, 87, 90, 93, 96–97, 166, 176; Crum, *Behind the Silken Curtain*, pp. 117, 130, 137.

26. Vida, *From Doom to Dawn*, p. 67; David B. Sachar, "David K. Niles and United States Foreign Policy Toward Palestine: A Case Study in American Foreign Policy," p. 21; Aydelotte Diary, April 19, 1946, Bauer *Flight and Rescue*, p. 202.

27. Aydelotte Diary, April 11, 1946.

28. *Ibid.*; Polk, *The U.S. and the Arab World*, p. 187; "Memorandum On The Administration of Palestine Under the Mandate," prepared for the Anglo-American Committee of Inquiry, February 1946, p. 6, box 5, file 2, Cunningham MSS.; Crossman, *Palestine Mission*, p. 114; *Commentary* (January, 1946), p. 68; Aydelotte to Earl G. Harrison, February 10, 1947, series 6, box 1, "Citizens Committee on Displaced Persons," Aydelotte MSS.

29. Phillips Diary, March 11, 1946; McDonald Diary, March 2, 1946; Crossman, "Chatham House Speech," June 13, 1946, Crossman MSS.; Crossman, *Palestine Mission*, pp. 102, 123; Crossman to wife, Zita, undated, Crossman MSS.; 30. McDonald Diary, April 1, 1946; Phillips Diary, April 1, 1946.

31. Phillips Diary, March 31, 1946; Crossman Diary, April 8, 1946; Buxton to Frankfurter, April 14, 1946, Frankfurter MSS.; Phillips, *Ventures in Diplomacy*, p. 445; CAB 128 #51 (June 20, 1946); Crossman, *Palestine Mission*, p. 168; Crossman to Attlee, April 22, 1946, with "Notes on Palestine Report of Anglo-American Committee," appended, PREM 8 302/XM 03323.

32. Crossman to wife, April 4, 8, 1946; W. F. Crick to Crossman, July 4,

1946, Crossman MSS.; Aydelotte Diary, April 3, 6, 7, 12, 16, 19, 20, 1946; Buxton to Frankfurter, April 19, 1946, Frankfurter MSS.

33. Buxton to Frankfurter, April 19, 1946, Frankfurter MSS.; Crossman to Attlee, April 22, 1946, PREM 8 302/XM 03323; Crossman Diary, April 8, 1946; Phillips Diary, March 31, April 14–April 18, 1946; Aydelotte Diary, April 16, 1946; folder 187, McDonald MSS.; Crum, *Behind the Silken Curtain,* p. 265; Hutcheson to Truman, n.d., folder, "Report of the Joint Anglo-American Committee of Inquiry on Palestine," OF 204b, Truman MSS. On April 3, 1946, McDonald wrote Bernard Baruch, "We are fortunate in the chairmanship of Judge Hutcheson, who has displayed an amazing power of comprehension and synthesis," Baruch MSS.

34. *Palestine,* pp. 1221–34.

35. Wilson, *Decision on Palestine,* p. 78; Crum, *Behind the Silken Curtain,* pp. 282–83; McDonald Diary, April 19, 20, 1946; Phillips Diary, April 20, 1946; Buxton to Frankfurter, April 19, 1946, Frankfurter MSS.; Bain, *March to Zion,* p. 108.

36. Crossman, *Palestine Mission,* pp. 188, 192; FO 371 52516/3634; Bauer, *Flight and Rescue,* p. 203; Lucas, *Modern History of Israel,* p. 205; Crossman to Attlee, May 7, 1946, PREM 8 302/XM 03323, Richard Crossman, *A Nation Reborn,* p. 79.

37. Crossman, *A Nation Reborn,* pp. 81–83; PRO CP (46) April 27, 1946; Crossman to Attlee, May 7, 1946, PREM 8 302/XM 03323; Crum, *Behind the Silken Curtain,* pp. 219–20; CAB 129 CP #258 (July 8, 1946), p. 6; CAB 128 #38 (April 29, 1946), *New York Times,* May 2, 1946; p. 1; FO 371 52520/4051, 51671/A1355.

38. I. F. Stone, "The Palestine Report," p. 564; Emanuel Celler to Richard Crossman, May 22, 1946, Crossman MSS.; JC, May 3, 1946, p. 10.

39. Chaim Weizmann to Clement Attlee, May 13, 1946, PREM 8 304; FO 371 52609/A2155; General Records of the State Department, NA, RG 59, box 1, memorandum of June 21, 1946.

40. FO 371 51671/A1355; Melvin I. Urofsky, *We are One! American Jewry and Israel,* p. 111; *Commentary* (June 1946), p. 69.

41. Robert F. Wagner statement on Anglo-American Committee report, April 30, 1946, box 733, folder 42, Wagner MSS.; "Reaction to the report of the Anglo-American Committee on Palestine," prepared by Public Attitudes Branch-Division of Public Liaison, Office of Public Affairs, Department of State, Phillips MSS.; FO 371 51671/A1355; Richard P. Stevens, *American Zionism and U.S. Foreign Policy, 1942–1947,* p. 145.

42. McDonald Diary, April 1, 1946; Buxton to Frankfurter, September 10, 1946, Frankfurter MSS.; copy of talk by Crossman, "The Palestine Report," given at Chatham House, June 13, 1946, Crossman MSS.; see also Bain, *March to Zion,* pp. 34–35, 37–38.

43. Joseph B. Schechtman, *The United States and the Jewish State Movement: The Crucial Decade: 1939–1949,* p. 176; Barnet Nover, "Bull of Bashan," Washington *Post,* June 13, 1946, p. 7; Maurice J. Goldbloom, "This Month

in History," *Commentary* (July 1946), 2:60; Zvi Ganin, *Truman, American Jewry, and Israel,* p. 75.

44. FRUS (1946) 7:592–605; *New York Times,* May 1, 1946, p. 13; October 15, 1946, p. 4; Washington *Post,* May 2, 1946, pp. 1, 2, May 3, 1946, pp. 1, 5.

45. "Comments on Anglo-American Committee's Recommendations," Cunningham MSS.; Crossman to *Times*[?] (London), May 25, 1946, copy in Crossman MSS.

4. PALESTINE, POLAND, AND POLITICS

1. FO 371 51671/A1661, 51608/A1700; PPP, June 14, 1946.

2. *Ibid.,* June 11, 1946; David B. Sachar, "David K. Niles and United States Policy Toward Palestine: A Case Study in American Foreign Policy," p. 32; John W. Snyder to James G. McDonald, July 17, 1946, McDonald MSS.; Dorr Memoir, pp. 172, 186.

3. CAB 128 #64 (July 4, 1946); Herbert Feis, *The Birth of Israel: The Tousled Diplomatic Bed,* p. 31; Crossman, *Palestine Mission,* p. 196; Dorr Memoir, p. 22; *New York Times,* August 4, 1946, p. 1; Schechtman, *The United States and the Jewish State Movement,* p. 165.

4. *New York Times,* July 26, 1946, p. 1; Schechtman, *The United States and the Jewish State Movement,* pp. 162, 165; CAB 128 #73 (July 25, 1946); FO 371 57756/WR2066; FRUS (1946) 7:656–61; Stevens, *American Zionism and U.S. Foreign Policy,* p. 152; Sachar, "David K. Niles," p. 38; box 5, file 2, p. 6, Cunningham MSS.; "Adventure In Diplomacy," p. 161, unpublished manuscript in box 5, Henry F. Grady MSS., Truman Library.

5. CAB 128 #73 (July 25, 1946); Howard M. Sachar, *A History of Israel,* p. 271.

6. Wallace Diary, pp. 4865, 4877; Dorr Memoir, pp. 269–70, 272, 274.

7. Abba Hillel Silver to Bernard M. Baruch, July 30, 1946, box 71, Baruch MSS.; Buxton to Frankfurter, August 9, 1946, Frankfurter MSS.; "The Truman Administration Record on Palestine," August 26, 1946, box 68, file 12, Wise MSS.; Ganin, "Diplomacy of the Weak," p. 190; Truman to Ed Flynn, August 2, 1946, PSF 184, folder (Palestine 1945–1947), Truman MSS.

8. American Jewish Conference, Minutes of the Interim Committee, April 2, 1946, July 12, 1946, Meir Grossman, Report to the Interim Committee, September 20, 1946, ZA; David R. Wal to Meir Grossman, July 23, 1946, General Files on Displaced Persons, JDC MSS.; John McCormack to Harry S. Truman, July 22, 1946, Truman to McCormack, July 24, 1946, PSF, box 184, folder (Palestine 1945–1947), Truman MSS.

9. Sachar, "David K. Niles," p. 1; Henderson Memoir, pp. 110–11; Rifkind Interview; Engel Interview.

10. FO 371 57717/WR2066; Margaret Truman, *Harry S. Truman,* p. 299; Wallace Diary, pp. 4864, 4876; Carol Eleanor Hoffecker, "President Tru-

man's Explanation of His Foreign Policy to the American People" (Ph.D. dissertation; Harvard University, 1967), p. 121.

11. FRUS (1946) 7:648; Urofsky, *We Are One*, p. 132; Kimche, *The Secret Roads*, p. 91; Sachar, "David K. Niles," p. 33; Sachar, *A History of Israel*, p. 26; CAB 128 #72 (July 23, 1946).

12. Safran, *Israel*, pp. 32–33; Mark Wischnitzer, *To Dwell In Safety: The Story of Jewish Migration Since 1800*, p. 280; FRUS (1946) 7:679n; *Stars and Stripes* (European edition), August 13, 1946, p. 1.

13. *Time*, July 15, 1946, pp. 36–37; Zachariah Schuster, "Between The Millstones in Poland," *Commentary* (August 1946), 2:110; JC, July 12, 1946, p. 1, July 19, 1946, p. 9; *New York Times*, July 6, 1946, p. 1; Hirshmann, *The Embers Still Burn*, p. 188; FRUS (1946) 6:479; Philip S. Bernstein to General Joseph T. McNarney, "Report on Poland," August 2, 1946, Bernstein MSS.; WJC items from the press, July 22, 1946, box 89, Wise MSS.

14. WJC items from the press, July 22, 1946, box 89, Wise MSS.; FO 371 57694/WR2335; Michael Checinski, "The Kielce Pogrom: Some Unanswered Questions," p. 60; JC July 19, 1946, p. 1, August 9, 1946, p. 1; "Displaced Persons and Infiltrees in the American Zones of Occupation in Germany," July 29, 1946, folder, "Immigration, D.P.'s, 1945–47," AJC MSS.

15. Crossman, *Palestine Mission*, 87; Samuel Lubell, "The Second Exodus of the Jews," p. 85; F. W. Buxton, "Report on Poland," February 16, 1946, "Report of Leslie L. Rood . . . on Visit to Poland," February 7–13, 1946, McDonald MSS.; "Displaced Persons and Infiltrees in the American Zone of Occupation in Germany," July 29, 1946, AJC MSS.; Robert Murphy to Secretary of State, January 23, 1946, State Department, Decimal File, RG 59, box C-525, NA; *Time*, July 23, 1946, p. 37; "Hearings Before the Anglo-American Committee of Inquiry," p. 32.

16. FO 371 57684/WR15; *New York Times*, January 3, 1946, p. 3, April 6, 1947, p. 52; JC December 21, 1945, p. 8, January 8, 1946, p. 9, February 1, 1946, p. 9, March 8, 1946, p. 1, May 3, 1946, p. 1, June 14, 1946, p. 8, July 12, 1946, p. 9, August 31, 1946, p. 1; Bauer, *Flight and Rescue*, p. 3; State Department, Decimal File, RG 59, box 5601, item 1-2946; Kimche, *The Secret Roads*, p. 87; Lucjan Dobroszycki, "Restoring Jewish Life in Post-War Poland," *Soviet Jewish Affairs* (1973), 3:66.

17. *Washington Post*, January 3, 1946, p. 1; *New York Times*, January 3, 1946, p. 1, January 4, 1946, p. 10; Bauer, *Flight and Rescue*, p. 98.

18. Jackson Memoir, pp. 190, 218–21; Attachment to letter no. 1498, September 5, 1946, JDC MSS.; *Stars and Stripes* (European edition), August 21, 1946, p. 1.

19. Dekel, *B'RIHAH*, p. 93; Sachar, *A History of Israel*, p. 268–69; FO 371 57684/WR98; *New York Times*, January 4, 1946, p. 12; Kimche, *The Secret Roads*, p. 88.

20. Kimche, *The Secret Roads*, p. 90; Louis Barish, ed., *Rabbis In Uniform*, pp. 51–52; Crossman, *Palestine Mission*, p. 83; Dekel, *B'RIHAH*, p. 93; Sachar, *A History of Israel*, p. 269; Bauer, *Flight and Rescue*, p. 262.

21. Vitales Report, p. 17; Ziemke, *The U.S. Army in the Occupation of Germany*, Lorimer, "America's Response to Europe's Displaced Persons," pp. 41–42, 80; "Occupation Forces in Europe Series, 1945–46, Displaced Persons," p. 196; MG Reports, January 20, 1946; JC December 7, 1945, p. 1; Crossman, *Palestine Mission*, p. 83; JDC Memo, p. 5; "Report of AJDC Staff Conference," October 21, 1945, p. 17, folder 11, DP Collection, Germany, YIVO; Proudfoot, *European Refugees*, p. 334; Grossman, "Refugees, DP's, and Migrants," p. 130; Pritchard, "Social System of a DP Camp," p. 18; Revercomb Committee, p. 12; "Displaced Persons: Poland," Subject File, Displaced Persons, box 234, UNRRA MSS.; Nathan Reich, "Europe's Jews Since V–E Day," p. 4; F. W. Buxton, "Report on Poland," "Report of Leslie L. Rood . . . Visit to Poland," McDonald MSS.; FO 371 57688/WR736; *New York Times*, August 8, 1946, p. 6.

22. FO 371 57696/WR2668; clipping file on Displaced Persons, Wiener Library, London; FRUS (1946), 5:178; JDC Memo, pp. 5–6; Dekel, *B'RIHA*, p. 82, Washington *Post*, August 10, 1946, p. 2; *Stars and Stripes* (European edition), October 23, 1946, p. 1; J. Hilldring to M. Leavitt, July 31, 1946, folder 2205, DP Collection, Germany, YIVO.

23. FRUS (1946) 5:153; Liebschutz, "Rabbi Philip S. Bernstein," p. 124; Cohen, *Not Free to Desist*, pp. 287–88; Harry S. Truman to Groucho Marx, October 8, 1946, Harry S. Truman to Walter George, October 8, 1946, PSF, folder (Palestine-Jewish Immigration), box 184, Truman MSS.; Proskauer, "Memo to AJC Members," October 7, 1946, folder, "Immigration, DP's, 1950," AJC MSS.; Lessing Rosenwald to Harry S. Truman, November 26, 1946, unprocessed material, box 1, "President Truman Correspondence, 1945–1946," ACJ MSS., Madison; Sidney Hertzberg, "This Month In History," *Commentary* (February 1946), 1:48; Sheldon Morris Neuringer, "American Jewry and United States Immigration Policy, 1881–1953" p. 276; PPP, 1945, pp. 572–76. See also Amy Zahl Gottlieb, "Refugee Immigration: The Truman Directive."

24. Brook, Friedlander, Gottlieb interviews; *New York Times*, December 29, 1945, pp. 1, 8; Revercomb Committee, pp. 26–27; Fulton Committee, p. 76; Speech by Irving M. Engel to the Conference of Jewish Social Welfare Agencies, May 23, 1951, box 22, DPC MSS.

25. FO 371 51606/AN35; John Lesinski to Harry S. Truman, January 30, 1946, PSF, folder (Palestine-Jewish Immigration), box 184, Truman MSS.; George H. Gallup, *The Gallup Poll*, 1:555; see also Bain, *March To Zion*, p. 58.

26. FRUS (1946) 7:645, 703; Dorr Memoir, p. 206; David Niles to Matt Connelly, July 15, 1946, Truman to Sol Bloom, July 23, 1946, PSF, folder (Palestine-Jewish Immigration), box 184, Truman MSS.

27. JC August 23, 1946, p. 6; *New York Times*, August 18, 1946, September 3, 1946, p. 3; *Stars and Stripes* (European edition), August 21, 1946, p. 3.

28. "The Truman Administration Record on Palestine," August 26, 1946, box 68, file 12, Wise MSS.; Neuringer, "American Jewry and United States Immigration Policy," p. 282; Eleanor Baldwin Tripp, "Displaced Persons: The Legislative Controversy In The United States, 1945–1950," p. 53.

29. FO 371 52568/2198; *Commentary* (July 1946), p. 60; *New York Times,* August 17, 1946, p. 12; August 21, 1946, p. 5; Washington *Post,* August 18, 1946, p. 4B.

5. THE FORMATION OF THE CITIZENS COMMITTEE

1. Engel Interview; Bernard Interview; Neuringer, "American Jewry and United States Immigration Policy," p. 282.

2. Minutes of the Interim Committee, American Jewish Conference, November 19, 1946, May 2, 1947, ZA; Minutes of the Executive Committee, American Jewish Conference, July 12, 1945, ZA; William S. Bernard to Henry Busch, March 17, 1948, box 104, folder "Relief Organizations—Citizens Committee on Displaced Persons, 1948–1950," ACJ MSS., Madison.

3. *New York Times,* September 29, 1946, p. 13; "Our Own Open Door," p. 468; "Send Them Here!," p. 36; PPP, October 4, 1946, p. 1162; Stevens, *American Zionism and U.S. Foreign Policy,* p. 155; JC, October 11, 1946, pp. 1, 6; Snetsinger, *Truman, The Jewish Vote,* p. 42; FO 371 51610/AN3901.

4. AJC Administrative Committee, Minutes, October 2, 1946, AJC; Cohen, *Not Free To Desist,* pp. 288–89.

5. Box 59, folder, "National Committee on Postwar Immigration Policy," NCWC MSS.; William S. Bernard, ed., *American Immigration Policy,* pp. xviii, 259; ACVAFS, "The Problem of Displaced Persons," mimeographed report of the survey committee on displaced persons of the ACVAFS, June 1946, pp. 57, 61, 74–75, AJC Library; "HIAS 1945 merger with National Refugee Service," box 5, National Refugee Service MSS., American Jewish Historical Society, Waltham, Mass.; folder, "National Committee on Post War Immigration Policy," AJC; Earl G. Harrison to Kathleen Hambly Hanstein, June 25, 1946, American Friends Service Committee MSS., Philadelphia; William S. Bernard to George J. Hexter, November 5, 1946, November 28, 1947, NCPI folder, AJC MSS.; Bernard to Hexter, October 19, 1948, IME MSS.; Joint Conference on Alien Legislation, National Committee on Post-War Immigration Policy, box 23, American Council For Nationalities Services MSS., shipment 3, box 23, Immigration History Archives, St. Paul, Minn.

6. Bernard Interview; ACJ Executive Committee Minutes, January 21, 1947, unprocessed material, box 2, folder, "Executive Committee Meetings, 1947," ACJ MSS., Madison; Lessing Rosenwald sent out a dozen letters of inquiry on November 13, 1946, unprocessed material, box 3, folder, "Immigration Program," ACJ MSS., Madison; Irving Feist to Elmer Berger, November 26, 1946, John G. Slawson to Elmer Berger, November 25, 1946, *ibid.*

7. Engel Interview.

8. Minutes of the AJC Staff Committee on Immigration, October 7, 1946, AJC.

9. Hirsh Interview; "Resume of minutes of Political Strategy Committee," April 17, 1947, folder, "Displaced Persons Citizens Committee, 1947, undated," box 6, IME MSS.

10. Lessing Rosenwald to Harry S. Truman, November 26, 1946, unprocessed material, box 1, folder, "President Truman Correspondence, 1945–1946," ACJ MSS., Madison; Engel Interview; Minutes of Immigration Sub-Committee Luncheon, November 5, 1946, Minutes of Immigration Committee Meeting, November 25, 1946, AJC; *New York Times*, November 17, 1946, p. 52.

11. Minutes of Immigration Sub-Committee Luncheon, November 5, 1946, AJC.

12. *Ibid.*

13. Earl G. Harrison to Abram Orlow, February 17, 1947, Harrison to Eleanor Roosevelt, April 2, 1947, box 3756, E. Roosevelt MSS.; Minutes of Immigration Committee, October 25, 1946, Selma G. Hirsh to IME, November 6, 1946, IME MSS., "Report of Immigration Committee," November 6, 1946, Minutes of Administrative Committee, November 6, 1946, AJC MSS.; George J. Hexter to Jacob Billikopf, July 28, 1948, IME MSS.; Neuringer, "American Jewry and United States Immigration Policy," pp. 306–7.

14. Minutes of CCDP Organization Meeting, n.d., *ca.* December 20, 1946, AJC.

15. *Ibid.*

16. Joseph M. Proskauer to Jesse Steinhardt and fifteen others May 9, 1947, CCDP files, "March-May '47"; Lessing Rosenwald to Irving M. Engel, December 29, 1947, folder, "Fund Raising 47–48"; Rosenwald to Engel, March 4, 1947, folder, "June-Dec., '47," AJC MSS. The situation was most clearly stated in a letter from Ely M. Aaron to Proskauer: "We are getting practically no help from the non-Jewish groups in raising funds," May 21, 1947, "Fund Raising," *ibid.* Of the first $47,000 collected for the CCDP, the Rosenwald family contributed $36,000 and non-Jews, $4,400. George Hexter to Proskauer, February 27, 1947, folder, "Nov. 46–Feb. 47." *ibid.*

17. Stratton Interview; *Congressional Quarterly Notebook* (May 5, 1948), 6:157–158; Stephen K. Bailey and Howard D. Samuel, *Congress at Work*, p. 247.

18. Lorimer, "America's Response to the Displaced Persons," p. 110.

19. Bailey and Samuel, *Congress at Work*, p. 247; Lorimer, "America's Response to the Displaced Persons," p. 110; folder, "Displaced Persons Misc. Material," box 24, and scrapbook, "Immigration Pamphlets and Notes," box 23, Stratton MSS.; shipment 3, box 7, shipment 6, box 7, American Council for Nationalities Services MSS., Immigration History Archives; W. S. Bernard to Cooperating Organizations, January 19, 1948, CCDP folders, AJC MSS.; folder, "Relief Organizations—Citizens Committee on Displaced Persons, 1948–1950," box 104, ACJ MSS., Madison. See also appendix C.

20. William S. Bernard, "Refugee Asylum in the United States," pp. 3–4.

21. Walter Dushnyck to IME, June 18, 1947, IME MSS.; "Do you Know That?" folder 2839, Kem MSS.

22. *Ibid.*

23. Minutes of the CCDP Executive Committee Meeting, February 21, 1947, CCDP folders, AJC MSS.; "Remarks concerning detailed criticism of

the Citizens Committee on Displaced Persons made by Miss Anna Lord Straus; prepared for . . . Mrs. Lillian Poses," folder, "Displaced Persons Citizens Committee, 1946, undated," IME MSS.

24. Stratton Interview.

25. *New York Times*, April 6, 1947, 4:7; Lt. Colonel Jerry M. Sage, "The Evolution of U.S. Policy Toward Europe's Displaced Persons: World War II to June 25, 1948," p. 67; Burnet R. Maybank to a constituent, January 16, 1947, Maybank MSS., College of Charleston, Charleston, S.C.; Harry S. Truman to David K. Niles, April 10, 1947, PSF, box 131, folder, "Niles, David K."; *Newsweek* (December 30, 1946), 28:23; Memo to chapter chairmen from Nathan Weisman of the AJC, March 20, 1947, CCDP files, folder, "March-May '47," AJC. Polls taken for the AJC showed a strong anti-immigrant sentiment in the United States; see Joseph M. Proskauer, "Memorandum On Immigration," October 7, 1947, folder on "Immigration, DPs, 1950," AJC MSS. Carl Hayden to Mrs. J. Forrest Ingle, April 3, 1947, box 42, folder 12, "D.P.'s from the Baltic Area," Carl Hayden MSS. The CCDP representative was told in Washington, *ca*. March 26, 1947, that a bill to aid DPs did not have "a chance of seeing the light of day this session." Shipment 6, box 8, folder, "F–Misc.," American Council For Nationalities Services MSS., Immigration History Archives.

26. Camilla G. Booth to William G. Stratton, May 26, 1947, Robert Zachary to William G. Stratton, June 4, 1947, and several others in folders "Out of State Corr against 2910," box 23, and "Displaced Persons, April thru June, 1947," box 22, Stratton MSS.; G. D. Minick to Senator Tom Connally, May 26, 1946, box 185, Connally MSS.

27. Herbert Lehman to Fred Van Devanter, June 25, 1947, General Correspondence, 1947, I, Lehman MSS.; John Ransom to William G. Stratton, June 10, 1947, folder, "Ill. Corr. against H.R. 2910," box 23, Stratton MSS.; *New York Times*, May 3, 1948, p. 20.

28. William S. Bernard to Reuben Resnick, December 2, 1947, Leo J. Margolin to Bernard, memo on "Propaganda Problems," n.d. *ca*. November 30, 1947, CCDP folders, "June-Dec. '47," AJC MSS.

29. *The State of the Union Messages of the Presidents* (3 vols.; New York: Chelsea House, 1966), 3:2498.

30. "Analysis of Revercomb Report on DPs," appended to letter from H. Graham Morison to John R. Steelman, February 25, 1947, OF 127, box 552, Truman MSS.; Phileo Nash to Leonard Dinnerstein, November 21, 1978; Engel Interview; Edwin G. Nourse to William G. Stratton, April 24, 1947, Raymond G. Foley to William G. Stratton, May 23, 1947, folder, "Displaced Persons II," box 23, Stratton MSS.

31. C. Irving Dwork to A. Leon Kubowitski, February 5, 1947, folder, "Post War Planning–Immigration to US, 1947" in World Jewish Congress MSS., New York City. This is the only reference to the WJC MSS. in New York City, all other references to WJC MSS. are to the papers housed in London. Dorr Memoir, p. 339.

32. *New York Times*, June 16, 1947, p. 7; "Seek Admission of 400,000

DP's," p. 84; IME to George Hexter, April 24, 1947, Hexter to Arthur J. Goldsmith, March 8, 1948, IME MSS.; Samuel McCrea Cavert to Aroos Benneyan, December 18, 1947, Displaced Persons folder in General Secretary's Files, 1947, Federal Council of Churches of Christ in America MSS., Presbyterian Historical Society, Philadelphia; Bernard Interview.
33. Engel Interview; Bernard Interview.

6. THE SCENE SHIFTS TO CONGRESS

1. Susan M. Hartmann, *Truman and the 80th Congress*, pp. 17, 42, 100, 184, 211, 213; Minutes of CCDP Executive Committee Meeting, February 7, 1947, CCDP folders (Nov. 46–Feb. 47), AJC MSS.; 80C1(S) *CR*, (July 21, 1947), 93(8):9476.
2. Hartmann, *Truman and the 80th Congress*, p. 103.
3. Tris Coffin, "A Man of the Good Old Days," p. 28; William Matthew Leary, Jr., "Smith of New Jersey," p. 100; Hartmann, *Truman and the 80th Congress*, p. 13.
4. Leo J. Margolin to Joseph Fanelli, April 25, 1947, copy in box 23, folder, "Displaced Persons II," Stratton MSS.; excerpt from address by Senator Robert A. Taft, Corvallis, Oregon, September 27, 1947, folder, "Displaced Persons, 1948," box 586, Taft MSS.; IME to Baruch Feldman, June 7, 1948; Goldthwaite Dorr to William Hallam Tuck, November 17, 1947, Tuck MSS.; Rosenfield Interview; Engel Interview.
5. Dorr to Tuck, July 26, 1947, July 31, 1947, November 17, 1947, Tuck MSS.; Cecelia R. Davidson to Joseph Joslow, August 7, 1947, General Files on Displaced Persons, JDC MSS.; IME to Charles J. Bloch, July 26, 1948; Engel Memoir, tape 2–8; Murray Frank, "Washington Notes," *The Chicago Jewish Forum* (Fall 1948), 7:62; Drew Pearson, "Washington Merry-Go-Round," Joplin *Globe* (Missouri), July 20, 1948.
6. *New York Times*, December 31, 1946, p. 4; Revercomb report, 80C1(S) *CR*, (March 25, 1947), 93(2):2520.
7. Washington *Post*, January 15, 1947, p. 12.
8. "Displaced Persons," p. 238; "Welcome Immigrants!," p. 86.
9. Robert J. Donovan, *Conflict and Crisis*, pp. 231, 234, 293; Lawrence Wittner, *Cold War America* (2d ed. New York: Holt, Rinehart & Winston, 1978), pp. 37–39.
10. Norman Podhoretz, *Making It* (New York: Random House, 1967), p. 135; Liebman, *Jews and the Left*, p. 59; Klemme, *The Inside Story of UNRRA*, pp. 291–92.
11. DPC Semi-Annual Report, February 1, 1949, p. 5; Scrapbook, vol. 19, p. 58, Vandenberg MSS.
12. Dorr Memoir, p. 343; Scrapbook, vol. 19, pp. 55, 58, Vandenberg MSS.
13. Marcus Cohen to Selma Hirsh, February 4, 1947, IME MSS.; Dorr Memoir, p. 375; see also Samuel McCrea Cavert to Helen A. Shuford, n.d.,

ca. June 1947, Displaced Persons folder in General Secretary's files, 1947, Federal Council of Churches of Christ in America MSS., Presbyterian Historical Society, Philadelphia.

14. Dorr Memoir, p. 376; "List of Proposed Witnesses for Hearings on Displaced Persons Bill," folder, "Displaced Persons Material," box 23, Stratton MSS.; Fellows Committee, pp. iii, 242, 445, 602; Samuel McCrea Cavert to Jack Wasserman, April 25, 1947, William S. Bernard to Cavert, June 18, 1947, Displaced Persons folder in General Secretary's files, 1947, Federal Council of Churches of Christ in America MSS.

15. Dorr Memoir, p. 206; Dorr to Col. Stanley Mickelson, July 2, 1947, Dorr to General Clarence Huebner, July 2, 1947, Tuck MSS.

16. Fellows Committee, pp. 127–28.

17. U.S. Displaced Persons Commission, *Memo To America,* p. 15; Fellows Committee, pp. 102, 108, 110, 250.

18. Fellows Committee, pp. 6, 9, 26, 172, 407; *New York Times,* July 3, 1947, p. 7, July 15, 1947, p. 15; folders "DP Bill" and "Displaced Persons Materials," box 23, Stratton MSS.; FO 371 66705/WR2854; Diary of H. Alexander Smith, July 13, 1947, Smith MSS.

19. Fellows Committee, pp. 602–6.

20. Helen A. Shuford to Becky Best, April 21, 1947, Shuford to Bernard, December 3, 1947, CCDP MSS., Immigration History Archives; Scrapbook— "Immigration Pamphlets and Notes," box 23, Stratton MSS.; Fellows Committee, pp. 38–39.

21. Bernard, "Refugee Asylum in the United States," p. 8; William S. Bernard to Leonard Dinnerstein, October 13, 1976 and October 5, 1977; Bernard Interview; *New York Times,* May 18, 1947, p. 29.

22. Dorr to Tuck, July 31, 1947, Tuck MSS.; Dorr Memoir, pp. 371–72; Memo to Members of CCDP from W. S. Bernard, "Summary of Testimony on H.R. 2910 on June 10, 1947," and "Summary of Testimony . . . on July 9, 1947," folder, "Relief Organizations—Citizens Committee on Displaced Persons, 1948–1950," box 104, ACJ MSS., Madison; Frank L. Chelf to George C. Marshall, July 9, 1947, folder (Sept., 1946–Aug., 1947), box 552, OF 127, Truman MSS.

23. Republicans Homer Ferguson (Michigan), Joseph H. Ball (Minnesota), John W. Bricker (Ohio), John S. Cooper (Kentucky), Wayne Morse (Oregon), Leverett Saltonstall (Mass.), and H. Alexander Smith (New Jersey), and Democrats Carl Hatch (New Mexico), and J. Howard McGrath (Rhode Island).

24. IME to Arthur Goldsmith, September 23, 1947; Dorr to Tuck, July 31, 1947, Tuck MSS.; Bailey and Samuel, *Congress at Work,* p. 24.

25. Folder, "DPs, 1950," box 30, Harley M. Kilgore MSS., Franklin D. Roosevelt Library; folder, "Displaced Persons, 1946–1947," box 586, Taft MSS.; Fellows Committee, pp. 40–44; *The DP Story* pp. 12–13; Denver *Post,* July 10, 1947, p. 8.

26. James Raymond Wilson to James R. Mead, July 28, 1947, American

356   6. CONGRESS

Friends Service Committee MSS., Philadelphia; Elizabeth W. and Chester L.
French to James P. Kem, July 25, 1948, folder 3917, Kem MSS.
    27. *New York Times*, July 7, 1947, p. 15; Bailey and Samuel, *Congress at
Work*, p. 247; *Congressional Quarterly* (January 1948), p. 19.
    28. PPP, 1947, p. 328; FO 371 66705/WR2854; Robert Lovett to Alexander
Wiley, July 26, 1947, S 1563, Docket 668, NA; JC, August 29, 1947, p. 1;
Dorr to Tuck, August 21, 1947, Tuck MSS.
    29. IME to William S. Bernard, July 1, 1947, July 23, 1947; FO 371
66705/WR2854; Dorr to John R. Steelman, July 11, 1947, box 552, OF 127,
Truman MSS.; Lt. Col. Jerry M. Sage, "The Evolution of U.S. Policy Toward
Europe's Displaced Persons," p. 41; IME to members of AJC, August 26,
1947, folder, "Immigration, Displaced Persons, 1950," AJC MSS.
    30. Dorr to Tuck, July 24, 1947, July 31, 1947, August 21, 1947, Dorr to
Lucius D. Clay, July 24, 1947, Tuck MSS.; Murray Frank, "Washington
Notes," *Chicago Jewish Forum* (Winter 1947–48), 6:131; *New York Times*, July
19, 1947, p. 12; "Goldberg" to H. Alexander Smith, n.d. *ca.* July 24, 1947,
Smith MSS.
    31. Copy of statement by Paul Griffiths of the American Legion, made on
radio station WEVD, New York City, October 12, 1949, in "Displaced
Persons" folder, box 34, Ives MSS.; H. Alexander Smith to John Paul Floyd,
February 20, 1948, folder, "DP's," box 96, Smith MSS.; Revercomb Com-
mittee, p. 1.
    32. Dorr to Clay, July 24, 1947, Tuck MSS.; Frank K. Schilling to Ugo
Carusi, February 9, 1948, folder, "Legislation–1948," box 22, DPC MSS.
    33. Dorr to Tuck, October 10, 1947, Tuck MSS.; FO 371 61956/E9459,
66673/WR3598.
    34. Revercomb Committee, pp. 11, 15, 16, 17, 19, 20, 23, 55, 56; Tuck to
Dorr, November 8, 1947, Tuck MSS.
    35. Dorr to Tuck, August 21, 1947, Tuck MSS.; *Congressional Quarterly*
(January 1948), p. 18; Fulton Committee, pp. 29, 82; *New York Times*,
November 16, 1947, p. 1; Julius Levine to Mr. Trobe, October 13, 1947,
General Files on Displaced Persons, JDC.
    36. Harry S. Truman to Watson B. Miller, November 6, 1947, PPF #3530,
Truman MSS.; Engel Interview; "Americanization chairman" of the Amer-
ican Legion in Detroit to Congressman Bartel Johnson, July 8, 1947, Robert
S. Halper to J. George Friedman, July 23, 1947, Nathan Weisman to George
J. Hexter, June 23, 1947, folder, "DP's, Veterans; Immig. Leg.," AJC MSS.
    37. Clipping from Tris Coffin's column, "The Washington Daybook,"
January 16, 1948, "Displaced Persons Citizens Committee—Congressional/
Washington Items, 1947/1948," box 6, IME MSS.; ACJ Executive Committee
Minutes, October 7, 1947, unprocessed material, box 2, "Executive Com-
mittee Meetings, 1947," ACJ MSS., Madison; *Newsweek* (May 10, 1948),
31:23; St. Louis *Post-Dispatch*, November 28, 1947, p. 2C; St. Paul *Pioneer
Press*, November 28, 1947, p. 12.
    38. Josephine Ripley, "The Climate Shifts on Immigration," p. 10; Bernard

Interview; Irving M. Engel to William S. Bernard, October 20, 1947, IME to AJC members, February 16, 1948; Minutes of the Executive Committee of the CCDP, October 3, 1947, Memos to William S. Bernard from Helen A. Shuford, November 20, 1947 and November 26, 1947, CCDP MSS., Immigration History Archives.

39. IME to Jerome J. Rothschild, October 21, 1947; *New York Times*, November 19, 1947, p. 3, November 21, 1947, p. 22; Dorr to Tuck, November 17, 1947, Tuck MSS.; Robert A. Divine, *American Immigration Policy: 1924–1957*, pp. 118–119.

7. CONGRESS ACTS

1. Eve Adams to Senator McCarran, February 15, 1948, in National Archives, Files of Senator McCarran, Immigration Subcommittee, Displaced Persons, S. 1563, docket 668.

2. Revercomb Committee, p. 26; Dorr to Tuck, December 27, 1947, Tuck MSS.

3. IME to J. R. McCrary, February 9, 1948, IME to Charles J. Block, July 26, 1948; Engel Memoir, tape 2–8; Murray Frank, "Washington Notes," p. 62; Samuel McCrea Cavert to Aroos Benneyan, December 8, 1947, Federal Council of Churches of Christ in America MSS.; Ugo Carusi to Marshall M. Vance, February 5, 1948, folder "Legislation–1948," box 22, DPC MSS.

4. Dorr to H. Alexander Smith, September 15, 1947, "Foreign Relations Committee–IRO, 1947," folder, "G. H. Dorr's Observations on DP Camps," box 95, Smith MSS.; IME to Benjamin F. Saltzstein, November 21, 1949.

5. Glen H. Smith, "Senator William Langer: A Study In Isolationism," pp. 128, 131–32, 167; Robert S. Allen and William V. Shannon, *The Truman Merry-Go-Round*, pp. 311–12; Rosenberger interview; Robert Griffith, "Old Progressives and the Cold War," pp. 341–42; folder 2, "Displaced Persons, 1947–1948," box 214, Langer MSS.; IME to Members of AJC Immigration Committee, December 10, 1948.

6. On the motion to include the *Volksdeutsche*, Ferguson, Kilgore, and Wiley voted with Langer; Revercomb, Donnell, Cooper, McCarran, and McGrath formed the majority in opposition. "Excerpts from Minutes of Meeting of Committee on the Judiciary Held on Monday, March 1, 1948, with regard to displaced persons legislation," folder 10, "Displaced Persons, 1949–1950," box 256, Langer MSS.; CR, 80th Cong., 2d. sess., vol. 94, pt. 5, p. 6894.

7. Langer to W. M. Palmer, March 29, 1948, folder 18, "Displaced Persons, 1947–1948," box 213, folder 8, "Displaced Persons, 1949–1950," box 256, Langer MSS.; *New York Times*, March 2, 1948, p. 12.

8. George Hexter to IME, March 2, 1948, IME to Mortimer Brenner, March 5, 1958, Thomas Downes to IME, March 12, 1948.

9. Revercomb Committee, pp. 50–52.

10. *American Jewish Year Book* (1948–49), 50:465; Revercomb Committee,

p. 12; Robert A. Divine, *American Immigration Policy*, p. 135; D. A. Davis to Mrs. W. S. Coffin, November 8, 1947, folder, Issues, "Displaced Persons," box 95, Smith MSS.; DPC *Semi-Annual Report*, February 1, 1949, p. 16.

11. Interview with Dr. R. Gogolinski-Elston, May 28, 1978, London; Tuck to Dorr, July 23, 1947, Tuck MSS.; folder on Palestine-Jewish Immigration, box 184, PSF, Truman MSS.; Kathryn Close, "They Want to Be People," p. 393.

12. *JDC Review* (August 1948), 4:52.

13. Samuel H. Flowerman and Maria Jahoda, "Polls on Anti-Semitism," p. 83.

14. IME to Henry M. Busch, March 12, 1948; *New York Times*, May 27, 1948, p. 24; Taft to Rosenwald, March 10, 1948, folder, "Displaced Persons Correspondence," March–April, 1948, IME MSS.; Scott W. Lucas to John H. Millett, April 29, 1948, folder 0437, box 32, Lucas MSS.; William Phillips to Henry Cabot Lodge, March 19, 1948, Phillips MSS.; William Green to A. W. Robertson, April 13, 1948, drawer 7, file 39, Robertson MSS.

15. Robert M. Lovett to Chapman Revercomb, April 15, 1948, RG 51, Budget, HR 2910, K8-11/47.1, NA; Sidney Liskofsky to Morton Thalhimer, August 19, 1948, folder, "Immigration, D.P.'s, 1945–47," AJC MSS.

16. Memo from H. Alexander Smith, Jr., re: Displaced Persons, April 28, 1948, Smith MSS.

17. Dorr to Tuck, April 15, 1948, Tuck MSS.; AP Clipping, May 26, 1948, series 14, box 24, "Scrapbooks, September 1947–March 1949," Wiley MSS.

18. Herbert Hoover to William Hallam Tuck, May 13, 1948, folder, "IRO; W. H. Tuck Scrapbook of Photos and Clippings," box 5, Tuck MSS.

19. 80C2(S) *CR* (June 2, 1948), (94) 5: 6868.

20. The Senators represented the following states:

Republicans	Democrats
Owen Brewster, Maine	Dennis Chavez, New Mexico
John W. Bricker, Jr., Ohio	J. William Fulbright, Arkansas
C. Douglas Buck, Delaware	Carl Hayden, Arizona
Harry P. Cain, Washington	Clyde R. Hoey, North Carolina
Arthur Capper, Kansas	John L. McClellan, Arkansas
John S. Cooper, Kentucky	Ernest W. McFarland, Arizona
Zales N. Ecton, Montana	Millard E. Tydings, Maryland
Ralph E. Flanders, Vermont	William B. Umstead, North Carolina
Albert W. Hawkes, New Jersey	
William E. Jenner, Indiana	
William F. Knowland, California	
Edward Martin, Pennsylvania	
Eugene D. Milliken, Colorado	
Clyde M. Reed, Kansas	
Robert A. Taft, Ohio	
Edward J. Thye, Minnesota	

Arthur H. Vandenberg, Michigan
Arthur V. Watkins, Utah
Kenneth S. Wherry, Nebraska
George A. Wilson, Iowa
Milton R. Young, North Dakota

21. 80C2(S), *CR* (May 20, 1948), 94(5):6184; *ibid.*, May 27, 1948, p. 6583; *ibid.*, June 2, 1948, p. 6869; *New York Times* March 2, 1948. David Schoenbaum of the University of Iowa provided me with the information about the constituent groups among the *Volksdeutsche*, Schoenbaum to Leonard Dinnerstein, May 28, 1981.

22. Wayne Morse to Jacob Billikopf, June 7, 1948, folder, "Displaced Persons Correspondence," June, 1948, IME MSS.; *CR ibid.*, May 25, 1948, pp. 6403–4, 6585, 6859, 6900, 6913–14; A. W. Robertson to William Thalhimer, June 8, 1948, drawer 7, file 39, Robertson MSS. Both Senators from Georgia (Walter F. George and Richard B. Russell), Louisiana (Allen J. Ellender and William C. Feazel), Mississippi (James O. Eastland and John L. Stennis), and Texas (Tom Connally and W. Lee O'Daniel) as well as Arkansas' John L. McClellan, Oklahoma's Elmer Thomas, South Carolina's Olin D. Johnston, and Virginia's Harry F. Byrd opposed the bill. The Senate debate is summarized in Divine, *American Immigration Policy*, pp. 121–24 and 127–28.

23. Press Statement released by the CCDP, June 7, 1948, folder, "Displaced Persons, Immig., 1946–1950," AJC MSS.

24. Dorr to Tuck, April 15, 1948, Tuck MSS.; Memo to AJC Immigration Committee on Fellows Bill from IME, April 23, 1948, folder "Displaced Persons Citizens Committee, 1948," box 6, IME MSS.; Tripp, "Displaced Persons," p. 127.

25. Tripp, "Displaced Persons," pp. 127–29; *New York Times*, April 30, 1948, p. 9, June 11, 1948, p. 3, June 12, 1948, pp. 1, 3, 16; Hartmann, *Truman and the 80th Congress*, p. 178; U.S. *House*, "Amending The Displaced Persons Act of 1948," p. 2.

26. Memo to CRC (National Community Relations Advisory Council) from George Hexter, June 25, 1948, folder "Displaced Persons, Immig. 1946–50," AJC MSS.; IME to Joseph L. Bacon, June 24, 1948, IME to Benjamin F. Saltzstein, November 21, 1949; George J. Hexter to Irving G. Rhodes, July 21, 1948, "DP Correspondence," box 7, IME MSS.; Smith Diary, June 13, 1948, June 15, 1948.

27. *House Report No. 581*, pp. 3, 4; Minutes of the CCDP Executive Committee, June 17, 1948, CCDP files, folder "48–50," AJC MSS.; *New York Times*, June 20, 1948; Emanuel Celler, *You Never Leave Brooklyn*, p. 96. The four who refused to sign the conference report were Senators Ferguson and Harley Kilgore (D., West Virginia), and Congressmen Celler and J. Caleb Boggs (R., Delaware).

28. PPP, 1948, pp. 382–84.

29. James C. Davis to M. F. Goldstein, August 1, 1948, folder "DP correspondence Aug.–Sept., 1948," IME MSS.

30. Tripp, "Displaced Persons," p. 146.

31. 80C2, *CR* (1948), 94(12):9020; "Discrimination By Law," p. 8; William Haber to Jacob Billikopf, June 18, 1948, Jacob Billikopf MSS. Penciled in, with the date June 25 added, is the comment: "The worst provisions of the Senate Bill have been retained. It is the most anti-Semitic Bill in US history."

32. Hirsh Interview; Will Maslow and George J. Hexter, "Immigration—or Frustration?" *The Jewish Community* (September 1948), 3:17; memo from "Marc" [Vosk] to "Sandy" [Flowerman] re: "DP Legislation," July 9, 1948, folder, "Displaced Persons Legislation," AJC MSS.; memo from George J. Hexter on DP legislation, n.d., *ca.* late June 1948, folder "Displaced Persons Citizens Committee–Congressional/Washington Items, 1948–1950," IME MSS.

33. Duker Analysis, pp. 2, 4.

34. Folder, "Displaced Persons, 1948," box 17, Daniel Reed MSS., Cornell University, Ithaca, New York.

35. Abraham Duker, "The DP Scandal Reviewed," *The Day* (Yiddish language, New York City), July 25, 1948; William S. Bernard and Abraham G. Duker, "Who Killed Cock Robin?—The DP Act Discussed," *The Day* (English magazine section) August 29, 1948; Abraham G. Duker, "Admitting Pogromists and Excluding Their Victims," p. 21.

36. Neuringer, "American Jewry and United States Immigration Policy, 1881–1953," pp. 308–9; George Hexter to Jacob Billikopf, July 28, 1948, folder, "DP correspondence, July, 1948," box 7, IME MSS.; Haber Report, December 20, 1948, "Reports of the Advisors on Jewish Affairs," AJC Library.

37. Duker Interview.

38. *The Council News,* July 1948, ACJ MSS., New York.

39. *New York Times,* June 24, 1948, p. 15, July 15, 1948, p. 15; 81C1(H), *CR* (June 2, 1949), 95(6):7170, 14499–500; Maslow and Hexter, "Immigration—or Frustration," pp. 17–20; Minutes of the CCDP Executive Committee, June 17, 1948, CCDP files, folder, "48–50," AJC MSS.; H. A. Smith to Joseph P. Chamberlain, June 2, 1948, Smith MSS.; Robert A. Taft to Benjamin S. Katz, June 28, 1948, folder, "Displaced Persons," box 967, Taft MSS.; Engel Interview, IME to Benjamin Katz, June 3, 1948, IME to Baruch A. Feldman, June 7, 1948, "Notes and Comments For Policy Committee," by W. S. Bernard, June 3, 1948, IME MSS.

40. Minutes of the CCDP Executive Committee, June 17, 1948, CCDP files, folder, "48–50," AJC MSS.; *New York Times,* June 24, 1948, p. 12; Neuringer, "American Jewry and United States Immigration Policy, 1881–1953," pp. 301–2; Cohen, *Not Free to Desist,* p. 291.

41. AJC, *42nd Annual Report,* p. 112.

42. Clipping, New York *Herald-Tribune,* July 15, 1948, folder, "DP Clippings, 1947–1950," IME MSS.; McCarran Committee, p. 47; Sidney Liskofsky to IME, August 13, 1948; Tripp, "Displaced Persons," p. 146.

43. Ilja M. Dijour, "Changing Emphasis In Jewish Migration," p. 77; clipping, January 15, 1949, Wiener Library, Clipping File.

8. RESETTLEMENT

1. DPC Report, February 1, 1949, p. 10; *New York Times*, August 3, 1948, p. 4; Lorimer, "America's Response to Europe's Displaced Persons," p. 220; McCarran Committee, pp. 1046, 1047, 1110; Charles H. Jordan to Moses A. Leavitt, May 24, 1950, JDC MSS.; Dorr Memoir, p. 392; Rosenfield interview; Bernard interview.
2. Rosenfield interview; folder, "History–USNA," box 19, DPC MSS.; Mr. Mohler to Mr. Mulholland, January 8, 1949, box 40, NCWC MSS.
3. E. M. O'Connor to Robert E. Brody, October 22, 1948, Harry Rosenfield to David Niles, September 13, 1950, folder, "Advisory Committee on Resettlement of Displaced Persons," box 2, DPC MSS.; Leo W. Schwarz to Joseph Schwartz, "Summary Analysis of JDC Program in the U.S. Zone of Occupation, Germany," January 13, 1947, folder 9, YIVO.
4. Ugo Carusi to Charles W. Tobey, May 5, 1949, folder, "Displaced Persons Commission, 1949–50," Tobey MSS.; "DP's Hired by Industry Prove Eager, Willing Workers," p. 24.
5. Clipping, *Christian Science Monitor*, November 6, 1948, folder, "Newspaper Clippings, Nov. 1948," box 25, Rosenfield MSS.; *New York Times*, March 3, 1949, p. 8.
6. Ugo Carusi to Alexander Wiley, December 10, 1948, folder, "Legislation–1948," box 22, DPC MSS.; W. Irwin to Senator H. A. Smith, "Memorandum—Displaced Persons—Interview with Mr. Fierst," November 29, 1948, Smith MSS.; *New York Times*, November 2, 1949, p. 20; Jane Perry Clark Carey, "The Admission and Integration of Refugees In The United States," p. 69; *Interpreter Releases* (January 3, 1949) 26:1.
7. John W. Gibson, "The Displaced Placed," p. 77; Thomas Cooley II to George Hexter, July 22, 1948, folder, "DP correspondence July, 1948," IME MSS.; *Facts on File* (1948) 8:284; *New York Times*, August 30, 1948, p. 3.
8. McCarran Committee, pp. 565–66; Charles H. Jordan to Moses Leavitt, February 8, 1950, May 24, 1950 folder, "Displaced Persons, 1950," JDC MSS.
9. Arthur Greenleigh to Argyle M. Mackey, September 27, 1951, Greenleigh to J. Howard McGrath, November 23, 1951, folder, "USNA 1948–49," box 55, DPC MSS.
10. Folder on Displaced Persons, box 12, NCWC MSS.; *The DP Story*, pp. 72–76; "End the DP Obstacle Race," *Christian Century* (January 19, 1949), 66:72.
11. McCarran Committee, pp. 493, 519–20; *New York Times*, March 23, 1949, p. 8; Lorimer, "America's Response to Europe's Displaced Persons," p. 223; Haber Report, November 18, 1948, in "Reports of the Jewish Advisors," AJC Library, New York *Herald-Tribune*, May 31, 1949, p. 4; folder,

"Conference–Chicago–January 18–19, 1952," box 14, DPC MSS.; DPC Report, February 1, 1950; *Interpreter Releases* (July 18, 1949), 26:230.

12. MG Reports (December 1945), p. 2; FRUS (1946) 5:147; "Report on Displaced Persons," p. 9, Smith MSS.; "Report—Relations With Military–D.P. #U.S.–2," p. 43, "Report–Field Operations–D.P. #U.S.–3," p. 7, box 799, UNRRA MSS.; Clark Report, p. 187; folder, "False Documents," box 46, DPC MSS.; Stoessinger, *The Refugee and the World Community*, p. 58.

13. *Stars and Stripes* (European edition), July 1, 1946, p. 1; folder, "Eligibility, Screening," box 66,484, UNRRA. Germany Mission. U.S. Zone, Office of the Director, 1945–1947. Displaced Persons. Racial Minorities; folder, "Screening & Eligibility–GENERAL," box 233, UNRRA, Executive Offices, Office of the General Counsel, Subject File, 1943–1946, Displaced Persons; "Report—Field Operations—D.P. #U.S.–3," p. 7, UNRRA; *Lithuanian Bulletin* (January–February 1947), 5:18.

14. UNRRA Incoming Message, March 22, 1947, box 233, UNRRA; Gitta Sereny to Jack Whiting, July 21, 1946, folder "Infiltree Reports, Feb. 46–Sept. 46," box 66,484, UNRRA; E. H. Ein et al., attached to Johannes Kaiv to A. H. Vandenberg, February 20, 1947, box 2, Vandenberg MSS.; McNarney to Commanding Generals, Third and Seventeenth Armies, April 4, 1946, Policy Book, box 169 3/3 OMGUS; *Lithuanian Bulletin* (January–February 1947), 5:18; "Report–Field Operations–D.P. #U.S.–3," p. 7, box 799, UNRRA; Lowell W. Rooks to John H. Hilldring, January 24, 1947, Rooks to Povilas Zadeikis, July 2, 1947, folder, "Screening & Eligibility–GENERAL," box 233, UNRRA.

15. McCarran Committee, pp. 835–37, 1088–89; folder, "False Documents," box 46, DPC MSS.

16. Ed Suter? (signature illegible) to Harry Rosenfield, November 1, 1950, cases attached to letter, folder, "Memo to Squadrilli," box 53, DPC MSS.

17. P. E. Brown to J. H. Whiting, August 2, 1946, folder, "Displaced Persons Camps–1 July," box 66,480 UNRRA; Dick (Senator Richard) Russell to Charles J. Block, April 4, 1950, folder, "Displaced Persons Correspondence, 4/1950–4/1953," box 7, IME MSS.; Heymont, "After the Deluge," p. 96; McCarran Committee, pp. 558–59, 1141, 1188; *DP Express*, December 10, 1947, p. 1; Charles H. Jordan to Rita Stein, March 13, 1950, folder, "Displaced Persons, 1950," JDC MSS.; interviews with Brook, Friedlander, and Gottlieb; clipping from Washington *Post*, February 4, 1950, Scrapbook no. 28, McCarran MSS.

18. R. H. Hillenkoetter to Ugo Carusi, April 7, 1949, folder, "Central Intelligence Agency," box 45, and Rosenfield to Harry W. Lielnors, folder, "Latvian Relief, Inc.," box 47, DPC MSS.; Rosenfield interview.

19. Celler Committee, pp. 145–46; folder, "Intelligence," box 173 1/3 OMGUS; Edward M. Glazek to Ugo Carusi, May 11, 1949, reprinted in McCarran Committee, p. 493, see also p. 521.

20. Revercomb Committee, p. 2; R. L. Fisher, "The Army and Displaced Persons," pp. 3–4; U.S. Senate, *United States Relations With International Or-*

ganizations, pp. 29, 32–33, 43; Fulton Committee, p. 19; Hirschmann, *The Embers Still Burn*, p. 234; *New York Times*, September 15, 1948, p. 30.

21. Genêt, "Letter From Aschaffenburg," p. 90; FO 371 66705/WR2854; Liebschutz, "Rabbi Philip S. Bernstein," p. 125; Kimche, *The Secret Roads*, pp. 217, 315; Stoessinger, *The Refugee and the World Community*, pp. 129, 130, 139; Haber Report, October 6, 1948, "Reports of the Advisors on Jewish Affairs," AJC Library; Hirschmann, *The Embers Still Burn*, p. 141; Frank Beswick, M.P., "Rescue For Refugees," *Spectator* (March 7, 1947), 178:235; *New York Times*, May 30, 1948, section 6, p. 42; JC, June 25, 1948, p. 1.

22. Sophia Podolsky, "Resettling the Reich's Refugees," *Sunday Record* (Bergen County, N.J.), April 22, 1979, p. E1.

23. FO 371 66673/WR3446, 66710/WR1284, 66711/WR1456, 66714/WR3628; George Leather, "'Westward Ho' and After," p. 659; Stoessinger, *The Refugee and the World Community*, pp. 114–15, 122–23, 125, 127; "Displaced Persons," p. 242; "Features of Post-War Migration," p. 5; JC October 31, 1947, p. 5; *New York Times*, November 9, 1947, p. 16.

24. Fulton Committee, p. 69; Gottlieb interview.

25. Hirschmann, *The Embers Still Burn*, p. 234; Stoessinger, *The Refugee and the World Community*, pp. 131–32, 144; Haber Report, October 6, 1948, "Reports of the Advisors on Jewish Affairs"; Fredericksen, *The American Military Government Occupation of Germany*, p. 80; "The Story of I.R.O." 10:32; "International Refugee Organization, 1948–1949," in folder, "Displaced Persons Commission," Elmer Thomas MSS., Western History Collections, University of Oklahoma, Norman; *New York Times*, May 19, 1948, January 15, 1949, June 10, 1949, p. 8; Pierce Williams to Harold Glasser, July 27, 1948, AJC MSS.

26. "Report on Displaced Persons," p. 11, Smith MSS.; Fisher, "The Army and Displaced Persons," p. 4.

27. Joseph C. Hyman to Jerome H. Kohn, September 9, 1948, General Files on Displaced Persons, JDC MSS.; Study no. 35; Kurt Grossman, "The Jewish DP Problem," Institute of Jewish Affairs, World Jewish Congress, 1951, pp. 35–36; JDC Memo, p. 1; *JDC Review* (April 1948), 4:25 (November–December, 1948), 4:1; *Wiener Library Bulletin* (1956), 10:32; Hal Lehrman, "The 'Joint' Takes a Human Inventory," pp. 19–20.

28. *New York Times*, March 14, 1949, p. 19; Isaac L. Asofsky, "HIAS Executive Director Reports on 10-Week Survey of Emigration Needs in Europe," pp. 2, 10, 12; "Executive Director Details HIAS Services," p. 4; Lewis Neikrug to Charles H. Jordan, December 4, 1948, JDC MSS.; folder, "USNA," box 19, DPC MSS.

29. Margaret Hickey, "Displaced Persons . . . From Refugee Camps To 'Grand Hotel,'" p. 261; Sidney Hertzberg, "The Month In History," *Commentary* (December 1946), 4:554; folder, "USNA Correspondence 1946–50," box 148, Central Jewish Federation and Welfare Funds MSS., American Jewish Historical Society, Waltham, Mass.

30. Arthur D. Greenleigh to Ed O'Connor, October 25, 1949, folder,

"USNA 1948–49," box 55, DPC MSS.; Lorimer, "America's Response to the Displaced Persons," p. 247; Lyman C. White, *300,000 New Americans*, p. 40; Lessing Rosenwald to Thomas H. Beck, April 24, 1948, unprocessed material, folder, "Collier's Weekly Article," box 4, ACJ MSS., Madison.

31. A-19, folder 7, "Displaced Persons, 1949–1950," box 256, Langer MSS.; Lorimer, "America's Response to the Displaced Persons," p. 231; Bruce Mohler to Thomas Mulholland, April 17, 1946, Rev. Patrick J. O'Boyle to Rev. Richard Flynn, May 9, 1946, extract from Mulholland memo of August 20, 1946, Memorandum from Miss Buckley to Mohler, April 30, 1946, Rev. Emil N. Komara to Bruce M. Mohler, October 4, 1946, unmarked folder, box 12, NCWC MSS.; Jane Carey cites the figure of 41,379 admitted under the Truman Directive, "The Admission and Integration of Refugees," p. 66; the DPC, in its final report, gave the figure of over 42,000, *The DP Story*, p. 7.

32. Loula D. Lasker, "Enter: the DP's By Legal Permit," p. 142; *New York Times*, January 16, 1948, p. 23; September 29, 1949, p. 31; clipping, New York *Herald-Tribune*, December 18, 1947, folder, "DP Clippings, 1947," box 7, IME MSS.

33. Folder, "USNA Correspondence 1946–50," box 148, Central Jewish Federation and Welfare Funds MSS.; "International Social Welfare," p. 54; "Protestants Are Failing Refugees," p. 541; "Immediate Action Needed by D.P.'s," *Christian Century*, p. 611; Helen G. Ormsbee to Dr. Julius Bodensieck, February 13, 1947, Displaced Persons folder in General Secretary's files, 1947, Board Minutes of Church World Service, May 19, 1948, Federal Council of Churches of Christ in America MSS.; *New York Times*, September 29, 1949, p. 31; folder, "History–NLC," box 19, DPC MSS.; David L. Lloyd to Samuel McCrea Cavert, July 2, 1952, Lloyd, "Memorandum for the Files," July 15, 1952, Cavert to Lloyd, July 15, 1952, Cavert to Harry S. Truman, September 12, 1952, folder 4, "Immigration—Memorandum & Letters Re," box 3, David L. Lloyd MSS., Truman Library; Joseph Chamberlain to H. A. Smith, February 4, 1949, Smith MSS.; folder, "State Committee Reports," box 36, DPC MSS.; "Welcome Immigrants!," p. 85.

34. Bruce Mohler to Thomas F. Mulholland, January 8, 1949, folder on Displaced Persons, box 12, NCWC MSS.; *New York Times*, October 31, 1948, p. 1; "America Gets First of 200,000 DPs," *Life*, p. 33; Jan S. Pargiello, "Let Us Give a Helping Hand to Polish D.P.s," pp. 13–14.

35. *New York Times*, November 2, 1948, and December 22, 1948, box 25, Rosenfield MSS.; *New York Times*, May 16, 1949, "News Clippings, 1949," box 27, DPC MSS.; Katherine M. Lenroot to Mrs. Ingeborg Olsen, November 16, 1945, folder, "Immigration Quota into the US," box 2, Rosenman MSS.; *The DP Story*, pp. 24, 245; see p. 62.

36. Boston *Daily Globe*, May 16, 1949, p. 1; *New York Times*, December 21, 1950, p. 8; Duker Analysis, p. 4.

37. W. B. Courtney, "Unwanted," *Collier's*, p. 60; folder, "News Clippings, 1949," box 27, DPC MSS.; boxes 81 and 82, in particular, are filled with pictures and clippings, DPC MSS.

38. Sidney Shalett, "How are the DP's Doing in America," p. 26–27; Quentin Reynolds, "God, Make Us Forget," pp. 50–51; Helena Huntington Smith, "Who Said Promised Land?," p. 19; *Ladies' Home Journal*, November, 1949, pp. 23, 261; Roger Butterfield, "We Live Again," pp. 163–68; "New Americans One Year Later," p. 11; "A Displaced Person Gets Placed," pp. 39–45; "New Life for DP's," p. 90.

39. Memo to officers of NRS [National Refugee Service] from Joseph E. Beck, executive director, July 1, 1946, American Friends Service Committee MSS.; *Journal of International Affairs* (1953), pp. 73–74.

40. *The DP Story*, pp. 250, 372; *Collier's* (July 2, 1949), pp. 19–20; "Exploitation of D.P.'s Must Be Stopped!" p. 699; Rudolph Heberle, "Displaced Persons in the Deep South," pp. 364, 375.

41. Clippings, John Bunker, "Many DPs in Bay State Seem in Unsuitable Jobs," *Christian Science Monitor*, n.d., *New York Times*, July 16, 1950, Lehman MSS.; *Journal of International Affairs*, p. 73; "Some Facts About The 'DP' Program," p. 68.

42. "D.P. At Home," p. 58; Celler Committee, pp. 101, 110; *The DP Story*, p. 301; reports by Jeremiah T. Chase, Hopewell H. Darnielle, Jr., and Raymond E. Elliott, Fall 1950 and Spring 1951, folder, "State Committee Reports," box 36, DPC MSS.

43. Arkansas, California, Colorado, Connecticut, Delaware, Georgia, Illinois, Indiana, Iowa, Kansas, Kentucky, Louisiana, Maine, Maryland, Massachusetts, Michigan, Minnesota, Mississippi, Nebraska, New Hampshire, New Jersey, New York, North Carolina, Oklahoma, Oregon, Pennsylvania, Rhode Island, South Carolina, South Dakota, Tennessee, Texas, Virginia, Vermont, Washington, Wisconsin, Wyoming.

44. Folder, "State Committee Reports," box 36, and "State Committees, General," and "Conference–Chicago–Jan. 18–19, 1952," box 14, DPC MSS.; *The DP Story*, pp. viii, 296, 302; Werner W. Boehm, "State Programs For Displaced Persons," pp. 489–90.

45. Reports by Chase, Darnielle, and Elliott, folder, "State Committee Reports," box 36, DPC MSS.

46. *The DP Story*, pp. 28–29.

47. Divine, *American Immigration Policy*, p. 132.

9. PAT McCARRAN AND THE AMENDED DP ACT

1. Bailey and Samuel, *Congress at Work*, p. 240.

2. *New York Times*, November 4, 1948, p. 2; William S. Bernard, "Displaced Persons Legislation," p. 5; Tripp, "Displaced Persons," p. 144; PPP, 1948, pp. 834, 852, 854–55, 867, 896; "America Gets First of 200,000 DPs," p. 33; Robert G. Spivak, "Members of New Congress Back Move to End DP Law Bias," *New York Post*, December 2, 1948, pp. 2, 47; Minutes of CCDP Executive Committee, December 10, 1948, IME to Herbert Bayard Swope, December 28, 1948, folder, "48–50," CCDP files, AJC MSS.

3. Alfred Steinberg, "McCarran, Lone Wolf of the Senate," pp. 89, 90,

92; "The Senate's Most Expendable," p. 18; Connie A. Kirby, "Amending The Displaced Persons Act of 1948," pp. 32–33; "Pooh Bah McCarran," Washington *Post*, August 30, 1949, p. 10; Robert Laxalt, *Nevada* (New York: Norton, 1977), p. 66.

4. Steinberg, "McCarran, Lone Wolf," p. 92; Edwards interview; Pat McCarran to W. J. Arnette, August 10, 1949, "S/MC/9/1," Itemized File, McCarran MSS.; McCarran interview.

5. Edwards interview; Bailey and Samuel, *Congress at Work*, p. 241; chapter draft on "Civil Aeronautics Authority," in Jerome E. Edwards' uncompleted, unpublished biography of Pat McCarran; Steinberg, "McCarran, Lone Wolf," p. 89.

6. Bailey and Samuel, *Congress at Work*, pp. 238 and 242; Tripp, "Displaced Persons," p. 163; IME to Morton G. Thalheimer, June 3, 1949; Steinberg, "McCarran, Lone Wolf," p. 92.

7. Rosenfield interview.

8. Rosenberger interview.

9. Marcus Cohen to IME, November 8, 1948; Bailey and Samuel, *Congress at Work*, p. 243; clipping, Washington *Post*, August 13, 1949, box 26, Rosenfield MSS.; McCarran interview.

10. Mobile *Press Register*, February 8, 1950, reprinted in 81C2(S) *CR* (February 28, 1950), 96(2):2460; "Public Opinion," July, 1949, in folder, "Displaced Persons. Immig. 1946–1950," AJC MSS.; 81C1(S), *CR* (October 14, 1949) 95(12):14493; John Thomas Taylor to Carl Hayden, October 18, 1949, W. C. "Tom" Sawyer to Hayden, August 23, 1949, folder, 12, box 28, Hayden MSS.; W. W. Hopper to Pat McCarran, July 14, 1949, "S/MC/9/1," Itemized File, McCarran MSS.; James J. Laughlin to Robert A. Taft, folder, "Displaced Persons," box 973, Taft MSS.; an Oklahoma City physician to Elmer Thomas, February 8, 1950, folder, "Displaced Persons Legis.," box 223, Thomas MSS.; Robert L. Halliday to Tom Connally, January 24, 1950, box 241, Connally MSS.

11. "Public Opinion," AJC MSS.; Celler Committee, pp. 93–116; Fort Worth *Star-Telegram* (morning edition), January 31, 1949, p. 6; flyers with excerpts from newspaper editorials, folder 6792, Kem MSS.; folder 81, Crump MSS.; Bailey and Samuel, *Congress at Work*, p. 248; George Xanthaky to J. H. McGrath, March 8, 1949, "Corres. Re Displaced Persons in Greece, 1949, Senatorial," box 20, McGrath MSS.; Theodore H. Hoffman to Burnet H. Maybank, February 28, 1950, Maybank MSS.; Celler Committee, pp. 15, 18, 39–42, 239; A-19, folder 4, Displaced Persons, 1949–50, box 246, Langer MSS.; form postcard from Ernest and Maria Mueller to Joseph P. Kem, Christmas, 1949, folder 6749, Kem MSS.; *New York Times*, August 6, 1949, p. 30; Edward M. O'Connor to Ugo Carusi, September 14, 1949, folder, "Legislation–1949," box 22, DPC MSS.; "Legislative Bulletin" of War Relief Services–NCWC, March 15, 1950, folder, "Resettlement," box 78, NCWC MSS.; Gretchen Klammek to B.B. Hickenlooper, August 6, 1949, folder, "Displaced Persons (General Legislation)," Topical Files, Hickenlooper MSS.; *The DP Story*, p. 29.

12. *The DP Story*, p. 29.

13. Abraham Hyman to Louis Barish, February 28, 1949, folder, "Displaced Persons, 1949," JDC MSS.; IME to Benjamin S. Katz, July 13, 1948, IME to Edward I. Kaufman, December 16, 1949; Neuringer, "American Jewry and United States Immigration Policy," p. 327.

14. Edward E. Swanstrom to Harry N. Rosenfield, February 14, 1949, folder, "Legislation–1949," box 22, DPC MSS.; *New York Times*, March 2, 1949, p. 13; CCDP Memo, March 28, 1949, folder "Relief Organizations–Citizens Committee on Displaced Persons, 1948–1950," box 104, ACJ MSS., Madison; WRS-NCWC proposals for a revised DP bill, n.d., box 20, McGrath MSS.; IME to Judge Proskauer, February 17, 1949, copy attached to letter from George Hexter to Lillian Poses, February 18, 1949, box 210, Baruch MSS.

15. Celler Committee, pp. 13, 14, 54, 127.

16. *Ibid.*, pp. iii–v, 24–29, 117, 120–21, 127; Divine, p. 133; PPP, 1949, p. 58; Lorimer, "America's Response to Europe's Displaced Persons," p. 172; Rosenfield interview.

17. Rosenfield interview; Celler Committee, p. 184; *House Report No. 581*, p. 15; copy of H.R. 4467 in Displaced Persons Commission Folder, 1949–50, Tobey MSS.; John Pillsbury to William Langer, March 3, 1950, A-19, folder 5, Displaced Persons, 1949–50, box 246, Langer MSS.; Divine, *American Immigration Policy*, pp. 133–34; folder, "Relief Organizations–Citizens Committee on Displaced Persons, 1948–1950," box 104, ACJ MSS., Madison.

18. *House Report No. 581*, p. 47; Divine, *American Immigration Policy*, p. 134.

19. "Latest News on Senate DP Legislation," attached to CCDP Memo, June 23, 1949, folder, "Relief Organizations–Citizens Committee on Displaced Persons, 1948–1950," box 104, ACJ MSS., Madison.

20. Tripp, "Displaced Persons," p. 154; *New York Times*, April 12, 1949, p. 1, May 2, 1949, p. 11; 81C1(S), *CR* (April 26, 1949), 95(10):5042; Lorimer, "America's Response to European Displaced Persons," p. 183; Marcus Cohen to John Slawson, November 11, 1949, folder, DPC Correspondence, "November, 1949–March, 1950," box 7, IME MSS.; folder, "Relief Organizations–CCDP," box 104, ACJ MSS., Madison.

21. Washington *Post*, June 24, 1949, p. 2; *New York Times*, June 24, 1949, p. 11.

22. McCarran Committee.

23. Irving Ives to Eleanor Roosevelt, August 12, 1949, folder, "Corresp. 1949, L–Z," box 37, U.S. Senate/Correspondence, Ives MSS.; U.S. Senate, Minutes of Majority Policy Committee, August 4, 1949, box 227, Lucas MSS.; *New York Times*, August 9, 1949, p. 5; Bailey and Samuel, *Congress at Work*, p. 249.

24. *New York Times*, August 11, 1949, p. 12, August 18, 1949, p. 15, August 20, 1949, p. 12, August 25, 1949, p. 12; Bailey and Samuel, *Congress at Work*, pp. 249–50; folder 0290, box 20, Lucas MSS.

25. Folder 0290, box 20, "Minutes of Majority Policy Committee," box 227, Lucas MSS.; 81C1(S), *CR* (September 12, 1949), 95(10):12769; clippings,

Legislative Daily, September 12, 1949, Washington *Post*, September 13, 1949, McCarran Scrapbook no. 28, McCarran MSS.; Marcus Cohen to John Slawson, October 5, 1949, DPC Correspondence, "August–October, 1949," box 7, IME MSS.

26. Pat McCarran to Tom Connally, October 7, 1949, box 241, Connally MSS.; Bailey and Samuel, *Congress at Work*, p. 251; *New York Times*, October 8, 1949, p. 3; folder, "Legislation–1949," box 22, DPC MSS.

27. 81C2(S), *CR* (October 14, 1949), 95(11):14491–99 passim; *New York Times*, October 16, 1949, p. 39.

28. Bailey and Samuel, *Congress at Work*, p. 252; *San Francisco Chronicle*, October 13, 1949, p. 1; *New York Times*, October 13, 1949, p. 1.

29. Bailey and Samuel, *Congress at Work*, p. 253; Daniel Seligman, "Congress and the DP's," p. 228; Lorimer, "America's Response to Europe's Displaced Persons," pp. 189–90; *New York Times*, October 14, 1949, p. 1, October 16, 1949, p. 1.

30. Bailey and Samuel, *Congress at Work*, pp. 256–57; Divine, *America's Immigration Policy*, p. 137; *Commonweal*, December 16, 1949, p. 288; Memo to DP Executive Committee from W. S. Bernard, October 16, 1949, "Notes on the Recommitment of the Celler Bill," folder, "Relief Organizations–CCDP, "box 104, ACJ MSS., Madison.

31. *New York Times*, December 8, 1949, p. 36, January 7, 1950, p. 8; 81C2, *CR* (January 6, 1950), 96:114.

32. Peter Peterson to Pat McCarran, January 6, 1950, cited in Edwards' unpublished manuscript on McCarran.

33. *New York Times*, January 11, 1950, p. 22, January 12, 1950, p. 4; "D.P. Opposition Hits New Low," p. 100.

34. McCarran Committee, pp. 553, 1145, 1174.

35. *Ibid.*, p. 553.

36. *Ibid.*, pp. 1141, 1145.

37. McCarran Committee, testimony of Edward M. Glazek, Donald W. Main, and Almanza Tripp, on pp. 485–514, 557–645, 647–722, respectively, passim, and pp. 527, 1132.

38. McCarran Committee, pp. 518, 519, 524, 528, 532, 535, 547, 550, 586, 650.

39. *Ibid.*, p. 845.

40. FRUS (1949) 1:404.

41. Bailey and Samuel, *Congress at Work*, pp. 258–59; Tripp, "Displaced Persons," pp. 193–96; Lorimer, "America's Response to Europe's Displaced Persons," p. 203; *New York Times*, March 25, 1950, p. 19; McCarran Committee, pp. 1066, 1072.

42. McCarran Committee, pp. 727, 756, 854.

43. *Ibid.*, pp. 907, 930–31, 1089, 1107.

44. Samuel Whitehead, "The Half-Open Door," p. 149.

45. McCarran Committee, pp. 1054, 1055, 1069; *New York Times*, March 16, 1950, p. 12.

46. *New York Times*, March 16, 1950, p. 12; McCarran Committee, pp. 1097–1100, 1113–14.

47. McCarran Committee, pp. 1122–23.

48. Bailey and Samuel, *Congress at Work*, p. 247; Lorimer, "America's Response to Europe's Displaced Persons," p. 198; Tripp, "Displaced Persons," pp. 191–92; *New York Times*, March 1, 1950, p. 15.

49. Clippings, Washington *Post*, February 1, 1950, March 1, 1950, McCarran Scrapbook no. 28, McCarran MSS.; *New York Times*, January 29, 1950, p. 11; Herbert H. Lehman to Ben Davidson, March 10, 1950, Washington Files, Legislative Drawer 3, J. C. C. Edelstein File, Lehman MSS.

50. Jacob Blaustein to George Hexter, February 10, 1950, DPC Correspondence, folder, "11/49–3/50," box 7, IME MSS.; *New York Times*, February 28, 1950, p. 19; Tripp, "Displaced Persons," p. 191; Bailey and Samuel, *Congress at Work*, p. 257; 81C2(S), *CR* (February 28, 1950), 96(2):2479.

51. 81C2(S), *CR* (February 28, 1950), 96(2):2476; Memo to CCDP Executive Committee from W.S. Bernard, re: "First Day of Debate on Displaced Persons Legislation," n.d., *ca.* March 1, 1950, folder, "Relief Organizations–CCDP," box 104, ACJ MSS., Madison.

52. Elmer Thomas to Sam M. Myers, March 13, 1950, folder, "Displaced Persons LG 10-13-49," box 223, Thomas MSS.; Bailey and Samuel, *Congress at Work*, p. 261; 81C2(S), *CR* (March 2, 1950), 96(2):2634; *New York Times*, March 3, 1950, p. 13, March 4, 1950, p. 8.

53. *CR*, vol. 96, p. 2737.

54. Bailey and Samuel, *Congress at Work*, pp. 260–61.

55. *Ibid.*

56. *Ibid.*; telegram from General Lucius D. Clay, et al., to Senator Elmer Thomas, February 22, 1950, folder, "Displaced Persons Legis," box 223, Thomas MSS.; Edward E. Swanstrom, et al., to Senator Burnet R. Maybank, February 22, 1950, Maybank MSS.

57. Bailey and Samuel, *Congress at Work*, pp. 264–65.

58. *New York Times*, April 6, 1950, p. 3. The fifteen who opposed were:

Republicans	Democrats
John W. Bricker, Ohio	Harry F. Byrd, Virginia
Harry P. Cain, Washington	Virgil M. Chapman, Kentucky
Guy Cordon, Iowa	Tom Connally, Texas
William E. Jenner, Indiana	Clyde R. Hoey, North Carolina
James P. Kem, Missouri	Spessard Holland, Florida
Kenneth S. Wherry, Nebraska	Olin D. Johnston, South Carolina
John J. Williams, Delaware	John L. McClellan, Arkansas
	John C. Stennis, Mississippi

59. Tripp, "Displaced Persons," p. 208; "A Pretty Picture," p. 23; *New York Times*, April 5, 1950, p. 16; New York *Herald-Tribune*, April 9, 1950, section 2, p. 5; Herbert H. Lehman to Irving M. Engel, March 13, 1950, IME MSS.

60. *New York Times*, April 6, 1950, pp. 1, 3; *Time*, (April 17, 1950), 23.

61. Bailey and Samuel, *Congress at Work*, p. 267; Tripp, "Displaced Persons," p. 204; Memo to Members of CCDP Executive Committee from W. S. Bernard, re: "KILGORE-FERGUSON SUBSTITUTE BILL WINS SMASHING VICTORY," April 5, 1950, folder, "Relief Organization-CCDP, 1948–1950," box 104, ACJ MSS., Madison.

62. Bernard interview; McCarran to Sister Mary Mercy (McCarran), April 7, 1950, "S/MC/2/3,1950," itemized file, McCarran MSS.

63. Bailey and Samuel, *Congress at Work*, p. 267; Tripp, "Displaced Persons," pp. 204–205; *New York Times*, April 7, 1950, p. 3.

64. "Minutes of the Majority Policy Committee," June 6, 1950, box 227, Lucas MSS.; *New York Times*, June 8, 1950, p. 14, June 17, 1950, p. 1; 81C2(H), *CR* (June 6, 1950), 96(6):8198.

65. *New York Times*, June 8, 1950, p. 4.

66. White, *300,000 New Americans*, p. 98; Lorimer, "America's Response to Europe's Displaced Persons," pp. 273–74; Memo from Ann S. Petluck to Migration Workers, November 16, 1949, folder, "Displaced Persons 1949," Reta L. Stein to Charles H. Jordan, April 7, 1950, Charles H. Jordan to Reta L. Stein, April 22, 1950, Jordan to Moses A. Leavitt, July 26, 1950, Memo to Ugo Carusi, Edward O'Connor, and Harry Rosenfield from Walter H. Bieringer, et al., August 21, 1950, folder, "Displaced Persons, 1950," JDC MSS.; *New York Times*, August 3, 1950, p. 13, August 8, 1950, p. 8, October 4, 1950, p. 21, December 5, 1950, p. 11, December 28, 1950, p. 10; Rosenfield interview.

67. Harry Rosenfield to Philip B. Perlman, February 1, 1955, post-presidential file, box 69, Truman MSS.

68. See appendix A, table 16.

69. *New York Times*, September 21, 1950, p. 1; "Security Through Chaos," *New Republic* (November 6, 1950), 123:7.

EPILOGUE AND CONCLUSION: THE DELAYED PILGRIMS AT HOME

1. Jacques Sandulescue, *Hunger's Rogues*, p. 347; "One Way We Buy Friends—And Get Our Money Back," p. 10; folder, "Last DP," box 56, DPC MSS.; *Facts on File* (August 6, 1953), p. 265, B3.

2. See appendix A, table 9.

3. Folder, "Germany Jewish Adviser—H. Greenstein," AJC MSS.; Herbert Agar, *The Saving Remnant*, p. 189; Kurt R. Grossman, "Refugees, DP's, and Migrants," p. 137; Hal Lehrman, "The Last Jews In The Last German Camp," pp. 3–4.

4. Lyman Cromwell White, *300,000 New Americans*, p. 75; *New York Times*, October 12, 1959, p. 3; OHHS, p. 11, Wiener Oral History Library.

5. Roger Butterfield, "Wisconsin Welcomes the Wanderers," p. 44; June Namias, *First Generation*, p. 144.

6. *Ibid.*, p. 46; President's Commission, pp. 888, 979; "Why Congress Is Split Over DP's," p. 18; folder, "State Committee Reports," box 36, DPC MSS. See also Joyce Williams Kushinka, "A Study of Assimilation Experiences of Jewish, Latvian and Ukrainian Displaced Persons." Kushinka traced the experiences of 24 DPs (8 Latvians, 8 Ukrainians, and 8 Jews) and found that most were engaged in occupations other than those recorded on their assurance forms when they first came to the United States, and that all had changed residences but none lived in ethnic neighborhoods. Kushinka also found that of the three groups, the Latvians were the most assimilated within American society.

7. President's Commission, pp. 682, 938; Gertrude Samuels, "Five Who Came Out of the Terror," *New York Times Magazine* (August 3, 1952), p. 51.

8. David Crystal, *The Displaced Person and the Social Agency*, p. 137; Dorothy Rabinowitz, *New Lives*, p. 203.

9. *New York Times*, October 12, 1959, p. 3; Rabinowitz, *New Lives*, p. 108; folder, "State Committee Reports," box 36, DPC MSS.; "Annual Report of the Lutheran Resettlement Service, 1949," folder, "History–NLC," box 19, DPC MSS.; form letter from I. George Nace, May 24, 1950, folder, "Displaced Persons–1950," box 18, Home Missions Council of North America, Inc., MSS., housed with Federal Council of the Churches of Christ In America, MSS., Presbyterian Historical Society, Philadelphia.

10. See Helen Epstein, *Children of the Holocaust*, passim.

11. Thomas O'Toole, "After 35 Years U.S. Begins a Serious Search for Ex-Nazis," Washington *Post*, August 17, 1980, p. A14; *New York Times*, November 22, 1979, p. B1, March 28, 1980, p. A22.

12. *Fedorenko* v. *U.S.*, 41 *Commercial Clearing House, Inc., United States Supreme Court Bulletin* (1981), B718.

13. *Ibid.*, pp. B722–B723. Justice Thurgood Marshall delivered the opinion of the Court. He was joined in the majority by Chief Justice Warren Burger, and Associate Justices William J. Brennan, Jr., Potter Stewart, Harry A. Blackmun, Lewis F. Powell, Jr., and William H. Rehnquist. Justices Byron R. White and John Paul Stevens dissented. Speaking for himself Justice Stevens observed, "Every person who entered the United States pursuant to the authority granted by the statute [the DP Act of 1948], who subsequently acquired American citizenship, and who can be shown 'to have assisted the enemy in persecuting civil populations'—even under the most severe duress—has no right to retain his or her citizenship." 41 *CCH S. Ct. Bull.*, B758.

14. Namias, *First Generation*, pp. 140–44, passim.

15. See Leonard Dinnerstein, "Antisemitism Exposed and Attacked (1945–1950)," *American Jewish History*, (September 1981) vol. 71.

16. Will Maslow and George J. Hexter, "Immigration—or Frustration?," *The Jewish Community* (September 1948), 3:17.

17. Stember, *Jews in the Mind of America*, pp. 121–22.

18. Hartmann, *Truman and the 80th Congress*, pp. 7, 42, 100, 211, 213.

19. Clipping, William Bernard to editor of *The Jewish Community*, October 27, 1948, p. 3, in CCDP folders, "48–50," AJC MSS.

APPENDIX A

1. *United States Relations with International Organizations.* III. *The International Refugee Organization.* 81st Cong., 1st sess. Senate Report no. 476. Committee on Expenditures in the Executive Departments. June 8, 1949.

2. W. S. Bernard to J. C. C. Edelstein, January 18, 1950, Lehman MSS.

3. Statistics on DPs furnished by Paul Baerwald to Myron C. Taylor MSS., Truman Library.

4. Displaced Persons Statistics, box 17, McGrath MSS.

5. Statistics on DPs furnished by Paul Baerwald to Myron C. Taylor, June 1947, box 3, Myron C. Taylor MSS., Truman Library.

6. *Ibid.*

SELECTED BIBLIOGRAPHY

Note: Some manuscript collections were unavailable to me. Abram Sachar refused to allow me to see the David Niles Papers which are in his possession. Two letters to Joseph B. Harrison for permission to see the papers of his father, Earl G. Harrison, went unanswered. The entries marked with asterisks indicate that Xerox copies were sent to me from these collections. I did not examine the collections.

MANUSCRIPTS

1. British Public Record Office, Kew, England
   Cabinet Papers, 1945–46.
   Foreign Office Papers, 1945–47.
   Minutes of the Cabinet Meetings, 1945–46.
   Prime Minister's Office Records, 1945–46.
   War Office Papers, 1945.
2. National Archives, Washington, D.C.
   Diplomatic Branch. The Displaced Persons Commission Mss.
   Modern Military Section. Civil Affairs Division, RG 165, Decimal File 383.7.
   —— RG 218 (U.S. Joint Chiefs of Staff), CCS 383.6.
   —— RG 331, SHAEF, G-5 Division.
   OMGUS (National Archives Record Center, Suitland, Md.) RG 260.
   Records of the State Department. RG 59. Decimal File, 1945–49. 840.48: Refugees.
3. Other Manuscript Collections
   American Council for Judaism. State Historical Society of Wisconsin, Madison, Wisconsin.
   —— New York, N.Y.
   American Council For Nationalities Services. Immigration History Archives, St. Paul, Minn.
   American Friends Service Committee. Philadelphia, Pa.

American Jewish Committee. New York City.

American Jewish Conference. Zionist Archives, New York City.

American Jewish Joint Distribution Committee. New York City.

Frank Aydelotte. Swarthmore College Library, Swarthmore, Pa.

Bernard M. Baruch. Seeley G. Mudd Manuscript Library, Princeton University, Princeton, N.J.

*Philip S. Bernstein. American Jewish Archives, Cincinnati, Ohio.

*Jacob Billikopf. American Jewish Archives, Cincinnati, Ohio.

Central Jewish Federation and Welfare Funds. American Jewish Historical Society, Waltham, Mass.

Citizens Committee on Displaced Persons. Immigration History Archives, St. Paul, Minn.

Tom Connally. Library of Congress, Washington, D.C.

Richard Crossman. Oxford University, St. Antony's College, Middle East Library, Oxford, England.

Sir Alan Cunningham. Ibid.

DP Collection, Germany. YIVO Institute of Jewish Research, New York City.

*Dwight D. Eisenhower. Eisenhower Library, Abilene, Kansas.

Irving M. Engel. American Jewish Committee, New York City.

Federal Council of Churches of Christ in America. Presbyterian Historical Society, Philadelphia, Pa.

Jules Feldmans. Hoover Institution, Stanford University, Palo Alto, Calif.

Felix Frankfurter. Library of Congress, Washington, D.C.

Laurence Frenkel. Hoover Institution, Stanford University, Palo Alto, Calif.

Henry F. Grady. Truman Library. Independence, Mo.

Kurt Grossman. Leo Baeck Institute, New York City.

Carl Hayden. Arizona State University Library, Tempe, Ariz.

B. B. Hickenlooper. Herbert Hoover Library, West Branch, Iowa.

Harold L. Ickes. Library of Congress, Washington, D.C.

Institute of Contemporary History and Wiener Library, London, England.

Irving M. Ives. Cornell University Library, Ithaca, New York.

James P. Kem. Western Historical Manuscript Collection, State Historical Society Manuscripts, University of Missouri Library, Columbia, Mo.

Harley M. Kilgore. FDR Library, Hyde Park, N.Y.

—— West Virginia University Library, Morgantown, West Virginia.

Fiorello H. LaGuardia. Municipal Archives, New York City.

*William Langer. The Orin G. Libby Manuscript Collection, Chester Fritz Library, University of North Dakota, Grand Forks, N.D.
Herbert H. Lehman. Columbia University, New York City.
David D. Lloyd. Truman Library, Independence, Mo.
Scott W. Lucas. Illinois State Historical Library, Springfield, Ill.
Vito Marcantonio. New York Public Library, New York City.
*Burnet R. Maybank. College of Charleston, Charleston, S.C.
Patrick McCarran. Nevada State Archives, Carson City, Nevada.
James G. McDonald. Herbert H. Lehman Papers, Columbia University, New York City.
J. Howard McGrath. Truman Library, Independence, Mo.
Henry Morgenthau, Jr. FDR Library, Hyde Park, New York.
National Refugee Service Archives. American Jewish Historical Society, Waltham, Mass.
William Phillips. Houghton Library, Harvard University, Cambridge, Mass.
Daniel Reed. Cornell University Library, Ithaca, New York.
*A. Willis Robertson. Swem Library, College of William and Mary, Williamsburg, Va.
Eleanor Roosevelt. FDR Library, Hyde Park, New York.
Franklin D. Roosevelt. Ibid.
Harry N. Rosenfield. Truman Library, Independence, Mo.
Samuel Rosenman. Ibid.
Richard B. Scandrett, Jr. Cornell University Library, Ithaca, New York.
H. Alexander Smith. Seeley G. Mudd Manuscript Library, Princeton University, Princeton, N.J.
William G. Stratton. Illinois State Historical Library, Springfield, Ill.
Robert A. Taft. Library of Congress, Washington, D.C.
Myron C. Taylor. Truman Library, Independence, Mo.
Elmer Thomas. Western History Collections, University of Oklahoma, Norman, Okla.
*Charles W. Tobey. Dartmouth College Library, Hanover, N.H.
Harry S. Truman. Truman Library, Independence, Mo.
William Hallam Tuck. Herbert Hoover Library, West Branch, Iowa.
UNRRA. United Nations Archives, New York City.
United Service for New Americans (USNA). American Jewish Historical Society, Waltham, Mass.
—— YIVO Institute for Jewish Research, New York City.

U.S. Catholic Conference (formerly National Catholic Welfare Conference). Center For Migration Studies, Staten Island, N.Y.
Arthur H. Vandenberg. Bentley Historical Society, University of Michigan, Ann Arbor, Mich.
Robert F. Wagner. Georgetown University Library, Washington, D.C.
War Refugee Board. FDR Library, Hyde Park, N.Y.
Alexander Wiley. State Historical Society of Wisconsin, Madison, Wis.
Stephen S. Wise. American Jewish Historical Society, Waltham, Mass.
Joel D. Wolfsohn. Truman Library, Independence, Mo.
World Jewish Congress. London, England; New York City.

UNITED STATES GOVERNMENT DOCUMENTS AND PUBLICATIONS

Army Talk #151. Prepared by Army Information Branch, Information and Education Division, War Department Special Staff. Washington, 1949.
Congressional Record. 1945–1950.
Fredericksen, Oliver J. *The American Military Government Occupation of Germany.* U.S. Army Headquarters, Europe: Historical Division, 1953.
House. "Amending The Displaced Persons Act of 1948." *House Report No. 581.* 81st Cong., 1st sess., 1949.
House. "Amending The Displaced Persons Act of 1948." *Hearings Before Subcommittee No. 1 of the Committee of the Judiciary on H. R. 1344.* 81st Cong., 1st sess., 1949.
House. "Displaced Persons and the International Refugee Organization," *Report of a Special Subcommittee of the Committee on Foreign Affairs.* Committee consisted of James G. Fulton, Pa., chairman, Jacob J. Javits, New York, Joseph L. Pfeifer, New York, with the collaboration of Frank L. Chelf, Ky. 80th Cong., 1st sess., 1947.
House. "The Displaced Persons Analytical Bibliography," *House Report No. 1687.* Prepared by a special subcommittee of the Judiciary Committee. February 27, 1950.
House. Abraham G. Duker. "Many Among DP's in European Camps are Collaborationists." Extension of remarks of Hon. Arthur G. Klein of New York in the House of Representatives,

August 2, 5, 6, 1948. *Appendix To The Congressional Record*, 80th Cong., 2d sess., 94(12): A4891–4892.

House. *Hearings Before the President's Commission on Immigration and Naturalization*. 82d Cong., 2d sess., Committee on the Judiciary, September 30, 1952–October 29, 1952.

House. "Permitting Admission of 400,000 Displaced Persons Into The United States," *Hearings Before Subcommittee on Immigration and Naturalization of the Committee on the Judiciary, H. R. 2910.* 80th Cong., 1st sess., June 4–July 18, 1947.

Military Government of Germany. *Displaced Persons, Stateless Persons and Refugees*. Monthly Report of Military Governor, U.S. Zone, 1945–1947. (no. 1 is August 20, 1945, the last, no. 27, is dated October 1, 1946–September 30, 1947—Cumulative Review. There were no issues numbered 8, 9, 10, 12, 14, 18, 20, 24 or 26.)

Senate. "Admission of Jews Into Palestine." *Senate Document No. 182.* 79th Cong., 2d sess., 1946. (Report of the Anglo-American Committee of Inquiry.)

Senate. "Displaced Persons," *Hearings Before the Subcommittee on Amendments To The Displaced Persons Act of the Committee on the Judiciary.* 81st Cong., Senate, 1st and 2d sess., 1949–1950.

Senate. "Displaced Persons In Europe," Report of the Committee On The Judiciary Pursuant To S. Resolution 137. *Report No. 950.* 80th Cong., 2d sess., March 2, 1948.

Senate. "Report To The Senate Steering Committee on the Possible Admission of Displaced Persons To The United States" (Revercomb Report). Reprinted in 80C1, *CR* 93(2):2507–20, March 25, 1947.

Senate. Committee on Expenditures in the Executive Departments, "United States Relations With International Organizations. III. The International Refugee Organization." *Report No. 476.* 81st Cong., 1st sess., June 8, 1949.

Trials of The Major War Criminals Before The International Military Tribunal. Nuremberg, November 14, 1945–October 1, 1946. 42 vols. Nuremberg, Germany, 1947.

U.S. Department of State. *Foreign Relations of the United States, Diplomatic Papers*, 1945–1948.

U.S. Displaced Persons Commission. *Semi-Annual Report To The President and Congress*, February 1, 1949, August 1, 1949, February 1, 1950, August 1, 1950, February 1, 1951, August 1, 1951.

—— *Memo To America: The DP Story.* Washington: U.S. Government Printing Office, 1952.

INTERVIEWS

William S. Bernard. New York City. June 28, 1977, November 15, 1979, November 7, 1980.
Benjamin N. Brook. Tucson, Ariz. November 5, 1978.
Abraham Duker. New York City. August 1, 1978.
Jerome E. Edwards. Reno, Nev. November 28, 1978.
Irving M. Engel. New York City. August 21, 1978.
William Frankel. London. April 5, 1978.
Henry M. Friedlander. Tucson, Ariz. October 10, 1978; San Francisco, December 28, 1979.
R. Gogolinski-Elston. London. May 28, 1978.
Amy Zahl Gottlieb. New York City. August 5, 1977.
William Haber. Ann Arbor, Mich. November 14, 1979.
Selma Hirsh. New York City. July 26, 1977.
Sister Margaret Patricia McCarran. Sparks, Nev. November 28, 1978.
Simon Rifkind. New York City. July 24, 1978.
Francis Rosenberger. Washington, D.C. July 31, 1978.
Harry N. Rosenfield. Washington, D.C. December 20, 1978.
John G. Slawson. New York City. October 25, 1978.
William G. Stratton. Chicago. October 29, 1980.
Bernard Wasserstein. London. April 6, 1978.

ORAL HISTORY

Columbia University Oral History Collection, New York City.
Goldthwaite Higginson Dorr Oral History Memoir
Sir Robert G. A. Jackson
Henry Wallace Oral History. Vol. 27.
Harry S. Truman Library, Independence, Mo.
McKinzie, Richard D., "Oral History Interview with Loy W. Henderson," June 14 and July 5, 1973.
William E. Wiener Oral History Library, American Jewish Committee, New York City.
"A Study in American Pluralism through Oral Histories of Holocaust Survivors"

"Oral History Memoir of Irving M. Engel"
Samuel I. Rosenman Oral History

BOOKS, PERIODICALS, AND ARTICLES

Acheson, Dean. *Present at the Creation.* New York: Norton, 1969.
Adlerstein, F. R. "How Europe's Lost Are Found." *The American Mercury* (October 1945), 61:485–91.
"Admission of Displaced Persons To The United States." *International Labour Review* (July 1948), 58:91–93.
Agar, Herbert. *The Saving Remnant.* London: Rupert Hart-Davis, 1960.
Allen, Robert S. and William V. Shannon. *The Truman Merry-Go-Round.* New York: Vanguard Press, 1950.
"Amend the Displaced Persons Act." *Christian Century* (January 5, 1949), 66:3–4.
"America Gets First of 200,000 DPs." *Life* (November 22, 1948), 25:33–37.
"American Committee For Resettlement of Polish D.P.'s." *The Polish Review* (December 25, 1949), 8:10.
"Among Ourselves." *Survey Graphic* (July 1948), 37:331.
"Anti-Semitism." *Life* (December 1, 1947), 23:44.
Arendt, Hannah. "The Stateless People." *Contemporary Jewish Record* (April 1945), 8:137–53.
Arnold-Foster, W. "Displaced Persons In Germany: UNRRA's Cooperation With The Armies." *Army Quarterly* (January 1946), 51:239–47.
—— "UNRRA's Work For Displaced Persons In Germany." *International Affairs* (January 1946), 22:1–13.
Asofsky, Isaac L. "HIAS Executive Director Reports on 10-Week Survey of Emigration Needs In Europe." *Rescue* (January 1947), 4:1–2, 9–12.
"Asylum in Britain and America." *New Republic* (August 30, 1943), 109:311–13.
Auerbach, Jerold S. "Joseph M. Proskauer: American Court Jew." *American Jewish History* (September 1979), 69:103–16.
Bailey, Stephen K. and Howard D. Samuel. *Congress At Work.* New York: Holt, 1952.
Bain, Kenneth Ray. *The March to Zion.* College Station: Texas A&M University Press, 1979.

Baram, Philip J. *The Department of State In The Middle East, 1919–1945.* Philadelphia: University of Pennsylvania Press, 1978.

Barish, Louis, ed. *Rabbis In Uniform: The Jewish Chaplain's Story.* New York: Jonathan David, 1962.

Bauer, Yehuda. *Flight and Rescue: BRICHAH.* New York: Random House, 1970.

Berger, Joseph A. "Displaced Persons: A Human Tragedy of World War II." *Social Research* (March 1947), 14:45–58.

Bernard, William S. "Displaced Persons Legislation." *The Polish Review* (December 25, 1948), 8:4–5.

—— "Refugee Asylum in the United States: How the Law was Changed to Admit Displaced Persons." *International Migration* (1975), 13:3–20.

Bernard, William S., ed. *American Immigration Policy: A Reappraisal.* New York: Harper, 1950.

Bernard, William S. and Abraham G. Duker. "Who Killed Cock Robin?—The DP Act Discussed." *The Day* (New York City, English magazine section). August 29, 1948.

Bernstein, David. "Europe's Jews: Summer, 1947." *Commentary* (1947), 4:101–9.

Bernstein, Philip S. "Displaced Persons." *American Jewish Year Book* (1947–1948), 49:520–32.

—— "Status of Jewish DP's." *Department of State Bulletin* (June 29, 1947), 16:1308–11.

Beswich, Frank. "Rescue For Refugees." *The Spectator* (March 7, 1947), 178:234–35.

Bethell, Nicholas. *The Last Secret: Forcible Repatriation To Russia, 1944–1947.* London: Andre Deutsch, 1974.

—— *The Palestine Triangle.* London: Andre Deutsch, 1979.

"Bevin's Remark Sheds Light," *Christian Century* (June 26, 1946), 63:795.

Bickerton, Ian J. "President Truman's Recognition of Israel." *American Jewish Historical Quarterly* (December 1968), 58:173–240.

Bierbrier, Doreen. "The American Zionist Emergency Council: An Analysis of a Pressure Group." *Ibid.*, (September 1970), 60:82–105.

Blanshard, Frances. *Frank Aydelotte of Swarthmore.* Middletown, Conn.: Wesleyan University Press, 1970.

Bliven, Bruce, "U.S. Anti-Semitism Today." *New Republic*, 117 (November 3, 1947), 16–19, (November 17, 1947), 20–23,

November 24, 1947), 21–24, (December 8, 1947), 18–21, (December 15, 1947), 22–24, (December 22, 1947), 16–18, (December 29, 1947), 22–25.

Blum, John Morton. *The Price of Vision: The Diary of Henry A. Wallace, 1942–1946.* Boston: Houghton Mifflin, 1973.

Blumenson, Martin. *The Patton Papers, 1940–1945.* Boston: Houghton Mifflin, 1974.

Boeher, Alexander. "The Atrocity of Mass Expulsions." *Christian Century* (April 9, 1947), 64:461–63.

Boehm, Werner W. "State Programs For Displaced Persons." *Social Service Review* (December, 1949), 23:485–94.

"Brazil's Failure to Provide Homes for Refugees." *World Report* (October 28, 1947), 16.

Butterfield, Roger. "We Live Again." *Ladies' Home Journal* (November 1949), 66:163–68, 195–97, 199.

—— "Wisconsin Welcomes the Wanderers." *Collier's* (July 14, 1951), 128:20–21, 44, 46–47.

"Campaign Starts." *Commentary* (December 1946), 2:553–54.

Carey, Jane Perry Clark. "The Admission and Integration of Refugees in the United States." *Journal of International Affairs* (1953), 7:66–74.

Carter, Henry. *The Refugee Problem in Europe and the Middle East.* London: Epsworth Press, 1949.

Celler, Emanuel. *You Never Leave Brooklyn.* New York: John Day, 1953.

Chandler, Alfred D. and Louis Galambos, eds. *The Papers of Dwight D. Eisenhower.* Vol. 6: *Occupation, 1945.* Baltimore: Johns Hopkins University Press, 1978.

Checinski, Michael. "The Kielce Pogrom: Some Unanswered Questions." *Soviet Jewish Affairs* (1975), 5:57–72.

Clay, Lucius D. *Decision In Germany.* Garden City, N.Y.: Doubleday, 1950.

Close, Kathryn, "They Want to Be People." *Survey Graphic* (November 1946), 35:392–95, 421.

Coffin, Tris. "A Man of the Good Old Days." *New Republic* (February 17, 1947), 116:28–30.

Cohen, Henry. "The Jewish 'Displaced Person.'" *Jewish Frontier* (March 1947), 14:26–29.

—— "The International Refugee Organization." *Jewish Frontier* (May 1947), 14:21–23.

Cohen, Michael J. "The Genesis of the Anglo-American Committee on Palestine, November 1945: A Case Study In The Assertion of American Hegemony." *Historical Journal* (1979), 22:185–207.

Cohen, Naomi W. *Not Free To Desist:* American Jewish Committee, 1906–1966. Philadelphia: Jewish Publication Society of America, 1972.

"Communications: Displaced Persons." *Commonweal* (March 1, 1946), pp. 502–4.

"Congress and the D.P.'s." *Social Service Review* (September 1948), vol. 22.

Congressional Quarterly Notebook (May 5, 1948), 6:157–58.

Cope, Elizabeth W. "Displaced Europeans In Shanghai." *Far Eastern Survey* (December 8, 1948), 17:274–76.

Courtney, W. B. "Europe's Hangover." *Collier's* (July 28, 1945), 118:18–19, 60–61.

—— "Unwanted." *Collier's* (July 17, 1948), 122:27–28, 60.

Cousins, Norman. "An Apology for Living," *Saturday Review of Literature* (October 9, 1948), 31:9–12, 54–58.

Crossman, R.H.S. "Mr. Bevin and Mr. Truman." *New Statesman and Nation*, (Special Supplement, 1947), 33:11–12.

—— *A Nation Reborn.* New York: Atheneum, 1960.

—— *Palestine Mission.* New York: Harper, 1947.

Crum, Bartley C. *Behind the Silken Curtain.* New York: Simon & Schuster, 1947.

Crystal, David. *The Displaced Person and the Social Agency.* New York: United HIAS Service, 1958.

Curtis, Dorothy E. "Nurse, There's Typhus in Camp." *American Journal of Nursing* (September 1945), 45:714–15.

Dallek, Robert. *Franklin D. Roosevelt And American Foreign Policy, 1932–1945.* New York: Oxford University Press, 1979.

Davie, Maurice R. "Immigrant And Refugee Aid." *American Jewish Year Book* (1947–1948), 49:223–36.

Davis, George W. "Handling of Refugees and Displaced Persons by the French M.M.L.A. (Section Feminine)." *Social Service Review* (1948), 22:34–39.

Davidowicz, Lucy S. *The War Against The Jews,* 1933–1945. New York: Bantam Books, 1976.

Davis, Franklin M. Jr. *Come as a Conqueror.* New York: Macmillan, 1967.

Dekel, Ephraim. *B'RIHA: Flight To The Homeland.* New York: Herzl Press, 1972.

DeNovo, John A. "The Culbertson Economic Mission and Anglo-American Tensions in the Middle East, 1944–1945." *Journal of American History* (March 1977), 63:913–36.
de Zayas, Alfred M. *Nemesis At Potsdam: The Anglo-Americans and the Expulsion of the Germans.* Rev. ed. London: Routledge & Kegan Paul, 1979.
DiJour, Ilja M. "Changing Emphasis In Jewish Migration." *Jewish Social Service Quarterly* (September 1950), 27:72–79.
"Discrimination By Law." *Rescue* (June 1948), 5:8.
"Displaced Person Gets Placed." *Life* (August 21, 1950) 29:39–45.
"Displaced Persons." *Congressional Quarterly Log for Editors* (July 8, 1948), 6:468.
"Displaced Persons." *Editorial Research Reports* (April 14, 1948), pp. 235–48.
"Displaced Persons." *New Republic* (September 15, 1947), 117:7–8.
"Displaced Persons Act—Its Interpretation and Administration." *Interpreter Releases* (July 18, 1949), 26:230.
"Displaced Persons in Germany." *Polish Review* (December 12, 1946), 6:3–4, 15.
Divine, Robert A. *American Immigration Policy, 1924–1952.* New Haven: Yale University Press, 1957.
Dmytryshyn, Basil. "The Nazis and the SS Volunteer Division 'Galacia.'" *The American Slavic and East European Review* (February 1956), 15:1–10.
Donnison, F. S. V. *Civil Affairs and Military Government, Central Organization and Planning.* London: Her Majesty's Stationery Office, 1966.
Donovan, Robert J. *Conflict and Crisis.* New York: Norton, 1977.
"D.P. Admissions Lag as Desired." *Christian Century* (November 16, 1949), 66:1348–49.
"D.P. At Home." *Time* (March 20, 1950), 55:57–58.
"D.P. Commission Makes Final Report." *Christian Century* (September 10, 1952), 69:1020–21.
"D.P. Opposition Hits New Low." *Christian Century* (January 25, 1950), 67:100–101.
"DP's Hired by Industry Prove Eager, Willing Workers." *Business Week* (July 16, 1959), pp. 22–24.
"DP's Find a Home in Brazil." *Saturday Evening Post* (February 26, 1949), 221:20–21.
Drutmann, D. "The Displaced Jews in the American Zone of Germany." *Jewish Journal of Sociology* (December 1961), 3:261–63.

Duker, Abraham G. "Admitting Pogromists and Excluding Their Victims." *Reconstructionist* (October 1, 1948), 14:21–27.

Duker, Abraham G., "The DP Scandal Reviewed." *The Day* (Yiddish language, this article in English; New York City), July 25, 1948.

Dushkin, Alexander M. "The Educational Activities of the JDC in European Countries." *Jewish Social Service Quarterly* (June 1949), 25:444–51.

Dushnyck, Walter. "European Refugees in Grave Danger." *America* (May 3, 1947), 77:125–27.

——— "The Importance of the Problem of Displaced Persons." *Ukrainian Quarterly* (1946), 2:285–88.

Dushnyck, Walter and W. J. Gibbons. "For a Positive Refugee Policy." *America* (June 21, 1947), 77:317–19.

Ebon, Martin. "No Peace for the Homeless." *Free World* (May 1946), 11:33–36.

Elliott, Mark. "The United States and Forced Repatriation of Soviet Citizens, 1944–1947," *Political Science Quarterly* (1973), 88:253–75.

Emanuel, Myron. "Back-Page Story." *New Republic* (February 17, 1947), 116:12–15.

"Emergency Refugee Shelter in the United States." *International Migration Review* (January 1945), 51:97.

"End the DP Obstacle Race." *Christian Century* (January 19, 1949), 66:72–73.

Epstein, Helen. *Children of the Holocaust*. New York: Putnam's, 1979.

Esco Foundation for Palestine, Inc. *Palestine:* A Study of Jewish, Arab, and British Policies. 2 vols. New Haven: Yale University Press, 1947.

"Executive Director Details HIAS Services." *Rescue* (February–March 1947), 4:4–5.

"Exploitation of D. P.'s Must Be Stopped!" *Christian Century* (June 8, 1949), 66:699–700.

Facts on File (1948), 8:284.

"Fair Immigration, Broader Resettlement Urged." *United Nations Bulletin* (February 1, 1948), 4:85.

Farago, Ladislas. *The Last Days of Patton*. New York: McGraw-Hill, 1981.

Fay, Sidney B. "Displaced Persons In Europe." *Current History* (March 1946), 11:199–205.

"Features of Post-War Migration." *International Labour Review* (July 1954), 70:1–15.

Feingold, Henry L. *The Politics of Rescue*. New Brunswick: Rutgers University Press, 1970.

Feis, Herbert. *The Birth of Israel*. New York: Norton, 1969.

Fensterheim, Herbert and Herbert G. Birch. "A Case Study of Group Ideology and Individual Adjustment." *Journal of Abnormal and Social Psychology* (October 1950), 45:710–20.

Fisher, R. L. "The Army and Displaced Persons." *Military Government Journal* (April 1948), 1:1–4, 24–25.

Flowerman, Samuel H. and Marie Jahoda. "Polls On Anti-Semitism." *Commentary* (April 1946), 1:82–86.

Frary, William T. "I Am Pleading For The Poles In Germany." *The Polish Review* (March 1949), 9:8–9.

Friedman, Paul. "The Road Back For The DP's." *Commentary* (December 1948), 6:502–10.

Friedman, Saul S. *No Haven for the Oppressed:* United States Policy Toward Jewish Refugees, 1938–1945. Detroit: Wayne State University Press, 1973.

Friedrich, Carl J. *American Policy Toward Palestine*. Westport, Conn.: Greenwood Press, 1971. Originally published by Public Affairs Press, Washington, D.C., 1944.

Fuchs, Lawrence H. *The Political Behavior of American Jews*. New York: Free Press, 1956.

Gallup, George H. *The Gallup Poll*. 3 vols. New York: Random House, 1972.

Ganin, Zvi. *Truman, American Jewry, and Israel, 1945–1948*. New York: Holmes and Meier, 1979.

"Gateway To Freedom." *Rescue* (October–November, 1948), 5:1–2.

Genêt. "Letter From Aschaffenburg." *New Yorker* (October 30, 1948), 24:86–91.

—— "Letter From Würzburg." *Ibid.* (November 6, 1948), 24:104–9.

Gershon, Karen. *Postscript*. London: Victor Gollancz, 1969.

Gibson, John W. "The Displaced Placed." *Journal of International Affairs* (1953), 7:75–81.

Goldfeder, Pinchas. "A Practical Scheme To Settle The DP's." *Commentary* (August 1948), 6:108–13.

Gottlieb, Amy Zahl. "Refugee Immigration: The Truman Directive." *Prologue* (Spring 1981), 13:5–18.

Griffith, Robert. "Old Progressives and the Cold War." *Journal of American History* (September 1979), 66:334–47.

"Grim Outlook for Europe's Refugees." *World Report* (September 30, 1947), pp. 18–19.

Gringauz, Samuel. "Our New German Policy and the DP's," *Commentary* (June 1948), 5:508–14.

Grossman, Kurt R. *The Jewish DP Problem.* Institute of Jewish Affairs, World Jewish Congress, 1951.

Grossman, Kurt R. "Refugees, DP's, and Migrants." Reprinted from *The Institute Anniversary Volume* (1941–1961). New York: Institute of Jewish Affairs, 1962.

Gruenberger, Felix. "The Jewish Refugees In Shanghai." *Jewish Social Studies* (1950), 12:329–348.

Gruss, Emanuel. "In A Camp for Displaced Jews." *Congress Weekly* (June 29, 1945), 12:12–13.

Halpern, Ben. *The Idea of the Jewish State.* Cambridge, Mass.: Harvard University Press, 1971.

Harrison, Earl G. "The Last Hundred Thousand." *Survey Graphic* (December 1945), 34:468–73.

Hartmann, Susan M. *Truman and the 80th Congress.* Columbia: University of Missouri Press, 1971.

Heberle, Rudolph. "Displaced Persons in the Deep South." *Rural Sociology* (December 1951), 16:362–77.

Hickey, Margaret. "Displaced Persons ... From Refugee Camps to 'Grand Hotel,' 1949." *Ladies' Home Journal* (November 1949), 66:261–62, 264.

Hill, Russell. *Struggle For Germany.* London: Victor Gollancz, 1947.

Hirschmann, Ira A. *The Embers Still Burn.* New York: Simon & Schuster, 1949.

Hoehler, Fred K. "Displaced Persons." In George B. deHuszar, ed., *Persistent International Issues.* New York: Harper, 1947, pp. 41–68.

Holborn, Louise W. *The International Refugee Organization.* London: Oxford University Press, 1956.

Horowitz, David. *State in the Making.* New York: Knopf, 1953.

Hulme, Kathryn. *The Wild Place.* Boston: Little, Brown, 1953.

Hurewitz, J. C. *The Struggle For Palestine.* New York: Norton, 1950.

Hurvitz, Nathan. "From a Soldier's Letters." *Congress Weekly* (October 19, 1945), 12:11, 13.

Huxley-Blythe, Peter J. *The East Came West.* Caldwell, Idaho: The Caxton Printers, 1968.

Hyman, Abraham S. "Displaced Persons." *American Jewish Year Book* (1947–1948), 49:455–473.

Ickes, Harold L. "Shepherds and Coyotes." *New Republic*, (September 5, 1949), 121:16.

"Immediate Action Needed by D.P.'s." *Christian Century* (May 18, 1949), 66:699–700.

"Immigration: Talk and the Closed Door." *Newsweek* (May 10, 1948), 31:23–24.

"International Social Welfare." *Survey* (February 1948), 84:53–55.

Information Bulletin of the American Council for Judaism, 1946.

Israel, Fred L., ed. *The War Diaries of Breckinridge Long*. Lincoln: University of Nebraska Press, 1965.

Janowicz, Morris. *The Professional Soldier*. New York: Free Press, 1960.

JDC Review. 1947–1949.

"Jewish Resettlement of D.P.'s." *Social Service Review* (March 1950), 24:101–2.

Johnson, Alvin. "Places For Displaced Persons." *Yale Review* (March 1947), 36:394–404.

Katz, Shlomo. "The Jewish 'Displaced Persons.'" *Jewish Frontier* (July 1946), 13:6–8.

"Keep the Gates Open." *Survey* (March 1946), 82:82.

Kimche, Jon. "British Labor's Turnabout On Zionism." *Commentary* (1947), 4:510–17.

Kimche, Jon and David. *The Secret Roads*. New York: Farrar, Straus, and Cudahy, 1955.

Klemme, Marvin. *The Inside Story of UNRRA*. New York: Lifetime Editions, 1949.

Koehl, Robert L. *RKFDV: German Resettlement and Population Policy, 1939–1945*. Cambridge: Harvard University Press, 1957.

Kranzler, David. *Japanese, Nazis and Jews:* the Jewish Refugee Community of Shanghai, 1938–1945. New York: Yeshiva University Press, 1976.

Kulischer, Eugene M. *Europe on the Move: War and Population Changes, 1917–1947*. New York: Columbia University Press, 1948.

Lane, Arthur Bliss. *I Saw Poland Betrayed*. Indianapolis: Bobbs-Merrill, 1948.

—— Letter to the Editor. *Polish Review* (December 25, 1948), 8:3.

Lang, Daniel. "A Reporter At Large." *New Yorker* (September 13, 1947), 23:86–97.

Laqueur, Walter. *A History of Zionism*. New York: Holt, Rinehart & Winston, 1972.

Lash, Joseph P. *Eleanor: The Years Alone*. New York: Norton, 1972.

Lasker, Louda D. "Enter: The DP's By Legal Permit." *Survey* (March 1949), 85:139–44.

Leather, George. "'Westward Ho' and After." *New Statesman and Nation* (December 8, 1951), 42:659–660.

Lehrman, Hal. "The 'Joint' Takes a Human Inventory." *Commentary* (January 1949), 7:19–27.

—— "The Last Jews In The Last German Camp." *Rescue* (Fall 1953), 9:3–4.

Levin, Moshe. "Meeting in Munich." *Furrows* (October 1945), 3:14–17.

Liebman, Arthur. *Jews and the Left*. New York: Wiley, 1979.

Lithuanian Bulletin (January–February 1947), 5:18.

Logan, Andy. "A Reporter At Large." *New Yorker* (July 17, 1948), 24:44–51.

Lubell, Samuel. "The Second Exodus of the Jews." *Saturday Evening Post* (October 5, 1946), 219:16–17, 76, 80–85.

Lucas, Noah. *The Modern History of Israel*. London: Weidenfeld and Nicolson, 1974.

Macardle, Dorothy. *Children of Europe*. Boston: Beacon Press, 1951.

McNeill, Margaret. *By the Rivers of Babylon*. London: Bannisdale Press, 1950.

Martin, David. "Jews, Christians—and 'Collaborators.'" *America* (January 1, 1949), 8:344–45.

—— "Not 'Displaced Persons'—But Refugees." *Ukrainian Quarterly* (1948), 4:109–14.

Martin, Jean I. *Refugee Settlers:* A Study of Displaced Persons in Australia. Canberra: The Australian National University, 1965.

Mayne, Richard. *The Recovery of Europe*. New York: Harper & Row, 1970.

Medlicott, W. N. *British Foreign Policy Since Versailles, 1919–1963*. London: Methuen, 1968.

Meinertzhagen, Richard. *Middle East Diary, 1917–1956*. New York: Thomas Yoseloff, 1959.

Merritt, Anna J. and Richard L. Merritt, eds. *Public Opinion In Occupied Germany:* The OMGUS Surveys, 1945–1949. Urbana: University of Illinois Press, 1970.

Miller, Aaron David. "The Influence of Middle East Oil on American Foreign Policy: 1941–1948." *Middle East Review* (Spring 1977), 9:19–24.

Millis, Walter, ed. *The Forrestal Diaries*. New York: Viking, 1951.

Morgan, Edward P. "They Seek a Promised Land." *Collier's* (May 4, 1946), 117:66–67, 83–84.

Morse, Arthur D. *While Six Million Died: A Chronicle of American Apathy.* New York: Random House, 1967.

Nadich, Judah. *Eisenhower and the Jews.* New York: Twayne, 1953.

Namias, June. *First Generation.* Boston: Beacon Press, 1978.

Nekrich, Aleksandr M. *The Punished Peoples.* New York: Norton, 1978.

Nevins, Allan. *Herbert H. Lehman and His Era.* New York: Schribner's, 1963.

"New Americans One Year Later." *Life* (December 26, 1949), 27:11–15.

"New Hope for Foehrenwald DPs." *JDC Digest* (July 1955), 14:4.

"New Life for DP's." *Newsweek* (June 27, 1949), 33:90.

Nicolson, Harold. "Marginal Comment." *Spectator* (November 22, 1946), 177:733.

"Non-repatriable." *The Economist* (August 24, 1946), pp. 286–87.

Nowinski, M. M. "The Polish American Congress Keeps Alive The Battle For Poland." *Polish Review* (July 31, 1947), 7:3, 15.

Nurkiewicz, Ignatius. "Facing The D. P. Problem." *Ibid.* (December 25, 1948), 8:8–9, 15.

Nussbaum, David W. "DP Camps Swarm With Pro-Nazis; IRO Shrugs It Off." *The New York Post Home News,* November 21, 1948, p. 5.

"One Way We Buy Friends—And Get Our Money Back." *Saturday Evening Post* (February 9, 1952), 224:10.

Ott, Jacob M. "The Polish Pogroms and Press Suppression." *Jewish Forum* (January 1946), 29:3–4.

"Our Own Open Door." *Commonweal* (August 30, 1946), 44:468.

Pargiello, Jan S. "Let Us Give a Helping Hand To Polish D.P.s." *Polish Review* (December 25, 1948), 8:13–14.

Parzen, Herbert. "President Truman and the Palestine Quandary: His Initial Experience, April–December, 1945." *Jewish Social Studies* (January 1973), 35:42–72.

—— "The Roosevelt Palestine Policy, 1943–1945: An Exercise in Dual Diplomacy." *American Jewish Archives* (April 1974), 26:31–65.

"Passport to Nowhere." *Journal of Home Economics* (May 1948), 40:262.

Pearson, Drew. "Washington Merry-Go-Round." *Joplin Globe* (Missouri). July 20, 1948.

Pelcovits, N. A. "European Refugees in China." *Far Eastern Survey* (October 23, 1946), 15:321–25.

Peterson, Edward N. *The American Occupation of Germany—Retreat to Victory.* Detroit: Wayne State University Press, 1978.

Phillips, William. *Ventures In Diplomacy.* Boston: Beacon Press, 1952.

Pickett, Clarence E. "Handling Displaced Populations In Occupied Territory." *Public Opinion Quarterly* (1943), 7:592–605.

Pinson, Koppel S. "Jewish Life In Liberated Germany: A Study of the Jewish DP's." *Jewish Social Studies* (1947), 9:101–26.

Podet, Allen H. "Anti-Zionism in a Key U.S. Diplomat: Loy Henderson at the End of World War II." *American Jewish Archives* (November 1978), 30:155–87.

Podolsky, Sophia. "Resettling the Reich's Refugees." The *Sunday Record* (Bergen County, N.J.). April 22, 1979, E 1–2.

"Polish Press In D/P Camps In Germany." *Polish Review* (February 7, 1946), 6:13–14.

Polk, William R. *The U.S. and the Arab World.* 3d edit. Cambridge, Mass.: Harvard University Press, 1975.

"Pretty Picture." *Time* (April 17, 1950) 55:23.

"Protestants Are Failing Refugees." *Christian Century* (April 27, 1949), 66:541.

"Protestants Fail the D.P.'s." *Ibid.* (April 27, 1949), 66:515–16.

Proudfoot, Malcolm J. *European Refugees: 1939–1952:* A Study in Forced Population Movement. Evanston, Ill.: Northwestern University Press, 1956.

Rabinowitz, Dorothy. *New Lives.* New York: Avon, 1977.

Reed, John C. "DP's Find Homes." *Social Order* (October 1954), 4:347–353.

"Refugee Problems U.S. Faces." *United States News* (July 18, 1947), 23:19.

"Refugees in the USA." *Survey* (January, 1946), 82:16–17.

Reich, Nathan. "Europe's Jews Since V-E Day." *Congress Bulletin,* Montreal, (December 1947), 4:4–6.

—— "The Last Million." *Survey* (April 1947), 83:110–112.

Renton, Bruce. "Europe in Flight. *Spectator* (November 30, 1951), 187:733–34.

"Resettlement of Refugees and Displaced Persons in the United States." *International Labour Review* (June 1953), 67:559–76.

Reynolds, Mary G. "New Horizons." *Americas* (August 1949), 1:2–7, 30–31, 44.

Reynolds, Quentin. "God, Make Us Forget." *Collier's* (March 26, 1949), 123:50–51, 54–55.

Rifkind, Simon H. *The Disinherited Jews of Europe Must Be Saved.* New York: American Jewish Conference, 1946.

—— "I Lived With The Jewish D.P.'s." *Congress Weekly* (April 12, 1946), 13:9–12.

—— "They Are Not Expendable." *Survey Graphic* (1946), 35:205–7, 234–36.

Ripley, Josephine. "The Climate Shifts on Immigration." *Commentary* (January 1948), 5:35–40.

Rogow, Arnold A. *James Forrestal.* New York: Macmillan, 1963.

Roosevelt, Kermit. "The Partition of Palestine: A Lesson in Pressure Politics." *Middle East Journal* (January 1948), 2:1–16.

Ross, Robert W. *So It Was True: The American Protestant Press and the Nazi Persecution of the Jews.* Minneapolis: University of Minnesota Press, 1980.

Sachar, Howard M. *A History of Israel.* New York: Knopf, 1976.

Safran, Nadav. *Israel: The Embattled Ally.* Cambridge, Mass.: Harvard University Press, 1978.

Samuels, Gertrude. "Five Who Came Out of the Terror." *New York Times Magazine*, August 3, 1952, pp. 12–13, 51–52.

—— "Passport To Where: A DP Story." *New York Times Magazine*, September 19, 1948, pp. 14, 62–63.

Sandulescu, Jacques. *Hunger's Rogues.* New York: Harcourt Brace Jovanovich, 1974.

Schechtman, Joseph B. *European Population Transfers, 1939–1945.* New York: Oxford University Press, 1946.

—— *The United States and the Jewish State Movement:* The Crucial Decade, 1939–1949. New York: Herzl Press, Thomas Yoseloff, 1966.

Schneider, Catheren M. "The Displaced Person as a Patient." *American Journal of Nursing* (September 1945), 45:690–92.

"Schools In The 'Displaced Persons Centers' of Germany." *School and Society* (December 15, 1945), 62:384.

Schwarz, Leo W. *The Redeemers: A Saga of the Years, 1945–1952.* New York: Farrar, Straus and Young, 1953.

"Screening DP's," *America* (December 1, 1948), 8:251.

"Seeks Admission of 400,000 DP's." *Catholic World* (April 1948), 167:84.

Segalman, Ralph. "The Psychology of Jewish Displaced Persons." *Jewish Social Service Quarterly* (June 1947), 23:361–69.

Seligman, Daniel. "Congress and the DP's." *Commonweal* (December 16, 1949), 51:286–88.

"Senate's Most Expendable." *Time* (March 20, 1950), 55:18.

"Send Them Here!" *Life* (September 23, 1946), 21:36.

Shalett, Sidney. "How are the DP's Doing in America?" *The Saturday Evening Post* (August 27, 1949), 222:26–27, 91–92.

Shuster, Zachariah. "Between The Millstones in Poland." *Commentary* (August 1946), 2:107–15.

Smith, H. Alexander. "The Displaced Persons Act—Unfinished Business." *Polish Review* (December 25, 1948), 8:3, 10, 14.

Smith, Helena Huntington. "Who Said Promised Land?" *Collier's* (July 2, 1949), 124:19–21, 57–58.

Smith, Jean Edward, ed. *The Papers of General Lucius D. Clay, Germany, 1945–1949*. 2 vols. Bloomington: Indiana University Press, 1974.

Snetsinger, John. *Truman, The Jewish Vote, and the Creation of Israel.* Palo Alto, California: Stanford University, Hoover Institution Press, 1974.

"Some Facts About The 'DP' Program." *Congressional Digest* (March 1950), 29:68.

"Special Committee on Refugees and Displaced Persons." *Department of State Bulletin*, April 21, 1946, pp. 664–65.

Spivak, Robert G. "Members of New Congress Back Move to End DP Law Bias." The *New York Post*, December 2, 1948, pp. 2, 47.

Srole, Leo. "Why The DP's Can't Wait." *Commentary* (1947), 3:13–24.

Stein, George H. *The Waffen SS*. Ithaca, N.Y.: Cornell University Press, 1966.

Steinberg, Alfred. "McCarran, Lone Wolf of the Senate," *Harper's Magazine*, (November 1950), 201:89–95.

Stevens, Richard P. *American Zionism and U.S. Foreign Policy, 1942–1947*. New York: Pageant, 1962.

Stoessinger, John George. *The Refugee and the World Community*. Minneapolis: University of Minnesota Press, 1956.

Stone, I. F. "The Palestine Report." *Nation* (May 11, 1946), 162:562–64.

—— *Underground to Palestine*. New York: Boni and Gaer, 1946.

"Story of I.R.O." *Wiener Library Bulletin* (1956), 10:32.

Swanstrom, Edward E. *Pilgrims of the Night*. New York: Sheed and Ward, 1950.

Thompson, Dorothy. "Refugees: A World Problem." *Foreign Affairs* (April 1938), 16:375–87.

Tolstoy, Nikolai. *Victims of Yalta*. London: Hodder and Stoughton, 1977.

Truman, Harry S. *Memoirs: Years of Trial and Hope*. Garden City, N.Y.: Doubleday, 1956.

Truman, Margaret. *Harry S. Truman*. New York: William Morrow, 1973.

"Truman Opens Gates To Refugees." *Christian Century* (January 2, 1946), 63:2.

United Nations. Economic and Social Council. *Report of the Special Committee on Refugees and Displaced Persons*. London, June, 1946.

"U.N. To Assume Resettlement Task." *United Nations Weekly Bulletin* (August 3, 1946), 1:13–15.

Urofsky, Melvin I. *American Zionism From Herzl To The Holocaust*. Garden City: N.Y.: Anchor Press/Doubleday, 1976.

—— *We Are One!* American Jewry and Israel. Garden City, N.Y.: Anchor Press/Doubleday, 1978.

Vernant, Jacques. *The Refugee in the Post-War World*. London: Allen and Unwin, 1953.

Vida, George. *From Doom to Dawn*. New York: Jonathan David, 1967.

Waldman, Morris D. *Nor By Power*. New York: International Universities Press, 1953.

Warburg, Miriam. "Jews in Europe Today." *Westralian Judean* (September 1946), 18:12–14.

Warren, George L. "Interaction of Migration Policies and World Economy." *Department of State Bulletin* (February 10, 1946), pp. 213–16.

Wasserstein, Bernard. *Britain and the Jews of Europe, 1939–1945*. London: Clarendon Press, Oxford University Press, 1979.

Weekly Review, 1946–1947. Publication of the American Jewish Joint Distribution Committee.

Weizman, Chaim. *Trial and Error*. London: Hamish Hamilton, 1949.

"Welcome Immigrants!" *Fortune* (December 1948), 38:85–86.

Werner, Alfred. "The New Refugees." *Jewish Frontier* (July 1946), 13:21–23.

White, Lyman Cromwell. *300,000 New Americans: The Epic of a Modern Immigrant-Aid Service*. New York: Harper, 1957.

Whitehead, Samuel. "The Half-open Door." *Nation* (February 18, 1950), 170:148–49.

"Why Congress Is Split Over DP's." *U.S. News* (March 31, 1950), 28:18–19.

"Why The Displaced Persons Cannot Return Home." *Polish Review* (October 10, 1946), 6:11, 14.

Williams, Francis. *Ernest Bevin.* London: Hutchinson, 1952.

Wilson, Evan M. *Decision On Palestine.* Stanford University: Hoover Institution Press, 1979.

Wilson, Francesca. "Displaced Persons—Whose Responsibility?" *Current Affairs* (June 28, 1947), #31. Carnegie House, London: Bureau of Current Affairs.

Wischnitzer, Mark. *To Dwell In Safety:* The Story of Jewish Migration Since 1800. Philadelphia: Jewish Publication Society of America, 1948.

Woodbridge, George. *UNRRA.* 3 vols. New York: Columbia University Press, 1950.

"World Relief Confusion." *Survey* (December 1946), 82:335.

Wycislo, Aloysius J. "The Catholic Program For The Resettlement of Displaced Persons," *Polish Review* (December 25, 1948), 8:6–7, 11.

Wyman, David S. *Paper Walls:* America and the Refugee Crisis, 1938–1941. Amherst: University of Massachusetts Press, 1968.

Ziemke, Earl F. *The U.S. Army in the Occupation of Germany.* Washington, D.C.: Center of Military History, 1975.

Zink, Harold. *American Military Government in Germany.* New York: Macmillan, 1947.

NEWSPAPERS

Deggendorf Center Revue. Deggendorf, Germany, 1945.

DP Express. Munich, Germany, 1947.

Jewish Chronicle. London. 1945–48.

The New York Times. 1945–50.

Stars and Stripes. Germany edition, 1945–46. European edition, July–September 1946.

The Times. London. 1945–48.

Washington Post. 1945–50.

UNPUBLISHED MATERIAL

American Council of Voluntary Agencies For Foreign Service. "The Problem of Displaced Persons." Report of the Survey Committee on Displaced Persons of the ACVAFS, June, 1946. Copy in Blaustein Library, American Jewish Committee, New York City.

Citizens Committee on Displaced Persons. "Releases, Memoranda, etc., 1946–1950," in loose leaf binder, *ibid.*

Emmet, Christopher. "Confidential Memorandum On Significance of Articles Attacking Non-Jewish D.P.'s *By David Nussbaum, New York Post, November 19, and 21, 1948*," in American Jewish Committee Archives, New York City.

Ganin, Zvi. "The Diplomacy of the Weak: American Zionist Leadership During The Truman Era, 1945–1948." Ph.D. dissertation, Brandeis University, 1975.

Haron, Miriam Joyce. "Anglo-American Relations and the Question of Palestine, 1945–1947." Ph.D. dissertation, Fordham University, 1979.

"Hearings Before the Anglo-American Committee of Inquiry," Washington, D.C. 2 vols. January 7–14, 1946. Copy in Zionist Archives, New York City.

Heymont, Irving. "After The Deluge: The Landsberg Jewish DP Camp, 1945." Letters to Mrs. Heymont. Copy in possession of the author.

Kirby, Connie A. "Amending The Displaced Persons Act of 1948." Seminar paper, Southwest Missouri State University, 1973. Copy in Truman Library.

Kishinka, Joyce Williams. "A Study of Assimilation Experiences of Jewish, Latvian and Ukrainian Displaced Persons." Ed.D. Rutgers University, 1979.

Leary, William Matthew, Jr. "Smith of New Jersey: a Biography of H. Alexander Smith, United States Senator From New Jersey, 1944–1959." Ph.D. dissertation, Princeton University, 1966.

Liebschutz, Thomas Philip. "Rabbi Philip S. Bernstein and the Jewish Displaced Persons." M.A. thesis, Hebrew Union College–Jewish Institute of Religion, May, 1965.

Lorimer, M. Madeline. "America's Response to Europe's Displaced Persons, 1948–1952: A Preliminary Report." Ph.D. dissertation, St. Louis University, 1964.

Neuringer, Sheldon Morris. "American Jewry and United States Immigration Policy, 1881–1953." Ph.D. dissertation, [Department of History,] University of Wisconsin, 1969.

Newman, Gemma Mae. "Earl G. Harrison and the Displaced Persons Controversy: A Case Study in Social Action." Ph.D. dissertation, [Department of Speech,] Temple University, 1973.

Pritchard, Anton A. "The Social System of a Displaced Persons Camp." Honors thesis, [Department of Social Relations.] Harvard University, 1950.

"Reports of the Advisors on Jewish Affairs to the United States Command in Germany and Austria, 1947–1950." Copy in Blaustein Library, American Jewish Committee, New York City.

Sachar, David B. "David K. Niles and United States Policy Toward Palestine: A Case Study in American Foreign Policy." Thesis, Department of History, Harvard University, March, 1959.

Sage, Jerry M. "The Evolution of U.S. Policy Toward Europe's Displaced Persons: World War II To June 25, 1948." M.A. thesis, [Department of Public Law and Government,] Columbia University, 1952.

Smith, Glenn H. "Senator William Langer: A Study In Isolationism." Ph.D. dissertation, [Department of History,] University of Iowa, 1968.

Statement of the Honorable Benjamin R. Civiletti Before the B'nai B'rith Luncheon Forum, Nov. 7, 1979, International Center, Washington, D.C.

Tripp, Eleanor Baldwin. "Displaced Persons: The Legislative Controversy in the United States, 1945–1950." M.A. thesis, Department of History, Columbia University, 1966.

INDEX

Contemporary American History Series

WILLIAM E. LEUCHTENBURG, GENERAL EDITOR

Lawrence S. Wittner, *Rebels against War: The American Peace Movement, 1941–1960*, 1969.

Davis R. B. Ross, *Preparing for Ulysses: Politics and Veterans during World War II*, 1969.

John Lewis Gaddis, *The United States and the Origins of the Cold War, 1941–1947*, 1972.

George C. Herring, Jr., *Aid to Russia, 1941–1946: Strategy, Diplomacy, the Origins of the Cold War*, 1973.

Alonzo L. Hamby, *Beyond the New Deal: Harry S. Truman and American Liberalism*, 1973.

Richard M. Fried, *Men against McCarthy*, 1976.

Steven F. Lawson, *Black Ballots: Voting Rights in the South, 1944–1969*, 1976.

Carl M. Brauer, *John F. Kennedy and the Second Reconstruction*, 1977.

Maeva Marcus, *Truman and the Steel Seizure Case: The Limits of Presidential Power*, 1977.

Morton Sosna, *In Search of the Silent South: Southern Liberals and the Race Issue*, 1977.

Robert M. Collins, *The Business Response to Keynes, 1929–1964*, 1981.

Robert M. Hathaway, *Ambiguous Partnership: Britain and America, 1944–1947*, 1981.

Leonard Dinnerstein, *America and the Survivors of the Holocaust*, 1982.

Lawrence S. Wittner, *American Intervention in Greece, 1943–1949*, 1982.

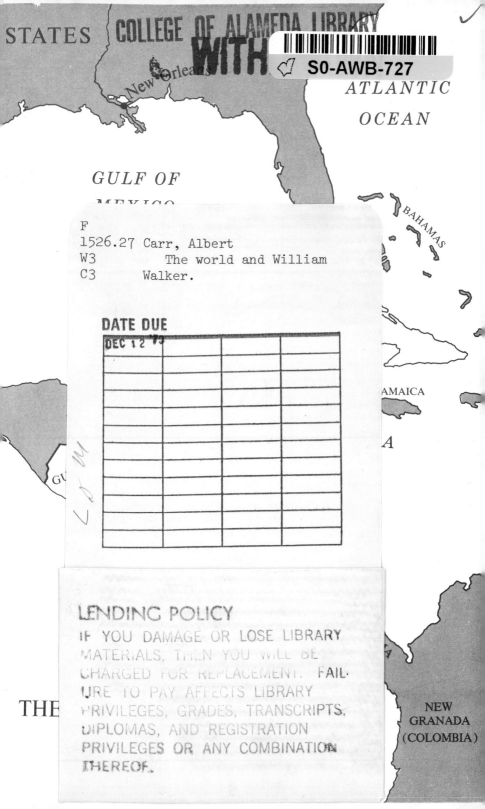

THE WORLD AND WILLIAM WALKER

Books by Albert Z. Carr

JUGGERNAUT: THE PATH OF DICTATORSHIP

MEN OF POWER

AMERICA'S LAST CHANCE

NAPOLEON SPEAKS

TRUMAN, STALIN AND PEACE

THE COMING OF WAR

JOHN D. ROCKEFELLER'S SECRET WEAPON

THE WORLD AND WILLIAM WALKER

ALBERT Z. CARR

THE WORLD AND WILLIAM WALKER

GREENWOOD PRESS, PUBLISHERS
WESTPORT, CONNECTICUT

Library of Congress Cataloging in Publication Data

Carr, Albert H   Z
    The world and William Walker.

    Reprint of the ed. published by Harper & Row,
New York.
    Bibliography: p.
    Includes index.
    1. Walker, William, 1824-1860. I. Title.
F1526.27.W3C3 1975   972.8'5'040924   75-18354
ISBN 0-8371-8328-6

Originally published in 1963 by Harper & Row, Publishers, New York

Reprinted with the permission of Mrs. Albert Carr.

Reprinted in 1975 by Greenwood Press,
a division of Williamhouse-Regency Inc.

Library of Congress Catalog Card Number 75-18354

ISBN 0-8371-8328-6

Printed in the United States of America

CONTENTS

v

PART TWO: The Shape of Destiny

PART THREE: All or Nothing

AUTHOR'S NOTE

In the years just prior to the Civil War, William Walker's name was read in countless headlines, and heard everywhere. Millions of Americans regarded him as their Man of Destiny, and a leading European periodical hailed him as "the rival of Washington"; while President James Buchanan ordered the United States Navy into action against him, and Horace Greeley attacked him with bitter invective. His prodigious career dazzled the country. Before he was twenty-five he had been a physician, a lawyer, and a crusading newspaper editor. At thirty-one he entered Nicaragua with only fifty-eight men, defeated armies of thousands, made himself general and dictator, and was elected president. People were thunderstruck by his temerity in challenging simultaneously the might of England, the power of the President of the United States, and the millions of Cornelius Vanderbilt.

This man with the pedestrian name painted his exotic adventures on so large a canvas, in such brilliant colors, and in so surrealistic a style that it is easy to miss their inner meaning. Through his story the politics of an age may be discerned. His achievements were intimately connected with great issues—whether the Civil War would be fought —where the canal connecting the Atlantic and Pacific oceans would be dug—whether Cuba and Central America would become part of the

vii

United States. The pattern of America's present-day relations with the Latin-American countries was largely set in Walker's time, and in spite of him. There is even perhaps in the background of the strange Walker saga a kind of Neanderthal anticipation of the dilemma in which the world finds itself in the mid-twentieth century.

In the intense agitation that he created, Walker himself, his human essence, his personality, all but disappeared from view. He became a historical enigma. In the literature about him, as it deals with the crucial passages of his life, such words as "baffling," "inexplicable," "incredible," repeatedly occur. The great volume of extreme propaganda for and against him, the myths and the legends created a distorting fog around his character, motives, and intentions. Viewing him as a political phenomenon or as a knightly hero or as a ruthless power-seeker, men lost sight of the human passions that drove him to storm the citadels of power and to defy the great forces that dominated the world of the 1850's.

It was in an effort to dispel some of the uncertainties about him that I began years ago to investigate the surviving documents of his life in cities that had known and reacted to him—New Orleans, Nashville, San Francisco, León, Washington, New York, London. Gradually a coherent and remarkable personality emerged from the record. In these pages I have tried so far as possible to let that record speak for itself. Dialogue passages are as reported in newspapers and magazines of the period, or, in one or two instances, as reconstructed from clear indications in the historical accounts.

A. Z. C.

Truro, Massachusetts

"How far high failure overleaps
the bounds of low success!"
—SIR LEWIS MORRIS

PART ONE

Overture for Bugles

《《 》》

"A great idea springs up in a man's soul; it agitates his whole being, transports him from the ignorant present and makes him feel the future in a moment. . . . Why should such a revelation be made to him . . . if not that he should carry it into practice?"

WILLIAM WALKER

I

THE GALAHAD COMPLEX

In Nashville, Tennessee, where Walker was born and raised, every literate and prosperous home had in its bookcase, alongside the Bible, Webster's Dictionary, and Marshall's *Life of George Washington,* half a dozen books by Sir Walter Scott. "The Sir Walter disease," as Mark Twain called it, was then rampant throughout the South. In the 1830's and 1840's everyone read pirated editions of *The Lady of the Lake, Ivanhoe, Marmion, The Talisman, Quentin Durward,* and the rest. *Ivanhoe* especially, according to Mark Twain, set the South "in love with dreams and phantoms." But popularizations of Malory's Arthurian legends also had a great vogue, and the chastity and dedication of Galahad were as much admired as the strength and nobility of Ivanhoe. It was a period that gave to its favorite books a devotion approaching reverence, with the result that the dreams of a generation of Southerners were shaped by medieval romance.

The yearning for the ancient glories of chivalry was more than a literary passion. Almost certainly, young people of Walker's day and place turned to Scott and the *Morte d'Arthur* out of psychological need, as a response to social conditions then prevalent. Contrary to a popular impression, the puritanical austerity of life in most parts of the

South was more extreme than in the North, and this was especially true of inland communities, such as Nashville, where the Protestant sects vied with each other in repressing the normal impulses of youth. Millions of youngsters like Walker had the virtues of male "purity" drilled into them by countless preachments from adolescence on, and were brought up believing that the sexual impulse, outside of the marriage bed, was the prompting of the devil. In this strict moral environment, anything that evoked the romantic mood was bound to reach deeply into the lives of the young. They wanted to idealize the relations between the sexes so as to be better able to resist the natural temptations of sensual pleasure and conform to the mores of the community. In emulating Ivanhoe or Galahad, unmarried young men found a psychological crutch with which to bear the dislocation of the reproductive instinct. Many a Southern youth, compelled to remain virginal too long, filled his mind with all the high and impossible traditions of chivalry and learned to make a virtue of abstention. It was easier to endure sexual frustration if one was living up to a grand conception of knightly honor, however illusory.

II

During Walker's childhood an ailing mother was his special care. In a memoir of the time, a friend of the Walkers' wrote, "I used often to go to see his mother and always found him entertaining her in some way." The chief form of sickroom entertainment was a reading from a favorite book. Many an afternoon, while his mother lay back on her pillows, Walker, reading in his soft Tennessee voice, must have evoked and been carried away by the mood of chivalry, in which any damsel in distress had a claim on the true knight, in which no honorable chevalier permitted a woman to be wronged if he could help her, in which one willingly gave up one's life for a friend, in which the feat of derring-do had the greater fame if the odds against one seemed hopeless. These were attitudes that stayed with him all his life.

He was not taken in by the absurdities of the chivalric manner—he was impatient of grandiose expressions of sentiment, elaborate rituals of courtesy and the naïve ferocity displayed by many Southerners in the defense of narrow points of honor. But when it came to questions of soldierly behavior and the claims of womanhood he was the romantic unalloyed. During his heyday as a conquerer, when he was leading an army of hardened soldiers of fortune to whom the looting of conquered cities and the raping of women seemed altogether reasonable, he many times risked his popularity by imposing unheard-of standards of personal restraint on his men. "On entering a town," wrote the poet Joaquin Miller, who served under him in Nicaragua, "he as a rule issued a proclamation making death the penalty for insulting a woman, for theft, or for entering a church save as a Christian should." Drunkenness among soldiers on duty was more heavily punished than in the United States Army. When his own brother, Captain Norvell Walker, got drunk on the eve of a battle, Walker publicly reduced him to the ranks; and at the most desperate point of his military fortunes he was capable of warning his men that he intended "to see properly punished, socially as well as legally, the intemperance which is calculated to bring the army into contempt and disgrace." He himself did not need to drink. For him danger was wine enough; it made him glow.

His youth in Nashville was painfully good. In sophisticated New Orleans, where the lively Creole tradition was strong, glossy young bloods kept mistresses, bedded slave girls, seduced coquettes, and slept with widows, but in the Walkers' circle in Nashville even talk of such libertinism was unthinkable. There were, of course, Nashville men who made concubines of their female slaves, but they were not likely to be found among the Disciples of Christ, the stern sect to which the family adhered. In such an environment the only chance for the sexual education of an adolescent boy was seduction by some bold and amorous girl, and what girl would bother with a lad who was short, slight, towheaded, freckle-faced, shy, bookish, and over-sensitive?

Doubtless before he reached manhood he had some kind of sexual experience—he lived for a year as a medical student in Paris. But if, as seems not improbable, his friends took him once to a brothel, he would have been repelled by the experience. There was nothing in his background to prepare him for frank nudity, bawdy talk, and casual sex. One can imagine him, after his first hopeless encounter with a laughing Parisian prostitute, flinging his cloak around him, stalking out into the night, and pacing the cobbled streets of the Left Bank, indignant, disturbed, unwilling to admit his frustration even to himself, determined more than ever to maintain his knightly ideals.

By his early twenties, although he had emancipated himself from fundamentalist religion, the ascetic pattern was firmly fixed in him. He had dissected many a corpse, he knew the physiology of sex, he was drawn to women; but sex, love, and marriage were in his mind linked in a romantic chain to a conception of beauty virginal and distressed, which needed him to rescue it and defend it. Then, in New Orleans, he met Ellen Galt Martin* and found the beauty, the virginity, and the affliction. She was a year younger than himself, twenty-three, desirable, intelligent—but a deaf-mute. The sight of beauty cut off from all the sounds of life must have called forth every protective impulse in Walker, made him wish to hold his shield before Ellen and by his personal force keep her safe from the hurtful world. He fell deeply in love.

The only extant picture of Ellen, a stylized painting, suggests a considerable charm: a high forehead, searching dark eyes, a heart-shaped, piquant face, firmly molded features, and a delicate sensuality of figure, so far as petticoats and pantalettes permit judgment. There is an alert look about her that accords with other testimony to the effect that she was exceptionally well-read and deeply interested in the questions of the day. After an attack of scarlet fever at the age of five had robbed her of both voice and hearing, her parents sent her to a school near Philadelphia which specialized in the teaching of handicapped children. On her return to New Orleans she revealed a spirited quality of mind that enabled her to share in the social life of the Martins, who were a well-to-do and prominent family. Ellen, says a family account, "used to go to balls and parties, carrying a tiny pad and pencil which she used to exchange lively repartee with many beaux."

In 1848, when Walker met her, her brothers had married and left home, and she was living with her widowed mother, Clarinda Glasgow Martin, in a large house fashionably situated. Among their acquaintance was a young lawyer and man about town, Edmund Randolph, who coming as he did of the noted Virginia family (his grandfather had been George Washington's Attorney General) had entrée everywhere; and Randolph, who had become Walker's closest

---

* Her name erroneously appears as Helen Martin in most of the Walker literature. New Orleans *Times-Picayune*, Sept. 26, 1937.

friend, brought him to the Martins' home. The result might have been predicted. Ellen responded to his love. No doubt they could read each other's feelings in eyes and expressions, in shy embraces, but their frustration at inability to communicate in speech must have been overwhelming. A book on the manual sign language for the deaf and dumb had been published not long before, and Walker spent long hours practicing its spectral routines, until he could read Ellen's patient fingers and gesticulate his way letter by letter through brief replies. It was a courtship charged with tenderness, urgency, and intense concentration.

Randolph was able to give Mrs. Martin the necessary assurances as to Walker's background and respectability, but beyond this, Ellen would have learned from her mother the striking facts about him that all New Orleans knew: that before he was twenty he was a physician with a degree from the University of Pennsylvania Medical College; that for two years he had traveled in Europe, pursuing his studies in Paris, Edinburgh, and Heidelberg; that he had put aside medicine in order to study law in New Orleans, and had practiced briefly and brieflessly as Edmund Randolph's partner; and that he had just given up the law to become an editor of the city's youngest newspaper, the *Crescent*. But she needed answers to a thousand questions, too many to be conveyed by sign language. Many a night Walker must have sat at his desk and dashed off, with ink and quill, the long letters that she craved. The written word came naturally to him—he was always fluent on paper, laconic in speech.

III

His father, James Walker, was a Scotsman born, who emigrated to Nashville, Tennessee, for the good reason that he had inherited property there from an uncle, and notably a prosperous dry-goods store. Soon he made a constructive marriage with the daughter of a well-known Tennessee family, Mary Norvell, whose father had been an officer in George Washington's army. Thereafter James Walker founded a commercial insurance company and became its president; and as one of Nashville's rising men, lost no time in building a substantial brick house in Nashville's best district. William was born there, the eldest of the four Walker children.

The stern spirit of Calvin and Knox was strong in the Walker home.

The Disciples of Christ maintained that a primitive and stark simplicity of worship and a literal adherence to the Bible was the only route to godliness. Religious conviction may account for the fact that James Walker would not own slaves. Too canny a businessman to let himself be called an abolitionist in a Southern community, he yet made it a point to employ as servants free Negroes to whom he paid wages—a practice not uncommon in the border states, where the example of Washington and Jefferson in freeing their slaves had not been ignored. To be sure, the economic condition of the free Negro was generally little better and sometimes worse than that of the slave, but for Negroes freedom was nevertheless the only word of hope. In any event William was brought up in a home with a nonconformist attitude toward slavery, and without firsthand experience of slave owning.

James Walker was not an unkind man, but he was a pietistic and austere father. The relationship between him and his eldest son evidently followed a classical pattern of authority and rebellion. In his early years, William was a difficult child and a reluctant schoolboy —avid for learning, but impatient of discipline. One guesses that the pride, the silence, and the tenacity that characterized him in later years were conditioned in him early by the bullying of larger boys— and most boys of his age were larger than he. From the very beginning his chief weapon in life must have been his fighting spirit. There is a certain type of small boy who is an insoluble problem to the lads of superior muscle who knock him down, because he never knows when he is licked; they cannot make him stop coming at them; they can never have an easy moment until they make peace with him. Walker the man created the impression of having been such a boy.

His father similarly gave way before him. When he was twelve, and James Walker pressed him to study for the ministry, William successfully resisted. In a time when fathers customarily selected their sons' careers, and in a household deeply dedicated to religion, his stubbornness must have shocked the older Walker, while for William the triumph of this, his first rebellion, opened a whole new vista of possibilities in life. Later, when he determined to leave Nashville, he had his way again. Perhaps his father was glad to get the rebel out of the house. His other children yielded easily to his authority.

William's first choice of a career was strongly influenced by his intense feeling for his mother. He was one of those boys who wish that they had been immaculately conceived. Mary Walker was a quiet woman, and during his school years William saw her stoically endure persistent pain which her physician was unable to diagnose or to ease. He was seized by a boy's dream of returning home as a master physician and effecting her cure; and the same dream may well have been the spur that thereafter speeded him through his schooling. Before he was ten he turned a psychological corner and became an exceptional student; he entered the University of Nashville at twelve, and graduated at fourteen, *summa cum laude*. This was, of course, less prodigious a feat than it would have been at Harvard or Yale. Nevertheless, to qualify for admission at the University of Nashville, Walker had to be fluent in Latin through Caesar's *Commentaries* and Cicero's *Orations,* and in Greek through the New Testament; while the compulsory courses at the university included algebra, geometry, trigonometry, and calculus; surveying, navigation, and astronomy; chemistry, mineralogy, and geology; logic, experimental philosophy, and natural history; Greek and Latin classics, rhetoric and belles-lettres; history, political economy, international and constitutional law; composition, criticism, and oratory. The University of Nashville's claim "to rank among the first institutions of learning in the Republic" and its pride in its library of 3,500 volumes and "the best mineralogical collections in the United States" were perhaps excessive, but it took its obligations seriously.

Religion was strongly stressed, with classes in theology and "moral training." Walker's class of twenty prayed twice every day in chapel, attended church on Sundays, and rose to hear a long benediction before every meal in the dining hall. But the puritanical spirit showed itself even more in that which was banned. The light indulgences known to college students elsewhere—balls, horseraces, cockfights, theaters—and such luxuries as dogs, horses, carriages, and servants—were strictly forbidden at Nashville. Even the study of music was permitted only as a special dispensation. It seems that Walker was allowed to practice fencing under a private master; the longing to handle a sword had been in him since childhood, and he had a wiry physique well suited to the art.

After his graduation, some months spent in reading medical books in the office of the family's physician, Dr. Thomas Jennings, confirmed his desire to pursue a career in medicine. He had no difficulty in entering the Medical College of the University of Pennsylvania, at Philadelphia, and in 1843 he graduated with his degree in medicine. He was then nineteen years old—certainly one of the youngest qualified physicians in the country.

The subject of his doctoral essay was "The Iris," and there is some reason to believe that Walker at this period became interested in mesmerism. His extraordinary eyes, "which burned with a cold grey fire," and to which some later attributed hypnotic power, were enough in themselves to attract him to a study of what was then called "mesmeric phenomena." The vogue for hypnotism to which the work of the controversial Dr. Mesmer had given rise in Europe had not made much headway in the United States, but the possible pain-relieving power of hypnosis was much debated among medical students, at a time when no effective anesthetic for use in surgery was yet available.

Although a career was waiting for him in Nashville, he showed no interest in pursuing it. His heart was set on further study, this time in Europe. Edinburgh, the Mecca of aspiring American medicos, seemed the obvious choice among foreign universities, and James Walker's family was in Scotland, but William elected to go to Paris. The faculty of the Sorbonne, where he attended lectures, may have been of less importance in his decision than the immemorial appeal of France for romantic spirits.

IV

The disillusionment that led Walker to give up medicine began in the hospitals of Paris. Balzac's novels portray the materialism, corruption, and cynicism that flourished under the last Bourbon kings, and medicine, no less than business and government, had become hopelessly reactionary. Of all Frenchmen, a wry wit said, physicians shrugged best. Except in those hospitals which served the wealthy, facilities were medieval, sanitation negligible, and methods ruthless. Infant mortality was far higher than in London; epidemics of contagious disease within hospitals were frequent; and human suffering under the surgeon's scalpel was beyond description. The conditions observed by Walker at nineteen made a mockery of his Hippocratic ideals; and the mood of the city, for all its surface gaiety, must have been equally trying for a young puritan who did not patronize brothels, drink, or gamble. The chief values of Paris for him lay in his exposure to French literature. Victor Hugo became one of his idols. His political ideas especially leaped ahead. But Parisian *politesse* also left its mark on him; his manners took on a formality and a subtlety which many Americans considered "sissified," and which, in his filibustering* days, startled those who, meeting him for the first time, expected to find a roughhewn swashbuckler.

Leaving Paris after something over a year, Walker attended medical lectures at Heidelberg. He seems to have had a gift for language; later he learned Spanish. A German source relates that he participated in the compulsory duels, with two-edged swords, of the student societies at Heidelberg, and emerged unscarred—no small tribute to his Nashville fencing master, if true; but this may be apocryphal. What other European centers he visited is uncertain, but finally he headed north for study at Edinburgh, spending some time in London on the way. His stay there apparently prejudiced him against the British. *Martin Chuzzlewit* was just then putting an additional strain on Anglo-American relations; and Walker, who had none of the American habits caricatured by Dickens—he did not get drunk, spit, swear, boast, murder the language, or regard money as the main thing in life—would have resented the patronizing style in which most Englishmen of the period spoke of his countrymen.

After a long, rough, transatlantic crossing he returned to Nashville, where he was received with all the admiration that a widely traveled young man with university degrees evoked in those days. "The most accomplished surgeon that ever visited the city," he was called. But there was bitter irony in his situation, for he found his mother not very far from death, wasted away, grey before her time, in pain most of her waking hours from "rheumatism" and "neuralgia"; and he could not pretend to know, any more than the family physician, how she should be treated.

The profession of medicine now seemed futile to him. He made a brief attempt to practice, but without zest. Although he never lost his interest in medical theory or his respect for dedicated physicians, he quickly realized that the dispensing of calomel, the administering

---

* "Filibuster"—from the Dutch *vrijbuiter*, freebooter.

of purges, and the obstetrics which filled the doctor's daily round were not for him. That he was tossing aside the fruit of years of study and a large financial investment, and bitterly disappointing his father, made no difference.

After his long absence, he must have felt himself something of a stranger in his family, holding views sharply different from theirs, and perhaps displaced from the center of his mother's affections by his two younger brothers and his sister. In any event, he was determined not to remain in Nashville. Of all the cities in the United States, New Orleans attracted him most, with its Creole glamor, its international flavor, and its metropolitan culture. Nowhere else in the South could there be found in one city theaters, opera, publishers, literary clubs, a variety of newspapers, and a famous cuisine. And it was easy to find a reason for going there. Having long since rejected the ministry, and having no inclination, or so it seemed, for military life, he was left with only one "gentlemanly" profession still open to him, the law. He would study law, and in New Orleans; the superiority of the Code Napoléon, as established in Louisiana, was a favorite conviction of romantic young Southerners.

His father's assistance, if it was forthcoming at all, was on a meager scale, for William as a law student in New Orleans had very little money. Two years of reading for the bar saw him qualified for practice. He was then twenty-three years old, and although hardly gregarious, had formed a wide and useful acquaintance. Edmund Randolph, a few years his senior, and who was Clerk of the United States Circuit Court, was closest to him. In type they were sharply different. Randolph was a cheerful blade, with a pretty quadroon mistress in a house on Rampart Street and a proper collection of gambling debts and bar bills. He evidently saw in Walker qualities needed to complement his own, for at his urging they opened a law office, as partners. But the firm did not prosper. Randolph was more interested in the pursuit of pleasure than in his practice, and although Walker was a fluent and effective speaker when he chose, he tended to be silent and enigmatic with strangers. His style could not have been inviting to potential clients; he dressed without regard to fashion, and made an unimpressive appearance. Standing only five feet, five inches, weighing less than 120 pounds, he seemed even younger than his years. If one did not observe his eyes, his face gave no special indication of latent force. A high unwrinkled brow under lank, light-brown hair; a long straight nose; a wide mouth, not unfriendly, but with a hint of the satirical in the quirked corners; an angular jaw—all this was familiar American physiognomy. Only the heavy-lidded eyes suggested the possibilities within him. Grey, brilliant, luminous, they seemed to penetrate the skulls of the men he talked to; they quickened the interest of friends, arrested strangers, and threw antagonists off balance.

In all probability he had given up the law in his heart, as he had given up medicine, even before he began to practice it. It would not have taken him long to discover that practitioners in the courts of New Orleans had to have as thick a skin as did physicians in the hospitals of Paris. A tight cabal of politicians controlled the municipal government, rigged the elections, hand-picked the judges, packed the juries, ran the police force, had keys to the jails, and made a mockery of the Code Napoléon. New Orleans' men of wealth came to terms with the political bosses in the usual financial way, but there was little justice and less mercy for the citizen without money who came up against the civic authority. As for serious municipal administration, it was conspicuous by its absence. No money was forthcoming for sanitary improvements, the draining of marshes, construction of sewers, repairs of the levees, paving of muddy streets, and the regular garbage collections needed to protect the city against recurrent epidemics. Gambling and vice flourished, however. Brothels, protected by the police, openly distributed handbills advertising their "virgins just in from the country" and "*filles de joie* trained in Paris."

Randolph, with his realistic outlook, was able to play the game, but Walker could no more accommodate himself to the chicanery of the city's courts than he could have patronized Madame Fifi's Select Cabaret. He had no real interest in the ordinary run of legal business. It was only the drama of the courtroom that attracted him. It is as impossible to imagine him sending out bills and pocketing fees as, in his medical guise, prescribing placebos or cultivating a bedside manner. He tasted medicine and law as most young gentlemen of his time tasted a brace of bottles of dubious wine, found them sour, and turned away.

The excuse that he needed to throw aside his new profession came early in 1848, when he was approached by two experienced newspapermen, A. H. Hayes and J. C. McClure, who had just resigned from the staff of the conservative New Orleans *Delta*. They were planning to publish a paper of their own, to be called the *Crescent*, and they were looking for a man to edit news from abroad and write on foreign affairs. Walker, with his European experience, his several languages, his classical education, and his medical and legal training, struck them as hopeful for their purpose. He could not have hesitated long before accepting. A newspaper would give him needed opportunity for self-expression, enemies to tilt against, and above all the chance to make his reputation. Time was moving fast. Educated young men in those days liked to quote Schiller's *Don Carlos:* "Twenty-four years old and still nothing accomplished for immortality!" Napoleon, Pitt, and Bolívar were not long dead, and their gigantic careers had already been in movement at twenty-four.

For an additional spur to his new enterprise, there was his need for Ellen. The nature of their relationship can best be imagined in the context of the age. His great ambition and knightly ideals, far from striking Ellen as absurd, would have had her warm encouragement. Beneath his reserved style she would have recognized a warm and generous spirit, and would have loved his pride, his kindness, his gentle manner. But these inexperienced and silent lovers were caught "between ascetic rocks and sensual whirlpools." For them the seeking touch of hand to hand, the brief caress of lips, were novel and exquisite sensations, which taxed their restraint. The problem was compounded by their silence. Without words there was no way for them to express ardor and reveal pulsing desire except by such physical trespass as would have violated the code in which they had been reared.

Marriage was their need and their hope; but that would have to wait until Walker could offer a suitable home and reasonable prospects. It was essential for him to prove himself a man of substance, one to whom Mrs. Martin need have no fear of confiding her daughter. The offer from the *Crescent* came at a propitious time. Although his first pieces, signed with his initial, W, were contributed experimentally, he was soon a full-time member of the paper's small staff. By March, 1848, he had given up his unclouded law office to become a journalist, with a small income but large aspirations.

II

FAR TO THE LEFT

Eighteen-forty-eight was a great year for American newspapers. Sensation followed sensation. It seemed that year as if the entire human species felt a spontaneous urge to burst its bonds. Everywhere discontent and frustration were suddenly translated into violence. The revolutionary furor first revealed itself in Paris, where in three days of street fighting republican insurgents toppled King Louis Philippe from his throne. From France the contagion spread swiftly eastward. The King of Prussia, his hair standing on end as he heard rumors of a new and frightening creed called Communism, felt compelled to grant a constitution to appease the grim crowds of Berlin. In Vienna, the Hapsburg emperor was saved only when Cossack cavalry sent by the Czar of Russia came to his aid; but even the feared Russians could not prevent Hungary, led by Kossuth, from achieving independence, or the Balkans from blazing in rebellion, while the entire north of Italy shook off the Austrian yoke. Spain held its breath as Spanish exiles from a bloody rule established bases in France from which to launch a civil war against the Bourbon monarchy. Starving men in Ireland vented their panic and grief in riots against the British government as they counted one fifth of all the Irish, a million and

15

a half people, dead or emigrated in three years of potato blight and famine. Even in dispirited Asia men were challenging established authority. The anti-imperial rebellion called Taiping, or Great Peace, began to make itself felt in China. Hardly a month passed in India without action by British troops to punish states and tribes foolhardy enough to contest the might of Queen Victoria.

All this passionate turmoil would soon subside. France would return to Napoleonism, kings and dictators everywhere would continue to reign, and liberals pursued by the secret police of their native lands would seek sanctuary abroad. Soon the Russian writer Alexander Herzen would write with a sigh from Paris, "It is a strange thing: since 1848 we have all faltered and diminished, we have thrown overboard all that mattered, we have shrunk back into ourselves." But while the year ran its course, anything seemed possible. The managing editor of the New York *Herald,* Charles A. Dana, reported from France, "I find that . . . socialism has gained very greatly. A shrewd observer, who is not a socialist, remarked to me the other day that the ultimate triumph of the new ideas was certain. The future will show whether he was a true prophet."

Of the great powers of Europe one alone escaped the revolutionary temblor—England. Not that the British people lacked cause for anger. Describing their condition, the London *Inquirer* said, "Misery and degradation confront you at every step. . . . It is absolutely distressing to sit by your fireside on account of the piteous objects who place themselves before your windows, exhibiting every mark of wretchedness and woe. . . . We have no plan . . . to remedy this great evil which pervades English society. We can only lament its existence."

A few daring spirits went so far as to advocate the abolition of child labor and the shortening of the factory work week from eighty to seventy-two hours, and workers assembled under the Chartist banner tried to demonstrate in the streets. But the British as a whole, although they wept over the plight of Oliver Twist and Little Nell, were at the same time so charmed and stimulated by recent triumphs of British arms, diplomacy, and commerce that Monday's protests were drowned in Tuesday's cheers. India was yielding undreamed-of riches. From romantic Cathay, too, great revenues were coming as millions of Chinese contracted the opium habit; for a few years earlier England's artillery had compelled Peking to permit the importation of the previously forbidden drug. Not merely an empire but the entire globe was being tapped by British commercial enterprise, backed by the world's strongest navy. American rivalry in trade, while energetic, was by no means alarming. The Atlantic stood between the Yankee factories and the European market; while the Cape of Good Hope route to the Orient gave England a long advantage in distance and time over American vessels compelled to go around Cape Horn. Gold poured into London from all quarters, including the United States, where British manufacturers had a huge market. In so congenial a situation, the mood of England's governing class was benign.

As for the United States, its people could hardly have cared less about the fall of kings and the overturn of governments abroad— except to agree, in general, that it served them right. Great events close to home that year were exalting the American state of mind. The surrender of the Mexican army under Santa Anna had enabled President Polk's administration to wrest nearly half of Mexico's territory from her, on pretexts so thin that some leading Americans— Daniel Webster and Henry Clay among them—were apologetic. But many on the contrary berated the President as a "Slow-Polk" for his failure to make all of Mexico forthwith a territory of the United States. At any rate, what was done was done; and then came the breath-taking news of vast deposits of gold in California, making every American a millionaire in his dreams, and setting off a burst of speculative enthusiasm on Wall Street. At the same time, American industrial genius was displaying its power on all sides. In Chicago, Cyrus McCormick had begun to manufacture his revolutionary reaper. In Philadelphia, Richard Hoe's steam-powered rotary press was turning out newspapers four times faster than had ever been possible before. Samuel Morse's electric telegraph now ran the length of the American coast from Boston to New Orleans.

Especially there were the railroads. With the aid of British capital, tracks were being laid from New England to the Mississippi, from the Great Lakes to the Ohio. Asa Whitney that year appeared before Congress to urge the building of a transcontinental line. President Polk made a treaty with the South American country of New Granada (Colombia) for the construction of a railroad across the Isthmus of

Panama, to transport passengers between the Atlantic and Pacific oceans. The steam locomotive was hope, it was wealth, it was the future. Monied men were buying railroad stocks, and every child aspired to be an engineer—except those who longed to be captain of a China clipper or pilot of a Mississippi steamboat.

Such a year of good news, military, mineral, and industrial, the American people had never before experienced. The country was on the move, growing, surging, rushing. But as 1848 drew to its close, beneath the shimmering surface of events was a current of deep concern. Unemployment was high, wages were low, and crime was mounting in the cities. Bitter old John C. Calhoun of South Carolina was saying that the slavery question "must be brought to a final decision," and that if the government attempted to prevent the spread of slavery to the West the question of Southern adherence to the Union might soon be vital. He went so far as privately to threaten the President of the United States with immediate secession. Horace Greeley in the New York *Tribune* ominously demanded, "Men and Brethren, how shall this great question be decided?" Yet there were men both North and South who still looked for gradual emancipation of slaves, to be achieved by nonviolent means.

II

With so much excitement to be had for a penny, newspaper circulation soared and advertising revenue multiplied. All over the country papers sprang up, and educated young men turned to journalism in increasing numbers as they recognized in the press a shortcut to influence, fame, and wealth. There were in the nation over 2500 dailies, weeklies and periodicals, as compared with 1500 in 1840—this for a population of 23,000,000. In New York the *Herald* alone had a circulation of almost 17,000 daily, and the *Tribune* not much less. Never before had the press exerted so much power. Columns of telegraphed news made it possible for the first time to shape the opinions of the American people quickly on a national scale.

Of all the infant newspapers of the year none had a better beginning than the *Crescent*. New Orleans was the metropolis of the South, the heart of the all-important cotton trade, the chief port for southbound shipping, and the focal point for news from Mexico. The

Crescent set out to offer its readers something more than they could find in the well-established *Picayune* or *Delta*—a broad and less specifically Southern view of the world. In their opening announcement, Hayes and McClure expressed the intention to establish "a general and accurate newspaper with enlarged and liberal views on subjects connected with commercial enterprise and agricultural industry." Here, for those able to read between the lines, was a daring hint of something less than enthusiasm for the institution of slavery. The *Crescent,* added the front-page editorial, "would discuss the great questions of State and National policy with impartiality and freedom"— or in other words, they would not necessarily support the prevailing Southern view of states' rights, among which the alleged right of secession was uppermost in men's minds. That so bold a stand might prove poor business the men who ran the *Crescent* recognized, but their venture, they said, would be "persevered in while there is any hope of success."

The generally lucid style of the *Crescent's* editorials stood in contrast to the murky and adjectival rhetoric then favored by many journalists in the South. Walker's contributions especially were distinguished by a certain intensity of feeling, indignation or enthusiasm. He respected facts—a trait instilled in him by his medical and legal training—but the main quality of his writing was its heat. At the same time, according to reporters who worked for him, he was a dependable and effective editor. One of them later described him as "very silent and very kind, with the look of a man bent upon a hard course of study, and a book always in his hand."

Almost from the first, the paper throve surprisingly, for its opinions were stimulating, its news coverage professional, its format creditable, and its writing superior. A New York journalist who visited New Orleans in 1848 remarked that "the *Crescent* is growing like Anak." After its first month it was able to thank its readers and advertisers "for support beyond what we had anticipated." A few months later one of the city's prominent lawyers and politicians, "Judge" J. C. Larue, bought an interest in the paper; and an editorial proudly said, "With a daily increasing subscription list and an advertising business which is extended with every number, the establishment of our paper is no longer an experiment: it is 'a fixed fact.' "

One of the *Crescent's* successful novelties was a first-page feature called "Sketches of the Sidewalks and Levees, with Glimpses into the New Orleans Bar (Rooms)." The author was a young journeyman printer—Walt Whitman—who had adventured to New Orleans from the North, and was entranced by the city. Although he earned his living in the *Crescent*'s pressroom, the abundance in him flowed constantly into reportage. He saw the colorful life around him with a poet's fresh and loving eye—the sensual excitement of the streets, the gay cries of the street vendors, the strong Negro women in their blue dresses and bright turbans, the beautiful quadroon girls paraded and guarded by watchful mothers, the half-starved grisettes of the seamstress shops, the elegant French restaurants with their noble wines, the drunken squalor of the rivermen's bars, the cotton, slave, and horse markets in and around the grand Hotel St. Louis, the love of Napoleonic glory, the streets named after Bonaparte's victories. All this he caught with a lightly satirical pen.

Perhaps Whitman's best piece for the *Crescent* was "Daggerdraw Bowieknife"—a violent lampoon of the professional duellist and bully whose type was then common in the city, and who, Whitman said, "would rather shoot a man than pay him what he owed him." Where Walker was preoccupied with large political issues, Whitman explored the troubled soul of the city, perceiving that its polite society of a few thousand people of means and education was merely a gloss over the broad, bawdy, and orgiastic life which teemed below. In no other large city in America—it was then third in rank after New York and Philadelphia, with a population, white and black, of 125,-000—did the ordinary citizen spend so much time in the pursuit of pleasure, in the forms of women, cards, alcohol, prize fighting, cock-fighting, and well-cooked food. Throughout its history, under Spanish, French, and American rule, New Orleans had always been a wide-open town. Perhaps its extreme sensual indulgence grew in part out of its acute sense of the chanciness of life. More than in most metropolises, to live in New Orleans was to live with peril—peril from Mississippi floods—peril from almost annual epidemics of cholera, the plague, and most dreaded of all, the yellow fever—peril from hooligans and thieves swarming in the dark streets at night—peril from brawling backwoodsmen and roistering boatmen on their drunken sprees—peril from venereal diseases that spread from scores of thriving brothels—economic peril from the violent movements of

IV

The extent to which Walker influenced the total editorial policy of the *Crescent* must be conjectural, but to judge by the internal evidence of content and style, his individual mark was all over it. A series of studies of French philosophers, including Pascal, Montesquieu, and Chateaubriand is probably attributable to his influence. His advanced intellectual interests were a source of pride to the newspaper. When, in October, 1848, he was invited to Nashville to deliver the commencement address at his university, choosing as his subject "The Unity of Art," the *Crescent* reported the event with satisfaction, and quoted from the Nashville press to make the point that "Mr. W. acquitted himself with great ability in composition and delivery."

This address,* reprinted by the University but long lost from sight, throws a revealing light on Walker at the age of twenty-four. "Were I called upon to state succinctly the object of University education," he begins, "I should say that it is the cultivation of art. . . . On the university depends, in great measure, the maintenance of good taste which is a chief and essential element of what we denominate civilization." Art he conceived broadly as the outward manifestation of man's spiritual life, embodied in beauty, truth, and virtue. The study of science, he said, far from being antagonistic to art, could contribute to the development of artistic perceptions, for "science teaches the principles on which the worlds were made, as well as the great mathematical truths . . . pointing to the invisible world, the world of spirit."

Of all the arts, it was heroic poetry that touched him most deeply. He saw Shakespeare and Milton as the poets of heroism, Byron as the hero of poetry. Byron's life he considered to have been lived artistically—"although he died young, yet was he old in fame and deeds." Life itself was an art form. It was only through the pursuit of the art of living that man, "half worm and half angel," could rise above the primeval. Man's artistic self found an outlet even in war—"the strongest and fiercest expression of patriotism"—and the artist in life must strive to achieve the "perfect and radiant countenance" of courage.

---

* Library of the Tennessee State Archives, Nashville.

He cautioned against letting petty proprieties and conventional ideas stifle the impulse to art. Aiming an ironic shaft at those "who are afraid of philosophy," he urged the reading of the poetry of Milton, with its inquiry into man's inner nature; and he even went so far as to remind his pious Tennessee audience that in *Paradise Lost* the most interesting and attractive figure is Satan of the "unconquerable will" and "immortal hate."

Walker's entire subsequent career may in some sense be regarded as an expression of these ideas. They gave the directional thrust to his life's trajectory. He had already begun to formulate the principles of heroic conduct by which he tried to live; from the ideal of Galahad to the ideal of Byron was a natural evolution for him. In his time, for a young man to strive for a life of Byronic grandeur was not considered absurd. The striving was its own justification.

Perhaps equally important, "The Unity of Art" reveals him as fully aware of many of the great seminal ideas of the age then taking root in Europe. This same awareness came out repeatedly on the editorial page of the *Crescent*. Walker almost certainly wrote a striking article called "The Wars of the World," taking its text from Thomas Hobbes, and asking speculatively, "Must men remain forever the slaves of their purely destructive propensities? Or are we yet but in the germ of being, and is it necessary to pass through the lower grades of existence before we can arrive at the higher and nobler states that await us [mankind] in the future?" This was a decade before Darwin published the *Origin of Species;* it would appear that someone on the *Crescent* had been reading the works of the earlier French evolutionists. Similarly it is likely that Walker, with his medical training abroad, was responsible for the publication in the *Crescent* of some advanced and original articles written by other physicians on the prevention and treatment of cholera and yellow fever. Appearing long before the investigations of bacteria by von Helmholtz and Pasteur were published, these articles hinted at the existence of such microorganisms, plainly spoke of "the animalcular theory of cholera and all diseases, with very few exceptions," and urged that sanitary measures be taken in "places favoring the development of insects which spread disease."

Late in December, 1848, one of the *Crescent*'s editors, and not improbably Walker, set himself to the composition of an article, such as newspapers have immemorially presented to their readers, appraising the significance of the year. "The year which has just completed its course . . . is crowded with events which will cause it to stand out in such bold relief that posterity will look back on it as the beginning of a new era." Europe was convulsed by revolutionary and democratic agitation. The United States stood as victor in war and proud possessor of vast new territories. Incalculable possibilities for the country had been opened up by the gold of California. The dream of riches was causing thousands of starry-eyed Americans to leave their homes and journey westward. In New Orleans the mood of excitement was caught in a local witticism: "Last year it was yellow fever, this year it's gold fever." The entire front page of the *Crescent* that New Year's Day was given over to descriptions of California and a map of the mining regions.

But the editorial concluded on a sobering note. A severe epidemic of cholera had broken out in New Orleans. "In the midst of these golden dreams . . . the cup of happiness is dashed from our lips. The returning pestilence has invaded our land, carrying . . . misery to many a heart." Over a thousand deaths had already been reported. Many New Orleans families were fleeing northward. Walker must have worried deeply about Ellen and her mother, who remained in the city. "Thus ends the Old Year, and begins the New with the souls of men flamed with the desire for gain and the Asiatic plague recommencing its deadly and terrible march."

III

"LET IT COME"

It was while he edited the *Crescent* that Walker took the specific political position on which he based his subsequent career. Like the majority of Americans in his time, he believed ardently in the nation's "Manifest Destiny" to establish its institutions and its power throughout the Western Hemisphere. With him, however, this conviction was not merely the product of wild and thoughtless chauvinism. He felt, as did many of America's political leaders, that the best chance for preventing the nation from tearing itself apart over the slavery issue was to rally the people in a common cause, with a moral justification. That cause, that justification, as he saw it, lay in the Monroe Doctrine. In 1849, the country learned that England had been almost contemptuously flouting the Doctrine by its actions in Central America. The London *Times* openly boasted that almost half of the isthmus was in British hands.

The point of contention that arrested Walker lay in a broad strip of land along the Atlantic coast of Nicaragua, a territory known as Mosquitia, or Mosquito. Belatedly, the United States had awakened to its strategic importance. Europe, however, had long believed that Nicaragua was one of the main keys to the world empire of the future.

More than a hundred years earlier, in 1740, a French scientist, La Condamine, had said as much before the Academy of Sciences in Paris and had proposed the construction of a canal in Nicaragua to connect the Atlantic and Pacific oceans. His paper came to the attention of the British Foreign Office; and while the French were still considering the matter, England sent warships to Nicaragua, then a possession of declining Spain, and hoisted her flag on the swampy east shore. The primitive Mosquito Indians offered no opposition. Always careful, the British then justified their action in diplomatic terms. A document was solemnly produced to show that in 1720 the "King" of the Mosquitos had voluntarily put his territory under the protection of the governor of Jamaica.

Spain protested; England shrugged; and so the matter stood for a century. But when the Central American states shook off Spanish rule, and under Bolívar's inspiration formed a Federation, Nicaragua felt emboldened to ask by what right the British governed in part of her territory. England's representatives in Central America decided that the old Jamaican authority would no longer serve. Accordingly they dressed a descendant of one of the former Mosquito kings in the uniform of a British major, formally crowned him King Robert Charles Frederick of the "Mosquito Shore and Nation," surrounded him with a court of "noble lords," and solemnly asserted his sovereign powers.

Here arose an unforeseen development; King Robert took his role seriously, and since he was fond of whisky and bright clothing, began to give away large tracts of his country to Yankee traders, in return for liquor and gay cotton prints. The British intervened, spirited the King away, and imprisoned him for the rest of his life, but not before he had signed (with an "x") a document appointing an Englishman as his regent, "in recognition of all the favors heaped upon him and his people by the English." Thereafter the country was ostensibly governed by a native Council of State, who provided a diplomatic screen for the British officers in the background.

All this was part of a larger British plan—to get rid of the Central American Federation, which, being democratic in tendency, was already under heavy pressure from the large Nicaraguan landholders of Spanish descent. Its destruction took some years, but in 1838 the Federation fell apart in a welter of civil war and confusion. This was the moment England had been awaiting. First she seized the east coast of Guatemala, known as Belize, and which she thereafter called British Honduras; next, she took possession of Cape Honduras, which lay just to the north of Mosquito; and finally she pushed the Mosquito protectorate southward. For it had now become clear that the best canal route across Nicaragua would utilize the San Juan River, close to the boundary of Costa Rica. A drowsy little town of grass-thatched huts, San Juan del Norte, lying at the mouth of the river, had taken on strategic importance. There, one day, appeared a party of armed Englishmen. Raising the Mosquito flag (which had a small Union Jack in its corner) they formally claimed San Juan in the name of the Mosquito King, and ordered the Nicaraguan customs officer of the port to leave. When he refused, he was forcibly taken off in a boat and abandoned miles away on an uninhabited shore. The Mosquito Kingdom was threafter alleged to run to the southern limit of Nicaragua, and even beyond into Costa Rica. San Juan del Norte was renamed with the brisk English syllables of Greytown, and would be so called until Walker, as the ruler of the country, restored its original proud, sleepy name.

II

As he grasped the story, Walker was incensed by the ignominy of the American position. The Monroe Doctrine might never have existed. True, almost every administration had made a gesture toward Nicaragua. Andrew Jackson in 1836 had sent a special agent to study the possibility of a Nicaraguan canal, but the man became involved in a shady transaction in Panama, and never even stopped off at Nicaragua. President Van Buren's agent, although he thought the canal feasible, warned that "capitalists will not sink their money in an unsettled and revolutionary country." After England's seizure of San Juan, when the American press raised some small outcry, Daniel Webster, then Secretary of State for President Harrison, sent one of his men to Nicaragua to report, only to have him roundly snubbed by the British, and return with nothing to suggest. Webster himself was seeking to avoid war with England over the noisy Maine and Oregon boundary disputes, and the buzzing of the Mosquito affair was understandably faint in his ears.

But England, with her eternal vigilance for weeds in her diplomatic garden, knew that the issue was far from dead. With the outbreak of the Mexican War in 1846, talk of a transisthmian canal mounted. Sooner or later, the British realized, Washington would challenge their presence in Greytown. Early in 1847 Lord Palmerston, then Foreign Secretary, took the precaution of writing to all agents of the Crown in Central America, requiring them to report "what authentic information they could obtain as to the boundaries claimed by the King of Mosquito," and also what in their opinion was "the line of boundary which Her Majesty's Government should insist upon as essential for the security and well-being of the Mosquito State." It was not really surprising that the boundaries established by this procedure reached south from Cape Honduras through Nicaragua and into Costa Rica, in full accord with previous British claims.

Nicaragua protested that there had never been, and still was not, a Kingdom of Mosquito; and in a mood of recklessness, sent troops into Greytown, who took prisoner every Englishman they could find. The British reply was the arrival of a naval squadron on January 1, 1848, and the landing of a strong force of marines, who quickly recaptured Greytown, reasserted England's authority "in the name of the Mosquito Indians," and marched inland toward Lake Nicaragua. This development shook the Nicaraguan government into hasty appeasement. A parley was held, a treaty was drafted, Nicaragua apologized and recognized the existence of Mosquito, if not British authority there.

James Buchanan was then Secretary of State, and his response to the British action was altogether in character. In a letter to the American minister to Nicaragua, he said, "The object of Great Britain in these seizures is . . . to obtain control of the route for a railroad and canal between the Atlantic and Pacific oceans," but he warned that "the government of the United States is not as yet determined what course it will take." During the ensuing year Washington made no progress toward a decision, and when the Taylor administration took office in 1849, the country's sense of frustration in the Greytown issue had grown into a major issue. Was England to be allowed to tear up the Monroe Doctrine? The question was asked repeatedly in the Senate, while many newspapers warned President Taylor that the nation would not tolerate supine timidity in the face of British aggression. Among them was the New Orleans *Crescent,* with Walker as editor of foreign news.

III

Walker did not as yet know—only a few people in Washington then knew—just why the United States after so long had begun to challenge the presence of the British in Mosquito. The fact was that his life was becoming intertwined with great forces of which he was not even aware. The springboard from which he was to leap to fame was being secretly shaped and set by men occupied with vast affairs—peace or war, millions made or lost—in London, Washington, New York.

The central figure in the Nicaraguan situation was a man who in type, conditioning, outlook, and purpose stood so far apart from Walker that they might almost have belonged to different species. Cornelius Vanderbilt was tall, strong boned, physically powerful, loud and blunt of speech, domineering. In his middle fifties, although white-haired, he was still a man spectacularly virile, who had produced thirteen children, all of whom he bent ruthlessly to his will; whose wife, having once been confined by him in an institution for the insane, lived in mortal fear of his temper; and whose mistresses were open secrets in the gossip of New York City. But his ruling passion was money. He was the economic man personified—practical, realistic, impatient of theory and philosophical speculation, contemptuous of legalism and sometimes of the law—a man who believed that the one test of sound business was the size of the profit, and who regarded wealth and power as interchangeable terms. "What do I care about the Law?" he is quoted as saying. "Hain't I got the power?" When he took monetary risks, he sought not only to add to his fortune, but to prove his mastery over men and circumstances, to glory in his strength and cunning as he crushed competitors and raked in his gains. Far more than Walker he was the true type of the freebooter, ferocious in attack, merciless in conquest. One of his contemporaries, describing a Vanderbilt operation in cornering a stock, wrote: "The stock flies up from 20 to 200, and for seven days the torturing screws are turned down tighter and tighter till the Stock Exchange rings with the clamor of his victims. . . . When summoned before a court . . . his memory fades out so completely that he forgets . . . even his own signature.

There is something magnificent in a career in which a million dollars is like a ten-cent piece taken by a shoe-blacking gamin. . . . He strips the street of five millions with the same nonchalance as he would win a hundred dollars at cards."* In 1849, Vanderbilt had as yet acquired no more than five or six millions—in itself a reasonable success for the poor boy who at the age of sixteen had gone into business as a ferryman—to which he added steadily through the profitable operation of a large fleet of steamboats on the Hudson River and Long Island Sound. It was from this business that he took his favorite title, "Commodore."

Like many another tycoon, he had discovered naked power to be a witch-woman of surpassing beauty and no inhibitions, and he could no longer be content with the commonplace grapplings of business. One of his mortifications just then was that a former competitor on the Hudson River, a man of almost equal aggressiveness and sagacity, George Law, had stolen a march on him. Founding the United States Mail Steamship Company, Law had prevailed on the government in Washington to grant him a subsidy of $290,000, for which he agreed to provide steamships to carry California mail between New York and Panama. A similar grant had been made to a San Francisco ship owner, who was providing comparable service between Panama and San Francisco. What irked Vanderbilt, however, was not the governmental bounty these men received, so much as their luck. Their contracts with the government had scarcely been signed when California's golden news arrived. From that moment, with the gold fever raging on the east coast, the passenger service from New York to San Francisco became a bonanza. Law's steamships were the largest seen up to that time on the Atlantic coast, and a berth in a crowded stateroom to Panama could command as much as five hundred dollars. It was estimated that each trip of a Law steamship from New York to its Panama port netted a profit of over $100,000, and in 1849 the line made the run thirty times. Even the hardships of the overland crossing of Panama, by oxcart, mule, or foot, with ever-present danger of brigands, sunstroke, fever, and snakes, did not deter many "fortyniners" who knew that by this route they might be in California five months sooner than if they went overland. To add to Law's windfall, work had been begun on a railroad across Panama, in which he had

---

* J. K. Medbery, *Men and Mysteries of Wall Street*, 1879, p. 155.

an interest, and which would still further increase the popularity of his steamship line.

Hearing of Law's triumph with huge Atlantic steamships, while he himself owned nothing more than riverboats, Vanderbilt asked himself the inevitable question: how could he, a late-comer, overtake his rival? He began to study maps of Central America, and they disclosed to him a possibility that seized his imagination. Panama, obviously, was the narrowest part of the Central American isthmus, but did that make it the best point for transit? Why not instead use Nicaragua, which would take 500 miles off the route to California? Let the Panama Railroad be built; it would require six or seven years to complete the track over the mountains that ran down the center of the isthmus there. And the railroad would soon become obsolete, if there were a canal through Nicaragua which would enable passengers, freight, and mail to go from ocean to ocean without having to be disembarked. Although on the map Nicaragua at its narrowest point looked three times as wide as Panama, it actually seemed to offer the better route for a canal, for Lake Nicaragua permitted unimpeded ship travel for nearly half the distance, and use could be made of the San Juan River, which flowed from the lake to the Atlantic. Construction of a canal east of the lake, he estimated, would be comparatively easy, requiring few locks. Only in the strip between the lake and the Pacific would there be difficulties, and this was a mere eleven miles.

The plan took shape: he would form a company to build the canal, and while it was in the building, he would create a line of steamships from New York to Nicaragua, and another from Nicaragua to San Francisco, with an overland transit of passengers between; he would not only collect mail subsidies, but by offering passengers the shortest route to California, he would scuttle George Law's scheme and make millions.

IV

Vanderbilt realized that before anything could be done, England would have to be persuaded into cooperation. If she remained adamant, it might require nothing less than a war to bring her to reason. Early in 1849, one of his associates went to Washington to explore the matter with the new Taylor administration. Suddenly the capital buzzed with talk of Mosquito, the sanctity of the Monroe Doctrine, and the comparative strength of British and American arms. It was a report of debate on Nicaragua in the United States Senate that caught Walker's attention. "If the war must come," he wrote enthusiastically in the *Crescent*, "then let it come!" Gone now were all pacifistic inclinations. "America will be found fighting where she has always been morally—at the head of the column of Progress and Democracy." He did not use the phrase "Alliance for Progress" but something similar was in his mind.

IV

THE ANGRY MAN

The death of Ellen Martin was a turning point in Walker's life.

A fever, followed by pneumonia—described by the attending physician as "congestion"—and all at once she was gone. The loss must have been the more shocking since by that time, April, 1849, the cholera epidemic had almost run its course, and she had appeared to be safe. Moreover he had just then begun to achieve the success which might have made their marriage possible. Only a few weeks earlier, his name had appeared on the *Crescent's* masthead as one of the publishers.

A Nicaraguan writer who investigated his years in New Orleans declares, "Walker, who held in his heart the love of two women only, his mother and Ellen, returned from the cemetery a spirit shattered; and sick with loneliness, threw to the winds all that he had. So ended the first phase of his life." This judgment has a somewhat operatic sound, but all the available evidence supports it. The extent to which he was shaken can be read between the lines of the *Crescent's* editorial page. For several weeks the characteristic Walker articles were missing from the paper, which in his absence almost ceased to comment on foreign affairs and the slavery issue. When he began to write again, his editorials sounded a new note of stridency and bitterness.

A month after Ellen's interment, the Mississippi rose and over-flowed the levees, flooding the city's cemeteries. A wild and ranting editorial cried out at the municipal authorities for their failure to protect the dead from watery desecration. Let the living, it said, look to their own spiritual salvation—"If we live basely and ignobly, not all great Neptune's flood can wash the stain from out our souls." A similar feverishness appeared in articles on events abroad. An attack on Louis Bonaparte, then President of the French Republic, for perverting the French revolution, was followed by a defense of Italian revolutionaries which in its radicalism could only curdle the blood of conservative readers. Followers of Calhoun in New Orleans were alienated by an article condemning the views of the apostle of slavery. "We do not," it said coldly, "rank among his admirers."

It was almost as if Walker was obsessed by a wild and joyless purpose to destroy the *Crescent*'s circulation, and as if he had infected his associates with his rage. Gauntlets were thrown down right and left. A sharp attack on the municipal government for making no effort to arrest men known to have committed murder was followed by a sudden slashing indictment of the powerful *Picayune* and the *Delta,* because they had failed to condemn graft in the state capital. When these formerly courteous rivals replied in kind, they evoked a snarl of outrage against "a petty clique, to whom the *Crescent* is an object of jealousy and hate." This was journalism in a very different tone from that of a year earlier. And the mood of anger alternated with Hugoesque and mystical flights of the pen, which heralded the emergence of the new Walker. "Unless a man believes that there is something great for him to do, he can do nothing great. Hence so many of the captains and reformers of the world have relied on fate and the stars. A great idea springs up in a man's soul; it agitates his whole being, transports him from the ignorant present and makes him feel the future in a moment. It is natural for a man so possessed to conceive that he is a special agent for working out into practice the thought that has been revealed to him. . . . Why should such a revelation be made to him, why should he be enabled to perceive what is hidden to others—if not that he should carry it into practice?"

What was that revelation? With Ellen gone, he had begun to

dream of himself at the head of that "column of Progress and Democracy" of which he had written, riding in the name of America's Manifest Destiny, diverting the passions of the nation from civil commotion to the uplifting of peoples from whom the benefits of civilization were being withheld by European imperialists. He felt an evangelical mission in which the highest ideals of the America of his time were fused—the spreading of democracy—the enhancement of the national power—the uplifting of downtrodden peoples—the prevention of fratricidal war.

II

For a controversial journalist, the South then held special hazards. Offended readers brandishing horsewhips were a recurrent spectacle in newspaper offices, and in spite of laws against duelling, challenges from rival editors were to be expected whenever they regarded themselves as insulted—a frequent phenomenon, since their thresholds of tolerance were low. Nevertheless, Walker had come through the year 1848 unscathed, unchallenged, and uncompromised in conviction. Perhaps the boyish look of him turned away wrath.

The change that came over him with Ellen's death expressed itself in a sudden urge to personal as well as journalistic violence. Soon afterward he fought a duel with an editor named Kennedy, the cause unknown. (It is probably no more than a coincidence that the physician who had attended Ellen in her mortal illness was also named Kennedy.) Neither man was wounded. The duelists, says the account, "met with pistols at twelve paces, exchanged shots, and retired, satisfied." There was also a contemporary story to the effect that an anonymous New Orleans journalist had challenged a man who insulted him to "a duel with the cholera"—that is, exposure to the disease by nursing its victims. This has the sound of a Walkerism. Later in the year, he is known to have administered a severe flogging to the editor of the Spanish newspaper, *La Patria,* for printed remarks that he considered offensive.

It was a stormy time for the *Crescent.* In the summer of 1849, the Cuban issue boiled to a crisis, when the Spanish consul in New Orleans was accused of complicity in the kidnaping of an American citizen. The abducted man was a Cuban revolutionary named Garcia-Rey, who had taken out naturalization papers. His story was that a ship's captain, one McConnel, had brought him against his will to Havana, where he was held incommunicado and subjected to beatings until diplomatic representations by American officials effected his release. On learning of the charge, the Spanish Government recalled its consul, but McConnel was arrested and brought to trial. For his defense he retained J. C. Larue, one of the *Crescent*'s proprietors and a noted attorney.

Ever since the days of George Washington and the great quarrel with Spain over the navigation of the Mississippi, tempers had always run high in New Orleans when Spaniards were suspected of transgression. Garcia-Rey's story was dubious—there were contradictory affidavits by the score—but the essential political fact was that Southern expansionist leaders promptly took up his case as their own. Here at last, so it seemed to them, was a "legitimate" reason for the immediate invasion and seizure of Cuba. Their philosophy was crisply summed up by General John A. Quitman, one of the ardent proponents of the plan. "Our destiny is intertwined with that of Cuba. If slave institutions perish there, they will perish here. Thus interested, we must act. Our government, already distracted with the slavery question, cannot or will not act. We must do it as individuals."

The time seemed especially right for the purpose, because a suitable man to lead an expedition against Cuba was then available. There had recently come to the United States a famous fighter for Cuban independence, General Narciso Lopez, a Venezuelan by birth, who had just met with Calhoun and had received secret encouragement from the fountainhead of Southern wisdom. A group of New Orleans extremists proposed to Lopez that he raise a small army in their city, transport it to Cuba, rally the Cubans to his revolutionary banner, drive out the Spanish governors, set up his own administration in Havana (retaining the institution of slavery), and then apply for the admission of the island to the American Union.

Recruitment was no problem. New Orleans was crowded with veterans returned from Mexico, restless, roving fire-eaters as ardent for adventure as their descendants would be for security a century later. For them, the conquest of the Caribbean appeared a natural and proper sequel to the Mexican campaign. Money was available. Although Lopez was careful to keep in the background, his agents printed bonds on the Cuban treasury, to be redeemed at par as soon as Cuba should become independent; these were offered at a few cents on the dollar, and were snapped up by speculators. Management of the enterprise was in the hands of the so-called Cuban Junta, which, according to the New York *Sun,* included some of the South's most distinguished men.

The only problem was publicity, or rather, its avoidance. During the summer of 1849, shipping for the expedition was secretly assembled at an obscure island in the Gulf of Mexico, just off the delta. It was imperative that federal authorities in New Orleans remain unaware of the rendezvous, or at least look the other way, until Lopez and his troops were on the seas, and beyond the danger of interception by the United States Navy. Otherwise the Taylor administration would feel compelled to invoke the Neutrality Laws against the expedition.

The *Crescent* had thrown itself into the Rey case (as the newspapers called it) partly no doubt because of Larue's active role as lawyer for the defense, but also out of conviction. It reaffirmed its stand against violation of the Neutrality Laws, and by implication against the expansion of slavery. Long editorials appeared denying the right of American citizens to retaliate for the alleged kidnaping by intervening in Cuban affairs. But the paper was inviting more punishment than it could return. In opposing the Lopez scheme it stood alone among the journals of New Orleans. The owners of the *Delta* were intimately connected with the Cuban junta, and the *Picayune* was of the same persuasion. Theirs was the popular side, and they made the most of the advantage. Daily they blasted at the *Crescent,* until the sheer weight of their invective caused the city to respond, and the *Crescent*'s circulation and advertising fell away.

Desperately, the *Crescent* fired its last remaining shot. In August, 1849, it published an article which made it impossible for Washington to ignore any longer the fact of the Lopez expedition. Under the heading "The Mysterious Expedition and the Laws," it described "mysterious gatherings designed for the invasion of the island of Cuba," and gave the exact location of the ships and encampments. Under such prodding, the Federal Marshals in New Orleans, with whatever reluctance, were compelled to act in support of the Neutrality Laws. Washington was notified, and United States Navy gunboats were ordered to prevent the Lopez expedition from sailing.

The intervention of the Navy was a victory, but a Pyrrhic victory for the *Crescent*. Torrents of abuse poured on its editors from all sides. They had, it was said, betrayed the South; they had befriended the Yankee abolitionists. Against attacks so virulent and sustained, the paper was defenseless. Hayes, the chief owner, had no illusions as to the outcome. To stay in business would have meant the putting up of more money and probably the fighting of more duels. Late in 1849 he suspended publication, and subsequently sold the name and the presses.

III

Now New Orleans no longer had any hold on Walker; he was loveless, jobless, and even friendless, for Edmund Randolph had succumbed to the spell of the Golden Fleece and had gone to California. In the autumn, Walker followed. Most of the wagon trains of the period assembled at Independence, Missouri, and took the Old Oregon Trail past Fort Laramie, Fort Bridger, and Salt Lake, over the Sierras to Sacramento and San Francisco; but references to the long journey are conspicuously absent from the the Walker literature. The eight or nine months spent in crossing two thousand miles of plains and mountains, through the lands of the Comanches, the Sioux, and the Blackfeet, he must have regarded as so much time lost from the pursuit of his destiny. If there were hardships endured, fights with Indians, and strange sights seen, they apparently impressed him so little that he never mentioned them in the brief accounts of his career that he subsequently gave to his associates. All that is known of this passage in his life is that in June of 1850 he appeared in San Francisco, sunburned and weather-beaten, an unimpressive figure in dusty old clothes and a broad-brimmed black hat, and almost penniless.

V

THE HIGHER DIPLOMACY

Late in 1849, Cornelius Vanderbilt initiated the enterprise for control
of which, a few years later, he would contend with the President of
Nicaragua, Walker. A company with a resounding name—the Ameri-
can Atlantic and Pacific Canal Company—was incorporated, and
Vanderbilt was careful to include in its management a lawyer, Joseph
L. White, who had intimate ties with the country's leading politicians.
White journeyed to Washington, and wheels began to turn.

A new minister to Nicaragua, George Squier, was appointed, Secretary of State John M. Clayton gave him a letter of instructions, the
nub of which lay in a single sentence: "We are willing to enter into a
treaty stipulation with the government of Nicaragua, that both governments shall forever protect and defend the proprietors who may succeed in cutting the canal and opening the water communication between the two oceans for our commerce." The "proprietors" whom
Clayton had in mind were Vanderbilt and his associates. Soon Squier
wrote that "Vanderbilt and Company has made a proposition to the
Nicaraguan government which, if I am correctly informed of its details, is most extravagant."

The "extravagant" offer consisted of a promise to pay $10,000 on signing of a suitable contract; $10,000 a year thereafter until completion of the canal; $200,000 of stock in the enterprise; and 20 per cent of the net profits of the canal. It was enough. The Nicaraguan Congress ratified a contract with Vanderbilt, and in the autumn of 1849, Squier was able to write to Clayton: "I have the satisfaction of informing the department that I have succeeded in accomplishing the objects of my mission to this republic. The commissioner of the 'American Atlantic and Pacific Canal Company' has concluded his contract."

II

England's chief agent in Central America, Frederick Chatfield, had observed the activities of Squier and Vanderbilt's agents with misgivings. Letters from him to Lord Palmerston in London warned that the Yankees were seriously negotiating with Nicaragua for a canal route. The possibility was obvious that the United States, by invoking the Monroe Doctrine, might encourage Nicaragua to seize Greytown, to assure an Atlantic entry for the canal. Whether or not war resulted, England would be at a disadvantage; her claim to Greytown was undeniably weak, and the place was impossible to defend against assault from the interior.

Palmerston, who was known for his bold diplomacy, responded pugnaciously. England's first need, he decided, was to preempt the Pacific end of the proposed canal route. His eye was on an island known as Tigre, owned by Honduras. Occupying a dominant position in one of the world's great natural harbors, the Gulf of Fonseca, it could give England more obstructive power on the west coast of Central America than could any other single spot. What he wanted now was a diplomatic excuse to justify occupation of this island. The specialists of the Foreign Office obliged him. With just such a purpose in mind, they had been nursing an ancient claim against Honduras for alleged mistreatment of some of Her Majesty's subjects by Honduran officials. Orders went to Chatfield, and simultaneously the British admiralty was instructed to move strong squadrons of warships to both sides of the isthmus.*

* R. W. Van Alystyne, "The Central American Policy of Lord Palmerston," *Hispanic-American Historical Review*, Vol. XVI, pp. 352-7.

Chatfield wasted no time. Hastening to Truxillo, the chief Atlantic port of Honduras, he demanded immediate settlement of England's claim. When the Hondurans denied the validity of the claim, Chatfield called their attention to the British battleships which were by then standing off Truxillo, with their guns trained on the town.

The American minister in Nicaragua, Squier, was a man of ability and resource. Sensing England's intention, he rushed to Truxillo with the draft of a treaty under which the United States offered to pay Honduras generously for Tigre Island and for permission to fortify certain mainland stations on the Gulf of Fonseca. As between the free-spending eagle and the threatening lion in these circumstances there was little choice, and the Hondurans hastily signed the Squier treaty.

The frustration of the British was expressed by the naval squadron which, just before sailing from Truxillo harbor, fired a single indignant cannon ball at the town. Chatfield, however, had only begun to fight. Riding westward across Honduras, to the Pacific, he met with the admiral in command of the British fleet which was by then anchored in the Gulf of Fonseca, and authorized him to seize Tigre Island "for debt" in the name of the Crown, to hoist the British flag, and put down a garrison. This the admiral did on October 16, 1849.

The shadow of war was now dark over Central America, but still Squier did not hesitate to assume responsibility. A terse note went to Chatfield, stating that England had unlawfully taken possession of land belonging to the United States and must evacuate Tigre immediately. When Chatfield, with the diplomatic equivalent of a sneer, refused, Squier issued nothing less than an ultimatum, requiring the British to withdraw from Tigre within six days. Otherwise, he said, their occupation of the island would be regarded by the United States as an act of aggression, and dealt with accordingly. But the British stayed where they were, and with the Union Jack still flying over Tigre, Chatfield reported the situation to London, Squier to Washington.

This was the situation when Vanderbilt prodded Clayton to take a positive stand on the Nicaraguan question. Specifically the financier wanted to know what the British would say to his contract with Nicaragua. The problem confronting Clayton was thus two-pronged. On the one hand he wanted to prevent a war if he could. At the same time he felt the obligation to advance the cause of an American-controlled canal in Nicaragua. The best hope, as the Secretary saw it, lay in the time-honored diplomatic technique—a club in the right hand and a gift in the left. If England were plainly confronted with the danger of war, and at the same time were offered a chance to share in the Nicaragua canal, she might just possibly consent to a peaceful compromise. At any rate, the idea was worth trying. In this spirit, he sent a message to the British minister in Washington, John F. Crampton, requesting him to call.

III

In the weeks that followed, a series of extraordinary dispatches went from Crampton to Palmerston.*

Washington, September 15, 1849
My Lord: Mr. Clayton having requested me to call upon him at the Department of State, said that he wished to converse with me frankly and confidentially upon the subject of the proposed passage across the isthmus, by way of Nicaragua and the river San Juan, with regard to which he had long felt a great deal of anxiety. . . . You know, he said, that the government have no majority in the Senate . . . and you can form an idea of the eagerness with which the party opposed to the government will avail themselves of the opportunity of either forcing us into a collision with Great Britain on this subject, or of making it appear that we have abandoned, through pusillanimity, great and splendid advantages. . . . He begged me to communicate the substance of what he had said to me to your lordship.

Washington, October 1, 1849
. . . I am the more anxious to report accurately to your lordship the substance of Mr. Clayton's remarks from the circumstance that the President . . . joined in our conversation. . . .

The junction of the two oceans by a canal, Mr. Clayton observed, was an object so important to the whole of the commercial world that . . . it should be made a bond of peace and good understanding, by being brought about by a combined effort, and for the general benefit of mankind. . . .

What the United States Government would now propose, therefore,

---

* *Documents and Correspondence Relative to a Trans-Isthmian Canal.* Compiled from the archives of the British Foreign Office and the U. S. Department of State and privately printed by the law firm of Sullivan and Cromwell, New York, 1900.

was this: That the United States . . . should propose, simultaneously with Her Majesty's Government, [a] treaty to Nicaragua . . . the great object of which should be to guarantee the safety of a company of capitalists, to whom a charter should be granted by Nicaragua. . . .

Mr. Clayton then recurred to the embarrassing position in which the friends of this great enterprise would be placed if Her Majesty's Government continued to support the Mosquito claim in opposition to the arrangement now proposed. . . .

Mr. Clayton considered that this question could never be amicably settled unless both Great Britain and the United States withdrew all claim to the territory of Nicaragua. . . . General Taylor cordially concurred. . . .

Washington, November 4, 1849

My Lord: I had the honor of forwarding to your lordship . . . the copy of a contract between an American company and the Government of Nicaragua for the formation of an interoceanic canal by way of the river St. John and the Lake of Nicaragua. . . . Mr. Clayton, although he approved of the general tenor of the contract, thought that some of the articles were objectionable . . . particularly those which require that all directors of the company and a majority of the shareholders shall be American citizens. . . .

Mr. Clayton now informs me that he has had a conference with the two principal directors of the company in question [Vanderbilt and White]; and that as he anticipated, he finds that no objection will be raised on their part so to modify the provisions of the contract as to remove from it anything of an exclusive nature.

I V

All was now clear to Palmerston. The United States government, on behalf of Vanderbilt, was seeking to entice England with an offer of shares in a nonexistent canal, or to coerce her by the threat of war into giving up a strategic position of great potential importance to her future.

Peace or war, then? England's trade with the Orient, vital to her prosperity, was already feeling the competition of the Yankee merchant marine. Let the Americans open a passage for cargo through the Central American isthmus and they would gain a significant advantage of distance and time in reaching the profitable markets of China, Southeast Asia, and the East Indies. The British government would not tolerate the building of a Nicaraguan canal unless England herself could control the route. It was for this reason, more than any other, that the British had held so tenaciously to the swamps of Mosquito for over a century. To share such a canal with others would be to give away one of the chief assets of the Empire, the strategic scheme of trade routes dominated by English guns. The Cape of Good Hope was British; so were the Falkland Islands that lay on the route to Cape Horn; and if there was to be another way for ships to Asia, it would have to be under the flag of England.

In Palmerston's view, Vanderbilt's proposal that England share in ownership of his canal company was naïve. Did the Yankee actually expect to get the benefit of British capital for a project which, in the final test, was bound to be more beneficial to the United States than to any other country?

It was only the Nicaraguan route across the isthmus that concerned Palmerston. The possibility that the United States would seek to dig its canal in Panama struck him as remote. Surveys made for the Royal Geographic Society left no doubt that, with the construction techniques then in use, the Cordilleran range in Panama presented insuperable obstacles to a canal; and he himself had flatly said as much to Parliament. As he saw the situation, Nicaragua was worth a war. "The desirability of obtaining so desirable a spot in the commercial world and freeing it from the competition of so adventurous a race as the North Americans" had been stressed in reports from men whom he trusted. His conviction was in part due also to no less a personage than Louis Bonaparte, then President of the Second Republic of France, and soon to be Emperor Napoleon III. In a pamphlet written some years earlier and published in London, Bonaparte had proposed to form a company to be known as *La Canal Napoléon de Nicaragua,* and had presented such an array of supporting facts and figures as to have a profound effect on British opinion. "The State of Nicaragua," he had asserted, "can become . . . the necessary route of the great commerce of the world, and is destined to attain *an extraordinary degree of prosperity and grandeur.*" For Palmerston, it was essential to make sure that the canal would not be dug unless England dug it, and that English businessmen would have an advantage in exploiting the Central American resources. If this policy meant war with the United States, then England would fight for her ocean supremacy as she had fought many times before.

Not that Palmerston wanted war. On the contrary, he was only too aware of its perils. The United States was now a far more formidable nation than it had been in 1812. Moreover, some of England's largest financial houses, notably the Rothschilds and the Barings, had large and profitable investments in American railroads, and were eager to see the peace preserved.

Palmerston had to consider, too, that a crisis with Russia over the spoils of the tottering Ottoman Empire was distinctly visible on the diplomatic horizon. If it should result in war between the western European powers and the Czar, and if the United States were to seize the opportunity to annex the Caribbean countries, England might be unable to do much more than protest. Consequently there was much to be said for finding a peaceful solution of the Central American problem. If diplomacy could serve to avoid war while keeping Grey-town and Tigre under England's control, let the diplomats by all means have their chance.

What if England were to strike a conciliatory pose, perhaps sending a new minister plenipotentiary to Washington specifically for the purpose of negotiating with Clayton—and without giving up anything, yet keep the peace? It would be a master stroke, and it would take a master of diplomacy to bring it off. But it was not unthinkable. And Palmerston knew the very man to whom such a mission might be entrusted.

V

While Walker was somewhere on the trail to Fort Laramie (one can imagine him sitting alongside the driver of a wagon, his face impassive, his eyes on the bleak horizon, saying a few courteous words now and then in his low voice, but absorbed for the most part in his thoughts and dreams), another strand in the web of his destiny was being spun in Washington, where Palmerston's emissary, Sir Henry Lytton Bulwer, had arrived. Elder brother of the novelist, Bulwer-Lytton, he had a well-earned reputation as a wily and successful gambler, both in diplomacy and at the tables. On December 24, 1849, Bulwer, in full dress uniform, presented his credentials as Envoy Extraordinary and Ambassador Plenipotentiary to President Taylor—a glittering Christmas present, as it were, from Great Britain to the United States. His was a spirit completely attuned to the majestic hypocrisies of British statecraft. In a brief, eloquent address he spoke of the Anglo-American community of interest. "I have entire confidence, Sir, that our two governments will act with the most perfect concord in carrying out this great design, and for my own part I unfeignedly assure you that I could not have a duty more congenial to my feelings." To which the President replied, "I hope, Sir, that your residence in this country will prove as agreeable to you personally as you have given me reason for believing that it will be honorable and advantageous, both for Great Britain and America."

Almost at once Secretary Clayton and the ambassador went to work on the draft of a treaty covering the problem of the Central American canal, setting the stage on which Walker was triumphantly to leap five years later. One of Bulwer's convictions was that nothing has greater value in diplomacy than "seizing the important point in an affair, the peculiar characteristic of an individual, the genius and tendency of an epoch." The important point in this affair was the Vanderbilt contract with Nicaragua; the essential characteristic of Clayton was his frankness, for he made no attempt to conceal his anxiety for the canal; and the tendency of the epoch was the widening of the breach between North and South, which gravely hampered the United States in its conduct of diplomacy. That he could play on these three keys to sound "Rule, Britannia," Bulwer was confident. He lost no time in telling Clayton that he could participate in the drafting of a treaty only with the proviso that the *status quo* in Central America should not be changed. The Mosquito question could not be considered, he said, "except to the limited extent determined" by the needs of the canal. These qualifications Clayton accepted without demur.

Every advantage in the contest went to Bulwer. Not that Clayton was incompetent—on the contrary, he was a successful lawyer and had been a useful senator; he thought clearly and talked well. His disadvantage was inherent in the situation, in the fact that he was emotionally involved with the Nicaraguan canal project. His interest was more than political, more than a matter of commitment to Vanderbilt and White. The canal had long been a favorite dream of his. Shortly before Bulwer arrived in Washington Clayton wrote to another American official that the subject of the canal had attracted his attention twenty years earlier, "since which time it has never

ceased to occupy my mind." To go down in history as the man who
made the canal possible was his ambition. In consequence, he was
eager—always a defect in diplomacy. He wanted something that only
England could give him, the freedom of the Nicaraguan canal route,
from a man who knew a dozen ways of denying a request while appearing to accede to it.

Six weeks later a draft of the treaty was complete. Its essence was
the agreement of the two powers that neither would seek exclusive
control of any canal built through Nicaragua, and a declaration that
neither would "assume or exercise dominion" over any part of Central America. In sending the draft to Palmerston, Bulwer wrote, "I
finally agreed to submit to your Lordship's sanction the enclosed project . . . its object being to exclude all questions of the disputes between Nicaragua and the Mosquitos . . . [except] as far as the ship
communication between the Atlantic and Pacific was concerned. . . .
As the matter now stands, it is clearly understood that Her Majesty's
Government holds by its own opinions already expressed as to Mosquito."

As Bulwer saw the issue, it hinged on the meaning of the word
"dominion." The treaty, he wrote, with his tongue unmistakably in
his cheek, left England "protecting" Mosquito, "but forbade the protection to be used for the purposes of dominion." Where did the one
end and the other begin? On this matter of definition, the treaty was
silent. What then had Britain conceded? Nothing.

The United States, however, had conceded a good deal. At one
point in their negotiation, Clayton conveyed to Bulwer, and without
more distortion than is usual in diplomacy, that it would be comparatively easy to bring all Central America into the American Union.
"There is not one of these five Central American states that would
not annex themselves to us tomorrow, if they could; and if it is any
secret worth knowing you are welcome to it—*Some of them have offered and asked to be annexed to the United States already.*"

Bulwer knew precisely how much value to place on this statement.
He was well aware that, as matters then stood, the North was unwilling to let the Central American republics, any more than Cuba, join
the United States under the domination of the South, while Southerners wanted them on no other terms. It was also obvious that Clayton wished to avoid a war for the isthmus, such as would almost

certainly result if the United States were to force the issue at once. Immediate annexation was therefore out of the question. On the other hand, if the Americans bided their time until England became involved in difficulties with Russia, they might well be able to establish hegemony over the isthmus without war; and in such an inviting situation, North and South might work out an accommodation in the matter. Unquestionably, Clayton's threat had some basis in reality; so that, in agreeing not to seek dominion in Central America, the United States was yielding up a useful counter in the game.

Even better, from England's standpoint, was the treaty's provision that the United States could not proceed with a Nicaraguan canal without British assent and participation. Bulwer did, however, make a friendly gesture in the direction of Vanderbilt. "I should state to your Lordship," he wrote to Palmerston, "that . . . a gentleman of great weight . . . considered that it would be only fair that the two governments should give an open and avowed preference by name to an American company. . . . This I objected to. . . . A sort of compromise was effected. . . ." The compromise was a clause giving a "priority of claim" to any company that already had a contract for the construction of the canal, and that had "made preparations and expended time, money and trouble on the faith of such contract." The name of the "gentleman of great weight" never appeared in the correspondence.

Bulwer had fulfilled his mission. He had negotiated a treaty which, while committing the United States, left England uncommitted; and so he told Clayton graciously that "Her Majesty's Government would freely undertake to obtain the consent of Mosquito" for the canal. By March, 1850, both sides were ready to proceed with ratification.

VI

As soon as Clayton showed the draft approved by Bulwer and himself to members of the Senate Foreign Relations Committee, he was sharply challenged. Was England, said the senators, to retain Mosquito? If so, ratification by the Senate was unthinkable. Knowing that England could not be persuaded to abandon her protectorate in Mosquito, Clayton was in a quandary. At last, however, a possible way out occurred to him. When he next saw Bulwer, he had with him the draft of a new clause to the effect that neither nation would "make use of protectorates or alliances for the purposes of . . . occupying, fortifying or colonizing . . . any part of Central America." Clayton reasoned that if England agreed to this clause, she would be virtually abjuring the use of force in Central America; and if she abjured the use of force, was that not for practical purposes equivalent to eventual withdrawal from Central America? And would not the Senate be willing on these grounds to ratify the treaty?

Bulwer, of course, understood perfectly well what was in the Secretary's mind. Reading the proposed clause, it struck him as having little practical significance in the light of other sections of the treaty. The loopholes in the document as drafted were large enough to permit a British fleet to pass through them if necessary—and if the new clause would serve to assure ratification of the treaty, he would not reject it. But neither was he willing to accept it out of hand. His agreement had to be made to look like the large concession that Clayton wanted to report to the Senate. Assuming an air of injured innocence, the ambassador gently reproved Clayton for inconstancy. But when the Secretary, in considerable distress of mind, threatened to jettison the treaty, Bulwer appeared to capitulate. "It is no use our trying to get around each other," he wrote to Clayton, "and it is in neither of our characters. . . . I now agree to all you have asked."

Clayton was elated. Writing to the American ambassador in London he said triumphantly that thenceforth the Mosquito protectorate would stand only "as the shadow of a name." There was a note of satisfaction, too, in the presidential message which accompanied the treaty when it was formally submitted to the Senate: "I found Great Britain in possession of nearly half of Central America, as the ally and protector of the Mosquito king. It has been my object, in negotiating this treaty, not only to secure the passage across the isthmus . . . but to maintain the independence and sovereignty of all Central American republics. The Senate will judge how far these objects have been effected."

Popular opinion, as reflected in the press, was sharply divided. Some papers praised the treaty as a masterpiece of high-minded statesmanship, by means of which war with Britain had been averted. Others saw it as a repudiation of the Monroe Doctrine. The New York *Herald* went so far as to assail Clayton as "weak" and "ignorant," and alleged openly that the treaty had been "concocted" by Joseph White for the Vanderbilt interests. But Clayton remained confident that his efforts would be vindicated by time. England, he assured the Senate, had in effect abandoned her policy of encroachment in Central America. The two great Anglo-Saxon powers were to join hands fraternally in the interest of commerce and enduring peace. And the senators, responding perhaps less to the Secretary's eloquence than to Joseph White's lobbying, rushed the treaty to a vote, and ratified it.

This was the moment for Bulwer to play the winning trump concealed in his hand. It took the form of a short note simply stating that he did not "understand the engagements of the convention to apply to Her Majesty's settlement at Honduras or its dependencies." As Clayton read, the icy touch of reality must have shocked him. The treaty did indeed say that the British would not occupy, fortify, or colonize any part of Central America. But what was Central America? It was merely a loose geographic term, like the Orient, or the Levant. Did it comprise all of the isthmus or only the five independent republics? Nowhere in the treaty was it defined. Not that Clayton had ever seriously hoped to bring British Honduras, a long-established Crown Colony, under the restrictions of the treaty. If England chose to regard this possession as distinct from "Central America," the United States could hardly object. But the real menace of Bulwer's note came in the word "dependencies." Why was it now for the first time introduced into the dialogue? Here was a distinct implication that England had decided to make her other Central American holdings dependencies of British Honduras, and in this way remove them also from "Central America" and free them from the restrictions of the treaty. If Mosquito were to become such a dependency it could be occupied and fortified as England chose, without technical violation of the treaty. Moreover, since the boundaries of Mosquito were largely undefined, as were, indeed, those of the five republics, there would be nothing to prevent "the King of the Mosquitos" from claiming still more Central American territory as part of his ancestral lands, as had been done in the past.

Clayton could envisage the storm that would be stirred up in Congress and the press if the suspicion arose that the treaty had accomplished no more than this. The resulting anger and ridicule might prevent the promulgation of the treaty, destroy the prestige of the administration, put an end to all hope for the canal, injure the investors who had bought stock in Vanderbilt's new companies, and conceivably lead to war. On the other hand, the Secretary could not afford to ignore Bulwer's note. An evasive tactic was his only solution. Writing to the Chairman of the Senate Foreign Relations Committee, he asked for that gentleman's personal concurrence in the view that the treaty was not intended to apply to British Honduras; but he carefully omitted any mention of "dependencies." In this way he succeeded in extracting from the innocent senator agreement that "the Senate perfectly understood that the treaty did not include British Honduras."

Thus reinforced, Clayton wrote to Bulwer acknowledging that "British Honduras was not embraced in the treaty," but declining "to affirm or deny the British title to their settlement or its alleged dependencies." As to the boundaries of the Central American states, he admitted that no alteration could be made in the treaty for the purpose of defining them, "without referring the same to the Senate." But perhaps in the future something might be done to remedy the omission?

To this feeble effort Bulwer replied with scarcely veiled sarcasm. "I understand that you do not deem yourself called upon to mark out at this time the exact limits of Her Majesty's settlements . . . but that you fully recognize that Her Majesty's title thereto will remain just as it was. . . . I now deem myself authorized to exchange Her Majesty's ratification of the treaty . . . for that of the President of the United States."

Clayton had in effect agreed to an amendment of the treaty without consulting the Senate. His painful awareness of his predicament found expression in a memorandum that he wrote and secretly deposited in the vault of the Department of State, together with Bulwer's decisive letter. "The written declaration from Sir Henry Lytton Bulwer was received by me. . . . I wrote him . . . carefully declining to affirm or deny the British title" [to their Central American possessions]. "The consent of the Senate to the declaration was not required and the treaty was ratified as it stood."

With an eye to patriotic symbolism, the anxious Secretary had selected July Fourth as the date for the formal signing of the treaty by President Taylor and Bulwer. The President's comments as he took his pen in hand showed simple and unfeigned pleasure in the event, leading to the surmise that Clayton had not told him of the hidden letter from Bulwer. No event more memorable had occurred in Taylor's administration, nor would occur, for a few weeks later the well-meaning old soldier was dead of the cholera.

The British view of the transaction was as clear and unambiguous as that of the Americans was hazy and obscure. The London *Times* called it "a contest in the use of terms," and had no doubt as to the victor. As soon as the signed treaty was in Palmerston's hands, he ordered a warship to Greytown, where marines were landed to perform yet another flag-raising ceremony, and to reassert once more the authority of "the Mosquito King." It was as well to remind all concerned that England had given up nothing.

In this way, "the convention between the United States of America and Her British Majesty for facilitating and protecting the construction of a ship canal between the Atlantic and Pacific oceans" became law. Its immediate effect was to prevent America from asserting her power at a point of high strategic importance to her interests. The nation now had no way in which to control the situation in Nicaragua except by privately organized military expeditions. The moment that the treaty was signed, Walker's spectacular adventure became possible.

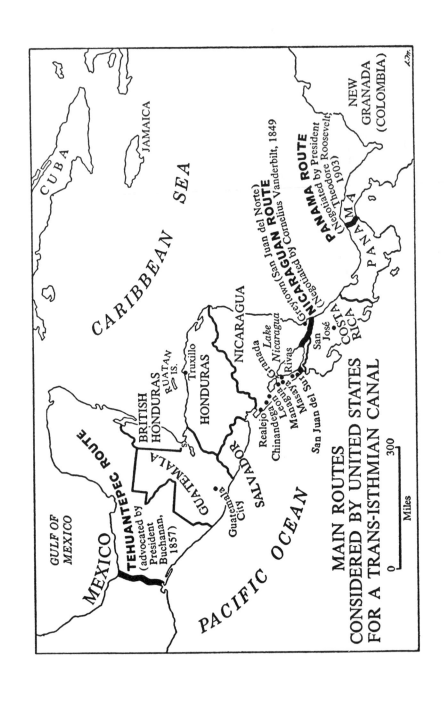

MAIN ROUTES
CONSIDERED BY UNITED STATES
FOR A TRANS-ISTHMIAN CANAL

GULF OF
MEXICO

MEXICO

TEHUANTEPEC ROUTE
(advocated by
President Buchanan,
1857)

GUATEMALA

Guatemala
City

SALVADOR

BRITISH
HONDURAS

RUATAN IS.

Truxillo

HONDURAS

NICARAGUA

Realejo
Chinandega
León
Managua
Masaya
Granada
Lake
Nicaragua
Rivas
San Juan Sur

San Juan del Sur

CARIBBEAN SEA

CUBA

JAMAICA

Greytown (San Juan del Norte)

NICARAGUAN ROUTE
(Negotiated by Cornelius Vanderbilt, 1849)

San
José

COSTA
RICA

PANAMA

PANAMA ROUTE
(Negotiated by President
Theodore Roosevelt,
1903)

NEW
GRANADA
(COLOMBIA)

PACIFIC OCEAN

0   300
Miles

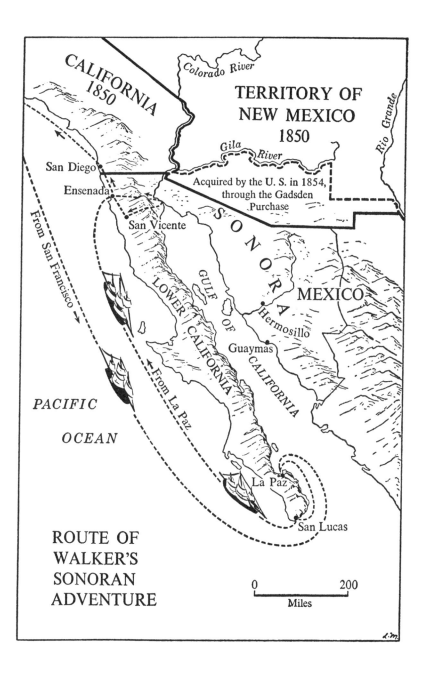

CALIFORNIA
1850

Colorado River

TERRITORY OF
NEW MEXICO
1850

Rio Grande

Gila River

San Diego

Ensenada

Acquired by the U. S. in 1854,
through the Gadsden
Purchase

San Vicente

S O N O R A

MEXICO

From San Francisco

Hermosillo

LOWER CALIFORNIA

GULF OF CALIFORNIA

Guaymas

PACIFIC

From La Paz

OCEAN

La Paz

ROUTE OF
WALKER'S
SONORAN
ADVENTURE

San Lucas

0   200
Miles

VI

THE MAN OF PRINCIPLE

Walker's first action on arriving in San Francisco was to seek out his old friend Edmund Randolph, who had by that time put down roots in the community; and through him he met John Nugent, the proprietor and editor of the youngest of the city's dozen newspapers, the *Herald*. Nugent gladly put him to work. The little paper was thriving, for every San Franciscan was avid for news. Like its bouncing competitors, the *Herald* charged twelve cents per copy, filled much more than half of its four pages with advertising, and published a "steamer edition," at one dollar per copy, for passengers on outgoing ships. Its chief problem was the shortage of newsprint, which had to be imported from the east, and which cost twenty times its price in New York. San Francisco's publishers had to accept what supplies they could get, however cheap, coarse, or discolored, and when ships failed to arrive on time, desperate printers would turn out editions on grey paper used to wrap Chinese tea, or on legal foolscap.

The *Herald*'s deficiencies of appearance, however, were more than offset by its vitality. It had a definite and usually liberal opinion about everything. It was for free trade and the right of divorce in unhappy marriages. It strongly opposed the introduction of slavery into California. It believed that the slavery issue in the Union as a whole could be settled without secession and civil war if extremists on both sides could be held in check. It quoted the London *Times*: "There can be no doubt that the anti-slavery feeling will eventually preponderate in the States to the extinction of the Southern institution; but the question will not be carried by the violence of the present agitators." It was eloquent on French culture and especially the theaters of Paris. It resented the American ambassador to England who, in an address in London, boasted that "We Americans are of the Anglo-Saxon race, reared in the Protestant faith." The *Herald* exploded into satire. "Wonderful! What geniuses we must be! Only think of it—to be of the Anglo-Saxon race!" What of the Celts and the French? What of the Catholics and the Jews? Were they not also Americans?

Two months after the Clayton-Bulwer Treaty was signed, news of it reached San Francisco and was published in the *Herald,* as in other newspapers. Taken at face value, it seemed a hopeful development, and editorial comment was favorable. But international diplomacy meant little to the San Franciscans of 1850. The great topic of the day was crime in their own midst. Wars and treaties were nothing by comparison. Even gold strikes had become secondary. Gangs of robbers and murderers, many of them from Australia's convict colonies, nightly roamed the city and made it a hell for the law-abiding. No respectable man, whatever arms he carried, could safely walk the street after dark. There was no room in the newspapers to deal with more than a few of the sensational murders, assaults, and burglaries that were committed every day. Most of the city's bars and taverns provided women as a sideline and, thus baited with liquor and lechery, served as traps for the unwary. As the *Herald* reported: "These ruffian resorts are the hot beds of drunkenness and the scenes of unnumbered crimes. Unsuspecting sailors and miners . . . are filled with liquor—drugged if necessary—until . . . they fall an easy victim. . . . Many robberies are committed which are not brought to light through shame on the part of the victim."

It could not be said that law enforcement had broken down, for it had never got started. In a few months of 1850 over one hundred murders were committed, without the execution of a single criminal. Worse: three times that year the city was devastated by fires which, it was shown, were deliberately started by the pestilential gang known as the Sydney Ducks to provide a rogues' festival of robbery and rape. The city was close to anarchy.

Shortly after Walker's arrival, the *Herald* began an anticrime crusade which made it a storm center, and which, as events showed, was largely his work. With his experience of the New Orleans courts, he quickly perceived that the essence of the terrifying situation lay in the alliance of the gangs with the crooked politicians who dominated the city, and who had the police and the judges under their venal thumbs. Nugent gave him a free rein. The first blast of the *Herald* was against the California Supreme Court, which from its seat in Sacramento set the tone of the entire judiciary of the state. "The Supreme Court," said an editorial, "has rendered itself ridiculous," by "flagrant stupidity," and by its toleration of "unprincipled and disreputable hangers-on" and "corrupt practitioners and pettifoggers." To this unexpected attack, the first of its kind to appear in the San Francisco press, the justices of the Supreme Court felt impelled to reply. Using the Sacramento City Council as their mouthpiece, they issued a strong diatribe against the *Herald,* as subversive of justice. Walker was now in his element. Happily he delivered an even harder thrust. On Christmas, 1850, he published an item headed "Personal," to express his feelings about the Sacramento Council. It began on a lofty note: "If an editor were to turn from his course to notice the abuse mouthed by corrupt officials . . . he would indeed be stooping". . . . However, to leave no uncertainty as to his opinions, he added that the Council was "a collection of knaves and blackguards."

For some weeks thereafter, under the heading of "Law Intelligence," the *Herald* published detailed accounts of miscarriages of justice in the courts, and seldom missed an opportunity to upbraid the authorities for failure to act against the criminals of the city. It had plenty of ammunition. The police force was an absurdity. Constables openly consorted with criminals. There was not even a jail in San Francisco. Even if the perpetrator of a crime was identified and brought to court he ran no risk. A little money or the right connection would always uncover a legal technicality to assure dismissal of his case. Or the jury would be packed with friends of the man on trial. Crime had become a way of life for hundreds of dangerous men and women, while the courts looked the other way.

It was a ringing editorial in the *Herald,* "A Way To Stop Crime," that first publicly advocated a Vigilante movement, although the word was not yet used. "A band of two or three hundred 'regulators,' composed of such men as have a stake in the town" was needed, said the *Herald,* "to drive the criminals from the city," if necessary with "a few examples of Lynch Law." Twice that week the advice was repeated, with full recognition of its dangers, and a somber warning: "Terrible is the retribution which our citizens will visit on the unworthy public servants who have reduced them to the necessity of defending themselves" against the criminal elements.

Other newspapers took up the idea of a Vigilante corps, until alarm at the prospect impelled the ruling politicians to make some gesture to public opinion. At the request of the district attorney, a Grand Jury of respectable citizens was impaneled to try to cope with the flood of crime. Taking itself seriously, it quickly found indictments against a number of known criminals, only to call forth a reprimand from the bench. The Chief Judge of the District Court, Levi Parsons, informed the Grand Jury that it could not indict except on evidence warranting conviction by a petit jury—which meant, for practical purposes, that it could not indict.

It was Parsons' misfortune that this instruction, which might have passed almost unnoticed in the scurry and cynicism of San Francisco life, fell under Walker's legally trained eye. Next day the *Herald* printed a little paragraph, signed "One of the People," and which said, "Whether his Honor, Judge Parsons, in this instance has laid down for the guidance of the Grand Jury, an incorrect rule of law, through haste, inadvertence or misapprehension it is immaterial to inquire." The fact remained, by every precedent of law a Grand Jury need not wait to indict until it had accumulated all the evidence required to convict in an ordinary court.

Judge Parsons, known for his pomposity, replied by an ill-advised blast from the bench. The *Herald,* he said, was a public nuisance and should be prosecuted as such by the county authorities. He then appeared personally before the Grand Jury and urged the indictment of the *Herald* for contempt of court; but the jurors refused to act. Walker seized the opening. In a biting editorial, "The Press A Nuisance," he said plainly that "the District Court instructs the Grand Jury to aid the escape of criminals. . . . No wonder that after laying down the law favorably to criminals the District Judge should declare

against the Press." This Walker concluded, was "judicial madness."
As for the charge of contempt, "The courts cannot be reduced much
lower than they have reduced themselves. If we were the Guardian
Angel of the District Judge we would whisper in his ear, Beware!"

A group of lawyers who were friendly to Parsons promptly held a
meeting at which the *Herald* was denounced on the ground that in
attacking the Judge it had attacked the courts and the process of
justice. Some even called for the paper's suppression. Thus fortified,
as he thought, Parsons took direct action. It was common gossip in
the city that the attacks on him had come from Walker's pen, and the
Judge issued a warrant for his arrest, on a charge of contempt of court.

I I

Walker's appearance before the court was reported in great detail by
the San Francisco press. The courtroom was crowded with partisans
both of the Judge and the accused. Edmund Randolph, already regarded as a leading light of the San Francisco bar, spoke for the defense. Handsome, impressive, combining aristocratic hauteur with a
touch of fire, he had the further advantage of being known as an
excellent shot—a significant asset in the profession of law in
the San Francisco of the 1850's. He began by requesting that the
charge against Walker be put into writing. Parsons said, "The objection is overruled," and so continuous were his interruptions thereafter that Randolph was unable to complete a sentence.

Finally he made himself heard, shouting that the Judge stood in
violation of the Bill of Rights of the California Constitution. "You are
liable to impeachment by the Legislature for your official conduct.
. . . The proceeding is monstrous!"

"Mr. Randolph!" yelled the Judge. "The Court cannot sit here to
hear itself abused and its proceedings characterized as monstrous!"

Randolph retorted, "I will then call your conduct monstrously
illegal, monstrously unjust—" An uproar arose among the spectators,
while Parsons, purple in the face, said that he could not tolerate
Randolph's "exceedingly disrespectful" language.

"I regret," said Randolph icily, "that the circumstances of the case
will not allow me to make an apology."

This was a word full of menace, for it brought the thought of a duel to every mind. Hastily Parsons said, "We do not ask for an apology."

The defense was then permitted to state its case—which was simply that Walker did not stand in contempt of court. If the Judge had a proper charge against him, it was libel, not contempt. "I admit that it" [the controversial editorial] "is a libel; there is pungency in it; and if the statements contained therein are true, the conclusion is inevitable that Levi Parsons is a corrupt man, a dishonest judge." The court rocked at this blast. A fist fight broke out among the spectators. Perceiving the danger of a riot, Parsons sought to terminate the hearing by demanding that Walker admit authorship of the editorial. The room quieted. "Yes," said Walker, "I wrote and published that article to promote—*and not obstruct*—public justice."

Parsons instantly replied, "Then I find you guilty as charged! The fine is five hundred dollars."

"I shall not pay it," Walker said quietly.

"Sheriff!" ordered the Judge. "This man is to be held in close confinement until the fine is paid."

The extraordinary excitement generated by the case reflected the public's awareness that for the first time the scandal of judicial corruption had been brought into the open. Walker had hardly been taken to a cell next to the Sheriff's office and locked up when placards began to appear all over the city: "Justice! Public Meeting! . . . to express opinions in regard to the decision of the Judge of the District Court." . . . That day 4,000 men gathered on the plaza before the court house and held a mass-meeting remarkable for its gravity and decorum. Edmund Randolph was the chief speaker. A great point of law was at stake, he said—the rights of Californians under the Constitution. Let there be no violence. "Mr. Walker has asked me to speak to you of the importance of avoiding violence. He said to me that he will not let himself be set free by violence."

Some of his listeners were disappointed. There were shouts: "Let's bring the Judge out here!" "Parsons resign!" "Set Walker free!" But Randolph maintained his calm and kept the crowd in check. A resolution condemning Parsons' action as "an unwarrantable exercise of power and violation of law" was formally proposed and carried in a voice vote. This resolution, it was agreed, would be delivered in writing to Parsons by a Committee of Ten. Meanwhile, Randolph would apply to the Superior Court of the city for a writ of *habeas corpus.*

Whatever else might be said of Parsons, he was a stern fighter for injustice, and he showed no sign of giving way to public pressure. For the following week, while the *habeas corpus* proceeding was being argued, most of the San Francisco newspapers allotted whole columns daily to the affair. The case was seen as a major test of the common law, as a defense of the public against judicial tyranny. Walker, from his cell, provided additional editorial matter for the *Herald,* referring to Parsons' "masterly inactivity" in dealing with crime, and adding, "The Judge is a stickler for contempt and he has succeeded in securing to himself an unstinted measure. . . . In trying to snuff out the *Herald,* his Honor has extinguished himself."

The judge of the Superior Court who had to consider Randolph's demand for a writ of *habeas corpus* was in an embarrassing position. To deny the writ would be to defy an aroused public opinion; to grant it would offend the powerful Parsons and his cronies. By this time, however, the case had attracted the attention of the entire state, and steps for the impeachment of Parsons were under way before the Legislature. Ten days after Walker's arrest, the writ was reluctantly issued by the Court, and he was set free. His first action was to publish "A Card" in the *Herald,* thanking those who had rallied to his cause, which was the cause "of the whole people of California." Of Edmund Randolph's arduous efforts he spoke with especial feeling. "It would be idle ceremony for me to return thanks"; this had been an unforgettable act of friendship. The recollection of that act would, five years later, profoundly affect not only Walker's destiny but that of a nation.

As the tumult died away, it appeared that the only real beneficiary of the affair was the *Herald.* Its circulation boomed; it enlarged its page size so as to accommodate more advertising and began to turn out a weekly newspaper in addition to the daily. But Walker was well aware that nothing had yet been accomplished for the city. Crime was unabated. The courts went on their accustomed way. The attack on Parsons and the judiciary, he felt, had to be pressed. Early in April, he appeared before a special committee of the Legislature in Sacramento to present a memorial on Parsons' instruction to the Grand Jury. The committee investigated the charge and recommended impeachment; and the impeachment proceedings moved as far as the floor of the Legislature. There, however, Parsons' political friends were able to intervene successfully; and after some desultory debate, the matter was dropped.

III

The San Francisco underworld had its own views on "the contempt case," as it was called, and it expressed them with ferocity. On the night of May 4, 1851, simultaneous fires broke out at a dozen points in the downtown business districts, producing a conflagration that totally destroyed twenty blocks of wooden buildings, among them the office and printing plant of the *Herald*. Under cover of the excitement the gangs swarmed into the city and robbed and looted to their hearts' content.

It was a night of terror and despair; and the hope that the Walker case had aroused went up in smoke. The *Herald* lost everything except its fighting spirit. A printing plant which had escaped the fire was put at Nugent's disposal, and he managed to resume publication three days after the fire, with anger bubbling from every page, calling for "a volunteer police." This time something was done, and men armed with rifles began to patrol the city. The entire press of the city was demanding action against the arsonists. The *Herald* went further. On June 5, it came out with an editorial headed, "The Organization of Crime in This State," in which it flatly asserted that the men who had set the fire were known to the authorities, and were receiving the protection of politicians, some of whom were Catilines aiming at nothing less than complete mastery of the city and the state. It was time, said the *Herald,* for "a general war on crime." The shocked and frightened public, however, was in no mood to harken to clarion calls. It was rumored that many respectable people were preparing to leave San Francisco.

The *Herald*'s charge of a major political conspiracy resting on a criminal base became more credible when, about three weeks later, with the rebuilding of the ruined district well under way, another great fire broke out, destroying even more of the city, again to the accompaniment of countless robberies. It was this devastating blaze that provided the immediate impetus for the formation of the first Committee of Public Safety, the Vigilantes, who would finally crush the gangs only to impose their own despotism.

I V

The *Herald* still held to its conviction that, before order could be established, the courts had to be freed from corrupt judges of the Parsons stamp. His docket was crowded with cases, yet he absented himself from the court for days at a time. "How long must we tolerate this man?" Walker demanded editorially. The same question, in reverse, was in Judge Parsons' mind, and he was in the better position to answer it. Among his friends was a notorious duelist, Graham Hicks, known for his deadly skill with the revolver. Several prominent San Franciscans had already fallen to his marksmanship. He was a small wiry man, not unlike Walker himself in build. Walker, said Hicks, had insulted "a friend of his," and would have to apologize or fight. Duelling was the most popular spectator sport in the city, and as soon as the challenge became known and the time of the meeting was set, a huge crowd turned out for the event.

The fact that Walker fought four revolver duels in his life without wounding a single antagonist led some to believe that his marksmanship was poor; but it would have had to be almost incredibly bad to achieve such a record, and other evidence points in the opposite direction. It is perhaps not unreasonable to believe that he had an aversion to this cold-blooded form of killing—that he deliberately shot into the air or the ground in the expectation that his opponents would follow his example. This practice was not unusual among the gentlemen of New Orleans, as a means of satisfying honor without bloodshed. In one of his duels, fought in San Francisco with W. H. Carter in the spring of 1855, at eight paces, Walker was wounded in the foot —an injury sufficiently unusual to suggest that Carter was shooting to miss or to inflict minimal damage after Walker had missed. In the Hicks duel, also fought at eight paces, Walker as usual got his shot off first, without effect. Hicks, however, felt no obligations to *noblesse*. His shot, intended to kill, went through the upper part of Walker's arm, near the shoulder, just missing the bone.

What followed made a great impression on the spectators. Showing no sign of pain, Walker motioned to Hicks that they should take a second shot, but before they could raise their guns again, the seconds intervened, and the duel was declared over.

Some later commentators on Walker's career professed to find in his several duels the signs of a bloodthirsty character, of a desperado, but it is safe to say that they misread both the man and his age. A contemporary of Walker's who sought to explain his outlook to a later generation stressed the atmosphere of the 1850's as an essential factor to be considered. "Men looked upon life from a more romantic viewpoint than they do now. There was more sentiment, more singing of songs . . . grace and gallantry. . . . Men had not outgrown the customs of their forefathers, and if they resorted to the *code duello* in defense of their honor, and the honor of women, they were moved by sincerity, and surrounded by traditions still too potent to be cast aside." The way in which a gentleman conducted himself in a duel in Walker's time was taken as a major test of character; the fortitude with which he bore the wound inflicted by Hicks and the anger that made him want to continue the duel gave him an instant reputation as a man among men. "A brave, highly educated and able man" with "a high moral and political position"* on all issues of the time, was the character attributed to Walker in the San Francisco of the 1850's. Men clustered around him.

---

* F. Soulé, J. H. Gihon, and J. Nisbet, *Annals of San Francisco*, 1855.

VII

MR. VANDERBILT FORGIVES
GREAT BRITAIN

Walker in the San Francisco *Herald,* quoting the New York press, commented enthusiastically on Commodore Vanderbilt's great enterprise in Nicaragua. He saw the canal as the key to the Americanization of the Caribbean. The interests of the great capitalist had begun to touch those of the inconspicuous journalist. With the signing of the Clayton-Bulwer Treaty, two new Vanderbilt corporations had sprung into life: the Nicaraguan Canal Company, which was to dig the canal under Anglo-American management; and the Accessory Transit Company, which would carry passengers across Nicaragua until completion of the canal. Talk of war died away. Even the New York *Herald,* which had been virulently anti-British, discovered that in the matter of Nicaragua the United States as well as the British had been at fault, "but an influence of common sense arose from . . . the London Exchange on the one side and Wall Street on the other."

San Francisco heard nothing but favorable news of the venture. Already the Accessory Transit Company was constructing shallow-draft steamboats to operate on the San Juan River and Lake Nicaragua.

Yet another Vanderbilt company, the Nicaragua Steamship Line, had ordered ships of unsurpassed size and speed to make the runs from New York to Nicaragua and from Nicaragua to San Francisco. An eminent engineer, Colonel C. W. Childs, had agreed to go to Nicaragua for Vanderbilt to make a detailed survey for the canal and an estimate of cost. And finally it was announced that Vanderbilt would go forthwith to England to negotiate with British financiers.

The success of the canal scheme was taken for granted. How could America and England, acting together, fail? All hopes seemed confirmed when copies of the *Times* of London arrived, praising the Vanderbilt project, and stating, "There is every prospect of the undertaking . . . being pushed to a successful issue." Vanderbilt's talks with the Rothschilds and Baring Brothers, said the *Times,* had resulted in "a satisfactory financial arrangement."

Vanderbilt's next concern was to bring the Accessory Transit Company to life while Colonel Childs was making his survey of the canal. Here he ran into difficulties. Engineers whom he had sent to Nicaragua had reported that the San Juan River, contrary to expectations, was not passable by steamboat, owing to five dangerous rapids along its course. The only hope for the transit route, they said, would be to dig small canals around these rapids. With his accustomed energy, the Commodore decided to see for himself. The first of his new ocean-going steamships, the *Prometheus*, was ready for him. It was a fast boat, but on this first voyage made no attempt at a speed record, for it towed behind it, on the ten-day run to Greytown, a small shallow-draft steamboat, the *Director*, designed for use on Lake Nicaragua.

I I

"The presence of the enterprising and indefatigable Commodore Vanderbilt," wrote Walker in the *Herald,* "will insure the perfection of all arrangements to make the transit connection complete." The tribute was merited. When the *Prometheus* docked at Greytown and Vanderbilt proposed to take the *Director* up the San Juan to the lake, he found himself up against a solid front of pessimism among his own employees. The boat would be wrecked, warned his engineers. No one had ever succeeded in getting a steamboat through the San

Juan. Vanderbilt brushed objections aside. He had come to take a boat up the river and he would do it. What followed left his men awe-struck. With Vanderbilt himself at the wheel, the *Director* headed up-stream as if possessed of a devil. "The Commodore," reported one of the crew, "insisted on 'jumping' all the obstacles, and tied down the safety valves, put on all steam, and compelled the little steamer to scrape and struggle over the obstructions into clear water again." At one point where the river dropped appallingly and the water boiled around huge protruding rocks, Vanderbilt taught the crew another lesson, by using heavy rope tied around trees to warp the vessel, an inch at a time, past the rapids.

On New Year's Day, 1851, the *Director* completed the 119-mile course of the river and entered Lake Nicaragua. The remainder of Vanderbilt's trip was equally full of achievement. By the time that he returned to Greytown he had laid out the complete transit route. From Virgin Bay, on the west side of the lake, a road was to be cut through the jungle to the nearest usable harbor on the Pacific, San Juan del Sur. To the east, the San Juan River was to be improved by blasting, and where that would not suffice for the passage of boats, a portage around obstinate rapids would take care of the problem. The Commodore gave orders: construct wharves in all of the Transit's harbors on seacoast and lakeshore; purchase mules and stagecoaches to carry passengers and their baggage; please the Nicaraguans by paint-ing the coaches in their national colors, blue and white; lay wooden planks all along the road through the jungle; buy land outside Grey-town and put up company offices—move, act, build! Then he boarded the *Prometheus* and made a record-smashing run back to New York.

From this moment all went as if by magic. Ocean-going steamships designed to Vanderbilt's specifications were constructed and sent around Cape Horn to handle the run between San Juan del Sur and San Francisco. He also ordered two small iron-hulled steamers to be built especially for the rocky San Juan River, and he named these, not inappropriately, the *John M. Clayton* and the *Sir Henry Bulwer*. A somewhat larger boat was sent to join the *Director* on Lake Nicara-gua. On July 3, 1851, one year precisely after the signing of the Clay-ton-Bulwer treaty, advertisements appeared in New York newspapers for the "New and Independent Line for California." All New York was excited. What could not Americans do when they put their minds to it? The New York *Herald* looked forward to the time "when the government and institutions of the United States will be extended over the whole of Mexico and Central America," as a result of the enterprise of such men as Vanderbilt and George Law. California was even more elated, if possible. The fastest ship-time from New York to San Francisco around Cape Horn had been fifty-one days. The new route through Nicaragua would shorten the trip to twenty-five days.

When the *Prometheus* sailed from New York for Greytown, Vanderbilt and a large party of guests were aboard her. Still his luck held. The passengers enjoyed the summer voyage, marveled at the lush scenery of the Nicaraguan coast, were hospitably received in Greytown, boarded the *Sir Henry Bulwer,* ascended the San Juan River with only minor difficulties, were transferred to the *Director,* crossed the lake to Virgin Bay, mounted mules (the stages being still undelivered), and rode eleven miles to San Juan del Sur, where one of Vanderbilt's big new ships, the *Pacific,* was waiting to take them aboard for the run to San Francisco. A letter received by the New York *Herald* from one of the passengers might almost have been written to Vanderbilt's order: "With good swift boats, gentlemanly commanders, and with scenery to attract the eye, studded with banana, orange, lemon, palm and a thousand varieties of trees, what shall deter the traveler from the United States in making a choice of this sure and practicable route?"

More steamships were coming from the ways for the Vanderbilt line, and by late 1851 it was in full competition with Law's Panama route. All the advantage now lay with the Commodore. California-bound passengers soon learned that they could save four days (days in which they might find a gold deposit before someone else got to it!) by traveling through Nicaragua. When Law tried to hold his position by warning the public in print against "melancholy detentions" on the Nicaragua route, Vanderbilt hotly countered with assertions that cholera was rampant in Panama. Law lowered his fares; Vanderbilt lowered his still more. On the early runs of the *Prometheus,* first-class passengers paid $400 per person, but month by month the price went down until at one point it stood at $150, while steerage passengers could make the voyage to San Francisco for only $45. At this stage, loud complaints were heard from passengers about crowded conditions, wretched food, and poor seamanship, but Vanderbilt could afford to shrug; his boats were traveling full, Law's half empty. Nothing could daunt the multitudes eager to reach the promised land of California by the shortest route, and the price war notwithstanding, Vanderbilt's profits were massive. The line was making three sailings a month out of New York, carrying up to 600 passengers at a time, while the San Francisco office was booking about 300 passengers per trip and obtaining large revenues from the shipment of eastbound gold. The gross revenues of the Nicaragua Steamship Line and the Accessory Transit Company in their first year of full operation were reported to be over $5,000,000, of which nearly 40 per cent was net profit. (Walker in that year of 1852 was lucky if journalism earned him a thousand dollars.)

III

San Francisco heard that the Commodore's Nicaraguan venture was dazzling Wall Street by its success and ingenuity. Accessory Transit did not even have to pay taxes to New York State, since, as its lawyers made clear to the courts, it was "a Nicaraguan enterprise." Where taxes were not concerned, however, the company was glad to wrap itself in the American flag. At one point friction arose with Nicaragua, whose government was so temerarious as to request the share of profits due it under its contract with the company. Vanderbilt claimed that there had been no profits, that a steamboat had been lost, that the outlook was bleak. This the Nicaraguans could hardly credit, since it was public knowledge that Accessory Transit had paid agreeable dividends to stockholders; and they sent two commissioners to New York to press their case. Vanderbilt refused to see them.

To every display of the Commodore's aggressiveness, the public responded with applause, and more than applause, with money. While the price of shares in Law's Panama Line was dropping on the exchange, Accessory Transit stock became a favorite of the bulls, rising in a few months from $18 to $50 per share. At this price, so it was later asserted, Vanderbilt disposed of most of his shares. But this was the least of his gains. It was the soaring of Nicaraguan Canal Company stock that set Wall Streeters agog. Coming on the market at $800 per share, it was first regarded only as an interesting speculation for the wealthy. Then, just at the time when the success of the

Accessory Transit Company had made Vanderbilt the darling of the financial community, came the awaited report from Colonel Childs. The sum of $32,000,000, said the colonel, would be enough to build a practicable lock canal on the Nicaraguan route; and what was more, his plans had been approved by engineers of the British and American governments. A wild rush for Nicaraguan Canal Company shares followed. Although the *New York Times* shook its editorial head, pointing out that the project still existed only on paper, and reminding its readers of the Mississippi Bubble, Wall Street paid no attention. Up and up went the price until in March, 1852, it stood at $3600 per share.

The precise details of the subsequent collapse were never revealed, but shrewd guesses were made. As soon as Colonel Childs returned from Nicaragua, Vanderbilt sent him with some financial advisors to London, to arrange for British capital in the venture. A few weeks later he held in his hands a letter, transmitted by Childs, from a partner of Baring Brothers, which knocked the props out from under his hopes. British finance would have nothing to do with the Nicaraguan Canal Company. As planned by Childs, the canal would be too narrow to accommodate large freighters, and the cost was excessive relative to the revenue that could be obtained from small passenger ships.

Whether or not the Barings' calculations were valid, whether or not Childs' plans for the canal could have been modified to meet their objections, hardly mattered. The fact, as George Squier, the American minister, plainly stated, was that all estimates of the cost of the canal were only guesses. He himself guessed $100,000,000 as being closer to the mark than Childs' figure. Any man of common sense, he said, could see that the canal's immense benefits would justify an outlay of $200,000,000, if necessary. Vanderbilt, too, understood this. He perceived between the lines of the British refusal its real significance. England simply did not want the canal. Her policy had not changed an iota; and since the Clayton-Bulwer Treaty, which bound her to nothing, effectively prevented the United States from proceeding without her, there would be no canal.

How long Vanderbilt knew of the Baring letter before he released it for publication no one could find out. The *Herald* made plain its conviction that he kept his information to himself until he had unloaded his shares at some $3600 each. With the announcement came panic. First by hundreds and then by thousands of dollars the price of the stock fell, until buyers could not be found at any price.

While regretting England's decision, Vanderbilt let it be known that he harbored no hostility toward her. Perhaps the reason for his forgiving attitude lay in the profit that he realized from his Wall Street transactions at this period. He was worth, so he told a friend, some eleven millions—which meant that he had doubled his fortune in three years. More, his money was so invested as to yield him a return of 25 per cent. He could afford to forgive those who had transgressed against him. In any event his original purpose was achieved. Nicaragua had replaced Panama as the favored route to California, and the stock of George Law's Panama Steamship Line was steadly dropping on the exchange.

Thus, after three years of high diplomacy and even higher finance, England and Vanderbilt were satisfied, but the American government found its position in Central America sadly worsened, and its hopes of a canal blighted. Senatorial inquiry to find out why the plan had foundered had a curious result, for it brought to light the letter from Bulwer that Clayton had hidden away, together with his secret memorandum. Aghast, Congress and the public realized how large Bulwer's diplomatic victory had been; and senator after senator arose to aver that he would never have voted for the treaty if he had known of this "outrageous betrayal." But betrayal or no betrayal, there the treaty stood, a firm barrier against closer relations between the United States and Central America. The one benefit that the nation had gained was the development of the Nicaraguan transit route, through which thousands of California-bound Americans continued to pour.

To Walker, as to many another American, the Clayton-Bulwer Treaty now seemed a terrible misfortune for the nation, an evil which it was the obligation of all men of spirit to resist and overcome. The fact that it may have served to avert a war with England was less important to him than the sharp limits which had been set on the expansion of American power to the south.

VIII

"A RASH AND DESPERATE UNDERTAKING"

A new opportunity had come Walker's way. A highly regarded lawyer, Henry P. Watkins, who had a practice in nearby Marysville and was involved in state politics, offered him a partnership. Walker was again restless. He had exhausted the possibilities of San Francisco journalism for challenge and recognition. Without much deliberation, he accepted Watkins' offer and moved to Marysville.

With Watkins looking after the business side of the practice, Walker was able to concentrate on the forensic battles which were the only aspect of legal practice that attracted him. A tribute to his rhetorical power came to him from Stephen J. Field, a colleague of the Marysville bar who later became a Justice of the United States Supreme Court, and who called Walker "a brilliant speaker." This was in his twenty-seventh year. It was not to be expected, however, that his temperament and ambition would permit him to take the slow, steady course to professional affluence and political preferment. Nor did anything in the society around him conduce to a settled life. "Those were the days when the ardor for adventure by land and sea was hot in the breasts of men." The one influence that might have made him give up his romantic dreams for conventional reality, the love of a woman, was absent. If there had been any chance of his finding a flesh-and-blood woman who could displace Ellen Martin's image for him, Marysville was the last place in which to seek her. The shortage of women there was even more acute than in San Francisco. Few newcomers to the town were able to find wives who had not first been prostitutes. Most men patronized the brothels; some became pederasts; more than one arrest was reported in the newspapers for "bestiality." In many instances, Walker's among them, the sexual impulse was suppressed—or rather, transmuted into other forms of action. His chance of emotional liberation had gone with the death of Ellen Martin. The extraordinary heat that he seemed to generate, so that every situation in which he found himself became incandescent and explosive, may well have had its psychological root in sexual abstinence. His maleness found its outlet in an assault, as it were, upon the political timidities of his environment. Frustration must nevertheless have tormented him. There is more than a hint in his life of the same psychic forces that caused Girolamo Savonarola, after a thwarted love affair, to become a monk, and by the intensity of his belief to make himself the master of Florence. One suspects that the tremendous outpouring of Walker's energy into work and the harsh monastic rigors and fatigues that he imposed on his waking life, and at which his friends marveled, were a way of exorcising the female images of night, and allaying the unresolved tensions of continence.

During his year in San Francisco he had met a remarkable personality who, in some ways, so much resembled him that they might almost have been brothers—a French nobleman, Count Gaston Raoul de Raousset-Boulbon. Raousset, like Walker, was a man with a chivalric and romantic stance toward life. Both were idealistic democrats in the French revolutionary tradition; both were imbued with and exalted by the idea of personal heroism. The Frenchman was some seven years older than Walker, similarly short and slender, and with a face distinguished by magnetic eyes. They also matched each other in energy, courage, education, and literary flair. Raousset while in Paris had founded and edited a radical newspaper, *La Liberté,* and had written an emotional novel, *La Conversion,* describing his transformation from aristocrat to democrat.

He had in fact tried his hand at even more professions than Walker: he had been a soldier in Algeria, and in California a miner, a fisherman, a hunter, a cattle dealer. It was in their attitude toward women that they differed most; if Walker was Galahad, Raousset was Don Juan. In France he had fought a number of duels over women, with a ferocity that earned him the sobriquet of *Petit Loup*. One of his literary fragments, a poem written on the eve of his departure from Paris as a penniless adventurer—he had dissipated a fortune on pleasure—caught the essential spirit of him. "My despairing heart runs from one to another; who knows if I shall live to be thirty, whether the future will be gay, or whether I shall be shot; only kiss me, Camille, kiss me."

Early in 1852, the California newspapers began to carry extraordinary news of Raousset. Despite his empty purse, he was the center of the French colony of San Francisco, where one man out of every ten was a Frenchman seeking adventure in adversity. One of their chief topics of conversation was the possibility of wresting from Mexico the southern region of Arizona, then part of the State of Sonora, and reputed to be rich in mineral wealth. A plan to this end quickly took shape in the Count's fertile mind. The population of Sonora was living in terror of the frequent raids southward from Arizona of the savage Apache Indians. It struck Raousset that if he went to Mexico City with the diplomatic support of the French government and offered to lead a French force into Sonora to suppress the Apaches, he might as a reward obtain from the Mexican government a concession to the gold and silver mines of Arizona. And after that, who knew what his power might become?

By the spring of 1852, it seemed that success was close. The rulers of Mexico were as well disposed to the French as they were resentful of Americans. A company was formed to operate the mines, with a suitable distribution of shares to certain Mexican officials; Raousset formally pledged himself to clear the Apaches out of Sonora; the government granted the new company rights to the Arizona mines; and all went with dreamlike precision. Hastening back to San Francisco, Raousset obtained the aid of the French consul in chartering a ship and raising an expeditionary force of 150 of his compatriots, and in May, 1852, sailed for Guaymas, the chief port of Sonora. Since they went nominally as "colonists," and at the invitation of the Mexican government, the American Neutrality Laws were not invoked to prevent their departure.

II

Walker viewed normal life, with its emphasis on security, with the impatience of a race horse hitched to a milk cart. Raousset's glamorous enterprise made the practice of law in Marysville seem insignificant and tawdry. Life in San Francisco had hardened Walker and the duel with Hicks had left more than a physical scar. His respect for the law had been corroded and cracked. The Neutrality Laws which, in his New Orleans days, had caused him to inveigh against General Lopez' filibustering designs on Cuba, now seemed to him merely a legalistic cover for the weakness and timidity of politicians in Washington, three thousand miles away. Were these ill-advised laws to be obeyed while France took Sonora? Was America, after winning the Mexican War, to stop short of one of the chief prizes of victory, the mines of Arizona? Confident of his vision of the American future, he regarded as ignorant and reactionary those laws which seemed to him to sacrifice the future to the present.

The fact that Raousset already had a contract with the Mexican government did not disturb Walker. It was generally thought that the Sonorans were disaffected and ripe for revolution. Why should not Sonora, like California, be given the benefit of American institutions? Why should not an American company, by making a contract with the Sonoran government, put itself in a position where it could either share Raousset's project or displace it?

Although Walker was for the most part soft-spoken, reticent, and thoughtful of demeanor, he was capable of flashing bursts of excitement that illuminated the projects in which he was interested, and made the people around him regard him as their natural leader. His enthusiasm for the Sonoran venture was so contagious that it won over his partner, Watkins, and several other prominent men. That spring of 1852 a group selected by Walker met to discuss the possibility of an American expedition to Sonora. Agreement was reached, money was found, and two of the men present were designated to go to Guaymas, their purpose to obtain permission from the Governor of Sonora to bring into the state a number of American "colonists." The hope proved futile. Before Walker's agents could reach Guaymas, Raousset had already come to terms with the Governor of Sonora. Owning a substantial block of shares in the French mining company, the Governor had no interest in any other expedition, and certainly not one composed of *gringos*. Walker's agents returned to Marysville disappointed, and he and Watkins had reluctantly to go back to their petty practice.

A few months passed and then the fever returned, as fresh news came of Raouset's expedition. It appeared that the military commander of Sonora, General Blanco, who had more actual power than the state's governor, had somehow been overlooked in the distribution of stock in Raousset's company. A San Francisco banking house, with its eye on the Sonora mines, hastily took advantage of the situation to bribe Blanco to its interest. If he would ignore the Mexican government's contract with Raousset, the bankers told him, he could sign one of his own with a new company to be formed for the purpose. Instantly it became Blanco's chief aim to wreck the French expedition. To this end he kept Raousset and his men dangling in Guaymas, on one official pretext or another, until idleness and disease began to take their toll, and supplies began to run short. When at last the Count was allowed to depart for the north his force was gravely enfeebled; and its situation was made worse by wholesale desertions of Mexican muleteers and guides. The wily Blanco then showed his hand by demanding that Raousset's company submit themselves to him and either become Mexican citizens or work as laborers at the mines under his command. Enraged, the French leader sought to organize a revolutionary movement among the Sonoran people, but without success. Finally in desperation he launched an attack against Sonora's capital, Hermosillo, a city of 12,000 where Blanco had a large garrison. In the battle that followed 243 Frenchmen stormed the adobe walls in the face of musket and cannon fire from 1200 Mexicans, took the town, and almost captured Blanco. But still unable to bring the natives to his side, and suffering from fever, Raousset was compelled at last to come to terms with the Mexican, and to leave Sonora.

If this was failure, San Francisco did not know it. On his return, Raousset was greeted as one of the heroes of the age. He further delighted his admirers when, in accepting the honors heaped upon him, he vowed to go back to Mexico. "I cannot live without Sonora," he said. With that he began to prepare for another and larger expedition.

Not to have been part of so stirring an adventure was more than Walker could bear. Early in 1853, he and his partner Watkins called on Raousset and offered their cooperation and services for the new attempt.

"Together," Walker told Raousset, "we would be far more than twice as strong. There are many in the United States who would stand with us and use their influence in our behalf."

Raousset listened courteously and with appreciation of Walker's intensity. "My friends," he replied, "what you say is perhaps true, but I cannot be associated with you. To be frank, Americans are so strongly detested in Mexico that your presence would destroy my chances."

Walker did not argue. With one of his rare smiles he said, "Then we must be rivals."

"So be it," said Raousset, and they shook hands warmly, while the prosaic Watkins looked on in admiration.

The Frenchman was basing his hopes on a report that a revolution had just brought to the Presidency of Mexico General Santa Anna, known to be friendly to France. This was the moment for another visit to Mexico City, to make a new and binding contract; and he would soon be on his way. Walker's plan was far more daring—nothing less than to introduce a force of Americans into Sonora, under the guise of colonists, and make himself master of the state, either with the cooperation of its politicos or without them. Sonora would then declare itself an independent republic, put itself under the protection of the United States, and give the mining concession to an American company, regardless of any contracts with the French signed in Mexico City.

This was also the reasoning of some of San Francisco's wealthy mining men, who were eager to speculate on the chance of a concession for the Sonora mines. Their need was for a leader who could dominate a fighting force recruited from among the adventurers of San Francisco, and at the same time outmaneuver the Frenchman, Raousset, and the Mexican Governor of Sonora. In the view of the San Francisco magnates, Walker's reputation for bravery, his burning conviction, his power of speech, and his legal and journalistic training outweighed his lack of military experience. They would provide him with the necessary backing and funds, they told him, if he would devote himself to the expedition.

Money was raised by the sale of bonds "secured" by the land which Walker expected to obtain in Sonora.

The Independence Loan Fund [the bonds read] has received of ———— ———— the sum of $500, and the Republic of Sonora will issue to him or his assigns a land warrant for one square league of land, to be located on the public domain of said Republic.

Signed, this first day of May,

William Walker,

Colonel of the Independence Regiment*

Sold secretly to selected purchasers, the bonds provided enough money to permit recruitment, the purchase of guns and supplies, and the hiring of a ship. Walker had brought Edmund Randolph and another close friend, Parker Crittenden, also a lawyer, into the project, and together they organized the expedition. He felt, however, that before sailing he needed firsthand information on the conditions that he would have to face; and a few days after Raousset-Boulbon left for Mexico City, the self-created colonel boarded a ship for Guaymas.

Walker found the Sonoran port less than hospitable. The Mexican authorities would not even have permitted him to remain if the American consul had not come to his aid. When he sent a message to the Governor of Sonora, asking permission to call on him, no reply was forthcoming for days. His time had to be spent largely in the small American colony of the town. There several American women spoke of their fear of the Apaches, who had been raiding close to the city, and they begged Walker to bring enough men to Sonora to assure their safety. In this way they provided him with the one ingredient that had been missing from his enterprise—the need of defenseless womanhood for his knightly protection.

The effect that Walker made at Guaymas in 1853, as he appeared in his new role as soldier and liberator, is preserved in an eye-

---

* *Alta California,* Dec. 1, 1853.

witness account. "His appearance was anything else than that of a military chieftain . . . unprepossessing . . . insignificant. . . . But anyone who estimated Mr. Walker by his personal appearance made a great mistake. Extremely taciturn, he would sit for an hour in company without opening his lips; but once interested he arrested your attention with the first word he uttered, and as he proceeded, you felt convinced that he was no ordinary person. To a few confidential friends he was most enthusiastic upon the subject of his darling project, but outside of those immediately interested he never mentioned the topic."*

Presently a message came to him from the Governor: if Walker would come to the capital of Sonora, Hermosillo, they would discuss the matter of colonization and the suppression of the Apaches. Walker smelled a trap. Too much time had gone by. Almost certainly the canny Governor had learned the real purpose of the Americans, and would find a way to dispose of their leader if he once got him in his clutches. The desired land grant would have to be sacrificed. The expedition could no longer hope to mask itself as a group of peaceful colonists; it would have to sail from San Francisco in violation of federal law and fight for Sonora from the moment of its landing. The prospect in no way dismayed Walker. Hastening back to San Francisco, he prepared for action. One hundred men had been recruited, and the brig *Arrow* was in readiness, with a cargo of guns, ammunition, food, and other stores needed for a campaign.

The San Francisco press knew Walker's intention, and encouraged him. *Alta California,* reporting the murder in Sonora of eighty people by Apaches in a single week, declared, "They cannot protect themselves, and the government cannot protect them." But the American military authorities saw the matter otherwise. On September 30, 1853, Walker's plan came to a sudden halt when the United States Army general in command at San Francisco ordered the *Arrow* seized on suspicion that it was to be used to violate the Neutrality Laws.

With Edmund Randolph as his attorney, Walker instantly filed suit to have the vessel released; but the outlook was dark and he did not intend to submit to any lengthy legal process. Instead, he

---

* T. Robinson Warren, *Dust and Foam,* 1858.

had another brig, the *Caroline,* fitted out for his purposes and, with as many of his recruits as could be hastily rounded up, secretly boarded the vessel, weighed anchor and stood out to sea before they could be intercepted. Forty-five men were with him. The date was October 8, 1853. Before he sailed he received news which must have heartened him. French rivalry no longer was a threat. Count Raousset-Boulbon had fallen out with President Santa Anna, had been forced to flee Mexico for his life, and was back in San Francisco.

III

Walker was being driven by idealism and ambition together—an irresistible combination when their thrust is in the same direction. He believed with all his heart that the democratic institutions of the United States offered hope to the peoples of the world and that there was an obligation on Americans to bring the light of democracy to their benighted neighbors. At the same time he held in his heart the heroic dream of world fame. All his secret aspirations were centered on the overcoming of enemies and victory in battle—but in the name of right, justice, and the United States.

He was undismayed by the appearance of absurdity. There was in him just that touch of fanaticism required to ignore public opinion when it ran counter to his own convictions. His true profession was heroism. Like Raousset, another incurable romantic, Walker could no more resist an opportunity to risk everything for a high purpose than a dedicated surgeon could refuse a chance to pit his skill against death. He had become an addict of danger. Regardless of the practical purpose of the Sonoran enterprise as conceived by his backers, to him from the beginning it had always been a personal test, a feat of arms against great odds, by which a man might overnight enter the ranks of glory for the sake of his country. His failure on this, his first try at war and conquest, was abysmal, it was grotesque; and yet it had about it something that was not of the time, a hint of ancient quest and knightly fortitude, a touch of grandeur that men recognized, and that in time caused the laughter and the sneers to die away, and Walker to emerge a larger figure than ever in the eyes of the California public.

In a broad political sense as well, the expedition was by no means fruitless. Although commentators have called it "an inexcusable raid on an unoffending people" and "a rash and desperate undertaking which needs the pen of a Cervantes to do it justice," the fact remains that it played a considerable, if indirect, part in the acquisition by the United States of 45,000 square miles of Mexican territory, an area as large as the state of Pennsylvania, and containing the valuable minerals coveted by California interests, as well as a desirable railroad route. This was the so-called Gadsden Purchase, which a few months later was incorporated with the territories of Arizona and New Mexico.

Walker's original strategic plan called for a landing near Guaymas, but he was compelled to change it. With fewer than fifty men, he could not hope to contend with the strong Mexican garrison at Guaymas. A suitable base of operations was needed at which to assemble additional recruits, promote a native insurrection against the Sonoran government, and finally launch an invasion. For this purpose he decided that his first conquest had to be the sparsely populated peninsula of Lower California, less than a hundred miles across the Gulf of California from Sonora. The *Caroline* accordingly put in at La Paz, the capital, and Walker landed his force. Without firing a shot they quickly made a prisoner of the Governor of the state, put him on board the brig, hauled down the Mexican flag over his house and raised in its place the flag of the "Republic of Lower California."

To the natives he gave assurance that his purpose was to lead a successful revolution for them against the tyranny of Mexico. Lower California, he stated in a proclamation, was "free, sovereign and independent." Its people no longer owed allegiance to Mexico. He himself would serve as President of the new nation until it was firmly established.

Subsequently his men beat back an attack from a small Mexican force, and captured a Mexican revenue cutter. There was danger that a major expedition might sail against Walker from nearby Guaymas, and not as yet wishing to face such a risk, he sailed north. The port of Ensenada, only one hundred miles south of the American border, struck him as a suitable place at which to marshal the reinforcements that he expected, and from which communication could readily be maintained with the United States. He took possession of the town without bloodshed, and issued a statement for the American people, elaborating his aims. Lower California, he said, had been shamefully neglected by the Mexican government. His purpose in creating the new republic was to develop the resources of the peninsula and "to effect a proper social organization therein." To accomplish this, it was first necessary to achieve independence from Mexico. He had therefore established a government of Americans to begin to administer the country. A list of "cabinet appointments" of chosen officers followed.

This large declaration, coming from a man of twenty-nine years and no military experience, and whose minuscule force consisted in the main of dockside toughs, undisciplined and untried, struck many Americans as ridiculous when they read of it. But it was more astute than Walker's contemporaries realized. He was gambling on sustained support from his backers in San Francisco. To show anything less than complete confidence would have been folly. Everything depended on the reinforcements and supplies that Henry Watkins was supposed to bring him. If the San Francisco newspapers failed to carry word, and bold word, of his achievements and purpose, the entire project might collapse from inattention.

While he awaited Watkins, he had to lead his men in his first serious battle. Two hundred Mexican soldiers, advancing from the north, entered Ensenada and laid siege to a house which he had selected as a fort. The defense was strong and competent, and after three days of bloody fighting, a bold sortie routed the attackers. The elation of victory did not last long, however. One morning soon thereafter the ship *Caroline,* on which most of Walker's provisions were stored, was seen to be hoisting anchor and making sail. Incredulously Walker and his men saw it put out to sea on a southward course, ignoring all his signals. Later it appeared that the crew had succumbed to the bribes of their prisoner, the Governor of Lower California, who had been left on board.

A few days later, the brig *Anita* put into the harbor, carrying Watkins and 230 men, full of zeal and expectation. Walker's first question was, what supplies had Watkins brought? The answer bore out his fears. The *Anita* carried guns and ammunition, but little food.

This was a terrible blow. As soon as the new men had disembarked, Watkins had to turn around and sail for California; everything depended on the speed with which he could return with a cargo of provisions. Meanwhile, with so many mouths to feed, Walker sought a way to obtain supplies without arousing the animosity of the rancheros by raids on their land. His scouts learned that a noted Mexican outlaw, Melendrez, whose camp was nearby, had considerable supplies of corn as well as cattle and horses; and in a surprise attack on Melendrez' camp, Walker seized this booty. His problem, however, remained acute. Reduced rations consisting entirely of beef and corn took a toll of his men's morale, already weakening from idleness and disease. They resented, too, the strict discipline that Walker enforced, especially his threat to shoot any man who robbed a house or raped a woman. The signs of impending mutiny were unmistakable.

IV

News of Walker's proclamation of independence had gone to Mexico City, and there it produced political consequences which were to deprive his venture, in American eyes, of its purpose. The Mexican government was then being pressed by the American minister, James Gadsden, to sell northern Sonora for $10,000,000 plus assurance that the Apaches would be prevented from raiding into Mexico. The price was felt by Mexican officials to be outrageously low, and the offer as a whole insulting, but they had to consider whether the United States, if balked, might not use force to compel submission. They had been shocked by Walker's raid on La Paz; now the news from Ensenada that Lower California had been declared independent under American rule seemed to presage disaster for Mexico. Fearing that Walker was secretly abetted by the American government, they came to the conclusion that if they did not consent to negotiate they might lose both the peninsula and Sonora, without compensation. The result was a provisional treaty hastily drawn and signed on December 31, 1853, in which Gadsden's terms were met. A separate letter from him assured the Mexican government that the United States regarded Walker as a violator of federal law, and would deal with him accordingly.

From this point, Walker's expedition lost its appeal for Americans. With the coveted mineral-bearing part of Sonora secured for the United States, who cared about Lower California, or about "effecting a proper social organization" in Sonora?

Adversity now multiplied its forms. A Mexican gunboat appeared off Ensenada and patrolled the coast to prevent further reinforcement of Walker's troops; and almost at the same time an American warship, the *Portsmouth*, anchored in the harbor. Its commander came ashore, met with Walker, gave him news of the Gadsden Purchase, and warned him: he could expect no further aid from his friends in San Francisco, and certainly none from the government of the United States.

The provisional treaty that Gadsden had signed with Mexico struck Walker as altogether unsatisfactory. Its chief defect was its failure to provide an outlet for the United States on the Gulf of California—a limitation certain to hamper the development of the American southwest, Mexico and Central America. The fact remained that Walker could do nothing about it. His military situation was desperate, and he admitted as much to his officers. The question was, had they any choice but to slink home to the jeers of San Francisco? Was there still a chance to convert humiliation into glory? If the venture was not to be abandoned, there was only one direction in which to move—Sonora. His staff agreed: any risk, however rash, was preferable to certain dishonor. So long as there was something still to try, self-respect demanded that they go on. Walker thought it barely possible, but nevertheless possible, that a Sonoran insurrection against Mexico could be fomented, would submit to his leadership, and bring the Gulf of California under American control. On this remote chance he now staked everything.

V

How does a foreigner make a revolution in a place where his countrymen are hated, where his motives are suspect, and when he is not even there? Walker conceived the idea of beginning with an assembly of disaffected elements in Lower California. Then, bolstered by popular support, he would cross the Colorado River into Sonora and try to win over enough natives to give momentum to his cause. In this hope, he issued another proclamation, asserting Sonora's independence from Mexico, with the status of an independent republic, like that of Lower California.

Food was a major consideration. This time there was no alternative to foraging. The regiment ranged the countryside around Ensenada, commandeering cattle and corn in the name of the revolution, and stirring up hot indignation among landowners. On the whole, there was little violence, and Walker's orders against pillage were respected. But the restrictions that he enforced on his men's behavior became increasingly aggravating to them as their situation deteriorated. Although his officers, who were in daily contact with him and felt the impact of his own conviction, remained steadfast, the morale of the soldiers in the ranks was cracking badly, and they needed only an excuse to show their resentment.

The crisis came when Walker, organizing the transport of supplies into Sonora, gave orders that horses which had been taken from the outlaw Melendrez were to be used for this purpose. A number of his men had come to regard these mounts as their own and they flatly refused to turn them over to their officers. Summoned to the spot, Walker was met by open complaints and even threats.

It appeared that the expedition was about to founder in turmoil and disgrace. Those of the men who were still loyal to Walker waited pessimistically to see what he would do. His response startled them. He ordered the bugler to blow assembly. Hesitantly, the men formed ranks and stood at attention. After a long moment of silence, he spoke to them in a ringing voice, and in courteous, restrained language.

"If any of you wish to leave the expedition, you are free to do so. I shall not compel anyone to remain who wishes to go. Those of you who wish to stay with me I shall ask to signify their loyalty by taking an oath of allegiance to the flag of Lower California. Let there be no misunderstanding. I shall expect the men who follow me to abide by the highest standards of military behavior. Those who wish to go can fill their pockets with rations and leave camp. I shall expect them to be gone within two hours. The American boundary is only a three or four days' march from here. Any of you who do not wish to take the oath of allegiance will step forward, put down your rifles, and go to the supply depot for rations."

About fifty of the men left the formation, and gathered in a group to one side, talking among themselves. Some were embarrassed and uncertain, others in a state of intense anger. Finally they decided on a course of action. Instead of accepting Walker's offer, they turned and began to walk away from the camp, their rifles still in their hands.

Walker's aide, Captain Timothy Crocker, known for his courage, rushed after the deserters and ordered them to drop their guns. When no one obeyed, he drew his pistol. A man snarled, "Go on, shoot, Captain. I dare you." Several rifles were aimed at Crocker. At this point, without waiting for orders, another of Walker's officers ran to a nearby howitzer, already loaded, and trained it on the mutineers, ready to fire if Crocker were shot. Walker shouted, "Hold your fire!" For a moment, no one stirred; then the sullen men turned their backs on Crocker and continued to walk away. Walker jumped on a horse, and rode after them. An eyewitness, reporting the subsequent scene, was astonished by the kindliness and calmness of his voice when he overtook them. "Men," he said, "you are going to need rations, and you had better go back for them. I shall not try to take your rifles from you, but you know as well as I do that they are badly needed, and they belong to the regiment. I ask you to leave them behind."

More than half of the men put their rifles down. Two or three expressed their frustration and rage by smashing the butts on nearby rocks before they turned away. Some went back for rations. The entire group crossed the American border safely, and were taken by steamer to San Francisco. It was largely from their bitter testimony that the American press formed its judgment of Walker at this time. He was accused of being excessively harsh with his men, and of believing that "might makes right." But better than anyone else, he had reason to know that might does not make right, for the might was always with others, not with him. In Lower California it was the men behind him who had the power, not he. All they had to do was snap their fingers at him, and he was finished. What he depended on, in the final test, was discipline, or the idea of discipline. In order to hold in check the self-assertive and unruly men who had volunteered for this adventure, he had to focus the full power of his personality on every breach of discipline. Boyish, slight, physically unimpressive, possessed only of an indomitable will and searching grey eyes, he held them by a thin thread. A single lapse in their respect for him would have been fatal. To command them, he had to make them fear, not so much himself, as the disciplined response of their comrades to his orders. In this he was surprisingly successful. After the mass desertion at Ensenada, he increased, rather than diminished the severity of his discipline, for he knew that the least relaxation would invite further mutiny from men to whom the least restriction was galling. The punctilio of military etiquette was not abated for an instant. Privates were expected to salute their officers. Men stood at attention when addressed by their superiors in rank. All were warned that the death sentence would be imposed on mutineers and deserters. In practice, however, this rule was modified. Of four men who subsequently deserted after having taken the oath of allegiance, only the leader was shot; the others were driven from the camp.

When he finally marched out of Ensenada Walker had to leave behind him many who had been wounded or were ill. His active force numbered only 130. Establishing temporary headquarters at San Vicente, some thirty miles south of Ensenada, he spent ten days in a diligent search for natives who might lend themselves to his revolutionary purpose. Finally he convened an assembly of 62 Mexicans, who were received in a setting as impressive as ingenuity, in that poverty-stricken land, could make it—complete with a guard of honor, a vestigial military band, and a display of the flags of the new republics of Sonora and Lower California. There were oaths of allegiance, cheers, the firing of field pieces. A written declaration of loyalty prepared by the assembly and addressed to Walker gave him sanction, as the leader of the revolution, for further foraging and requisitioning of provisions.

When at last, leaving a small garrison in San Vicente, he led his shrunken regiment on the 200-mile march eastward to the Colorado River, they drove a herd of cattle before them. It took two weeks of wearisome struggle to climb up the rugged trails of the Sierras and down again almost to the mouth of the Colorado. By this time they were in rags, and their boots were worn through; Walker himself had lost one boot, and had improvised a kind of sandal in its place, giving a special touch of the grotesque to his emaciated little figure. Exhausted though they were, they had no choice, he said, but to go on. Somewhere in that arid countryside they found wood with which to build rafts. The great question was whether the cattle could be made to swim across the river, which ran wide, deep and swift. An hour later they had their answer; the men and some bags of corn crossed safely, but such cattle as could be driven into the river were swept away and perished.

They were, then, in Sonora, and finished; almost without food, almost without shoe leather, totally without hope. Seventy miles up the river, they knew, was Fort Yuma, under the American flag. Half of the men did not stop for Walker's decision, but deserted and started their northward trek at once. The others waited for their commander to lead them in the same direction. To their considerable resentment, he refused. A skinny hollow-eyed scarecrow standing among scarecrows, he maintained his military dignity, saying that he would give his orders at the right time; and somehow he kept his hold on them.

Three days later he knew that he could expect no aid or comfort from the Sonorans. His half-starved, bearded men lined up at his order, and in silence heard him say that they would march back to San Vicente, for the comrades who had been left there could not be abandoned to the Mexicans. From San Vicente they would go north again across the desert to the United States. Grimly they listened, and obeyed—recrossed the river, and laboriously began to climb the stony mountain trails behind their leader.

VI

May 8, 1854, was Walker's thirtieth birthday. This was the day on which, with the thirty-four men who were all that remained to him, he staggered toward the American military post across the border in California. The last thirty miles had been under the hot desert sun, without food and almost without water. Continuous harassment by the Mexican outlaws commanded by Melendrez, and who rode, jeering, just beyond bullet reach, added the final note of irony to that march. But even now, with his exhausted, parched, and starving little troop at its last gasp, the preservation of dignity was important to Walker. Presenting himself to the American military commander at San Diego, and holding himself erect, he said formally, "I am Colonel William Walker. I wish to surrender my force to the United States."

He was arraigned before the Federal Court in San Francisco on an indictment by a Grand Jury, charged with violation of the Neutrality Laws. His partner, Watkins, had already been tried under the same auspices, convicted and fined $1500—a light penalty, as the judge pointed out, since the chief interest of the court was vindication of the law. Filibustering, as seen by public opinion, was a doomed profession. Walker's rival, Count Raousset-Boulbon, had failed in yet another attempt to enter Sonora with a military force, and was soon to face a Mexican firing squad. Major General John E. Wool, newly appointed to the command of the Department of the Pacific of the United States Army, had made public an order from President Pierce: "You will, to the utmost of your ability, use all proper means to detect the fitting out of armed expeditions against countries with which the United States are at peace, and will zealously cooperate with the civil authorities in maintaining the Neutrality Laws." It was Wool's watchfulness that had brought Watkins into court. *Alta California* exulted in the demonstration that the courts of San Francisco had done "what New York and New Orleans failed, discreditably failed, to do"—upheld the federal law against filibustering. All the auguries seemed to be against Walker when, with Edmund Randolph again at his side, he heard the clerk of the court read the charges, and answered, "Not guilty."

The trial was put off for four months, and he was set free on Randolph's recognizance. In spite of his failure and the gibes of the newspapers, Walker's reputation, it appeared, was far from shattered. The loyal men who had returned with him from Mexico, whatever their resentments of him as a martinet, had no fault to find with him as fighting man, and the San Francisco press began to change its tune. Even his insistence on preserving his military dignity under conditions of despair was now seen in a sympathetic light. Everywhere he went he was a center of respectful attention. His friends, especially Watkins and Randolph, urged him to enter politics, and sufficiently persuaded him so that he returned to Marysville, as a base of candidacy for public office.

Delegates were then being chosen for the Democratic State Convention of 1854, and "Mr. Walker of Yuba County" was among those elected. When the Convention met in the Baptist Church of Sacramento, on July 18, he was one of its prominent figures, although still under indictment.*

VII

Nothing in which Walker participated was ever quiet, and the Convention was no exception. The chief issue of the time was the contest for control of the State Democratic Party between David C. Broderick, President of the State Senate, who came from New York City and was an ardent free-soiler and strong antislavery man, and United States Senator William M. Gwin, formerly of Mississippi, a Southern fire-eater who never stopped urging the introduction of slavery into California. Walker from the first was a Broderick man and, when he arrived at the Convention, his faction, which had a slight majority, at once made him Chairman of the Platform Committee, Chairman of the Committee to Nominate Permanent Officers, and Keynote Speaker. Nothing could more have outraged Gwin's followers. Not only did they refuse to let the Convention be organized unless the slavery interest was given equal representation, but they backed their refusal by setting up their own separate committees. Noisy confusion and turmoil prevented the Convention from making any progress on its first morning, and there were even threats of violence from Gwin's supporters, most of whom came from the South, and were quick to turn to guns when tempers flared. In their eyes Walker was a traitor to his Southern origin.

When, on the afternoon of the first day, he rose to speak, the hall was tense. He had hardly begun when a Gwin man yelled that he was nothing but a tool of Yankee abolitionists. Bedlam broke out while Walker waited quietly on the platform. Suddenly a shot was heard. Later it was reported that a nervous delegate had been handling his pistol to make sure it was loaded, and that it had accidentally gone off, but at the time it was believed the shot was aimed at Walker. The effect was cataclysmic. Several delegates

---

* H. S. Hoblitzell, *Early Historical Sketch of the City of Marysville and Yuba County,* 1876.

jumped out of the windows, others engaged in fist fights, while Broderick's men rushed to protect Walker. Eventually quiet was restored, but as soon as Walker tried to resume his speech, he was again hooted down by the Gwin element. Thus the first day's session ended.

Overnight an arrangement was made that the Gwin and Broderick factions would meet the next day in separate halls, and try to negotiate a compromise. Walker, never more mild and reasonable then when he was the center of turmoil, was appointed as chairman of a "Committee of Compromise and Reconciliation" for his group, and led his associates to a meeting with their opponents. The result was predictable. Gwin's people rejected all compromise; one man even went so far as to propose, in a formal motion, that Walker be thrown out of a window. On that note the Convention fell apart.

IX

THE OPENING OF THE GATE

Walker's first experience in practical American politics was his last. He never ran for office. For a time after the Convention he busied himself with political journalism, contributing regularly to the *Democratic State Journal* of Sacramento, a Broderick organ. But soon there entered into his orbit a new personality, who was to have a determining influence on his subsequent career. This was Byron Cole, a well-to-do, ambitious, and sophisticated young man, who had recently come to San Francisco from New England, and had bought control of a declining conservative newspaper, the *Commercial-Advertiser*, so as to have a vantage point from which to seek out greater opportunities. Cole, who had covered the Democratic Convention for his newspaper, saw in Walker's gift of leadership a magic ingredient which, in combination with his own connections, might achieve great things, and he invited Walker to return to San Francisco as editor of the *Commercial-Advertiser*. The post itself appealed to Walker less than other journalistic openings that were available to him, but Cole was able to add compelling inducements. From the first it was Manifest Destiny, rather than journalism, that linked the two men.

Cole's voyage to California had been by way of Nicaragua, and

93

what he saw there had convinced him that the country was ripe for American intervention. The alternative was sustained chaos. Civil war was almost continuous. The rapid alternation of dictatorship and revolt was like the pulse of a feverish patient, sick with despair. In a period of six years, fifteen presidents had held power, their capitals shifting between Granada in the south, where the aristocratic party known as the Legitimists had its base, and León in the north, the stronghold of the Democrats. The country was beautiful to look upon and rich in natural resources; it had valuable lumber—mahogany, cedar, Brazilwood—in inexhaustible quantities; it produced gold, silver, copper, lead, iron, sulphur; its plantations grew cacao, sugar, cotton, indigo, tobacco, maize, wheat, rice, and a hundred fruits, vegetables, and spices; cattle were abundant; but the people had been ravaged beyond endurance by poverty, war, and disease. Repeated conscription of males into the warring armies of the politicos was a major source of misery. Women outnumbered men three to two, in some villages five to one, while the population remained almost static, at some 250,000.

The current revolution was an attempt to oust from the Presidency Fruto Chamorro, the formidable leader of the Legitimists. Supported by wealthy rancheros and, behind the scenes, by the British government, Chamorro had forced his way to the Presidency in order to prevent the Democratic government from forming a new liberal federation with Honduras and San Salvador; and he had changed the Nicaraguan constitution to give himself dictatorial powers. The desperate Democrats, foreseeing their doom, had promptly set up a rebel government in León. Other Central American states, in which there was an almost identical division of parties, threw their influence into the struggle. Honduras, with a liberal administration friendly to the United States, supported the Democrats; while Costa Rica, where the British enjoyed great influence under a conservative government, gave active aid to Chamorro.

In the early months of 1854, the hopes of the Democrats had been lifted by a substantial military reinforcement from Honduras. But England's agents in Central America soon managed to reverse the trend. Their strategy was simple and effective. Guatemala, where there was a conservative regime, was encouraged to threaten neighboring Honduras with war, with the result that the Honduran government hastily withdrew its soldiers from Nicaragua in order to strengthen its own defenses. This was an almost mortal blow to the Nicaraguan Democrats. It appeared unlikely that they could long sustain themselves against the attack which the Legitimists could be counted on to launch as soon as their army was sufficiently strong.

The situation as outlined by Cole inflamed Walker's imagination, and revived in him the vision of the "column of Progress and Democracy" about which he had written in New Orleans. The United States and especially California, had a great stake in Nicaragua, with its overland Transit and its potentialities for a canal. If British domination of the isthmus was to be prevented, America could not afford to delay in asserting its democratic leadership. The indifference of President Pierce's administration to England's manipulation of the Central American governments was rapidly destroying the prestige of the United States among them. Neutrality Laws or no Neutrality Laws, the Democrats of Nicaragua deserved American support, and the United States could not afford to withhold it.

What if a band of privately organized American fighting men undertook the task? They might turn the tide of the Nicaraguan struggle, and compel action by Washington. An O'Higgins had rescued Chile from Spanish oppression; a Walker might save Nicaragua from native tyranny. Under friendly tutelage from the North, Nicaragua might set a shining example of economic creativity for the entire isthmus. She might even become the center of a Caribbean alliance with close ties with the United States.

The prospect, with its potentialities of glory and its idealistic aspect, was irresistibly attractive to Walker, as for more practical reasons it was to Byron Cole. If the Democratic effort failed, Cole was aware, the government of Honduras would almost certainly go down with it and be replaced by a pro-British regime. In that event American business interests in Honduras would be imperiled—and Cole was one of the owners of the Honduras Mining and Trading Company, which was about to exploit a large tract of mineral-bearing lands. He was eager for action to protect his interests, and no sooner had Walker accepted the proffered post on the *Commercial-Advertiser,* than the publisher embarked on a ship for Nicaragua, to explore the situation.

I I

It was autumn of 1854, and Cole had not yet returned, when Walker stood trial on charges of having violated the Neutrality Laws in his Sonoran enterprise. He came before the federal court as editor of a respectable newspaper and a figure of considerable prominence. Addressing the jury in his own behalf, he began with an appeal to their sense of fair play. The Neutrality Laws he believed to be injurious to the country, and probably unconstitutional, but if they were to be regarded as law, then the courts had an obligation to prosecute equally all who were believed to have violated them. Yet none of the Frenchmen who had gone to Mexico with Count Raousset-Boulbon had been brought to trial. Why should the government choose Americans for punishment? The point was particularly effective for the jury owing to the circumstance, perhaps prearranged, that some of the Frenchmen who had been associated with Raousset's ill-starred adventure were sitting in the courtroom, scot-free, as Walker spoke.

Primarily, however, Walker rested his belief that he was not guilty on the moral aspect of his case. The people of Sonora were notoriously oppressed by a corrupt government and were virtually without protection against the raids of the terrifying Apaches. When he had been at Guaymas, Mexicans as well as Americans, women as well as men had urged him to return. He had felt a call that transcended mere legalistic niceties. "It was then that I took my decision and made my plan, which, had it not been for the interference of the government, might have succeeded," he told the jury.

His failure he attributed to the federal authorities. When they prevented the sailing of the whole body of men who had volunteered to accompany him, when they deprived him of needful stores and field-pieces, all began to go awry. As a result, "I found myself at sea with only forty-five men, and with so few followers I was compelled to land in a sparsely settled region. Some sort of flag had to be raised to protect us." They had been able to sustain their long ordeal in Lower California and their nightmare marches across the mountains and desert only by the consciousness that "right and humanity" were on their side. "The Pilgrim fathers came to a savage land, rescued it from savages and made it an abode of civilization." Was there not always a moral sanction for men who sought to emulate them?

The federal prosecutor, District Attorney Inge, would have none of this. Scoffing at Walker's claim to a humane purpose, he said that regardless of whether he had intended to protect the Sonorans against Apaches or to loot the country, the expedition had violated the Neutrality Laws and Walker was guilty. The judge obviously shared this view of the case, for his summation of evidence and charge to the jury were distinctly unfavorable to Walker. The jury, however, consisted of men in whom the expansionist spirit of the age and the belief in America's Manifest Destiny were stronger than merely legal considerations. After only eight minutes of deliberation, they returned with a verdict of not guilty. Some of the San Francisco newspapers were concerned; Watkins, who was only an agent of Walker's, had been found guilty, while Walker himself was acquitted; was this justice? But the *Herald* replied that Watkins was Watkins, and Walker was Walker, and this seemed to be sufficient answer.

Walker's reputation, which five months earlier had been shattered by failure, now rose intact and brighter than ever. It was rumored that a new Walker expedition, its goal as yet unknown, was in the making, and men eager for adventure sought him out and offered their services in whatever project he might be planning.

III

By late October, Cole was back in San Francisco, bearing with him a signed letter from the Provisional Director of the Democratic rebel government, Francisco de Castellon. If Cole would bring three hundred men to Nicaragua to serve in the Democratic army, the letter said, they would receive regular pay and land grants after Castellon became head of the national government. To Cole's disappointment, Walker found the letter useless. To attempt to raise an expedition with no better legal ground than it contained would lay them open to immediate arrest for violation of the Neutrality Laws—and with little hope, this time, of escaping conviction. The need, he told Cole, was for a formal grant of a substantial tract of land in Nicaragua and for permission to colonize it—a contractual document which would say nothing of a military purpose. If Cole could obtain such a grant, "something might be done with it," Walker said. Even then, if the federal authorities insisted on probing beneath the surface of the contract, the expedition might not be allowed to sail.

Cole had begun to count heavily on Walker, and he was impelled to make another voyage to Nicaragua. By this time his connection with the *Commercial-Advertiser* had become so tenuous that he saw no purpose in maintaining his interest in the newspaper, and he sold it. Simultaneously, Walker resigned as editor and accepted a similar position in Sacramento, with the *State Democratic Journal.* He was still regarded as a promising political figure, for whom high public office in California was a distinct possibility. Two months passed. Then, early in 1855, Cole sent from Nicaragua a contract, signed by Castellon, and meeting Walker's specifications. This time his efforts bore fruit. On receipt of the contract, Walker at once gave up his post with the *State Democratic Journal* and returned to San Francisco to prepare for his next adventure. He had been given the key to political advancement, and he threw it away with a shrug, as a married man might throw away the key to a prostitute's room; he was in fact married to danger, and he regarded politics as prostitution.

The decisive question for him was whether, in view of President Pierce's recent proclamation against filibustering, Major General Wool would accept Castellon's colonization grant as sufficient justification for the sailing of an armed force from the port. The prospect was by no means hopeful. Wool had achieved much publicity by urging the prosecution of the French consul in San Francisco on the ground that he had aided the filibustering expedition of Raousset-Boulbon. Although a jury had failed to convict the consul, it seemed likely that the general's policy in respect to future expeditions would be stern. District Attorney Inge, still smarting from his defeat at Walker's hands in the trial resulting from the Sonora affair, was not likely to be cooperative. Nevertheless, having gone so far with Cole, Walker was obligated to try to convince Inge and Wool that the fighting men he planned to recruit would be no more than peaceful colonists on their way to a foreign land. Everything would depend on their willingness to let themselves be deceived.

IV

In the period when Walker was practicing law in Marysville, Commodore Vanderbilt had taken it into his head to go abroad; and the impulse that removed him from New York and from active supervision of his affairs introduced a radical change in the unfolding pattern of events, and gave a dramatic new turn to Walker's life story. The repercussions of Vanderbilt's decision were felt finally in the attitude of District Attorney Inge toward Walker's enterprise.

Between Vanderbilt and total success in life there stood, to his way of thought, only one obstacle—the social barrier. In spite of his great wealth, he and his family had not been able to escape the stigma of the *parvenu*, had never been able to penetrate the high society of the period. The invitations that they most desired were withheld from them, and they had to find their friends in families whose riches were as recent as their own. This was intolerable, and he conceived a plan for dealing with the problem. Believing that the surest key to the locked door of aristocracy is fame, and that the short cut to fame is publicity, he decided to generate such publicity as no mere millionaire before him had ever received. He would compel the bows of New Yorkers who professed to regard him as a vulgar money-man, by first compelling the respectful attention of the entire world.

For his instrument, he decided on a steam yacht, which was designed to his specifications in 1852. The *North Star,* 2500 tons, 270 feet long, cost him half a million dollars to build and half as much again to operate each year. Engineered to perfection, with an interior in which marble flooring, granite columns, rosewood paneling, and frescoed ceilings created the effect of a luxury hotel, it was by far the largest and most elaborate pleasure craft seen in American waters up to that time. Even before it was completed in 1853, Vanderbilt announced an intention that delighted New York's sensation-hungry newspapers. With his family and a few friends and retainers, he would take the *North Star* on a gala transatlantic voyage such as no American had ever previously undertaken. It was easy to envisage the stir his magnificent boat would make in the ports of England, France, Italy, Russia—tangible proofs for haughty European eyes of the potentialities of American enterprise. Everyone could imagine the brilliant receptions that would be given on board for the aristocracy of Europe, the enviable invitations received in return. Thereafter, the Commodore calculated, even the proudest New York homes would be open to the Vanderbilts—while the huge advertisement could hardly fail to benefit his business interests.

He had to consider, however, that the trip as planned would

consume the better part of half a year. What of the companies that he managed? On this score, as always, his decisions were bold, simple, and profitable. The subsequent deal, when its details became known, made other millionaires quiver with envy. By this time, Vanderbilt had got rid of those in Accessory Transit who were capable of offering resistance to his will, and a puppet board of directors obligingly met his terms. Almost overnight he sold to the company the ships of his Nicaragua Line for $1,500,000, resigned from the presidency, opened his own office as exclusive New York agent for the company, and took as his emolument no less than 20 per cent of the company's gross receipts—this for continuing to manage the ships—plus an agent's commission of 2½ per cent of all passenger fares.

At a later time, the arrangement was criticized as an outrage against business morality, but Vanderbilt calmly maintained that it was no more than his due as founder and moving spirit of the Transit. By this stroke he relieved himself of responsibility, added to his fortune and assured himself of an enormous income without giving up power. It was a neat, compact plan. He not only ate his cake and had it; he also sold it.

A problem remained—who could properly manage the affairs of Accessory Transit while he was abroad? Two strong and capable executives were needed—one in whose hands he could safely leave the New York headquarters, the other to look after the San Francisco end of the business. Searching his acquaintance, he turned to Charles Morgan, a prominent shipowner, almost as well-known as Vanderbilt himself, and whose Morgan Line dominated the traffic between New York and the ports of the Gulf of Mexico. When Morgan, in return for a share in the commissions earned by the New York agency, consented to serve as Vanderbilt's deputy, the Commodore was flattered. In addition, Morgan was able to settle the question of the California agency. He had formed a connection with a redoubtable man of business, Cornelius K. Garrison, who had made a fortune as a banker in Panama, and who was at that very time planning to establish a banking house in San Francisco. It was Morgan's suggestion that Garrison be invited to New York and induced to manage Accessory Transit's affairs on the West Coast. So it was arranged; Vanderbilt was impressed by Garrison; and a sufficient inducement was found for him in a contract at a salary of $60,000 per year, placing Garrison among the highest-paid men in the United States.

V

The cruise amply fulfilled Vanderbilt's hopes. While everything that Walker did was the wild gamble of a moneyless man, his only stake his life, Vanderbilt's least venture was expensively planned in detail. He did indeed experience one or two snubs from British aristocrats, but these were more than balanced in his eyes by a reception given in his honor by leading Americans in London. There he met many of the great political and social figures of England, and after that, the rest was easy. Admiring descriptions of his career and his yacht appeared in the British press and were circulated throughout the world. The London *Daily News* compared him favorably with Cosimo de Medici, and added, "It is time that *parvenu* should be looked upon as a word of honor. . . . It is time that the middle classes should take the place that is rightfully theirs in the world that they have made." In Paris, men of prominence respectfully approached Vanderbilt with business proposals; in Italy he sat for a portrait bust by America's most noted sculptor, Hiram Powers; in Russia the Czar himself took an interest in the *North Star* and gave Vanderbilt the use of one of the imperial carriages. From first to last, the cruise sparkled like the gem of self-assertion that it was. But it had its flaw. Letters from New York which came to Vanderbilt just before he sailed for home told of maneuvers by Morgan and Garrison to oust him permanently from control of Accessory Transit. Under Morgan's leadership, the company had canceled its contract with the Commodore's agency, on the ground that it had proved "impossible to obtain a statement of accounts" from Vanderbilt. There was even a suggestion that he had defrauded the company. A new agency, owned by Morgan, now handled all Transit business in New York, and took the commissions which the Commodore regarded as his own; while Garrison had allied the West Coast operation with Morgan.

In the last days of the voyage Vanderbilt burned with a desire for revenge. Knowing his temper, Wall Street held its breath as the *North Star* was reported steaming back to New York. When, in September, 1853, the *Herald* commented that "trouble is expected upon the return of Commodore Vanderbilt," the sophisticated chuckled at the dry understatement. A few days after his return, Vanderbilt addressed to Morgan and Garrison one of the shortest and most famous letters in the history of business. "Gentlemen," it said, "You have undertaken to cheat me. I won't sue you, for the law is too slow. I'll ruin you. Yours truly, Cornelius Vanderbilt."

To many, the threat, which was published, sounded like bombast. Morgan and Garrison were men of wealth, power, and driving energy comparable with Vanderbilt's own. Within six months of his arrival in San Francisco, Garrison had been elected Mayor of the city, while his administration of the company on the Pacific side was an unqualified success. Morgan had similarly proved an efficient manager of the business in New York. The service on the Nicaragua Line, everyone agreed, had never been so satisfactory, the profits of Accessory Transit had never been so high. The price of the shares had risen 50 per cent above what it had been at the time of Vanderbilt's retirement from the presidency, and the sentiment of the investment community was largely with Morgan.

The courts of New York soon swarmed with lawyers in *Vanderbilt vs. Accessory Transit Company, C. Morgan and C. K. Garrison.* So numerous were the charges and countercharges, so confused the records of account, so complex the issues uncovered, that the public soon came to agree with the *Herald's* prediction that "no one would ever get at the bottom of this mysterious, mixed-up matter." Vanderbilt himself regarded the litigation merely as a harassing action against his enemies. It was on a direct, frontal attack that he was counting. Early in 1854, he organized a new line of steamships, which included the famous *North Star,* to carry passengers to San Francisco by way of Panama—the very route that he had formerly decried. His new service, called the Independent Line, was designed for one purpose only—to divert passengers from the Nicaragua Line—and it made much of the fact that the transisthmian railroad in Panama was almost completed. The Independent Line offered rates even lower than those which had marked Vanderbilt's earlier price war with George Law. For $100, plus the railroad fare, a man could travel "first class" all the way to California, while steerage cost no more than $30.

From the moment that the Independent Line's advertisements

appeared, saying flatly that "passengers will be guaranteed to arrive in San Francisco ahead of the Nicaragua Line," its ships were crowded. Whether it could make money with rates so low was debatable, but Vanderbilt knew more than one way to turn a dollar. Before Wall Street got wind of his scheme he sold short many thousands of shares of Accessory Transit stock. Never was a speculative profit more certain. The falling off of business on the Nicaragua Line was accompanied by a steady decline in the price of Accessory Transit shares on the exchange. To add to bearish sentiment, the New York press published reports of serious fighting in the latest of Nicaragua's long series of revolutions, further inclining passengers to look to Panama, and investors to sell their Accessory Transit shares. As a result Vanderbilt was able to buy in his "covering" shares at a substantial gain. Morgan and Garrison were his targets, but his hard thrusts at them were also damaging the Panama Line which Law had founded. Wall Street soon began to gossip that the Commodore had "done it again." All his enemies were in retreat.

Morgan and Garrison were particularly hard hit when, in the summer of 1854, the Accessory Transit Company, now their property, ran into trouble with obstructive British officials in the port of Greytown. In resentment, the company persuaded the American Navy to bombard the sleepy little town*, and the news caused a further diversion of the Caribbean passenger traffic to Panama.

The immediate beneficiary of the affair was Vanderbilt, for the price of Accessory Transit stock, already depressed, took a further drop. At this point, instead of selling, he began to buy the stock in large quantities. His purpose now was to regain control of the company; and Morgan and Garrison, alarmed, sought a compromise. Accessory Transit, they said, would pay Vanderbilt's claim for moneys due him under his agency contract, if he in return would sell his Independent Line to the company and agree to retire from isthmian shipping. "A settlement," reported the New York *Tribune,* "has been amicably arranged." "Amicably" was hardly the appropriate adverb. No victory that was less than complete could slake Vanderbilt's thirst for revenge. Morgan and Garrison still had the

---

* *Wheeler Scrapbooks,* Vol. II, p. 10, Congressional Library. W. O. Scroggs, *Filibusters and Financiers,* New York, 1916, Ch. 7.

Accessory Transit Company, which he had founded. Quietly he continued to accumulate the company's shares.

Mayor Garrison, still in charge of Accessory Transit's office on the West Coast, sensed that the Commodore would soon make another attempt to recapture the company. Garrison was a man of resource and daring, to whom defeat, especially public defeat, was as intolerable as it was to Vanderbilt. Like Vanderbilt, he had fought his way up in the world from lowly beginnings, and he too understood the techniques of power. San Francisco was under his thumb. He was the idol of the Vigilantes and the collaborator of Broderick, the state boss, in plucking the political plums of the time. Almost as much as he valued his $60,000 salary from Accessory Transit he valued his reputation as a consistent winner. His position was strong, for his contract with the company meant that Vanderbilt could not easily dispose of him; and through a San Francisco banking house in which he and Morgan were partners he had access to considerable financial resources. Given a weapon with which to fight, he could bring to bear enough money and influence to give pause even to Vanderbilt.

The hint that a weapon might be found came to Garrison late in 1854 from a Sacramento publisher who had a slight acquaintance with Walker. This man, Parker H. French, combined an almost total lack of scruple with a fertile imagination, enormous effrontery, and a persuasive tongue. He had learned of Walker's talks with Cole about Nicaragua; he knew of Garrison's struggle with Vanderbilt; and without Walker's knowledge, he appointed himself go-between.*

Garrison was interested, but he was too canny to act hastily or impulsively. He could not afford to have it said that he was in any way connected with a violation of the Neutrality Laws. If Walker could succeed in reaching Nicaragua and establishing himself there—in itself an unlikely assumption—that would be time enough to consider an approach to him. He dismissed French with a curt message. He wished "to have nothing to do with such enterprises as he supposed Walker to contemplate." Nevertheless, from this moment, he took a friendly if distant interest in Walker's plans; and his influence in San Francisco being what it was, the danger that District Attorney Inge would stop Walker from taking an expedition to Nicaragua became negligible.

---

* William Walker, *The War in Nicaragua,* Mobile, 1860, Ch. 5.

VI

An even more roundabout stream of circumstance, originating in Madrid, played on the mind of General Wool, who had the intention and the physical power at his command to prevent Walker from defying the Neutrality Laws. A few years earlier Spain had raised to aggravating heights Cuba's tariffs on American goods entering the port of Havana and had imposed onerous new rules on American shipping. At that time Cuba was America's third largest export market, taking large quantities of such products as flour, corn, pork, and dried fish; the drastic decline in exports, resulting from the new tariffs, was felt especially by Southern businessmen.

Secretary of War Jefferson Davis, who had inherited Calhoun's mantle as chief spokesman for the South, and who wanted to see Cuba annexed for political reasons, promptly demanded action against Spain, even at the price of war. He did not believe that, in the final test, England or France would stand by the Spaniards. Many influential Englishmen, in fact, were already reconciled to the annexation of Cuba by the United States. The London *Spectator,* speaking for a large segment of British opinion, had said openly that it would be "a fatal mistake" to pledge England "to uphold the perishing interests of Spain."

President Pierce, as was his habit, put the problem in the hands of his Secretary of State, William Marcy. A shrewd man, stronger and keener than Pierce, and allied to large business interests in New York, Marcy was noted for his frank defense of the spoils system which he had helped to introduce into American politics. For practical purposes, he and Davis ran the administration through a series of superficial compromises, while the fundamental cleavage between North and South grew steadily more dangerous.

The specific measure advocated by Davis with respect to Cuba was suspension of the Neutrality Laws. This move in his plan was to be followed by a new and this time powerful filibustering expedition, which, coinciding with a popular Cuban revolution, would drive out the Spaniards, without providing a pretext for British and French intervention. Thereafter a friendly Cuban regime would seek statehood in the Union. Davis' great fear was that, unless the island was quickly brought into the United States, Spain might abolish Negro slavery there—a development which could wipe out the political value of the acquisition for the South, and would intensify the agitation over slavery in the United States.

Marcy held back from the naked use of force, and urged that an attempt be made to purchase Cuba from Spain. The annexation would then appear to be a national, rather than a Southern solution of the problem. Reluctantly, Davis consented, stipulating only that the negotiation with Spain be entrusted to a Southerner. The assignment went to Senator Pierre Soulé of Louisiana, a Frenchman born, and a man of great personal charm, if otherwise unfitted for diplomacy. As minister to Madrid, he was instructed by Pierce and Marcy to offer Spain "a reasonable sum" for Cuba, up to $130,000,000. This much was known at the time; what was not discovered for another seventy-five years was that Soulé's orders contained also a secret clause, stating that if Spain proved unwilling to sell, "you will then direct your efforts to the next most desirable object, which is to detach that island from the Spanish dominion and from all dependence on any European power."*

VII

Soulé turned out to be a diplomatic disaster. Medieval notions of personal honor and a tendency to resort to arms at the least slight caused him to be regarded as the wild man of Madrid's diplomatic colony. Within a few months of his arrival in Madrid, he had seriously wounded the French ambassador in a duel, and had hopelessly antagonized Spain's Foreign Minister, Calderon, with whom he was supposed to negotiate. Under the circumstances, "to part with Cuba," Calderon told Spain, "would be to part with national honor." In Havana, Spanish authorities expressed Madrid's anger in action, by seizing an American ship, the *Black Warrior,* and confiscating its cargo, on the pretext that the vessel had violated technical regulations of the port.

A great diplomatic to-do followed. Marcy instructed Soulé to demand a $300,000 indemnity from Spain for the *Black Warrior,* but the fire-eating minister was not content to follow orders; he converted

* A. A. Ettinger, *The Mission to Spain of Pierre Soulé,* 1932, p. 412.

his note into an ultimatum, giving Spain forty-eight hours to comply. The effect was to revive the spirit of the Spanish government, which replied by sending 6000 soldiers to reinforce its garrison in Havana.

By now most of the American press was demanding strong action by President Pierce—repeal of the Neutrality Laws, a blockade of Cuba, an invasion in force. "In the course of the thick-coming events Cuba is bound to be admitted to the Union," the *New York Times* told its readers. Southerners were so convinced that the Neutrality Laws would be suspended that General John Quitman of Mississippi openly began to organize a filibustering expedition of gigantic proportions. To add to American confidence, the Crimean War had begun; England and France were hotly engaged in Russia, and had veered away from support of Spain if it involved war with the United States. In Parliament the influential Richard Cobden made a stir when he plainly declared, "In the present state of feeling no great regret would be felt if the Americans were to get possession of Cuba."

In all the decades during which the eyes of America's leaders, from Jefferson on, had been fixed yearningly on "The Pearl of the Antilles," there had never before been so promising an opportunity for its annexation. That the moment was not seized was due to the peculiar political position in which President Pierce found himself. At the time of the *Black Warrior* crisis the Senate was being torn by strife over the Kansas-Nebraska bill,* and sectional animosities were inflamed to the kindling point. Pierce, who had to think about renomination by the Democratic Party in 1856, had chosen to conciliate Southern opinion by declining to take a firm stand against the dangerous measure, and in so doing had stirred up deep resentment in the North. Under the circumstances, if he had given way to the South on Cuba as well, he would have lost most of his Northern support in the next Democratic Convention.

At one point, in an effort to extricate himself from his dilemma, he tried to use Cuba as a bargaining point with Southern senators. Had they been content to see Kansas and Nebraska enter the Union as free states, under the terms of the Missouri Compromise, their reward might well have been the suspension of the Neutrality Laws

---

* Urged by Southerners, this bill left to the settlers of Kansas and Nebraska the decision as to whether slavery should be permitted in their territories. It was generally assumed that Kansas at least would become a slave state. The bill became law in the spring of 1854.

and the annexation of Cuba. They were, however, determined to have both the island and Kansas. This was their undoing, and Pierce's. The South's threat to secede from the Union, unless the rich lands of Kansas were opened to the slave trade and Southern domination, was met by firm determination on the part of most Northern senators not to move against Cuba.

While the debate raged, the opportunity passed. In May, 1854, Spain altered the entire complexion of the affair. Suddenly she announced that thenceforth the slave trade would be banned in Cuba, and hinted at eventual emancipation of the island's Negroes. No move could have been better calculated to harden the split in American opinion and paralyze the administration. Many in the North who had favored acquisition of Cuba so long as the move appeared to be directed against Spanish tyranny now became intensely aware of the moral problem involved, and took a fixed stand against any steps to annex the island.

Then, while Congress was trying to find its footing in the tangled affair, Havana announced that the *Black Warrior* and its cargo had been released. This done, the United States had no choice but to regard the incident as closed. The danger of war, President Pierce told Congress, had passed, and he warned that violations of the Neutrality Laws would be severely punished. At Marcy's orders, General Quitman was arrested and compelled to give bond to assure his compliance with the law.

The relation of the Cuban affair to the Kansas-Nebraska bill was well understood by the press. On June 1, immediately after the passage of the bill, the conservative Northern view of the matter was expressed by New York's *Courier and Enquirer.* "There was a time when the North would have consented to annex Cuba, but the Nebraska wrong has forever rendered annexation impossible." Marcy himself privately wrote, "The Nebraska question has sadly shattered our party in all the free states and deprived it of that strength which was needed and would have been much more profitably used in the acquisition of Cuba."

Walker, then editing the *Democratic State Journal* in Sacramento, also felt impelled to declare himself on the issue. In a revealing editorial he wrote, "Events are justifying the foresight of the Southern men who opposed the Kansas-Nebraska bill. The South . . . has lost instead of gaining by the act. . . . A few hot-headed and narrow-minded men have persuaded the South into a course she already begins to repent of. . . . It is now too late to repent. . . . Ultra-slavery men are the most active and efficient agents abolitionists can have in the Southern States. The true friends of the South are those who repudiate the ideas and acts of the South Carolina school."* At this stage, his views on slavery were identical with those which he had expressed while editing the New Orleans *Crescent* five years earlier—against its expansion and against secession.

VIII

President Pierce's political position was becoming hopeless, and the real party leaders, Marcy and Jefferson Davis, lost no time in seeking to assert their influence over the Presidential election to come in 1856. Both men recognized that James Buchanan was a strong candidate. As Secretary of State under Polk, he had cautiously avoided serious offense to either Northern or Southern prejudices. Where slavery was concerned he professed to be neutral. Even if he was not a strong swimmer in the political currents of the time, he could tread water with the best.

Buchanan's fitness for the Presidency, as Davis saw it, would be determined largely by his willingness to declare himself favorable to the Southern aspiration for Cuba and Kansas. Marcy's position was less definite. He himself had a hankering for the Presidency. Nevertheless his interest as a leader of the Northern wing of the party and as its chief dispenser of patronage required a Democratic victory in 1856, no matter who the candidate. The first need was to make Davis feel that either Buchanan or himself, Marcy, might be acceptable to the South, in terms of Cuban policy. This seems to have been the main motive behind the extraordinary developments that followed.

The three chief American envoys in Europe, Buchanan, Soulé, and the minister to France, John Mason, were instructed by Marcy to meet on the continent and come to a joint recommendation for the administration's policy with respect to Cuba. The meeting took place in October, 1854, at Ostend, Belgium. Out of it came the notorious document known as the Ostend Manifesto. If Spain re-

---

* *Democratic State Journal,* Sacramento, Cal., Aug. 12, 1854.

fused to sell Cuba, said the Manifesto, and if the island in her hands constituted a threat to the United States, "then, by every law, human and divine, we shall be justified in wresting it from Spain if we possess the power."

Although the Manifesto was supposed to be secret, its contents became known to European journalists even before the official version reached Marcy in Washington. England's newspapers professed to be outraged by the flagrant immorality of the document. The London *Times* said that if the policy expressed in the Manifesto were seriously entertained by the American government, it would justify a declaration of war. America's antislavery press was equally loud in denunciation. The New York *Post* called the Manifesto "atrocious!" Horace Greeley's phrase for it in the influential *Tribune* was "a Manifesto of brigands," and he demanded its repudiation by Pierce.

The violence of the adverse Northern reaction shocked Marcy, and in self-protection he bluntly renounced the Manifesto that he himself had invited. Its first effect, however, was to revive the attack of Jefferson Davis and others on the Neutrality Laws. Although he had been thwarted on the Cuban issue, Davis now developed a strong interest in the possibility that one or more filibustering expeditions might head for Nicaragua. He saw that if a private military force should succeed in Nicaragua, the entire position of the United States in the Caribbean might be altered. The Neutrality Laws might be swept into the discard, and the government compelled after all to seize Cuba and fight Spain. As Secretary of War, Davis was officially committed to rigorous enforcement of the Neutrality Laws, but as a practical politician he knew how large the gap is between the avowal of a law and its implementation. To that gap he now directed his efforts. Rumors of a possible expedition from California to Nicaragua were already current. A remarkable letter from Davis to General Wool in San Francisco now made clear his wish that the general temper zeal with discretion where the Neutrality Laws were concerned.

"Doubtful questions," wrote Davis, "may arise in regard to the powers vested in the President to enforce our neutrality laws, and the extent to which he may devolve authority for that purpose upon military officers. These laws have not yet received at all points a full judicial consideration. It is understood from the language of the Supreme Court that the President may authorize a general in command to use his command directly against the violators of these laws, and without the interposition of the civil authorities. But the court were also of the opinion that this 'high and delicate power' ought only be exercised when 'by the ordinary process of exercise of civil authority, the purpose of the law cannot be effectuated,' and when military or naval force is necessary to ensure the execution of the laws."*

This letter was understood by Wool as implying that he was to invoke the Neutrality Laws against filibusters only if the civil authorities requested his intervention. Consequently, when Walker approached Wool early in 1855 to ascertain his views on the expedition, the general was suddenly all affability. He declared frankly that the instructions of the Secretary of War left him no authority to interfere unless San Francisco's District Attorney requested him to do so. Privately the old soldier went even further, grasping Walker by the hand, and saying, "Not only will I not place any hindrance in your way, but I wish you the greatest success!"

The civil power of the city, with Mayor Garrison setting its tone, was equally obliging. District Attorney Inge, after inspecting Walker's contract with Castellon, made no effort to probe beneath its surface. The contract in itself contained no violation of law, and he saw no reason to invoke interference by the Army with Walker's movements.

The train of great events that Commodore Vanderbilt had set in motion five years earlier, when he sought to construct a canal in Nicaragua, had at last intersected Walker's curious orbit. Through the instrumentality of Jefferson Davis and General Wool, through Cornelius Garrison and District Attorney Inge, he was being given a chance to make history.

---

* House Exec. Doc., 88, 35th Cong., 1 Sess., pp. 98-100.

PART TWO

The Shape of Destiny

《《 》》

"We have again and again called Walker a hero.
. . . We are obliged to recognize a persistence, an endurance,
a resolute heroism which merit a higher place in human
esteem that can be ceded to all the knights errant of history
and Faërydom. . . . The difference is that ours is a nineteenth century hero. . . . Who knows how soon he may
replace the laurel of the hero with the diadem of a king?"
Harper's Weekly, JANUARY 31, 1857

X

"THE IMMORTALS"

The failure of Walker's Sonora expedition notwithstanding, hundreds of the adventurers and soldiers of fortune in whom San Francisco abounded, as well as its derelicts, offered themselves for his service. From among them he chose with a shrewd eye for courage and endurance. His enthusiasm and conviction about his new venture were infectious. He had been studying a detailed description of Nicaragua's history, geography, and people, by the former American minister, George E. Squier, and it significantly aided recruitment. In addition to arresting facts, the book was full of charming little vignettes of Nicaraguan life. Squier had been especially susceptible to the charm of the lissome, glossy-haired native girls, "of all shades from white to ebon black, straight as arrows, lithe yet full-figured, with quick, mischievous eyes"—flirtatious, full of animal spirits, and dressed in vividly colored skirts and scanty blouses that often revealed as much as they concealed when the girls raised their arms to balance red water jars or baskets of fruit on their heads. One passage in his book was picked up by the newspapers—a scene in which Nicaraguan soldiers, seeing some girls swimming nude in a river, sought to scare them to the beach by shouting, *"Lagartos! Lagartos!"* ("Alligators!"). Another anecdote described the negotiation of an infatuated young Bostonian with a village priest for the hand of his "niece"—all unaware that it was customary to find in the household of many a *padre* a young and pretty girl designated as the *sobrina*—a niece only by courtesy. A little sketch by Squier of a bare-bosomed beauty rolling tortillas similarly attracted attention by its frankness. In woman-starved California, the sexual possibilities of Nicaragua must have excited almost as much masculine interest as the prospect of winning rich lands in Walker's service. Squier pointed out that the owners of the great Nicaraguan plantations, drawing princely incomes from the land, lived a life of feudal satisfactions such as could not be found in the United States. An aristocrat with a hundred thousand cacao trees or so might obtain from this crop alone some $30,000 per year, free of all taxes; master of his workmen, he would be impeded only by his own conscience in his access to their women folk.

To those who, like Walker, needed an idealistic purpose in any adventure, he was able to speak of the benefits that Nicaraguans themselves would gain from peace, democracy, and American civilization. A number of the men who joined him brought exceptional experience and abilities to the expedition. One was a physician, Dr. Alexander Jones, who had already tasted high adventure in a hunt for buried treasure in the Indian Ocean, and who yearned for further action in a world of danger. Another was Achilles Kewen, who had fought alongside General Narciso Lopez in his attempt to liberate Cuba, and whose brother Edward was prominent in California politics. Colonel C. C. Hornsby had served with distinction in the Mexican War, and had visited Nicaragua; he too threw in his lot with Walker. So did Major Frank Anderson, another noted veteran of the Mexican War, and Timothy Crocker who, as Walker's aide, had undergone the miseries of the campaign in Lower California, and was nevertheless still loyal to him. A high proportion of the other recruits were miners and prospectors who had been disappointed in the gold fields, and were ready to try their luck elsewhere.

The limiting factor in Walker's effort to prepare his expedition was money. His own meager resources were soon exhausted. Influential friends did their best for him, among them Edmund Randolph, now married and a pillar of San Francisco society. Another favorable voice was raised for Walker by California's favorite son, Colonel John C. Frémont, who, running against Buchanan in 1856, would be the first Republican candidate for the Presidency of the United States. But the funds at Walker's disposal fell far short of his need. A ship had to be chartered; arms, equipment, and food had to be bought. Each additional recruit increased the cost of the expedition—which, it was plain from the first, would have to travel on a shoestring. He was hampered, too, in raising money by the wound in his foot sustained in his latest duel, and which resulted in a painful if temporary limp. When all was done, Walker was unable to pay for many of his purchases; he could afford no better boat than an unseaworthy old brig named *Vesta*; he had no money with which to hire a crew; the only captain available to him was a drunken ne'er-do-well; and he could put aboard only fifty-eight men. It was these men who, a few months later, were celebrated by the entire press of the nation as "The Immortals."

II

The element of the absurd which was so often present in Walker's undertakings, and which generally arose from his refusal to admit the hopelessness of the odds against him, materialized on the *Vesta* just before it was due to weigh anchor. A revenue cutter, the *Marcy,* came alongside, and San Francisco's sheriff, with a party of deputies, boarded the *Vesta* and ordered it attached for debt. A storekeeper who had extended credit to Walker had changed his mind, and was demanding immediate payment. Until it was forthcoming, the brig might not leave port. To make certain of Walker's compliance, the sheriff seized the *Vesta*'s sails and carried them onto the dock.

One of the newspaper accounts of the incident stated that Walker showed "profound anger"—a display of emotion unusual for him. He suspected that the development was a stratagem of District Attorney Inge, who, while unwilling to block the expedition openly and thus incur the displeasure of Mayor Garrison, might well have resorted to a legalistic trick to express his enmity. Walker acted, however, with restraint and prudence. Cautioning his restive men not to interfere with the sheriff, he limped ashore, sought out the trouble-making storekeeper, and quietly pointed out the hazards that would be run by the man whom his recruits might hold responsible for the failure of the expedition to sail. It was a cogent argument, and the creditor hastily agreed to lift the libel on the ship.

But Walker's problem was far from solved. A more serious threat awaited him on the *Vesta*. The sheriff, in his absence, had prepared a bill of costs for his own part in attaching the brig, and wanted three hundred dollars before he would release it—a sum so far out of Walker's reach as to imply the end of the expedition. At this moment, only one thing was clear to him. The *Vesta* had to sail, and soon. Many of his men, irked by the delay, were becoming unruly and dangerous. Another day's idleness could mean violence, the disintegration of his force, and an end to all his hopes. The sarcasms of the newspapers, too, as they reported his plight, had to be cut short before they weakened the chances of raising future reinforcements.

"It is almost night," he said quietly to the sheriff. "I shall not be able to get the money until morning."

Pleased that Walker had not questioned his exorbitant demand, the sheriff said that he would wait.

"However," Walker went on, "you will not be paid unless the sails are brought back on board immediately. Legally, you had no right to remove them. If necessary, I shall ask the court for a ruling."

The sheriff, uncertain of his legal position, and with his mind fixed on the three hundred dollars, was not disposed to argue the point. The return of the sails seemed to him to involve no risk. Not knowing that the creditor's libel on the ship had already been lifted, he thought that the cutter *Marcy,* still alongside, would continue to guard the brig; and it did not seem likely that the *Vesta* would sail without a crew. He assented to Walker's request. A deputy, he said, would spend the night on the brig, and he himself would be around to collect the money in the morning.

With the sails once more on board and the sheriff gone, Walker courteously invited the deputy, one Purdy, to join him in a drink. Together they went to his cabin. Once inside, Walker fixed Purdy with a cold grey eye. "The *Vesta* is going to sail, Mr. Purdy," he remarked in the low-pitched drawl that, in him, always signified high tension. As the deputy gaped at him, he pointed to a table. "There, sir," he said, "are champagne and cigars." From his pocket he drew a pair of handcuffs which he placed alongside the bottle. "And there are handcuffs and irons. Pray take your choice."* Purdy, who had been a member of the California legislature, was inclined to be philosophical; and he settled down in a chair with the bottle. Excusing himself, Walker locked the cabin door behind him and went aboard the *Marcy* to show its commander proof that the ship had been cleared to leave port. This done, and finding the officer friendly, he asked a favor of him. Would the *Marcy's* crew help in bending on the Vesta's sails—a task for which Walker's own men were untrained? Sailors from the *Marcy* came over the brig's side, and by midnight the work was completed.

As soon as the *Marcy* had gone, Walker signaled the shore. A steam tug for which he had previously arranged came alongside, took the *Vesta* in tow, and brought it to a point well outside the harbor. Just before the tug cast off, deputy Purdy was put aboard her, to raucous cheering from Walker's recruits. Then, spreading her sails, the *Vesta* stood out to sea.

III

Six weeks later (the *Vesta* had sailed a slow, stormy, and erratic course) Walker landed at Realejo, the northernmost port of Nicaragua, close to the revolutionary capital of León. The wild and piratical look of the bearded Americans did not prevent heartening displays of friendliness by the people who lined the streets of the shabby little town. Men cheered, women waved, everyone smiled at the newcomers who were to help the Democrats of the north against their enemies, the Legitimists. A formal welcome from an officer of the Leónese army was followed by the appearance of a gentleman of British birth, Charles Doubleday, who knew Nicaragua well and who offered his services to Walker—a valuable acquisition. Doubleday, who served thereafter as an officer in Walker's army and wrote a book about his experiences, described the impression that the American made on him: "He exercised a magnetic attraction . . . such as is rarely witnessed." Testimony to the same effect came from Joaquin Miller, who in one of his poems spoke of Walker as having "a piercing eye, a princely air, a presence like a chevalier." His

* *Harper's Weekly*, 1857, Vol. I, p. 332. New York *Herald*, June 2, 1855.

appeal for them was obviously much more than a matter of eyes and bearing. Their response and that of many another to Walker was of the kind that idealism alone is able to evoke in educated and sensitive men. Regarding himself as an apostle of American democracy and with unshakable faith in the justice of his cause, Walker radiated the intense glow of the true believer. There was already in him that touch of fanaticism, later to become more apparent, which all men respect as a source of power, and which, in so soft-spoken and courteous a personality, was all the more effective.

IV

From the first, Walker felt the fascination of the unique Nicaraguan landscape. He had read of the great green plain bordered in the far distance by low emerald hills and a belt of black towering volcanoes, by great blue lakes and a vast rain forest, but everything exceeded his expectation. The brilliant contrasts of raw color under the blazing sun and the dreamlike splendor of the soft tropic night generated in him a sensuous excitement that he never lost. "You felt," he wrote, "as if a thin and vapory exhalation of opium, soothing and exhilarating by turns, was being mixed at intervals with the common elements of the atmosphere." He was as infatuated with the country as if it had been a woman. There was languid music even in the names of the towns, which ran from north to south, on or close to the Pacific coast: Realejo, Chinandega, Corinto, León, Managua, Masaya, Granada, Rivas, San Juan del Sur. But his enthusiasm was held within himself. Outwardly he remained altogether the military man —crisp, definite, authoritative. His first order was a warning to his men of stern punishment if they disturbed the peace of Realejo. It is some measure of the respect in which he was held that those hard-bitten adventurers, who had been confined to a wretched little vessel for six weeks, and who were now quartered on the town, contented themselves with some drinking of *aguardiente* and a little singing in the taverns (which also served as brothels) and refrained from looting, rape, and street brawls.

The day after his arrival, Walker rode to León for his first interview with the Provisional Director of the revolutionary regime, Castellon. The first summer rains had come, and everything that grew was green. He had the sense of traveling in an ocean of verdure, through avenues of huge tropical trees meeting overhead, past high hedges of red-flowered cactus, and sudden clumps of coconut palm, mango, and banana trees. All around him the rich fields bespoke fertility, and mules laden with produce and browsing herds of cattle added to the picture of a bountiful land. On this ride Walker may have glimpsed the ageless and serene Indian villages where, among the thatch-roofed huts and green-fruited calabash trees, broad-hipped women, naked to the waist, smoked their *cigarros* as they went about their chores; where small boys ran naked except for straw hats and little cigars, and where only a dozing policeman, wearing a sword and with an old blunderbuss at his side, suggested the high civilizing influence of government.

León, a city one-third the size of San Francisco in 1855, was an impressive contrast to that wild boom town. Dignity and tradition were the essence of the Democratic capital. At the center of each municipal district was a church and a plaza, the core of community life and of the markets, while at the city's heart was a venerable cathedral, facing the grand plaza and the government buildings. As he passed the cathedral, Walker noted that its stone walls were heavily scarred with bullet pocks, marks of past revolutions in which the great building had been used as a fortress. A few days later, he would meet the dominant personality of León, the purple-robed Bishop, a man of exceptional intellect and experience, who was well disposed to Walker from the beginning. One of the Bishop's favorite remarks was, "Nicaragua needs only the aid of the United States to become an Eden of beauty and the garden of the world."

V

Walker could hardly have come at a more fortunate moment for his purposes. The hopes of the Democrats were waning fast. A strong Legitimist army under the most famous of Nicaraguan commanders, General Ponciano Corral, was preparing to march on León from the south. Castellon, grey and anxious, received the American as a drowning man clutches at a log. Through his embraces and compliments Walker perceived a faltering spirit and incipient despair, and he came at once to the conclusion that Castellon "was not the man to control a revolutionary movement or to conduct it to a successful issue." On the surface, however, they established an amicable understanding. Castellon proposed and Walker agreed that the Americans would be constituted a separate corps—*La Falange Americana*—the American Phalanx. To Walker's request that he be given an additional two hundred Nicaraguan soldiers there was no demur. His next and crucial demand, however, produced an immediate crisis. This was for authority to sail south in the *Vesta* and occupy the Transit route. As he himself later wrote in *The War in Nicaragua*, "It was a fixed policy with Walker to get as near the Transit as possible, in order to recruit from the passengers . . . and to have the means of rapid communication with the United States. . . . It was idle for them [the *Falange*] to waste their energies and strength on a campaign that did not bring them toward the Transit road."

It was not Castellon, but his military commander, General Muñoz, who objected. Muñoz was a tall, handsome, and haughty egotist, by no means incapable, but exceedingly jealous of his prerogatives. Resplendent in a blue uniform with red lining and much gilt, he eyed Walker's drab clothing and slight figure with unconcealed disdain. The *Falange*, he insisted, should remain in the vicinity of León to defend the capital against probable attack. Walker replied quietly that it would be unwise to submit his men to the corrosive temptations of garrison life. "Nothing so much tries the firmness of men like those in the *Falange* as inaction." They had to an extreme degree, he said, "the characteristic American thirst for action and movement."

An argument took shape. Muñoz' strategy was based on the traditional concept of war in Central America, in which victory went to the side that successfully stormed the enemy's capital. Usually the hard fighting took place at the very center of a besieged city, its grand plaza and cathedral. The defenders would sacrifice the countryside and outlying sections of the city in order to entice the enemy into its heart, where fortification and supply gave an advantage to the besieged. A decade earlier a Legitimist army, having failed to capture León, had sacked and burned a thousand dwellings on the outskirts—an atrocity the memory of which still inflamed the passions of the Leónese. Nevertheless, Muñoz saw no alternative but to prepare for another such campaign.

Walker barely concealed his impatience. The strategy of siege made for long, inconclusive, and highly destructive fighting, and was altogether at odds with his temperament. Swift attack, the seizure of lines of communication, the shattering of enemy morale, and the rout of his army were the essence of military success, his reading had taught him. The Americans had not come to Nicaragua to be cornered in a city. The victory could not be won by waiting for the enemy to come north. The Democratic army had to take the initiative, and he and his men were prepared to be the spearhead of the attack.

This line of reasoning left Muñoz cold. "I must first consider the safety of the capital," he said. "That is my responsibility."

"And my responsibility," said Walker, "is to maintain the fighting power of my men and win the war."

The Nicaraguan drew himself up. "It should be understood," he snapped, "that the decision lies with the Commander in Chief—subject, of course, to the wishes of the Provisional Director."

There was a moment's silence; then Walker turned to Major Kewen, who stood next to him. "Mr. Kewen," he said, "will you show the general, on this map, the plan of campaign that we have discussed?" Muñoz tried to brush Kewen aside, but the diversion served Walker's purpose; he was able to take Castellon slightly apart from the others and say to him in a low voice, "Let me speak frankly. If General Muñoz is to give me orders, I cannot serve you."

"But," Castellon protested, "he is the commanding general."

"Perhaps that explains the perilous position of your government," said Walker.

The merits of the case aside—and there was much to be said for Walker's stand—the urge to rebel against constituted authority was growing stronger in him. No man had ever commanded him. He had sprung directly to his colonelcy from the freedom of civilian life, without ever having served in an army. An order from another was a sting, arousing all his combativeness. His challenges were invariably aimed at the men who issued orders, men more powerful than himself. It had been Judge Parsons; now it was Muñoz; soon it would be Vanderbilt. It had once been his father.

One senses that power for Walker was more than a psychological, it had become a biological need. Like other ascetic romantics of exceptional energy, ability, and idealism—John Knox, Savonarola, Robespierre—men who cut themselves off from sexual womanhood and rejected possession of things—Walker had left himself only one direction in which to discharge his masculine potential—domination. The democratic cause was still his purpose and his justification, but the burning pressure within him was to rule. Although he had been in León only a day, already he had generated controversy. But his calculation was sound. Castellon did not dare risk the withdrawal of the Americans. Reluctantly, apologetically, the Provisional Director turned to Muñoz and said, "General, I think we should give Colonel Walker the opportunity he asks."

"As you wish," said Muñoz icily, and making a formal bow to Walker, left the room.

VI

A man who had made as many enemies as Walker could not be unduly disturbed at making another, but from this moment he sensed that Muñoz' influence would be used to destroy him, and he was right. Instead of the two hundred Nicaraguans promised him, he received, after a long interval, only half that number. Supplies needed at Realejo were so slow in arriving as seriously to delay the departure of the *Vesta*. By the time Walker landed his force near the Pacific end of the Transit road, valuable days had been lost, and he soon had reason to believe that advance word of his plan had gone to the enemy through an agent employed by Muñoz.

His first objective was the inland town of Rivas, a Legitimist base near Lake Nicaragua which had to be taken before the Transit could be held. Simple caution dictated that a surprise attack be made at night, but his native guides proved untrustworthy and the crucial hours of darkness were lost in following a circuitous route through the rain forest. A heavy downpour, with continuous flashes of lightning overhead and treacherous mud underfoot, further impeded the march. When the rain ended, and the moon could be glimpsed through the thick foliage, the spectral effect of the black gigantic tree trunks, the heavy branches, the creepers and vines, and a sense of the wild animal life around them made some of the men uneasy; and they began to sing, low-voiced, the favorite tunes of California: "Oh, Susanna" and "Hail, Columbia!" Walker always enjoyed the singing of his troops. Few as the men were, they made a formidable showing. "The felt hats of the *Falange,*" he observed, "showed, in their drooping brims, the effect of the night's rain, and thick heavy beards gave to most of the body a wild and dangerous air." Wearing dark trousers and shirts, booted, carrying pistols and Bowie knives in addition to rifles, the Americans formed a sharp contrast to the barefooted Nicaraguans, who wore straw hats and once-white cotton pantaloons, and were armed with old-fashioned muskets and machetes. Their common purpose showed on their hats, where red ribbons signified their Democratic allegiance.

As a result of the delay, the *Falange* was compelled to advance on Rivas in broad daylight. Walker's own description of the march strikes an almost lyrical note. "Every now and then market-women, with baskets on their heads, and just come from Rivas, would gayly greet the soldiers. . . . Such of the men as spoke any Spanish would waste all the terms of endearment they could muster on the girls, who seemed pleased. . . . When, however, the command reached the summit of a hill . . . a scene of beauty and splendor drew them from everything else. Though the order was to march in silence an exclamation of surprise and pleasure escaped the lips of all. . . . The lake of Nicaragua lay in full view and rising from it, as Venus from the sea, was the tall and graceful cone of Omotepe. The dark forests of the tropics clothed the side of the volcano. . . . The beholder would not have been surprised to see it waken at any time. The first glimpse of the scene made the pulse stand still; and the *Falange* had scarcely recovered from its effects when the command was halted in order to prepare for the attack."

At noon on June 29, 1855, as the *Falange* advanced on Rivas for its first battle, it became evident to Walker that he had been betrayed. The enemy force awaiting him behind barricades was far larger than he had been given reason to expect, and it was under the command of a notorious Honduran general, Santos Guardiola, who had come to Nicaragua to aid the Legitimists. Guardiola was known—with reason—to all Central America as "The Butcher," and the terror of his name was enough to weaken the morale of Walker's Nicaraguan troops. At the first fire they fled without making even the pretense of a stand, leaving 55 Americans opposed to over 500 of the enemy.

In the first few minutes of fighting six of Walker's men were killed

—among them two of his chief aides, Crocker and Kewen. Hard-pressed, the *Falange* fought its way to a large house and held off the enemy by accurate rifle fire from the windows. The men's fighting spirit was heightened by rage, for they saw five of their wounded comrades, unable to reach the house, done to death on the streets by sadistic bayonets. After four hours of sporadic shooting, the enemy losses exceeded those of the *Falange* ten to one. Now, however, the Legitimists received reinforcements, including a cannon, and with this advantage were able to approach the improvised fortress and set it on fire.

The last hope of the Americans who were still on their feet was to break through the enemy lines, and at Walker's signal, with a wild yell, they charged out of the house by an unguarded door. The movement was so unexpected and their marksmanship so effective that the nearest of the Legitimist troops turned and fled, while the rest were momentarily paralyzed. Retreating through the streets of Rivas, beating back their pursuers with deadly bullets, the Americans were able to make their way into the forest and at last back to the coast. A few hours later, weary and disheartened, they were again on the *Vesta*, sailing north.

Curiously, the defeat at Rivas did not diminish, but rather reinforced, Walker's sense of destiny. Like many a soldier who comes unscathed from a stricken field, he may have gained a kind of strength from the simple fact that he was alive when so many were dead. It has often been noted that repeated survival of great dangers breeds a sense of invulnerability, a secret feeling that one is favored by the gods. After the battle his men saw in him, to their amazement, not chagrin and worry, but a confidence and assurance that sprang wholly from within him, for there was certainly nothing in their circumstances to warrant it. He spent the days of the voyage back to Realejo tending their wounds, seeing that they rested, reviving their morale, and drafting a report for Castellon.

The primary purpose of the report, which he sent by messenger from Realejo, was to break the hold of General Muñoz on the Democratic army. The general, it said bluntly, had acted in bad faith; and he, Walker, would leave Nicaragua with his men at once unless Castellon investigated the sources of the apparent treason which had led to the defeat at Rivas. The response was much as Walker anticipated.

Castellon, although unwilling to challenge Muñoz, begged Walker not to leave, but to bring his force to León, where fears of a Legitimist attack were thickening.

In the two weeks of fruitless correspondence that followed, Walker gave the appearance of sulking in his tent, but as soon as his men were fit to march he appeared to yield to Castellon's entreaties, and headed for León and a showdown with Muñoz. Fresh encouragement had come to him in the arrival of Byron Cole, who had just returned from Honduras, and who brought with him another valuable man. This was Bruno von Natzmer, a former Prussian cavalry officer, who knew Nicaragua as well as any foreigner. Their presence made Walker feel a little less the loss of Crocker and Kewen. Natzmer confirmed a point of considerable military importance that had begun to come home to Walker. The ordinary Nicaraguan, though he feared the North Americans, feared even more being conscripted into the armies of his own country, and would take far greater risks to escape the recruiting sergeant than he would ever run in battle. "There is scarcely any labor a Nicaraguan will not do," noted Walker, "in order to keep out of the clutches of the press-gang." He laughed at the Nicaraguan generals for their "inveterate habit of catching a man and tying him up with a musket in his hand to make a soldier of him." The only natives that he cared to have in his army, from this time on, were volunteers.

VII

Walker was beginning to sense the mercurial and wide-ranging temperament of the Central American, with his insistence on *dignidad* and his love of the flamboyant, with his religiosity and his superstition, with his hot courage and, in many instances, his cold treachery. Especially there was no mistaking the hostility that lay just beneath the surface of the Nicaraguan's formal courtesy to the *gringo*. It expressed itself in many ways, from the studied indifference of Nicaraguan aristocrats to the suppressed mockery of a guide, when, as Walker's men came through a forest, they were showered with excrement by a band of chattering monkeys. The monkeys, said the guide with a straight face, for some strange reason performed that trick only on North Americans.

Walker was not unduly surprised, on returning to León, to find that although Castellon's professions of friendship were unabated, he was willing to deliver the *Falange* to the mercies of Muñoz. The general had put forward a new proposal—let the American force be broken into small units and distributed among the Nicaraguan regiments. As soon as Walker became convinced that Castellon was about to support Muñoz on the issue, he decided to take his men out of León to a safer spot. But horses and oxcarts were needed, and when he sent a requisition for them to Castellon, it was ignored. An hour later Muñoz marched a strong Nicaraguan force into quarters directly opposite those of the Americans, as if daring them to attempt a move; and for a time it appeared that the *Falange* would have to fight its way out of León.

Walker then wrote an ultimatum to Castellon: "Remove your troops within an hour or we will consider them a hostile force and act accordingly." The threat succeeded. Rather than face the prospect of battle within his own ranks, Castellon agreed to exert his authority over Muñoz. The Nicaraguan troops were ordered away from the danger spot, horses and oxcarts were provided, and the Americans were allowed to leave the city.

There remained Muñoz to be dealt with. The plan in Walker's mind was open defiance of the general—in effect, a mutiny within the revolutionary army—supported by the populace of the countryside, where Muñoz, as a ruthless conscriptor of men, was highly unpopular. Chance, however, made this drastic action unnecessary. A small Legitimist force appeared south of León, and Muñoz, leading his troops in a raid against it, was mortally wounded. His death freed Walker to develop his own strategy.

He had selected the city of Chinandega, not far from León, as his headquarters, while he prepared his next move, for the Chinandegans were known to be dissatisfied with the do-nothing policies of Castellon. The people were hospitable enough, but the morale of his own men caused him serious concern. In their view, the expedition had come to a dead end. Supplies of cartridge metal were so low that they were compelled to range the countryside for objects made of lead—a futile search, which they could not even enliven by loot or women without incurring severe punishment. Their interest in Walker's purpose was fading fast. What they wanted was to enjoy such Lotus pleasures as the country afforded—to sprawl in the green tropic shade, pluck fruit from the trees, dally with the Indian girls who preened themselves under their hard masculine stares. Chinandega was one of the many Nicaraguan towns where the dearth of males made women exceptionally responsive. In such an atmosphere Walker's insistence on frequent drill, long hours of duty, and high standards of personal behavior provoked bitter feeling. Two of his men deserted.

Spirits began to revive, however, when a contest between Walker and an English merchant in Chinandega solved the ammunition problem. This gentleman, Thomas Manning, had been a former British consul; and he bore himself so proudly and at the same time was so shrewd a man of business that no Nicaraguan dared oppose him. He professed to regard Walker and his enterprise with contempt. When it was learned that he and he alone in the area owned enough lead to provide a fresh supply of bullets for Walker's men, and an officer went to his house and proposed to purchase the metal, Manning rebuffed him in strong language. Walker recognized that his reputation among the Nicaraguans and the Americans alike might hinge on the outcome of the matter, and he felt more tension than showed in his own report. "A small guard was sent with orders to take the lead, paying a reasonable price. Thereupon the Englishman declared . . . that if the guard entered his house he would run up the British flag and put his house under the protection of the British government. The officer, uncertain how to act, returned . . . for orders; and being told that no foreign resident, except the representative of the sovereignty of his country, had a right to fly a foreign flag, he was ordered to enter the house; and in case the British colors were shown over it, to tear them down and trample them underfoot, thus returning the insult offered to the Republic of Nicaragua by their display. The native authorities, accustomed to yield to the wishes not only of British consuls but even of British merchants, were utterly astounded at these orders. On the Englishman, however, the orders produced a wholesome effect; for he immediately gave up the lead . . . for the use of the Americans." Manning conceived a considerable respect for Walker, and a little later congratulated him warmly on his successes.

A more important result of this affair was its part in bringing Walker a potent new friend—José Vallé, a pure Indian of vast bulk, robust personality, and great influence, who had been a colonel in the Democratic army before a serious wound forced his retirement. Walker's boldness and vigor appealed to him; intensely loyal to the Democratic cause and a shrewd judge of fighting men, he saw in the American far more hope for his party than in the vacillating Castellon, and gave him undeviating allegiance. Walker on his part conceived a hearty liking for Vallé, whose vitality, keen intuition, and emotional force made him a natural leader of men. "With a certain rude eloquence," Walker described him, "he was accustomed to stir the hearts of the people with a recitation of the wrongs they had suffered from the Legitimist government." Nor was Vallé's influence confined to the men. He was a performer on the guitar, an instrument which, with its yearning sounds and female shape, was particularly satisfying both to the lusty player and the women who listened to him. The practical political value of Vallé's musical talent comes out in Walker's comment on his new ally. "When he took the guitar in hand he would carry the women away with his songs of love or of patriotism; and the control he exercised over the women was not to be despised in a country where they serve to some extent the use of newspapers, at the same time scattering news and forming opinion."

VIII

Vallé proceeded to recruit a force of Indian field hands and town workers—volunteers, for Walker barred conscripts—to serve under the American with himself as their captain. When word of this activity reached Castellon, he promptly sent Vallé a peremptory order to disband his troop. No one bothered to reply. Instead, Walker led his Americans to Realejo and boarded the *Vestà,* where they were joined a few days later by Vallé and his Nicaraguans. Hot on their heels came another message from Castellon: Walker was to bring the *Falange* back to León.

This was serious, for Castellon was one of those essentially weak public men who need occasionally to taste raw power, as a kind of political aphrodisiac. If disobeyed, he might well use the one effective weapon at his disposal—declare his contract with the Americans void, thus destroying their legal justification for being in the country, and reducing their status to that of mere freebooters. Walker decided that the *Falange* must leave Realejo before such an order could arrive. The moment was hardly propitious, for cholera had broken out on shipboard, and was taking a heavy toll of Vallé's men, but Walker, after imposing stringent sanitary regulations on the American troops, gave orders to sail. Not one of the *Falange* came down with cholera on this voyage, in spite of its presence all around them, and the epidemic among the Nicaraguans was held in check—facts suggesting that Walker's medical training was proving its military value. It was at this time that his men, impressed by his care for their welfare, took to calling their thirty-one-year-old commander—behind his back—"Uncle Billy."

Again the *Vesta* bore southward, and three days later was anchored in the harbor of San Juan del Sur. There Walker heard news which revealed the full extent of the trial that lay ahead. The Legitimists had not been deceived as to his purpose, and 600 of their best troops were approaching under the command of The Butcher, Guardiola, who had sworn a sacred oath to drive the *falanginos* into the sea. Walker had not read his military historians for nothing. It was essential to occupy a favorable strategic position, and one that would command the Transit, without delay. A forced march brought him and his men, now comprising 50 Americans and 120 natives under Vallé, to Virgin Bay, the Transit harbor on Lake Nicaragua. They were eating breakfast and spreading their blankets when the advance guard of Guardiola's army, which had found their trail, attacked their pickets. These pickets, Nicaraguans all, proved the courage and the reliability of the native volunteer, as distinguished from the native conscript. Their cool, disciplined, and staunch defense of their posts gave Walker time to deploy his troops in strong positions, on rising ground, with their backs to the lake, and in possession of the buildings owned by Accessory Transit.

With no retreat possible, and with the knowledge that they could expect no quarter from the enemy, the *falanginos* and Vallé's men made their bullets count. After hours of rifle fire, the Legitimists fled. Sixty of them were found dead after the fight, but not a single American was killed, and only two of Walker's Nicaraguan allies. He himself had a close call, for he was struck in the throat by a spent bullet, and another shot cut through a packet of letters from Castellon, which were in his coat pocket. His readiness to expose himself to enemy fire and the dash with which he led a charge won him unstinted admiration from his men. The Leónese troops were even more impressed, however, by the care that he took to preserve the lives of the enemy wounded—an innovation, for the stricken Nicaraguan soldier left behind in a retreat could usually count on being shot or bayoneted by his captors.

For Walker, the battle of Virgin Bay, his first military victory, was a turning point. He could not know how widely and with what enthusiasm it would be reported in the United States, but the effect in Nicaragua was all that his heart could desire. The country was deeply stirred by the Democratic triumph, which was enhanced by the fact that the dictator, Chamorro, had been stricken by cholera, and was dead—a passing which to many seemed an omen of Legitimist doom.

From León, too, came encouragement. There Walker was hailed as a hero, the man who had defeated The Butcher. Castellon also had fallen a victim to the cholera epidemic, and his successor wrote Walker that a company of Nicaraguan volunteers was on its way to serve as reinforcement. Even better, in American eyes, was the arrival of a Transit vessel from San Francisco, with 35 recruits for the *Falange;* while local representatives of the Accessory Transit Company, who had viewed Walker with distrust, were suddenly affable and cooperative.

His army now consisted of nearly 250 men—enough, he considered, for a major offensive. The audacity of his next move, if it had not succeeded, would have made him a laughing stock among military strategists. It was nothing less than the capture of the Legitimist capital, the old city of Granada. Using the tactics of surprise, he embarked his force on a steamboat of the Transit Company, landed at night at a point near Granada, advanced under cover of darkness, attacked at dawn, scattered the city's garrison within a few minutes, and took possession of the government offices. There was little bloodshed. "The encounter," said Walker lightly, "could scarcely be dignified with the name of an action." No triumph in battle could have been more effective. Overnight, from being a military adventurer at the head of a tiny force, he had become, for practical purposes, the dominant man of the nation; for the life of Nicaragua centered in the fertile lands that stretched from Granada to León, and to hold both cities was to hold the country.

His first order, as usual, was a warning to his men against looting, rape, and brutality. Resentment among the Americans was multiplied in his Leónese companies, most of whose men had seen their families suffer at Legitimist hands, and who dreamed of revenge. The heavy punishments with which he proposed to enforce his discipline caused mutinous murmurings, and for a time even his staunch comrade-in-arms, the Indian Vallé, was enraged at him.

IX

Shortly after entering the city, Walker paid his respects to the American minister to Nicaragua, John H. Wheeler, and at the legation found a large number of Granadan women and children who had sought the protection of the American flag. Amazed by his boyish appearance and gentle manner, they begged him for mercy, only to find, incredulously, that he regarded himself as their protector. Among the women to whom Wheeler presented him was one who particularly caught his attention—Doña Irena Ohoran, an unmarried woman of mixed Spanish and Irish blood (her name had once been spelled O'Horan), who was one of the leaders of Granadan society and a power in Legitimist politics. A few years older than Walker, diminutive, and with a face that radiated intelligence, she touched a responsive chord in him. When she offered her house, one of the finest in Granada, to serve as his headquarters, he instantly accepted. Under her guidance he glimpsed the beauties of Granada. It was a city of only 15,000, much smaller than León, but proud. Through green avenues of palm and orange trees one could see the vast blue sheet of Lake Nicaragua, stretching a hundred miles to the south, and where great seafish, the shark, the swordfish, the tarpon, were found in fresh water. Irena Ohoran pointed out volcanic islands in the distance, inhabited by idol-worshiping Indians, hostile to all whites. There was the beautiful Cathedral of Guadalupe, the grand plaza, and the market place— empty, now; but tomorrow, when the people understood that Colonel Walker intended them no harm, the shutters on the shops would come down and hundreds of market women would appear with their colorful baskets of fruit and vegetables. The shops were the best in Nicaragua, offering cottons from England, jewelry from Spain, silks and wines from France.

As for the social life of Granada, it was extremely active. The wide houses in the fashionable streets were more elegant than they looked from the outside. Built low in order to withstand earthquakes, almost every house had its patio and its garden of gay flowers, and many had rooms large enough for a ball. Granadans loved to dance, and orchestras of six, or even ten, violins and guitars were available. But the best entertainment of all was in the streets. In the cool of the evening the ladies, in their finery, would sit at their windows while in the wide avenue the *caballeros,* mounted on their best horses, would come in brilliant colors and wide-brimmed hats, guitars in hand, to serenade their favorite señoritas, display their horsemanship, and exchange gossip from house to house.

The horses and riders were as good as any in the world, and there was many a race in the Nicaraguan style. At the crack of a pistol, two young men would start out holding hands, and race until one was dragged from his horse: broken bones, sometimes broken necks resulted. Of other sports, too, there were plenty—especially cockfighting, the national pastime. Bullfighting was prohibited by law, but bull baiting was permitted—nearly as exciting, when ambitious youths tried to ride the maddened creatures. Men could gamble, too, at a casino, or in the billiard rooms. Theaters were lacking, but sometimes British variety acts—tumblers, singers, clowns—would appear, and one could occasionally ride out to the country to see villagers perform *una sagrada función*—a kind of morality play—very amusing to the sophisticates of the town. In no other small city in Central America did the gentry live so carefree a life. Servants were abundant and cheap. There was much wealth in Granada, derived largely from the great cacao and sugar estates nearby; and every year many Granadans went to Europe to study or travel.

Walker was well aware that the life described by Irena Ohoran was that of a few hundred families only. He did not need to be instructed in the condition of the poverty-ridden workers of the town, or the Indians of the countryside, serfs doomed to incessant labor and to premature death. He had seen their rickety hovels, usually shared with chickens, with dirt floors, mildewed walls, and beds consisting of the stretched hide of a cow. In those dwellings, the chief luxury was the candle. It not only gave illumination but also yielded soft balls of wax, which, when rubbed on the body were a reasonably efficient way of removing the ticks which bored into human skin and were regarded as a worse plague than the scorpions and the snakes.

Among the Granadans Walker became more popular with every hour, the more so because Legitimist propaganda had created an image of him as a bloodthirsty and lecherous buccaneer—and worse, a Democrat—from whom no mercy could be expected. When he set free a large number of political prisoners who had been chained in a medieval dungeon, crowds gathered in the streets to cheer him—crowds composed, it was noted, largely of poor folk who had made their way to the city's center, curious to see their new conqueror, a *gringo* and a Democrat. It was clear to everyone that he was much under Doña Irena's influence, which showed on the very day following his victory. This was a Sunday, and he attended eight o'clock mass at the Cathedral of Granada, where he listened to a sermon counseling "peace, moderation, and the putting aside of revolutionary passions." Afterward he called to his side the parish priest who had delivered the sermon, Padre Augustin Vijil (later to be minister to the United States), and publicly approved his sentiments.

This was the first move in Walker's policy of conciliation toward the Catholic Church. He needed, and knew that he needed, the great influence of the clergy on his side. His enemies abroad, as well as in Nicaragua, spread reports that he encouraged his men to desecrate shrines and churches; there was even a legend that he buried gold and jewels looted from the holy places of the country, but such stories were later found to be fabrications designed to discredit him. In his "Fifty-Three Articles of War By Which the Army of the Republic of Nicaragua Shall be Governed," Article I read: "It is earnestly recommended to all officers and soldiers to attend divine worship, and any officer or soldier who shall in any way behave with impropriety in any place of divine worship shall be punished according to his offense by sentence of a court-martial."

At one point, the Church authorities of Granada granted him a loan of 1000 ounces of silver bullion, certainly without expecting to be repaid. The reality of Walker's relationship to the Church in the early days of his regime is suggested by a letter written to him on November 26, 1855, by the Vicar-General of the See of Nicaragua: "I congratulate your excellency on the victory obtained in favor of liberal principles. . . . I congratulate my country, for she will now come out of the ruins in which she has been sunk for more than thirty years." At the time, the Vicar-General was under the impression that Walker was dissociating himself from the extreme Democratic partisans. Later, when Walker's political activity began to deviate sharply from the preferences of the Church, most of the clergy of the country turned against him, but the issues between them were those of political ideology, not of religion.

Even the British, it would appear, regarded him in those first months as a hopeful figure. A letter from Thomas Manning, with whom Walker had quarreled in Chinandega only a few weeks earlier, and who had been appointed England's Acting Vice-Consul in Nicaragua, said, "As an eyewitness of all the horrors and events which have occurred since May, 1851 [the outbreak of the current Nicaraguan revolution], nobody can better appreciate than myself the re-establishment of order and quiet. . . . Be persuaded, Sir, that the government of Her British Majesty will be disposed to sympathize with you." In London, the highly regarded *Economist* was even willing to concede all Central America to Walker and the United States. "We could not hinder the ultimate absorption by the Anglo-Saxon republicans of Central America if we would—and we are by no means certain that we should."

XI

THE HOT SUN OF NICARAGUA

Whether or not Walker actually fell in love with Irena Ohoran, his men gossiped freely about them. Her popular nickname in Granada was La Niña, the little one, and by the time rumor had worked its way through the ranks of the American force, La Niña Irena had been distorted into "Nila Mairena." Under this name she later appeared as a figure of mystery in American writings about Walker. The men sensed, however, that this was no ordinary affair of the flesh. Between the lines of his own comments on La Niña much can be read. Initially he described her as "a quick and minute observer, with all the gravity and apparent indifference of the native race . . . fertile in resources for sending intelligence to her friends. She had rendered much service to the Legitimist party in days past; and even the stern nature of Fruto Chamorro owned her sway and yielded to her influence, when all others failed to move him."

There soon appears in his account, however, a strong hint of something more than respect for her political talents. He discovered that she had a highly placed lover. "The private relations," wrote Walker in a vein of extraordinary bitterness, "which it is said, and probably with truth, existed between her and D. Narciso Espinosa, a leading man among the Legitimists, enabled her to breathe her spirit into the

137

party after the death of Chamorro." His feelings about Espinosa, whom he described as "a man without principle and without honor," were tinged with a personal resentment such as he displayed toward no other Nicaraguan. It took the form finally of an accusation of complicity in an alleged Legitimist plot against the new regime. What was the evidence against Espinosa? Walker himself admitted that it was only "vague and uncertain," yet he had the man forcibly deported from Nicaragua. Such unusual heat in him suggests emotions at work which were more than political. From this time, the connection between Walker and La Niña became merely formal.

Prior to the Espinosa incident, however, Irena helped to steer Walker through the maze of Nicaraguan politics and to indoctrinate him in the techniques of political warfare, Central American style. In so doing she may well have influenced fundamental decisions. A major strategic problem then confronted him—and more than strategic, for it touched the core of his philosophy. Was he a Democratic partisan, the role implied by his contract with Castellon, or was he seeking to reshape Nicaragua in a new way? There was a common impression in the United States that the partisan armies of Central America represented no more than the personal ambitions of the warlords who led them, and that party programs counted for little, but Nicaraguans knew better. The Democrats had espoused far-reaching reforms in land rents, peonage, and trade, and contemplated a revival of the old Central American Federation. The Provisional Government at León and the Leónese troops in Granada were counting on Walker to secure their control of the country. Anything less than total victory over the Legitimists, in their view, would be an invitation to a renewal of civil war. Similarly the Democrats and Liberals of the neighboring republics regarded Walker with high hope. The San Salvador newspaper, El Rol, on January 2, 1856, defended Walker against attacks by conservative elements, stating boldly that "this much-decried invasion of Nicaragua by the North Americans is but an invective and a calumny of the aristocratic party." It was the belief of many throughout the isthmus that unless Walker succeeded in re-establishing the Central American Federation under Democratic rule, nation would continue to fight nation, party would continue to fight party, and the people would be doomed to incessant warfare and inevitable retrogression.

The issue could not be long postponed. Already the Liberal regime in Honduras had been driven from power, and the ousted President, Trinidad Cabañas, who had unhesitatingly sent troops to fight alongside the Nicaraguan Democrats in their time of need, was asking Walker for similar aid. Could he, should he rescue Honduran democracy? This was the question Walker had to decide.

He fully accepted the view that the five Central American republics ought to be consolidated. The Great Seal of State that he designed for the Nicaraguan government showed five volcanoes in a close cluster, with the sun rising behind the first, and the legend *Dios—Union— Libertad*. In the flag that he adopted (two broad horizontal stripes of azure blue and a white stripe between) the center was dominated by a five-pointed red star. But a political conception was one thing, military reality another. He was less misled than the enthusiastic Democrats by the appearance of his triumph. The Legitimist power could not easily be broken. Its army, under General Corral, still occupied strongly fortified positions on the Transit route, and was much larger than the forces at Walker's command. And throughout Central America, behind the conservatives and the aristocrats, stood not only the prevailing influence of the Church, but also that of England.

Part of Walker's case against England was her indifference to the condition of the people. He pointed out that although her protectorate over the Mosquito Indians had lasted for over a century, "still they have not made any progress toward civilization." The British government did not forget for a moment, however, the interests of England's magnates in the mines of Guatemala and Honduras, and the mahogany of Nicaragua and Costa Rica. The Legitimists of Nicaragua were openly called "the British party," and Costa Rica's aristocratic government was reorganizing its army with the aid of a British Captain (later Colonel) John Cauty.

It was obvious to Walker that a successful democratic revolution in Central America could take place only if it were strongly supported by the United States. But the administration of President Pierce, far from encouraging the Nicaraguan Democrats, showed a strong bias in favor of the Legitimists; it had recognized Chamorro in spite of his flagrant suppression of democratic rights. The Accessory Transit Company, too, had been content with Chamorro, so long as he did not interfere with their operations. Against this background, Walker took it for granted that a strongly partisan position would invite an attack in overwhelming force from all sides.

In the upshot, the strategy that he chose was a painful disappointment to his Democratic friends. To bring peace to the country was his first purpose, he announced, and this could be done only by compromising the differences between the two parties and establishing a coalition government. His Leónese soldiers muttered, but for the Granadans this was pleasant news. All at once Walker was a favorite of the Legitimists. Receptions given in his honor by Irena Ohoran and others were attended by the wealthiest and most aristocratic families of the city, who now regarded Walker as the only barrier between them and the vengeance of the Democrats. Every honor was accorded him; when he entered a room men and women rose and applauded. The Granadans were in fact awed by his ability to control both the hotheaded Leónese troops and the bearded *gringos*. When one of the Americans in a drunken fog wantonly shot and killed a Nicaraguan boy, and Walker had him court-martialed and executed, the city felt that here at last was a military man dedicated to justice.

II

The American's driving energy also impressed Nicaragua. His working hours were from six o'clock in the morning until ten at night, his only recreation a daily horseback ride. Confronted with a thousand problems of the moment, he nevertheless found time to plunge into new and ambitious projects, among them the establishment of an official newspaper. One of his Californians had been a printer and editor; they imported a press and some fonts of type from San Francisco, and were able to improvise a remarkably competent weekly, *El Nicaragüense,* partly in English, partly in Spanish. From the beginning it was one of Walker's major tools, through which he interpreted his purpose to the Granadans and the world. Copies went regularly to the United States, inviting Americans to share in the exotic pleasures and bright future of beautiful Nicaragua; and the influence of the paper on the American press, which quoted it extensively, played a large part in bringing nearly one thousand recruits to Walker's service in the year that followed. Political opinion was similarly shaped. *El Nicaragüense* made it clear that Walker was no mere freebooter or dangerous revolutionary, but the "regenerator" of a much abused and unhappy nation. The effect showed in many American newspapers as skepticism steadily gave way to approval. The influential *Alta California*, which had for a time jeered at the filibuster ("What a hero Walker has become! William the Conqueror, Cortez and Pizarro are but the forerunners of a greater, the destined conqueror of Central America!"), soon was soberly admitting to San Francisco that "Walker, in his campaign in Nicaragua, has certainly exhibited a good degree of skill, perseverance, energy and a vast amount of policy," and complimented him on "the considerable degree of ability" shown in his newspaper.

He was especially successful in surrounding his name with an aura of predestination. There was an old legend among the Nicaraguan Indians, that the people would some day be brought into the light by a redeemer, who would be recognized by his grey eyes. Walker had come across this legend in his reading; under the circumstances, he may even have been inclined to believe it. *El Nicaragüense* left no doubt that he was "the grey-eyed man of destiny." "Last week," reported the newspaper, "we saw in Granada a delegation of Indians, who rarely visit the city, who desired to see General Walker. They were charmed by his gentle reception, and offered to him their heartfelt thanks for their liberation from oppression and for the present state of quiet of this country. They laid at his feet the simple offerings of their fruits and fields, and hailed him as 'Grey-Eyed Man' so long and anxiously awaited by their fathers." Newspapers throughout the United States seized on the story, and for a year it was a rare newspaper article about Nicaragua that did not refer to Walker's grey eyes.

Even the sophisticated European mind was caught by him. British periodicals, which then habitually shrugged at America's politics and public figures, felt constrained to report Walker's actions and statements with close attention, mentioning his name more frequently than they did the President of the United States. Spain's government made him the subject of repeated and anxious notes to its representatives in Washington, London, Paris, Mexico, and Havana. In France, Emperor Napoleon III requested a special memoir on Walker from his Minister of Foreign Affairs. The *Revue des Deux Mondes* published a major article on the significance of his achievements, ranking him among the great political figures of the age, "the rival of Washington." Other journals circulated the rumor that Walker was by birth a French aristocrat and a formidable lover of women, and for a time he was the talk of Paris.

Europe was fascinated not so much by the dramatic fact that, with a handful of men, Walker had swiftly conquered a country and become its dictator, as by the practical implications of his action. Was the United States entering on its imperialistic phase? Accustomed to the ways of their own governments, the statesmen of England, France, and Spain found it almost inconceivable that he could have undertaken such a project, not to say succeeded at it, without undercover support from Washington. The British especially could not believe that he stood alone, and expecting him momentarily to receive recognition and aid from Washington, were tentative and cautious in their first dealings with him.

III

As the strong man of a Central American republic, Walker suffered from the serious liability of a puritanical upbringing. Instinctively the Nicaraguans felt him to be at the polar extreme of temperament from themselves. He might sympathize with their sorrows, but could never enjoy their pleasures, the stronger force binding men together in daily life. Cockfighting, Granada's favorite sport, he privately considered detestable. He did not even laugh, he hardly smiled. That there was an ironic humor in Walker is shown by many passages in his writings, but to him ready displays of mirth were a sign of weakness. He had read Hobbes, who perceived that laughter at its core expresses a sudden feeling of superiority, and he chose to discipline that feeling within himself. His serious manner was not the pose of a man with a romantic sorrow, nor was it the dour style of his Scottish forebears: it expressed the ascetic determination to live at the highest level of self-control of which he was capable. To most Nicaraguans, this was incomprehensible. They respected his ability to control other men, but they were baffled by his insistence on controlling himself. In their feudal world, full of visible misery, imminent pain and sudden death, it was altogether sensible to conciliate those stronger than oneself, take advantage of the weaker, and freely indulge such pleasures of the flesh as were available, while one could. If North American civilization meant a way of life less sensuous than that to which they were accustomed, they wanted none of it. Even the style of Walker's dress struck them as bizarre. Who ever heard of a dictator who wore an ordinary blue coat with cheap dark pantaloons and a black felt hat with a partisan red ribbon, and who moreover carried no arms except in battle?

The chief problem that Walker faced, very simply, was that he wanted to regenerate Nicaragua, and that Nicaraguans did not wish to be regenerated—or, more precisely, the gentry and the clergy wished things to stay as they were, and the unschooled poor, the Indians and half-breeds, aspired to no more than a little more food and clothing. Long experience with Indian gods and Spanish rulers had destroyed hope. To most of the Nicaraguan people it seemed that the difficulties of their lives could only be made worse by radical change. Politically, they lived in a jungle world of passion without principle; they were not in favor of anything; they were merely against everything; their attitude might be described as anti-ism. They would follow a revolutionary leader to help him destroy an oppressive government, but as soon as the new government was established, it in turn became their enemy, for it represented the hated power of the law. Every attempt in the past to bring modern improvements to the country had been fiercely resisted. A few years before Walker's arrival in the country, a wealthy Nicaraguan plantation owner of singular progressivism and benevolence had imported from the United States machinery for the refining of sugar, with the consequence that the machinery was promptly wrecked and he was murdered by workers of the countryside, who had been told that their livelihoods would be destroyed by the new methods.

Temperament aside, Walker showed himself a shrewd judge of popular feeling. He said little about his plans for the country. When the municipal council of Granada drew up a petition urging him to assume the Presidency of Nicaragua, he reproved them in terms perfectly calculated to allay Legitimist anxieties. They had no right, he said, to make the offer, nor he to accept it; much more appropriate would be the election of such a man as the Legitimist Commander in Chief, General Corral, with a government drawn from the best men of both parties.

This move was highly approved by the Americans in Granada as well as by the Legitimists. Minister John Wheeler was so impressed by Walker's bearing that he offered to go to Rivas, where Corral had his headquarters and to serve as intermediary between the two—and this although Walker had no legal status in the United States. Wheeler was an amiable and impressionable man, himself a former soldier, who regarded Walker as a great man, a rare combination of military virtues and intellectual refinement. Presently his hero-worship would express itself in a remarkable collection of Walkeriana. But in attempting to negotiate with Corral, he exceeded both his authority and his talents. Corral, a man of personal force and conviction, regarded him as Walker's tool, insulted him, and declared his intention to pursue the war against the Democrats.*

More effective than Wheeler's intervention was Irena Ohoran's subterranean influence among the Legitimists. How she persuaded Corral is not clear, but just when the situation seemed most dangerous, a letter from him arrived at Granada, offering to receive Walker for private talks. Doubtless to Irena's surprise, Walker now resisted her. If Corral wished a meeting, he said, it would have to take place in Granada; for he sensed that the first overt move of conciliation on either side would be read as a sign of weakness.

Just when he needed it, a way to exert pressure on Corral was unexpectedly put into his hands by a twisting chain of events. A contingent of recruits from California had just arrived in Nicaragua, and its leaders, acting without Walker's knowledge, and even before they had reported to him, decided for their own aggrandizement to seek battle with Legitimist forces on Lake Nicaragua. Commandeering a Transit steamer, they fired on a fortress overlooking the lake, and controlled by Corral. The result was disastrous. Not only were they forced by bombardment to scurry back to safety, but they provoked the Legitimists to reprisals in which a number of innocent Transit passengers, including women and children, were massacred.

The crisis was the more serious because Walker needed the services of the American officers who had ordered the attack, and on whose cooperation depended the arrival of future reinforcements from California. With them he went no further than stern reproof; most of his wrath was directed at the Legitimists, on the incontestable ground that their assault on the Transit passengers had been cruel beyond

* Senate Exec. Doc. 68, 34th Cong., 1 Sess.

military need. In an angry pronouncement, he called for the punishment of those Granadans who, because of their opposition to the idea of a unified country, had urged General Corral to maintain his armed resistance. These Legitimist conspirators were "morally responsible" for the tragedy of the Transit passengers, Walker declared; and the guilt was especially heavy in the instance of one Mateo Mayorga, a former Legitimist cabinet minister. Mayorga, who had earlier been arrested on suspicion of treason but released on parole at the request of John Wheeler, and was actually living in Wheeler's home, had taken advantage of Walker's indulgence to intrigue against him and encourage Corral. Walker had him taken into custody, submitted the facts to a court-martial which quickly found Mayorga guilty of conspiracy to foment civil war, and turned him over to a firing squad.

When Mayorga was led to the plaza and publicly executed, the Leónese soldiers cheered, and Legitimists trembled. Who would be next? Was this the beginning of the Democratic reign of terror that they had feared? At the height of the agitation, Walker sent a message to Corral. From this moment, he vowed, all the Granadan families of officers of the Legitimist army would be regarded as hostages for the good behavior of Corral's soldiers. The effect was magical. With one voice Corral's officers urged him to make peace; and he went immediately to Granada.

IV

Outside Granada, Corral was met by Walker with a mounted escort, and at a stately pace they rode together to the city's center. Walker later recalled the enthusiasm of the Granadans at the spectacle. "As they passed, the doors and windows of the houses were filled with women and children, dressed in the bright colors of the country and smiling through tears at the prospects of peace." During the ride, the two men exchanged enough courtesies so that by the time they reached Government House the tension between them had been somewhat relaxed. In the ensuing conference, Walker allowed himself to appear at a disadvantage. Corral was empowered to speak officially for the Legitimist Party, but the American had been given no such authority by the Democratic regime at León, and he was careful to limit himself to such statements as befitted "the colonel commanding the forces occupying Granada." Accordingly, he let Corral "develop freely the terms he desired, saying little by way either of objection or of amendment. . . . The treaty, as signed, was nearly altogether the work of Corral."*

It was a reasonable document. Establishing a Provisional Government, naming as President an elderly and respected gentleman of conservative views, Don Patricio Rivas, making Corral Minister of War, it pleased the Legitimists; while the Democrats were to be satisfied by constitutional reforms, for which they had been contending; and Walker was given the post of Commander in Chief of the army. In the fact that he, who had been totally without military experience a year or so earlier, now assumed the rank of general, his critics in the United States later professed to find proof of unbridled vanity, but it is difficult to see how he could otherwise have commanded an army already loaded with generals.

A few days later word came from León approving the treaty and confirming the peace. All the bells of Granada rang out. The Legitimists especially were elated by what they felt to be a diplomatic triumph, for what, after all, was a mere constitution as compared with the power of administration? Corral was overheard to call out to Irena Ohoran, as he rode past her house one evening, "we have beaten them with their own game-cock!" This piece of gossip filtered back to Walker from his Leónese officers and widened the rift between him and La Niña.

Corral's jubilation, however, was premature. From the outset, he misread Walker's character. He had expected to find a bully who would attempt to dominate him, trick him, or even humiliate him, in order to gain ascendancy. Discovering instead a quiet and courteous little man, with a profound respect for law, he was unimpressed. He himself had a tall and majestic presence, and this fact may have contributed to his feeling that Walker could be reduced to a subordinate role. His error was soon made plain to him. Walker had based his calculation on the insights which he had recently gained into the mind of the Nicaraguan conscript, and events proved him right. With the announcement of peace, the Legitimist garrisons in the towns, consisting largely of Indians and *mestizos* longing for their homes,

---

* William Walker, *The War in Nicaragua*, p. 125.

melted away; and Walker, as Commander in Chief, did nothing to interfere with their desertion. Within a few weeks Corral's authority over the army had become merely nominal; the real power of compulsion now rested with the *Falange,* and Walker lost no time in exercising it.

A question arose as to the selection of a cabinet officer responsible for relations with the other Central American republics. To Corral's resentment, Walker insisted that the post go to the most celebrated and ardent revolutionary among the Democratic generals, Maximo Jerez, who was also an intellectual with a degree in law, and with whom Walker had conversed at length in León. Such an appointment meant to Corral a major threat to his control of the administration and to the gentry of the entire isthmus. If the extreme Democrats were to have control not only of the army but also of intergovernmental communications, they might well be able to promote revolutions in countries north and south. At all costs Jerez had to be kept out of the cabinet, and Corral said hotly and flatly that he would not serve in the same government with the Leónese. Walker replied simply, "Then we must refer the matter to the President." All Granada by this time was aware that President Rivas regarded the American as Nicaragua's only hope for peace, and never opposed him.

Corral awoke too late to Walker's force of leadership. Although he did not resign from the cabinet, he felt that the Legitimist cause was lost in Nicaragua. His misgivings were strengthened by the evident determination of the Leónese soldiery to maintain their partisan solidarity. Walker had issued an order requiring troops of both parties to remove from their hats the colors of their political faiths, the red ribbon of the Democrats, the white of the Legitimists, and to wear instead the blue ribbon of the nation, with the device, NICARAGUA INDEPENDENTE. The Legitimists obeyed, but the red ribbon remained on most of the Democratic hats. This persistence of the revolutionary spirit Corral considered an evil augury. It was, he felt, only through the intervention of other countries that he and his friends could now be saved.

In that conviction, he wrote an impulsive letter to the new dictator of Honduras, and sent it off by secret messenger. Coming from the Minister of War of the Nicaraguan government to the head of another state, this letter was the stuff of treason unmistakable. "My esteemed friend: It is necessary that you write to friends to advise them of the danger we are in, and that they work actively. If they delay two months, there will not then be time. Think of us and of your offers . . . Nicaragua is lost; lost Honduras, San Salvador and Guatemala, if they let this develop. Let them come quickly, if they would find allies here."

Some historians have seen in this letter a warning against seizure of the isthmus by Walker for the United States, but there is more reason to believe that Corral's great fear was the triumph of the Democrats throughout Central America. Unfortunately for him, the messenger whom he chose to carry this dangerous missive had strong grievances against the Legitimists. Instead of taking the letter out of Granada, he promptly put it into the hands of a Leónese officer, and within the hour it was being read by Walker, together with two other notes of the same kind penned by Corral. The situation thus created, while in one way to Walker's advantage, also confronted him with an ugly problem. That Corral had to be exposed and punished was evident, but the man was much loved in Granada. Imprisoned, he would be a center of conspiracy; executed, a martyr to whose memory thousands would rally; while a light penalty would stir bitter resentment among the Leónese troops, who might even suspect Walker of supporting the Legitimists against them.

In a grim mood, Walker notified President Rivas that an emergency demanded an immediate cabinet meeting, and Corral, not scenting danger, attended. To the assembled ministers Rivas said, "General Walker has something of grave consequence to tell us." Walker put the fatal letters in front of Corral and asked, "Did you write these, General?"

Corral turned pale, but bearing himself with dignity, admitted authorship of the letters, which were then read aloud to the cabinet. "President," said Walker to Rivas, "I charge General Corral with treason, and request you to order his arrest." Rivas nodded unhappily; a Leónese officer who had been waiting outside the door was summoned; Corral gave up his arms and was placed in confinement.

V

Corral's crime, committed as a civilian official, called for a civilian trial. The new government, however, had not yet established a civil court, and it was apparent, moreover, that no Nicaraguan could be

William Walker in 1857 (from an old print)

Walker's great love, Ellen Galt Martin, "in costume for a fancy dress ball" (from a portrait in oils)

Walker leading the final charge at the first battle of Rivas (from *Leslie's Illustrated Newspaper*)

Cornelius Vanderbilt

One of Vanderbilt's Lake Nicaragua steamboats (from *Leslie's Illustrated Newspaper*)

This issue of Walker's official newspaper, appearing before he became President, sought to reassure American opinion as to the stability and pro-American character of his regime. It states that Walker, although not President, "is the government of Nicaragua as Louis Napoleon is the government of France."

A serial biography of Walker, "The Man of Destiny," was featured in New Orleans shortly after his election as President of Nicaragua.

Victory of Walker's schooner *Granada* over the Costa Rican warship *Once de Abril* (from *Leslie's Illustrated Newspaper*)

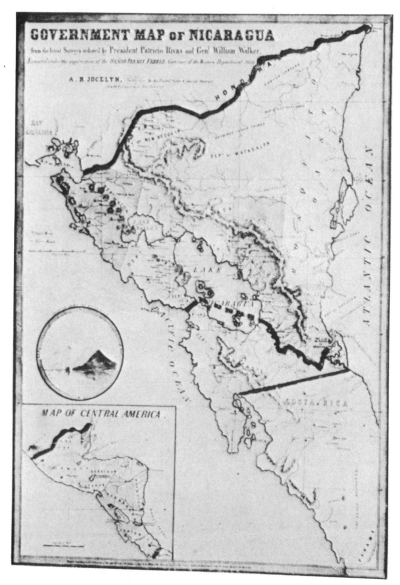

The Transit route, on a map prepared at Walker's instructions to show Nicaraguan ownership of territories in dispute with Costa Rica and Honduras.

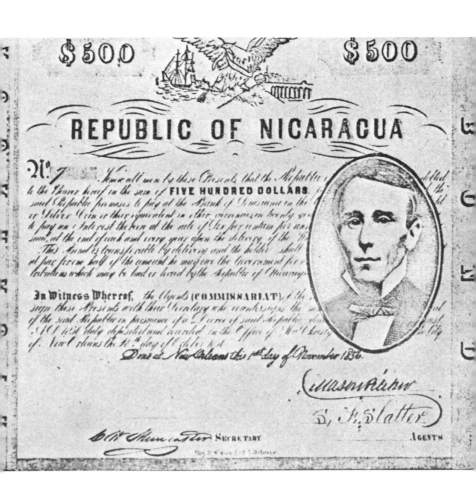

One of the bonds issued by Walker in 1856, after
he became President of Nicaragua

Captain Callender Irvine Fayssoux, Commander of Walker's "Navy"
(from *Leslie's Illustrated Newspaper*)

Major General Charles
Frederick Henningsen
(from an old print)

Pierre Soulé
(from a portrait)

A military order, written by Walker to Captain Fayssoux of the warship *Granada* at a time of desperation. It reads: "Come to this place as soon as possible. I desire to consult you on an important matter."

Walker's draft of his response to an irresponsible challenge to a duel from a former officer in his army, Col. S. A. Lockridge, who felt himself insulted by a passage in Walker's book, *The War in Nicaragua*. The note, addressed to Lockridge's second, says, ". . . I did not intend to impugn the honor or courage of Mr. Lockridge. When I aim to make charges against the character of any man, let me assure you it shall be in words not easily misunderstood."

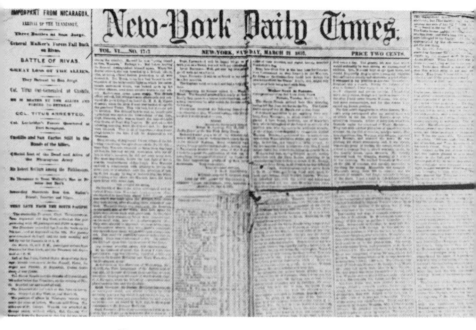

Full pages of leading newspapers devoted to Walker's exploits were not uncommon in the late 1850's. The *New York Times* saw in Walker's victory at Rivas, in 1857, a major change in his fortunes. The New York *Herald,* in 1860, sent a special correspondent to accompany Walker on his last expedition.

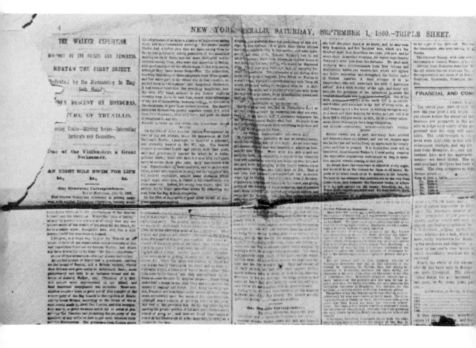

President James Buchanan (from a daguerreotype)

THE BEWILDERED OLD WOMAN.

A famous cartoon of the year before the outbreak of the Civil War.
Lost in a graveyard, Buchanan protests, "Sakes alive! I know no North,
no South, no East, no West—no Nothing!"—and tries to conceal the
Ostend Manifesto.

expected to be impartial in the matter. The Cabinet therefore decided on a court-martial to be composed entirely of American officers. No time was lost; the trial was conducted fairly, the verdict was guilty, the sentence "death by shooting." But the court was unanimous in urging Walker to show clemency to the prisoner.

The burden was now altogether his. No matter what the decision, it could only harm him; that was evident. In the end he fell back on the principles of John Knox and his Scottish forebears, on belief in the value of the cautionary example. How could the treaty of peace which he and Corral had solemnly sworn to uphold "continue to have the force of law if the first violation of it—and that by the very man who had signed it—was permitted to pass unpunished? . . . Mercy to Corral would have been an invitation to all Legitimists to engage in like conspiracies."

The word went out—Corral was to be shot. Immediately there was a great outcry in the city. Priests and notables begged Walker to remit the sentence. "The night before the fatal day," he himself related, "the daughters of Corral, accompanied by many of the women of the city, came with sobs and anguish and tears" to plead for their father's life. At such a moment a man of Latin blood, a Bolívar or a San Martín, might have let himself be carried away by pity, might have commuted the sentence, and endeared himself, at least briefly, to the populace. But Walker, congenitally averse to emotional displays, sought to remain detached. "He who looks only at present grief, nor sees in the distance the thousand-fold sorrow a misplaced mercy may create, is little suited for the duties of public life," he wrote in self-justification. Nevertheless, he was deeply disturbed by "such entreaties as the daughters of the prisoner pressed," and he "closed the painful interview as soon as kind feeling permitted." An effort on Corral's behalf by Irena Ohoran was equally fruitless.

The execution of the Legitimist general, on November 8, 1855, left Walker the undisputed master of the Nicaraguan government. But locks of hair from Corral's corpse and handkerchiefs dipped in his blood were preserved in many a Granada home, symbols of a revenge to come. Where Walker had been feared, he was suddenly hated. A people accustomed to the hot cruelty of rage could not be expected to comprehend the lucid and cool cruelty of reason. If Walker had shrieked out a denunciation of Corral and personally stabbed him they would have understood him better and felt closer to him; but they could not forgive his dispassionate and unshakable judgment that the man had to die.

VI

So long as Corral lived, the dominant conservative groups of Central America had reserved judgment on the Rivas regime, but with his death they concluded that Rivas was a mere figurehead for the revolutionary Democrats led by the Americans. Walker made earnest efforts to allay their animosity. A circular letter went to all four of the other isthmian republics, declaring Nicaragua's peaceful purposes, and asking for their friendship. Only little San Salvador replied in kind. In Guatemala, Honduras, and Costa Rica the letter was ignored, while their official newspapers made unbridled attacks on the Rivas government. At this stage, hundreds of Nicaraguan Legitimists began to cross into Costa Rica, seeking asylum and offering their services in a war against the Americans; and the equivalent party in Costa Rica, the *Serviles,* demanded that their nation mobilize.

A new decision faced Walker—attack, or wait to be attacked? General Jerez, whose presence in the cabinet had precipitated the Corral crisis, urged him to seize the initiative. Central American democracy was indivisible, he told Walker, and he outlined a bold plan. Rally the Democrats of the entire isthmus. Mobilize a large Democratic army. Send troops, Americans among them, to restore Cabañas to power in Honduras. Move swiftly against the Costa Ricans. Remove the Nicaraguan government to León. Begin to fight. Walker was tempted but unconvinced. To recruit a substantial force of volunteers would take months; he had no faith in Nicaraguan conscripts; he had only a few hundred Americans behind him; and with so small a force he saw only one way to win a simultaneous war against Costa Rica, Honduras, and the Nicaraguan Legitimists. That was to persuade the United States government to cooperate in sending him recruits and supplies in quantity. "Let the enemy strike the first blow," he told Jerez, for if he appeared to be the aggressor he might alienate the sympathies of the American people, on whom he counted for final victory.

To one concession he agreed. Cabañas was invited to Granada to present his case in person, and was received with all respect. He was one of those dedicated revolutionaries who, out of love for humanity, was ready "to embrace Liberty upon a pile of corpses." But Walker remained adamant in the face of the Honduran's plea—a decision that would later rise to haunt him. The high-minded Cabañas and the fiery Jerez felt betrayed. It seemed to them, as Jerez later wrote, that Walker was seeking not a Democratic victory, but personal power, and in this conviction they left Granada angrily and rode north to the protection of León.

Walker was learning some bitter truths of power: that every significant decision of the ruler makes a new enemy, and that every significant enemy imposes a new decision; that although support at best grows only arithmetically, opposition may well grow geometrically. In spite of the confusion of forces around him he saw his situation more clearly than did most of his advisers and critics. In the end, everything would depend on the aid, the men and the money, coming to him from the United States. If that aid were sufficient, he would be able to federate the republics of the isthmus, bring them under "the civilizing influence of the American people," and introduce democratic institutions. Otherwise Central American democracy was a lost cause.

The British government shared this view. As the London press made clear, the big question at the Foreign Office about Central America was whether Walker, in addition to popular and Congressional support, had the backing of President Pierce. If so, it would be difficult to prevent Walker from succeeding. London noted that President Pierce had asked Congress for a discretionary fund of three million dollars to be used in the event of a rupture with England, and that a bill calling for construction of ten new warships was being sped through the Senate. Untimely British intervention in Central America might trigger a costly and undesirable war, at a time when England's taxpayers were still groaning over the expense of the Crimean muddle.

Fortunately, from the British standpoint, the American minister in London, James Buchanan, seemed almost eager to support England's position and was using his influence in Washington to that end. His attitude was especially significant because he was bound to be a strong candidate for the American Presidency in 1856. As an astute politician, he was aware that behind the scenes British influence would be a weighty factor in the presidential preference of the wealthy, conservative and powerful businessmen of New England and New York. In a private letter to Lord Clarendon, the British Foreign Minister, in whose friendship Buchanan took great satisfaction, the American had written that "the friendly offices of the two governments will be required to put things to rights in Central America," and his only worry over his stand seemed to be "What will Mrs. Grundy say? . . . That Buchanan has made a capitulation."*

The Foreign Office judged that it would be wise to watch and wait and strengthen the Costa Rican army until the signs of Washington's intentions could be read more clearly, or until Buchanan became President. Instructions to that effect went out to England's diplomatic agents in Central America, while a secret shipment of British guns was sent to Costa Rica. Although that nation's dominant political figure, President Mora, was eager to move on Granada, his British advisers counseled delay. For the time being Mora had to confine himself to statements denouncing the American Phalanx—or Rangers, as Walker had renamed them. "They have come to Central America to seek in our wives and daughters, our houses and our lands, satisfaction for their fierce passions, food for their unbridled appetites." When this diatribe was read in Granada by Walker's men, who were growing more and more restive under his strict discipline, it provoked a good deal of satirical laughter.

---

* *Buchanan Papers,* Pennsylvania Historical Society, Philadelphia (Holograph letter of Jan. 2, 1855).

XII

MEPHISTO AS ENVOY

Two months before Corral's execution, just prior to the battle of Virgin Bay, when Walker's star was flickering uncertainly, an old acquaintance had boarded the *Vesta* in the harbor of San Juan del Sur—the former Sacramento publisher and promoter, Parker French —he who claimed to have the ear of Cornelius Garrison. French had something to say that arrested Walker's attention. If Walker would give him the necessary authority, he would return to San Francisco, recruit seventy-five men, and bring them to Nicaragua on an Accessory Transit steamer, at the company's expense.

Although Walker was aware of a cloud around French's reputation, he knew nothing specific to his discredit—and San Francisco was a city full of forgotten pasts. Whatever else the man might be, he was a personality. One-armed—he had lost the other years before in a Mexican adventure—he cultivated the style of a soldier of fortune. He had a handsome, Mephistophelean head, and wearing a beard like that of Napoleon III, whom he somewhat resembled, and talking with the glib charm of a P. T. Barnum, he evoked so much interest that one almost forgot to distrust him. Dubious though he was of the man, Walker saw no reason to refuse his offer. French

153

thereupon returned to San Francisco, while Walker went on to victory at Virgin Bay.

For some weeks there was no communication between them. Soon after the conquest of Granada, however, French landed in San Juan del Sur at the head of a company of volunteers, as promised. In addition, he brought tidings so hopeful as to make all else secondary. The friendship of Garrison for Walker's enterprise, he said, was not to be doubted, even though it could not appear on the surface. The Transit Company, eager to see the situation in Nicaragua stabilized, stood ready to carry without charge as many as 500 additional recruits to Nicaragua. What was more, money was available to meet Walker's pressing needs. The new General Agent of the company in Nicaragua, C. J. McDonald, who had just arrived from San Francisco, could put $20,000 at Walker's disposal.

These were magical words in Walker's ears. The problem of pay and supply for his men gave him no peace, for the Nicaraguan treasury was empty. They spoke of French's reward for bringing the company's aid to Walker. If the promised cooperation from Accessory Transit materialized, French said, he would hope to be made Nicaragua's minister to Washington.

Walker was taken aback. He knew how much depended on his selection of an envoy to the United States. His intention was to send a trustworthy Nicaraguan, who might appear to speak for his people. The fact remained that French seemed able to speak for Garrison. Without his good offices the Provisional Government might collapse from sheer inability to pay and feed its troops. Putting first things first, he agreed to French's demand.

Mephistopheles, bargaining for Faust's soul in return for his favors, insisted on a pledge signed in blood, but French, surer of his man, accepted Walker's spoken word. Together they went to McDonald, who turned out to be a cautious Scot, carrying credentials signed by Garrison. He confirmed French's statements. The company, he said, wished success to Walker because it wished to see the Transit route kept open. A loan was perfectly feasible. There was at the moment in Nicaragua, on the way to New York, a large shipment of privately owned California gold bullion. If Walker could provide reasonable security, $20,000 worth of the bullion would be extracted from the shipment, and turned over to him. The owners of the bullion would receive instead drafts for $20,000 on Charles Morgan, the Transit Company's agent in New York, whose credit was unimpeachable. As for security, that presented no problem. Under the terms of its charter, the company owed the Nicaraguan government certain sums, the amount still in dispute. Let the $20,000 borrowed be subtracted from that debt. Thus the loan would be instantly repaid.*

A few days later, the necessary papers had been signed, and the gold was turned over to Walker. That it was tendered him in the interest of Garrison and Morgan was obvious, but no effort had been made to commit him. No one could say that he had been bought. There had been no dishonorable bargain. The initiative remained with him, to act as the best interests of the Nicaraguan government demanded. As if to assert this view, he dispatched two Nicaraguan emissaries to New York, to demand that the company settle all remaining obligations due his government.

Now there was French, waiting for his reward. There was only one honorable way for Walker to extricate himself from his pledge— by giving the man a post even more attractive to him than that of envoy. A cabinet seat was open, the Ministry of *Hacienda,* with authority over landed estates and responsibility for finding revenue. This French consented to accept in lieu of the Washington mission. Almost at once he distinguished himself by confiscating property and goods on a scale that aroused nationwide resentment. "His rapacity," Walker commented ruefully, "made him dreaded by the people," and it became urgent to get him out of the country without delay. Thus, although beset by doubts about him, Walker was forced back to his original promise.

His hope was that the Pierce administration, even if less than happy with the appointment of French, would be well disposed. American newspapers were highly encouraging as to Marcy's intentions. Although he was being urged by Nicaragua's neighbors to ban shipments of arms to Walker, he had resisted them, saying that he "would not infringe the sovereign rights" of Nicaragua. How could this be interpreted, if not as a hint that the Rivas government would soon be recognized? All that French would have to do would be to present his credentials, keep quiet, and stand by.

* William Walker, *The War in Nicaragua,* Ch. 5.

The American press and the people as a whole were unmistakably on Walker's side, regarding him as the avatar of the nation's destiny. Wherever he looked in the autumn of 1855, the horizon was rosy with hope. He felt sufficiently secure so that he invited his younger brothers, Norvell and James, to join him and share his success.

II

Some common-sense perceptions that men need in order to function in a commercial society were markedly lacking in Walker. He had no talent for the small and continuous compromises that are the building blocks of security. He did not hesitate to make enemies of those who might have helped him, if their conduct failed to conform to his code of gentlemanly behavior. He felt obliged to fulfill his promises, no matter how inconvenient. The claims of friendship he regarded as taking precedence over his own interests. It is no wonder that many practical men of affairs were outraged by him. Wherever his large strategic requirements came into conflict with his personal code of honor, the strategic requirement was sacrificed, and not because he was blind to it. This was not so much bad judgment as antijudgment. He was often called ambitious, but it would have been more correct to say that he was not ambitious enough, or perhaps that his ambition, like Caesar's, should have been made of sterner stuff. Whether any statesman has the moral right to put personal honor ahead of the needs of his government is a moot question, but Walker did, or tried to. He actually seemed to take seriously the views which he had put forward in his address on *The Unity of Art,* seven years earlier—to regard heroic behavior as a form of the aesthetic in life, more important than mere success.

This attitude, which showed in his unwillingness to break his word to French, almost immediately afterward led him deeper into danger. Not long before, another expedition had left the United States for Nicaragua, commanded by Colonel Henry Kinney of Texas. The colonel claimed the right to colonize a piece of Nicaragua about the size of the State of Maine, and including Greytown and most of Mosquito. This claim was based on a deed which the former Mosquito "King," Robert Charles Frederick, had granted to an American trader, and which Kinney had acquired. Persons close to President

Pierce were backing him financially, and worked to have the Neutrality Laws suspended in his favor. The Accessory Transit Company,
which was counting on Walker to protect its interests, regarded Kinney
as a potential nuisance, and tried to prevent his sailing, but without
success; and it fell to Walker to deal with the problem.

Kinney was anathema to Walker—partly because he sought to
colonize Nicaraguan territory on the basis of a claim which had no
legality in Nicaraguan eyes; partly because Kinney, in Greytown,
had power to interfere with Walker's Atlantic communications; partly
because his venture, clearly heading for failure, was likely to discredit
American influence among Nicaraguans. Kinney was ill, the ship on
which he had set out from the United States had been wrecked, and
he himself lacked essential qualities of leadership. With a few followers he had gone through the motions of establishing a "government" in Greytown, but its emptiness was evident from the beginning.
The hopelessness of his situation was plain to everyone but himself.
Finally, his men urged him to seek an alliance with Walker, and the
unhappy colonel sent three of them to Granada for the purpose.

Walker greeted them courteously, but on hearing the proposal that
he join forces with Kinney, he let his indignation show. Kinney, he
told them, had no right to be in Nicaragua. He could only be regarded
as an enemy of the Nicaraguan government. "Tell Governor Kinney,
or Colonel Kinney, or Mr. Kinney, or whatever he chooses to call
himself, that if I ever lay hands on him on Nicaraguan soil I shall
surely hang him!"

The threat snapped the slender cord of loyalty that linked Kinney's
men to him. They conferred briefly, and then they said, "General,
we have no wish to return to Greytown. We would like to join your
army."

It seemed to everyone that Walker had scored an effortless triumph.
But impotent as Kinney was, he yet had one thing that Walker
needed. He could count on the friendship of the White House, and
especially of Sidney Webster, President Pierce's private secretary.
Another of his financial backers was Caleb Cushing, the Attorney
General of the United States. Two of Walker's high-ranking officers,
who had known Kinney in the States, came to the conclusion that
the interests of both men required an accommodation, and in this
belief they made a journey to Greytown, and urged the Texan to go

to Granada himself and talk with Walker. They would, they told him, pledge their honor for his safety. Under the impression that their invitation had Walker's approval, Kinney accepted.

Meanwhile, Walker had prepared a decree declaring all of Mosquito, including the lands claimed by Kinney, to belong to Nicaragua. Just after this document had been made public he heard, to his astonishment, that Kinney was in Granada. His first impression was that the Colonel had come to surrender and seek a place in the Nicaraguan government and on this assumption he agreed to a meeting.

When Kinney entered his office, Walker was cold but not hostile. It came to him as a shock to hear the proposal that their two governments mutually recognize each other, and that he use his army, if need be, to protect Kinney in his possessions. Incredulous, he merely stared. But tenacity was Kinney's strong point, and long experience in fighting Indians and bamboozling settlers on the Texas frontier had given him a certain shrewdness and crude verbal power. "He had acquired," Walker said of him, "that sort of knowledge and experience of human nature derived from the exercise of the mule trade." Sprinkling his talk with profanities of which he himself was unconscious, unaware of the disdain with which he was being listened to, he ignored Walker's rejection of him. He had a right to be in Mosquito, he asserted. His claim had been paid for in hard cash. His syndicate had so far spent over a hundred thousand dollars on the colonization project. How could Walker reasonably expect them to abandon it?

This argument Walker shrugged aside. "You can't survive another month," he pointed out, "without the protection and aid of the Nicaraguan government. Why should I help you? What do you offer in return?"

Kinney's reply was definite. He could bring to Nicaragua a large number of American colonists; he was in a position to negotiate a loan in the United States; and most important, he could do more than anyone else to secure American recognition for Walker.

These were cogent points, and despite his prejudice against the man, Walker hesitated, adjourning the meeting until next day. For some hours it appeared that an alliance of sorts might after all materialize between them. But Kinney was a man who could not even sniff the fumes of the heady brew of power without losing his common sense. Flushed with hope and lacking in sensitivity, he committed an offense which, in Walker's eyes, was unpardonable. He had hardly left Walker when he sought a private meeting with President Rivas and set about to discredit his rival. Walker's army, he told Rivas, would eat up the country like a plague of locusts. Himself he presented as a man of peace and of business, without political ambitions. Colonization—agriculture—new blood—these were the needs of Nicaragua. One American colonist was worth five soldiers to the country.

Rivas, unimpressed, answered that Nicaragua, faced with the threat of invasion, looked to General Walker. He dismissed Kinney; and to assure that Walker, if he heard of the meeting, would not misunderstand its nature, he sent him a detailed report of Kinney's remarks and his own replies.

Even now, if Walker had chosen to dissemble he might easily have kept Kinney dangling without a commitment, until he had made use of the man's connection with Pierce, but this he could not bring himself to do. When the optimistic Kinney presented himself the next morning, Walter's voice and words were soft and restrained, but deadly. "I wish no further communication with you, Mr. Kinney," he said. "You have used improper methods in discussing government affairs."

Kinney, a big man, stood for a moment speechless before the slight figure of his adversary, and Walker added, "I have ordered your arrest."

"Arrest!" shouted Kinney. "You can't do that! I came here on a guarantee of safe-conduct."

This was news to Walker, but on inquiry, he found that such a pledge had actually been given. Thereupon he changed his order from one of arrest to deportation, and Kinney was taken back to Greytown ignominiously, under armed guard. He left the country soon afterward.

III

News of the breach between Kinney and Walker reached Washington some little time before French arrived to present his credentials to

Secretary of State Marcy. He came with a great fanfare of personal publicity. Walker was then the darling of the American press, and French was able to bask in his light. People believed, erroneously, that he was one of the fifty-eight Immortals, a one-armed hero, a paladin. His name was heard everywhere. Newspapers in New York and Washington urged Marcy to receive him promptly and with honor. But the ambassadors of England, France, and Spain were making strong representations against recognition of the Walker government, and Marcy felt it advisable to wait. When French requested an audience he was told that "those who were instrumental in overthrowing the government of Nicaragua were not citizens belonging to it." Marcy's view was that the country should be represented by one of its own nationals. He went on to convey that a free election showing that Rivas and Walker were supported by the Nicaraguan people might influence the attitude of the United States.

Leading publicists at once rallied to French and berated the administration. The New York *Daily News* contended that Marcy's alleged reason for denying recognition to Walker was meretricious on the face of it. The real reason, said the *News,* lay in the investments made by members of the Pierce administration in the Kinney claim. In California, another motive was found—the fact that Walker had supported antiadministration candidates for high office. In Ohio, Marcy was accused of playing England's game. Walker's own reply, when the news of Marcy's action reached him, was a vigorous editorial in *El Nicaragüense,* praised by the *New York Times* as "reasoning sustained to a high degree of ability." Its essence was a reminder that American independence had been won with the aid of foreigners— Lafayette, De Kalb, Steuben. The Rivas government, Walker said, represented the only hope of Nicaraguan independence and democracy, and was entitled to American aid. As for a free election, the Provisional Government was prepared to hold one in the very near future.

A number of newspapers pressed home the argument, and there were signs that Marcy was beginning to weaken under Congressional prodding. It was plain that the American public cared little about the merits of the Nicaraguan revolution. They regarded it as a kind of athletic competition, and they wanted the Americans to win; that was all.

Marcy had, in fact, left a door open for retreat, in the event that public opinion forced his hand. If the promise of a free election had been coupled with a modicum of discretion on the part of French, the issue could quickly have been resolved in Walker's favor. But French's ego made him indifferent to his obligations. He set up such an anti-Marcy clamor in the Press that the Secretary in self-respect could not modify his stand. The Kinney story especially was French's stock in trade. His accusations were so open that Webster and Cushing, not to say Pierce and Marcy, had to counter them with blows of their own. Cushing, as Attorney General, set in motion an investigation of French's past as the best means to justify Marcy's rejection of him.

Still exuberant, French went to New York, where he found the welcome that had been denied him in Washington. His suite at the St. Nicholas Hotel was a favorite gathering place of reporters, for he was lavish of champagne and cigars, and every day he had something new and exciting to tell about the iniquities of the Pierce administration, the bravery of the Immortals, and the importance of his own contributions to Walker's success. In one respect only did he serve Walker. He obtained a promise from Charles Morgan to transport recruits for Nicaragua from New York, as from San Francisco. With an eye on the Neutrality Laws, "emigrants" would be shipped for only twenty dollars per head, and no cash would be demanded. As in the case of recruits carried from San Francisco, the cost would simply be deducted from the company's debt to the Nicaraguan government. This policy was continued after Vanderbilt ousted Morgan from the Accessory Transit Company.

So far as the Commodore was concerned, there was every reason to assist Walker to stabilize Nicaragua. French was encouraged to place advertisements of a seemingly innocuous nature in New York's newspapers—"Wanted: ten or fifteen young men to go a short distance out of the city. Single men preferred. Apply at 347 Broadway, corner of Leonard Street, Room 12, between the hours of ten and four. Passage paid." The same newspapers carried glowing reports from Nicaragua and excerpts from *El Nicaragüense* on the opportunities awaiting Americans there—the beauty, fertility, and resources of the country, the broad lands available to settlers, the low cost of living, and the charm of the señoritas—until the imagination of Manhattan's footloose males had been thoroughly aroused. Nothing was said of cholera, dysentery, mosquitoes, flies, or the chiggers that burrowed into human flesh and were the torment of Walker's troops.

Hundreds of men were interviewed by French and accepted as "emigrants." Soon all New York knew what was in the wind. Newspapers reported that in California Walker's agents were swamped by volunteers. A riot broke out at San Francisco's docks, when so many passengers sought to board a Transit steamer for Nicaragua that nearly 300 had to be left behind. New Orleans also was bursting with enthusiasm. There a distinguished Cuban fighter for independence, Domingo de Goicuria, was busily recruiting 250 men, many of them Cubans, for service in Nicaragua, and Vanderbilt had assured him of a Transit ship to carry them to Greytown.

I V

The federal government felt compelled to make another effort to enforce the Neutrality Laws. Attorney General Cushing demanded that the District Attorneys of the great ports put an immediate stop to the recruitment and transportation of men for Walker. To assist them, he gave the press his accumulated facts about French's past. A startled public learned that French had been incontestably guilty, not many years before, of forgery and embezzlement. Worse, in the days of the gold rush, he had defrauded and victimized thousands of emigrants en route to California by wagon train. A Senate report bore evidence to his misdeeds, and a pamphlet called *The Sufferings and Hardships of Parker H. French's Overland Expedition* had been privately printed in 1851.

Newspapers which had been lauding French were silenced. The New York *Mercury* spoke the disgust of many when it said, "In bitterness of spirit, let us exclaim, with Sir Harcourt Courtly, 'Will nobody take this man away?'" The abuse heaped on French was as pungent as former praise of him had been saccharine. Heavy criticism was aimed at Walker also for having chosen such a man as his envoy. Nevertheless, to the extent that French was Walker's representative, he still had support. The *New York Times* reminded Marcy that "it is not Captain French, of questionable antecedents, who solicits the ear of our government, but the agent of a sovereign power," and the *Sun* commented that "eminently bad men, morally, hold high places in the governments with which we maintain friendly relations. International morals are not so pure that there need be any squeamishness in admitting Colonel French to the diplomatic circle."

French employed all the tricks his ingenuity could conceive, and they were many, to put Nicaragua-bound recruits on board the Transit steamships without giving the government firm legal grounds for interference. A favorite device was to have the men come on board singly, and mingle with California-bound passengers, of whom there were always a considerable number, and who were always glad to pretend that Walker's men were their sons and brothers. The frustration of federal officers, who knew the filibusters were there and yet were unable to distinguish them from their companions with any certainty, was compounded by the open derision of the passengers. Steamer after steamer was able to sail from New York loaded with "emigrants" to Greytown, while crowds on the dock cheered the name of Walker and booed any mention of Pierce. New York's District Attorney obtained Grand Jury indictments against French; he even had him put under arrest, but this move proved so unpopular that the order was hastily rescinded.

French, however, had not reckoned on the depth of Walker's anger over his behavior, and especially over his statements about Pierce and Marcy. A curt letter came to him from Granada. His commission as minister was revoked. A new envoy had been appointed to Washington—the Nicaraguan priest, Augustin Vijil, who had steadfastly supported Walker from the beginning. With this news, French lost his hold on all that remained to him of public approval, and when he left New York the newspapers hardly bothered to dust their editorial hands of him. He went to Nicaragua, to hear from Walker's own lips that there was no place for him in the country. French was wise enough not to argue, and boarded a ship for New Orleans. There he gave out that he was on secret business for Walker, and roamed the South, delivering lectures on Nicaragua to large audiences. Returning to New York, he sought to promote a new steamship venture, asserting that in spite of everything he was still Walker's trusted friend. So persistent was he that El Nicaragüense was finally compelled to publish a statement by Walker that "French has no connection whatever with this government; . . . he is at present engaged in doing the [Nicaraguan] administration all the injury his genius is capable of."

XIII

MR. VANDERBILT IS OUTRAGED

In November, 1855, Cornelius Garrison, reading letters from Morgan in New York, knew that the moment of crisis was at hand. Wall Street sources left no doubt that Vanderbilt's purchases of Accessory Transit stock were rapidly bringing the company under his thumb, and that at the next stockholders' meeting he would take over.

Although Garrison's contract with the company had some years to go, he was highly vulnerable, not only because of past opposition to Vanderbilt, but perhaps even more because of certain irregular transactions of the company's San Francisco office—transactions which he was unwilling to submit to Vanderbilt's scrutiny. But in Garrison's philosophy there was always more than one way to skin a tiger, even if his name was Vanderbilt. He and Morgan had sketched out a plan by which the Commodore might be made the butt of Wall Street for a change, instead of its hero, and some of his millions squeezed out of him.

Everything now depended on one man, Walker. Experience as a politician and banker had made Garrison a shrewd judge of character. It was clear to him that Walker's motivations differed sharply from those of the run of men. Conversations in Nicaragua reported by C. J. McDonald and Parker French had so far brought nothing more from Walker than formal appreciation of Garrison's aid. The time had now come to get a definite commitment from him.

With such a man, Garrison sensed, a crude appeal to the pocketbook would not serve. You cannot bribe a knight-errant. But you can always appeal to his knightliness. Garrison accordingly began his campaign by retaining the services of two of Walker's oldest friends, Edmund Randolph and another well-known San Francisco attorney, Parker Crittenden, offering them shares in large future profits if they would go to Nicaragua on his behalf. Their specific assignment was to persuade Walker to seize the properties of the Accessory Transit Company in the name of Nicaragua, and turn them over to Randolph, who would form a new company to be headed by Garrison and Morgan. A legal justification for such a move could be found in the fact that Accessory Transit over the years had refused to admit its sizable debt to Nicaragua.

It was the plan of Morgan and Garrison, if they could win Walker's consent, to sell the stock of Accessory Transit short in huge quantities and make a Wall Street killing when the news broke. But nothing of this was to be said to Walker. Randolph and Crittenden were to emphasize that the new company would accept a charter far more favorable to Nicaragua than that held by Vanderbilt, a contract that would assure frequent and regular shipping service from the United States; and that cooperation in providing the recruits and supplies needed by Walker would be unstinted. He was to be told, further, that if he would not agree, Morgan and Garrison would no longer feel an obligation to make efforts on his behalf. With so cogent an argument, Randolph and Crittenden saw no reason why they should not accept the mission. At the last moment, the Mayor suggested that they take with them his son and trusted aid, W. R. Garrison.

I I

In December, 1855, Cornelius Vanderbilt, once more at the helm of Accessory Transit, was feeling expansive. Having accumulated all the necessary stock, he had ousted Morgan from the company and regained the presidency. The company's shares had thereupon bounded upward and had added at least a million to his wealth. With Walker in Nicaragua, the Transit route was secure; and his success might open up not only Nicaragua but the entire Caribbean to American capital. There could be no doubt that the independence of Cuba was one of Walker's major objectives. Why else was the noted Cuban revolutionary, Domingo de Goicuria, recruiting for him in New Orleans? One of Vanderbilt's first actions after assuming command at Accessory Transit had been to confirm an order previously issued by Morgan to send a company ship to New Orleans to transport Goicuria and his men to Greytown without asking cash payment. Vanderbilt expected to begin negotiations with Walker soon over the amount of the Transit's debt to Nicaragua, and he anticipated that his bill for the ocean fares of Walker's recruits, plus the filibuster's gratitude, would offset most of the obligation. Goicuria's gratitude could be expected to have similar dollar value if and when he and Walker succeeded in wresting Cuba from Spain.

At Granada, Walker received a message from Goicuria, who said that if Walker and he were in agreement on future strategy, he would bring to Nicaragua 250 fighting men. One thing only the Cuban wanted to determine. Could he count on aid not only in the overthrow of the Spanish tyranny in Cuba, but in support of Cuban independence against any aggressive tendencies that the United States might display?

Walker was able to reply, with complete truth, that to aid in the liberation of Cuba had always been one of his dreams. He believed that the best interests of the United States would be served by the independence of the Caribbean nations, which, under efficient and honest administration, would benefit from the availability of American capital, business enterprise, and trade.

A memorandum of agreement was drawn up and signed. Goicuria was to aid Walker in "consolidating the peace and the government of the Republic of Nicaragua." Walker on his part would "assist and cooperate with his person and his various resources, such as men, in the cause of Cuba and in favor of her liberty."*

---

* W. O. Scroggs, "William Walker's Designs on Cuba," in *Mississippi Valley Historical Review*, 1914, Vol. I, p. 199.

III

While Goicuria and Walker were negotiating for the future of Cuba, Randolph, Crittenden, and young Garrison arrived in Granada, together with a hundred new recruits. It was a joyous moment for Walker, able to receive his oldest friend against a background of power and fame. That evening he entertained the three San Franciscans at a dinner attended by President Rivas and the entire cabinet; and the next day he met privately with Randolph.

Subsequently reporting Walker's action in seizing the Transit, some American newspapers said that in accepting Garrison's offer he displayed impulsiveness and ignorance verging on idiocy. Walker himself made no defense of his action. But his decision was far from impulsive or ignorant. Several weeks earlier word has come to him from San Francisco that some kind of stock-rigging deal was in the wind.* There was nothing in this to tempt him. No one could read the New York newspapers, as he had done for years, without being aware of Vanderbilt's tremendous power. That he was wary of any commitment to Garrison and Morgan shows in their recourse to Randolph. He appreciated the aid he had received from Garrison, but he did not misunderstand it or overvalue it. Sooner or later it would all be paid for by Nicaragua through reductions of Accessory Transit's debt.

New York newspapers telling of Vanderbilt's bid for recapture of Accessory Transit reached Granada before Randolph's arrival. The practical question that Walker had to consider was whether he would be better off to cooperate with the legal head of the company, Vanderbilt, or to throw in his lot with the men whom Vanderbilt had defeated. While only that question was before him, he remained neutral. He wanted the good will of the company regardless of the identity of its head. The dangers that would follow defiance of Vanderbilt were unmistakable. But when Randolph came to him, the situation suddenly changed. This was the man of all men to whom he was devoted, the friend who had more than once come to his rescue, helped him, saved him.

A realist, a Napoleon, would have had no hesitation in sacrificing

* William Walker, *The War in Nicaragua*, p. 149.

the friendship to political advantage—would have played for time, put off the decision until Randolph grew tired of waiting. Not so Walker. The saying that "a friend in power is a friend lost" did not apply to him. Given his attitude toward life, he could deny Randolph nothing—the point on which Garrison counted. Walker's motivation in the matter was described enigmatically by himself. "The friendship between Randolph, Crittenden, and Walker was of a character not to be expressed by words; but the existence of such a sentiment between these three is essential for an understanding of the perfect confidence which marked their acts in reference to the Transit."

The press was mystified by what seemed to be a totally irresponsible action on the part of a man who, until then, had conducted his affairs with considerable skill. What it could not know was that, reasoning from Walker's special premises, his decision was in fact entirely logical. His life had never been guided by the canons of success, but by the canons of personal honor, in which the claim of friendship was paramount.

He was not unaware of the economic motivations of politics. Rather he rejected them. It was this apparent indifference to the realities of American life that prompted Horace Greeley to call him "the Don Quixote of Central America." The Knight of La Mancha did not seem more wrong-minded and absurd to his contemporaries than Walker in the eyes of the great magnates of the 1850's. It was not merely that he dared to defy Vanderbilt. He was defying the onset of a new age. He was tilting at the unshakable windmill of the money-power.

His own description of his private meeting with Randolph, while formalized, hints at the forces at work in him. "Randolph informed Walker that he and Crittenden had carefully examined the charter of the Accessory Transit Company, and were both clear and decided in the opinion that it had been forfeited. . . . After due reflection, Walker was entirely satisfied . . . that the agreement with Garrison was the means, and at that time the only means, for carrying out the policy vital to the Rivas administration. True, neither the President nor the cabinet knew of the means whereby their objects were accomplished; and it was in fact highly necessary to the success of the measures that they should be known to as few persons as possible. After Randolph and Walker had agreed on the terms of a new transit grant, a copy was sent to Garrison at San Francisco, McDonald being the bearer of it. W. R. Garrison went to New York for the purpose of informing Charles Morgan of the arrangements which had been made, and were about to be made, while Randolph remained at Granada. Nothing was said to Rivas of the new transit contract."

Walker's failure to fulfill his responsibility to Rivas was heavy on his mind. When the President was informed of the affair, he exclaimed indignantly that Walker had consented to "the sale of the country." This Walker did not deny. Instead, ruefully, he said, " 'The sale of the country,' in Rivas' use of the term, was a foregone conclusion . . . the only way to get into the country a force capable of protecting it, not only from domestic but from foreign enemies. . . . Whoever desires to hold Nicaragua securely must be careful that the navigation . . . is controlled by those who are his staunchest and most reliable friends." He did not, however, attempt to explain why he had broken with Vanderbilt when the latter was cooperatively providing free passage for recruits.

As Richard III for a kingdom, so for friendship Walker was ready to "set his life upon a cast," and "stand the hazard of the die."

IV

At the end of February, 1856, the stock of the Accessory Transit Company sold at $23 a share, in a rising market. Early in March, the *New York Times* reported that Morgan, "lately in the administration of the company, was selling the stock [short] much as Vanderbilt had done after the latter had lost control." Vanderbilt eagerly grasped what seemed to him a heaven-sent opportunity to corner the stock and squeeze a fortune out of his enemy, and he bought as heavily as Morgan was selling, holding the price close to its peak level. Then, on March 12, news from Nicaragua that Walker had annulled the Accessory Transit charter, and had issued a new charter to Edmund Randolph, precipitated a wild rush on Wall Street to sell Transit shares. That day the price of the stock dropped four points, and it continued to fall until the shares were selling at $13 each. At this price Morgan covered his short sales, for a profit estimated at close to a million.

Incredulous at the first reports of Walker's action, once Vanderbilt was sure of the facts he let out his rage in private and public. The great question in New York's financial community was: what had possessed Walker to do such a thing? Regretfully the well-informed *Herald* remarked that "the great mass of the American people deeply sympathize with the present government of Nicaragua and will regret that its gallant head has perilled its hitherto bright prospects. It will be seen that it is in Mr. Vanderbilt's power to kill off the new government by opening another route and thus cutting off Walker's communications with San Francisco and New York."

The accuracy of this forecast soon became evident. Morgan had neglected to organize the new line of steamships on which Walker was counting, and for six vital weeks no steamers sailed from New York with the men and supplies essential to Walker's security. Efforts made by Garrison to keep Accessory Transit steamers running from San Francisco to Nicaragua proved fruitless when a Vanderbilt agent arrived with orders that all of the company's ships out of California were to be routed to Panama, where their passengers would be transferred to the Atlantic side by railroad. The Commodore was moving simultaneously on many fronts. When his letters demanding intervention by the United States brought only a cold reply from Secretary of State Marcy, the millionaire promptly turned to England. His agents rushed to London and to the Caribbean to invoke the aid of British diplomacy and warships in blocking the Transit entry at Greytown. Still another agent went to Granada, where he talked secretly with President Rivas, in an effort to produce an open break between him and Walker. Simultaneously Vanderbilt brought suit for $500,000 against Garrison, on a charge of fraud, and another, for $1,000,000 against Morgan, Garrison, and Walker, alleging trespass, conversion, and dispersal of the company's goods, and fraudulent conspiracy to interrupt and molest the corporation.

The force of these moves produced a prompt effect on Morgan and Garrison. Content with their stockmarket killing, they had gone through the form of purchasing the new transit charter from Randolph; now they offered to sell the new charter, with its privileges, to Vanderbilt. He flatly refused. His duty, he replied, was to protect the stockholders of the old company, and he wrote a letter to the New York *Herald* to explain his virtuous stand. "Mr. Garrison called on me and . . . intimated that if I would participate with him and Charles

Morgan . . . we could make a good business of it to the exclusion of the Transit Company. I told him he must clear up his character as regards his conduct toward the company. . . ." This was no doubt accurate, but it was far from being the truth. The great financier had in fact found it possible to extract a cash profit from the situation. His order to withdraw his ships from Nicaragua and enter the Panama run created consternation among the other Panama lines. Recognizing his nuisance value, Vanderbilt promptly offered to withdraw his ships from competition, on payment by the Panama lines of a monthly "subsidy" of $40,000 (later, $56,000) a month. The agreement was too close to blackmail to be put into writing, but it was made orally, and carried out.*

---

* *Harper's Weekly*, 1859, Vol. III, p. 114.

XIV

"YOU STAND ALONE"

Walker, in 1856, stood at a focal point of history, where great political and economic forces converged: the need of the United States for a short ocean route to California—the determination of England to prevent the Americans from building an interoceanic canal that would give them an advantage in trade with the Orient—the drive of New York capitalists to control the Central American isthmus—the dream of Manifest Destiny shared by millions of Americans—the urge of the South to annex Cuba and the Caribbean lands—the unending struggle of Central America's peons against feudal serfdom. The importance that the world attributed to his venture is suggested by the enemies that he made. These included, in addition to Vanderbilt, the conservative wing of the American Congress; the Nicaraguan Legitimists; the governments of Costa Rica, Honduras, and Guatemala; England; and less overtly, Spain and France. In the immensity of their power he found a wry satisfaction. He still hoped for victory, but a defeat by hostile forces of such magnitude would at least be no disgrace.

Almost at the moment when his defiance of Vanderbilt was shocking informed circles in New York, a number of speeches sharply

172

critical of him were made in the United States Senate, while British enmity was not confined to words. The chances of intervention on Walker's behalf by the Pierce administration had diminished, England calculated, to the point where her Central American friends need no longer be restrained. State papers which were not made public until many years later revealed that Great Britain's War Office at this time arranged a grant of arms to Costa Rica to combat "the troops under Mr. Walker, against whom you may have to defend yourselves."

These British arms included, in addition to 2,000 rifled muskets equipped with sights and superior to those used by Walker's men, a million rounds of ammunition and much other equipment.* This became known to Walker when a messenger carrying official mail to San José was intercepted and letters from the Costa Rican consul in London were found containing evidence that the British Foreign Secretary, Lord Clarendon, had personally authorized the shipment of arms which emboldened Costa Rica to go to war. "When I was telling Lord Clarendon," wrote the consul, "that Costa Rica already had an army of eight hundred men on the frontier, he was much pleased, and said that was a proper move . . . and that is the reason for their giving us the muskets."

To a letter from the Costa Rican government requesting naval support as well, the Foreign Office replied that a cruiser would visit Costa Rica "to protect British interests." Actually, a large squadron comprising some of England's finest warships began to range both coasts of Central America. Reported the New York *Daily News,* a pro-Walker organ, "The British Ambassador at our Federal Capital, having been in due form interrogated regarding the aggressive posture of the . . . British fleet off San Jan del Norte declines communicating any explanation."

Thus encouraged, at the beginning of March, 1856, President Mora of Costa Rica issued an order of mobilization calling for an army of 9000 men "to take up arms for the republic of Nicaragua" against what he maintained was an American invasion; and without waiting for a formal declaration of war, a substantial force equipped with British guns advanced into Nicaragua. Advising Mora, it subse-

---

* British State Papers, Vol. XVI, pp. 784-5, 794-6.

quently became known, were agents of Spain and France, as well as of England.

To this invasion the Nicaraguan government responded with a declaration of war. Let the world note, said President Rivas, that his country had been attacked without provocation. More to the point was a statement personally issued by Walker—the affirmation of political principles that Jerez had earlier urged him to make. Throwing off all claims to impartiality as between Democrats and Legitimists, he made a frank appeal to the revolutionary elements of the entire isthmus. He had been invited to Nicaragua by the Democrats, he said, and he and his men had never ceased to struggle for the principles of the revolution. True, he had held his Democratic friends in check, he had sought to conciliate the Legitimists, he had tried to establish friendly relations with the antidemocratic governments of neighboring countries, but all his advances for the sake of peace had been repulsed with scorn. Now the country was being attacked. Let it be so. He and his American followers were joined with Nicaraguan Democrats in eternal opposition to *Servile* governments throughout Central America, and they would resume and wear forever the red ribbon of democracy.

Walker's belief in democracy was by no means inconsistent with his urge to power. For him, as for the world of his time, the institutions of the United States could be equated with democracy. To extend these institutions to another people, as he hoped eventually to do in Central America, was to serve the democratic cause. His opponents assumed that his professions of democratic faith were dictated by cold expediency. To the conservatives his aim seemed to be "absolute and exclusive domination of the country" in the interest of the United States.* The fact remained that in 1856 Walker's reaffirmation of democratic allegiance was accepted by many Nicaraguans. Native volunteers continued to serve in his army. His popularity among the poorer classes was noted more than once. The most dedicated of the Democratic leaders, Maximo Jerez, agreed to join the new Rivas cabinet as Minister of War.

For all the turbulence he created, one comes at the core of his thinking to a sudden quiet perception of a truth to which America

---

* R. Obregon Loria, *La Campaña del Transito,* San José, 1956, p. 58.

did not awaken until he had been dead a century—that a great power best serves its own interest by lifting poor and primitive peoples into the light of productive civilization. At a time when economic assistance to other countries on a national scale was unheard of, it was only by capitalistic enterprise and the introduction of equitable institutions that exploiting nations could help the exploited make progress, as the United States later did in the Philippines. It is not to be mistaken that, left to their own devices, the Central American peoples experienced a lowering of their standards of living and social condition after Walker's day, not an advance.*

Horace Greeley might consider him a power-hungry pirate, Wall Street an agent of cunning capitalists, but he thought of himself as the head of a revolutionary army, fighting against the feudal owners of the isthmus in the name of democracy. As proof of his Democratic good faith he not only brought Maximo Jerez into the government, but gave two other cabinet posts to Democrats of Jerez' choice; he authorized the transfer of the seat of government from Granada to León; and he had the government announce an early presidential and congressional election, to be held by popular vote.

To him the shocking thing was that although England did not hesitate to support her reactionary aims in Central America with arms and supplies, the government of the United States, calling itself democratic, refused to see the significance of the struggle that he was waging. *Harper's Weekly* remarked that the treatment of Walker by the American government was very like that of John Knox and John Wesley by the Church of England. It was a comparison the more apt because of the psychological similarity of Walker to the great religious reformers. Like them, he never complained about the injuries inflicted on him by enemies, but the calumnies of his own countrymen left a scar. He had ridden out under the banner of democracy into a world full of danger, seeking dragons to slay, and his feelings about the castigation of him by Marcy and Buchanan were like those of a knight who, while on a great quest, heard that he had been blackballed and barred from the Round Table.

---

* A. G. Frank, "The Economic Development of Nicaragua," in *Inter-American Affairs,* 1955, Vol. VIII, No. 4.

II

In the ensuing military campaign, which comprised only two battles, Walker's forces lost both, and his reputation as a general was permanently damaged, yet he emerged as the victor and a greater hero than ever in the eyes of the American public. The first battle took place at Santa Rosa, south of Lake Nicaragua, where the enemy vanguard was encamped, and where the Costa Ricans swore death to every American on whom they could lay hands. Walker's situation was deteriorating rapidly. Another cholera epidemic, then in its initial stage, coupled with widespread dysentery and fevers, had reduced his American effectives to only 600. He himself was down with fever and a painful swelling of the face. In an effort to conserve his men for what he could not doubt would be a long struggle, he determined to send against the Costa Ricans initially a battalion of four companies: one composed entirely of Frenchmen recently arrived from San Francisco; one of German immigrants out of New York; one of Nicaraguans, and one of raw American recruits. A question immediately arose: who was to command this polyglot force? Walker's choice could hardly have been worse if he had been delirious with fever, as some thought he was. His attention centered on a German named Louis Schlessinger, an educated and plausible man whom he had previously used on diplomatic missions, and who spoke all of the four essential languages. Totally untrained and psychologically unfit for military leadership, Schlessinger failed to scout the territory into which he was advancing, and was surprised by the enemy in force. At the first fire the undisciplined company of Germans broke and fled, followed by the French, with Schlessinger himself among them. For a few minutes the Nicaraguans and Americans held back the enemy but, after a hundred men had fallen, joined the rout, leaving their wounded to summary execution at the hands of the jubilant Costa Ricans.

News of this shocking defeat came to a Granada already unnerved by the terrors of cholera, and was followed closely by rumors that a Honduran army was about to join in the attack on Walker. The resulting wave of panic swept up many Americans as well as Nicaraguans. Scores of recent arrivals from New York who had not yet enlisted in Walker's force begged to be sent home. Even his veterans were dispirited, especially since a number of his best officers had been stricken by cholera. Efforts to revive morale were unavailing before the despondency evoked by the spectacle of half-starved fugitives from Santa Rosa straggling in with reports of Schlessinger's incompetence and Costa Rican savagery. Schlessinger himself was arrested, court-martialed and condemned to be shot as a coward, but managed to escape, some thought with the secret connivance of Walker, whose own responsibility in having selected so untried a man for a military command was manifest. To his friend and most stalwart defender in the United States Congress, Senator John Weller of California, Walker wrote in a vein of grim realism: "We have great moral odds against us. . . . I may not live to see the end . . . but if we fail, we feel that it will be in the cause of honor."

Most imminent and acute of all the dangers confronting Walker was the likelihood that the enemy, now numbering 4,000, would occupy the all-important Transit route and block the way for American reinforcements. To forestall this move, although he was still weak from his illness, he took personal command of the 500 Americans left to him, and led them south to the town of Rivas, the scene of his defeat a year earlier, astride the western segment of the route. There he put all his energy into a revival of the health, morale, and discipline of his troops.

"Woe betide the luckless wretch who unfitted himself for duty in that dread presence on the eve of battle," wrote one of his officers. It was at this time that Walker publicly reprimanded his brother Norvell, and reduced him from a captaincy to the ranks, for having participated in an all-night carouse against orders. Thereafter he paraded his restive men in the plaza of Rivas, and briefly addressed them. It was a typically Walkerian performance. Thinner than ever, pale and feverish, his drab clothing hanging from him like a scarecrow's slops, he sought to give his men a vision of themselves as heroes.

"Let me try," he said, "to place before you the moral grandeur of the position that you occupy. You stand alone in the world, without a friendly government to give even its sympathy, much less its aid. You have nothing to support you in this struggle except the consciousness of the justice of your cause. Those who should have befriended you have maligned you. . . . I would not conceal from you the great peril and the urgency of the danger in which you stand." They heard him in silence. But "the words . . . had the desired effect and created a new spirit among them," Walker wrote. "It is only by constant appeals to the loftier qualities of man that you can make him a good soldier; and all military discipline is a mere effort to make virtue constant and reliable by making it habitual."

III

The news grew worse. President Rivas reported from León that in spite of his efforts to conciliate the Hondurans, they were about to invade Nicaragua and attack Granada. Walker now had to consider whether he dared do battle with the Costa Ricans on the Transit route; for even if he won against the heavy odds confronting him, his losses were almost certain to be large, and his army would be unfit to meet the Hondurans. His decision was to return to Granada until Nicaraguan reinforcements then being organized in León could reach him.

No sooner had he reached Granada than further word came: the rumors from Honduras were false. An invasion from the north was not anticipated in the near future. Shaken by this disclosure of the weakness of President Rivas as a source of intelligence, Walker turned back toward the Transit, but too late; the Costa Ricans had taken advantage of his withdrawal to occupy the towns of Rivas and Virgin Bay, where they seized the buildings of the Transit Company and wantonly killed nine of its American employees.

In such a situation, failure to attack would be equivalent to slow suicide. As Walker saw it, his only hope lay in forcing the Costa Ricans out of their strong position in Rivas. Despite the small size of his force and his lack of artillery, he determined on an immediate assault. The first hours of the battle went well for him. Driving into the streets of Rivas in an unexpected circular movement, his men trapped and shot down large numbers of the enemy, and forced the rest, nearly 2000, into the center of the town. There for a time the exchange of fire continued heavily in favor of the Americans, with five Costa Ricans falling for every one of Walker's soldiers. But he lacked the manpower needed to maintain his advantage, and his casualties, killed and wounded, rose to 120, one quarter of his total command. The fall of night enabled him to withdraw his men, the movement being carried out in utmost silence, and when with daylight the Costa Ricans prepared to resume the battle they found to their astonishment that the Americans were gone, carrying their wounded with them.

Some of Walker's own associates thought the end had come, as they again retreated northward toward Granada, but they did not reckon on the imponderables of war. Costa Rica soon began to hear the truth about her heavy losses at Rivas, and after General Mora's bombast the long casualty lists came as a shock. Even worse was the appearance of the cholera in his army, in an especially virulent form. It was not to see thousands of its young men destroyed within a fortnight that his nation had heeded the call to arms; and the epidemic, which had begun to spread throughout Costa Rica itself, was blamed on the war. When a spontaneous demonstration demanding the return of the army and verging on revolt broke out in San José, Mora decided to hasten back to his capital with such troops as were fit to march.

Suddenly, amazingly, the Americans heard that Rivas, Virgin Bay, and the Transit once more lay open to them. There came a note from the commander whom Mora had left in Rivas, begging the indulgence of Walker for the stricken hundreds of Costa Ricans whom he would find there. The first reaction in Walker's camp was a roar of protest; was the shooting and bayoneting of wounded Americans to go unrequited? Nevertheless, when Walker issued an order that the troops respect the conventions of war among civilized peoples, it was obeyed. The enemy sick were tended; those who recovered were repatriated, and those who died were given formal burial. Even the most anti-American of Costa Rican historians had to admit, "In regard for the truth, we must say that Walker treated with humanity the soldiers whom he found in Rivas."*

This display of humanitarianism in the midst of despair and horror caught the imagination of the American people, and proved to be Walker's most effective political instrument, more than offsetting his

* J. Perez, *Memorias,* II, p. 51.

loss of military prestige. Nation-wide approval greeted reports of scenes in the improvised hospitals of Rivas, where he personally inspected the wounds of enemies and provided them with such care as could be found. The press, which had begun to grow cool at news of his defeats, took him again to its editorial heart, praised him for his forbearance and generosity, rejoiced in the fact that the tide had turned for him, and even saw in the ravages of the cholera, which had brought Mora's campaign to its abrupt end, the beneficent favor of Providence for Americans, recalling the fate of the Assyrian when he came down like a wolf on the fold.

"*Los Yankis,*" exulted the *Daily News* of New York, "are not monsters of rudeness and cruelty, as the designing slanders of European bureaucracy describe us, but . . . have burst their way like a fertilizing torrent through the barriers of barbarism. . . . Nicaragua is at peace." British journals too were impressed, the London *Post*, no friend to Walker, going so far as to see in him "a certain resemblance to the chivalry of the middle ages . . . the Normans in their palmy days"; while the influential *Saturday Review* told England that "if Walker . . . should eventually annex Central America to the United States, it may be doubted whether European statesmen have any longer a motive for interfering."

In May, 1856, Walker, regarded as doomed two months earlier, was again in full command of the situation. Costa Rica and Honduras appeared to have lost their stomach for war. Legitimist insurrectionists had been put down by Nicaraguan troops under the command of Vallé and Goicuria. Some reinforcements and supplies from America were again reaching Greytown on a steamer belatedly supplied by Morgan. And most important, American sentiment for Walker was making itself heard more and more loudly in political circles. A speech in the Senate on May 1, 1856, by Senator Weller of California was widely reported. "There is no man whose character has been more shamefully misrepresented in this country than General Walker. I have known him for several years on the Pacific Coast as a quiet, unobtrusive and intelligent gentleman of uncommon energy and decided character. His integrity—his honor—was never impeached in any quarter. After being invited, he went to Nicaragua—not as a 'freebooter'; he did not go there for plunder. He neither coveted their lands nor their money, for no one has less of the sordid feeling than General Walker. He was actuated by a high and honorable ambition —a patriotic desire to aid in establishing free institutions in Nicaragua, and ultimately confederate, in a peaceable manner, the Central American states into one great republic. This was his ambition—this was the object he sought to accomplish. Many gentlemen of the highest character residing on the Pacific, actuated by the same motives, rallied under his banner. It is a great mistake to suppose these men are desperadoes and freebooters!"

IV

Like any political man, Walker was perpetually striving to make rational decisions in an irrational framework. Whether his judgment was good or bad in a given instance mattered less than the ever-changing and unpredictable pattern of circumstance in which he worked and which more than anything else determined the outcome of his actions. A man shooting from the hip at a mile-high eagle had as good a chance of hitting his target as Walker to overcome the hostility of the Pierce administration by anything that he might purposefully do. Only great luck, some favorable concatenation of events could change the President's attitude toward him. That luck was his in the spring of 1856, when his mercy to the Costa Ricans at Rivas was affecting American sentiment. The Platform Committee of the Democratic Party was then at work drafting the principles on which the party's choice of a presidential nominee would presumably be made. Prominent in the Committee was Pierre Soulé, who had never forgiven Marcy and Pierce for their "betrayal" of him in the matter of the Ostend Manifesto. Regarded as a leading light of the American expansionists, he was determined to revive the spirit of the Manifesto in the Democratic platform. The soaring of Walker's reputation—"the noble Walker," Soulé called him—provided the former ambassador with precisely the opportunity he sought; and almost singlehanded he drafted a plank for the platform that, he hoped, would alter the nation's policy not only toward Walker's effort in Nicaragua, but with respect to Spanish and British provocations throughout the Caribbean.

"The time has come for the people of the United States to declare themselves in favor of free seas, and progressive free trade throughout the world. . . .

"Resolved, That the great highway . . . marked out for free communication between the Atlantic and Pacific oceans . . . would be secured by a timely and efficient exertion of the control which we have the right to claim over it. . . . No power on earth should be suffered to impede or clog its progress. . . .

"Resolved, That, in view of so commanding an interest, the people of the United States cannot help but sympathize with the efforts which are being made by the people of Central America to regenerate that portion of the continent which covers the passage across the inter-oceanic isthmus."

Soulé in effect was saying that only a candidate who would agree to back Walker and the Ostend Manifesto would get the majority of the Southern delegations at the Convention which was to assemble in Cincinnati in June—a warning to Buchanan, and an invitation to other hopefuls. Buchanan was playing a subtle game. To Southerners he spoke of his satisfaction in his part in the Manifesto, to which he had made considerable contributions. But in the North and in British circles he let it be known privately that Soulé, "a regular bird-charmer," had hypnotized him into signing the document, and that he was in fact out of sympathy with it. No one could be sure precisely where he stood in the matter.

The first candidate to yield to Soulé's pressure was President Pierce, who still dreamed of succeeding himself in the White House. For once overriding Marcy, and ignoring protests from Costa Rica, Honduras, and Cornelius Vanderbilt, on May 14, 1856, he recognized the Rivas government of Nicaragua, in the person of its new minister, Padre Augustin Vijil.

No one could have been more surprised by the new turn of events than Padre Vijil himself, who from the moment of his appearance in Washington had been subjected to insults and vilification. A gentle and idealistic soul, a former lawyer turned priest, eager to serve the cause of peace and the popular welfare, he was dismayed by the intensity of feeling against Walker that he encountered wherever the influence of Great Britain, the Central American conservatives, or the Catholic hierarchy was felt. Most of Washington's diplomats ignored him, the Vanderbilt-oriented press abused him, and the Archbishop of Baltimore rebuked him: "Is it possible that a Catholic priest should come to this country to labour against his Church and his native land?" It took the President's acceptance of his credentials to make Vijil realize that Walker's strength lay not in Washington but in the country at large.

In New York City a mass meeting, attended by thousands, was held to celebrate the recognition of Walker, with gigantic signs reading NO BRITISH INTERFERENCE ON THE AMERICAN CONTINENT! and ENLARGE THE BOUNDS OF LIBERTY! At this meeting, another contender for the Democratic nomination joined the pro-Walker camp—Lewis Cass, United States Senator from Michigan. In a letter read to the cheering crowd he said, "I am free to confess that the heroic effort of our countrymen in Nicaragua excites my admiration. . . . The difficulties which General Walker has encountered and overcome will place his name high on the roll of distinguished men of his age. . . . A new day, I hope, is opening upon the states of Central America. Our countrymen will plant there the seeds of our institutions, and God grant that they may grow up into an abundant harvest of industry, enterprise and prosperity."

These developments were not lost on the British, who supposed that recognition of Walker would be followed by open American aid to him. It was the easier for England to believe this, since she herself was secretly aiding his enemies. As evidence of the seriousness with which he viewed the situation, Lord Palmerston ordered 20,000 troops to Canada, and staged a great naval review, to which the American minister in London was pointedly invited. A wave of war talk rose again on both sides of the Atlantic. The London *Post* warned that "no one can tell to what consequences the success of filibustering in Central America may lead. . . . We must be prepared to defend our possessions." Advocates of a direct American challenge to England, over Nicaragua, were prominent at the Democratic Convention in Cincinnati. There, after hot debate, Soulé's Nicaraguan plank was incorporated in the party platform to loud cheers.

Most of the Southern delegates at the convention gave their votes to Cass or Pierce. The Northern states, however, felt safer with the always-uncommitted and exquisitely cautious Buchanan, and as many had foreseen, he emerged with the nomination. With the ineffectual

Millard Fillmore as the American Party (Know-Nothing) candidate, and the newly born Republican Party gambling wildly on General Frémont of California, it was not difficult to foresee where the victory would lie in the coming November. At this stage there was still a widespread impression that once Buchanan was in the Presidency he would reveal himself as an expansionist, call what was generally assumed to be Palmerston's bluff, and give Walker all possible aid and encouragement.

XV

THE PRESIDENT

In Nicaragua, too, 1856 saw a presidential contest, and it achieved a degree of turbulence remarkable even for Latin America. In the early spring, when southern Nicaragua was in the throes of war, there was an election in the region around León. A head of state was chosen from among three candidates—Rivas, standing as a moderate, Jerez, representing the radical wing of the Democratic party, and Mariano Salazar, a wealthy merchant turned army officer, who had achieved considerable popularity by fiery speeches and judicious expenditure. The returns favored Salazar by a slight margin. After Walker had re-established order in the south, however, Rivas demanded that Granada and the districts to the east and southwest of Lake Nicaragua, where most of his own strength lay, be polled. Instantly trouble began.

The Granadans were agitated by the realization that no matter which of the three candidates was elected, they would be subordinate to hated León. Even Rivas was committed to the northern center as Nicaragua's capital. The alarms of war had not abated the rivalry of the two cities by an iota. They had been brought into uneasy truce only by the American, Walker. If there was to be a new

President, said many in Granada, let him too be a candidate. Let there be a completely new election.

Against this proposal Rivas, Salazar, and Jerez all three took a firm stand. They had no doubt as to the outcome of an election in which Walker was a contestant. Not only the Granadans but even some of the Leónese could be expected to vote for him. Withdrawal of the Costa Rican troops had made him a national hero. In Granada he was followed by cheering crowds wherever he went. When he visited León with some of his American troops the city went wild with enthusiasm. Feasts were given, songs were written in his honor, "women of every age and condition" thronged around him with blessings for having protected their homes. News of Padre Vijil's recognition by President Pierce added to his stature in the public eye. He was the successful man, and the people, realizing that further attacks on their country from south and north were probable, looked to him and his *gringos* to protect them.

The intensity of feeling with which Rivas opposed the idea of a new election took Walker aback. He came to the conclusion that pressure from Vanderbilt's agents and from the British-dominated Guatemalan government had begun to sway Rivas. In no other way could he account for the proposal that the elderly President blurted out during their meeting in León—that Walker, in order to appease Nicaragua's neighbors, reduce by half the size of his American force. Sensing conspiracy in the air, he replied only that he would consider such an idea when Nicaragua was able to pay the men discharged, in accordance with their contract, which promised them substantial grants of money and land at the end of their service.

Walker noted, too, that "the face of Jerez had a cloud over it." One evening Jerez came to Walker's residence in León to discuss the future of the Nicaraguan legation in Washington, for Father Vijil had asked to be relieved of the post. Thinking that Jerez wanted the appointment for himself, Walker promptly offered his approval, and Jerez seemed pleased when he took his leave. Within the hour he returned, however, to ask uneasily, "My appointment to the United States is then decided on?" Walker caught the intimation. The offer, Jerez felt, might be designed to get rid of him. To reassure him, Walker said, "I will support the appointment, Don Maximo, only if you desire it." But Jerez still showed suspicion, and Walker realized that no words of his could restore their former amity.

Salazar also became a potential source of trouble, for it transpired that he had used his army position to make profitable contracts for himself as a merchant, at the expense of the state. Walker, calling him to account, turned him into a powerful enemy. "There were many," he wrote of this period of tension, "desirous of exciting popular passions and prejudices against the Americans . . . to destroy the confidence of the people in the naturalized Nicaraguans." He and most of his men had long since become citizens of their adopted state.

II

At a cabinet meeting, when Rivas' ministers debated whether or not to call a new election, all except one of them stood opposed. Walker listened in silence. Central American historians, dealing at length with this moment in his career, concluded that he was animated wholly by ambition, but this view misses the fact that he could have made himself President long since had he so chosen. He himself had established and maintained the Rivas government in power. The Presidency, for him, was certain to be an embarrassment, giving fresh ammunition to his enemies in Washington. There is no reason to doubt his own statement that his motive in insisting on a new election with himself as a candidate was to assure the protection of his American followers. "All things tended to show that in case Nicaragua was invaded . . . the Americans might find the machinery of the government they had created and sustained turned against themselves," he wrote. "Hence, unless disposed to carry Rivas off a prisoner—and thereby the whole moral force of his government would have been lost —it was necessary for the welfare of the Americans that a new election should be called." He could no longer control the government from behind the scenes—and not to control it would have been to betray the army that had loyally fought for him.

At the decisive cabinet meeting, having listened patiently to every opinion, he turned to Rivas and quietly requested him to decree a new election. Threats were unnecessary; all knew that the issue had been reduced to a test of power, and there could be no doubt as to where the power lay. Yielding, the President signed the decree.

The next day, leaving an American garrison under Natzmer in the city, Walker rode south toward Managua, midway between Granada and León. Rivas went to considerable lengths to convey that he was reconciled to Walker's policy. "The President and many others of the chief citizens . . . accompanied him [Walker] several miles on his journey; and at parting Don Patricio [Rivas] affectionately embraced the general-in-chief, remarking with moist eyes that he could be depended on in any emergency." But Walker had not gone twenty miles when the political storm hanging over León broke. Suddenly the unfounded rumor spread that the entire cabinet was about to be arrested by Natzmer, and as if convinced of its truth the President and several of his ministers took horses and fled northward. Chief fomenter of the trouble was Salazar, who rode through the city proclaiming that the Americans were about to assassinate the Nicaraguan leaders. The unfounded accusation was especially effective in the poorer sections of the city, where the poverty-ridden were easily stirred to demonstrations and riots. Large numbers of ragged and perpetually hungry men came out of their huts, some of them armed, and began at Salazar's urging to throw up barricades in the streets near an arms depot guarded by American troops.

The crisis mounted fast. Natzmer, believing his soldiers were about to be attacked, ordered his small force to occupy the towers of the Cathedral of León, and prepare to defend themselves. Promptly an order came to him from Jerez, as Minister of War: the Americans were to evacuate the Cathedral, and would be replaced by Nicaraguan troops, who would maintain order in the city. Natzmer hesitated. Disobedience might be construed as mutiny, but he feared to expose his men to attack in the streets. Hastily he sent a fast rider to Walker with Jerez' order and a request for guidance.

As Walker saw the matter, "the designs of Rivas and Jerez were now apparent . . . Jerez had given the order to Natzmer, supposing it would not be obeyed, thereby hoping to make the movement against the Americans turn on their disobedience to a lawful authority." Unwilling to have the breach between himself and the Leónese occur on such an issue, he ordered Natzmer to withdraw his men from León immediately, and join him on the road to Granada.

III

In a bitter proclamation Walker told Nicaragua that Rivas had betrayed his faith as President by inviting the troops of other nations, Guatemala and San Salvador, into Nicaragua. Of this there was factual evidence. "Conspiring against the very people it was bound to protect, the late Provisional Government was no longer worthy of existence. In the name of the people I have therefore declared its dissolution."

A new Provisional President was appointed—a Nicaraguan who had held responsible government posts and whose headquarters were in Granada. Rivas, from León, replied in kind, calling Walker a traitor, depriving him of his command and summoning the country to take arms against the Americans.

Sunday, June 29, the election was held. As tabulated in *El Nicaragüense,* the ballots gave Walker an overwhelming majority— almost 16,000 out of a total vote of 23,000, and out of some 35,000 eligible to vote in the entire nation. These figures were obviously incredible, since no ballots were cast in the heavily populated area in and around León. In this respect, the Granadans who ran the election for Walker followed the national custom. Nicaraguan elections were traditionally almost as dishonest as those held in New York or San Francisco at the same period. Of the country's small male population only a small fraction had the qualifications and the interest needed to vote. Most of those who did vote were townsmen of the middle class, shopkeepers and artisans, for few in the rural districts would make the tedious journey to town merely to replace one politico by another. The total vote was generally too small to be convincing, and the standard procedure of the controlling party was to inflate the size of its victory, so as to create the impression of a popular choice.

To the Granadans the outcome of the election was a relief; what would have happened if a Leónese had become their ruler? The city turned out *en masse* for the inaugural, and the streets were filled with cheering multitudes. *"Viva el Presidente! Muerte a los enemigos del orden!"* To the splendor-loving Latin American multitude Walker's drab personal appearance must have been sadly disappointing. The thirty-two-year-old undersized President was dressed in a rusty black coat, baggy trousers, and a black felt hat—looking, in the words of a reporter for the New York *Tribune,* like "a grocery keeper from one of the poorer localities of the Sixth Ward." Nevertheless, there was a sufficiency of pomp—a parade, martial music, flags, a church service, a solemn ceremonial oath. Later Walker addressed a great crowd assembled in the plaza of Granada. A rumor that he would utilize the occasion to seek to annex Nicaragua to the United States had been widely circulated, and representatives of the press and consuls of the great powers were present in considerable numbers. To the general surprise, the crux of the speech was a warning of Nicaragua's intention to control her own destiny at any cost, and a denial of the rights of other powers, "either neighboring or distant," to occupy or dispose of any part of her territory. The firing of a twenty-one-gun salute put exclamation points after this proud asseveration.

An inaugural banquet, attended by fifty leading Nicaraguans and Americans was equally a success. In deference to Walker's personal preference, all toasts were drunk in light wines—a sensible precaution, since no fewer than fifty-three were offered. Walker himself proposed a toast to President Pierce, but the most enthusiastic response greeted a toast by one of his officers to "Uncle Billy." It brought a hearty laugh from Walker—a phenomenon sufficiently rare to cause comment in the press.

IV

Two days later he announced the formation of his cabinet, consisting entirely of Nicaraguans—who were backed, however, by American deputies. As reform followed reform, it was quickly seen that his intention was to Americanize the country, even while retaining its independence. English was introduced into the courts as a legal language "of equal value" to Spanish. Currency values were brought into line with the American dollar. Bonds bearing six per cent interest were printed, to be offered for sale through agents in the United States. Military scrip in dollars was issued to meet current expenses. But the most important changes came in fiscal policy. The Nicaraguan government had in the past drawn its chief revenue from high tariffs on imported staples, such as cloth, wines, knives, plows, and the like, an arrangement which had made prices oppressive for the poor. These commodities Walker put on the free list, while duties on other items were sharply limited in order to encourage trade.

The government, Walker declared, must henceforth look for income to sources which previously had been exempt from taxes. All retailers were to be licensed, and to pay a licensing tax to the government. Manufacturers (the chief, almost the only "manufactured" product of Nicaragua was the national alcoholic beverage, *aguardiente*) were similarly required to pay heavily for the privilege of doing business. Lands which had been in the possession of disloyal persons—those who had assisted the enemies of the Republic—which meant Nicaraguan Legitimists who had supported the Costa Rican invasion—were to be confiscated and sold. Of such estates there were several score, including some of the richest in the country. These announcements, reminiscent of measures introduced by Robespierre in the radical years of the French Revolution, brought howls of pain from Nicaragua's conservatives, and considerable criticism in the United States.

The seizure of the large estates was a major element in Walker's program of Americanization. It was the only way, he believed, to attract American capital to Nicaragua. Every piece of land which the government believed itself justified in taking was to be appraised by a Board of Commissioners, and unless the owner appeared within forty days to show cause why it should not be sold, the sale would be made to the highest bidder. The first of these auctions, held in Granada late in September, 1856, comprised over forty estates. Properties listed—ranches, houses, crops, and animals—were appraised at $753,000, and the auction was publicized by newspapers in New York, New Orleans, and San Francisco.

The seizure of the estates outraged Nicaragua's propertied class, but it also deeply disturbed the tenant farmers and hired hands of the countryside. Whatever the hardships of their lives, they had no desire to exchange their familiar masters for strangers and *gringos*. The unpopularity of Walker's land policy was evident from the first. He was not in a position, however, to alleviate the blow. Time was running out. With the Leónese against him and troops from San Salvador and Guatemala likely to join them at any time, and with England prodding Costa Rica to a resumption of the war, prompt American support more than ever was his only hope. If money, men, and supplies were not soon forthcoming from the United States in quantity, defense against the impending odds would be hopeless. The rich farms of Nicaragua were bait which he deliberately dangled before the eyes of Americans in order to lure them to Nicaragua and the defense of his government. "It may be," he later wrote, "that the reorganization in Nicaragua was attempted too soon, but . . . the Americans were driven forward by the force of events."

V

He was seeking to strengthen his army, and he even established a rudimentary navy. This initially consisted of a single schooner, owned by Walker's Leónese enemy, Salazar, who had begun to trade with Costa Rica under an American flag to which he had no claim. When the schooner put into the harbor of San Juan del Sur, Walker's men promptly seized it. Two small cannon were put on board, it was renamed the *Granada,* and was placed under the command of a remarkable young sailor of fortune, Lieutenant Callender Fayssoux, a handsome, bearded young Missourian who had distinguished himself with the Cuban expeditions of Narciso Lopez five years earlier. Resembling Walker in pride of bearing and determination, Fayssoux quickly justified Walker's faith in him. A British man-of-war, the *Esk,* hailed him on the seas, and its captain, Sir Robert McClure, ordered him to come aboard and exhibit the commission under which he sailed the *Granada,* "flying a flag unknown to any nation." Fayssoux bluntly refused, and threats to sink his ship could not make him obey McClure's order.

Walker, reading Fayssoux's report of this incident, resolved not to let it pass. Some days later McClure visited him in Granada to arrange for the safe departure of some British subjects then in the city. Walker did not rise or even suggest that the Englishman be seated. Instead, looking at him coldly, he said, "I hope, sir, that you have come to apologize for that affair of the schooner. Your conduct to Lieutenant Fayssoux was unbecoming an Englishman and a British officer. I shall make a report of it to your government, demand an investigation, and insure an explanation."

McClure found that he would be unable to transact his business until he apologized, and he finally consented to do so. From this time on, Fayssoux was Walker's favorite among his officers.

Another temporary lift to Walker's prestige came from the American minister in Granada, Wheeler. A belated letter from Secretary Marcy informed Wheeler that the credentials of the Nicaraguan minister Vijil had been accepted, and instructed him to establish diplomatic relations with the Nicaraguan government. So far as Marcy knew when he wrote this letter, the President of Nicaragua was Rivas. Wheeler did not bother to wait until the Secretary could reconsider the matter in the light of Walker's assumption of the Presidency. Instead, he hastened to Walker with the news that he would immediately recognize his government on behalf of the United States. At a subsequent ceremony, Wheeler took it on himself to threaten Great Britain, by implication, with war. "The government of the United States," he told Walker, "hopes to unite cordially with you in the fixed purpose of preventing any foreign power that may attempt to impede Nicaragua's progress by any interference whatever. The great voice of my nation has spoken. Its words must not be unheeded."

VI

The hopes kindled by Wheeler's action soon fizzled out. Its chief effect was to precipitate an open break between the Pierce administration and Walker. Pierce, now a lame-duck President, no longer had any motive to support Walker against Marcy's wishes. Marcy was thus able to rebuke Wheeler in caustic terms, and recall him to Washington; and he was equally sharp in denying an interview to the new minister whom Walker had sent to replace Vijil.

So far as the American government was concerned, Walker was now an outlaw whose head was forfeit to any one of his myriad enemies who could capture him. Was there then any hope? One man on Walker's staff thought there was—the Cuban, Domingo de Goicuria, then a brigadier general in Walker's service. Nearly sixty years old, a man of broad experience and common sense, he was impatient of Walker's romanticism. He himself cut a romantic figure— he wore a flowing grey beard which he had vowed never to shave until his country should be free from Spain—but the idea of compromise did not disturb him. Walker's willingness to fight Vanderbilt and his determination to make no concessions to British power struck Goicuria as unreasonable in a man whose own country had abandoned him. Why should Walker not abandon the United States? It seemed possible to Goicuria that England could be made to see Nicaragua under the new regime, not as an American bastion, but rather as a buffer against any move by the United States into the Caribbean. Only a month earlier Benjamin Disraeli had made a speech in the House of Commons, suggesting that England might cease to contest the Americanization of Nicaragua if the United States would give up the aspiration to Cuba—an idea full of encouragement for the Cuban independence movement.

Walker believed that if he could hold out for some eight or nine months, until Buchanan won the Presidential election and assumed office, all might yet go well. He had received no indication that Buchanan would ignore the plank in the Democratic platform calling for support of the American effort in Nicaragua. His need was for time, and any expedient that might win him time was worth trying. In this frame of mind, he agreed to let Goicuria make a diplomatic effort on his behalf, and appointed him minister to England with a twofold mission: first, to negotiate a loan in the United States; and thereafter to proceed to London to see what he could do. In furtherance of his approach to England, he gave the Cuban a letter carefully concocted to produce the impression that, as between England and America, he was neutral. "Make them [the British] see that we are not engaged in any scheme for annexation. You can make them see that the only way to cut the expanding and expansive democracy of the north is by a powerful and compact southern federation based on military principles."

This was one of those letters, familiar in diplomacy, which, while ostensibly containing secret instructions, are actually intended to be shown privately to statesmen on the opposite side, in order to carry conviction—a card in the diplomatic game, accepted by Goicuria in this sense. Walker evidently felt the need to reassure Goicuria's Cuban friends as well as the British of his intentions with regard to Cuba, for he added, "Cuba must and shall be free, but not for the Yankees. Oh, no! That fine country is not fit for those barbarous Yankees.

What should such a psalm-singing set do in the island?" This was the tone in which Latin Americans were accustomed to talk of the *gringo;* the style is curiously inconsistent with Walker's, and it is not unlikely that the idea and phrasing were suggested by Goicuria.

VII

In his first port of call, New Orleans, Goicuria was badly jolted. The public might feel enthusiasm for Walker, but Southern men of means felt none whatever for Nicaragua's bonds. Aside from the precariousness of Walker's situation, they could not overlook his unsatisfactory stand on slavery. Such hope as remained of raising money on the requisite scale lay in New York, and Goicuria went north without delay. But there the situation was even more disillusioning. Financiers merely smiled at the suggestion of a loan for Walker. With Vanderbilt to contend with? And with Morgan and Garrison already backing away from their contract to supply ships for the Nicaragua run? No one would touch the proposition. The men with whom he talked showed moreover a distressing cynicism about Walker's motives. It was well known in Wall Street that Randolph stood to gain a personal fortune from the deal with Morgan and Garrison. Would anyone in his right mind doubt that Walker himself was to be similarly paid? Goicuria defended his chief against the imputation; on this ground, at least, he knew his man. Walker might be corruptible in other ways, it might be that the need to hold power was already corrupting him, but no one cared less for personal wealth.

The Cuban was seized by a tremendous idea. Since Walker's government could not survive without a loan, and since a loan could not be obtained against the weight of Vanderbilt's enmity, there was only one way out. He would approach the Commodore. Impetuously, without waiting for instructions from Granada, he called on the millionaire and boldly stated his proposition—restoration of Vanderbilt's privileges in the Transit route, in return for a loan.

The Commodore was interested—more, amenable. The destruction of Walker was turning out to be a costly business—and his admiration had been stirred by the man's courage and persistence. All he wanted was Walker's capitulation; that assured, he was disposed to be generous. A loan of a quarter of a million dollars to Walker was discussed—one hundred thousand to be paid on the day when Vanderbilt restored ship service to Nicaragua, the balance within a year thereafter.

Overjoyed, Goicuria hastened to write Walker the great news. He could not resist, however, adding to his letter the reports that he had heard of Randolph's personal stake in the deal with Morgan and Garrison. This proved a fatal error. He did not understand that where Randolph was concerned Walker would hear no criticism. A month of uncertainty followed while the letter went to Granada and was answered. The reply when it came was like a whip across Goicuria's face. "You will please not trouble yourself further about the Transit Company. As to anything you say about Mr. Randolph, it is entirely thrown away on me."

So curt a rebuff the Cuban could not endure, and he wrote Walker in terms which put them still farther apart. It was evidently useless, he said, for him to proceed to England. If the comparatively friendly American government had refused to receive Walker's envoy, there could hardly be hope of British recognition—until at least the present Nicaraguan government had proved its stability by a decisive victory over its military enemies. In icy language, Walker responded that if Goicuria chose to resign from his mission, another would go in his place; and he spoke bluntly of his concern over rumors that the Cuban had become an agent of Vanderbilt's.

At the same time, Walker revoked Goicuria's commission as a brigadier general in the Nicaraguan army, and an item to that effect appeared in *El Nicaragüense.* New York's newspapers, especially the *Herald,* pressed Goicuria to explain, and unable to contain his anger, he released for publication that part of his correspondence with Walker which bore on his attempt to regain the good will of Vanderbilt. The entire nation focused on the controversy. The Vanderbilt faction gleefully cited the letters as proof that Walker was either a fool or a hireling of Morgan and Garrison's, while friends of Walker denounced Goicuria as Vanderbilt's cat's-paw. Edmund Randolph, who was then seriously ill and confined to his bed in the Washington Hotel on Broadway, published in the *Herald* a paid notice which delighted readers: "In the Transit business Don Domingo de Goicuria is an intruder, with a dishonest and treacherous intent, and knowing the import of the language I use, I shall remain here until one o'clock

tomorrow and longer if it is the pleasure of Don Domingo de Goicuria."

The duel of pistols was averted, but the duel of words went on. It
was at this stage that the wrathful Cuban scored his most telling
blow, by publishing Walker's secret letter of instructions for his
mission to England. Readers of the *Herald* learned that, contrary to
the general expectation, Walker had no intention of bringing Nicaragua
and Cuba into the United States—that he intended rather to bar the
way to American expansion—that he regarded Yankees as "a psalm-
singing set" not fit to control the Caribbean lands. The purpose for
which the letter had been written was not explained.

Some years later the Cuban privately expressed regret at having allowed the Walker correspondence to be published, for its effect on
Walker's reputation was enduring and deadly. The floodgates were
opened to vicious abuse of Walker from American, as well as from
British and Central American sources. He was condemned as un-
patriotic and false to the interests of the United States. He was called
a cold-blooded martinet indifferent to human suffering. The *Atlantic
Monthly* published a savage piece by a deserter from Walker's army,
who, writing under a pseudonym, complained that General Walker,
"instead of treating us like fellow-soldiers and adventurers in danger
. . . bore himself like an Eastern tyrant—reserved and haughty—
scarcely saluting when he met us, mixing not at all." A scurrilous
pamphlet called "The Address of the Seven Prisoners," ostensibly
written by seven of Walker's soldiers "captured by the Costa Ricans at
Santa Rosa," received wide attention. As Mora's captives, asserted the
authors, they had been freer and better treated than as Walker's
soldiers. Later it was learned that only three of the seven signatories
were Americans, and that one of these, a drummer boy, knew no
more of the document than that it had been shown to him by a deserter, that he had refused to sign it, and that his name had been used
without his knowledge.

XVI

THE MOMENT OF FALSEHOOD

With the November election coming closer, James Buchanan, as the candidate of the Democratic Party, had to make up his mind about Walker and Nicaragua. The scope of the decision went far beyond American interests in Central America. In the words of an authoritative interpreter of the diplomacy of Buchanan's administration, the President recognized that "the only way to avert civil war . . . was to unite North and South by a common foreign policy of a nature to arouse national feeling."* There was one means by which he might hope to rally North and South to a common cause—abrogation of the Clayton-Bulwer Treaty and reassertion of the Monroe Doctrine. This was precisely the policy for which Walker stood. But it was not easy to predict how the British would react to such a challenge; and Buchanan, aside from his anglophilia, was temperamentally incapable of taking the risks inherent in an adventurous foreign policy.

There was also another reason, one which came to light only later, why he preferred to adopt a hands-off policy toward Nicaragua. His close friend and political manager, Senator John Slidell of Louisiana,

---

* L. Einstein, "Lewis Cass," in *American Secretaries of State*, (S. F. Bemis, ed.), Vol. VI, p. 302.

and the junior Senator from Louisiana, the financier Judah P. Benjamin, were actively interested in promoting an interoceanic railroad and canal route across the Tehuantepec Isthmus of Mexico. Buchanan himself certainly had no financial interest in this venture. He was a wealthy man, scrupulous in the observance of proprieties, patriotic in every ordinary sense. He had a habit, however, of convincing himself that expedients comfortable for himself coincided with the nation's benefit. With Slidell and Benjamin opposed to governmental support for Walker and the Nicaraguan Transit, it was not to be expected that Buchanan would move in the opposite direction.

To Soulé, Buchanan's attitude was a crass betrayal, and he wrote the President-to-be an incredulous letter. "It could not be that one so high as you in the estimation of your country . . . has thus belied what I shall not cease to consider one of the proudest acts of his life" [the Ostend Manifesto]. But the ardent Creole recognized that his party's nominee would do nothing to give pain to his friends in Washington or London. Walker consequently stood in the gravest peril. The London *Times* shared this view, for it contentedly commented that if Buchanan had not been nominated, "Walker's government, founded upon the strongest anti-British feeling, would have been able to . . . set the current of feeling [in the United States] against us. As it is . . . we may look forward to an early and satisfactory settlement of the dispute."

Only one card remained in Soulé's hand, and he now played it. Announcing that he was going to Nicaragua to confer with Walker, he boarded ship in New Orleans and on October 20, 1856, arrived in Granada. The main reason for his visit, as stated in *El Nicaragüense,* was to advise Walker as to methods of floating a loan in the United States. So far as it went, this statement was accurate. It was Soulé's advice, which Walker accepted, not to attempt to combat Vanderbilt's influence in New York, but to handle the loan entirely through agents in New Orleans. Twenty-year bonds, paying six per cent, in the amount of $500,000, and secured by one million acres of public lands would be issued; and at the same time Walker put on the market other public lands at low prices for purchasers in the Southern states. It was obvious, however, that these formal moves in themselves meant nothing. The wealthy men of the South, the great majority of whom were plantation owners, had no interest in acquiring lands or making investments in a country which excluded slave labor. In their view efficient cultivation of the tropical crops which Nicaragua produced was possible only with slaves, either Negroes brought into the country, or Nicaraguan Indians. The burden of Soulé's message was that if Walker wanted Southern support, he would have to pay for it in the one form which the South's aristocracy would accept—the introduction of slavery in Nicaragua. This was the only door of survival still open to him—"the only way in which he could secure the countenance and aid of the Southern politicians who . . . dominate in the government of the United States."*

If Parker French was Mephisto to Walker's Faust, Soulé was Lucifer himself. A man of fiery temperament, vivid imagination, and great verbal power, he had a gift for evoking dreams and inspiring visions. The temptations that he put before Walker must have been grand of scope and eloquent of description. Anyone could foresee that the South would separate from the Union before long. On which side would Walker be? From which country, the Northern rump of the United States or the Southern confederacy could he expect support? To which would he, a Southerner, want to give support? Nicaragua and the Caribbean might well become the key to the survival of Southern civilization.

In his journalistic days Walker had taken what was then termed the "conservative" position on slavery—against its expansion, and less overtly, in favor of its gradual elimination by law and economic measures. When he had been a small boy, advocates of this stand were numerous even in the South. Of some 125 antislavery societies in the United States in the 1820's, nearly three fourths were south of the Mason-Dixon line. Many Southerners hoped to prevent the frightful economic and social problems of sudden emancipation by encouraging state-by-state abolition. In the North, too, gradualism had vigorous support. Several prominent businessmen urged that Northern capital be used to construct railroads and factories in the South, to demonstrate the benefits of free labor while breaking down dependence on a plantation economy. Others (including a radical Whig Congressman named Abraham Lincoln) thought that Congress should authorize the government to compensate slaveholders who emancipated their

---

* Congressional *Globe*, Jan. 14, 1858. Speech of the Hon. Frank P. Blair, Jr., of Missouri, on Soulé and Walker.

slaves. Dr. William Ellery Channing, the noted Boston minister, urged Daniel Webster to reassure the South that "we consider slavery as your calamity, not your crime, and we share with you the burden of putting an end to it." Unfortunately, this view had little appeal for the Northern taxpayers who would have had to contribute funds to share the burden of emancipation. Although as late as 1848 it was thought that the border states would soon abolish slavery, and the New Orleans *Crescent,* with Walker as editor, openly made such a prediction, no practical steps to this end were taken. In Washington, shrewd politicians professed to be "neutral" on slavery. Inertia sat in the White House, term after term. When all the pious oratory was vaporized, it could be seen that the residual choice offered the South was in reality no choice at all—or, more accurately, a choice of evils so appalling that rational selection between them was impossible. Southerners could sacrifice themselves for the higher morality and the nation by giving up their slaves and voluntarily plunging into bankruptcy and social chaos, or they could continue to oppose the entire trend of world thought and eventually fight against the superior military force of the North. The human paradox was—and is—that men so closely identified their own survival with the persistence of their institutions, that they preferred to die rather than submit to changes in their way of life. The institution, becoming a symbol of life, invited death for its sake. As usual when the only chance of peace depended on the willingness of men to give up an institution that they had been taught to revere, there was no chance of peace.

The voices of peace and good will grew faint. By 1856 the Southern "ultras" and the militant Northern abolitionists were dominating public opinion. It was becoming rare to find any informed American who did not grimly believe that the time had passed for a peaceful solution. As the threat of civil war came closer, Southern gradualists were faced with the wrenching need to choose between beloved Dixie and the claims of an uneasy social conscience. For most of them loyalty to the homeland was the stronger emotion, and they found themselves struggling to preserve an institution that in their secret thoughts they regarded as an evil and a misfortune.

In Walker's case the issue was even more painful. His last hope of success in Nicaragua was at stake. The situation as Soulé presented it must have been crystal clear. Walker could maintain an antislavery stand and go down with his men to sure disaster, or he could flee Nicaragua and seek discreditable asylum abroad, or he could abjure his former political views, link himself to the land of his origins, and perhaps rise to further triumphs with the aid of his own people.

II

He was being torn apart by the same forces that were tearing apart his country. He had to fight the Civil War within himself five years before it began. His effort to preserve his intellectual integrity showed in the weeks that it took him to make up his mind. His first response was an attempt at compromise. Early in September he issued a decree which, in effect, established a system of forced labor for all Nicaraguans who were adjudged guilty of vagrancy, or who failed to fulfill the terms of their labor contracts with employers. This decree did not in fact materially change the status of the Nicaraguan farm worker, who while technically free lived actually in a state of feudal serfdom. In effect, Walker was reassuring American purchasers of Nicaraguan estates as to the availability of workers.

If he hoped to avoid further concessions, he was mistaken. A change in the military situation forced his hand, when word came that a strong army, representing Guatemala, San Salvador, Honduras, and the Leónese Nicaraguans was being mobilized for attack on him. At this time, Walker had not yet committed himself on the slavery issue. Several days went by in which he must have been close to despair. Later there were those who said that as a matter of cold reason, such as he had brought to bear on the fate of Corral, he should have taken his own life rather than sacrifice a principle under duress. But the urge to triumph over adversity was still strong in him, and in any event, suicide in his view was morally unthinkable, a coward's solution, especially when the survival of his American soldiers was involved with his own. He could not abandon his men, whatever political convictions he might be compelled to abandon.

On September 22, he issued the decree which was to brand him as a slavery man. It did not mention slavery. Its essence was a declaration that certain provisions of the Nicaraguan Constitution were null and void. One of these had prohibited the introduction of slaves into the country.

The thing being done, he had to find a justification with which he could live. The poorest and most numerous class in Nicaragua, the Indian workers of the Nicaraguan plantations, he wrote in a letter to an American Congressman, had been exploited by the great landowners and the town tradesmen until their economic and social condition was worse than that of most slaves in the United States. Slavery under the American system would actually be a step upward for them, the best way of freeing them from perpetual indebtedness. In Nicaragua, he conveyed, slavery would not be the end of democracy, for there was no democracy there. His decree provided a practical means, as he saw the matter, by which Americans could be induced to come to Nicaragua as planters and to introduce the democratic institutions required to begin the regeneration of the country.

But when all was said, he knew what he had done to his moral position in the eyes of the Nicaraguan people. He had been popular among the Indians largely because he spared them from the horrors of military conscription. Now he was bound to lose them. One of his letters to Congressmen admitted that in revoking Nicaragua's decree of freedom he "was opposed by the whole body of native inhabitants."

Some of his antislavery admirers were loath to believe that their hero could overnight shift his position so radically. The former American minister to Nicaragua, George Squier, wrote a letter to the London *Times* denying that Walker really intended to introduce slavery in Nicaragua. But from this time on, Walker's chief allies were Southern ultras. He who had refused to be served by conscripts and who had never owned or wished to own a slave could find support only among the slavery men.

It was later rumored that he had from the first been an agent of the slavery interest, and he deliberately lent credence to this notion. Rather than admit that he had changed his politics and chosen survival at the expense of principle, he preferred to appear as a man who had always been secretly dedicated to the Southern cause. Once he made his fundamental concession, he went to extremes to have it thought that in his heart he had never doubted the virtues of slavery, and so had no need to be convinced by Soulé. To his earlier writings on the subject he never referred.

In a long and tortured chapter in *The War In Nicaragua,* written just before the outbreak of the Civil War, he sought to find some solid intellectual ground on which to stand before the peoples of the Americas as a proslavery man and avowed racist; but in spite of himself, his inner doubts showed through. In one strange, confessional passage, he implied that if he had realized how resentful the Northern reaction to the slavery decree would be, he might not have issued it. "It is true the author of the slavery decree was not aware, at the time it was published, of the strong and universal feeling which exists in the Northern States against Southern society. He did not know how thoroughly anti-slavery sentiments prevail in the free-labor states." Again, he could not bring himself actually to denounce the anti-slavery position. Apropos of a speech by Senator Seward on the unsound economics of slavery he wrote, "It is impossible not to approve the force and vigor of his thoughts and language. The writer deems it a great error, on the part of Southern men, to attempt to belittle the intellect, or depreciate the motives of the leaders of the anti-slavery party."* His efforts to convey that the establishment of slavery in Nicaragua had been his intention from the first may have deceived some; but one of his officers, who observed him closely during the crucial period of his decision, had no doubt that "the subject [slavery] took root and form in the mind of General Walker in the summer of 1856."

III

The concerted attacks on Walker in the United States, resulting from his slavery decree and the Goicuria affair, came at a time when his military position was rapidly worsening. Over 2,000 troops had been put into the field by the alliance of the Northern republics. Costa Rica was preparing to renew her war on Walker from the south. Thirteen British warships manned by 2500 men had arrived in the harbor of Greytown. Against these forces Walker had only one ally —the cholera, which, while it depleted his own ranks, took a much heavier toll from enemy troops, and temporarily paralyzed them. In every other respect—with only 600 men, with no new recruits to be expected, facing serious shortages of food and ammunition—he was

* William Walker, *The War in Nicaragua,* p. 264.

at a hopeless disadvantage. For readers of American newspapers the allied advance toward Granada in September and the first reports of the fighting presaged his imminent doom. At Masaya, on the allied route to Granada, his troops suffered a severe repulse, and had to fall back on the capital; but before he could reach the city, a strong Guatemalan column had invested it, murdered a number of American civilians, and seized all the munitions and food supplies they could find.

Everyone thought he was finished. It came both to Nicaragua and to the United States as a stunning surprise when, in a battle on October 13, exactly one year after his original seizure of the city, he drove the enemy out of Granada, inflicting heavy losses, and re-established his authority in the capital.

XVII

MR. VANDERBILT TAKES HIS
REVENGE

After Walker's unexpected recapture of Granada, a strange rumor
began to circulate in the financial district of New York. Behind the
scenes a powerful and unexpected well-wisher was working for him—
the only man perhaps capable of coping with Walker's enemies at
home—the great "Liveoak" George Law, Panama shipping magnate,
railroader, multimillionaire, and a man who harbored heavy personal
grievances against Vanderbilt. It had struck Law that neither the
Garrison-Morgan combine nor Vanderbilt's company any longer had
a firm legal hold on the Nicaraguan Transit route. If aid initiated by
himself were to enable Walker to win his war, would he not reward
his benefactor with the privileges of the Transit, and would not Vanderbilt writhe? This appears to have been the reasoning behind the
moves made by Law in the summer of 1857.

He knew, or thought, he knew, how to rescue Walker from his dark
military situation. Among Law's friends in New York was one of the
world's most renowned soldiers of fortune—the Swedish-born
Charles Frederick Henningsen, a blond Viking of a man, scarcely

206

forty years of age, who had distinguished himself in wars in Spain, in Russia, and notably in the Hungarian revolution, where he had become one of the chief officers and close friends of the famous Kossuth. The author of several much-praised books on military strategy, his talents went still further: he was an able journalist, a novelist of wit and repute, and the husband of a wealthy and aristocratic Georgian beauty. Henningsen had from the first taken a deep and admiring interest in the youthful Walker's struggle and had come to the belief that with a few hundred more men, some mortars and howitzers, better rifles, and adequate supplies, the American could yet beat back his foes and conquer the isthmus. When he mentioned his views to Law, the financier instantly proposed that they join forces. It was the kind of adventure that Henningsen could not resist. Law had bought several thousand army muskets with a view to their use in Nicaragua, and he offered these to Henningsen together with $20,000 for the purchase of artillery and ammunition.

Henningsen's first move was to supervise the conversion of Law's muskets into Minié rifles, the most advanced body-arm of their time, and which had never before been produced in the United States. When this news reached Vanderbilt, he countered by having Goicuria, whose connection with him was still not generally known, approach Law and ask, as if on Walker's behalf, for part of the accumulated arms, ostensibly to be taken to Nicaragua by himself. For a time Law believed in the Cuban's good faith, but on making inquiries he perceived Vanderbilt's shadow in the background, and brushed the proposal aside.

The landing of Henningsen in Greytown early in October, 1856, was widely acclaimed by the American press as a possible turning point in Walker's fortunes. Boats of the Accessory Transit Company brought him and his armament to Granada, where they were joyfully welcomed by Walker and his men; and within two weeks the Swede had organized and trained two effective companies of artillery and one of sappers and miners. His impact on the little army was considerable, and Walker wrote that he "never had reason to regret the confidence" that he placed in Henningsen. From the first his knowledge, skills, and competence were so manifest that even when his commission as Major General put him above other veteran commanders in rank, jealousy was diluted with respect.

Henningsen willingly accepted Walker's leadership, and later wrote articles for New Orleans and Nashville newspapers, paying high tribute to Walker's intelligence, modest bearing, and force of character. The curious composition of the little army also impressed the Swedish adventurer. In explaining the ability of Walker's soldiers to sustain battle against appalling odds, he wrote, "Such men do not turn up in . . . everyday life. I was on the Confederate side in many of the bloodiest battles of the late [Civil] war, but I aver that if at the end of that war I had been allowed to pick 5000 of the bravest Confederate or Federal soldiers I ever saw, and could resurrect and pit against them 1000 of such men as lie beneath the orange trees of Nicaragua, I feel certain that the thousand would have scattered and utterly routed the 5000 within an hour. All military science failed, on a sudden field, before assailants who came on at a run, to close with their revolvers, and who thought little of charging a battery, pistol in hand." He calculated that for each 100 men in Walker's army, 137 wounds had been received in the course of their 1856 campaign, without diminishing their fighting spirit. The extraordinary number of educated men who were risking their lives in Walker's service similarly surprised him. "I have heard two greasy privates disputing over the correct reading and comparative merits of Aeschylus and Euripides. I have seen a soldier on guard incessantly scribbling strips of paper, which turned out to be a finely versified translation of the Divina Commedia." Products of American universities fought side by side with famous duellists and adventurers, among them the legendary Colonel Thomas Henry, one of the original "Immortals," and Frederick Townsend Ward, later a general of the Chinese army.

The very same qualities that made practical men of affairs turn from Walker drew to him the idealistic youths, the poets, and the soldiers of fortune. The small band of Americans who followed him to Nicaragua produced no fewer than six books about his venture, as well as numerous articles and a considerable amount of poetry. Although his men found it hard to understand his motivation, one thing at least was clear—he was indifferent to material reward, not interested in having, owning, or getting.

The army's morale was remarkable, and contrary to statements by Walker's Northern critics, he was revered by his men, who recalled an occasion on which he had given his horse to a wounded soldier, while he himself trudged thirty miles on foot. Similarly, Henningsen praised the discipline of the army, and discounted frequent charges of pillage and rape against Walker's troops. Much of the adverse criticism aimed at the Americans on this score was due to the depredations of thirty men, who in July, 1856, arrived from Texas in a body, and who turned out to be a robber gang urgently wanted by United States authorities. Deserting almost immediately after arrival, and wearing the uniforms of Walker's Rangers, they wandered through the Nicaraguan countryside in search of loot, leaving a trail of misery behind them, and carefully avoiding Walker, who had sworn to hang them if they fell into his hands.

Another striking feature of Walker's operation observed by Henningsen was the good will shown him by the poorer folk of the countryside. Even the "slavery decree" did not materially affect the attitude of the Nicaraguan Indians toward Walker in the first months of his war with the allies. Their feeling was undoubtedly due mainly to the fact that, unlike their native commanders, he never conscripted them for military service—a dispensation which filled them with gratitude amounting almost to reverence. The company of Nicaraguans who remained in his service to the end, and whom he regarded as equal to any of his troops in courage and loyalty, were all volunteers.

It was the propertied and their retainers, the *calzados,* the wearers of shoes, numbering perhaps one tenth of the Nicaraguan people, who regarded Walker as their natural enemy. The change that took place in the popular attitude toward him came only in the late stages of the war, when appalling shortages of food compelled his men to forage. Unlike Walker himself, who ate sparingly and almost indifferently of whatever rations came to hand, they were accustomed to consume far more provender than did the typical Nicaraguan. Not content with a diet of *tortillas* and plantains, they seized grain, cows, horses, mules, and chickens as they found them, ravaging the countryside for miles around their camps. Word of such depredations spread quickly, and before the war's end country folk and town dwellers alike had come to regard the appearance of Walker's bearded Rangers as a disaster. When Henningsen first came to Nicaragua, however, his chief's reputation among the common folk was considerably higher than that of any Central American general.

II

Three weeks after Henningsen's arrival, a strong Costa Rican army crossed into Nicaragua and moved north to occupy the Transit route west of Lake Nicaragua. Simultaneously a Leónese column marched south to join the Guatemalans and Salvadoreans for another attack on Granada. With 600 men Walker had to fight a war on two fronts against nearly 5000. A sudden attack drove the Costa Ricans out of San Juan del Sur, but this did not help him much. Compelled to leave a garrison of 250 men to hold the Transit route, he had only 300 effectives with which to resist the northern allies, who were strongly fortified in the town of Masaya, some twenty miles north of Granada.

The allied army had every advantage except one—artillery. The great question for Walker was how far mortars and howitzers could offset weakness in numbers. His only hope lay in a bold strategy. The enemy had to be shattered in a single battle. He and Henningsen wasted no time before beginning the attack on Masaya. Within an hour, however, they realized that their main asset was hollow. The fuses of their mortar shells were too short, and the explosions were taking place harmlessly in the air, instead of on the ground. To retreat would have invited pursuit in force; they had no choice but to try to take Masaya by assault, relying on Henningsen's trained sappers and miners to dislodge the allies from their strongholds. For a time success seemed possible. In three days of sleepless effort they pushed the Central Americans into the center of Masaya, and pressed them hard. A few hundred fresh troops, had they been available, could conceivably have compelled the surrender of the entire allied army, and made Walker the master of Central America. But exhaustion was taking its toll. With a third of his men killed or wounded, and the rest staggering from weariness, there was nothing for them to do but abandon the attack and drag themselves back to Granada. A strong sortie by the enemy would have finished them. It was their good fortune that the losses of the allies were so heavy, and their commanders so shaken by their close call, that they did not follow up their advantage.

There was worse to come. Although a few days of recuperation somewhat restored the morale of Walker's men, their extreme fatigue and the primitive conditions of their hospitals, where flies and vermin abounded, made them excessively vulnerable to the most dangerous enemy of all, cholera. An epidemic broke out, raging at a new peak of mortality, and claiming as one of its victims Lieutenant James Walker, the filibuster's youngest and favorite brother. As each day took the lives of two or three per cent of his force, Walker's surgeons warned him that unless he evacuated Granada every American there would be dead within six weeks.

Granada had to be abandoned, and under Walker's personal direction the sick were moved across Lake Nicaragua, first to one desolate place, then to another, in an effort to find safety and tolerable conditions. Their miseries and fatalities increased with each day. The horrors of this hopeless flight from disease shook Walker as had nothing before in his experience, for among the evacuees were a number of women, some of them wives of Americans who had come to Nicaragua as to a promised land. He, the defender of womankind, had no internal defense against their sufferings and reproaches—any more than he could forget that he had lured his brother to his death.

It was at this point of psychic turmoil that he had to make a decision which was bound to confirm to the outside world his reputation for ferocity. The allies, anyone could foresee, would soon occupy Granada, and the moral, as well as the military effect of the move would be disastrous. Holding both Granada and León, they would hold the core of Nicaragua. No hope would remain for Walker's army. To destroy the city would be to send up cries of horror from all Central America, but to leave it intact would be suicidal. So, at least, Walker and Henningsen reasoned. It fell to Henningsen, with 300 men, to undertake the task of razing Granada after first evacuating the native population. Amid further scenes of misery and tragedy, the shocked and wretched Granadans, such as still remained in the city, were removed by boats of the Transit Company to points along the shores of Lake Nicaragua, while the grim work commenced.

Part of Granada was still intact when the allied army surrounded the city and commenced a three-sided assault on Henningsen's small force. Through four days of incessant fighting, firing from adobe houses and public buildings, the Americans stood them off, their marksmanship taking a great toll of life. An illustration of the battle in an American magazine suggests the scene: the plaza under the pale blazing sky, everything starkly outlined in sunlit white and angular black shadow, a wretched rubble of buildings in the background, puffs of musket smoke coming from the few that remained standing, and white-clad Guatemalan corpses sprawled in the tawny dirt.

Henningsen's problem was complicated by the fact that the strongest position in the city, Guadalupe Cathedral, had been seized by the enemy. To leave it in their hands, he realized, would be fatal. It had to be taken by storm; but could he afford the resulting losses? To make matters more difficult, his men uncovered in one of their improvised fortresses a large store of liquor, and their discipline, already faltering from exhaustion and desperation, disintegrated. In the middle of the battle, half of them were stupefied by drink. Nevertheless, at a lull in the fighting the tireless and inspired Henningsen was able to rally enough volunteers to drive the enemy out of the cathedral. A few hours later he had crowded into it his entire force, now reduced to 200 men able to fight, together with the mutilated, the sick, the drunk, and some scores of women and children, many of them Americans, who still remained in the city. Their ordeal, marked by instances of extraordinary heroism and self-sacrifice on the part of women as well as men, provided sensational material for American journalists.

Presently General Zavala, the Guatemalan commander, realized that Henningsen was depending on supplies brought to the wharves of Granada by Walker's lake boats, which were also his only means of escape. For a time Zavala was deterred from attacking the wharves by uncertainty as to the size of the force which had been left to protect them, and which was strongly barricaded. Then fortune played into his hands. One of the defenders of the all-important area was a Venezuelan whom Walker had rescued from a Granadan dungeon a year earlier. Since then his gratitude had thinned away, and now he deserted and revealed to Zavala that there were only 27 men between him and command of the lake front. The storming action that followed wiped out the Americans in the little garrison to a man, and isolated the remainder of Henningsen's force.

With Walker's boats unable to reach the city, food supplies in Guadalupe Cathedral soon ran so low that men and women had to subsist on small rations of mule meat and decayed flour. Ammunition reserves also were dwindling fast. To provided shot for their field pieces Henningsen's artillery officers made holes in the sand, filled them with scraps of iron, and poured melted lead over them to form an approximate ball. Their situation seemed beyond hope. Zavala, however, was not in a position to follow up his advantage. His losses had been staggering, and in order to regroup his forces he temporarily broke off the attack. Instantly Henningsen ordered his men to proceed with the firing of Granada. Their effort culminated in a final explosion of powder trains which demolished the center of the city. Simultaneously a successful attack by Walker regained command of the wharves, and Henningsen was able to withdraw his troops and the noncombatants under his protection. His flair showed in his last gesture on leaving the ruined city, when he raised an improvised flag in the rubble, bearing the legend AQUI FUÉ GRANADA—"Here was Granada."

The unexpected success of the Americans in sustaining the siege, the burning of the city, the terrible mortality among the allies, the rejoining of Henningsen's force with Walker's, and the continued ravages of disease so shook Zavala that he hastily ordered a retreat to Masaya. The Costa Ricans also thought it wise to pull back, relieving the pressure on the Transit route. Quarrels between the allied commanders still further diminished the possibility of an effective attack on Walker. All at once his generalship, which had been sharply questioned by the American press, seemed vindicated.

Of major importance was word from San Francisco that a hundred well-armed recruits were on the way to join him. At this stage, he had to meet a new threat, when a large and well-armed brig of British origin appeared outside the harbor of San Juan del Sur, flying the Costa Rican flag, and manned by a large Costa Rican crew. Its obvious purpose was to blockade the port and prevent the landing of reinforcements. Walker's hopes rested on the little schooner *Granada,* with its 28 men and two guns. A two-hour sea fight ensued, in which Captain Fayssoux, by brilliant seamanship and accurate gunnery, sank the enemy vessel, and added compassion to victory by rescuing from the Pacific nearly half of the brig's 114 sailors. Almost immediately afterward, the ship from San Francisco arrived with Walker's recruits.

The Americans were further heartened by word that several hundred fighting men were on their way to Greytown from New Orleans. In spite of everything that England, Vanderbilt, and the Central American coalition had done to destroy him, it still appeared possible that Walker might re-establish control over Nicaragua.

III

To Vanderbilt it was unthinkable that his aims should be frustrated by a few hundred Americans led by the man who had dared to confiscate his property, and who was supported by his commercial foes. In his opinion Walker's Central American enemies had failed to grasp the strategic realities of their situation. To try to defeat the man's army of daredevils in direct battle would take too long and cost too much. The way to break Walker's resistance, he was certain, was simply to cut his lines of communication across the isthmus. So long as the filibuster held the Transit route and the boats of the San Juan River and Lake Nicaragua, he could be supplied by Law or by Morgan and Garrison; but without the route and the boats, he could soon be starved out and put at the mercy of the Central Americans.

Late in November, 1856, two of Vanderbilt's men traveled on his fastest ship to Costa Rica, where they held secret talks with President Mora. One of them was an American, Sylvanus Spencer, an old-time employee of Vanderbilt's, eminently suited to the task before him. He had at one time served as engineer on the Transit boats, understood every detail of their operation, knew their crews personally, and had navigated the San Juan River many times. With Spencer was an enigmatic Englishman, William R. C. Webster, an agent of the British government who apparently was assigned to Vanderbilt for the mission to Costa Rica, and who coordinated Spencer's operations with those of Captain Cauty, the chief British military officer in Costa Rica, and with the Central American army in the north.

In their arrangement with Mora, Spencer and Webster agreed to aid him to recapture and hold the Transit route while the northern allies destroyed Walker's army. In return, Vanderbilt would expect Mora's influence on the next Nicaraguan administration to be used to grant him anew the title and privileges of the Transit. Word of the agreement went to Vanderbilt from Spencer, and on December 25, 1856, the financier gave a Christmas remembrance to stockholders of the Accessory Transit Company, in the form of a notice in the

New York *Herald:* "Present appearances indicate a realization of my hopes that the company will be speedily restored to their rights, franchises and property upon the isthmus of Nicaragua."

Action followed swiftly. Within two days, Costa Rican troops led by Spencer, in a series of cleverly planned surprise attacks, had seized most of the Transit steamers and Spencer had assured the loyalty of the boats' officers and crews for his service by judicious use of a fund provided by Vanderbilt. Another Costa Rican column under the command of Captain Cauty invested a key fortress on the eastern shore of Lake Nicaragua, where Walker had not been able to leave more than a skeleton garrison. At Greytown, a British man-of-war prevented 400 well-armed American recruits who had arrived from New Orleans from recapturing one of the riverboats and steaming upstream to join Walker. Across the isthmus, at San Juan del Sur, British ships bottled up the harbor where the ship *Granada* rode at anchor. The joy of the Costa Rican government over these events spilled into a proclamation to its army: "The main artery of filibusterism has been cut forever. The sword of Costa Rica has severed it."

Under the Costa Rican flag, the Transit steamers swiftly concentrated the forces under Spencer and Cauty near the Transit route and they seized the crucial lake town of Virgin Bay before Walker, in his camp at nearby Rivas, had even been informed of the invasion. At the same time, the allied army at Masaya again advanced southward to form the upper jaw of the pincer movement in which he was now almost trapped. But in spite of their enormous advantage in manpower, they did not attack in force. The new plan was to bring the Americans to their knees by starvation. For four bitter months the siege continued, while hunger, thirst, disease, and boredom sapped the strength of Walker's men. And this was not the whole tally of his burden. He was concealing from his men two pieces of disastrous news. A letter from California had revealed that Garrison and Morgan had surrendered to Vanderbilt, and would no longer provide any aid for Nicaragua; and the effort of one of his trusted officers, Colonel S. A. Lockridge, to bring in the Americans stranded at Greytown had been conclusively thwarted by the British.

Walker fell sick of a fever, and to his sickbed came word, in March, 1857, that 160 of his men, who might in other days have fought off a thousand of the enemy, had been routed by a body of only 200 allied troops on the road west of Rivas. This demonstration of the extent to which the army's morale had deteriorated was more than he could bear. Dragging himself to his feet, he assembled his men on the plaza of Rivas and tried with words to revive their courage. "We are engaged in no ordinary warfare. . . . We have come here as the advance guard of American civilization. . . . Are we to be driven from the country merely because we were not born on its soil? Never! Never!"

His hold on them was still strong, for a few days later 400 of them followed him into a desperate attack on 2000 Guatemalans. In this battle his wild and reckless exposure of himself to enemy fire awed even those who thought they knew him. He seemed to be saying, with Marc Antony, "I'll make death love me!" But the bullet that might have honorably extricated him from his dilemma did not strike. In spite of feats of extraordinary valor on the part of his men, the attack failed, and Walker had to move back swiftly to Rivas. At one point during the retreat he was thought to be wounded, when a burst of musket fire from a house made his horse rear; but he relieved the alarm of his troops when he brought the horse under control, and drawing his revolver, fired a few deliberate and, as it were, symbolic shots at the window from which the bullets had come. Then with a wave of his hand, he motioned the column forward.

Twice his troops repulsed attacks by the Costa Ricans, but the victories were empty. The situation worsened from day to day. Rumors of the Garrison-Morgan betrayal had begun to spread among his men. Provisions were steadily diminishing, and foraging raids on the countryside had become unproductive. Henningsen, looking at the small hunk of mule meat that was counted as dinner, remarked "A little more of this and we'll have to eat the prisoners." Walker's own mood had become fatalistic. He no longer cared to submit his men to pitched battles which, even if won, could not save them; and daily exchanges of fire with the enemy were producing more casualties than he could stand. In a letter to Edmund Randolph, Walker told him that of some 800 men in Rivas, only 332 were fit for duty, and 224 were sick or wounded.

The last battle came on April 11, 1857, when Zavala, having learned of conditions in Rivas, grew overconfident, and mounted a surprise assault with nearly 2000 men, most of them raw conscripts from the farms of Guatemala. The result proved that Walker was still to be reckoned with. The open advance of the enemy was met with such withering rifle fire from behind barricades that 700 of the attacking force were killed or wounded, as against 9 American casualties. "It was with a feeling almost of pity for these forced levies," wrote Walker, "that the Americans were obliged to shoot them down like so many cattle. The Guatemalan officers cared no more for their men than if they were sheep."

Even now he still nourished a last secret hope of victory. The cholera, which had saved him before, was again decimating the enemy. Both the Guatemalan and the Costa Rican troop camps were daily losing scores of men to the disease. He felt that in another few weeks panic might yet compel them to lift the siege. Everything depended on such spirit as remained in his own army. It was dwindling fast. No longer was Walker "Uncle Billy" to his troops; many, especially among the recent arrivals, had begun to see him as a heartless fanatic, forcing them to fight in a lost cause that was meaningless for them. Eating their repulsive mule meat, they muttered to each other, where was the high adventure, where the rich lands, where the beautiful women for which they had journeyed to Nicaragua? In the period of inaction that followed the slaughter of the Guatemalan conscripts, morale steadily sank.

It was at this stage that General Mora of Costa Rica executed his most telling stroke. Recognizing that the struggle had become one of morale in both camps, he proclaimed that his former "no quarter" policy had been abandoned. Instead, he offered protection, food, liquor, and free passage home to any American who would come across the lines and give up his arms. Nothing could have more painfully shaken Walker's men. Not only a number of soldiers in the ranks but several officers stole away from their quarters on the very night of Mora's proclamation. One of the officers even appeared the next day on the enemy barricades, calling to his former comrades to join him and share in the meals, tobacco, and *aguardiente* that Mora was providing.

Daily the wave of desertions mounted until as many as twenty men a day were being lost. What followed was pure Walker. Calling his remaining force together, he told them that any soldier who wished to leave his service would be given his passports, so that he could cross the enemy lines without being regarded as a deserter. Probably no other tactic could have stiffened the backs of those unhappy men. Five soldiers among them who asked for their papers were hooted by their comrades as they left; and one who tried to turn back was intercepted by Walker himself, and was made to go on. The remaining troops, fewer than 200, laughed, cheered, and returned to their weary routines and wretched rations.

I V

Early in 1857, President Buchanan found himself under increasing pressure to bring the Central American embroilment to an end. Senator Benjamin and his associates were eager to begin active negotiations with Mexico for the Tehuantepec route, and were handicapped by the uncertainties over Nicaragua. Commodore Vanderbilt was disturbed by indications that the Costa Rican government, having put its flag on the Transit steamers, had no intention of letting them go. Action was needed, and it took the form of the arrival at San Juan del Sur of a powerful American sloop-of-war, the *St. Mary's*, and Commander Charles N. Davis, with official instructions to "take such steps as circumstances required for the protection of American citizens" in Nicaragua, and perhaps unofficial instructions to put an end to the war by any means that came to hand.

A shrewd man, Davis began by negotiating with General Mora to allow the removal of American women and children from Rivas under the protection of the American flag. A truce was declared for this purpose, and while it was still in effect, he suggested to Mora and the northern allies that they permit at the same time the departure of Walker's army. They were delighted to comply. Subsequently Mora admitted that in another twenty days his losses resulting from cholera would have compelled a cessation of the war. The only stipulation that he made was that he was to receive all of Walker's artillery and munitions. On April 30, Davis wrote Walker a letter, carried to him under a flag of truce by one of Mora's officers. Its essence was that the situation was hopeless, and that Walker would be well advised to surrender himself and his men to the United States, represented by Davis. If this offer were not accepted, Davis went on, he would seize the *Granada* at San Juan del Sur, thus cutting off the last marginal hope of escape.

The threat infuriated Walker; at the same time it made him see the futility of further resistance, and he replied that he was ready to negotiate the terms of capitulation. Conferences followed, distinguished chiefly by his determination to assure the safety of those Nicaraguan soldiers who had continued to serve in his army; he would sign no agreement that did not allow them to go peacefully to their homes. Nor did he have any intention of letting the Costa Ricans benefit from his artillery. The articles of surrender, while calling on him to deliver his field pieces, did not say that they had to be in firing order; and Henningsen and his officers proceeded systematically to wreck all mortars and howitzers, as well as an arsenal that they had constructed.

On May 1, 1857, at five o'clock in the afternoon, Walker addressed his men for the last time. His brief remarks were in a vein not likely to give much comfort to his dispirited and hungry followers. The tone was defiant, the ideas remote from their present miseries. One suspects that it was only by remoteness and detachment that he had been able to sustain his own morale during the siege; if he had identified himself with his men, their misery would have destroyed him. Now he told them that he and they must part "for the present." They had "written a page of American history which it is impossible to forget or erase. From the future, if not from the present, we may expect just judgment." He then thanked the officers and men who had served under him, and stood aside while General Henningsen explained the terms of the surrender and the order of march. Walker and his staff would go to San Juan del Sur, and deliver themselves to Commander Davis aboard the *St. Mary's*. The remainder of the army and the noncombatants would be taken over the Transit route to Greytown, to board another United States warship, the frigate *Wabash*, Commodore Hiram Paulding in command.

The fact that Walker and his higher officers were Davis's prisoners apparently did not come home to many of his men. Nor were they interested in the plans already in his mind for the future, and which required his return to the United States at the earliest moment. To the newer recruits especially, those who knew him least and had not felt the impact of his personality, the overriding fact was that he was leaving them at the low point of their lives. His departure, abrupt and seemingly unemotional, was to them the climax of a nightmare. From the moment when they saw him ride away their accumulated resentments gathered force. They felt toward him as the remnants of Napoleon's Grand Army felt when he left them on the retreat from Moscow. High politics meant nothing to the disheartened men in the ranks of Walker's army. They had endured hunger, festering wounds, fevers, flies, chiggers, lice, dysentery; they had lived in a miasma of blood, foul smells, fear, and disease; they had seen their friends, and even American women and children, suffer and die in Nicaragua; and now their leader, the man for whom they had risked everything, had deserted them: so they felt. He and his officers rode horses; they had to walk—or hobble, if they were wounded—the miles that lay between Rivas and Lake Nicaragua. He was in the hands of Americans; they were left to the mercies of the Costa Ricans. Rage grew in them on the slow boat journey across Lake Nicaragua and down the San Juan River to Greytown. Although Mora's troops refrained from obvious violence, they missed no opportunity to pilfer such belongings as the Americans still had, and to humiliate them; and such food as was offered them was barely edible. When at last they staggered on board the *Wabash,* the ship's officers were shocked and filled with pity by their plight, and the voyage home, through a stormy sea, was a long hymn of hate to Walker.

V

A crisis developed after Walker boarded the *St. Mary's,* for Commander Davis insisted on the surrender of the *Granada.* This had not been provided for in the articles, but when both Walker and Fayssoux demurred, Davis threatened to sink the vessel then and there, and trained his guns on the little ship. After a bitter protest, Walker wrote an order to Fayssoux—"Deliver the *Granada* to the United States." The sense of injury that he felt was compounded when Davis turned the vessel over to the Costa Ricans, and he subsequently expressed grim satisfaction when incompetent seamanship under the Costa Rican flag caused the doughty little schooner to be wrecked and lost.

In all, 2500 American fighting men had served under Walker in Nicaragua—never more than 800 in any one engagement—against enemy forces estimated by Henningsen at 17,000. Of the total American enlistment, 1000 had died of wounds or disease, 700 had deserted, 250 had been discharged, and 80 had been captured by the enemy. Henningsen, a trained military observer, believed that about 5800 Central Americans must have been killed or wounded in battle during the war, but how many had died of disease he could not guess.

The press of the world made much of the surrender. The London *Times* regretted that Davis had not left Walker and his "armed rabble" to be exterminated by the Costa Ricans, and Greeley's *Tribune* echoed the sentiment. But Walker had his defenders. Senator Toombs of Georgia expressed outrage at the administration's behavior in the matter, telling the Senate that Walker "had been driven out of the Presidency of Nicaragua . . . by a foreign invasion, aided by Commander Davis of the United States Navy." *Harper's Weekly* took the position that Walker's defeat was due primarily to Vanderbilt and Spencer, and surprised its readers by implying that it would be a good thing for Central America if Walker could come to terms with the Transit Company and assume again the Presidency of the country.

VI

The next moves on the Washington chessboard were predictable. The Costa Rican minister announced that his country had a legitimate claim to the Nicaraguan Transit, and planned to participate in its future control. Vanderbilt protested. Buchanan said that legality must be observed. Senator Benjamin and an associate left Washington for Mexico City, with the intention of concluding a contract for the Tehuantepec Transit route.

At this point, as so often during his administration, Buchanan's hopes of achievement collapsed at the first challenge. Neither he nor Benjamin expected that Pierre Soulé would forestall them in Mexico. Savagely indignant at the wrecking of his hopes for Nicaragua, the father of the Ostend Manifesto was determined to frustrate Buchanan by every means at his disposal. The Mexican officials responded to his political skill and eloquence, and Benjamin's negotiation swiftly lost momentum and came to a stop.

Here was a new embarrassment for the President. If an American transit could not be established in Tehuantepec, then the Nicaraguan route took on renewed importance. Belatedly he raised the question of its future with England. An almost plaintive letter went to his friend Lord Clarendon. "I think you ought to keep your protégés in Central America in better order. I wish I could induce you to believe that the interest of the United States in that region is the very same with your own. Your special favorite Costa Rica is now endeavoring to convert her patriotic assistance to her sister state against the filibusters into a war of conquest, and she modestly claims the right to sell the Transit route to the highest bidder."

Buchanan then added, in his first draft of the letter, as preserved in his files, the sentence, "To this I shall never submit." However, he characteristically struck out the word "never," and the letter as it went to Clarendon read merely, "To this I shall not submit." Then, on a sighing note, the President lamented, "Both of our countries and the world would have been better off if the Clayton-Bulwer treaty had not existed."

PART THREE

All or Nothing

《《 》》

"That his success would have inured to the benefit of civilization, few, perhaps, in view of the present condition of Central America, will be so rash as to deny."

W. O. SCROGGS ON WALKER,
in *Filibusters and Financiers*

"Had he been successful, the Civil War might have been postponed, might never have been fought, or might have had another result."

LAWRENCE GREENE ON WALKER,
in *The Filibuster*

XVIII

A NAME TO CONJURE WITH

He had gone to Nicaragua in the name of democracy and the Nicaraguan Democrats had turned against him. He had begun with a sense of America's mission to the world, and the government of the United States had rejected him. He had stood for the gradual elimination of slavery, and now the world knew him as a slavery man. His purpose had been twisted until all the idealistic essence had been wrung out of it. He could no longer hold on to his Byronic conception of himself. But to the average American he was still the hero of heroes. This fact first came home to Walker in the wild welcome that awaited him at New Orleans, where he landed on May 27, 1857. Word had come from Washington that, on order of the President, no charges would be preferred against him for violation of the Neutrality Laws; he was a free man. A cheering crowd was on the wharves; men surrounded him, lifted him to their shoulders, bore him to a waiting carriage, formed a procession, and marched behind him to the sumptuous St. Charles Hotel, where rooms had been reserved for him. So numerous and persistent were the people in the street outside that he was compelled to appear on the balcony of his apartment and make a short speech. This was not enough; his admirers entered the hotel and refused to leave until they saw him again.

He came down to the rotunda, mounted a table, spoke of his pleasure in being back in New Orleans, and promised that he would give a full account of his experiences at a mass meeting then being organized. Finally the crowd dispersed, to read newspapers which blazoned the hero's return over their front pages. When adjectival journalism gave out, editors filled their columns with panegyrics from readers in prose and verse. One lady of the city provided fifteen stanzas on the theme of Walker's greatness: "All hail to thee, Chief! Heaven's blessing may rest on thy battle-scarred brow" . . . and so forth. Women especially found irresistible the combination of his fame and his boyish appearance. Letters written to him by one enamored girl were still extant a century later. When one night he arrived late to see a play and was recognized, female throats accounted for a large share of the frenzy with which he was greeted. The show stopped, actors and audience applauded him, the orchestra struck up the Star-Spangled Banner, and he was cheered for ten minutes. "Never," commented a French writer, "was a monarch returning from victory more acclaimed by a people delirious with happiness."

At the mass meeting, held in the open two nights later, he stood on a platform surrounded by flags of the United States and Nicaragua, and spoke for two hours, making no secret of his intention to return to Central America and complete the task he had begun. The New Orleans press reported his oration as a *tour de force,* an oral history of his career on the isthmus, and an explanation—pointing bluntly at Secretary Marcy, Commodore Vanderbilt, and the British government —of the reasons why he had not succeeded. In speaking of President Buchanan, however, Walker was reserved; already arrangements were being made for a talk between them at the White House. One newspaper wondered whether he was planning on a political future in the United States. If so, the popular base for it was established. His was a name to conjure with.

II

Walker could not have been unmindful that all the cheering was being done by men whose politics he had opposed a few years earlier. Like others whose guiding principle has crumpled under pressure, he could achieve forgetfulness only by doubling the intensity of his new conviction, and hypnotizing himself with its repetition. Journeying north-ward, he asserted in every speech not only that the introduction of American civilization in Central America was the road to salvation for the United States, but that Southern institutions had to prevail there. Memphis took him to its heart. In Louisville, where he visited his sister, Mrs. Alice Walker Richardson, the press accorded him the tributes reserved for the mighty. In Cincinnati, Democratic politicians made much of him. Even in cynical Washington, where he arrived on June 12, he generated extraordinary interest. Newspapers reported that in a long and private conference at the White House he had given the President his version of events in Nicaragua, and had strongly pro-tested the actions of Commander Davis, especially with respect to the seizure of the *Granada*. It was Walker's position that if it had not been for Davis's interference, the Central American armies would have disintegrated; while the morale of his own men would have been sus-tained by the knowledge that a route of retreat was open to them. He made these charges first orally, then in writing.

Some months later, in a speech at Mobile, Walker said that the President in this meeting had not only heard him with attention but had actually encouraged him to make another attempt to conquer Nicaragua. Friends of Buchanan's scoffed, and accused Walker of outright fabrication; yet it would not have been out of character for the President to make remarks which Walker could have interpreted as encouragement. Buchanan was not the man to offend a visitor who had so strong a hold on public opinion as Walker had in the summer of 1857. According to an Assistant Secretary of State who served under him and had frequent opportunities to observe him, the Pres-ident was far from being the amiable weakling so often portrayed. Rather he was "cold and calculating, with a clear head but no heart . . . with a habit of indirectness that at times became almost falsehood and a wariness that sometimes degenerated into craftiness."* It would have been nothing for Buchanan to drop hints of sympathy and understanding without actually committing himself—hints that would have been the more effective because Walker as yet knew nothing of the President's commitment to the Tehuantepec project.

With a strong revival of inner confidence, Walker went on to the

* "Narrative of W. H. Trescott," in the *American Historical Review*, Vol. XIII, p. 547.

culminating point of his triumphal tour, New York. There even New Orleans' hullabaloo was exceeded. A committee of admirers met him in New Jersey and escorted him by boat to Battery Park, where in spite of rain a large crowd awaited him, and where he accommodated them with a short speech. At his hotel, hero-worshipers and reporters besieged him from dawn to midnight. It was his intention to spend his time conferring with members of his Nicaraguan staff who had assembled in New York, but his schedule was torn apart. When he went to Wallack's Theatre as the guest of General and Mrs. Henningsen, the ensuing uproar was quieted only when the orchestra struck up "Hail, Columbia." Walker was compelled to speak to the audience from the Henningsens' box, and beg their attention for the play they had come to see. At its end, the press of people outside the theater was so thick and persistent that he and the Henningsens could hardly reach their carriage. When he finally got to his hotel, it was to discover a brass band waiting for him, and he had to submit to an hour-long serenade.

So ruthless an invasion of his privacy was more than he could bear. Three days after his arrival he secretly left the hotel and secluded himself in a friend's house, the address of which was known only to a few intimates. There he set about the business on which he had come. This was nothing less than the formation of a secret "Central American League," with branches in the main American cities, each under the charge of a trusted officer, to raise funds, recruits, and supplies for a second expedition to Nicaragua. Henningsen was in charge of the New York branch. One after another his key men took their instructions from Walker, as from the general of an actual army, and departed. "We meet again at Philippi," Henningsen was reported as saying to them.

Walker's decision to hide himself from New York's reporters did him no good in their eyes. Perhaps he had forgotten that the fury of a journalist frustrated exceeds that of a woman scorned. During the preceding days, most of the city's newspapers had written of Walker with respect. Notwithstanding his quarrrels with Vanderbilt and Goicuria and his slavery decree, he had been credited with extraordinary talents. Now the press readily seized the first opportunity to turn against him. Several newspapers criticized him sharply for impugning the motives of Commander Davis, who after all "had saved him." A more serious attack followed, when Commodore Paulding's frigate *Wabash,* carrying 140 refugees from Nicaragua, including 13 women and 5 children, arrived in New York harbor. Many were sick; all were gaunt from long privation, and desperate with uncertainty as to the future. The reporters who visited the *Wabash* came away with enough in their notebooks to wreck a dozen reputations. As seen by the poor wretches on the *Wabash,* Walker was cruel and heartless. Paulding added a touch greatly appreciated by the press when he said that Walker's men were so covered with lice when they left Greytown that the ship had become infested, and its personnel had to "bathe in rum." This was a story to kindle the eyes of an editor. A dozen acidulous articles ate away Walker's prestige. The *Herald* admitted that the woes of the refugees might have been dictated by events beyond his control, but it was up to him to prove it. The press accused him of lack of compassion, of cold cynicism, and finally of moral cowardice, for reporters had been unable to locate him. He had "sneaked away," said the *Tribune.* The fact was that he had become indifferent both to popular praise and journalistic condemnation. Events would speak for him, or nothing would.

III

It was not a good time in which to raise money. A financial panic which had shaken the City of London was suddenly echoed in Wall Street; stock prices collapsed, credit tightened, business fell off, men lost their jobs, and a cloud of pessimism settled over the country. The Dred Scott decision and reports of violence between slavery men and free-soilers in Kansas added to the general disquiet. Many promises of support came to Walker, but they were seldom backed with cash. Nevertheless, he made some progress. He had gone to New Orleans, where, keeping out of the public eye, he found enough money to enable one of his secret agents to purchase a steamship, the *Fashion,* and a cargo of arms and military stores. Recruiting was no problem; many young Southerners were eager to serve under Walker, despite all the hardships his previous army had endured. The essential question was that which he had faced two years earlier in California— whether the Neutrality Laws would be enforced against him. It was soon answered. Buchanan's administration showed every sign of antagonism. Particularly significant was the fact that the new Secretary of State, Lewis Cass, who a year earlier, when he hoped for the Presidency, had backed Walker and "the rights of Americans to emigrate and take their arms with them," had reversed his stand. In subservience to Buchanan, Cass now ordered federal authorities in all port cities to be on guard against the departure of any filibustering expeditions.

On November 10, 1857, federal marshals appeared at Walker's house and arrested him. He made no protest. In the court hearing that followed, the New Orleans federal attorney showed evidence that the *Fashion,* which was advertised to depart for Nicaragua, had taken on board an extraordinary quantity of supplies such as would be required in a military campaign. That the passengers would be filibusters recruited by Walker was the prosecution's case, and the judge thought it good enough to remand Walker for trial, setting bail in the amount of $2000. There was no actual proof, however, that the *Fashion* had violated any law. Walker being ashore, and none of his men on board, the ship was allowed to weigh anchor and steam away.

With Pierre Soulé as his lawyer, Walker found bail and, released from custody, proceeded to execute a plan carefully devised for that very situation. Mobile, even more than New Orleans, was sympathetic to his cause, and it was unlikely that any federal officer there would seriously seek to stop him. Ignoring the fact that he was on bail, he and a few members of his military staff boarded the daily mail boat from New Orleans to Mobile. At every stop they were joined by additional small groups who had quietly left New Orleans well in advance, and by the time they reached Mobile Bay the boat was crammed with Walker's men. Among them were six of the original Immortals.

They found the *Fashion* anchored far out in Mobile Bay, where it had taken on a cargo of arms, and they boarded her without interference. The final test lay ahead. A cutter drew alongside and federal officers came on board. They had been instructed, they said, to inspect the steamer, its passengers, and the cargo. Solemnly they performed their duty, but carefully managed to see no arms, no sign of Walker or his officers, no suspicious circumstance of any kind. With 270 men on board, including such famous veterans as Colonels

Hornsby, Anderson, Natzmer, and Henry, and Commander Fayssoux, the *Fashion* was given her clearance for Nicaragua; and a telegram from Washington, ordering pursuit of the ship, was mysteriously lost before it reached the federal officer to whom it was addressed.

I V

Buchanan was then engaged in an attempt to persuade England to scrap the Clayton-Bulwer Treaty—something that England was determined not to do. Walker's flaunting of the Neutrality Laws not only made the President look foolish, but was interpreted by the British ambassador, Lord Napier, as proof that the United States had imperialistic designs in Central America, and stood in violation of the treaty. Otherwise would Walker not have been prevented from sailing? Buchanan hastily assured Napier that he intended to uphold the treaty until it was abandoned by mutual agreement. He then declared war on Walker. An order went to his Secretary of the Navy, Isaac Toucey: intercept the *Fashion*. Soon afterward, Buchanan sent his first annual message to Congress, and urged the enactment of legislation which would "be effectual in preventing our citizens from committing such outrages" as Walker had perpetrated. Walker's expedition could "do no possible good to the country" but was certain to "injure its interests and its character."

The unaccustomed vigor of the President's attack on Walker had a shrewd political purpose. Although Buchanan professed personal aversion to slavery on moral grounds, he had found it politically expedient to favor the slavery interest in Kansas. To justify his policy, the President had arrived at a strict and sterile interpretation of the Constitution which enabled him to maintain that the slavery problem in Kansas and elsewhere could be dealt with simply by "proper administration of the law." His position in Kansas had excited unrealistic expectations in the South and extreme abolitionist agitation in the North. Irreconcilables on both sides were increasing their power. But having won over the Southerners in Congress with his Kansas policy, Buchanan had to deal with the heavy fire then being aimed at him by the Northern press. His need was to show himself to the North, if he could, as, after all, neutral on slavery. Walker provided the perfect instrument. He was backed by slavery men; in attacking him, therefore, the President seemed to be attacking slavery, a position calculated to mollify Northern critics. And it was a safe tactic in the South, for Southern leaders in Congress were so eager to keep Buchanan's Kansas policy unchanged that they were unwilling to make a strong effort on Walker's behalf. It was politic and it was easy for Buchanan to condemn him unrestrainedly.

But the wording of Secretary Toucey's order to the Navy's Caribbean Squadron, calling for Walker's interception, was so vague as to create uncertainty in every officer who received it. One of them went so far as to request enlightenment from the Secretary: was he to "seize a suspicious vessel in a foreign port?" Or, rather than risk so illegal a proceeding, should he merely prevent the passengers from going ashore? And what if the passengers claimed to be only peaceful travelers? Toucey's reply doubled the doubt. A naval officer could not act, of course, merely on suspicion. There must be no interference, of course, with lawful commerce. Of course, there should be no violation of the soil of other nations. But if a vessel "was manifestly engaged" in filibustering, it should be intercepted and prevented from landing its men and arms. How this was to be done the Secretary did not say, but the sloop-of-war *Saratoga,* Commander Frederick Chatard, was ordered to the harbor of Greytown.

Walker, who foresaw that some such move would be made, seemed to his companions on the *Fashion* strangely unconcerned, as if he had an inner knowledge of events to come. So certain was he of success that he had even brought with him the editor of *El Nicaragüense,* John Tabor, several new fonts of type, and the Great Seal of Nicaragua, which he had carried away with him. The nine days of the voyage from Mobile were spent in organizing his force and drilling his men. His strategy had been thoroughly worked out. The first essential was the capture of the Transit steamers on the San Juan River and the small fort, Fort Castillo, which dominated the entry from the river into Lake Nicaragua. To try to move up the San Juan from Greytown, however, was hopeless; the Transit boats would be forewarned and would simply escape to the lake. Surprise was of the essence, and Walker knew how to achieve it. A fork of the San Juan known as the Colorado, which reached the sea at a desolate spot some miles south of Greytown, was known to be unguarded. Before attempting to land at Greytown, the *Fashion* would put down a company of picked men under Colonel Anderson at the Colorado, with three boats; this force would row upstream, seize the first Transit vessel encountered, capture the other steamers as they came down the San Juan, disembark at Fort Castillo under cover of the Costa Rican flag, and disarm the unsuspecting garrison. The steamers would then be sent back to bring the rest of Walker's troops up the San Juan and across Lake Nicaragua. Before an army could be mobilized against them they would take Virgin Bay, Rivas, and San Juan del Sur. By that time reinforcements already being organized by Henningsen in the United States would have arrived, they would sweep north to Granada, Masaya, Managua, and León, and Nicaragua would once more be in American hands.

True to this plan, the *Fashion* skirted Greytown harbor and in a drenching rain reached the mouth of the Colorado unobserved. After seeing Anderson and his men on their way, Walker ordered the ship to stand out to sea, and cruise slowly along the coast through the night, timing its approach to Greytown for broad daylight the next morning—an hour when, presumably, no filibustering ship would dare to run the *Saratoga*'s guns.

V

At seven o'clock on the morning of November 24, 1857, Commander Chatard of the *Saratoga* saw the steamship *Fashion* come into Greytown harbor, with fifteen passengers or so on deck. When he hailed the ship, an officer on the vessel called back something that could not be distinctly heard, except for the word "transit." Knowing that the Vanderbilt interests intended to reclaim the Transit property, Chatard came to the conclusion that this was the purpose of the party on board the *Fashion,* and he made no effort to interfere with its progress. A few minutes later, when the steamer tied up at a wharf, he had the shock of his life. All at once the *Fashion*'s decks were crowded with laughing men, carrying rifles, and leaping ashore.

Chatard's orders gave him no right to use force against the filibusters once they had landed. Only if they offered violence against members of his ship's company could he justify the use of his guns to coerce these Americans on foreign soil. To provoke some hostile action by Walker now became the purpose of the humiliated Commander, and in this he showed considerable ingenuity. Sailors went ashore to prevent Walker's men from occupying the buildings of the Transit Company, thus compelling them to bivouac in the open, exposed to the steady tropical rain. Officers of the *Saratoga*, disregarding Walker's sentries, strolled through his camp, some of them not even in uniform, inviting a challenge. More malevolently, the ship's gunners were ordered to use an area only a few yards from Walker's camp for cannon practice.

Understanding Chatard's strategy, Walker ordered his restive men to ignore all provocations, and quietly moved his camp to safer ground while awaiting news from Anderson. He was not, however, submissive under Chatard's pressure. The commanding officer of the *Saratoga*'s squadron, Commodore Paulding, was known to be at his Panama station on his flagship, the *Wabash,* and Walker sent the *Fashion* off to find him, with a letter detailing Chatard's offenses. Almost at the same time, a fast British mail boat put into Greytown, and Chatard took advantage of her presence to write Paulding on his own account. With his official report went a personal and highly emotional note which later figured in a Congressional investigation. He could not explain how he had allowed Walker to dupe him. "Somehow or other I was spellbound. . . . I beg you, Sir, in the most earnest manner, to come here and advise me. I am in a very cruel state of mind, and look gloomily to the future." He had reason for his gloom; Secretary Toucey, on hearing of his lapse, suspended him.

At Walker's camp, days of incessant rain passed with no word from Anderson. Mud, insects, boredom, and anxiety were telling on the men. Walker himself began to sit up of nights at a campfire, waiting for a signal from the river. On the afternoon of the twelfth day, when confidence was ebbing fast, a native canoe appeared on the San Juan, with one of Anderson's men sitting comfortably in the stern with a rifle, while two Costa Ricans, his prisoners, worked the paddles. The news that he brought sent the camp into a wild demonstration of joy. Anderson's expedition had been a total success. Without the loss of a single man, he had captured the river steamers and Fort Castillo; and although navigational problems had delayed the steamers, they were on their way to Greytown. In a day or two Walker and all his men would be able to start up the river.

The revival of spirits did not last long. Before a river boat could arrive, the frigate *Wabash* steamed into the bay, and anchored as close as it could to Walker's camp. Shortly it was joined by another American ship, the *Fulton,* and by two British men-of-war. With the *Saratoga* these ships among them carried over 200 guns. Pinnaces plied back and forth and the commanders were entertained at dinner by Commodore Paulding aboard the *Wabash.* The Commodore, a large, robust, and ambitious man, had been excessively aggravated by the thought that a United States Navy vessel, and a ship of his own squadron to boot, should be held up to derision. When British officers suggested that the ships of both nations join in taking Walker prisoner, he refused; he wanted Walker's scalp for himself.

His first move was to have small boats from the *Saratoga* go up the San Juan, ostensibly for fresh water, but actually to establish a blockade of the river. When two of Walker's chief aides, Hornsby and Fayssoux, arrived on board the *Wabash* to make a formal protest against this proceeding, he shrugged their words aside, and gave orders that they were not to be allowed to leave ship. They would be joined, he told them, by Walker and all his men, whom he would shortly make his prisoners.

Three hundred marines were sent ashore to take up a position that would prevent the filibusters from moving inland, and the ships swung their broadsides toward the camp. Walker could clearly see the gunners take their battle stations and train their cannon. Some of his men, unable to bear their disappointment, begged him to fight, but he refused to permit so senseless a sacrifice of life. He still bore his head high; no one observing him could have guessed that all his hopes had become ashes in his mouth. When a boat put off from the *Fulton,* in it one of Paulding's officers, Captain Engle, Walker went courteously to meet him. They shook hands, and Walker listened quietly while Engle read a note from Paulding. He and his men would board the Navy ships and be taken back to the United States, or they would be fired upon by sea and by land. As a sign of his surrender he was to lower the Nicaraguan flag that flew over his camp.

Walker merely said to Engle, "I surrender to the United States," and ordered his men to break camp. Of the two, Engle appeared the more emotional. "General," he said to Walker, "I am sorry to see an officer of your ability employed in such a service. Nothing would give me greater pleasure than to see you at the head of regular troops."

The cup of Walker's bitterness ran over when, at that very moment, one of the delayed river steamboats appeared with some of Anderson's men aboard, ready to begin the movement of his troops upstream. He had to watch while the boat was seized by Paulding's marines, and the men taken prisoner.

Having carried the day without opposition, Paulding was disposed to be considerate. Another officer came ashore to reassure Walker that, once on board, he and his officers, instead of being treated as prisoners, would have quarters suited to their rank. A polite oral reply from Walker acknowledged this gesture, and added that he did not seek privileges beyond those given his men. This message, garbled in transmission, came to Paulding as a blunt rejection—"General Walker asks no special benefits"—and deeply offended him. His next communication was a sharp command to Walker to embark immediately on the *Fulton,* to which the Commodore had transferred his flag.

A few minutes later Walker stood in Paulding's quarters, hearing himself addressed in a tone and in terms that no man had dared to use to him since he had been a boy in his father's house. He and his men were a disgrace to the United States. They had dishonored their country. They were no better than pirates and murderers. For the first time Walker's self-control cracked under the edge of suppressed rage and the weight of failure. With a curious mingling of satisfaction and sympathy, the tall, handsomely uniformed Commodore saw tears come to the eyes of the shabby little man whom all the world knew. So much, at least, is suggested by a letter that Paulding wrote to his wife. "This lion-hearted devil, who had so often destroyed the lives of other men, came to me, humbled himself, and wept like a child. You may suppose it made a woman of me, and I have had him in the cabin since as my guest. We laugh and talk as though nothing had happened, and you would think, to see him with the captain and myself, that he was one of us. He is a sharp fellow and requires a sharp fellow to deal with him. I have taken strong measures in forcing him from a neutral territory. It may make me President or may cost me my commission."

Paulding's uneasiness at the possible consequences of his actions grew when the *Fulton* arrived at its Panama base. He had accepted Walker's pledged word to proceed to New York by passenger ship and give himself up to the United States marshal there; and his desire to conciliate his prisoner before they parted expressed itself in numerous courtesies. Pointing out that five days would elapse before the next steamer would leave for the United States, he invited Walker to remain for this period in his comfortable cabin on the *Fulton,* rather than take up quarters in a flea-infested hotel of the town. Walker declined; he would not even share another meal with his captor. It was too much to expect that he could forgive the only man who had pierced the armor of his self-control. From this moment they resumed their enmity.

VI

Two distinguished lawyers and an Army general, all friends of Walker's, accompanied him when he offered himself for arrest to the United States marshal in New York. An ironic aspect of the situation lay in the fact that the marshal himself was one of Walker's great admirers—Captain Isaiah Rynders, a leader of Tammany Hall who had taken a large part in organizing public support for Walker. An arrest, Rynders said, was out of the question, since he had neither warrant nor official instructions. A conference followed, and out of it came a decision that he and Walker would go to Washington and present the problem to the administration. By that time impatient reporters were pushing their way into the marshal's office and demanding a statement from Walker. He gave them one that made headlines the next day. Paulding had invaded the territory of a friendly nation and insulted its flag. The government of the United States had an obligation to remedy his gross error. This it could do by returning him, Walker, and his men to the place from which they had been forcibly removed. On this note, leaving the reporters agape, he departed with Rynders for Washington.

Walker's departure had infuriated Buchanan; his return embarrassed him. Paulding had unmistakably exceeded his authority. Southern indignation promptly flared into mass meetings where Paulding was denounced in passionate terms and his condign punishment demanded. A resolution passed in New Orleans urged that the government not only return Walker's expedition to Nicaragua but indemnify it for losses "sustained from capture, detention and privation of liberty and property," and several senators volunteered to initiate Congressional action to that effect.

Increasingly the issue took the form of a personal contest between Walker and the President. As always, Buchanan moved with great caution. When the filibuster appeared in Washington, Cass quickly announced that there was no reason to keep him in custody. Walker staked his case on a long letter to the President, which he made public. His expedition had been justified, he insisted, in law and morality. He was the president-in-exile of a foreign government which had been recognized by a former President of the United States. It was his right and his duty to Nicaragua to seek to re-establish that government in power, with or without the aid of the United States. "Some have told you, I know, that I am a man 'without faith and without mercy'; but from the beginning to the end of my career in Nicaragua, I challenge the world to produce a single violation of public faith."

For Paulding's methods he expressed not so much resentment as disdain. "Far more grievous than the surrender . . . was it to be told that we were there to the dishonor of the United States. . . . There were men on that sandy beach, Mr. President, who had carried your flag aloft [in Mexico] amidst the thickest of the foe . . . who had led your soldiers across the continent in the path of duty and honor. . . . I call for the justice it is your high prerogative to bestow.

"But permit me to conclude by adding that . . . no extreme of illegal interference—no amount of hard words and unjust epithets— can deter us from following the path which is before us."

The day on which this letter appeared, January 4, 1858, the Senate passed a resolution calling on the President for "the correspondence, instructions and orders to the United States naval forces on the coast of Central America, connected with the arrest of William Walker and his associates." Buchanan was now compelled to reply, and he did so in a communication of considerable ingenuity. "In capturing General Walker and his command . . . Commodore Paulding has, in my opinion, committed a grave error. It is quite evident, however . . . that this was done from pure and patriotic motives." The President, having thus made clear his intention to let the Commodore off lightly, quickly moved to safer terrain. On a note of reassuring, if empty, prophecy, he said, "The tide of emigration will flow to the South. . . . Central America will soon contain an American population which will confer blessings and benefits upon the natives and their respective governments." Therefore, he implied, Walker and his methods were not needed. He went on to say he believed in the "Manifest Destiny" of the American people to dominate in the Western Hemisphere, but "no administration can successfully conduct the foreign affairs of the country in Central America . . . if it is interfered with at every step by lawless military expeditions set on foot in the United States."

A tumult of debate followed in both Senate and House. Conflicting resolutions were introduced, one calling for official punishment of Paulding, another for the presentation to him of a gold medal for his action in Nicaragua. For days all other business stood still while Walker and Paulding were each roundly criticized and staunchly defended. Fifteen senators made speeches, covering every aspect of the controversy. The question was raised, how was it that Paulding, if he regarded Walker and his men as "outlaws who had . . . left our shores for the purpose of rapine and murder"—the Commodore's words in his own defense—how was it that he had made Walker his close companion on the *Fulton,* taken meals with him, addressed him always as "general," and accepted his parole of honor for his return to New York? The question went unanswered.

The hardest attack on Walker came from Senator Slidell of Louisiana, Buchanan's great friend, who asserted at great length that Walker was a bloodthirsty pirate who merited no consideration from his country. In the end, the weary senators and the President arrived at a compromise. All resolutions were dropped. While Paulding was mildly censured by the Secretary of the Navy and temporarily relieved of his command, Walker was given no encouragement. When all was done, the administration still stood firmly against him; the Congress was divided as before.

VII

From the reception that he received as he journeyed South from Washington, one would have thought that Walker came with renewed laurels of conquest, instead of as a man who had twice failed of his purpose and had been roundly castigated by the President and many senators of his country. In Richmond and Montgomery, where every honor was heaped on him, he reminded his audiences that before leaving New Orleans for Nicaragua he had been arrested and put on bail; he was returning now to insist that he be tried for violation of the Neutrality Laws. At Mobile, he made a major address on the issue between Buchanan and himself. It was in this speech, delivered on January 25, 1858, that he brought into the open Buchanan's support of the Tehuantepec scheme, and Soulé's part in thwarting it.

The style of the Mobile speech and of the letters which Walker wrote on the Davis and Paulding affairs suggests the profound psychological change that had taken place in him. The former note of high-mindedness, the alleviating flashes of ironic humor have given way to hot indignation and cold legalism. While he regarded himself as a missionary for Americanism and democracy, his personality had color and warmth, but he seemed motivated now mainly by a demonic drive to fulfill "his destiny." At the age of thirty-three the only possibility of life that interested him was his return to Nicaragua.

But perhaps for that very reason his power to lift an audience to its feet was never greater. The Mobile speech was an immense success, a devastating exposure of Buchanan's inconsistency. The President's stand, Walker asserted, had nothing to do with principle. Surely the co-author of the Ostend Manifesto was not the man to defend the Neutrality Laws! It was not filibustering as such that aroused Buchanan's wrath, said Walker. What the President really resented was his, Walker's, alliance with Soulé, who had blocked the Tehuantepec project. The administration was perfectly willing to encourage filibustering attempts elsewhere than in Nicaragua. The Secretary of War, John B. Floyd, had actually urged Henningsen to aid a revolution in Mexico and incite a war with Spain, so as to provide a pretext for the annexation of Cuba. Therefore Buchanan's attacks on Walker had nothing to do with principle. They were to be understood simply as a matter of low politics to serve the interests of the President's friends in Tehuantepec; and Walker was fully justified in his defiance.

The public seized excitedly on this revelation. Floyd, who could not deny that he had met with Henningsen, contended that the statements attributed to him were false. The abolitionist North believed him; the South preferred to believe Walker, and became even more convinced that he had spoken truth when Henningsen went to Mexico to offer his services to a revolutionary movement in that country.

The practical result of the Mobile speech promptly showed in the Alabama legislature. Deeply impressed by Walker's arguments, the state granted a charter to the Mobile and Nicaragua Steamship Company, known to have been incorporated by Walker's supporters. Simultaneously the Central American League was revived, under the name of the Southern Emigration Society, and its branches throughout the South again took up the task of raising funds and finding recruits for Walker. Contributions were at first slow, for even ardent supporters now understood the weight of the odds against Walker. He had finally to undertake an extensive lecture tour, and this proved more successful. Listening to him, Southern audiences became convinced that Nicaragua was the key to their future security, and they responded with substantial donations to the cause. "General Walker," declared a newspaper after one of his speeches, "could raise a million dollars in Dallas County [Alabama] to Americanize Central America."

Even after two failures he still retained his luster. It was not the sad loyalty for a fallen idol, not the loyalty of nostalgia, that Southerners gave him, but a vibrant faith that he would yet achieve his purpose. When he stood trial in New Orleans he made the federal prosecutor appear feeble. An impassioned speech in his own defense outweighed in the minds of the jury both the evidence against him and an adverse charge by the judge; ten jurors out of twelve voted for acquittal. Intent on complete vindication, he demanded a new trial, but the government declined to prosecute further. On leaving the courtroom he declared openly that he would soon return to Nicaragua and "eat Christmas dinner in Granada."

XIX

THE DARK LIGHT OF HOPE

The strategic moment, Walker felt, could not be far away. Knowing Central American politicians, he was convinced that it would not be long before Costa Rica, holding the Transit, and the new Nicaraguan government were at daggers' points, and that a determined invasion would find only faltering and feeble resistance. In the early months of 1858, the press was astir with rumors of another Walker expedition, and this time it seemed that Buchanan would be unable to stop it. The President's hold on the Southerners in Congress had been seriously weakened by events in Kansas. In spite of his inclination to favor the Southern interest in the territory, resistance to slavery by "free-soil" settlers from the North had become so vigorous and so much blood was being shed, that Southerners had begun to lose hope. Kansas was no longer an effective lever with which Buchanan could push the South into acceptance of his anti-Walker measures. A major split in the Democratic Party and a revolt in Congress threatened the President if he sought to interfere with the new and powerful Walker expedition which, as widely rumored in the press, was in preparation. Walker himself went to Washington, where, after conferring with senatorial supporters, he wrote enthusiastically in a private letter that the administration would either "yield to the voice of the country in regard to our affairs," or face catastrophic Congressional reprisals.*

Buchanan, however, had by no means exhausted his repertory of political devices in his contest with Walker. There was yet one way in which criticism of his Nicaraguan policy could be silenced and Walker frustrated once and for all. That was to send to Nicaragua, with the consent of its new government, a strong force of American marines, who would occupy the Transit route and render meaningless and hopeless any attempt by Walker to land an expeditionary force. To this end Buchanan, through Secretary of State Cass, now addressed himself. The fact that his new policy ran counter to everything he had said and done in connection with Nicaragua since taking office did not trouble him.

The first step in Buchanan's plan was to aid an American company to gain control of the Transit concession. No one was any longer sure where legal title to the Transit lay. Nicaragua owned the route, Costa Rica held it; but the positions of Vanderbilt, and of Morgan and Garrison were obscure. The latter two made a bold effort to reassert their claim. It seemed to them that since Costa Rican troops held the boats and occupied most of the route, the key to the outcome lay with President Mora, and their problem was only to find an agent who could exert the necessary pressure on him. W.R.C. Webster, who had been instrumental in organizing the alliance against Walker, was an obvious choice; he had the advantage of being British and had a claim of sorts on Costa Rican gratitude. The fact that he was in Vanderbilt's employ was not a serious deterrent for Morgan and Garrison, who knew the uses of money. Webster broke with Vanderbilt, entered their service, traveled to Costa Rica with ample funds at his disposal, and within a short time was able to report success. Mora, always generous with his signature on documents that could be repudiated, had given him the desired contract.

Buchanan, however, did not trust Morgan and Garrison, largely owing to their previous connection with Walker. He quickly wrote to Lord Clarendon in London that Costa Rica "had got hold of the greatest scamps as purchasers" of the Transit route and plainly conveyed his feeling that Mora should be discouraged from any thought

* Fayssoux Collection (ms.) No. 66, Jan. 5, 1858.

of executing the contract he had given Webster. England cooperatively intervened, and from this time Morgan and Garrison ceased to
be serious contenders for the prize.

Vanderbilt had bitterly, hotly, and publicly protested the Morgan-
Garrison contract, and it was generally thought that their failure
would be his success. He, after all, controlled Accessory Transit Company, which held a contract with Nicaragua for the route; but with
his innate contempt for the law, he was unwilling to take his stand
on a merely legal claim. He wanted to get physical control of the
Transit first, and argue about legality later. To this end he began a
secret intrigue with a high-ranking Costa Rican general. This proved
a poor tactic. Agents of the State Department reported the plot to
Washington, and Buchanan was incensed to the point where he refused to give the Commodore diplomatic support. Instead he turned
to a new contestant for the Transit—Vanderbilt's former associate,
Joseph L. White, godfather of the Clayton-Bulwer treaty, and a
political manipulator of great skill and experience. With some wealthy
associates, White had accumulated the worthless shares of the old
Atlantic and Pacific Ship Canal Company. Thus he had acquired the
original canal concession granted by Nicaragua, which gave his claim
to the Transit a certain air of legality. More important, he had persuaded the new Nicaraguan government to grant him secretly a provisional contract covering both overland transit and canal. Here was
the opportunity that the President sought to put an end to filibustering and regain popularity among the expansionists. He set Secretary
of State Cass to work negotiating a treaty with Nicaragua under
which the United States would have the right to use military force, if
necessary, to protect "persons and property conveyed over the
route," as operated by White. Objections from Vanderbilt were dis-
regarded.

To Lord Clarendon, Buchanan wrote that British interests would
be protected, that the new treaty, known as the Cass-Irissari Convention, in no way threatened her rights or violated the intent of the
Clayton-Bulwer treaty, and that the Costa Ricans would have no
cause for complaint. "Great Britain and the United States, while
treating them [the Costa Ricans] justly and even liberally, ought to
let them know that this transit shall be kept open and shall never
again be interrupted."

II

At this juncture the Nicaraguan kaleidoscope was shaken again, and a totally new pattern emerged. To Buchanan's consternation, Nicaragua at the last moment rejected both the Cass-Irissari Convention and the White contract, and announced that the concession for the canal and Transit route had been granted, not to an American, not even to an Englishman, but to a Frenchman, one Félix Belly; and that in this grant Nicaragua and Costa Rica had acted in concert, as joint owners of the route.

The American press and Congress howled with anger. The weakness of the American government had lost the greatest prize in the Western Hemisphere, the isthmian canal route, to a European power —with all that that implied for the Monroe Doctrine and the future of the United States. There was talk of war with France. Was it for this that the President had rejected Walker? Buchanan was scourged even by newspapers which had been friendly to him. To make matters worse for the President, the tone of the Nicaraguan announcement was offensive in the extreme. Monsieur Belly, who represented a Parisian syndicate, was trading on the anti-*gringo* sentiment of the isthmus. Fluent in Spanish, vivacious, eloquent, with a talent for bravura, he was able to excite and persuade the Central American mind as could no Anglo-Saxon. He knew how to convey, without actually saying, that he was a trusted agent of Napoleon III, and that the wealth and arms of imperial France stood behind him. Why, he asked President Mora of Costa Rica, and the new president of Nicaragua, Martinez—why should they yield the Transit to the *gringos*? Instead, let them confer the rights to the route on a company of Europeans who shared their religion and their culture. Assured of protection by the French, and of a large share in the profits, their countries could grow rich, put an end to American pressure, and be free at last of William Walker.

This last point especially carried great weight with Mora and Martinez, who lived in dread of Walker's return. With a shrewd eye for theater, the Frenchman brought them together in the bullet-pocked town of Rivas, on the Transit route, to work out an agreement, and the resulting documents were made public on May 1, 1858, the first anniversary of Walker's surrender to Commander Davis. Most sensational of their productions was a joint Manifesto declaring the belief of the two Presidents that a new filibustering expedition against Central America was being organized in the United States, and requesting England and France not to leave them "at the mercy of barbarians." A separate declaration empowered Belly to arrange for the stationing of "European vessels of war" on the Central American coast.

Buchanan protested in language which for him was surprisingly strong. The Manifesto was an insult, he told Nicaragua and Costa Rica. The United States would not permit Nicaragua's contract with Belly to interfere with rights to the Transit already acquired by American citizens. If a canal were built, it would have to be a free and safe passage for all nations, and controlled by no one nation. The American government under no conditions would tolerate the stationing of French warships at the entry points of the canal or in it. To this the Central American presidents replied with much polite reassurance, but without in the least changing their minds; while Belly took ship for Paris, expecting to return with the approval of Emperor Napoleon III and all the necessary funds.

But like everyone else in the tangled business, he was doomed to disappointment. The French government shrugged him aside, partly because it was then deeply involved in a European crisis, partly because Belly's backers were out of favor at the imperial court, and partly because Napoleon was thinking vaguely of promoting his own long-dreamed-of Nicaraguan canal company. The one hope for Belly now lay in the possibility that American financiers and the Buchanan administration, recognizing his hold on the Central American leaders, would overlook his previous attacks on the United States, come to terms with him, and give him support. In this feeble hope he embarked for New York; but at the very moment of his arrival, the *Herald* was running a front-page dispatch from Paris under the headline DISAVOWAL OF M. BELLY. The myth of his power was exploded, and with it went all expectation that he would ever dig his canal.

III

With Belly's failure, every advantage in the contest for the Transit reverted to Vanderbilt. The bewildered Nicaraguan government was easily persuaded by his agents to declare invalid all previous contracts for the route, and to restore the concession to the original owner, the Accessory Transit Company. General applause greeted this news in the American press. Several newspapers confidently predicted that the Commodore would promptly move with his much-admired energy to reopen the Nicaraguan route and bring peace and prosperity to Central America. Buchanan himself now favored the Vanderbilt cause. The Commodore could at least be counted on to oppose Walker's return to Nicaragua.

But weeks went by, and Vanderbilt took no action. When queried as to the causes of the delay, he referred gravely to the physical deterioration of the Transit route. New steamboats would have to be built and bridges restored. Silting at the mouth of the San Juan River had seriously impaired the channel at Greytown harbor. The road west of Lake Nicaragua was in need of repair. Large new sums of capital would have to be invested—and the company was already in debt to Vanderbilt personally for loans made in the past. He would of course do what he could, but it was all very, very difficult.

Then, in June, 1858, light dawned on the press and the public, when word leaked out of Vanderbilt's arrangement with the Panama lines. Merely for withholding his ships from competition on the Panama run, he had been receiving $480,000 a year. Now he had yet another lever, the threat of renewed service to Nicaragua, with which to squeeze the Panama shipping magnates even harder. Rather than compete again with the Nicaraguan Transit, they had agreed to raise their payment to Vanderbilt by 40 per cent, to $56,000 a month.

Gone was any hope that the Accessory Transit Company would resume business—this despite the fact that the Commodore had urged the stockholders of the company to hold on to their shares. Over a million "blackmailing" dollars had gone into the Commodore's private pocket, more than he had lost on Accessory Transit stock two years earlier, and he was not a man to relinquish lightly so good a deal.

In the United States Senate, Robert Toombs of Georgia, one of Walker's staunch adherents, brought out the facts. "You give $900,000 a year to carry the mails to California," he told his fellow-senators, "and Vanderbilt compels the contractors to give him $56,000 a month to keep quiet. . . . He is the Kingfish that is robbing those small plunderers that come about the capital." The *New York*

Times compared Vanderbilt with "those old German barons who, from their eyries along the Rhine, swooped down upon the commerce of the noble river."

Prodded by the government and by public opinion, the Panama lines finally terminated their arrangement with the great financier. Only then did his interest in the Transit revive. Presently he wrote a letter to Buchanan: he understood that a new minister to Nicaragua, Alexander Dimitry, had been appointed, and would like to see him before he left the country, to discuss the reopening of the enterprise. "The route cannot be put into operation unless I do it myself." Evidently thinking it best to allay any suspicion that he might be planning further blackmail of the Panama lines, the Commodore added, "The only object I have in this matter is to further the wishes of your administration and to gratify my own feelings, as I have been heretofore so much identified with this particular route." Buchanan's reply was immediate and courteous. "Mr. Dimitry will be in New York tomorrow night. . . . I commend him to your kind attention."

A few months later, Vanderbilt informed Washington that he was planning a trip to Nicaragua, and Buchanan provided him with a personal letter addressed to Dimitry. "This letter will be delivered to you by Commodore Vanderbilt. He is about to . . . open the Nicaragua route. . . . I know no man in the United States who is so able and so willing to open it speedily as he is himself. This is an object the accomplishment of which I have much at heart. . . . This is in my opinion the wisest and most advantageous course the government of Nicaragua can pursue. . . . It is my desire therefore, that you should, as a private individual, exert yourself . . . for Mr. Vanderbilt."

The trip, however, never materialized. It was plain to Vanderbilt that the importance of the Nicaragua overland route was diminishing. Its troubles had created public suspicion of it, and California-bound travelers had become accustomed to the Panama service. Accessory Transit could never again be the bonanza it had been a few years earlier. As for a canal, the chances that it could be dug in the face of British opposition, and with the Clayton-Bulwer treaty still in effect, were as poor as they had ever been.

Besides, Vanderbilt's own interests were shifting. Now in his mid-sixties, he was still eager to prove his powers, and his mind was turning to great new ventures—transatlantic ocean liners, the railroads of the northeast, Wall Street warfare on a grand scale. He was through with Nicaragua. Those who continued to dream of a Nicaraguan canal and of the Transit route's revival recognized that everything would depend on Walker's next expedition.

IV

The leaders of Central America had come to believe the legends they had helped to create, in which Walker was seen as another Tamerlane, combining an insatiable thirst for blood with military genius—the implication being that they, having triumphed over this "military tactician of epic proportions," were the more deserving of their people's gratitude. In Nicaragua especially dread of Walker had been so sedulously cultivated by officials and priests that the prospect of his return evoked a nation-wide shudder. When the New Orleans *Delta* erroneously stated that Walker was in San Francisco, recruiting a thousand men for an invasion of Nicaragua's west coast, President Martinez was seized by panic. Bitter against America and disappointed in France, he turned to England for aid. Would she provide naval protection for Nicaragua's coasts and cope with Walker if he landed? The British were glad to comply. The opportunity was ready-made to extend their control of Central American resources and markets at the expense of the United States. All that was necessary was to keep the Clayton-Bulwer treaty in operation, Buchanan in his customary permissive state, and Walker out of Nicaragua, while British diplomats made the necessary arrangements.

The new British strategy hinged on an ostensible act of generosity, a voluntary yielding up of Central American territory. The first move in their gambit was an interview with Buchanan, solicited by Lord Napier, the British ambassador. The insight of the British into Buchanan's psychology had been shown in their selection of Napier as minister to his administration. He was an aristocrat of great astuteness and much charm; and the President was highly susceptible to displays of friendship by England's titled diplomats. With a light and delicate touch, Napier shaped Buchanan's mind to the views of Whitehall. He began by referring to the agitation in Congress for unilateral abrogation of the Clayton-Bulwer treaty. What were the President's views in the matter? Buchanan replied that he considered the treaty "a fruitful source of misunderstanding" but on the other hand it was a binding agreement, and "no attempt by Congress against it would have any countenance from him."

So far, so good; Napier now advanced another pawn. In recognition of the purport of the treaty, his government contemplated certain territorial concessions, long urged by the United States, to the republics of the isthmus. England was prepared at last to give Mosquito back to Nicaragua, and to return to Honduras certain islands off her Atlantic coast, seized by the British years earlier. Assuming that the President would welcome these moves, London would like to send out a special commissioner "to carry the Clayton-Bulwer treaty into execution . . . by separate negotiation with the Central American republics, in lieu of negotiation with the federal government" [of the United States].

Buchanan now stood at a crossroads of decision, but he chose not to see it. He could not have been oblivious to the ulterior motives that lay behind England's unusual philanthropy. It was apparent that the British no longer needed to maintain and pay for protectorates in Mosquito and the Bay Islands. They had been seized primarily to prevent the Nicaraguan canal from being dug; with the Clayton-Bulwer treaty in effect, they added little to England's position. Far more important to the British were valuable mining, forestry, and commercial rights (some of them formerly held by Americans), which the grateful Central American governments could be counted on to grant England in return for these territories; and long-range strategic benefits which would accrue from the establishment of pro-British governments up and down the isthmus.

Buchanan, if he felt a touch of skepticism within him, was not so inconsiderate of Lord Napier's feelings as to voice it. Instead, he expressed satisfaction at England's attitude. He said that "to him it was indifferent whether the concessions contemplated by Her Majesty's Government were consigned to a direct engagement between England and the United States, or to treaties between England and the Central American republics. The latter method might in some respects be even more acceptable to him."*

Napier doubtless understood the willingness, even eagerness, with which the President accepted his proposal. Although both houses

---

* *The Buchanan Papers*, ms. letters from Napier to Clarendon, Oct. 22, 24, 1857.

of the Congress were Democratic, antagonism to Buchanan was then so intense as to threaten the collapse of his legislative program. He urgently needed to be able to show the Congress and the country some constructive result of his statesmanship that would restore his prestige. If the people would accept England's concessions as a retreat on her part, the President would receive credit for it, and be strengthened accordingly.

In further recognition of England's gesture, Buchanan assured Napier that the United States had no territorial designs on Central America. "What could we do with such a people? We could not incorporate them; if we did, they would tear us asunder."

Napier said he could understand the President's view, but he believed "some Americans did contemplate the creation of colonies or dependencies" on the isthmus.

"That could not happen," insisted Buchanan. "We can only annex vacant territory." He had evidently forgotten his signature on the Ostend Manifesto, and he could not of course foresee the annexation of Hawaii, the Philippines, and Puerto Rico forty years later.

It was not long, however, before Buchanan was smitten by misgivings, for the British in Central America negotiated treaties so favorable to themselves as gravely to prejudice American interests. Disturbed, the President protested to Clarendon in a private letter that the new agreements were not "in the spirit of the Clayton-Bulwer treaty." He disliked especially a pledge given by England to "the great and mighty Republic of Nicaragua," assuring her of protection against filibusters. Buchanan felt that Nicaragua should have asked the United States to provide such protection. Soon afterward, the naval officer in command of America's Caribbean squadron informed Nicaragua, in a pride-swallowing note, that he would be glad to patrol her harbors to prevent filibusters from landing. The invitation was not forthcoming. A systematic patrol of Nicaragua's coasts by British warships went into effect, without American participation.

V

Walker's hopes of landing another expedition in Nicaragua were gone. Commanders of American warships might be reluctant to fire on a ship of his on the high seas, and lacking authorization from Nicaragua, might find it difficult to prevent him from landing or to pursue him, once landed; but the British, it was safe to say, would not be so inhibited. In view of Buchanan's attitude, they would feel no qualms in destroying filibusters at sea or on land. If there was to be another Walker expedition, it would have to be based on a new strategy, and this he began to work out in the autumn of 1858. He would aim not immediately at Nicaragua, but at Honduras, where he would not be expected; and having made a landing there, would establish a strong base. A revolt by Honduran Liberals was then gathering force; he would collaborate with it, defeat the existing regime, establish the Liberals in power, and with a friendly government at his back, drive south into Nicaragua.

He still had enough funds at his disposal to charter a ship and take an expedition out of the country. The question now was, would he be able to clear a ship from a Southern port? Could Washington exert enough influence on port officials in Mobile and New Orleans to prevent his sailing? The answer came in the curious indirect way of politics.

At that moment all Latin America shared and enjoyed the feeling that the United States was, after all, a paper eagle. This feeling was intensified when British warships in the Gulf of Mexico began to stop American merchantmen suspected of being slavers, and even fired on one or two which disobeyed their orders. Not since 1812 had so much humiliation been heaped on vessels flying the flag of the United States. The British, who were apparently testing the extent of Buchanan's tolerance, this time touched its limit, for he found the courage to lodge a protest and to send naval vessels to protect the country's shipping. Thereupon England acknowledged that her navy had no right to search American vessels in time of peace, and discontinued the practice.

If England had deliberately tried to revive Buchanan's prestige in the United States, she could have found no better means. The American public was all at once delighted with him, for had he not compelled perfidious Albion to respect the American flag? Was this not proof, after all—especially when taken together with England's return of Mosquito to Nicaragua—of bold and forceful statecraft on the part of the administration? A number of senators who had been extremely annoyed with Buchanan once more veered to his side. Without opposition he was able to staff the Gulf ports with federal officers on whom he could rely not to connive with Walker at evasions of the Neutrality Law.

The effect of this move by the President was fully felt by Walker late in 1858, when he assembled 300 men and a cargo of munitions at Mobile, and chartered a steamship to take them to Nicaragua as "peaceful emigrants." The new Collector of the Port, Thaddeus Sanford, flatly refused clearance, and the District Attorney summoned Walker before a Grand Jury, charged with conspiracy to violate the law. As usual, Walker spoke to the jurors in his own defense, and the old magic held. Gazing into the teeth of the evidence, the Grand Jury solemnly adjudged them false teeth, and exonerated him. But the expedition had been irretrievably damaged. His men, warned by United States marshals of their impending arrest, scattered to their homes, his ship was seized, and its cargo of munitions was confiscated.

Buchanan's campaign against Walker had turned out to be the single most successful effort of his administration.

XX

THE EASING OF PAIN

Close to the end of his resources, and with his chances of success steadily diminishing, Walker could not afford a long delay before trying again. Within a few days of his Grand Jury appearance, his veteran officers were scouting the Southern states to find yet more recruits and money for him. This time only about 100 men agreed to serve, and their quality, it was noted, was poorer than in the past. One of his chief aides, Doubleday, described them as "mostly of the class found about the wharves of Southern cities, with here and there a Northern bank cashier who had suddenly decided to change his vocation." Men of schooling or political conviction were few among them.

He had no money with which to charter a steamship, and this time his hope of taking an expedition out of Mobile centered on a sailing vessel, the schooner *Susan,* owned by one of his friends. On a December day the *Susan* put into harbor, and her owner asked for clearance, not to Central America, but merely to Key West. It was refused. Port Collector Sanford had no doubt of the true destination and purpose of the voyage, and he could not be budged. For a day or two it appeared that this expedition too would disin-

tegrate before it could sail. One move alone was still open to Walker
—defiance of the federal government—and he was desperate enough
to try it. The *Susan* left Mobile without clearance papers. Walker's
intention was to follow on another boat. But the *Susan* came to
grief on a reef off British Honduras, and its company were brought
back to Mobile by a British warship. Their return, on New Year's
Day, 1859, struck a curious note of triumph. The people of Mobile were so pleased by the British action that the failure of the
filibusters' mission was almost ignored. The city's leading men tendered a banquet to the officers of the warship and lauded them in
warm speeches, with toast after toast to Anglo-American, or more
correctly, Anglo-Southern friendship. Walker was not present. The
changing mood of Mobile, the last stronghold of filibusterism, could
not have been lost on him.

I I

There was no reason to believe that another effort to take an armed
force to Central America would prove more successful than the
last. On the contrary, the barriers against him were rising fast. Was
he so committed to his dream as to rule out every other possibility
of a career? If he had been willing to forego military adventures
and enter politics, he might still have opened up new and impressive possibilities for himself. But to Walker the current excite-
ments that were provoking the South to secession and war—the
bloodshed in Kansas—John Brown's slave-liberating raids into Virginia—the agitation in the North for higher tariffs inimical to Southern interests—all this was the shadow of doom. As before, the one
hope that he could see was the conquest of Central America in
the face of European opposition, as a rallying point for the entire
nation. All his efforts were still concentrated on this last declining
chance, which was linked to his inner need to regain the power
he had lost. For him the remaining alternatives were success or
death.

A new strategy for outwitting the federal government occurred
to him, and he and Henningsen obtained George Law's backing
for it. A hundred men would be placed on board a schooner, the
Granada, and cleared for Panama by way of Cuba with California

as their eventual destination. The port authorities at New Orleans could not deny the right of American citizens to go from state to state. He himself meanwhile would travel to Cuba, wait for the *Granada* to put into Havana harbor, and board it. The expedition would proceed to Panama and cross the isthmus. A steamship would be waiting for them on the Pacific side. Since there were comparatively few British warships patrolling the west coast of Nicaragua, Walker had no doubt that he could effect a landing there, and maintain a strong position until reinforcements, to be recruited in California, could join him.

A single aide, Colonel Bruno von Natzmer, was with him when he embarked on one of Law's Panama Line steamships, for which Havana was a port of call. His departure was observed, and a newspaper reporter, guessing part of the truth, concocted a story to the effect that Walker was going to Panama, and would proceed to California in order to recruit an army there. This report, published the very day of Walker's sailing, was a deadly misfortune for the plan. Federal authorities were alerted to the danger of permitting any vessel bound for Panama to carry what might be a filibustering expedition, and refused clearance to the *Granada*. Walker hastily tried to overcome the effect of the news story, by telling Havana correspondents that he was indeed going to Panama, but only "to take the English steamer for Southampton, intending to try what I can do in Europe." But it was too late to draw red herrings across his trail. On learning that his men had been taken off the *Granada* and dispersed, he returned to New Orleans.

If the piece of paper, a clearance certificate with an official signature on it, that stood between him and his purpose could not be obtained in one way, then it would have to be got in another. Fayssoux concentrated on winning over key officials in the office of the port of New Orleans, and finally reported success. Elated, Walker took the next step, a journey to New York, where he and Henningsen persuaded George Law to provide the funds needed for yet another expedition. By September, 1859, all was ready. A hundred Southerners were again waiting for the word to take ship with him. A Panama Line steamer, the *Philadelphia*, left New York for New Orleans with cases of guns and ammunition in its hold, and in a secret compartment an even larger quantity of arms. A second ship, the *St. Louis,* was to follow with 200 recruits from New York in the familiar guise of "emigrants." The expedition, as planned, was the largest ever assembled for Walker.

As soon as the *Philadelphia* docked in New Orleans, requesting clearance for Panama, most of the New Orleans contingent left the city on a small boat, intending to board the steamer unnoticed, just before it entered the Gulf. At first, all went well; the port inspectors examined the *Philadelphia,* found no contraband, and approved the sailing. At the last moment, however, high federal officials, including Buchanan's Secretary of the Treasury, Howell Cobb, took a hand, and formal clearance was refused. A company of soldiers from the garrison at Baton Rouge were sent down river to arrest Walker's men; the *Philadelphia* was twice searched until all the arms aboard had been found and confiscated; the ship itself was seized; and its sister-vessel, the *St. Louis,* was not permitted to leave New York. Cobb wrote to Buchanan: "You will be gratified to learn that the Walker expedition has *in all probability* been frustrated by the energy of our officers." It is some indication of the alarm still created by Walker's name in official quarters that even with the ships sequestered and the men under arrest, the Secretary was not quite sure that the expedition had been thwarted.

III

The loyalty that Walker evoked from the men who knew him best was a strange, if not a unique, phenomenon. He had managed to instill into his veterans—Henningsen, Anderson, Natzmer, Doubleday, Thomas Henry, Fayssoux, and others—his own feeling that to fight again in Central America was the only goal worth striving for. Those hard-bitten soldiers of fortune no longer sought fortune, for there was obviously none to be won in Walker's service. The ideals of democracy and Manifest Destiny with which some of them had begun had drained out through their wounds, but like him, they still believed that the future of the South and the prevention of civil war depended on the expansion of American institutions into the Caribbean. And there was still in them a determination, such as many a soldier has known, not to be thwarted by politicians and speculators. They had not yet had their fill of adventure. They wanted to fight again at the side of a man whom, for all his failures, they regarded as a great hero and a high-minded gentleman. So long as ships, guns, and recruits could be found, they would not desert him. After the dangers that they had survived with Walker, what else could they hope to do in life that would not seem pale and trivial by comparison?

The former sources of Walker's funds had dried up. George Law had concluded that the firmness of the federal government and the strength of British naval patrols in the Caribbean made the chance of taking another expedition to Central America too small to consider. To Southern magnates it also was evident that contributions to Walker's cause could no longer be regarded as a sound investment. He had, however, an invisible asset—his journalistic talent. In the autumn of 1859 a publisher offered him a contract for a book based on his experiences, and he spent the winter writing it. His hope for its success is suggested by a letter that he wrote to Fayssoux, reporting that the book was to be published in New York and Mobile simultaneously, and that the publisher expected to sell 20,000 copies in Alabama alone.

The haste of the writing shows repeatedly in the 430 pages of the volume, yet it is in many ways a remarkable production. Modeled in its third-person narrative after Caesar's *Commentaries,* it describes in clean and vigorous prose, with touches of classical scholarship, his adventures in conquest and the purposes that motivated him. Factually, the book is so accurate that even Central American historians to whom Walker was the great enemy accepted it as a reliable source of data. But Walker's passion for truth was at odds with the practical need to raise money for a new expedition, and much of the book was an effort to reaffirm his devotion to the South and to convince readers of the importance of Nicaragua to the future of Southern institutions.

The most remarkable feature of *The War in Nicaragua* is its impersonal restraint, which stands in sharp contrast to the highly emotional quality of his writing ten years earlier. It is as if Walker had deliberately censored every word that might reveal his feelings. The only expressions of pleasure come in his descriptions of landscape and of the bravery of his men in battle; the only regrets are for comrades lost; the only contempt is for the pusillanimity of American politicians. His attitude toward enemies is that of a gentleman whose hat has been accidentally knocked off by a passer-by—a slightly disdainful acceptance of an unpleasant fact. Probably his sharpest barb is a Dantesque reference to President Mora, who had just been banished from Costa Rica by a rival. "Let us pass Mora in exile, as Ugolino in hell, afar off and in silence."

Only a man habituated to monastic self-control could have written so exciting a story in so reserved a style. As he wrote, images full of pain must have come to his mind. He had been close to a world-shaking triumph, and where was it? Recollections of his own errors, of the bravery of his comrades, and the treason of those whom he had believed friends must have filled his heart, but only a cool and proud distillation of them reached paper. It seems a reasonable presumption that no writer of a personal memoir could suppress so much of himself unless he was seeking at a deeper level to suppress some unbearable admission. For Walker no admission could have been more bitter than that of failure. He had set out to be a Galahad, a Byron, a Bolívar—and he found himself at the age of thirty-five regarded as a tool of the slavery ultras, a fanatic with a lost cause.

He had been totally defeated, but he could not bring himself to say so. For him, failure was guilt—a guilt which overshadowed all the other guilts of his life, and they were many: the guilt of the hero who had betrayed his ideals, of the commander who had spilled the blood of others uselessly, of the man who had failed to use his procreative powers, perhaps of the boy who, loving his mother too much, had rejected his father. One of the mementos of this passage of Walker's life is a little note scrawled by his father about the time the book was published, and in which the relationship between them can perhaps be sensed. Addressed to Captain Fayssoux, it reads: "When you hear from my son, any information in regard to his health and movements will be acceptable to me—with kind regards to yourself, I remain very truly yours, James Walker."

As Walker wrote his story, and exposed himself to the terrors of memory, the need to be forgiven must have grown in him, for he could not forgive himself. It is not surprising that he turned that winter to religion, the one source from which he might yet win forgiveness. Significantly, the religion to which he gave himself was not that of his father, but Roman Catholicism, the faith which strict Tennessee Protestants of the 1850's most feared and hated.

The name of the priest who indoctrinated and prepared him was not revealed by the press. Some thought that the impulse to Catholicism had taken root in him years earlier in Nicaragua, under the inspiration of his gentle friend, Father Vijil. Following the news of his conversion, he was widely accused of cynical pretense. Was it not obvious, newspapers asked, that he hoped by becoming a Catholic to placate the Church in Central America and win new adherents there? Or perhaps to extract more money for his expeditions from the Catholic community of New Orleans? This view presupposes a naïveté in Walker that goes beyond credibility. He knew only too well how high the odds against him had become. The forces working in him at this stage of his life went far beyond ambition. Friends who were with him during the period of his conversion had no doubt of his sincerity. This was perhaps the logical conclusion for the man who had taken pride in his "unconquerable will." Only the religion of absolution could ease his pain.

XXI

ALL OR NOTHING

In April, 1860, the last springtime of peace before the great holocaust, Walker went to Louisville to visit his sister Alice, the one living member of his family to whom he was close. On his return to New Orleans, he found the bearded Fayssoux waiting for him in a state of excitement, with hopeful news. An Englishman had come from the Caribbean to seek Walker out, and in his absence had confided his mission to Fayssoux. He spoke, he said, for most of the British community on the large island of Ruatan, in the Bay of Honduras, where he was a substantial merchant. Ruatan was one of those islands which England had arbitrarily appropriated years earlier, and which she now proposed to turn over to Honduras in return for commercial concessions on the mainland. The transfer was to be consummated late in July, 1860; but many Englishmen on the island had agreed that, rather than submit to Honduran rule, they would seize the government office as soon as the British flag was lowered, set up an independent government, and defy Honduras. Would Walker assist them?

The prospect of action had a tonic effect on Walker. At once he began to conceive a grand scheme in which the liberation of

Ruatan was only the first step. With the island at war with Honduras, he would be justified in attacking the mainland and allying himself with the country's Liberals, who were in revolt under the leadership of the former president, Trinidad Cabañas. To be sure, Cabañas had no reason to feel friendly toward Walker, who in his Nicaraguan days had refused to help him; but four years had elapsed since then, and the necessities of war could be counted on to bridge the rift between them. There would be no more talk of slavery. Together they would overthrow the Honduran dictatorship and establish Cabañas as president. Walker would then recruit an American army, descend on Nicaragua and Costa Rica, appeal to the democratic elements, call for aid from the United States, and make a last attempt to achieve the great goal, Central American federation.

Within a week a small party of chosen men were on the way to Ruatan, traveling as ordinary passengers on a cargo boat, to study the situation. Walker himself, under the name of Williams, went to the island in June. After conferring with his Ruatanese allies, he established a secret supply depot on an uninhabited island not far away, with the fairy-tale name of Cozumel—this to avoid British interference with the landing of cargo on Ruatan. A message was sent to Cabañas, then said to be recruiting a rebel army of Hondurans in Salvador, to alert him to the new prospect, and to urge him to join forces with Walker in eastern Honduras in late August.

Returning to New Orleans, Walker took charge of the main body of the expedition, nearly a hundred men, who were to sail from Mobile in a schooner, the *Taylor,* with port clearance arranged by Fayssoux. Another schooner, loaded with supplies, sailed from New Orleans with a party under the command of a noted Alabama soldier, Colonel A. F. Rudler. But the plan had a fatal flaw— it could not be kept secret. The British sponsors of the intended coup disclosed it to friends in the government, in the futile hope of enlisting their cooperation, and from that moment Walker's chances of taking Ruatan were negligible. England was intent on completing her deal with Honduras, in which the island was a minor item; and she did not intend to let Walker return to Central America if she could help it. To block him was an easy matter. All that was necessary was to postpone the transfer of Ruatan to Honduras.

It was a safe assumption that so long as the Union Jack flew over the island, Walker would not attempt to land there. The strategy of delay was proposed to the Honduran government and eagerly accepted, as the best way to keep Walker out of their country.

Walker, as yet unaware that he had been outmaneuvered, ordered the *Taylor* to head for his supply base on Cozumel. The little island was by no means paradise, for the rainy season had begun early, but the men believed that they would have only a few days to wait before the British colors were struck on Ruatan. They would then take to their boat, make a landing, seize the government, and prepare for the invasion of Honduras. At Cozumel they were joined by a correspondent for the New York *Herald* who had got wind of the enterprise. He was greatly impressed; the expedition he described as "a fine-looking set of men," and Walker as "a silent, thoughtful man," "a wise leader"—"gentlemanly," with "cool determination."

A dull, wet week passed—and England still held Ruatan, with a warship in the harbor and a battalion of marines ashore. Walker's chief concern at this point was that Rudler's boat, which carried most of their ammunition, had failed to appear. Seeking to find Rudler and to maintain morale, Walker ordered the expedition onto the *Taylor* and sailed the surrounding seas. The blows of fate now became heavier. When finally Rudler and his men appeared off Ruatan, it was in a vessel other than the schooner in which they had set out. Their boat, together with its all-important cargo, had been seized by the British when necessity compelled a stop at a British port on the way to Ruatan.

With the entire expedition now aboard the *Taylor,* Walker continued to cruise off the Honduran coast. After a few more days, the painful truth became obvious: the British were determined to outwait him. Before Honduras took possession of Ruatan, his supplies would be gone.

He was trapped. The Ruatan project was finished. To return ingloriously to the United States would invite only mockery. What was left? Cabañas. True, without Ruatan Walker had little to offer the Honduran revolution—but that might be remedied. A wild scheme took shape in his mind—a way of making a grand gesture of defiance to the powers that were frustrating him, and at the same time, if he were lucky, of gaining enough military power to make an alliance with him worth Cabañas' while. He shared his idea with his men. The chance of success was slight, the risks were mortal; he would have no man follow him except by free choice. None refused. The extent to which his faith in his destiny and his urge to live had dwindled was known to no one but himself.

His proposal was nothing less than to storm and capture a great stone fortress, dating from the days of Cortez, that guarded the busy Honduran port of Truxillo. This done, they would take the town, join Cabañas, and win the country. Sailing in darkness, they made a landing three miles north of Truxillo and before daybreak were on the march. But some fishermen saw them, and before they reached the fort the alarm had been given. The fort's garrison was small, consisting only of some thirty Hondurans, but they had the advantage of artillery and walls, and once they were alerted, everything seemed to favor a successful defense.

I I

Walker's tactics at Fort Truxillo were based on his intuition of the Central American soldier, who usually shot at the nearest target and found it a strain to reserve his fire. Six men, willing to face the probability of death, volunteered to go forward to draw the first cannonade. If the Hondurans could be decoyed into firing their artillery prematurely, the main assault would be made from another direction before the guns could be reloaded and reaimed.

At dawn, the action began. It was one of those heavy, wet, dispirited tropical mornings in which even the birds and the monkeys are still. The hill leading to the fort was covered with slippery grass, and the grey stone walls above, with the mouths of the cannon visible in the embrasures, looked huge and formidable. Walker gave the signal. As the six volunteers broke from cover and ran forward, yelling and beckoning to an imaginary force behind them, every Honduran cannoneer discharged his load of grapeshot and canister at them. Three of the men were instantly killed, the other three badly wounded. Under the haze of smoke, the rest of Walker's force rushed the fort, ignoring a few panicky rifle shots. To hoist each other over the walls the Americans formed human pyramids, and as they jumped down on the other side the Hondurans took to their heels and fled.

Citizens of the town of Truxillo, who had climbed a hill nearby to view the battle, as at a spectator sport, saw with amazement the lowering of the Honduran colors hardly fifteen minutes after the first shots had been fired. Over the fort Walker raised the flag he had brought with him—the colors of the old Central American federation, symbolizing union and democracy. He was determined that the victory be recognized as the first battle in a democratic revolution, not as an act of piracy. Within an hour he was in Truxillo, reassuring the people that they would not be molested.

One of the first buildings in Truxillo occupied by Walker's men was the customhouse of the port, through which Honduras received most of its imports. Since the customs in most Central American countries were the main source of revenue for their governments, Walker believed that by cutting off the Truxillo duties he could inflict serious injury on the Honduran regime. With this end in view, he declared Truxillo a free port—an action also calculated to please local merchants. What he did not realize, however, was that England had an agreement with Honduras, under which all customs revenue from Truxillo was assigned to the British government for payment of an old debt.

When one of Walker's officers and a squad of men entered the building, the Honduran customs officials had already disappeared. There disappeared also, at this time, some $3000 which had been kept in a locked box, awaiting transfer to the British inspector who periodically visited the port. Whether the Hondurans had taken this money with them when they fled, or whether it had been misappropriated by the Americans could never be ascertained. The one certainty was that its removal provided the British with a legitimate pretext for intervening with military force.

Unaware as yet of the trouble which the seizure of the customhouse invited, Walker set himself to win the confidence of the local population. A proclamation to the citizens of Truxillo told them that he had not come to make war on the people of their country, but only on their government, "which stands in the way of the interests, not only of Honduras, but of all Central America." The people could rely on him to protect their rights, "both of person and of property." The tone of his statement was mild and placatory.

III

News of the victory at Truxillo, in spite of the tiny force engaged, produced a stir in the United States. An entire page of the New York *Herald* was headed: THE WALKER EXPEDITION—SUDDEN DESCENT ON HONDURAS—CAPTURE OF TRUXILLO. Much was made of the fact that Walker had established a hospital in Truxillo, and was himself assisting his surgeon in caring for the soldiers wounded in the battle, Hondurans as well as Americans. It seemed that the press was about to revive his heroic glamor. The American public was led to believe that he was well on his way to the conquest of the isthmus. Exultant Southern newspapers told readers that Walker and a hundred Americans in a fort with cannon and plenty of ammunition were equivalent to a Central American army of thousands.

Walker himself held no such illusion. He knew that, cannon or no cannon, unless supplies came to him promptly he could easily be starved out. Already it was reported that a strong Honduran force was approaching Truxillo. Everything would depend, as it had depended from the beginning, on his success in joining Cabañas, and making the revolution their common enterprise. There were rumors in Truxillo that the old Liberal was not far away, but no one could say where.

To try to locate Cabañas' camp, Walker chose the most experienced jungle fighter on his force, Colonel Thomas Henry, who set out with a Honduran guide, and was gone for several days. On his return, before reporting to Walker he stopped at a Truxillo tavern for a few drinks to offset his fatigue. He was by nature a pugnacious man—the survivor of a dozen duels, twenty battles, and many wounds—and liquor invariably accented his belligerence. When he climbed the hill to the fort, his mood was dangerous. Unable to find Walker in his quarters, he waited briefly, smoking a cigar, and then began to search the fort. The door to one room—the powder magazine—was closed, and he pushed it open. Inside was a squad of men preparing charges for the fort's cannon, and loose gunpowder was scattered on the floor. The young lieutenant in charge pointed to Henry's cigar and ordered him out. Nothing more was needed to inflame the wrath of a man spoiling for a fight. Cursing, Henry struck the lieutenant and tried to grapple with him. In a panic, the young man leaped back and pulled a pistol from his belt, and when the colonel rushed him, fired blindly. The bullet struck Henry in the jaw, carrying away the lower part of his face, a wound so hideous that even the most hardened veterans of battle were shocked by the sight.

In great pain, Henry was taken to the hospital, where the surgeon gave him morphine, before sending for Walker. The message on which Walker's hopes rested now lay in the mind of a drugged man, whose wound made it certain that he would never be able to speak again. Walker waited at the bedside and himself performed such surgery as might help to save Henry's life; but the lack of needed antiseptics made for a dark prognosis.

While Walker was waiting for Henry to regain consciousness, he was faced by still worse trouble, with the arrival at Truxillo of the British warship *Icarus,* Captain Norvell Salmon. Within a few hours a sailor brought Walker a curt message: he was to surrender, lay down his arms, and restore the money which had been in the customhouse when his men took possession of it, and which was the property of the British crown. This was Walker's first intimation that the money had been stolen.

The problem now was to prevent Captain Salmon from shelling the fort and landing marines. Still hoping for news of Cabañas from Henry, Walker played for time. His hastily written reply to Salmon said, "I cannot, under the circumstances, regard it as dishonorable to lay down my arms to an officer of the British crown"; but he asked Salmon to particularize his terms for a surrender, and to investigate the facts surrounding the alleged theft.

Henry had meanwhile opened his eyes and recognized Walker. A slate was put into the hands of the voiceless man, and he managed to scrawl a few words, apparently enough to convey some faint notion of Cabañas' whereabouts. Walker's choice was painfully clear. On the one hand, there was the will-o'-the-wisp chance of finding the jungle encampment of the Liberal rebels, who might or might not be willing to accept him. On the other hand, there was the opportunity to surrender safely to the British. Salmon's second note, which arrived some days later, was specific, if supercilious: the Americans would have the protection of the British flag when they laid down their arms. They would then leave the country on a schooner; and Walker himself would have to make good the money stolen from the customhouse by someone in his service. The note also pointedly remarked that 700 Honduran government soldiers had taken up a position just outside Truxillo.

Salmon's haughty tone may have influenced Walker's decision. Three times before in his life he had been compelled to surrender to officers of the American Army or Navy, and once he had wept at the necessity, but to bow to an Englishman was an even more crushing prospect. Consulting with his officers, he found them ready to follow him in a last desperate effort. Word went to Salmon, postponing until the next day a final reply to his demand for surrender.

While his men were spiking the guns of the fort and destroying all munitions they could not carry with them, Walker visited the hospital to say goodbye to the wounded and to leave a message for Salmon, asking that they be protected against Honduran vengeance. One of the filibusters later described Walker's farewell to the dying Colonel Henry. The gangrene in Henry's wound was spreading rapidly, maggots had appeared in the rotting flesh of his wound, and his voiceless suffering was agonizing for the men around him to see. There was a cup near him, and when Walker, after a few words, turned to go, he squeezed Henry's shoulder, and left alongside the cup a full bottle of morphine. Then, turning abruptly, he strode away. The others watched as Henry painfully reached for the cup, emptied the bottle into it, and forced the drug down his gullet. Before dying, he pulled his blanket over his graveyard face.

IV

Silently, before dawn, the men left the fort and, with a Honduran guide, followed a jungle track not far from the Atlantic coast, moving southeast toward the place in which Cabañas had last been seen. As soon as their flight became known in Truxillo, a strong force of Honduran soldiers set out after them. Twenty-four hours later, as the filibusters were about to ford a stream, the pursuers caught up with them and opened fire, wounding twenty men at the first volley.

Walker rallied the rest, and they managed to beat off the attack. In this engagement he sustained a flesh wound in his cheek, his first injury in all the battles in which he had fought in Central America. Carrying their wounded with them through narrow, twisting jungle trails they pushed on, until they came to the banks of a broad river, the Rio Negro, where a friendly tribe of Carib Indians provided shelter for them. Here their guide, after conferring with the Caribs, gave Walker an encouraging report. A day's journey toward the coast, on the banks of the Negro, they would find Cabañas and his men.

With Walker's long experience of treason in all forms, suspicion must have hammered at him and become near-certainty when the guide disappeared. Nevertheless, he decided to make the indicated move, for his men were subsisting entirely on bananas, the wounded men were in distress, and nothing was to be gained by tramping aimlessly through the jungle. He commandeered the Caribs' canoes, and they drifted downstream, until a few miles from the coast they saw signs of a deserted encampment. Whoever had been there, Cabañas or another, had long since gone.

As they got out of their canoes, they were attacked by waiting Honduran snipers. What saved them was the presence of some rotting barricades, from behind which they were able to defend themselves. A week of sleepless nights and hopeless days ensued. The camp was located in a swampy region, and the insects, the fetid odors, the drenching bursts of rain, the burning sun, and the incessant rifle fire reduced the hungry little band to a state of misery in which the only relief was an occasional successful shot at a Honduran. Several of the men were killed, others wounded. Walker himself came down with fever, which he tried to ignore. Moving from man to man behind their defenses, guiding their rifle fire, shifting their positions as necessity required, tending the wounded, he did what he could, until fatigue began to close down on them, like a fog. It was with a sense of mingled despair and relief that, nine days after the fighting began, he saw two British boats coming up the river, manned by British sailors, with Captain Salmon sitting stiffly in the bow of the lead boat. As the Hondurans ceased firing, a sailor got out of the boat, advanced to the camp, and gave Walker a message. The Captain wished him to come at once to his boat, prepared to surrender his force.

The last military decision of Walker's life was in some ways the easiest. His urge to resist was gone. The only gesture that he made to his reputation as he walked to the shore was a conscious straightening of his shoulders and lifting of his head.

Salmon was a big man, with a ruddy complexion and a booming voice—almost a caricature of his type. "Sir," he began, "I demand that you surrender to me immediately."

"To whom do I surrender?" asked Walker.

"To an officer of Her Majesty's Government. And you may thank me, too"—pointing at the Honduran soldiers in the distance —"that you have a whole bone in your body and that your men leave here alive."

Something in Salmon's manner must have aroused Walker's distrust, for he repeated his question in a slightly different form. "Do I understand you to say, sir, that my surrender would be to a representative of Her Majesty's Government?"

"Yes," said Salmon, "to me."

"Under these circumstances," Walker replied, "I surrender to you, Captain." He handed his sword and pistol to Salmon, and turning, ordered his men to deliver their guns and knives to the British marines. That was all.*

He and Colonel Rudler were taken immediately to the *Icarus,* the rest of the men following in other boats. As soon as all were on board, Salmon ordered the ship to proceed at full steam to Truxillo. There, he announced, they would be handed over to the Honduran authorities. Walker's men would be protected by the British flag, but the fate of Walker himself, and Rudler, would be left to the Hondurans.

Walker was at first incredulous, then disdainful. The correspondent of the New York *Herald* boarded the *Icarus* at Truxillo, and before leaving the ship Walker dictated a short statement to him.

* New York *Herald,* Sept. 28, Oct. 4, 1860. *Harper's Weekly,* Vol. IV, p. 647.

On board the Steamer *Icarus*
Sept. 5, 1860

I hereby protest before the civilized world that when I surrendered to the captain of Her Majesty's Steamer *Icarus,* that officer expressly received my sword and pistol, as well as the arms of Colonel Rudler, and the surrender was expressly made in so many words to him, as the representative of Her Britannic Majesty.

William Walker

That was the last flicker in him of the urge to survive. He was ripe for death and knew it. At thirty-six, he had exhausted the possibilities of romantic heroism; knights-errant must die young. Asceticism had deprived him of the best reason for enduring the pain of failure— the woman and the child. He knew that the world was tired of him, and he was tired of himself. The Hondurans who took him to the fort that he had stormed not long before and put him in an improvised cell found him courteous and tractable. He did not really wish to resist the end that he could foresee. His only request was that a priest be sent to him. The priest, later interviewed by Joaquin Miller, said that Walker told him, "I am prepared to die. My political career is finished."

His chief concern was to have the priest intercede with the Honduran government for the security of his men. "I alone made the decision to attack Truxillo. They knew nothing of it." It was, he felt, altogether unfair that Colonel Rudler should share his fate. When after a few days a Honduran officer came to him to say that he would be executed the next morning, he asked at once about Rudler, and was relieved to hear that the Colonel's sentence had been commuted to a limited imprisonment.

Many concocted versions of Walker's execution appeared in the American press, including "last words" which it is virtually certain that he never uttered. What is known is that at eight o'clock on September 12, 1860, flanked by two priests, he was led by a company of soldiers to a ruined wall, on the outskirts of Truxillo, followed by a large and jubilant crowd of Hondurans. He ignored the laughter and jests around him. His bearing was calm and resolute, and he seemed to give his attention wholly to the words of the priests. The soldiers formed a line around the square in front of the wall, as the last rites were administered. When the priests had concluded and withdrew, Walker stood erect, facing the soldiers impassively and without speaking. A squad of Hondurans stepped forward, aimed, and at an officer's command, fired. Walker was apparently dead when he fell. A second squad then advanced and fired another volley at the body, after which the officer walked forward, put his pistol to the head of the corpse, and pulled the trigger, mutilating the face beyond recognition. The crowd cheered, the troops marched off, and the priests removed the body, with the help of some Americans who had come off a ship in Truxillo, and who paid for a coffin. The interment was conducted with a Catholic service at an isolated spot. Afterward the Tennessee Historical Society, of which Walker was an honorary member, attempted to bring the remains to Nashville for burial, but the Honduran government refused permission. Captain Salmon, with a shrewd eye for British relations in Central America, gave Walker's sword to Nicaragua. There was considerable criticism of him in the United States for his mortal deception of Walker, but the British government winked at the episode and it did not interfere with his subsequent career.

V

The blaze of interest that centered on Walker while he lived contrasts curiously with the oblivion that overtook him in the grave. As abruptly as he had come to the world's notice, he dropped out of it. Perhaps the same thing would have happened to Napoleon if he had been trapped in Egypt, or to Clive if he had been defeated at Plassey. But the speed with which Walker's fame evaporated had something of the same phenomenal quality that marked him all his life. The coming of the Civil War, with its new crop of heroes, was no doubt mainly responsible for the country's readiness to forget him, but there may have been also another, more subtle reason—the way of thinking and feeling for which he stood. Men of business had then begun to take possession of the United States; their special outlook and mentality was becoming dominant throughout the North and in parts of the South; and their standards of judgment were more and more regarded as identical with law, morality, and good government. Walker's entire career was a romantic challenge to economic man, his personality wholly antithetic to the great powers then about to reshape the American way of life. By his enemies is a man known, and Walker contended with the money-master, Cornelius Vanderbilt, was abandoned by the artful friend of wealth, Buchanan, and was castigated by the leading advocate of the economic virtues, Greeley.

A concerted and final attack on his reputation by the abolitionist press was in the making when he died. Its tone was set by Greeley in the New York *Tribune*. A long editorial, which appeared before news of the execution had reached the United States, called Walker "impudent" — "imbecilic" — "idiotic" — "insane" — "cowardly" — "contemptible" — "a vagabond" — "pestilent creature" — and found it "inexplicable that men should follow him." His death, the editorial plainly conveyed, would be a godsend. Even in that age of easy slander, this was remarkable. President Buchanan echoed Greeley's sentiments. In a message to Congress in December, 1860, when the nation was rocking toward civil war, he took time to express pious satisfaction in Walker's disappearance from the national scene. "I congratulate you on the public sentiment which now exists," he told Congress, "against the crime of setting on foot military expeditions within the limits of the United States, to proceed from thence and make war upon the people of unoffending states with whom we are at peace. In this respect a happy change has been effected since the commencement of my administration." Buchanan had chosen to forget that he himself had once advocated the forcible annexation of Cuba, that he had been elected on a Democratic platform which called on the administration to support Walker, and that he had received him at the White House with every civility and courtesy. His remarks were in fact an echo of statements made by the press of England, where Walker's death was regarded with unalloyed pleasure. On both sides of the Atlantic, official opinion took the stand that he had been simply a troublemaker; and the Northern interpretation of history which dominated American thought after the Civil War accepted this view.

The *New York Times* saw Walker otherwise. "Whatever hard things may have been said of General Walker—and much, we doubt not, would have been left unsaid had his fortune been more propitious— he was at least no vulgar adventurer, either by birth, habits, or education, or the honourable purposes with which he set out in life. His parentage was unsullied, his private walk and temperance unquestioned, his learning profound, and his original aims, however subsequently misdirected by an unchastened ambition, such as commended him to success, while enlisting the esteem of numerous friends. Even those who deny him all claim to military skill or political sagacity as a leader, pay the highest compliment to his moral force and personal integrity. Without these his first failure as an adventurer must inevitably have been his last."

Until the flame of his natural genius was quenched by despair, Walker had the glow of an idealist as well as the heat of a hero. *Harper's Weekly* observed that he failed because, instead of seeking to win support from the wealthy and influential, he relied only on himself. The real tragedy, *Harper's* commented, lay in the rejection of him by the American government. "Had William Walker been an Englishman or a Frenchman, he would never have become a 'filibuster,' but would have found ample scope for his extraordinary talents in the legitimate service of his country."* It was the kind of epitaph that Walker himself might have desired.

---

* It is impossible not to wonder what would have happened in Central America if President Pierce or Buchanan had chosen to support Walker in the first flush of his conquest, and before he made his fatal concession to the South. Would the flow of American capital and enterprise to the isthmian republics have enabled them to make more progress in the century that followed? It seems safe to say that they could hardly have made less. Would England have gone to war with the United States over Nicaragua in 1856? There is considerable reason to doubt it. Would American concentration on Central America and the construction of a canal there have eased the internal schism in the United States? Would Walker have been justified in his belief in the possibility of averting civil war by rallying the nation to an expansion of democratic institutions and productivity overseas? It may be noted that echoes of the idea persist in mid-twentieth-century politics. At a time when, as Adlai Stevenson has said, the world itself is threatened with civil war, there are not a few who feel that the most realistic hope of peace lies in the diversion of the energies of the great powers away from direct confrontation and to an effort to bring underprivileged peoples into "the column of Progress and Democracy" of which Walker wrote.

BIBLIOGRAPHY

Among manuscript collections consulted in the writing of this book two were of especial importance: the *Fayssoux Collection,* at the Middle American Research Institute of Tulane University, New Orleans, and the *Buchanan Papers,* Pennsylvania Historical Society, Philadelphia. The *Clayton Papers* in the Congressional Library and manuscript archives of the United States Department of State and the United States Navy Department dealing with Central America in the 1850's also provided valuable data.

Documents and Correspondence Relative to a Trans-Isthmian Canal, privately printed by the New York law firm of Sullivan and Cromwell in 1900, contributed greatly; and the *Wheeler Scrapbooks,* a large collection of newspaper clippings in five volumes, at the Library of Congress, were a significant source of material.

Contemporary newspapers in every city in which Walker stayed for an appreciable time were consulted. Among the more essential were: for the years 1848–49, the *Crescent, Delta,* and *Picayune* of New Orleans; for 1850–55, the San Francisco *Herald, Alta California,* and the *State Democratic Journal* of Sacramento; for 1856–60, the *Herald, Tribune,* and *Times* of New York, the *Delta* and *Picayune* of New Orleans, and *El Nicaragüense.* For official views of Walker between 1855 and 1860, the *Congressional Globe,* and for Anglo-American Relations, the *London Times* were indispensable.

Fresh insights into Walker's psychology were afforded by his published

275

address, *The Unity of Art,* in the Library of the Tennessee State Archives at Nashville. Prior to 1962, this pamphlet was incorrectly attributed. Among the books listed below, *Filibusters and Financiers,* by W. O. Scroggs, by the thoroughness of its documentation greatly aided the search for useful sources and provided numerous interpretive clues. Walker's own book, *The War in Nicaragua,* is, of course, a primary source.

BOOKS

Adams, James Truslow, *America's Tragedy,* New York, 1934.

Alemán Blaños, G., *Centenario de la Guerra Nacional de Nicaragua contra Walker,* Guatemala, 1956.

Alfaro, Olmedo, *El Filibustero Walker en Nicaragua* (Pamphlet), Panama, 1932.

Alvarez, Miguel, *Los Filibusteros en Nicaragua,* Granada, 1944.

"An Officer in the Service of Walker" (Anon.), *The Destiny of Nicaragua,* Boston, 1856.

Andrews, Wayne, *The Vanderbilt Legend,* New York, 1941.

Asbury, Herbert, *The Barbary Coast,* New York, 1933.

———, *The French Quarter,* New York, 1936.

Atkinson, E., *Cheap Cotton and Free Labor,* Boston, 1861.

Atlantic and Pacific Ship Canal Company, *Terms of the Contract Between the State of Nicaragua and the Company* (Pamphlet), New York, 1849.

Bailey, Thomas A., *A Diplomatic History of the American People,* New York, 1944.

Bancroft, H. H., *History of Central America,* San Francisco, 1887.

———, *History of Mexico,* Vol. IV, San Francisco, 1888.

Bass, J. M., *William Walker* (Pamphlet), Nashville, 1898.

Belly, F., *A Travers l'Amérique Centrale,* 2 vols., Paris, 1860.

Belt, Thomas, *The Naturalist in Nicaragua,* London, 1874.

Bigelow, John, *Breaches of Anglo-American Treaties,* New York, 1917.

———, *Retrospections of an Active Life,* New York, 1909.

Bonaparte, Louis Napoleon, *A Project to Connect the Atlantic and Pacific Oceans* (Pamphlet), London, 1846.

Bulwer, Sir H. Lytton, *Historical Characters,* London, 1867.

Caldwell, R. G., *The Lopez Expeditions to Cuba,* Princeton, 1915.

Chase, H. and Sanborn, C. W., *The North and the South: A Statistical View,* New York, 1856.

Choules, J. O., *The Cruise of the North Star,* New York, 1854.

Christy, D., *Cotton Is King,* New York, 1856.

Claiborne, J. F. H., *Life and Correspondence of John A. Quitman,* 2 vols., New York, 1860.

Clapp, Theodore, *Autobiographical Sketches,* Boston, 1858.

Comegys, J. P., *Memoir of John M. Clayton,* Wilmington, 1882.

Croffut, W. A., *The Vanderbilts and the Story of Their Fortune*, New York, 1882.

Crowe, Frederick, *The Gospel in Central America*, London, 1850.

D'Auvergne, E. B. F., *Envoys Extraordinary*, London, 1937.

Davis, Richard Harding, *Real Soldiers of Fortune*, New York, 1906.

Doubleday, C. W., *Reminiscences of the "Filibuster" War in Nicaragua*, New York, 1886.

Einstein, L., "Lewis Cass," in *American Secretaries of State* (S. F. Bemis, ed.), New York, 1928.

Ettinger, A. A., *The Mission to Spain of Pierre Soulé*, New Haven, 1932.

Field, S. J., *Personal Reminiscences of Early Days in California* (Privately printed), 1893.

Gámez, J., *Historia de Nicaragua*, Managua, 1889.

Gándara, M. M., *El Gobernador y Commandante General de Sonora a Sus Habitantes* (Broadside), Hermosillo, 1853.

Greeley, Horace, *The American Conflict*, 2 vols., Hartford, 1864–66.

Greene, Lawrence, *The Filibuster*, Indianapolis, 1937.

Hall, A. H., *The Manhattaner in New Orleans*, New Orleans, 1851.

Hittell, J. S., *California*, 3 vols., San Francisco, 1878.

Hoblitzell, H. S., *Early Historical Sketch of the City of Marysville and Yuba County*, 1876.

Jamison, J. C., *With Walker in Nicaragua*, Columbia, Mo., 1909.

Keasbey, L. M., *The Nicaragua Canal and the Monroe Doctrine*, Philadelphia, 1896.

Lambertie, R., *Le Drame de la Sonore*, Paris, 1856.

Lane, Wheaton J., *Commodore Vanderbilt*, New York, 1942.

Learned, H. B., "William Marcy," in *American Secretaries of State*, New York, 1928.

Letts, J. M., *California Illustrated*, New York, 1852.

Lévy, Daniel, *Les Francais en Californie*, San Francisco, 1884.

Manning, William R. (ed.), *Diplomatic Correspondence of the United States*, vol. 4, Washington, 1932.

Meade, Rebecca Paulding, *Life of Hiram Paulding*, New York, 1910.

Medbery, J. K., *Men and Mysteries of Wall Street*, New York, 1879.

Melendez Ch. Carlos, *Ideario politico de Walker*, San José, 1956.

Montúfar, L., *Walker en Centro America*, 2 vols., Guatemala, 1887.

Naval Affairs Committee (House), "Arrest of William Walker by Commodore Paulding" (Pamphlet), Washington, 1858.

Neumann, Alfred, *Strange Conquest*, New York, 1954.

——, *Gitterwerk des Lebens*, Los Angeles, 1951.

Nicaise, Auguste, *Les Filibustiers Américains*, Paris, 1860.

Nichols, R. F., *Franklin Pierce*, Philadelphia, 1931.

Obregon Loria, Rafael, *La Campaña del Transito, 1856–57*, San José, 1956.

Oliphant, Laurence, *Patriots and Filibusters*, London, 1860.

Olmstead, F. L., *The Cotton Kingdom*, New York, 1862.

O'Meara, James, *Broderick and Gwin*, San Francisco, 1881.

Perez, J., *Memorias . . . de la guerra contra los Filibusteros*, Managua, 1857.

Perkins, Dexter, *The Monroe Doctrine, 1826–67*, Baltimore, 1933.

Polk, James K., *Diary of James K. Polk*, 4 vols., New York, 1910.

Powell, E. A., *Gentlemen Rovers*, New York, 1913.

Ratterman, Elleanore, *Documents* (ed. by W. O. Scroggs), Nashville, 1916.

Rauch, Basil, *American Interest in Cuba, 1848–1855*, New York, 1948.

Rhodes, J. F., *History of the United States, 1850–4*, Vols. 1-2, New York, 1902.

Ripley, E. M., *Social Life In Old New Orleans*, New Orleans, 1921.

Rippy, J. F. *The United States and Mexico*, New York, 1926.

Roche, J. J., *The Story of the Filibusters*, London, 1891.

———, *Byways of War*, Boston, 1901.

Rollins, Clinton (Arturo Ortega, trans.) (Sp.), *William Walker*, Managua, 1945.

Scroggs, W. O., *Filibusters and Financiers*, New York, 1916.

Shuck, O. T., *Representative Men of the Pacific*, San Francisco, 1870.

Smith, J. H. *The War with Mexico*, New York, 1919.

Soulé, E.; Gihon, J. H.; and Nisbet, J., *Annals of San Francisco*, San Francisco, 1855.

Squier, E. G., *Nicaragua*, 2 vols., New York, 1852.

Stout, P. F., *Nicaragua, Past, Present and Future*, Philadelphia, 1859.

Sullivan and Cromwell, *Documents and Correspondence Relative To A Trans-Isthmian Canal* (Privately printed), 4 vols., New York, 1900.

Thomas, Jane H., *Old Days in Nashville*, Nashville, 1897.

Tinker, E. L., *Gombo—The Creole Dialect* (Pamphlet), Worcester, 1910.

Truman, Ben C., *The Field of Honor*, New York, 1884.

U. S. Senate, *Speeches on William Walker* (Pamphlet), 1858.

Walker, William, *The War in Nicaragua*, Mobile, 1860.

———, *Letters of General Walker* (Pamphlet), New York, 1858.

———, *Mexico and Central America: The Problem and Its Solution* (Pamphlet), New Orleans, 1858.

Warren, T. Robinson, *Dust and Foam*, New York, 1859.

Weller, J. B., *Remarks on Nicaraguan Affairs*, Washington, 1856.

Wells, William V., *Walker's Expeditition to Nicaragua*, New York, 1856.

———, *Explorations and Adventures in Honduras*, New York, 1857.

Wencker, Friedrich, "William Walker, der Diktator von Nicaragua," in *Ungekrönte Könige*, Vienna, 1934.

Williams, M. F., *History of the San Francisco Vigilance Committee of 1851*, San Francisco, 1911.

Williams, M. W., "John Middleton Clayton," in *American Secretaries of State* (S. F. Bemis, ed.), New York, 1928.
Wilson, Edmund, *Patriotic Gore,* New York, 1962.

PERIODICALS

The following periodicals contain articles of exceptional value relating to Walker, his times, or the later course of Central America's development:

Academia de Geografia e Historia de Nicaragua (*Revista*), Managua, 1946, t. 8, no. 3. ("William Walker trata de explicar por qué se esforzó en renstabler la esclavitud en Nicaragua").
American Historical Review, Vol. VII, pp. 709-750 (L. M. Sears— "Slidell and Buchanan").
 Vol. X, pp. 792-811 (W. O. Scroggs—"William Walker and the Steamship Corporation in Nicaragua").
 Vol. XLII, p. 497 (R. W. Van Alstyne, ed.,—"Anglo-American Relations 1853–59").
Annual Report of the American Historical Association, 1911, Vol. II, p. 447 ("The Correspondence of . . . Howell Cobb").
Arizona Historical Review, 1935 ("William Walker's Invasion of Sonora").
Atlantic Monthly, Vol. IV, p. 665 ("A. Absalom").
Blackwood's Magazine, 1856, Vol. LXXIX, pp. 314-316 ("The Destiny of Nicaragua").
Harper's Weekly, 1857–60 (frequent editorial comment, 1857–60, in Vols. I, II, III).
Hispanic-American Historical Review, Vol. XVI, pp. 352-357 (R. W. Van Alstyne—"The Central American Policy of Lord Palmerston").
Huntington Library Quarterly, 1944, Vol. VII, pp. 153-166 ("Bandini's Account of William Walker's Invasion of Lower California").
Inter-American Affairs, 1955, Vol. VIII, No. 4 (A. G. Frank—"The Economic Development of Nicaragua").
Journal of Modern History, Vol. XI, pp. 157-161 (R. W. Van Alstyne— "British Diplomacy and the Clayton-Bulwer Treaty").
Mississippi Valley Historical Review, Vol. I, p. 199 (W. O. Scroggs— "William Walker's Designs on Cuba").
Pacific Historical Review, 1933, Vol. II, pp. 194-213 (R. K. Wyllys— "The Republic of Lower California").
Political Science Quarterly, Vol. VIII, p. 22 (S. Webster—"The Ostend Manifesto").
Proceedings of the South Carolina Historical Assn., 1947, p. 9 (W. H. Patterson).
Putnam's Magazine, April, 1857, pp. 425-435.

Revue des Deux Mondes, August, 1856 (A. Assolant—"Walker et les Aventuriers Américains").

Sociedad de Geografia e Historia de Guatemala (Revista), 1957, t. 30, No. 1-4, pp. 7-92 (V. Rodriguez Beteta—"Transcendencia de la guerra nacional de Centro America").

Sunset Magazine, Vol. XVI, p. 564 (Poem and article by Joaquin Miller).

ACKNOWLEDGMENTS

I am deeply indebted to several friends who read the manuscript of this book at various stages of its development and provided helpful criticism: Phyllis Duganne (Mrs. Eben Given), O. Rudolph Johnson, and Richard Johnson. Dr. Sandor Rado generously reviewed my findings on Walker's psychology and made a number of stimulating suggestions. I must express, too, my gratitude to the staff of the Boston Athenaeum for many valuable services during the final year of research.

A.Z.C.

INDEX

About the Author

The nature of power and its impact on the men who wield it have long been a major interest of Albert Z. Carr. Previous books of his have dealt with Napoleon Bonaparte, Joseph Stalin and John D. Rockefeller.

Trained as an economist, during World War II Mr. Carr was assistant to the Chairman of the War Production Board and subsequently a White House adviser, serving on missions to England, China, Japan and other countries. After the war, as a director of the Inter-Allied Reparation Agency, he worked on the problem of German reparations. He also served as a consultant to President Truman during his 1948 campaign for reelection.

Mr. Carr's literary career began with short stories and articles contributed to leading magazines. A number of his stories have been made into motion pictures. In the fields of history and biography he has published eight books, which include *Juggernaut: The Path of Dictatorship, The Coming of War,* and *Men of Power.*

UNITED

Rio Grande

MEXICO

*PACIFIC
OCEAN*

WILLIAM WALKER

0   300
Miles